PRENTICE HALL

In Association with
CLOSE UP®
FOUNDATION

Civics

Participating in Government

James E. Davis

Phyllis Fernlund

Prentice
Hall

Needham, Massachusetts
Upper Saddle River, New Jersey
Glenview, Illinois

★ About the Authors

James E. Davis

Executive Director, Social Science Education Consortium, Boulder, Colorado. He received his Ed.D. in social science education from the University of Colorado, Boulder. An active NCSS member for over thirty years, and a former social studies teacher, he has developed curriculum materials and teacher resources for both elementary and secondary levels.

Phyllis Fernlund

Dean of the School of Education at Sonoma State University. She received her B.A. and M.A. from the University of Illinois, Urbana, in the teaching of history and her Ph.D. in education from Northwestern University. A former high school social studies teacher, she has developed curriculum and professional development materials for K–12, business, and higher education.

About the Close Up Foundation

The Close Up Foundation is the nation's leading civic education organization. Since 1971, Close Up has been a leader in the social studies field, reaching millions of students, educators, and other adults. The Foundation's mission of informed participation in government and democracy drives its experiential civic education programs in Washington, D.C., for students and teachers, as well as its television programs on C-SPAN and its award-winning publications and videos. Close Up's work represents a multidimensional approach to citizenship education by increasing community involvement and civic literacy—one student, one citizen, at a time.

ISBN 0-13-062867-0

3 4 5 6 7 8 9 10   05 04 03 02

Program Reviewers

Content Consultants

Jeff Blaga
Social Studies
    Department Chair
William Horlick High School
Racine, WI

John R. Doyle
Administrative Director,
    Division of Social Sciences
Miami-Dade County Public
    Schools
Miami, FL

Pat Easterbrook
Social Studies National
    Consultant
Fayetteville, NC

Rita Geiger
Director of Social Studies
Norman Public Schools
Norman, OK

Michal Howden
Social Studies National
    Consultant
Zionsville, IN

Tom Ilgen
Jones Professor of Political
    Studies
Center for Policy, Politics, and
    Economics
Pitzer College
Claremont, CA

Kathy Lewis
Social Studies National
    Consultant
Fort Worth, TX

Dr. John P. Lunstrom
Professor of Social Science
    Education
Florida State University
Tallahassee, FL

Jack C. Morgan
Director, Center for Economic
    Education
University of Louisville
Louisville, KY

Richard Moulden
Social Studies National
    Consultant
Federal Way, WA

Chuck Schierloh
Social Studies Consultant
Lima City Schools
Lima, OH

Donald Schwartz
Professor
California State University,
    Long Beach
Long Beach, CA

Heather S. Watkins
Lead Social Studies Teacher
South Oldham High School
Crestwood, KY

Joseph Wieczorek
Social Studies National
    Consultant
Baltimore, MD

Service Learning Consultant

Maria Elena Keenan
Educational Specialist
Miami-Dade County Public
    Schools
Miami, FL

Internet Consultant

Leslie Lee
Social Studies Teacher
Miami-Dade County Public
    Schools
Miami, FL

Reading Consultant

Lois Huffman, Ph.D.
Content Area Reading
    Specialist
North Carolina State
    University
Raleigh, NC

Constitution Consultant

William A. McClenaghan
Department of Political Science
Oregon State University
Beaverton, OR
Author, *Magruder's American
Government*

Block Scheduling Consultant

Barbara Slater Stern
Assistant Professor
James Madison University
Harrisonburg, VA

Economics Consultants

Arthur O'Sullivan
Professor of Economics
Oregon State University
Corvallis, OR

Steven Sheffrin
Dean, Division of Social
    Studies
University of California, Davis
Davis, CA

Contents

CLOSE UP
FOUNDATION

iv

CLOSE UP
FOUNDATION

CLOSE UP
FOUNDATION

CLOSE UP
FOUNDATION

UNIT **6** The American Legal System   **388**

Reference Section

on Primary Sources

Primary sources selected by the editors of the Close Up Foundation

PEOPLE *MAKE A DIFFERENCE*

Famous and ordinary Americans who have contributed to their community and country

BELIEFS *IN ACTION*

Respected Americans who have set an example by acting on their beliefs

ISSUES *THAT AFFECT YOU: Citizens and the Courts*

Explorations of important court cases that have affected our communities

DECISION MAKING SKILLS

Step-by-step lessons to learn and practice decision making skills

SOCIAL STUDIES SKILLS

Step-by-step lessons to learn and practice social studies skills

Graphs, Charts, and Tables

Graphs, Charts, and Tables (continued)

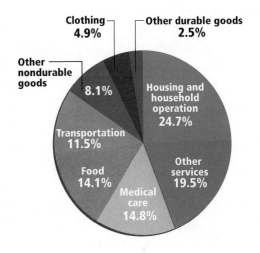

Maps

Foundations of Citizenship

Why Study Civics?

Let us say this much to ourselves, not only with our lips but in our hearts. Let us say this: I myself am a part of democracy—I myself must accept responsibility. Democracy is not merely a privilege to be enjoyed—it is a trust to keep and maintain...I am an American. I intend to remain an American...I will sustain my government. And through good days or bad, I will try to serve my country.

—**Stephen Vincent Benét**

As you read these words written by the twentieth-century American poet Stephen Vincent Benét, do they make you think about what it means to be an American? As Americans, what do we believe about our country, our government? How do we know what to expect from our government? How do we know what is expected of us?

These are all questions that can be addressed by the study of civics. If you look up the word civics in a dictionary, you will see that it is related to the word citizenship. Civics is the study of the rights and duties of citizenship. This is an especially important subject in the United States, where citizens' participation has been essential in maintaining our system of government since the founding of the country more than 200 years ago.

What's Ahead in Unit 1

In Unit 1 you will be taking a look at the ideas and beliefs that Americans share. You will begin to learn what it means to be an American citizen and what rights and responsibilities citizens share.

A Portrait of Americans

Citizenship and You

Meet three American citizens, each with a unique and interesting story.

My name is Peter Ky. I am eighteen years old. I was born in Vietnam, and I came to the United States with my family in 1991. In 1997 we all became American citizens. We have a family-owned restaurant in San Francisco, California. I work in the restaurant when I am not going to school.

I am Bernice Kelman. I am eighty-one years old. I grew up on a farm in western Kansas. My father, who came to this country from Scotland, and my mother, who was born in Germany, homesteaded a farm near Dodge City, Kansas, in 1918. I live nearby in the small town of Sublette.

My name is Doris Hollingsworth. I am forty-four. My great-grand-parents were slaves on a plantation near Augusta, Georgia, and my father was a construction worker in Atlanta. I live in Tucker, Georgia, a suburb of Atlanta, and I work for a large company as a computer analyst.

Despite their differences, Peter, Bernice, and Doris have an important thing in common—they are all American citizens.

What's Ahead in Chapter 1

In this chapter you will read about the many different kinds of people who are Americans and about some of the important ideas and values that bind us together as a nation and as a people.

Section 1 Who Americans Are

Section 2 America: A Cultural Mosaic

Section 3 The Values That Unite Us

Keep It Current

Items marked with this logo are periodically updated on the Internet. To keep up-to-date, go to **www.phschool.com**

Citizen's Journal

Write a paragraph describing yourself, like the ones written by Peter, Bernice, and Doris. Include your age, where you were born, information about your family's background, and anything else you think is important.

Who Americans Are

SECTION PREVIEW

Objectives

- Summarize where Americans live.
- Describe how Americans' jobs are changing.
- Explain why there are more older Americans.
- Describe why Americans are known for their diversity.

Building Civics Vocabulary

- Americans are known for their diversity, or differences.

 Focus

What if a visitor from another country asked you, "Who are Americans?" How would you answer that question? As you can see from reading about Peter, Bernice, and Doris, not all Americans are alike. We live in different places and work at different jobs. We are different ages and come from different backgrounds. Gathering information about all these characteristics can help to make a portrait of the American people.

Where We Live

Americans live in almost every kind of terrain the world has to offer. We live in high mountains and on broad prairies. We live in warm, tropical climates and in areas with frigid winters. From Alaska to Texas, and from the Hawaiian Islands to the coast of Maine, the United States is a vast and varied land.

When Peter Ky goes home, he climbs three flights of stairs to his family's apartment in San Francisco, a city of 746,000 people on the shore of the Pacific Ocean. Doris and her husband and daughter live in a condominium in Tucker, Georgia, a suburb of Atlanta with a population of about 26,000. Bernice's home is in Sublette, Kansas, a small farming town of 1,400 people.

Americans on the Move In the early days of our country's history, most people lived on farms or in small towns that hugged the eastern seacoast. Gradually, as more and more people came to the New World seeking land and jobs, our population spread out across the continent.

When Bernice was a little girl in the 1920s, one out of three Americans lived on a farm, as she did. Gradually, people began to concentrate in urban areas, or cities, where jobs were available in factories and offices. Today, four out of five Americans (about 217 million) live in urban areas, as do Peter and Doris.

Americans have not only moved from farms to cities. They also have been moving from the North and the East toward the South and the West, settling in warm-weather states such as Georgia, Florida, Texas, Arizona, and California. This region, which is called the Sunbelt, has been the fastest growing area in the nation in the last several decades.

Facts & Quotes

A Land for Everyone

We recognize our country in the words of Woody Guthrie's famous song, "This Land is Your Land."

This land is your land,
this land is my land,
From California,
to the New York Island,
From the redwood forest
to the Gulf Stream waters,
This land was made for you and me.

POPULATION DENSITY

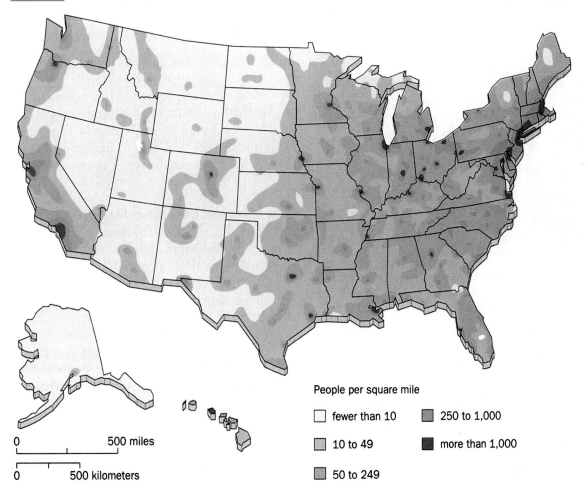

People per square mile

☐ fewer than 10

☐ 10 to 49

☐ 50 to 249

☐ 250 to 1,000

■ more than 1,000

0 ———— 500 miles

0 ———— 500 kilometers

While the population of the South and West is growing rapidly, the Northeast remains the most densely populated region. **Regions Into what population density category does most of the West fall?**

What Work We Do

Americans have always worked hard. The first settlers from Europe supported themselves by scratching farms out of the wilderness in Virginia and Massachusetts. Since then, we have cultivated land on both coasts and in the fertile plains and valleys across the continent. We have built houses, stores, factories, and office buildings. We have laid out roads, canals, railroads, and airports.

We have manufactured a vast array of products and sold them at home and in countries around the world. We have founded banks, insurance companies, colleges, and hospitals.

The American Work Force Our work force is made up of about 60 million women and 70 million men working in nearly 30,000 different occupations. Many people in your age group join the work force by

Many teenagers enter the work force for the first time when they take part-time or summer jobs. A large percentage of these jobs are service jobs.

taking jobs. Before they graduate from high school, many of today's students will have had the experience of working at part-time and summer jobs.

A hundred years ago, most Americans worked in farming and manufacturing. The development of modern farm machinery and the increasing use of electronic technology in our factories, however, has brought about a change.

By the year 2006, nearly 75 percent of American workers are expected to hold service jobs. In a service job, a person makes a living by providing a service for other people. Your doctor, your teacher, your dentist, and the person who fixes your family's car are all engaged in service jobs.

How Old We Are

To answer the question, "Who are Americans?" you will need to include some information about how old we are. At

different times in our history, the percentage of people in different age groups has varied. The bar graph on this page illustrates this point.

In 1850 more than half of Americans were children. Forty-four percent were in the 20–59 age range, while a very small percentage were of retirement age. How had those statistics changed by 1999?

More Older Americans There are several reasons for the changes in the percentage of the population in each age group. One reason is that improvements in medical care have increased our life expectancy. More and more Americans are living past age sixty. The average person in your age group today can expect to live to be about seventy-six.

Another reason for the changes in the age of our population is the "baby boom" that occurred between 1946 and 1964. During

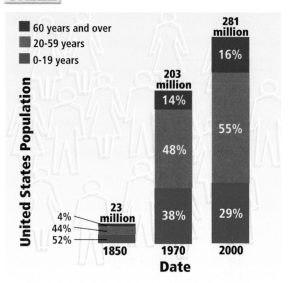

GRAPH SKILL   **THE AGES OF AMERICANS**

- 60 years and over
- 20-59 years
- 0-19 years

United States Population

Date

Source: U.S. Census Bureau

The population of older Americans is increasing rapidly. **Diversity** What percentage of Americans was under 20 years old in 2000?

Older Americans make up an increasingly large part of our population. At the same time, the number of children per family is going down.

these years, many American couples had three or more children. Today, the large number of people born during the baby boom has swelled the ranks of Americans in the 36 to 54 age group. Your parents, in fact, are likely to be baby boomers. Although there are more adults of child-bearing age than ever before, they are having fewer children than did people of their parents' generation. This is one reason why the percentage of younger people in our population has declined.

Population experts predict that by the year 2050, when the members of the baby boom generation will be senior citizens, the number of people sixty-five years of age and

older will have more than doubled. That means that more than one in four Americans will be age sixty-five or older. How do you think our country might change as a result of the aging of our population?

Where We Have Come From

Americans are a people who are known for their diversity, or differences, from each other. Our diversity is reflected in our different jobs, home towns, and ages—and especially in our backgrounds. Our backgrounds differ because we are from many different countries and belong to different races.

Peter Ky and his family have been Americans for only a few years. Like their ancestors, the Kys were born in the Southeast Asian country of Vietnam and grew up speaking a Vietnamese language, eating Vietnamese food, and observing the customs of that country. The Kys now think of themselves as Americans whose background is Vietnamese.

Doris's ancestors lived in Africa and were brought to this country as slaves to work on cotton and tobacco plantations. Doris's family has lived in America for almost 300 years, so she considers herself to be an American of African background.

Bernice has a mixed background. Her father was born in Scotland and her mother, in Germany. Bernice is not unusual. Many Americans have ancestors from more than one country or of more than one race.

As you explore what it means to be a citizen of this nation called the United States, it will be useful to look more closely at the diversity of our backgrounds and learn how that diversity contributes to who we are as a people.

Section 1 Assessment

1. **Define** diversity
2. What region of our country has grown the fastest in the last 30 years?
3. What is a service job? Give five examples of service jobs.
4. Why do older Americans now make up a greater percentage of our population than they did in the past?
5. **Analyze** What are some of the important ways in which Americans are diverse?

America: A Cultural Mosaic

SECTION PREVIEW

Objectives
- Explain why people from other countries come to America.
- Identify the five major groups of Americans.
- Describe how diversity has affected American society.

Building Civics Vocabulary
- **Immigrants** leave one country to start a new life in another.
- Unfair treatment of a group of people is **discrimination.**
- **Racism** is the belief that one race is superior to others.

 Focus

America was built by a nation of strangers. From a hundred different places they have poured forth … joining and blending in one mighty and irresistible tide. The land flourished because it was fed from so many sources—because it was nourished by so many cultures and traditions and people.

—*President Lyndon B. Johnson, 1965*

America has often been called a nation of **immigrants,** people who move from one country to make their homes in another. Immigrants brought to America the customs and traditions of their homelands as well as their hopes and dreams for a better life. As you read, think about some of the ways in which diversity has both strengthened our nation and caused difficulties.

Until 1943, Ellis Island in New York Harbor was the "Gateway to the New World" for millions of European immigrants.

European Americans

Among the first immigrants to the lands that became the United States were Europeans seeking religious freedom, political freedom, and opportunities to have their own farms and businesses. In the 1600s and 1700s they came mostly from England, Ireland, and Scotland, bringing their language—English— and their traditions of government, which would deeply influence the future nation.

Many settlers also arrived from Germany, France, the Netherlands, and Scandinavia. A majority of these immigrants were Protestants, although Catholics and Jews also found a haven in the young society.

The years between 1830 and 1920 saw the arrival of waves of Central and Eastern Europeans, including Germans, Slavs, and Russians. Denied political and economic freedom at home, these immigrants, many of them Jews, sought new opportunities in the United States. Meanwhile, Irish, Italians, Greeks, and others suffering from crop failures and lack of adequate farm lands also immigrated in large numbers.

Although European Americans came from the same continent, these immigrants were in

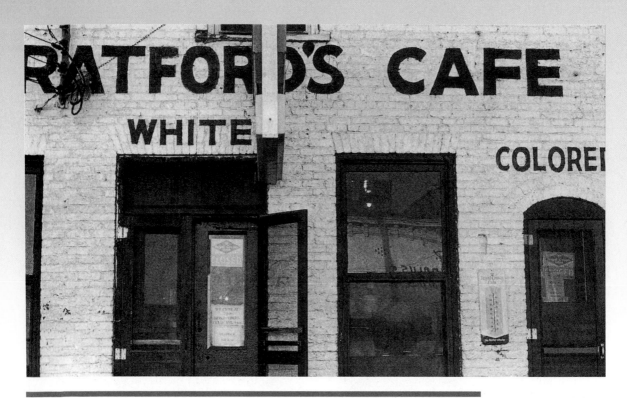

Separate doorways for blacks and whites are a thing of the past. However, black Americans still suffer from other forms of discrimination today.

many ways more diverse than they were alike. For example, they had grown up under different forms of government, and they spoke many different languages. They ranged from highly educated to unable to read or write, and they were accustomed to very different kinds of food, music, and clothing styles. They had different forms of worship. They celebrated different holidays—or the same holidays in different ways.

Immigrants from different European countries tended to settle in different parts of the United States. That is why you may still hear German spoken in Pennsylvania farm towns, attend a Norwegian church in Minnesota, or sit down to a Polish dinner in Chicago.

Although the waves of immigrants from Europe have dwindled in comparison with the past, European Americans still make up the largest segment of our population.

African Americans

Unlike immigrants who came to America by choice, African Americans did not come here voluntarily. Their African ancestors were brought to this country as slaves, beginning in early colonial times and continuing until the slave trade was ended in 1808.

Struggle for Equality The burden of two hundred years of slavery has been a difficult one. Although slavery was ended legally in 1865, it has taken a long time to change the way African Americans are treated.

Both by law and by custom, African Americans have suffered from discrimination, the unfair treatment of a group of people compared with another group. Because of discrimination, black Americans have not always had the same rights and opportunities as white Americans.

For many years, in various communities and states, African Americans were barred from voting, from attending schools with white students, and from living in neighborhoods with whites. Many restaurants, hotels, and theaters had signs warning "For Whites Only." Even public buses had seats reserved for whites, with black riders having to sit or stand in the back.

Discrimination is the result of racism, the belief that members of one's own race are superior to those of other races. Laws and practices that discriminate against blacks have been outlawed in the United States, but less visible kinds of discrimination persist in our society because of racism.

Since the era of slavery, courageous African Americans have struggled against racism and sought to obtain equal treatment for their people. From the 1960s to the present, inspired by the example of leaders like the Reverend Dr. Martin Luther King, Jr., African Americans in all parts of the United States have called attention to the unequal treatment that their people have received. As a result, opportunities in education, jobs, and housing have expanded.

However, equal treatment for all is a goal that has not yet been completely achieved. Many African Americans live in poverty due to lack of opportunities.

Hispanic Americans

Hispanic Americans share a common heritage from Spanish-speaking countries. (The Latin name for Spain is Hispania.) Many also share a common religion, Catholicism. Hispanic Americans can be of any race. As our nation expanded in the 1800s, it added areas that had been settled mostly by Spaniards and later by people from Mexico, then a Spanish colony. The inhabitants of these regions—including the present-day states of Florida, Louisiana, Texas, Arizona, New Mexico, and California—became American citizens.

 U.S. POPULATION BY GROUP, 2000

Group	Population (in millions)	Approximate Percentage of Total
European American	217	69%
African American	36	13%
Hispanic American	35	13%
Asian American	12	4%
Native American	4	2%

Note: Percentages may not add up to 100 due to rounding.
Source: U.S. Census Bureau

 Americans come from every continent. **Diversity Approximately how many Native Americans lived in the United States in 2000?**

Today, people from Mexico and the Spanish-speaking countries of Central and South America and the Caribbean make up one of the largest groups immigrating to the United States. Fleeing economic hardship and political persecution at home, they have come seeking better jobs and lives for themselves and their families.

Finding Opportunities Making a place for themselves in this country has been easier for some Hispanics than for others. Those with training in business or other professions have often made the quickest adjustment.

Other Hispanic immigrants find the transition to a new land difficult. Like many European immigrants who came before them, many of these newcomers do not speak English and do not have the skills they need to support themselves in our complex, technologically oriented economy.

Furthermore, like African Americans, they often feel the effects of racism. As a result, many Hispanic Americans can find only low-paying jobs.

Like immigrant groups in the past, and like African Americans, Hispanics are beginning to work together to improve their opportunities. Hispanic labor leaders are pressing for better working conditions, while voters are electing Hispanics to political offices, where they can represent the interests of these new Americans.

Asian Americans

Among the first Asians to come to America were young men from farm villages in southeastern China. They had heard tales of the discovery of gold in California in 1849 and came to North America to make money to send home to their families.

Like others lured by the gold rush, many Chinese set up small businesses to supply the miners' needs. Later arrivals found work building the railroads of the West and working on farms and in fisheries. As Japanese workers began to arrive, they also prospered in farming and business.

Exclusion of Asians The success of these Asian immigrants bred resentment and racism among other groups, who accused the Asians of taking away jobs by working for lower wages. As a result of such protests, laws were passed in 1882 and 1907 prohibiting any further immigration from China and Japan.

The last of these Asian "exclusion" laws were repealed in 1952. Since then, Asians have been coming to the United States in increasing numbers. After 1972, immigrants from the Southeast Asian countries of Vietnam, Laos, and Cambodia began arriving, driven from their homes by the effects of wars and revolutions.

At present there are over ten million Asian Americans living in the United States. Their numbers have nearly doubled in the last ten years. They speak many different languages and practice a number of different religions—including Christianity, Buddhism, Hinduism, and Islam.

Like Hispanic and African Americans, Asian Americans vary greatly in their educational backgrounds, and thus in the kinds of jobs they can hold. Trained scientists and engineers have made significant contributions to the nation's progress in medicine, physics, and electronics. Meanwhile, other Asian immigrants often struggle to find ways to support their families.

Native Americans

Not all Americans are immigrants or descendants of immigrants. People had been living on the North American continent thousands of years before Columbus and later explorers reached America. Today, descendants of these original inhabitants of our country call themselves Native Americans or American Indians.

These people were themselves very diverse, made up of many groups with differing languages and traditions. Some groups relied on farming, while others hunted, fished, and gathered wild plants to feed and clothe themselves. A few groups built large cities, and others lived in villages or moved from place to place. Different groups had different religious beliefs, and they cultivated different art forms, including pottery, painting, wood carving, and basketry.

When the first European settlers came to our shores, Native Americans often welcomed them and helped them adapt to the unfamiliar conditions they found. As more and more settlers arrived, they began to compete with the Native Americans for farm land and hunting grounds.

Although Native Americans fought for their lands in many bloody battles, they were gradually pushed west, often onto land that was not suitable to their traditional way of life. By the late 1800s, wars with settlers and the effects of the unfamiliar diseases the set-

Actress Promotes Native American Pride

Do you recognize Irene Bedard? Even if you have never seen her face, you may know her voice. She performed the speaking voice of Pocahontas—the Indian who helped English settlers in Virginia—in two popular animated films. This Native American actress also has another well known voice—one which speaks out for Native Americans in the arts.

Bedard, of Inupiat Eskimo and Canadian Cree heritage, grew up in Alaska. She recalls that as a child she watched neighborhood children playing cowboys and Indians. "Nobody wanted to be the Indians because they were the bad guys. This image of Native Americans was one children picked up very early from movies and TV."

After attending drama school in Philadelphia, Bedard moved to New York City where she acted in many plays and helped start a theater company that presented plays by and about Native Americans. "We started the group," says Bedard, "because we were frustrated by very stiff, unrealistic depictions of Native Americans in movies, TV, and other media."

Bedard has starred in several movies, including

Lakota Woman, which tells the story of a 1973 Native American protest at Wounded Knee, South Dakota. "What was so great about *Lakota Woman*," says Bedard, "was that it showed the character's pride in her culture and depicted Native Americans today."

As Bedard gains experience and fame, she continues working to draw attention on the richness of Native American culture. Bedard believes that as more Native Americans have a chance to write and produce their own movies, there will be "more films about who we are now, who we were, and who we have always been."

Active Citizenship

In what ways has Irene Bedard worked to promote a greater understanding of her heritage?

tlers brought with them had taken their toll, and many thousands of Indians had died. Today, about two million people are Native Americans, a very small percentage of the population of what was once their homeland.

Living in Modern America Trying to balance their religious and social traditions with efforts to support themselves in our modern society poses a great challenge to Native Americans today. They are meeting

Just as thousands of tiles fit together to form a mosaic, so all the diverse individuals and groups in the United States fit together to form our nation.

this challenge in a number of ways. For example, some groups are developing oil and other mineral resources on their lands, while others are building tourist businesses. Many groups are pressing the government for greater control of their reservation lands and for payments for lands illegally taken from them when treaties were broken.

Many Native Americans realize that to prepare themselves for the future, they must overcome the handicaps of poverty and lack of education. Thus, there has been a steady increase in the number of Native Americans seeking higher education in business, medicine, law, education, and other professions, through which they can contribute to the progress of their people and their nation.

The American Identity

In this description of Americans, you have again seen that we are a very diverse people. America is often called a "melting pot." This term reflects the idea that people from all over the world came here and melted into American society, giving up the heritage of their native lands. Most immigrants participate in the American way of life.

However, many immigrants have continued to speak their native language in their homes and with friends, and to follow their native customs. You can see evidence of these diverse customs in the wide variety of international foods we can buy. Throughout the year, parades celebrate the special days of different nationality groups: St. Patrick's Day for the Irish, Columbus Day for the Italians, Chinese New Year. Radio and television stations broadcast in a variety of languages.

Such examples of our cultural differences make clear that Americans have not melted together to form one identity. Instead of giving up our separate cultures, we have retained parts of them and, in the process, have enriched American culture as a whole.

The American Mosaic Have you ever seen a piece of mosaic (moh ZAY ik) artwork? A mosaic is made of small tiles of different sizes, shapes, and colors. When they are all fitted together, these diverse tiles create a whole picture.

Like mosaic tiles, all the diverse individuals and groups in the United States fit together to form a whole nation. Thus, when we ask ourselves, "Who are Americans?" we may answer that they are part—not of a melting pot—but of a mosaic in which each different tile is an essential part of the picture. That picture is American society.

Section 2 Assessment

1. **Define** immigrants, discrimination, racism
2. List and explain four reasons why people from other countries came to America.
3. What are the five major groups of Americans? What do members of each group have in common?
4. **Apply** Think about your school and community and what you see in newspapers and magazines and on television. What evidence can you find that American society is a mosaic made up of contributions from many cultures?

The Values That Unite Us

SECTION PREVIEW

Objectives
- Describe how American values continue to attract immigrants.
- Define the basic values that unite us as a nation.
- Explore why our society does not always reflect our ideals.

Building Civics Vocabulary
- **Beliefs** are ideas that we trust are true.
- **Values** are our standards of behavior.
- With **equality**, everyone has the same rights and opportunities.
- **Freedom** is the opportunity to make personal and public choices.
- Every American has the right to **justice**, or fairness.

 **Focus**

Each American is part of the cultural mosaic that makes up American society. As you have learned, we are a diverse people. Despite our differences, we have survived as a nation for more than two hundred years. What unites us as one people, one nation?

Americans are held together by certain shared beliefs and values. Beliefs are certain ideas that we trust are true. Values are our standards of behavior. Values help us decide how we should act and how we should live our lives. They are the guidelines for how we should treat each other. Shared beliefs and values form the glue that keeps our cultural mosaic together.

Equal Respect: The American Dream

The beliefs and values on which our nation was founded have attracted many of the immigrants who have chosen to make their homes in the United States. Peter Ky remembers when his father first spoke of leaving Vietnam:

66 *My father was discouraged by how hard life was for us in Vietnam. We had so little freedom and so few opportunities to improve our lives. My father said that in America, people were treated with respect and dignity. We would have a chance to make a good life for ourselves there.* 99

Mr. Ky's dream of a better life in America is based on a basic American belief: that everyone, regardless of age, sex, race, wealth, opinions, or education, has worth and importance. We believe that all people—unique tiles in our cultural mosaic—deserve the same chance to realize their full potential and to contribute their talents and ideas to society. In other words, every person has the right to be treated with equal respect.

Basic American Values

The American belief that all people deserve equal respect is supported by three basic values: equality, freedom (sometimes called liberty), and justice. To see what these values mean, consider the experiences of Doris Hollingsworth. Doris, an African American woman, often relied on these three values to support her efforts to gain equal respect as a computer analyst, which is traditionally a white, male occupation.

Equality Equal respect is based on the belief that every person can contribute to society. In order to make this contribution, each person must have the same rights and opportunities in life as any other person. The condition of everyone having the same rights and opportunities is called equality.

Doris Hollingsworth learned that even though equality is one of our basic values, equal opportunity is not always available in America. She recalls:

66 *Job hunting was tough at first. I thought I'd never get that first interview. Then, when I walked into the room, the interview committee—all white men—looked at me and then at each other as if to say, "We knew she was a woman, but black, too?"*

Facts & Quotes

Equality, Freedom, and Justice

Throughout our history, Americans have cherished the three basic American values. We read about them. We recite them. We even sing songs about them. Here are some lines that may be familiar to you. Do you know where they come from?

1. "let freedom ring"
2. "all men are created equal"
3. "with liberty and justice for all"
4. "the land of the free"
5. "sweet land of liberty"
6. "to establish justice...and secure the blessings of liberty"

Answers: 1. "My Country 'Tis of Thee," **2.** Declaration of Independence, **3.** Pledge of Allegiance, **4.** "The Star-Spangled Banner," **5.** "My Country 'Tis of Thee," **6.** Preamble to the Constitution

I didn't get the job, and I have a strong feeling that my being a black woman had something to do with it. **"**

Doris's experience is not uncommon. Even though discrimination because of race or sex is against the law, it still affects the lives of many people.

In this chapter you have learned just how varied the backgrounds, lifestyles, and occupations of Americans can be. Everyone has different skills and abilities. You may be a natural at math, for example, while your friend's greatest talent is on the soccer field.

Our opportunities in life may be limited by our abilities. Your friend may be less likely to get a job as a math teacher than you are. Our opportunities may also be limited by our energy and interests. Although your friend could have a career as a soccer player, he or she might not like training so hard and traveling so much. However, our race, sex, religion, background, and opinions should not be used to deny us an equal chance to succeed in life.

Doris, confident of her ability and training, knew she had the right to an equal opportunity. Says Doris:

"*I didn't give up. I had interviews at many companies. Then I finally landed a job with a company that judges me by the quality of my work, not by the color of my skin or by my sex. It feels good to work where I'm treated as an equal.* **"**

Freedom When you try to define freedom, you may explain that it means having the ability to say what you want, go where you want, choose the friends you want. Doris knows that freedom also means being able to choose where you want to work and with whom. She says:

"*Thinking back on that first interview, I know I wouldn't have accepted the*

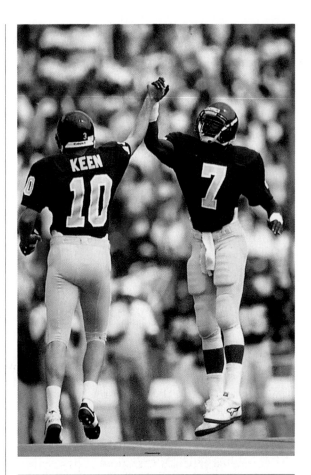

Working and playing together on the football field, these athletes have an equal opportunity to develop their talents and skills.

job even if it had been offered to me. I just didn't feel comfortable with the men on that committee. It was good to know that I was free to look for a job that I felt better about. **"**

If you believe in equal respect, you give the same freedoms to others that you expect for yourself. However, you must not be so free in your actions or beliefs that you interfere with someone else's freedom.

For example, you are free to listen to music you like. However, if you walk down the street playing your favorite CD at full volume, you may interfere with the right of other people to stroll quietly or listen to their own music. Can you think of another situation in which your freedom is limited because of respect for others' freedom?

Justice The third basic value, justice, can also be thought of as fairness. Equal respect includes the idea that every person deserves to be treated fairly. For example, you should not be paid more or get better grades or a better job because of your race, sex, or connections to powerful or well-known people.

Justice, however, does not require that people always be treated the same. In the work place, for example, people with greater skills and experience are rewarded with more pay or responsibility than those with fewer skills or less experience. Differences in pay are considered fair if they are based on differences in skill and experience.

When Doris was hired, she became the newest employee in the company. She made less money than employees who had worked there longer and were more experienced. As Doris continued to work for the company, she gained experience and showed her ability to do a good job. Her pay was then raised to match that of people with equal experience and performance.

Citizens and the American Ideal

The glue that holds American society together is our shared belief in equal respect and in values such as equality, freedom, and justice. These beliefs and values form an ideal, or model, of the kind of nation we want the United States to be. We judge our society by how well we are living up to this ideal.

An Imperfect Society Our history and the headlines in our daily newspapers show that we do not always achieve our ideal. Peter Ky found that his first few years in the United States were sometimes difficult. In Vietnam he had been told that everyone in America enjoyed freedom and equality. However, he found out that this statement did not always represent the truth.

Peter recalls something that happened when he was nine years old and had been in his new homeland for only one year.

> **❝**I was out in the street playing with some kids. Two older boys began choosing teams for kickball. The other kids begged to be picked. My English wasn't so good, so I kept quiet. Finally, I was the only one left to be picked—and I was the only Asian in the bunch. The two boys stared at me. "You take him," one said, pointing at me. "Forget it," the other replied. "I don't want him on my team." He looked at me. "What's the matter?" he jeered, "Don't you speak English?" Then he pulled at the corners of his eyes, to make them slanted, and laughed. I ran home cry-

Although the society around them is imperfect, young people like these can live the American ideal by treating each other with equal respect.

*ing. That was my first experience
with racism. I'll never forget it.
Never.* 🙴

Peter Ky's story illustrates that, while our nation is held together by the belief in equal respect for all, everyone does not live according to this ideal. The difference between the ideal of equal respect and its reality shows us the work that still needs to be done to ensure that the rights of all Americans to equality, freedom, and justice are protected.

Extending the Chapter

Global Views

Americans represent a mosaic of peoples from nearly every land. If each of us traces our roots back in time, we may end up in a Chinese city, an Italian seaport, an African village, a Mexican town, or any of a thousand other places. Compared to American Indians, who have called this home for over 10,000 years, other Americans are newcomers. Whether our ancestors arrived 400 years ago or 4 years ago, most came from somewhere else.

People are still leaving their homelands in search of better lives. Many are refugees from wars or have fled to escape persecution. Others look for jobs in nations with booming economies. While many come here, others go to countries such as Germany or Saudi Arabia.

Any country that accepts many immigrants faces the challenge of fitting them into its society. Immigrants contribute to a country's economy and culture, but the host country must provide services such as housing, transportation, medical care, and education. A healthy economy makes it easier to provide such help. But if many citizens are unemployed, they may resent immigrants as competitors for jobs and government services.

Despite the problems that arise, immigration brings many benefits. Immigrants' skills and hard work improve the economy, as new ideas, products, and technologies are exchanged. The host country is enriched by a greater variety in music, dance, literature, and film.

Although many other countries have a mosaic of peoples, no other nation is as varied as ours—shaped by native peoples, slaves, immigrants, and their descendants. Diverse backgrounds have often led to conflict, but we have unity as a country because we share common political, legal, and economic systems. These systems reflect the shared values and ideals that hold us together as a nation. The benefits that come from the ideal of equal respect make it possible for diverse individuals to live and work together.

How to MAKE A GOOD DECISION

Picture yourself in the following situation: You leave school on Friday, thinking about a long report that is due Monday. Suddenly some friends remind you that the money for the school candy sale has to be turned in on Monday. When they ask if you can help sell candy, you say that you are not sure because you have homework to do. They reply, "Well, let us know when you are through making up your mind."

"Making up your mind" is another way of saying "making a decision." You make decisions, or choices, every day. Some, such as deciding what to have for breakfast or which movie to see, are not very important. Others, as in the situation above, should be carefully thought out. Unfortunately, people sometimes put little thought into making important decisions. They might choose friends or school activities almost as quickly as they pick a cereal for breakfast.

Explain the Skill

Important decisions should be carefully thought out because the quality of your life may depend on them. Good decision making is a process that includes two main parts:

Choosing: Setting a goal—deciding what it is you want, and then selecting the best way to achieve it.

Taking Action: Planning how to take action and then doing what you planned.

Making good decisions is an important part of being a citizen because your choices may affect your family, friends, relatives, neighbors, fellow students, and other people in your community.

Analyze The Skill

You have read that we are largely a nation of immigrants. In the following account, Carlos Lopez, an immigrant from Latin America, explains how he and his wife decided to move their family to the United States. Think about what specific steps they went through in making their decision.

Food was scarce in our town, and prices were going up fast. Conditions at the sugar company where I worked were very bad. When we went on strike, many of us were put in prison. My wife, Maria, joined a group that was protesting cruel treatment of prisoners and worked for my release. After opponents of this group killed several members, Maria was terrified. She feared that our house was being watched and that our children might be hurt.

We wanted our children to live comfortably, to get a good education, to have opportunities to earn a good living, and to enjoy peaceful lives. We had to decide how to achieve these things. After I was released from prison, we listed options and carefully considered each one.

One option was to stay where we were, hoping that conditions would change. Maria could earn money by washing clothes. However, there was no work for me. I could have joined a group fighting against the government, but I refused. Even though they promised to provide food and protection for my family, I did not believe in using violence.

If we moved to the city, I would have a better chance of finding a job. However, in the city people who protested cruel treatment of prisoners were threatened and often killed. We had already received death threats.

A third option was to move to the United States. The journey would cost us our home and all our savings, and we would leave behind our friends. Also, our children might have difficulty learning English, and we might have trouble finding jobs. Still, we knew that Americans were friendly to people like us. Also, Maria and I already knew some English, and our children would have a chance for a good education and a prosperous life. We decided to move to the United States.

After deciding what to do, we had to plan how to do it. To get money, I sold our furniture. Maria wrote to some American friends who agreed to help us get permission to enter the United States. We figured out how to travel there and where to live.

We thought we could stay in our country while waiting to hear from our American friends. However, when we were questioned about our protests, we feared that any delay would cost us our lives. Therefore we traveled to Mexico.

After many weeks our permits to stay in Mexico were about to run out, and we still had not received permission to enter the United States. I contacted our American friends, who arranged for us to meet government leaders in Washington, D.C. After describing our problem, we were granted permission to live in the United States.

Now that we are living in America, we have looked back at how we decided to come here. We realize now that we did not think about the possible effects on our relatives. We worry that the same people who threatened our lives might threaten theirs. Our relatives face a long struggle for equal respect and justice.

If we had to make the decision over again, we would consider the effects on our relatives. However, we would probably still make the same choice. In the United States we have the best chance of being treated equally and fairly. We have found jobs and are living with friends until we can find a place of our own. School is hard for our children, but they are learning quickly. Our goal of giving our children productive, peaceful lives has been achieved.

Skill Assessment

Now that you have examined how Carlos and Maria Lopez made their decision, answer the following questions.

1. What goals did they set? What caused them to set these goals?
2. What options did they consider as ways to achieve their goals?
3. What actions did they take to achieve their goals?
4. In considering the first option, which did Carlos and Maria identify? Explain your answer. **(a)** only good points **(b)** only bad points **(c)** good and bad points
5. In considering the second option, which did Carlos and Maria identify? Explain your answer. **(a)** only good points **(b)** good and bad points **(c)** only bad points
6. In considering the third option, what did Carlos and Maria decide? Explain your answer. **(a)** the good points outweighed the bad points **(b)** they would automatically choose it because the other options were unacceptable **(c)** they should seek the advice of their relatives
7. In taking action to achieve their goals, which of the following did Carlos and Maria not do? **(a)** adjust their plan when the situation changed **(b)** decide what they needed in order to get out of the country **(c)** postpone making plans about where to live in the United States
8. Describe the two main parts of decision making.
9. To make good decisions, there are a number of steps you should take. Name one of them and explain why it is important.

How to **READ A BAR GRAPH**

Use the *Simulations and Data Graphing* **CD-ROM** to create and interpret graphs.

In this chapter, you read about some of the ways the American population is changing. Bar graphs provide an excellent way to present population data in a visual and easy-to-read format.

Explain the Skill

When you read a bar graph, first determine the subject of the graph by reading its title. Read the title of the bar graph below—The Birth Rate, 1910–2000. The birth rate is the number of babies born each year per 1,000 women.

What is being measured by this graph? To figure this out, study the graph's labels. Bar graphs usually have labels on both the vertical axis (up-and-down) and horizontal axis (side-to-side). On this graph, the number of births is shown on the vertical axis.

The Birth Rate, 1910–2000

Source: U.S. Bureau of the Census and National Center for Health Statistics

The horizontal axis identifies the years covered by the graph. Each bar in the graph represents the average number of births that occurred in a given year. In 1970, for example, an average of 18.4 babies were born each year for every 1,000 women.

Analyze the Skill

"What conclusions can I draw from this graph?" To answer this question, study the height of the bars in the birth rate graph. The height of the bars will reveal trends, or patterns that occurred over a long period of time. Overall, you can draw the conclusion that the birth rate fell during the first third of the twentieth century, then rose during the middle third, then fell again in the last third, reaching a low point at the end of the century.

Skill Assessment

Use the bar graph on this page to answer the following questions.

1. During what year shown on the graph did the birth rate fall to its lowest level? How does the birth rate during this year compare with the highest rate?
2. Between 1930 and 1945 the United States went through the Great Depression and World War II. How did these events affect the nation's birth rate?
3. After World War II ended in 1945, the United States experienced a baby boom, or rapid rise in the number of babies born. About how long did the baby boom last?
4. Looking at the graph as a whole, would you say that the birth rate has generally gone up or down since 1910?

CHAPTER 1 ASSESSMENT

Building Civics Vocabulary

The vocabulary terms in each pair listed below are related to each other. For each pair, explain how the two terms are related.

Example: *Freedom* is related to *justice* because both are basic American values.

1. *immigrants* and *diversity*
2. *freedom* and *values*
3. *discrimination* and *equality*

Reviewing Main Ideas and Skills

4. Describe three ways in which the population of the United States has changed over the years. Explain why each type of change has occurred.

5. Explain how the experiences of people in each of the following groups are both similar and diverse. **(a)** European Americans **(b)** Hispanic Americans **(c)** Native Americans

6. What are some ways that African Americans, Asians, Hispanics, and Native Americans have been treated unfairly?

7. **How to Make a Good Decision** Suppose you have to decide what to do during the upcoming summer. How would you go about making this decision?

8. **How to Read a Bar Graph** What can you determine by reading the labels on the vertical axis and horizontal axis of a bar graph?

Critical Thinking

9. **Drawing Conclusions** What are the advantages of immigration and diversity? The disadvantages?

10. **Analyzing Ideas** Why is racism in conflict with the ideal of equal respect?

11. **Linking Past and Present** Which three basic values have helped the United States survive for over 200 years? How have they helped unite Americans?

Writing About Civics

12. **Writing a Speech** Suppose you are running for school president and you have to give a speech on the subject "Why is it important to treat each person with respect?" Write a short speech dealing with this issue. Use at least four of the following terms: freedom, justice, equality, discrimination, immigrants, diverse.

Citizenship Activities

13. **Your Local Community** Visit your local supermarket and find the international or foreign foods section. Make a list of all the foods you see that are associated with a different country. Group these foods according to their country of origin.

 Take It to the NET

Access the **Civics: Participating in Government** Internet site at **www.phschool.com** for the specific URLs to complete the activity.

Explore online information on your state's population. Has it increased or decreased over the last fifty years? Create a chart showing any changes in the population of your state over the last fifty years. How might this change affect your state? If the population of your state has not changed significantly, explain why this might be so.

CHAPTER 2

American Society and Its Values

Citizenship and You

On September 11, 2001, Americans reacted with horror when terrorists struck at targets in New York City and near Washington, D.C. Using hijacked commercial airplanes as their weapons, the terrorists crashed into both towers of New York's World Trade Center and plowed into part of the Pentagon—the headquarters of the nation's Department of Defense. A fourth hijacked plane crashed in a field near Pittsburgh, Pennsylvania. Approximately 3,000 people lost their lives in these attacks.

Americans responded to the tragedy with an outpouring of support for the victims, their families, and the rescue workers at all three sites. Many gave blood or donated money and supplies to relief agencies. The country stood united in its grief. As American citizens struggled to make sense of the terrible events and mourned the losses, a new sense of patriotism and unity swept the nation. American flags appeared on homes, cars, businesses and public spaces. Signs with the words "United We Stand" appeared. Both the flags and the slogan became symbols of the nation's determination to seek justice, uphold American values, and emerge from adversity strengthened and whole.

What's Ahead in Chapter 2

Following the terrorist attacks, Americans came together in groups to support each other and to offer help. In this chapter you will read about why people belong to groups and how groups influence what we believe and how we act.

Section 1 **Groups and Institutions**

Section 2 **Family, Religion, and Education**

Section 3 **The Economy**

Section 4 **Government**

Keep It Current

Items marked with this logo are periodically updated on the Internet. To keep up-to-date, go to **www.phschool.com**

Citizen's Journal

Many people found that the events of September 11, 2001, deepened their appreciation for their country and its values. Write a paragraph in which you describe the American values that are most important to you.

Groups and Institutions: Meeting Needs and Sharing Values

SECTION PREVIEW

Objectives
- Explain why people form groups.
- Describe the five major social institutions.

Building Civics Vocabulary
- **Rules** are specific expectations of what our behavior should be.
- **Socialization** is the process of learning how to participate in a group.
- **Social institutions** are systems of values and rules that determine how our society is organized.

Focus

Everybody has needs. For example, people have physical needs for such things as food and shelter. They have emotional needs such as the desire for love and companionship. They have spiritual needs for answers to questions about the purpose of life and what happens after death.

People form groups to satisfy many of their physical, emotional, and spiritual needs. Of course, simply being born makes you a member of some groups, such as your family, a particular religion, and a nation. You are required to join other groups, such as a school, and you choose some groups, such as clubs and circles of friends. In any case, groups meet particular needs in people's lives. By looking at an informal group—a group of friends—it may be easier to understand how groups meet our needs and how they influence our values.

As you read, it is important to remember the difference between values and rules. Values are standards that guide our behavior. Rules are specific expectations about what our behavior should be. Rules are based on values. Because our society holds the value that education is important, for example, our schools have made certain rules that help students become educated.

A Group of Friends

Peter Ky's best friends are Alex and Carol. The three of them spend a lot of time together. They have this to say about their friendship:

Peter:
I trust Carol and Alex. They've helped me when I've been down. They listen and let me be myself.

Carol:
These guys make me laugh. But I also know that when things get bad, they'll be there to help me out.

Alex:
Without Peter and Carol, I'd have no one to go to the beach with or to call for biology notes.

As a group, Carol, Alex, and Peter's goal is to provide each other with companionship and a sense of belonging. This goal can be expressed as a value: it is important to be a good friend. The group has two other values: it is important to help your friends, and you should let members be themselves.

These values are the basis of unwritten rules—friends take time to listen to each other, and friends share expenses. Following these rules ensures that Alex, Carol, and Peter remain friends and thus continue to meet their needs for companionship and a sense of belonging.

A group of friends shares common values and rules of behavior. A new member will need to learn these rules.

Becoming a Group Member The process of learning how to participate in a group is called socialization. Socialization also means learning to accept the values of a group and learning the rules for behavior within it. A new girl in school, Melissa, went through the process of socialization when she joined Peter, Alex, and Carol's group.

Melissa met Peter, Alex, and Carol in biology class, and she quickly became a regular in their group. The friendship ran into trouble in one area, however. "I was kind of thoughtless when they first met me," remembers Melissa.

On one occasion, Melissa agreed to meet her new friends at the beach at two o'clock. She did not take the meeting time seriously and finally showed up just before four. Alex tells what happened next:

“*She was so cool about being late, it really got us mad. We had been worried about her. Peter had to be back at work by five o'clock. Our afternoon was ruined. We told her that if she was going to be late, for no good reason, she could go to the beach alone next time. Then she got mad and stormed off.* ”

Without realizing it, Melissa had run into one of the group's important values: being a good friend means being considerate. One of the rules based on this value is that everyone should show up for activities on time. Melissa had broken this rule, which brought her into conflict with the group.

Melissa missed her friends. "I called them," relates Melissa. "I told them that I was sorry and that I would really try to watch the clock better." Melissa's need for friendship led her to accept the group's values and to agree to change her behavior. By socializing new members, groups can continue to meet their members' needs.

Groups, then, have a powerful influence over your behavior and beliefs. Think of all the groups to which you belong, such as friends, teams, and clubs. Much of your life is shaped by these groups.

Institutions That Affect Us All

Although groups are important, they do not satisfy all of our needs. For example, they do not provide food or products such as clothing and houses. They do not make laws or help govern our society.

These functions, which groups are unable to perform by themselves, are taken care of by social institutions, systems of values and rules that determine how our society is organized. Five major social institutions in our society are the family, religion, education, the economy, and government.

Every society needs these five institutions in one form or another. Social institutions not only satisfy needs and teach values, they also provide a framework within which groups and organizations can exist.

Your family, for example, is a group. This group is part of the institution of the family, which provides the framework for how a family is set up and how it works in our society. Parents do not just make up the ideas that they will raise their children and that they will have the power to make rules for their children's behavior. These ideas come from the institution of the family.

In Chapter 1 you learned that shared values make it possible for Americans to live and work together as a society. It is through the process of socialization in our five social institutions that we learn those values.

Section 1 Assessment

1. **Define** rules, socialization, social institutions
2. What are some of the reasons that people join groups?
3. What are the five major social institutions?
4. **Apply** Think of several groups to which you belong. What needs of yours does each group meet?

Family, Religion, and Education: Society's Training Grounds

SECTION PREVIEW

Objectives
- Identify ways that families meet their needs.
- Explain why religious groups are important to many people.
- Describe why our society provides schools.

 **Focus**

The institutions of the family, religion, and education play very important parts in shaping the behavior and the values of the members of society. As you read this section, think about how these institutions affect you and the people you know.

The Family: Your First Institution

The family is the most basic institution in any society. From birth you depend on your family to provide you with food, clothing, and shelter, and to give you a sense of security and belonging. Your family also teaches you many of the values you need to participate in society and contribute to it.

What is a family? Many Americans think of the typical family as a husband at work and a wife at home with two or three children. Today, however, only about one in twenty American families fits that picture.

Many changes have taken place in the American family over the past century. Families are now smaller. As the cost of raising and educating children rises, and as more women work outside the home, couples are deciding to have fewer children, or none.

Even the typical family structure of father, mother, and children is changing. Because divorce is increasingly common, and more unmarried mothers are choosing to raise their babies alone, many families consist of a single parent—either a mother or a father—and one or more children. Some families are "blended families" made up of adults and their children from previous marriages. Children whose parents are not able to care for them may become part of other families through adoption or foster care.

Almost any arrangement of children living with adults who meet their physical and emotional needs can be considered a family today. That family plays a very important part in preparing the children to take their place in society.

Meeting Needs Imagine moving to a distant country where the people speak a language you do not understand. You cannot read the billboards, street signs, or newspapers; they are written in a language that uses an alphabet completely different from your own. The air is filled with sounds and smells you do not recognize. You feel completely confused.

Peter Ky had this experience when he first arrived in San Francisco. "Coming to America from Vietnam terrified me at first," Peter remembers. "Everything was so strange. I couldn't talk to anyone. I didn't know how to act." Luckily, he was not alone. "I had my family. We gave each other a lot of support. And we made it. We survived."

Peter's comments illustrate that your happiness depends on whether or not you feel secure. Feeling secure includes believing that you are safe and that you will be protected and cared for. You also need to have a sense of belonging, which is the knowledge that you are important and that no one else could take your place.

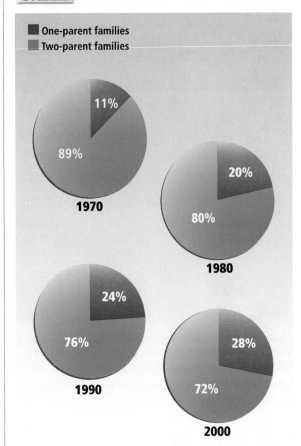

GRAPH SKILL FAMILIES WITH CHILDREN UNDER 18

■ One-parent families
■ Two-parent families

1970: 11%, 89%
1980: 20%, 80%
1990: 24%, 76%
2000: 28%, 72%

Source: U.S. Bureau of the Census

The percentage of one-parent families rose during the last 30 years of the twentieth century. **Diversity What percentage of families with children under 18 had two parents in 1980?**

Your family can meet these needs. It can provide you with a safe, secure environment in which to grow and learn. It can act as an "anchor point"—a support base—while you learn to become an independent, contributing member of society.

There are many types of families in the United States. A growing number of families are made up of one parent with several children.

Rules of Daily Life The family is the first group to which you belong and from which you learn many of the rules that govern daily life. Here is a list of some of the rules that a teenager might learn at home:

★ *Do* take out the garbage.
★ *Do* keep your room clean.
★ *Do* be polite to adults.
★ *Do* finish your homework.

★ *Do not* use bad language.
★ *Do not* leave the kitchen a mess.
★ *Do not* let the dog loose.
★ *Do not* use the phone too much.

Such rules reflect a set of values that parents think their children ought to live by: being responsible, clean, and respectful of others.

Every teenager has experienced punishments for breaking such rules. Being "grounded" for staying out too late is probably a familiar one. Of course, there are rewards for following the rules, too, such as praise from your parents, and being given more freedom.

How the Family Benefits Society The rules of conduct you learn at home do not disappear when you step out the door. For example, your parents have taught you to put trash in the garbage can rather than let it pile up on the floor. Society has created similar rules called laws. If you toss your soda can out of the car window, for instance, you are breaking the rule against littering.

This simple example illustrates the point that rules established within the family often reflect the values held by society as a whole. In a real sense, the family benefits society by serving as a kind of training ground for adults-to-be.

Religion: A Source of Support and Guidance

Although not everyone in America belongs to a religious group, the institution of religion plays an important part in our society, as it has in societies throughout history. Religion meets important individual needs, such as the need for comfort in times of sorrow, and the need to find answers to spiritual questions about the meaning of life and death.

Like the family, religious groups can also give people a sense of belonging—in this case a feeling of being part of a community of people who have similar goals and similar ways of looking at life. Religions provide people with moral standards that they can use to judge right from wrong and to decide how they should live their lives.

Two Friends Inspire Their Community

One morning in 1989 two suburban women sat in a fast-food restaurant in Raleigh, North Carolina, waiting for their sons to finish a soccer game. As Jill Staton Bullard and Maxine Solomon watched, workers threw out dozens of unsold breakfast meals. "All that good food wasted," Solomon remembers saying.

But the friends did more than just talk. Together Bullard, who is Christian, and Solomon, who is Jewish, founded the Interfaith Food Shuttle. "In the beginning," said Bullard, "we just wanted to get this great food to people who needed it."

The women began picking up donations and delivering them to a downtown soup kitchen. At first, though, they found only two restaurants willing to give them leftover food. Most feared a loophole in North Carolina's Good Samaritan

law that made them responsible if anyone became ill from eating the food.

In 1992 Bullard worked to convince the state legislature to insure protection of food donors. Once the law was changed, donations of food increased. Over time, not only other restaurants, but grocery stores, airlines, hospitals, hotels, and even the farmers at the state's huge Farmer's Market have joined the Food Shuttle's pick-up program.

Volunteers now collect as much as 10,000 pounds of perishable food a day, distributing it to over 150 food pantries, soup kitchens, homeless shelters, and community centers in local housing projects.

"As it has grown, the Interfaith Food Shuttle has lived up to its name," says Solomon. "We depend on our regular volunteers from church and synagogue youth groups to bag groceries and distribute food."

"Our religions teach us to respect the dignity of every human being," Bullard adds. "Religious faith involves hope and when we give of ourselves to help others, that is certainly a hopeful act."

Active Citizenship

How do the actions of Jill Staton Bullard and Maxine Solomon reflect their religious values?

A Sense of Community Bernice Kelman cannot imagine life without her church. It helps to draw the members together, giving them a sense of belonging to a community that can support them in times of trouble. Bernice says:

❝ *Church keeps us busy. We have services on Sunday and on Wednesday evening. We have youth groups for the kids, women's circles, even a men's choir.*

We know we can count on each other, too. Last year the Smith family lost everything—their house, barn, and crops—in a tornado. At church the following Sunday, we took up a collection. The next week, members of the church rebuilt the Smith's barn. **99**

Bernice Kelman's church provides its members with support. It is a place where members can meet to observe their faith together as one community. The church community gives each member a place to turn when times are bad.

Bernice recalls how religion has helped members of her church cope with unexpected tragedies by giving them comfort and a deeper understanding of life and death:

66*I remember when the Ramsey boy died of cancer. The whole congregation was upset. Our minister, Reverend Williams, showed us that the Ramsey boy had lived a good life, and that we should remember this more than his death. Reverend Williams helped us see that his death had brought us all closer together.* **99**

Rules to Live By Every religion has a moral code that establishes expectations for people's behavior and helps them judge right from wrong. These moral codes can be general guides for behavior, such as the Golden Rule: "Do unto others as you would have them do unto you." They can also include very specific rules, such as "Thou shall not kill," and "Thou shall not steal," two of the Ten Commandments found in the Bible.

A religious group can exert a powerful influence on its members to live according to its rules. Each religion has punishments for those who stray from its moral path. One form of punishment is to withdraw the emotional and spiritual support the group

Demonstrators express their opinions about abortion. Differing religious values can cause conflict in our diverse society.

provides. An individual can also be threatened with punishment after death.

People who follow the rules of their religion are rewarded by the acceptance and approval of the group. Most religions promise faithful members some kind of reward after death. Obeying religious rules and embracing the values they reflect also give people confidence that they are "living right": living lives that are moral and good.

How Religion Affects Society Many of the rules that guide people's behavior in our society are written into laws. However, the members of Bernice's church were not required by law to give money and to work to replace the Smiths' barn. They acted out of their belief that charity—helping others who are less fortunate—is good.

Charity, sympathy, and loyalty to friends and family are values that cannot be written into laws. However, when people live their lives according to such values, the whole society benefits. By teaching values, and by passing them on from generation to generation, the institution of religion makes an important contribution to American society.

Conflicting Religious Values

The diverse people who make up the cultural mosaic described in Chapter 1 belong to many religious groups. In fact, more than 1,200 different religious groups can be found in the United States today.

Not all of these religious groups share the same values and rules. If one religious group tries to impose its values on the rest of society and make everyone follow its rules, serious conflicts can arise. In the United States today, disagreements about such issues as the teaching of evolution are often based on the values of different religious groups.

As we debate such issues, we face the challenge of balancing two of our most important rights: freedom of speech and freedom of religion. One test of whether or not we as Americans are living up to our ideal of equal respect is whether members of religious groups can act according to their own beliefs and values while still respecting the right of others to hold different beliefs.

Education: More Than ABC's

Think back to your first days in elementary school. There were dozens of new rules to learn. You had to come on time, raise your hand to be called on, stand in line, and sit quietly at your desk. There were new names to remember and new games to learn. Soon you were practicing your ABC's, counting, and learning to write with a pencil.

Many of the rules and skills were new to you. You had not needed to know them to get along in your family and your neighborhood. However, as you moved into the larger world outside family and neighborhood, your needs began to change. To fit into that larger world, you needed to learn new skills and rules. The institution of education exists to meet those needs.

Why People Need Education

When Doris Hollingsworth was a little girl, she dreamed of growing up to be a firefighter and riding on a big red fire truck with its siren screaming. At age ten, Peter Ky could not decide between being a fisherman and an astronaut. Bernice Kelman was sure that nursing would be the best job for her.

Whatever your dreams might be, you, like every young person, have hopes for a career that uses your skills and talents, that provides you with a comfortable life, and that gives you a sense of being a worthwhile person. To achieve this goal, you will need at least a high school education.

Education is increasingly important in our society. Because we live in a time of rapid technological change, more and more of the available jobs require a great deal of knowledge or a special skill. It is in school that you will learn most of the skills and knowledge that will prepare you for your life as a working adult.

The institution of education has another important effect on you. School is one of the first places where you meet people from different backgrounds and with different values. As a member of a family, you are exposed mostly to people who share your values and live by the same rules you do. In school you begin to recognize the importance of listening to others' opinions and respecting their ideas and abilities.

Meeting Society's Needs

While the institution of education is meeting the needs of individual students, it is also serving our society. Society needs to train its citizens to do work. Without trained workers, how could our businesses and industries provide the products that we want? Who would run the banks, insurance companies, hospitals, and all the other services of our complex society?

In addition, our society needs to prepare its citizens to live together as a nation. The children who enter our schools are as diverse as American society itself. The values and customs they bring from home often differ from those of their classmates and are sometimes in conflict with them.

Society has entrusted the schools with the task of teaching young citizens the rules and values by which Americans are expected to live. Our schools offer us a knowledge of our history, culture, and government. They teach us a common language by which we can communicate with our fellow citizens. Our schools transmit society's ideal of equal respect and the values of freedom, equality, and justice that support it.

Schools also teach us to think critically, form opinions, make judgments, and solve problems. The institution of education gives us the opportunity to examine our own beliefs while exposing us to new ideas.

As you have learned, any group that wants to continue to exist must teach its values and rules to its members. It is through the institution of education—our schools and colleges, our teachers, our textbooks—that American society assures that this country will continue to be a free, democratic nation.

Education's Rewards What are the rewards offered by the institution of education? Getting good grades can be rewarding and so can getting a satisfying job. However, the rewards of your education can go far beyond grades and paychecks.

By the time you finish high school, you may have spent the better part of 13 years in school. As you walk across the stage to pick up your diploma, what rewards will you recognize? You will probably have some good memories and close friendships as well as some practical and academic skills. Perhaps, too, you will leave school with a better sense of who you are and how you can contribute to American society.

Section 2 Assessment

1. How does the family benefit the individual and society?
2. What needs do religious groups meet for the people who belong to them?
3. What do children gain from the institution of education?
4. **Analyze** How do the institutions of the family, religion, and education differ in the needs they meet and the ways they help society? What do they have in common?

The Economy: Satisfying Wants

SECTION PREVIEW

Objectives

- Identify the human wants that our economy meets.
- Describe the freedoms we have in our economy.
- Explain how citizens benefit from the American economy.

Building Civics Vocabulary

- Physical products like food and clothing are called **goods.**
- **Services** are jobs you pay to have done.
- **Wants** are desires for goods or services.
- The system for producing and distributing goods and services is the **economy.**
- **Consumers** use goods and services.
- A place where goods and services are exchanged is a **market.**
- The amount paid for a good or service is its **price.**
- **Money** is anything you can use to pay for goods and services.

Focus

Imagine that one day you are baking desserts and the brownie-like bar that comes out of the oven is incredibly delicious. You get an idea: why not make a huge batch of these bars and trade them for things that you need? Surely no one could resist the taste of your new creation, which you call the Wonderbar.

Filling a box with Wonderbars, you take off for Jane's farm. Jane agrees to exchange a dozen eggs for one Wonderbar. Then you are off to the tailor to trade him thirty Wonderbars for a pair of pants. You have

provided yourself with food and clothing. Such physical products are called goods.

Your next stop is Danny's Handyman Shop. You ask Danny to fix your television and repair your flat bicycle tire. Danny agrees to perform these services—work you will pay to have done—in exchange for two dozen Wonderbars.

You have just exchanged, or bartered, your Wonderbars to satisfy your wants, or desires for goods and services. Some of your wants, such as food, clothing, and shelter, are essential for your survival. Others, such as a television or bicycle that works, may not be essential, but they make your life more enjoyable.

The American Economy

Just as you, Danny, and Jane found a way to get what you wanted, every society has a system for producing and distributing goods and services to fulfill people's wants. This system is called an economy. Like the other institutions you have been learning about, the institution of the economy is organized to meet needs, which in this case means responding to people's wants. It also has a set of rules and expectations for its members.

Characteristics of Our Economy As participants in our economy, we play several roles. Each of us is a consumer, a person who uses, or consumes, goods and services to satisfy his or her wants. Most people are also workers. They provide the skills and the labor necessary to produce goods such as Wonderbars and televisions, or to provide services such as television repair and Wonderbar shipping.

A place or situation in which an exchange of goods or services takes place is called a market. In some markets, such as stores or shops, people meet face-to-face to exchange what they have for what they want. In other markets, such as stock exchanges, buyers and sellers never meet, but make transactions using complicated accounting systems.

The amount you must pay for a good or service in a market is its price. You used the barter system when you exchanged your Wonderbars for eggs, pants, and repair services. Although bartering is one way to pay for what you want, people usually use money. Money is anything, from beads to coins to checks, that is generally accepted as payment for a good or a service.

American Economic Freedoms

Like all institutions, our economy has rules that its participants must follow. These rules reflect some of the important values that Americans have agreed upon. One value, freedom, forms the cornerstone of our economy, or economic system. Built into this system are rules protecting five important freedoms.

Freedom to Buy and Sell You have the freedom to sell your Wonderbars to anyone you wish. You are also free to charge whatever price you think you can get for them. In addition, every person has the freedom to buy or not to buy your Wonderbars.

Freedom to Compete You are free to make and sell Wonderbars. At the same time, other people are free to compete with you, trying to make and sell more or better dessert bars.

Freedom to Make a Profit If people are willing to pay more for your Wonderbars than it costs you to make them, then you will earn a profit. Freedom to earn a profit on what they make and sell encourages people to produce goods and services.

Freedom to Own Property Your Wonderbars are your property, and you own them until you agree to sell them. The right to own your own property and to buy and sell and use it as you wish is a basic rule of the American economic system.

Freedom to Choose an Occupation

You are free to pursue any career you wish. Of course, whether you are successful will depend on whether there are jobs available in that career and on whether you have provided yourself with the proper training and skills.

In addition to protecting freedom, the rules of our economic system are based on the idea of fairness. If you make an agreement to do a job, sell a product, or pay a worker, for example, you may not break it. Furthermore, you may not make a product that does not work and claim that it does.

You and America's Economy

Not everyone has the job he or she wants, and most people cannot buy all the goods and services they would like. There are also people in our country who are very poor. On the whole, however, our economic system succeeds. The goods and services we desire are produced, distributed, and sold. We have the freedom to try to achieve our dreams—to have careers and lifestyles of our own choosing. In these ways, we benefit from the institution of the economy in the United States.

Section 3 Assessment

1. **Define** goods, services, wants, economy, consumer, market, price, money
2. How does our society benefit from having an economic system?
3. Make a list of the economic freedoms Americans have.
4. **Apply** Think of a recent day in your life. Did you have wants for goods and services? Were they fulfilled? How? Describe how our economic system affected you on that day.

Government: Meeting Society's Needs

Objectives

- Explain why we need a government.
- Define three common forms of government.
- Analyze how laws affect citizens.

Building Civics Vocabulary

- In a **monarchy,** all or most of the power is in the hands of a king, queen, or emperor.
- A **dictatorship** is a government controlled by one person, called a dictator.
- In a **democracy,** the power is shared by all the people.

 Focus

Do you think the following scenes could take place in the United States?

- ★ Suddenly, in the middle of the night, soldiers rush into your home and arrest your parents. You never see them again.
- ★ A president and other officials appoint themselves to office and stay in power as long as they want.
- ★ Religion is outlawed. Churches and temples are locked and barred.

These scenes are an everyday reality for people in many countries. Individuals live in constant fear because their rights are not protected. For them, government is the enemy.

Life in the United States is different. Our government was formed to protect our rights and to ensure that events such as the ones just described do not occur. Like the other institutions you have been reading about, the

By preventing crime and protecting community safety, police officers help government maintain law and order in our society.

American institution of government reflects the shared values of the country's members.

The Need for Government

Without government, life would be disorganized. There would be no order to the way roads were built or towns and cities planned. People would disagree about ways to settle arguments and deal with crime. We would have no proper way to defend our nation from attack.

Law and Order Government makes and enforces laws that protect rights and ensure that people's lives can proceed in a peaceful, orderly way. Through courts, our government can also settle disputes and punish law breakers.

Security Government provides for our common defense against outside attack by maintaining armed forces and weapons. Our government makes treaties with other countries in which both sides agree to keep the peace or to help each other in case of attack.

Public Services Government provides services we need but cannot depend on private businesses to provide. Such services include building and maintaining roads, sewers, and schools.

Maintaining Other Institutions
Government can help to maintain the other institutions in society. For example, in the United States, government protects our freedom of religion, pays for our schools, and provides hundreds of services for families, from health care to issuing marriage licenses.

Forms of Government

There are many forms of government that can provide the order, security, and services that a society needs. In the world today, monarchy, dictatorship, and democracy are three of the most common forms of government.

Monarchy A monarchy is a form of government in which all or most of the power is in the hands of one individual, the monarch. The monarch's authority is hereditary; it stays in the family, usually being passed down to a son or daughter. King, queen, and emperor are some of the titles that have been given to monarchs.

Monarchies were once the most common type of government in the world. Today, however, real monarchies—in which the monarch holds all the power—are rare. An example of such a modern-day monarchy is the kingdom of Saudi Arabia.

Dictatorship A dictatorship is a government controlled by one person, called a dictator. A dictator is different from a monarch because a dictator usually takes power by force, rather than by inheriting it.

Historically, dictators have usually come to power when an existing government is weak or has lost the support of the people.

Dictators are frequently military leaders. They rely heavily on the support of the armed forces and the police to maintain them in power. Their actions are not limited by laws or legislatures. Military dictatorships of the twentieth century include Germany under Adolf Hitler and Iraq under Saddam Hussein.

Democracy A third form of government is a democracy, a system in which the power is shared by all the people. Democracy means "government by the people." By voting and by choosing representatives, the people decide how their government will meet their needs and protect their rights and freedoms.

The United States was the first modern democracy. Since our nation was founded, countries in all corners of the world have adopted democratic forms of government. Many countries that were once monarchies have become democracies. Most of these countries, such as Great Britain and Japan, still have monarchs with ceremonial duties, but real power is held by democratically elected representatives. Countries with this form of democratic government are often called constitutional monarchies.

Laws: The Rules of Government

Laws are the formal rules that govern our behavior in society. The most basic and important laws of our nation are written down in a document called the Constitution. The Constitution tells what the government can and cannot do, and lists the rights guaranteed to states and to citizens. In the United States, governments at the town, county, state, and national levels can make laws, as long as these laws are not in conflict with the basic laws in the Constitution.

Laws influence nearly everything we do, from driving a car and voting in elections to getting a fishing license and disposing of garbage. By following our laws, we ensure that rights are protected and order maintained in society. What are some of the laws that affect how you ride your bicycle or skateboard?

Breaking laws can lead to very specific punishments. The seriousness of the punishment depends on the seriousness of the crime. For example, if you were to break the speed limit or litter, you would probably have to pay a fine. If you were to rob a bank, you could spend years in jail.

Changing the Laws In a democracy, the citizens have a right to express their opinions and work with others to try to make laws they think are needed. They can also try to change laws they think are unfair or harmful to society.

Our government responds to our demands, but only when it hears them. The opinions of the people do make a difference when they are made known to lawmakers and government officials.

Section 4 Assessment

1. **Define** monarchy, dictatorship, democracy
2. What are four important needs that the institution of government meets? Give an example of how each need is met.
3. In each of the three most common systems of government, who has the power to make decisions?
4. **Synthesize** Think of four laws that affect you. How would society be different if those laws did not exist?

Extending the Chapter

Historical Views

Social institutions provide the framework for our lives. They meet our most important physical, emotional, spiritual, and economic needs. Their values shape our own personal values, and their rules determine how we behave much of the time.

Because they reflect a society's most basic values, the institutions of the family, education, and religion change very slowly if at all in most societies. Forms of government and economic systems, however, can sometimes change very quickly.

A sudden, drastic change in a government is called a revolution. In a revolution, a government is overthrown by force and a new government is established. Often the new government orders major changes in the economy. Revolutions often occur when many people in a society believe that the government and economy are not meeting their needs.

As you know, the United States was created as a result of a revolution that began in 1775. Since then, however, our government and economy have changed only gradually. Even though many Americans have at times sharply disagreed with the way the government and the economy were working, we have never had to face another revolution. We are fortunate that our government was carefully designed to be flexible and responsive to the demands of its citizens.

How to CHOOSE BETWEEN OPTIONS

"I don't know. What do *you* want to do?" "I can't make up my mind. You decide." "What a boring day. I can't think of anything to do."

Do those statements sound familiar? At times we rely on other people to make choices for us, or we wait for something to happen so that we do not have to make a choice. Although frequently we must let others make decisions that affect us, sometimes we let them decide simply because it is "easier" or "safer." Unfortunately, the more we do this, the less control we have over our lives.

Often people let others decide because they feel that they cannot make good decisions themselves. Making good decisions, though, is mainly a matter of taking your time and following a careful process. This lesson will help you understand the first part of that process: choosing.

Explain the Skill

The following guidelines will help you choose a way to achieve your goal.

1. **State your goal clearly.** Determine exactly what you want to happen. That is, set a clear goal that points you in a direction, rather than a fuzzy goal that will not help you make a decision. Decide how you will be able to tell whether you have reached your goal.
2. **Identify options, or possible ways of achieving your goal.** Brainstorm a list of as many options as you can. Do not judge each option right away. Remember, one idea may lead to another.
3. **Think about the possible consequences, or effects, of each option.** For each option ask, "If I do this, what will probably happen?"

4. **Judge each option.** Identify which consequences are good and which are bad.
5. **Choose the best option.** Compare the good and bad points of each option to determine which option is best.

Analyze the Skill

The following account describes how a student named Janice worked with other student council members to choose a way to achieve a goal. As you read, look carefully at how they followed some specific steps of the decision-making process.

I was angry. Our school was looking like a garbage dump. Students wrote all over the desks and left wads of paper on the classroom floors. The bathroom mirrors and walls were covered with graffiti. Lunch tables were littered with wrappings and leftover food.

I brought my complaint to the other members of the student council, who agreed that the messiness of the school campus was a big problem. We talked about what we wanted to achieve. "We want to have a clean campus," said one council member. "Obviously, that is our goal." Soon we realized, however, that our goal was more specific than that. We wanted to deal with the *cause* of the problem, that is, to get students to recognize the importance of keeping the school clean. Therefore, we stated our goal more clearly. Chris, the student council president, wrote it on the chalkboard: *Goal: To get most students to willingly help keep the school clean.*

Next we considered what we could do to achieve that goal. We made a list of possibilities. No one judged any of the options while we brainstormed. Chris made a chart on the blackboard listing them.

After that we looked closely at each option and considered what might happen if we tried it. For instance, we thought that Jerry's suggestion of having student monitors might work for a while. However, in the long run we would probably have trouble finding enough volunteers to go on patrol. I found it hard to sit through the discussion on each option because I thought it was obvious that giving out spirit buttons was the best choice. But, as you will soon see, I am glad that I was patient.

GOAL: To get most students to willingly help keep the school clean	
Option	**Consequences**
Student Monitors	Will not cost money + Might quit soon −
Professional Guards	Will be expensive − Will be effective + Students will resent them −
Spirit Buttons	Will not cost much money + Having a reward will get students to volunteer +
Detentions	Will not cost any money + Will be difficult to assign fairly −

Our faculty advisor said that we had an impressive list but wanted to know how we were going to determine which option was best. We told her that we would look at the possible results of each option, using plus and minus signs to rate each consequence.

In looking at the options, we kept our goal in mind. Some possibilities, such as hiring guards, would help keep the campus clean but would not encourage students to take responsibility themselves. Our goal was to have the students keep the campus clean because they *wanted* to, not because they were forced to.

Most council members liked my idea of handing out spirit buttons as a reward to students who help keep the school clean. However, some thought that buttons were not enough of a reward. Then Karen came up with a clever idea: letting students cash in the buttons to get discounts at the cafeteria or on tickets for dances, athletic events, and other activities. We decided that passing out buttons that students could cash in was the best option.

Skill Assessment

1. Why did the students decide that their goal should not be only "to have a clean campus"?
2. How did the student council's goal lead them to reject the option of hiring guards?
3. In making their choice, what were the members of the student council *not* influenced by? Explain your answer. **(a)** the importance of students taking responsibility **(b)** the need to raise money for cleaning up the school **(c)** the long-term effects of the option they chose
4. Which of the following was *not* an important part of the process the student council went through in making their choice? Explain your answer. **(a)** the advice they received from the principal **(b)** the chart they created **(c)** their willingness to consider all the options.
5. Why is it important to define your goal clearly?
6. Explain how to judge options when making a decision.

How to READ A STATISTICAL TABLE

 Use the *Simulations and Data Graphing CD-ROM* to create and interpret graphs.

In this chapter you read that dropping out of high school can seriously limit your job opportunities and earning potential as an adult. The Fact & Quotes feature on page 34 lists several statistics showing that dropouts are often unemployed and usually earn less money than high school graduates. Another way to display this kind of information is in a statistical table.

Statistics are collections of information in the form of numbers. Statistics are easier to analyze if they have been displayed in an organized way. Statistics can be displayed in a graph or in a statistical table as shown below.

Education and Annual Earnings

Level of education completed	Mean yearly earnings in 2000	
	Men	Women
Less than 9th grade	$18,281	$10,561
9th-12th grade no high school diploma	$24,987	$12,729
High school graduates	$33,272	$18,499
Bachelor's degree or more	$72,427	$38,781

Source: U.S. Bureau of Labor Statistics and Bureau of the Census

Explain the Skill

When reading a statistical table, first read the title of the table to find out the kind of information the table is showing. The table above is entitled "Education and Annual Earnings."

Next, study the table's headings. Each column and row has its own heading. Once you understand the headings, you are ready to find specific information on the table. To find a particular statistic, choose the column and row that interest you. Where the column and row meet, you will find the statistic you are looking for.

Analyze the Skill

Suppose you want to use the table on this page to answer the question: What is the average yearly salary of a man who is a high school graduate? Find the column that gives information about average yearly earnings for men. Then find the row that shows information for high school graduates. Follow the column down and row across until they meet, then read the data at this point. You will find that men who are high school graduates earn an average of $32,647 per year.

Once you have read some of the statistics listed on the table, you can begin to draw conclusions about what the table shows. You can answer questions like these: How does a person's level of education affect his or her earning potential? On average, who earns more, men or women?

Skill Assessment

Study the statistical table on this page to answer the following questions.

1. What is the purpose of this table?
2. Which group earns the least per year?
3. Which group earns the most per year? How do the earnings of this group compare with the earnings of the lowest-paid group?
4. Compare the highest-paid group of women with the lowest-paid group of men. What do you notice?
5. What are two conclusions that you can draw from this statistical table?

CHAPTER 2 ASSESSMENT

Building Civics Vocabulary

The vocabulary terms in each pair listed below are related to each other. For each pair, explain how the two terms are related.

Example: *Social institution* is related to *economy* because the economy is a social institution that meets the needs of individuals.

1. *socialization* and *rules*
2. *goods* and *wants*
3. *money* and *price*
4. *monarchy* and *dictatorship*

Reviewing Main Ideas and Skills

5. Explain the reasons why members of a group must learn and obey the group's rules.
6. How does a child benefit from the institution of the family?
7. What benefits do individuals and society receive from the institution of religion?
8. Why does our society need schools?
9. What is the basic purpose of an economic system?
10. **How to Choose Between Options** Suppose you are a member of the camping club at your school and you want to raise money for a camping trip to a national park. Come up with several fundraising options and list the positive and negative aspects of each.
11. **How to Read a Statistical Table** Study the statistical table on page 11. What is the subject of this table? According to the table, what percentage of the U.S. population is Asian American?

Critical Thinking

12. **Drawing Conclusions** Pick one group to which you belong. What are some of the group's rules and rewards? What happens when you break the rules? Why are rules important to your group?
13. **Analyzing Ideas** Select one of the economic freedoms: freedom to buy and sell, to compete, to make a profit, to own property, or to choose an occupation. How might your life be different if you did not have that freedom?

Writing About Civics

14. **Writing an Essay** Review the five major social institutions described in this chapter. Which has had the greatest effect on shaping your values? Explain your choice and give examples of values you have learned.

Citizenship Activities

15. **Your Local Community** In groups, choose a recent day and analyze your activities as consumers in our economic system. Make a chart of the wants for goods and services that you had during that day. Note whether or not these wants were fulfilled.

 Take It to the NET

Access the **Civics: Participating in Government** Internet site at **www.phschool.com** for the specific URLs to complete the activity. Explore volunteer organizations online and find two or three that exist in your area. Find out what projects they are working on. Prepare an oral report describing their activities.

The Meaning of Citizenship

Citizenship and You

The Pledge of Allegiance first appeared in 1892 in a magazine called *The Youth's Companion*. The original Pledge, attributed to Francis Bellamy, stated: "I pledge allegiance to my Flag and the Republic for which it stands; one Nation indivisible with liberty and justice for all." In 1924, "my Flag" was changed to "the Flag of the United States of America." Congress officially recognized the Pledge in 1942 and added the words "under God" in 1954.

> *I pledge allegiance to the Flag of the United States of America, and to the Republic for which it stands, one nation under God, indivisible, with liberty and justice for all.*

Keep It Current

Items marked with this logo are periodically updated on the Internet. To keep up-to-date, go to **www.phschool.com**

What's Ahead in Chapter 3

In this chapter you will learn about citizenship: who has it, what rights and duties it involves, and how Americans of all ages can fulfill its responsibilities.

Section 1 **What It Means to Be a Citizen**

Section 2 **The Rights, Duties, and Responsibilities of Citizens**

Section 3 **Citizenship and Our Other Roles in Society**

Citizen's Journal

Write a paragraph explaining your understanding of what citizenship means. After you have studied the chapter, reread your paragraph. Write a new paragraph explaining how your understanding has grown.

What It Means to Be a Citizen

SECTION PREVIEW

Objectives
- Examine who can be an American citizen.
- Explain what it means to hold the office of citizen.

Building Civics Vocabulary
- A **citizen** owes allegiance to a country.
- A **naturalized** citizen has gained citizenship.
- An **alien** is a citizen of one country who lives in another.
- Citizens elect **representatives** to government offices.

 **Focus**

Bernice Kelman lives in Sublette, Kansas, in the United States. She is a citizen of her town, her state, and her nation. A citizen is a person with certain rights and duties under a government. Citizens' rights include the right to express an opinion and the right to protection under the laws. Duties include obeying laws and paying taxes. Each of us is a citizen of the town, state, and nation in which we live.

Who Is a Citizen?

The word *citizen* also has a special meaning. Our Constitution says that a citizen of the United States is a person who by birth or by choice owes allegiance to this nation.

You are legally an American citizen if any of these statements is true.

★ You were born in the United States or its territories. (This is true even if your parents were not citizens, unless they were living in the United States as representatives of a foreign government.)

★ At least one of your parents was a United States citizen when you were born.
★ You have been naturalized, which means you have gone through the process of becoming a citizen.
★ You were under age eighteen when your parents were naturalized.

Naturalized Citizens When Peter Ky's family came to this country from Vietnam, they were considered aliens. An alien is a citizen of one country who lives in another country. As aliens, the Kys had many of the same rights and duties as American citizens. However, they could not vote or hold government office.

In order to become American citizens, Peter's parents went through a process called naturalization, which is described in the chart on the next page. They learned English, studied the history of the United States, and learned the important values, laws, rights, and duties of citizens.

In Chapter 2 you learned that socialization is the process of learning the rules of a group or institution to which you belong. You might think of the process of naturalization as our government's way of socializing aliens who want to become American citizens.

Because Peter was less than eighteen years old at the time his parents became naturalized citizens, he automatically became a citizen, too. The history, civics, and government classes he studied in school socialized him as they are socializing you: teaching you the rules and the benefits of being a citizen.

Naturalized citizens have all the rights and duties of citizens by birth except the right to be President or Vice President. Once you are a citizen, you will always be a citizen except in a few special cases. For example, a person can decide to give up citizenship, or become a citizen of another country. In addition, citizenship may be taken away from a person who is convicted of trying to overthrow the United States government by force.

CHART SKILL **THE NATURALIZATION PROCESS** People who wish to become citizens must meet certain requirements and take a test. **Diversity In what subjects must applicants demonstrate ability and knowledge?**

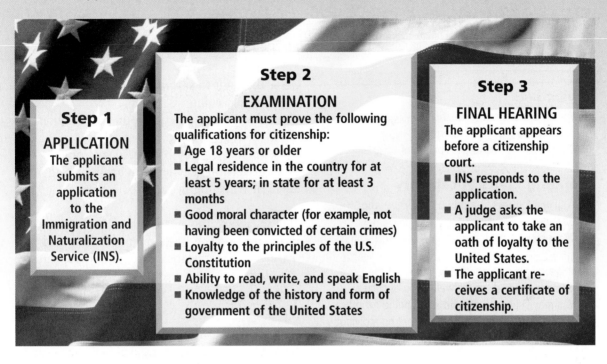

Step 1

APPLICATION

The applicant submits an application to the Immigration and Naturalization Service (INS).

Step 2

EXAMINATION

The applicant must prove the following qualifications for citizenship:
- Age 18 years or older
- Legal residence in the country for at least 5 years; in state for at least 3 months
- Good moral character (for example, not having been convicted of certain crimes)
- Loyalty to the principles of the U.S. Constitution
- Ability to read, write, and speak English
- Knowledge of the history and form of government of the United States

Step 3

FINAL HEARING

The applicant appears before a citizenship court.
- INS responds to the application.
- A judge asks the applicant to take an oath of loyalty to the United States.
- The applicant receives a certificate of citizenship.

The Office of Citizen

Being a United States citizen has a unique meaning. In this country, each citizen holds a very important position of authority. As Abraham Lincoln observed, ours is a government "of the people, by the people, and for the people." He meant that our government can operate—make laws, build roads and bridges, collect taxes, fight wars, make agreements with other countries—but only if we citizens want it to. When we say that the power of our government is based on "the consent of the governed," we mean that the citizens have the power to decide what our government will and will not do.

As citizens, we elect representatives, people who are chosen to speak and act for their fellow citizens in government. We elect members of Congress as well as the President, city council members, mayors, governors, and many of our judges. They have the power to make decisions and to pass laws.

However, our representatives hold office only as long as we want them to. We delegate—or lend—our power to them. The real power belongs to us. In a way, therefore, each of us holds an office, too—the "office of citizen." In our society, that is the most important office there is. As citizens we hold it for life.

Section 1 Assessment

1. **Define** citizen, naturalized, alien, representatives
2. What are the qualifications to be a citizen?
3. What is the "office of citizen"?
4. **Analyze** How is the office of citizen similar to that of an elected official? How is it different?

The Rights, Duties, and Responsibilities of Citizens

SECTION PREVIEW

Objectives
- Describe the rights of American citizens.
- Analyze the duties of citizens.
- Define some of the responsibilities of citizenship.

Building Civics Vocabulary
- A **jury of peers** is a group of citizens who decide a court case.
- **Witnesses** have information helpful in trying a case.
- It is a citizen's responsibility to uphold the **common good,** or the well-being of society.
- You may support a **candidate** running for office.
- The **rule of law** is the concept that no individual is above the law.

 **Focus**

Here is a riddle: How is holding the "office of citizen" like having a driver's license?

Having a license gives you certain rights. Your rights include the right to drive on public roads and highways, and the right to park where the law allows.

Of course, as a driver you also have duties. Your duties, which are required by law, include observing traffic signals and signs and obeying the speed limit and other rules of the road. In addition to your duties, you have responsibilities. They can be summed up this way: You are expected to drive in a way that will not endanger others and that will protect the safety of other drivers, cyclists, and pedestrians.

Have you figured out the answer to the riddle? Holding the "office of citizen" is like being a licensed driver because in both situations you have important rights, duties, and responsibilities.

Rights of Citizens

Can you name some of the rights of American citizens? Here are some that may be most familiar to you.

- ★ the right to vote and to hold elected office
- ★ the right to say what you think in speech or in writing
- ★ the right to practice your own religion
- ★ the right to have a fair trial
- ★ the right to be protected by your government when you are working or traveling in other countries

These rights, and our other rights as citizens, are based on the fundamental beliefs and values we Americans share: equal respect, freedom, equality, and justice. Our rights are guaranteed to us by our Constitution and protected by our laws and our courts.

Duties of Citizens

Just as a licensed driver has certain duties that go with the right to drive, citizens have duties, too. These duties include

- ★ obeying the laws
- ★ defending the nation
- ★ serving on a jury or as a witness in court
- ★ paying taxes
- ★ attending school

By performing each of these duties, we, as citizens, support our government's efforts to meet our needs as a society.

Obeying the Laws   Your family and your classroom have rules that keep them running in an orderly way. As you know, a society's formal, or written, rules are called laws. Some laws are to keep us from hurting each other. They range from laws requiring drivers and bicycle riders to stop at stop signs to laws against murder and armed robbery.

When we obey laws, we respect the rights of others. Some laws protect the right of individuals to determine who can use their private property.

Other laws establish the rules for making agreements and for settling disagreements in a fair and peaceful way. If Bernice Kelman hires Mr. Carey to paint her house, they might draw up and sign a written contract. A contract is a document that states how much Bernice will pay and how long it will take Mr. Carey to finish the job. Both Bernice and Mr. Carey have a legal duty to live up to the contract. If either of them thinks the other has broken the contract, the law gives them the opportunity to take the case to court.

We also must obey laws that protect citizens' rights. For example, the right of equal opportunity is protected by laws. Do you remember when Doris Hollingsworth was applying for a job? If an employer refused to hire her because of her race or religion, the employer would be breaking the law.

In a democracy, no individual—even the President—is above the law. This concept of a government of laws, rather than of men and women, is called the rule of law. Officials must base their decisions on the law, not on personal opinion. If an official breaks the law, he or she must be treated like any other citizen. Our laws are also public, and citizens know the basic law of the land. This is an important protection against government tyranny.

Defending the Nation Helping our country defend itself against threats to our peace and security is another important duty of citizens. The United States maintains armed services even in peacetime. In this way, the nation can defend itself in case of attack and can help other countries protect themselves.

When you are eighteen years old or older, you may volunteer to serve in the army, navy, air force, or marines. In addition, young men must register for military service when they reach age eighteen. Registering does not mean that they will have to serve in the armed forces, but it does mean that they can be

Men and women who volunteer for the armed forces can learn valuable skills while working to defend the nation.

called to serve when there is a national emergency. A man whose moral beliefs prohibit him from fighting may ask to be considered a conscientious (kahn shee EN shus) objector. If his request is approved, he will be assigned to some other kind of public service, such as working in a hospital.

Serving on a Jury or as a Witness

One of the basic rights of citizens is the right to a fair trial. In our legal system no person may be found guilty of a crime unless that guilt can be proved "beyond a reasonable doubt." We believe that the best way to determine a person's guilt or innocence is to conduct a trial in an open manner, with citizens participating in the process.

Experts, such as lawyers, police officers, and psychologists, may play an important part in a criminal trial—the process of trying to prove that an accused person did or did not commit a crime. However, experts do not make the final decision as to innocence or guilt.

A judge does not make the final decision, either, unless the accused person gives such permission. Instead, our Constitution guarantees that anyone accused of a crime may have the case decided by a jury of peers, a group of ordinary citizens who hear the case and decide whether the accused person is innocent or guilty.

During the trial, the lawyers may need the help of witnesses to prove their case. Witnesses are people who have seen events or heard conversations related to the crime, or who have special information that may help determine the guilt or innocence of the person on trial.

Criminal trials are not the only ones that use witnesses and juries. People may also ask a court to decide cases in which they think their rights have been violated or they have been treated unfairly. If Bernice Kelman and Mr. Carey cannot settle their dispute over the housepainting job, for example, they have the right to ask for a jury to hear the case. They may also call witnesses to help them—such as a neighbor who can testify that Mr. Carey did not finish painting the house when he agreed to.

As you can see, juries and witnesses play an important part in assuring that a trial is fair. Because Americans have a right to a fair trial, it is the responsibility of all adult citizens to serve as jurors and act as witnesses when they are called to do so.

Paying Taxes   Are you a taxpayer? A few students your age earn enough money at part-time jobs or through savings accounts or investments that they must pay income tax to the government. Many more of you pay sales taxes on items you buy, such as books, clothes, and CDs.

As an adult, you will probably pay other taxes as well, such as property taxes on land and a house or building that you may own. Through taxes our local, state, and national governments raise money to pay for the services that citizens ask them to provide.

Attending School Did it ever occur to you that every time you go to school you are performing one of your duties as a citizen? Although age requirements vary from state to state, children are usually required to attend school from age five or six to at least age sixteen.

As you discovered by reading about the institution of education in Chapter 2, our society depends on our schools to teach young citizens the knowledge and skills they need as they are growing up and when they become adults. One purpose of school attendance laws is to make sure that young people are prepared to support themselves and to contribute to our economy.

Another important task of the schools is to give students the knowledge, skills, and experiences they need to carry out the duties and responsibilities of the "office of citizen." If we, as citizens, are to continue to govern ourselves, uphold our values, and protect our rights, each of us must be educated about our history, our government, and the workings of our society. It is to the schools that our society has entrusted this important task.

Responsibilities of Citizens

As citizens of this democracy, we not only have duties, but responsibilities as well. Unlike duties, responsibilities are fulfilled by choice—they are voluntary. However, even though we are not required by law to fulfill our responsibilities, doing so is just as important a part of being a citizen as performing our duties.

The Common Good The basic responsibility of every citizen is to contribute to the common good, or the well-being of all members of society. Contributing to the common good means acting in ways that protect the rights and freedoms of other Americans and that make our communities, our states, and our nation good places for all of us to live.

All the other responsibilities of citizenship are part of contributing to the common good. They include the many ways we participate in our political process. For example, as citizens we vote for people who will represent us in government, and some of us agree to hold elected or appointed office ourselves. We also work alone or with others to influence government policies and decisions.

Facts & Quotes

A Citizen's Words

Being a responsible citizen is not always easy. An African American mother in New York City explains why she has made the effort:

> " I'm not like all these other[s] you see in the neighborhood,... doing nothing for their community, doing nothing for nobody. That's not for me. When I see something wrong, I speak up. I get involved.... That's why I ran for the school board.... I couldn't let [them close our schools]. I had to do something about it. Some'll tell you I'm a big-mouth, and maybe I am. But the way I see it, people who don't look out after anything, who only think of themselves, are really missing out on life.... It's hard being involved. The meetings are long, and it takes you away from your kids.... [But] while I was looking out for me, I was looking out for everybody else, too. Especially those kids. "

From *Best Intentions* by Robert Sam Anson

Barbara Jordan

Barbara Jordan never let difficulties keep her from achieving her goals. She was a Texas state senator, a member of Congress, and a college professor. Each success was, to Jordan, "just another milestone."

Barbara Jordan grew up in Houston, Texas, during the time of segregated schools. In high school, Jordan won her school's "Girl of the Year" award for academic excellence and contributions to community projects.

In 1956, Jordan entered Boston University School of Law, where she met the challenge of being one of only two African American women in her class. Upon graduating in 1959, Jordan returned to Houston to practice law, eager to use her free time in community service. After volunteering with the Democratic party in the 1960 election campaign, she declared that she "had really been bitten by the political bug."

Politics, Jordan decided, offered the best opportunity to make government respond to the needs of the people. Therefore, she decided to run for political office. In 1966 Barbara Jordan passed another milestone when she became the first African American woman ever elected to the Texas State Senate.

Jordan's next goal was a seat in the United States House of Representatives, which she won in 1972.

During three terms in the House, she earned respect for her hard work and thoughtful decisions. In 1976, she was honored by being invited to give the opening speech at the national convention of the Democratic party.

Jordan decided not to run for re-election in 1978, but her work in politics was far from over. As a speaker, writer, and teacher, she continued to influence Americans of all ages and backgrounds. She told her students that every American should take citizenship seriously, because "the stakes are too high for government to be a spectator sport."

Recognizing Viewpoints

Jordan told her students that citizenship is a serious responsibility. Explain how she followed this advice in her own life.

Voting The right to vote is one of the basic rights of American citizens. It is also one of our most important responsibilities. We vote for representatives at all levels of government, from President of the United States to members of the local school board.

In addition, in our states and our local communities citizens are often asked to vote on issues. We may be asked to make decisions about such public issues as building schools, changing taxes, or protecting wilderness areas.

To make good decisions and vote wisely, citizens have the responsibility to inform themselves. You can get information by reading, asking questions, and discussing the candidates and issues with other people. It is always important, when preparing to vote, to try to separate facts from opinions, and to try to base your decisions on reasons and not on personal likes and dislikes.

Holding Government Office

The people who agree to hold government office are fulfilling another important responsibility of citizenship. They have accepted the responsibility of learning about the issues and trying to make decisions that are in the best interests of the people they represent.

Citizens who hold office include our elected city council members, mayors, governors, and state and national representatives and senators. They also include appointed officials, such as members of local water boards and planning commissions, as well as advisors to the President.

Election Campaigns

Although there are age requirements for voting and for holding political office, most of the voluntary responsibilities of the "office of citizen" do not depend on age. One of the important ways to fulfill the responsibilities of a citizen is to help a **candidate**—a person running for office— with his or her election campaign.

You may be aware that getting elected to government office is not always easy. Often the candidate must face stiff competition. Listen to Bernice Kelman:

  ❝*When my father ran for election to the Kansas state House of Representatives, our neighbors really helped out. They wrote letters, made phone calls, and knocked on doors, telling people about my father and what a good representative he would be for our area.*

When my father gave speeches, his campaign workers were there, handing out information. And on election day they went around, reminding people to vote and even driving them to their voting place. Thanks to them he was elected. ❞

There are a number of ways that, as a teenager, you might help a candidate. They include carrying a campaign sign at a rally, stuffing envelopes with information to send to voters, and making phone calls to encourage people to vote for your candidate.

Influencing Government

Another way you can fulfill the "office of citizen" is to work to get the government to take action in a cause you believe in. Citizens of any age can influence the government by expressing their opinions in letters to elected representatives and to newspapers, and by speaking at city council and school board meetings.

You can also join or create an organization with a goal of influencing government actions. Here is Peter Ky's experience:

  ❝*At home and in our restaurant, my family has always been very careful to recycle bottles, cans, and newspapers. We have read that if we don't save our resources, the earth may run out of them.*

Last year some friends and I noticed that the trash cans in the school lunchroom were overflowing with cans and bottles that kids had thrown away. We talked to the principal about it. He suggested that we organize a committee and look into ways to set up recycling at the school.

We talked to kids at other schools in the city, and they organized recycling committees, too. Then we went to the school board and asked them to provide special bins for cans and bottles. The committees are working out details with the school board now, and we hope to have our recycling project underway soon. 🗣

Peter and his friends convinced their government representatives—in this case, the members of the school board—to take an action the students thought was important for their community. They did it by forming an organization and working together.

Serving the Community Not all of the responsibilities of citizenship are directly connected with government. Each of us is responsible for doing whatever we can to make our communities better places to live in.

When you listen with respect to the opinion of a person who disagrees with you, and when you make a new student feel welcome in your school or pick up a candy wrapper someone else dropped on the sidewalk, you are acting as a responsible citizen. You are fulfilling the "office of citizen" by contributing to the common good.

Section 2 Assessment

1. **Define** jury of peers, witnesses, the common good, candidate, rule of law
2. List at least four rights of American citizens.
3. What are four duties that every American is required to fulfill at some time?
4. What are three of the responsibilities of citizenship?
5. **Analyze** Choose one of the responsibilities of citizenship and explain how fulfilling it helps contribute to the common good.
6. **Evaluate** Do you think it is possible that conflicts can arise between an individual's personal and civic responsibilities? Why or why not? Explain.

Citizenship and Our Other Roles in Society

SECTION PREVIEW

Objectives
- Explore social roles, and the way they affect people's behavior.
- Examine the ways people play the role of citizen.

Building Civics Vocabulary
- **Social roles** are roles that people play in real life.

 **Focus**

Doris Hollingsworth leads a busy life. Here is how she described a typical day:

❝*This morning at breakfast I was looking through the newspaper to find out what the mayor had had to say about the need for more stop signs at the intersections near the school. Then my daughter rushed in, asking if I would drill her for her French vocabulary test. I barely had time to rinse out my coffee cup before I heard a horn tooting outside. It was my carpool. I really had to dash.*

At work I had a conference with my boss and then sat down with three co-workers to decide how to organize our new project. Luckily, by noon, things had calmed down, and I had time for lunch with two old college friends.

After work I picked up a few groceries at the supermarket. When we finished dinner, my husband and I watched a ballgame on TV. Then I finished the reading assignment for my class tomorrow evening. Finally, the two of us took a stroll around the neighborhood before we turned in for the night. 99

In the course of her day, Doris acted as a citizen, a family member, a member of a social group, a worker, a friend, and a consumer. She also acted as her own person—herself—in making choices throughout the day.

Playing Social Roles

When you think of the word role, you may think of an actor playing a role in a film or play. Doris plays roles, too. However, her roles are called social roles, which are roles people play in real life. The chart on this page shows seven types of these social roles.

When Doris helped her daughter with her homework, she was playing the mother role. Having dinner, watching television, and taking a walk with her husband were part of her wife role. The roles of mother and wife are both part of Doris's family member roles.

As a carpool member and a student, Doris was playing social group roles. The social groups of which we are members can range in size from small to large. Two people painting a poster for the school dance make up a social group. Other examples of social groups are all students, all workers, and all women.

When she was reading the newspaper, Doris was playing the citizen role by informing herself on a government issue. She played a worker role when meeting with her boss, a friend role at lunch with old friends, and a consumer role when she shopped for groceries. Finally, as she played all her roles, Doris was also playing the self role. She was guided by a sense of who she is as a person.

Our Many Social Roles Like Doris, you play many different social roles in the course of a day and in the course of your life. Some roles you play because you were born into them. Some you play because you are required to play them. Some roles you choose for yourself.

You were born into your family, where you may play several roles: son or daughter, sister or brother, grandchild, cousin, and so on. At this point in your life, you are required to be a student. Therefore, you are playing a role as a member of that social group. Later, you may be required to pay taxes and serve as a juror, which are citizen roles. Roles you choose now may include being a friend, being a member of a club, and being a consumer.

Roles as Expected Behaviors

In each of your roles you behave differently. What causes you to act the way you do when you are playing a certain role? Partly, your behavior is determined by a set of expectations that people have of how someone in that role should act.

CHART SKILL

THE SEVEN SOCIAL ROLES
Every citizen plays different social roles in society. **Diversity To which social groups do you belong?**

consumer
friend
citizen
self
social group member
worker/student
family member

A cheerleader, for example, is expected to wear school colors and to jump, dance, and lead the crowd in school cheers. A member of the marching band is expected to wear a uniform and to know the music and the marching formation. If you want to be a member of a group, you will make an effort to learn the expected behaviors for that group.

The way you play a role also depends on how you want to play it and on the kind of person you are. People who know you begin to expect certain behaviors from you when you play your roles. A brother may always grumble when it is his turn to do the dishes. On the other hand, he may be the kind of brother who volunteers to do the dishes for his sister when he sees that she has too much homework.

Changing Roles

You may notice that sometimes a person plays the same role in different ways, depending on the situation. In Chapter 2 you read about Peter Ky and three of his friends. For Peter, playing the role of friend to Carol, Alex, and Melissa includes acting sympathetic, sharing biology notes, and going to the beach. Peter plays the friend role differently with Jerry. Jerry and Peter both like to read science fiction novels, and when these two friends get together, it is often to swap books and talk about their favorite authors.

Roles can also change over time. Bernice Kelman has been a daughter and a wife. However, since the death of her parents and her divorce, she no longer plays those roles.

The way Bernice plays her role as a mother has changed, too. Once she fed her babies and changed their diapers. Later she helped them make Halloween costumes, attended their track meets and school plays, and made sure they had finished their homework. Today her children are adults, living in other states. She now writes them letters, sends them presents on their birthdays, and gets together with them for family reunions.

Overlapping Roles

As you think about your many roles, you will realize that sometimes you are playing more than one at the same time. In such cases, you can say that two or more of your roles overlap.

When Peter gets together with Carol, Alex, and Melissa to study for a biology test, he is playing two roles, friend and student, at the same time. When he fulfills his father's expectation that he will recycle their restaurant's bottles and cans, he is performing the son's role in his family. At the same time, he is playing a citizen role, serving the common good by protecting the environment.

Bernice's roles of daughter and citizen overlapped when she helped her father in his election campaign. In Doris's job as computer programmer she fulfills roles as both a worker and a family member since her salary helps support her family.

Conflicting Roles

Sometimes it is easy to play more than one role at a time. At other times, however, you find that the demands of your roles are in conflict with each other. Consider the following situations:

★ You want to go to the school dance, but you have already agreed to take a babysitting job that night.
★ Your best friend manages to get tickets to a rock concert tomorrow, but your stepmother reminds you that your grandmother is arriving for a visit.
★ It is your night to cook dinner for the family, but your big term paper is due in the morning.
★ You do not need a new pair of jeans, but everyone you know is buying the latest style.

In each of these cases, two of your roles are in conflict, forcing you to make a difficult decision. In the first case, your social group role is in conflict with your worker role.

What roles are in conflict in the other situations? How will you decide what to do?

Making choices in situations like these is not easy. It requires you to think about the consequences of each possible behavior. Often, being aware of the values that guide your behavior in each role can be helpful. For example, it may help you to choose whether or not to buy the popular jeans if you realize that you are weighing the value "it is not good to spend money on items I do not really need" against the value "being accepted by the social group that wears the latest fashions is important to me."

Level of Participation

As you play your social roles, you will often have to make choices about how actively you want to participate in a role at any given time. These choices, too, are based on your values and your sense of what is most important to you at the time. If you think that there are not enough social activities at your school, what can you do? You can do nothing, or you can get a group of students to help you plan a dance, hire a band, sell tickets, and decorate the gym. The course of action you choose will depend on how much time and energy you are willing to devote and how important it is to you to achieve a certain result.

You have a choice about your level of participation. However, you must realize that you will have to take the consequences of participating or deciding not to participate. In the case of the school dance, if you do nothing, you will have no activity, or perhaps someone else will plan an activity you do not enjoy. If you choose to take an active role, you are likely to have the kind of school activity you enjoy. Most people find that when they participate fully in a role, they feel satisfaction and get a better sense of who they are.

Many teenagers volunteer as part of their citizen role. This girl works with a group that provides information and advice to other teenagers.

Playing the Citizen Role

Earlier in this chapter, you learned the importance of the "office of citizen" in American society. In fulfilling that office, you are playing a very important role: the citizen role.

Some of the behaviors that people expect of citizens in our society include obeying the laws and paying taxes. These are the required duties of citizenship. The rest of the behaviors we expect of citizens are the voluntary activities, such as voting, running for office, and organizing to influence government actions.

Choosing Citizen Activities
For some people, playing the citizen role has high priority. When faced with a conflict between roles, they choose to devote more of their time and energy to the "office of citizen." These people, when they are students, are the ones who take leadership roles in student government. They plan the school activities and work with the administration and the school board to solve

school problems, as Peter Ky did with the recycling program.

Adults for whom the citizen role has high priority may run for government office. They may volunteer to serve on boards and committees that study government problems or plan for parks and recreation. They may devote much of their time to helping with political campaigns or working for organizations that try to influence government decisions.

Other people spend less time playing the citizen role. Some are satisfied simply to keep informed, to vote, or perhaps to give money to support candidates and issues.

As with your other roles, you cannot always participate in citizenship activities as actively as you might want to. For example, Peter Ky would like to be more active in student government. However, he knows that at this stage in his life, he needs to spend most of his time studying and helping in his family's restaurant.

Doris Hollingsworth has her hands full as a wife, mother, worker, and student. She says that she has very little time to devote to political activities just now.

Contributing to the Common Good

Being a responsible citizen is not limited to participating in political activities, however. Earlier in this chapter you learned that the overall responsibility of every citizen in the United States is to contribute to the common good. Many people are making such a contribution to the common good when they play roles that they may not think of as citizen roles.

For example, Bernice Kelman helps at the church thrift shop. The money the shop raises goes to buy medicine and food for elderly people in the community. In this way, Bernice is contributing to the common good while playing a role in a social group in her church. In addition, helping others makes Bernice feel good about herself.

Facts & Quotes

A Nation of Volunteers

According to a study by the Independent Sector of Washington, D.C.:

★ About 109 million American adults participate in some form of volunteer work.
★ About 56 percent of all Americans spend an average of 3.5 hours a week in volunteer work.
★ Americans spend about 19.9 billion hours of their time volunteering in a given year.
★ Volunteers provide a range of services, including serving food, making repairs, organizing events, and working with children.
★ Some of the major reasons why people volunteer include:

1. They like the opportunity to do something useful.
2. They enjoy the work.
3. The work helps people in need.
4. Volunteering supports their moral values.

When Bernice was secretary to the superintendent of schools, she was playing a worker role. However, the work she did supported the town's efforts to educate its children. Therefore, Bernice was contributing to the common good in her role as worker. Although neither of these activities is political, they both make Bernice's community a better place to live.

Setting Priorities for Citizenship How much time and energy will you devote to fulfilling your responsibilities as a citizen? This decision is one that you will make again and again in your life. Each time, that decision will be influenced by the other roles you are playing and how important they are to you. It will also be influenced by the stage of your life, by your values, and by your particular talents and interests.

Playing the citizen role in a political way may not always be a high priority for you. However, as a citizen you share the responsibility of all Americans to protect the basic values that unite us as a people and as a society. Therefore, if you choose never to play the citizen role, you are giving up your right to have a voice in your government and to make a difference in your community.

Section 3 Assessment

1. **Define** social roles
2. Describe two situations in which you play the role of student differently.
3. Give an example of a situation in which you play two overlapping roles.
4. What happens when a person's roles come into conflict with each other? Give an example.
5. Give two examples of how people behave when playing the citizen role.
6. **Synthesize** What do you think might happen in your community if no one chose to perform the voluntary activities of the citizen role?

Extending the Chapter

Global Views

In this chapter you have been learning about what it means to be an American citizen. Do citizens of other nations have the same rights, duties, and responsibilities as we do? The answer to that question depends upon the type of government a nation has.

You might be a citizen of a nation governed by an absolute monarch, such as Saudi Arabia; by a dictator, such as Libya; or by a group or political party that has complete authority to make and enforce the laws, such as China. The government of that nation might provide the services you and its other citizens need. It might protect the rights it thinks its citizens should have.

As a citizen of such a nation, you might be loyal to it and willing to defend it against its enemies. However, the nature of your citizenship would be very different than it is in the United States. You would be a subject—a citizen who must abide by the government's decisions but who has no legal power to try to change them or to choose different government officials.

The citizens of the United States deliberately took the power into their own hands. They created a government system in which the people, rather than a monarch or dictator or ruling party, have the final power.

Therefore, as citizens we must take the responsibility to be well informed and to participate in government by holding office, by voting, and by working to make sure that everyone's rights are protected and that everyone's voice is heard.

In a speech he gave in 1952, Adlai E. Stevenson, a candidate for President, said:

As citizens of this democracy, you are the rulers and the ruled, the lawgivers and the law-abiding, the beginning and the end.

With these words, he summed up the meaning of American citizenship.

How to TAKE ACTION

"Well, did you do what you said you were going to do?" Often, many of us have to answer "No" to this question.

Good decision making is not just a matter of choosing what to do. You have to plan how to do it and then do it. Otherwise you will be like someone who goes bowling and aims well but does not follow through. Your good decisions will roll into the gutter.

The Decision Making lesson in Chapter 2 showed you the steps involved in the first part of the decision-making process: *choosing* which way to reach your goal. This lesson will focus on the second part of the decision-making process: taking action—doing what needs to be done to reach your goal. Creating a plan of action and following through with it are necessary in good decision making.

Explain the Skill

One way to make an action plan is to follow these steps:

1. **State your action goal.** Your action goal is to carry out the decision you just made.
2. **Identify resources (what will help you) and obstacles (what you will have to overcome).** Knowing what you can use and what problems you might face will help you decide what has to be done.
3. **List what you have to do to achieve your goal.** Think about who will do what and when it will be done.
4. **Carry out your plan.** Check each step you take to see if what you are doing is getting you toward your goal. If necessary, change your plan.
5. **Judge how well your plan worked.** Identify the results of what you did, including

any unexpected results. Determine what you might do differently if you used the plan again.

Analyze the Skill

On page 40, you read about how the student council at Janice's school chose a way to achieve a clean campus. Now you will see how the members of the student council put their choice into action.

Everyone was pleased with our decision to give buttons as rewards to students for helping to keep the school clean. However, before we had finished congratulating ourselves, the student council president reminded us that we were not done yet. "I know this button idea looks great," Chris said. "But we still have to make it work. We have to make sure that the buttons will get most students to keep the campus clean." So with that the student council got down to business.

First, we thought of what could help us in putting our idea into action. Debbie thought that we might be able to use the Pep Club's button-making machine and get free poster paper from the art teacher. But there were also some possible problems to deal with. For instance, as Rob warned, students might complain that exchanging buttons for ticket discounts was unfair to people paying full price. If enough students thought that the plan was unfair, it would fall apart very quickly.

Now that we knew what would be useful and what might get in the way, we were ready to list things we needed to do, including using the available help and dealing with problems. Sharon and Raul would ask the principal for permission. Then Debbie would talk with the Pep Club president about using the button-making machine. Karen would develop a colorful button design.

To get students to support the idea of exchanging buttons for discounts, Tim and Rob would make rules showing that the buttons could be easily earned by any student. Eventually, our list of tasks covered everything from signing up teams and clubs as clean-up sponsors to recruiting students who would hand out buttons.

As our plan went into effect, we held several meetings to discuss our progress. Chris kept everyone's job flexible. For example, at first my task was to make morning announcements encouraging students to keep the campus clean. As the clean-up campaign got rolling, however, I began writing weekly reports for the school paper on the progress of the clean-up.

After a few weeks we knew that our plan was a success. The campus was free of litter, and the bathroom mirrors shone. Students were taking more pride in the school. There were also some results we had not expected. For example, instead of losing money by giving discounts to button holders, the school actually made more money. People who had complained about high ticket prices were now going to more dances and athletic events. The crowds were bigger than ever! We had helped school spirit in more ways than one.

One day Chris called us all together for another meeting and said, "Okay, our plan is working. Now what can we do to make it even better?" Diane suggested using several different button designs for variety. Then Ken came up with the idea of earning money for the school by recycling drink cans instead of throwing them in the trash. Right away we began thinking about how to include those suggestions in our clean-up plan.

Skill Assessment

Now that you have read about the students' plan, answer the following questions.

1. What was the student council's action goal?
2. What did the students think might help them? What was one of the problems they expected? Explain.
3. Name at least three actions the student council took. Explain why each action was important.
4. What was the main sign of the plan's success? Explain your answer. **(a)** attendance at dances and athletic events **(b)** the support of the principal and teachers **(c)** the clean campus
5. What did the student council do after judging how well their plan worked? Explain. **(a)** made changes in it, **(b)** decided that it was no longer necessary, **(c)** started a new project
6. How does the *acting* part of the decision-making process differ from the *choosing* part?
7. Explain why *acting* in decision making means more than just "doing something."

How to READ A NEWSPAPER

In this chapter you read a description of one day in the life of Doris Hollingsworth, a busy working mother. Doris describes reading the newspaper during her breakfast "to find out what the mayor had had to say about the need for more stop signs at the intersections near the school."

Doris was performing one of her responsibilities as a citizen—keeping herself informed about public issues. A good way to do this is to become a regular newspaper reader. Newspapers can provide you with a wealth of information about your community, state, nation, and world.

Explain the Skill

People who enjoy reading the newspaper regularly become familiar with the sections of their favorite newspaper. For example, most newspapers cover major news stories in a front section. This section may also include the editorial pages. Editorials express points of view on events and issues. Readers' opinions appear here in the form of letters to the editor.

Other sections may cover local news, sports, business, entertainment, lifestyles, food, and gardening. The classified section may have listings of job openings, housing for sale and rent, and items for sale.

Analyze the Skill

The front page of most newspapers has an index like the one on this page to help readers find specific information. In this index the letters and numbers refer to sections and to page numbers in a section. The comics, for example, are on D-7, or on page 7 in section D.

If Doris were looking through an index like this one for the mayor's comments on

Index

Business	C-1	Movies	D-2
Books	D-4	National News	A-2
Classified	E-1	Sports	F-1
Comics	D-7	Television	D-5
Editorials	A-10	Weather	B-10
Local News	B-1	World News	A-5

stop signs, she would have several options. The topic might be considered a major news story. If so, it could be covered on the front page or within the front section. On the other hand, it could be covered under Local News, which begins in section B on page B-1. Or it might appear in the Editorials, on page A-10. The mayor could have written a letter to the editor, or the topic could be the subject of an editorial piece by the newspaper.

Skill Assessment

Study the newspaper index shown above to answer questions 1–3.

1. Where might you look for information about the following topics? **(a)** a new plan to improve parking in your city **(b)** what readers think about the parking plan **(c)** racial problems in South Africa **(d)** where to buy a used bicycle **(e)** how cold it will be tonight **(f)** a debate in Congress about the President's recent health-care proposals
2. What is a likely name for section D?
3. In which two sections could an important local news story be located?
4. How does using an index help you to find an article in the newspaper?

CHAPTER 3 ASSESSMENT

Building Civics Vocabulary

Match each numbered vocabulary term with the lettered word or phrase most closely related to it. Then explain how the items in each pair are related.

Example: *Social roles* is related to *friend* because being a friend is one social role you might play.

1. *naturalized*   (a) "office of citizen"
2. *the common good*   (b) trial
3. *jury of peers*   (c) immigrant
4. *candidate*   (d) election

Reviewing Main Ideas and Skills

5. Describe the process of becoming a naturalized American citizen.

6. Explain what is meant by "government of the people, by the people, and for the people."

7. Choose three rights of citizens. Which basic values do they reflect?

8. Choose one of the five duties of citizens and explain why we are required to fulfill it.

9. Describe two ways that a person under age eighteen can fulfill the voluntary responsibilities of citizenship.

10. Give an example of a role you were born into, a role you are required to play, and a role you have chosen for yourself.

11. **How to Take Action** Suppose there is a shelter for homeless people in your community. You have decided to help it raise money. How would you formulate a plan of action to carry out your decision?

12. **How to Read a Newspaper** In which section of the newspaper would you find an article about plans to build a new local mall?

Critical Thinking

13. **Defending a Position** In a democracy, the office of citizen is the most important office there is. Do you agree with this statement? Explain why or why not.

14. **Predicting Consequences** Suppose that someone said to you, "Why should I bother to vote? My one vote won't make a difference." How would you answer that person?

Writing About Civics

15. **Writing for a Newsletter** You have been asked to write an article for a newsletter for new citizens. In one paragraph, explain why contributing to the common good is an important responsibility of citizenship.

Citizenship Activities

16. **Working in Groups** With three or four classmates, make a chart listing all the social groups each of you is a member of. Which social group memberships do all the people in your group have in common?

 Take It to the NET

Access the **Civics: Participating in Government** Internet site at **www.phschool.com** for the specific URL to complete the activity.

Study the data and charts about voter registration and voter turnout in your state. How many registered voters have turned out for recent presidential elections? Has the number increased or decreased? Write a sentence summarizing the trends in voter turnout in your state. Then write a paragraph explaining what you believe are the reasons behind these trends.

My American Dream

Dan Helfrich was a sixteen-year-old student at Loomis Chaffee Academy in Connecticut when he portrayed candidate George H. W. Bush in a mock presidential election. That experience gave him a new perspective on how our government works. He reflected, "I realized that politics was a lot more intricate [complex] than I thought."

Before you read the selection, find the meanings of these words in a dictionary: idealistic, proverbial.

If I had a wish one day, it would be that the government would take more seriously their influence on the lives of the people in their country....My wishes are real idealistic ones—that everyone would be represented in government and that the events that happen in Washington, D.C., and big-time politics would be more representative of the population in this country.

The American dream—that is everyone is gonna be free and someone can come over from Ireland when there was a potato famine and have equal opportunity—that's what I consider the proverbial American dream. But my American dream is that everyone else's American dream would come

true and that there wouldn't be so much underlying prejudice in this nation. My American dream is to see an African American in the White House. I think that would be a great thing. It would show me how far we have come....

The country is going in the right direction, but history will tell you that things take a long time to work themselves out. The abolition of slavery is a huge accomplishment for history, and it's a huge accomplishment that African Americans and women have the right to vote today—that took a real long time. And those are changes that we take for granted too. A lot of

progress has been made since the Revolutionary War, or since the days when Columbus came....

I have a good feeling about the future. The people of my generation are more outspoken and more in tune with what's going on, and I'd like to think that when the people of my generation are in the position that the people in politics are in today, they're going to be more sensitive and more representative of the people of our country. I think a lot of progress has been made in that regard. But more and more needs to be done; you can never say that's good enough. You gotta be looking to get a step ahead.

Source: Marcia A. Thompson, ed., Who Cares What I Think? American Teens Talk About Their Lives and Their Country (Alexandria, Va.: Close Up Foundation, 1994), pages 191–204.

Analyzing Primary Sources

1. What is Dan Helfrich's personal "American dream?"

2. According to Dan Helfrich, what kinds of progress have been made in American history?

UNIT 1 ASSESSMENT

Reviewing Main Ideas

1. Is it possible to treat another person with equal respect even if you find that he or she has opinions or values different from your own? Explain your answer, giving examples.

2. What does it mean to you now to play a citizenship role in the United States? How do you think you might answer this question when you are an adult?

3. Explain how each of the following activities contributes to the common good. **(a)** voting in an election **(b)** recycling newspapers **(c)** expressing your views in a letter to the editor **(d)** treating a person with equal respect

4. Match each social role listed below with the social institution that most affects you when you are playing that role.

1. son or daughter	**(a)** the economy
2. student	**(b)** government
3. citizen	**(c)** the family
4. consumer	**(d)** education

Summarizing the Unit

The tree map below will help you organize the main ideas of the unit. Copy it onto a separate sheet of paper. Review the unit to complete the graphic organizer by adding examples for each of the boxes in the bottom row. (The first one is done for you.) Then write a short essay that answers the question posed by the graphic organizer's title.

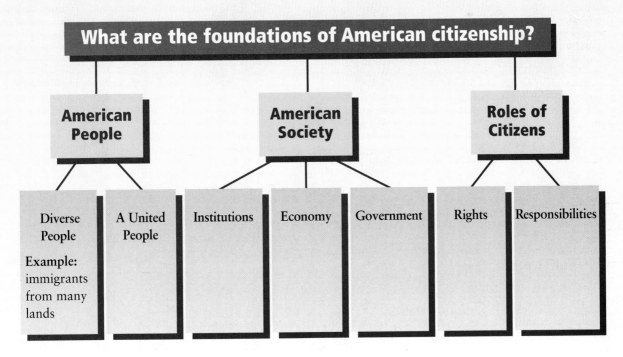

What are the foundations of American citizenship?

- **American People**
  - Diverse People
    - Example: immigrants from many lands
  - A United People
- **American Society**
  - Institutions
  - Economy
  - Government
- **Roles of Citizens**
  - Rights
  - Responsibilities

Creating a Lasting Government

Why Study Civics?

A government of our own is our natural right. It is infinitely wiser and safer to form a constitution of our own in a cool, deliberate manner, while we have it in our power, than to trust such an interesting event to time and chance.

—**Thomas Paine,** *Common Sense,* **1776**

Thomas Paine wrote the pamphlet *Common Sense* at the very start of the Revolutionary War. His goal was to urge Americans to fight for freedom from England and to establish a new kind of government—a government that belonged to the people. This dream became reality with the founding of the United States of America and the adoption of our Constitution. As Americans, we truly have "a government of our own." And the more we know about this government and how it was formed, the more we can do to lead our nation into the future.

What's Ahead in Unit 2

Unit 2 will explore the origins of our government. You will see how the colonists' beliefs about citizenship and government led to the creation of the Constitution that has guided our nation for more than 200 years.

America's Political Heritage

Citizenship and You

The date was November 11, 1620. A lone ship, the *Mayflower*, lay anchored off the rugged Massachusetts coast. Aboard the vessel were 102 passengers, many of whom were Pilgrims seeking religious freedom. Others had made the stormy two-month voyage from England mainly to seek wealth.

Whatever had drawn these travelers to North America, one thing was clear—they would all have to work together to survive the approaching winter. Order had to be established. Laws had to be made. The men gathered in the ship's main cabin and emerged with the Mayflower Compact—a signed agreement to make and obey "just and equal" laws for the "general good of the colony."

In a world in which most people had laws imposed upon them, this agreement was a bold step toward self-government. The rights and responsibilities of citizens continued to expand as the colonies grew, leading to the founding of the United States of America— a nation governed by its citizens.

What's Ahead in Chapter 4

In this chapter you will explore the origins of the American belief in government by consent of the people—a rare form of government in the history of the world.

Section 1 **The Colonial Experience**

Section 2 **Roots of American Government**

Section 3 **Moving Toward Nationhood**

Keep It Current

Items marked with this logo are periodically updated on the Internet. To keep up-to-date, go to **www.phschool.com**

Citizen's Journal

Suppose you were helping to write the Mayflower Compact in 1620. What is one right that you would want the agreement to protect? Write a paragraph explaining your choice.

The Colonial Experience

SECTION PREVIEW

Objectives

- Describe the role colonists played in their government.
- Define the rights and responsibilities of colonial citizens.
- Identify the freedoms that early colonists struggled to gain.
- Explain why many colonists became dissatisfied with royal governors.

Building Civics Vocabulary

- Traditions passed down from generation to generation make up our **heritage.**
- A **legislature** is a group of people chosen to make laws.
- A **charter** is a document giving permission to create a government.
- **Tyranny** is abuse of power.

Focus

Many of the American traditions you read about in Unit 1 took root during the colonial period. The values and experiences of the settlers in the 13 English colonies make up an important part of our heritage, the traditions passed down to us from generation to generation.

A Voice in Government

From the beginning, citizens in the 13 colonies were used to having a voice in their government. It was one of their rights as citizens of England. In each colony, citizens could elect representatives to the legislature, a group of people chosen to make the laws. This gave them a degree of self-government that was rare in the world at that time.

The beginning of representative government in America can be traced back to the year 1619, when the colonists of Virginia elected representatives called burgesses. This first colonial legislature, the Virginia House of Burgesses, was soon followed by other legislatures as more colonies were founded.

The right to elect members of their legislature, however, did not give colonial citizens complete control of their government. They were still subject to the authority of England, whose monarch established each colony through a charter, a document giving permission to create a government. Any colony that seriously challenged England's authority might be stripped of its charter and become a royal colony under the control of the monarch, who appointed a royal governor.

Facts & Quotes

Voting in the Colonies

A colonist did not cast his vote in the privacy of a voting booth as voters do today. Instead, he voted in full view of the candidates and other voters. One historian gives a picture of voting day at a county courthouse in Virginia:

" At a table sat the sheriff, the candidates, and the clerk. The voters came up one at a time to announce their choices, which were recorded publicly. Since anyone present could always see the latest count, a candidate could at the last minute send supporters to bring in additional needed votes. As each voter declared his preference, shouts of approval would come from one side and hoots from another. The favored candidate would rise, bow, and express thanks to the voter. "

In theory, England had final authority over the colonies, and the English governor could reject laws passed by colonial legislatures. However, throughout the 1600s and early 1700s England was busy fighting wars, and had little time to pay attention to colonial laws. Thus the colonists played a large role in governing themselves.

Preserving Rights Used to having a voice in government, colonial citizens resisted any efforts to ignore their rights or to weaken their legislatures. Typically those efforts were made by colonial governors, who were usually appointed to their posts rather than elected, and who generally represented England's interests rather than those of the colonists. Some also represented proprietors— wealthy nobles or merchants who had been granted charters.

From time to time, the legislatures became involved in power struggles with colonial governors and proprietors. For instance, the Virginia House of Burgesses declared that the governor could not tax citizens without the legislature's consent. Similarly, in 1641 the Massachusetts legislature passed laws protecting basic rights, such as trial by jury.

Citizenship in the Colonies

Many of our American rights and traditions can be traced back to the colonial period. However, being an English citizen in the 1600s and 1700s differed in some important ways from being an American citizen today.

First of all, most people who can now vote in our country would have been denied that right in the English colonies. Usually only white men who owned a certain amount of land were allowed to vote or hold office. A common belief was that they were the people most affected by the laws. Also, only a wealthy man was thought to have enough education and free time to become involved in politics.

In no colony could enslaved persons vote. Colonial laws not only denied them the right to vote, but also treated them as property.

COLONIAL SETTLEMENT BY ETHNIC GROUP IN 1770

America's cultural mosaic can be traced to the colonial period. Over half of the colonists were non-English. **Movement How many different ethnic groups were represented in South Carolina in 1770? What were they?**

This metal engraving of Harvard College was made in 1767 by Paul Revere, who later became one of America's most famous patriots.

rather than as people. The European colonists wanted rights for themselves, but they denied rights to the Africans who were forced to come to the colonies as slaves.

Although it is important to recognize that relatively few people in the colonies were allowed to vote, we should also remember that citizens in most nations and colonies during the 1600s and early 1700s did not have any rights. The English colonies in America were among the few places in the world where citizens actually participated in their government.

The Common Good Colonial citizens, like citizens today, had a responsibility to work for the common good. They helped their communities in various ways, such as serving on juries and becoming members of the local militia, or volunteer army.

Citizens also served their communities by supporting education. For instance, the Puritans in New England set up a public school system to make sure that people could read and understand the Bible. Harvard College, the oldest university in the United States, was founded by the Puritans in 1636. In the middle and southern colonies, where there were few public schools, parents usually sent their children to private schools or taught them at home.

Some Roots of Freedom

We Americans have many freedoms. Among these are freedom of the press, freedom of speech, and freedom of religion. Such individual freedoms, however, were unknown for most of human history. They became part of our heritage mainly through the efforts of the colonists.

Greater Religious Freedom The colonists lived at a time when religion was closely tied to government in most parts of the world. All English citizens, for instance, had to pay taxes to support the Anglican church as the official Church of England. Many colonists, including the Pilgrims on the Mayflower and the Puritans who founded the Massachusetts Bay Colony, had left England because they were persecuted for disagreeing with the Anglican church.

Although the Puritans had fled persecution in England, they denied religious freedom to those who disagreed with them. They forced a minister named Roger Williams to leave their colony after he criticized church leaders. In 1636, Williams founded the colony of Rhode Island, whose charter promised that no colonist would be punished "for any differences in opinions in matters of religion." Before long, other colonies were also allowing religious freedom.

An engraving (right) shows Andrew Hamilton boldly defending freedom of the press. Also shown is an early issue of John Peter Zenger's paper.

Actually, the colonists' definition of "religious freedom" differed from our definition today. They usually meant that a person could belong to any Christian church, such as the Presbyterian or Anglican churches. They did not mean freedom for members of non-Christian religions. Nevertheless, considering the world in which they lived, the colonists were taking an important step—one that would eventually lead to freedom of religion for all Americans.

A Call for Freedom of the Press When colonial newspapers appeared in the early 1700s, they became an important source of information. Freedom of the press, however, did not exist in England or in the English colonies. Under English law, a publisher was not allowed to criticize the government.

One of the earliest arguments for freedom of the press was made in 1735 in a crowded New York City courtroom. On trial was John Peter Zenger, the publisher of a newspaper called the *New York Weekly Journal*. Zenger had printed articles accusing the New York governor of abusing his power by accepting bribes and interfering with elections. Furious, the governor had burned copies of the newspaper and had jailed Zenger, accusing him of trying to stir up rebellion against the government.

Zenger's lawyer, Andrew Hamilton, argued that Zenger was innocent if what he had written was true. Hamilton declared that freedom of the press was a basic right:

> "*The question before the court is not of small nor private concern. It may in its consequence affect every free person that lives under a British government. It is the best cause. It is the cause of liberty, the liberty both of exposing and opposing arbitrary power by speaking and writing truth.*"

After hearing Hamilton's argument, the jury left the room to discuss the case. When the 12 jurors returned, the spectators leaned forward in their chairs. A member of the jury stood to announce the verdict.

"Not guilty," he declared. Loud cheers filled the packed courtroom. Zenger was released from jail and went back to publishing his newspaper.

Although the verdict freed Zenger, it did not change English law and therefore it did not actually guarantee freedom of the press in America. However, the Zenger case did inspire other colonists to continue the fight for freedom of the press and to criticize governors who abused their power.

Signs of Discontent

By the mid-1700s, England had tightened its control over the colonies, making most of them royal colonies. Like Zenger, many colonists were angry at royal governors who used power without regard for citizens' rights. Some governors ordered citizens' homes to be searched without warning.

Zenger's lawyer had spoken of "arbitrary power," or abuse of power—which was more frequently called tyranny. As people complained about royal governors, the word *tyranny* was increasingly used throughout the colonies. A growing number of colonists began to wonder whether England might eventually try to strip them of their rights and silence their voice in government.

Section 1 Assessment

1. **Define** heritage, legislature, charter, tyranny
2. Why were colonial citizens able to influence the laws that governed them?
3. Compare English citizens in the colonies with American citizens today.
4. How are some of our freedoms rooted in the colonial period?
5. **Evaluate** Consider the geographic diversity of the thirteen original colonies. How did this diversity influence the colonists' economic, social, and political lives? Explain.

Roots of American Government

SECTION PREVIEW

Objectives

- Examine the connection between American government and governments in ancient Greece and Rome.
- Explain how the English tradition of government influenced Americans.
- Identify the ideas of European writers who influenced the development of American government.

Building Civics Vocabulary

- In a **direct democracy,** laws are made directly by the citizens.
- A **republic** is a government in which citizens elect representatives to make laws.
- **Natural rights** are rights that people are born with and that no government can take away.
- Dividing government power among branches is called **separation of powers**.

 Focus

To understand how our country began, we must recognize that the American colonists had the benefit of other people's experiences and ideas about government. John Adams, who eventually became one of the founders of our nation, urged his fellow colonists to look to the past for inspiration:

“*Let us study the law of nature; search into the spirit of the British constitution; read the histories of the ancient ages; [think about] the great examples of Greece and Rome; set before us the conduct of our own British ancestors.*”

This Roman coin, minted in 137 B.C., shows a citizen voting by dropping a ballot into a box. Roman ballots were wooden or stone tablets.

Looking to Ancient Greece and Rome

What did John Adams mean by "the great examples of Greece and Rome"? First of all, he was thinking of the ancient Greek city of Athens. For hundreds of years, Athens and other Greek cities had been ruled by all-powerful kings. In time, the Athenians came to believe that the wisdom of all the citizens together was superior to the wisdom of one ruler.

The Athenians created the world's first direct democracy, a form of government in which laws are made directly by the citizens. The citizens of Athens met regularly to discuss ways to make life better for their community. Centuries later some American colonists practiced direct democracy by holding town meetings to vote on local issues.

While town meetings mirrored Athenian-style direct democracy, the colonial legislatures resembled a representative form of government established in ancient Rome. In 509 B.C., the Romans founded a republic, a government in which representatives were elected to make laws. Instead of being ruled by a monarch, citizens of the Roman republic elected representatives called senators, who conducted the business of government. As in Athens, citizenship in Rome was limited.

The English Tradition

The people in the English colonies saw the democracy of Athens and the republic of Rome as noble examples of governments designed to prevent tyranny. Unfortunately, those governments eventually gave way to government by force. The voices of citizens were replaced by the commands of monarchs, who often abused their power.

After the end of the Roman republic, government by the people disappeared for hundreds of years. Then, in the year A.D. 1215, a dramatic conflict took place in England—a conflict that changed the course of English history and laid the groundwork for the type of government we have today.

The Magna Carta For centuries, monarchs had ruled with complete authority over the English people. Instead of being citizens with rights, the people were subjects—they were subject to the monarch's command. Although some monarchs used their powers in a wise and just manner, other monarchs were tyrants who stirred resentment among their subjects.

By the early 1200s, English nobles had become strong enough to challenge royal power. In 1215 they forced King John to sign the Magna Carta, or Great Charter, which listed rights that even the English monarch would not have the power to take away. Among these rights were the right to a fair trial and the right to travel freely.

The Magna Carta was an important step in gaining basic freedoms for all English people. For the first time the monarch's power had been limited. Although the document was intended to protect only nobles, the rights it listed were eventually given to all English citizens—including the colonists.

King John is surrounded by nobles and church leaders who forced him to sign the Magna Carta. A monument stands at the site of the signing.

The English Bill of Rights Once the monarch's power had been limited, a representative government soon followed. By the late 1200s, a legislature called Parliament was well established in England. Over the centuries, Parliament gradually became more powerful than the monarch.

In 1689, Parliament passed the English Bill of Rights, which further limited the power of the monarch. For example, the king or queen would no longer be able to limit free speech in Parliament or to collect taxes without Parliament's approval.

The English Bill of Rights listed the rights of all English citizens, not just nobles. It included ideas that would later find a place in our government. One is that everyone, even government leaders, must obey the law.

Another is that all people have the right to a trial by jury and the right to make a formal petition, or request, to the government.

By stating the rights of English citizens, both the Magna Carta and the English Bill of Rights provided protections against tyranny. The colonists in America treasured these protections of their rights.

Relying on Reason

After reading the quotation from John Adams at the beginning of this section, you may have wondered what he meant by urging his fellow colonists to "study the law of nature." Actually, he was echoing what a number of European writers were saying during the 1600s and 1700s: that people have the power of reason, the ability to think clearly. By using reason, these writers argued, people can recognize their natural rights, rights they are born with and that no government can take away.

One writer who particularly inspired the colonists was the Englishman John Locke. He argued that representative government is the only reasonable kind—that government exists for the people, not people for the government. According to Locke, the purpose of government is to protect natural rights—the rights to life, liberty, and property. Any government that abuses its power by interfering with those rights should not be obeyed.

Many colonial leaders were also inspired by the ideas of the French writer Montesquieu (mon tes KYOO). Since they knew that power could lead to tyranny, they liked his proposal for separation of powers, dividing government power among legislative, executive, and judicial branches. The legislature would only make the laws; the executive, such as a governor, would only enforce the laws; the judges would only interpret the meaning of the laws. Such a system would

The writings of John Locke (1632–1704) had so much influence that he has sometimes been called "the intellectual ruler of the eighteenth century."

guard against tyranny because no government official or branch of government could gain too much power.

Section 2 Assessment

1. **Define** direct democracy, republic, natural rights, separation of powers
2. Describe which traditions in colonial government can be traced back to ancient Greece and Rome.
3. What did the colonists inherit from the English tradition of government?
4. What ideas of Locke and Montesquieu were important to the colonists?
5. **Compare** What similarities do you think the colonists saw in the Greek, Roman, and English traditions of government?

Moving Toward Nationhood

SECTION PREVIEW

Objectives
- Describe how and why colonists organized to oppose English rule.
- Summarize the arguments in the Declaration of Independence.
- Describe the state and national governments Americans established after winning independence.
- Analyze reasons why many Americans wanted a stronger national government.

Building Civics Vocabulary
- A written agreement to make and obey laws is a **compact**.
- A **constitution** is a written plan of government.
- A constitution needs **ratification**, or approval, before going into effect.

Focus

If the colonists had inherited their tradition of representative government from England, why did they become dissatisfied with English rule? Why did relations between the colonies and England get worse, eventually exploding into the war that led to American independence? Answering these questions involves looking first at how tensions developed between England and the colonies over the issue of representation in government.

A Clash of Views

England believed that Parliament represented all English citizens—including the colonists. The colonists, on the other hand, believed that they were only represented by their own legislatures. The colonists pointed out that they could not vote for members of Parliament and that no colonists were members themselves. They also noted that, unlike the colonial legislatures, Parliament had little understanding of the colonists' needs.

The colonists and the English government also had opposing views on colonial trade. Parliament permitted the colonies to trade only with England. The colonists wanted the freedom to sell their products to any country.

Despite these sharply differing views, many colonists still considered themselves loyal English citizens. In fact, they helped England defeat France in the French and Indian War, which ended in 1763. The colonists celebrated the victory, not knowing that their loyalty would soon be tested by new taxes forced on them by the English government.

A 1765 tax on stamped paper, which had to be used for official documents, enraged colonists. Here they burn stamped paper in protest.

"No Taxation Without Representation"

Facing huge war debts, Parliament decided to squeeze money out of the colonies through taxes, mainly on trade goods. Outraged, the colonists protested that they should not be taxed unless their own representatives approved such taxes. The colonists believed, following the ideas of John Locke, that taxation without representation was taking people's property without their consent. Soon the cry of "no taxation without representation" was heard throughout the colonies.

To make people pay the taxes, Parliament gave the governors greater power. Colonists accused of breaking tax laws were thrown in jail. Parliament ignored petitions protesting the taxes and the governors' actions, claiming that it had the power to make laws for the colonies "in all cases whatsoever." The cloud of tyranny seemed to be growing darker.

Steps Toward Independence

At first the colonies did not join together in protesting Parliament's actions. Having quarreled with each other in the past over boundaries and trade, they were not used to working toward a common goal. To inspire cooperation, some colonists organized Committees of Correspondence to pass news from colony to colony about how England was violating colonists' rights. Eventually many of the colonial legislatures saw the need for a united response to Parliament's threats. They called for a congress, or formal meeting, of representatives from all the colonies.

In 1774, delegates from 12 colonies met in Philadelphia for the First Continental Congress. The delegates hoped to convince the English government to respect colonists' rights. To pressure Parliament, they pledged to cut off all trade with England. Then they agreed to meet the following year if the situation did not improve.

Thomas Jefferson, at age 33, was chosen to draft the Declaration of Independence. He is shown here, presenting the document to the members of the Second Continental Congress.

Far from improving, the situation got worse. By the time the Second Continental Congress met in 1775, colonists in Massachusetts were already fighting English soldiers. Delegate Patrick Henry argued for independence, stating that the war had already begun and that there was no turning back.

Many colonists feared independence, however. Even if they fought and won, they thought, what future would they face without the security of being part of a strong nation like England?

The writings of Thomas Paine changed many people's minds. In 1776, Paine published his pamphlet titled *Common Sense,* in which he presented his argument:

> *To be always running 3,000 or 4,000 miles with a tale or a petition, waiting four or five months for an answer which, when obtained, requires five or six more [months] to explain it in, will in a few years be looked upon as folly and childishness—there was a time when it was proper, and there is a proper time for it to cease. There is something absurd in supposing a continent to be perpetually governed by an island. England [belongs] to Europe. America to itself.*

The Declaration of Independence

With popular support for separation from England increasing, the delegates to the Second Continental Congress finally voted for independence. However, they still had to convince some Americans of the wisdom of a break with England. The delegates also wanted to tell European countries why the colonies deserved to be free. Therefore, they appointed a committee to write a declaration of independence. Among the committee members were Thomas Jefferson, Benjamin Franklin, and John Adams. Jefferson was asked to do the actual writing.

The ringing phrases of the Declaration of Independence capture many of the colonists' beliefs about natural rights:

> *We hold these truths to be self-evident, that all men are created equal, that they are endowed by their Creator with certain unalienable rights, that among these are life, liberty, and the pursuit of happiness.*

As did John Locke, Jefferson described these rights as "unalienable"—meaning that no government has the power to take them away.

Further reflecting Locke's views, Jefferson described the purpose of government:

> **"** *...to secure these rights, governments are instituted among men, deriving their just powers from the consent of the governed.* **"**

In other words, the people give power to their government as long as it protects their rights. If a government abuses its powers, the people may change it or do away with it:

> **"** *...whenever any form of government becomes destructive of these ends, it is the right of the people to alter or to abolish it, and to institute [create] new government.* **"**

Jefferson then listed the ways in which England had ignored the colonists' rights as English citizens—proof that England was trying to rule the colonies with "absolute tyranny."

The Declaration concludes with the signers pledging to support it with "our lives, our Fortunes, and our sacred Honor." Adopted by representatives of the colonists in Philadelphia on July 4, 1776, the Declaration of Independence proclaimed that "these United Colonies are and of right ought to be, Free and Independent States."

The full text of the Declaration of Independence can be found on pages 86–87.

Organizing a New Government

Now that the colonies had become "free and independent states," each of them had to organize a government of its own. Because the colonies had been established by charters, people were used to the idea of having a written plan of government. People also remembered that the *Mayflower* passengers had made a compact, a written agreement to make and obey laws for the welfare of the group.

State Constitutions The newly independent states wanted to continue this tradition of basing governments on written agreements. Therefore each state created a constitution, or plan of government. By creating written constitutions, the states were clearly spelling out the limits on government power. Some state constitutions also included a list of citizens' rights, such as trial by jury and freedom of religion.

To help guard against tyranny, each state constitution limited the number of years a governor could hold office. The states wanted to make it clear that a governor could not be like a king who holds office for life. As a further protection against abuse of power, each state used Montesquieu's idea of separating government into legislative, executive, and judicial branches. Of the three branches, the legislature was given the most power because it most directly represented the interests of citizens.

The Articles of Confederation

Although the states were united in opposing England, they were still 13 separate governments. During the war against England, the delegates to the Second Continental Congress debated how to form a national government.

The delegates faced a difficult task. Conflicts with the English king and Parliament had made the colonists fearful of giving power—especially the power to tax— to a central government. Also, the states disagreed on how many representatives each one should have in the government. Large states like Virginia wanted the number of representatives to be based on population. Small states like Rhode Island were afraid that the large states, with more representatives, would then have too much power. They argued that each state should have the same number of votes.

In 1777, after long and heated debate, the Continental Congress drew up a plan

Black Patriots Memorial

Every year millions of tourists visit Washington, D.C., our nation's capital. Almost all of them spend some time viewing the monuments that honor Presidents Washington, Jefferson, and Lincoln. Most also stand in respectful silence at the Vietnam Veterans Memorial.

Wayne Smith, director of the Black Patriots Foundation, hopes to see another stop added to this marble and bronze tour of our nation's history. A Vietnam veteran, Smith heads the drive to build the Black Patriots Monument, a memorial to the 5,000 African American soldiers, sailors, and civilians who helped win the American Revolution. "Right now," says Smith "their role is a part of the nation's invisible history. No one disputes that African Americans fought courageously

throughout the Revolutionary War. But this part of history wasn't really recorded by men who viewed African Americans in equal terms."

The struggle to build the memorial has been a long one. In 1986, Maurice Barboza, who founded the Black Patriots Foundation, won the approval of Congress and President Reagan to construct the memorial.

Two years later Congress set aside a site for it on the National Mall, just 300 yards from the Vietnam Memorial.

The biggest hurdle to the memorial's construction has been finding the $7.8 million needed to create the 90-foot-long bronze sculpture. But with widespread support from individuals, foundations, corporations, and Washington, D.C. area school children, Smith believes the memorial will soon become a reality. "The Black Patriots Memorial will serve as a touchstone for racial harmony, ennobling us all," he says. "It will be a place that all Americans can be proud of."

Active Citizenship

According to Smith, why would the Black Patriots Memorial be important for all Americans?

---

for a loose confederation, or alliance of independent states. This compact, known as the Articles of Confederation, called for a national legislature in which each state would have one vote.

There would be no executive or judicial branches of government, mainly because the state legislatures feared that these branches might try to take power away from them.

In 1787, Daniel Shays' army of farmers marched on a government arsenal. The Massachusetts state militia opened fire, forcing the farmers to retreat.

The national legislature, known as Congress, was given power to declare war, make treaties with foreign countries, and work out trade agreements between states. However, it was *not* given the power to tax or to enforce any laws it made. Therefore, most of the power would remain with the states.

Before the Articles of Confederation could go into effect, they needed the ratification, or approval, of all 13 states. At first it seemed the states would reject the plan because many state legislatures still did not trust a central government. Even while fighting the Revolutionary War, it took four years for the states to agree on a plan of government. Finally, the states realized that they had to cooperate or lose the war. The Articles were ratified in 1781.

A Limping Government

You know the story of how the patriots under General George Washington won our independence in the Revolutionary War. However, after winning the war the new government had to face another challenge: a struggling economy. Congress and the states had borrowed money to buy war supplies.

Now they could not pay off these huge debts because they did not have enough gold and silver to back up their printed money. Many Americans and foreigners lost confidence in the value of American money.

Another problem was that the new Congress had no power to regulate trade with England. Americans were buying most of their manufactured goods from England because prices were low. American merchants could not sell their goods as cheaply as the English. Congress could not help because it did not have the power to raise the prices of English goods by taxing them. Furthermore, England no longer allowed Americans to trade with English colonies in the British West Indies, one of the most important markets for American crops and manufactured goods.

Shays' Rebellion Many farmers slid into debt, largely because they could not sell their crops to the Caribbean colonies. Farmers in Massachusetts faced an added problem. To pay its war debts, the state legislature had sharply raised taxes on land. Many farmers who were unable to pay the taxes faced loss of their farms. Local courts threatened to sell the farms and use the money to pay the taxes.

In 1786, hundreds of angry Massachusetts farmers, led by a former war hero named Daniel Shays, stormed into courthouses to disrupt court business. Congress did not have the power to force other states to help put down the uprising. Massachusetts had to use its own state militia to crush the rebellion.

Newspapers quickly spread word of the violent clash, which shocked people throughout the states. Many Americans called for a stronger national government, one that would keep law and order and solve the economic problems that had led to Shays' Rebellion. George Washington thought that the Articles of Confederation had weakened Congress, leaving it unable to keep order, raise money through taxes, or deal effectively with European nations. He wrote, "The Confederation appears to me to be little more than a shadow without substance."

Most Americans agreed that the 13 proud and independent states would have to face the challenge of establishing a stronger government. Their future was at stake.

Section 3 Assessment

1. **Define** compact, constitution, ratification
2. Why did the colonies rebel against England?
3. After declaring independence, how did the Americans organize their state and national governments?
4. Why did many Americans think that the national government under the Articles of Confederation was too weak?
5. **Analyze** How did their experience under English rule make it difficult for Americans to form a strong national government?

Extending the Chapter

Historical Views

Building on the English tradition, our ancestors established a government that was unique in its time. Nowhere else was there a government so dedicated to protecting the rights of citizens. The American example inspired other revolutions against tyranny, most notably the French Revolution of 1789. The days of powerful monarchs were numbered.

Although the nineteenth and twentieth centuries saw the decline of powerful monarchs, they did not see the end of tyranny. Monarchs are not necessarily tyrants and tyrants are not necessarily monarchs. Tyranny simply refers to any cruel and unjust use of power by a government. Hitler's Nazi dictatorship is an example of a tyrannical government of the twentieth century. Two of the most notorious dictators of the second half of the twentieth century were Idi Amin of Uganda and Pol Pot of Cambodia, both of whom brutally killed hundreds of thousands of citizens who opposed their governments.

The success of our representative government in the United States continues to demonstrate that government by consent of the people provides the best protection of citizens' rights and the best defense against abuse of power. As long as citizens control their government by carefully electing its leaders, they can prevent it from ever controlling them.

How to **READ A POLITICAL CARTOON**

As you read in this chapter, American colonists considered freedom of the press to be one of the most important freedoms. Colonists began struggling for this right decades before the outbreak of the American Revolution.

Freedom of the press extends not only to words, but also to graphics such as political cartoons. Political cartoons are usually found on the editorial pages of newspapers. These cartoons are often funny, but they communicate a serious message.

Explain the Skill

Political cartoons often get their point across through symbols—drawings of people, animals, or objects that stand for something else. Therefore, to understand a political cartoon, you need to know what event or issue the cartoonist is illustrating.

Begin by studying the drawing. Ask yourself: Who or what is this a drawing of? If the drawing is of an animal, what does the animal represent? Then read the caption that goes along with the drawing. Once you understand what event or issue the cartoon is referring to, and you have studied the cartoon's drawing and caption, you are ready to figure out the cartoon's message.

Analyze the Skill

On this page is a cartoon created by Benjamin Franklin in 1754. Many historians think that this was the first political cartoon to appear in an American newspaper. At the time this cartoon was printed, war had just broken out between France and England. Representatives from many of the English

colonies were gathered to discuss this question: Should the colonies join together to fight against the French? Franklin's cartoon illustrates his point of view on this issue.

With this background information in mind, study the cartoon's drawing and caption. Pay special attention to the initials, such as N.Y., N.J., and S.C., that are written above each section of the snake and think about what these initials stand for. Now you are ready to interpret the message of the cartoon.

Skill Assessment

1. In this cartoon, what does the snake stand for? How can you tell?
2. What do you think Franklin's message was?
3. Do you think this cartoon communicates his message effectively? Why or why not?
4. Look in a current newspaper and find a political cartoon. Write a short explanation of what the cartoon is showing and what point the cartoonist is trying to make. Bring the cartoon into class and share it with your classmates.

CHAPTER 4 ASSESSMENT

Building Civics Vocabulary

The vocabulary terms in each pair listed below are related to each other. For each pair, explain what the two terms have in common. Also explain how they are different.

Example: A *legislature* and a *monarch* are similar because they both make laws. They are different because a legislature is elected and a monarch inherits power.

1. *compact* and *constitution*
2. *direct democracy* and *republic*

Reviewing Main Ideas and Skills

3. How did self-government become part of our heritage as Americans?

4. Explain why few people in colonial America had the rights of citizenship.

5. Explain how each of the following influenced American government. **(a)** the governments of ancient Athens and Rome **(b)** the history of English government **(c)** the ideas of Locke and Montesquieu

6. Describe the view of government expressed in the Declaration of Independence.

7. Why did many Americans want a stronger government than the one created by the Articles of Confederation?

8. **How to Read a Political Cartoon** Look again at the cartoon on the previous page. Read the caption "JOIN OR DIE." Think of a new caption—one that could be used in place of this one. Make sure your caption does not change the cartoon's message.

Critical Thinking

9. **Applying Information** Give one example from the text and one example of your own to support the statement "Tyranny is still alive in our time."

10. **Linking Past and Present** Explain how freedom of religion in the colonies differed from freedom of religion today.

11. **Defending a Position** Do you think the American Revolution was unavoidable? Explain your answer.

Writing About Civics

12. **Writing a Dialogue** Write a dialogue between a citizen of colonial America and a citizen of the United States today. Have them compare citizenship then and now.

Citizenship Activities

13. **Working in Groups** Working in small groups, put on a mock trial of John Peter Zenger like the one described in this chapter. Include the following roles: John Peter Zenger, Andrew Hamilton, the governor of New York, the governor's lawyer, witnesses, and a judge. The rest of the group will be the jury.

 Take It to the NET

Access the Civics: Participating in Government Internet site at **www.phschool.com** for the specific URLs to complete the activity.

Research the documents that predated the Declaration of Independence, such as the Magna Carta and the Mayflower Compact. Select three and create a chart that explains how they helped shape our government.

In Congress, July 4, 1776

THE UNANIMOUS DECLARATION OF THE THIRTEEN UNITED STATES OF AMERICA,

When in the Course of human events, it becomes necessary for one people to dissolve the political bands which have connected them with another, and to assume among the Powers of the earth, the separate and equal station to which the Laws of Nature and of Nature's God entitle them, a decent respect to the opinions of mankind requires that they should declare the causes which impel them to the separation.

We hold these truths to be self-evident, that all men are created equal, that they are endowed by their Creator with certain unalienable Rights, that among these are Life, Liberty and the pursuit of Happiness. That to secure these rights, Governments are instituted among Men, deriving their just powers from the consent of the governed, That whenever any Form of Government becomes destructive of these ends, it is the Right of the People to alter or to abolish it, and to institute new Government, laying its foundation on such principles and organizing its powers in such form, as to them shall seem most likely to effect their Safety and Happiness. Prudence, indeed, will dictate that Governments long established should not be changed for light and transient causes; and accordingly all experience hath shown, that mankind are more disposed to suffer, while evils are sufferable, than to right themselves by abolishing the forms to which they are accustomed. But when a long train of abuses and usurpations, pursuing invariably the same Object evinces a design to reduce them under absolute Despotism, it is their right, it is their duty, to throw off such Government, and to provide new Guards for their future security.—Such has been the patient sufferance of these Colonies; and such is now the necessity which constrains them to alter their former Systems of Government. The history of the present King of Great Britain is a history of repeated injuries and usurpations, all having in direct object the establishment of an absolute Tyranny over these States. To prove this, let Facts be submitted to a candid world.

He has refused his Assent to Laws, the most wholesome and necessary for the public good.

He has forbidden his Governors to pass Laws of immediate and pressing importance, unless suspended in their operation till his Assent should be obtained; and when so suspended, he has utterly neglected to attend to them.

He has refused to pass other Laws for the accommodation of large districts of people, unless those people would relinquish the right of Representation in the Legislature, a right inestimable to them and formidable to tyrants only.

He has called together legislative bodies at places unusual, uncomfortable, and distant from the depository of their Public Records, for the sole purpose of fatiguing them into compliance with his measures.

He has dissolved Representative Houses repeatedly, for opposing with manly firmness his invasions on the rights of the people.

He has refused for a long time, after such dissolutions, to cause others to be elected; whereby the Legislative powers, incapable of Annihilation, have returned to the People at large for their exercise; the State remaining in the mean time exposed to all the dangers of invasions from without, and convulsions within.

He has endeavored to prevent the population of these States; for that purpose obstructing the Laws for Naturalization of Foreigners; refusing to pass others to encourage their migration hither, and raising the conditions of new Appropriations of Lands.

He has obstructed the Administration of Justice, by refusing his Assent to Laws for establishing Judiciary powers.

He has made Judges dependent on his Will alone for the tenure of their offices, and the amount and payment of their salaries.

He has erected a multitude of New Offices, and sent hither swarms of Officers to harass our people and eat out their substance.

He has kept among us in time of peace, Standing Armies, without the Consent of our legislature.

He has affected to render the Military independent of and superior to the Civil power.

He has combined with others to subject us to a jurisdiction foreign to our constitutions, and unacknowledged by our laws; giving his Assent to their Acts of pretended Legislation:

For Quartering large bodies of armed troops among us:

For protecting them, by a mock Trial, from Punishment for any Murders which they should commit on the Inhabitants of these States:

For cutting off our Trade with all parts of the world:

For imposing Taxes on us without our Consent:

For depriving us in many cases, of the benefits of Trial by Jury:

For transporting us beyond Seas to be tried for pretended offenses:

For abolishing the free System of English Laws in a neighbouring Province, establishing therein an Arbitrary government, and enlarging its Boundaries so as to render it at once an example and fit instrument for introducing the same absolute rule into these Colonies:

For taking away our Charters, abolishing our most valuable Laws, and altering fundamentally the Forms of our Governments;

For suspending our own Legislature, and declaring themselves invested with Power to legislate for us in all cases whatsoever.

He has abdicated Government here, by declaring us out of his Protection, and waging War against us.

He has plundered our seas, ravaged our Coasts, burned our towns, and destroyed the lives of our people.

He is at this time transporting large Armies of foreign mercenaries to compleat the works of death, desolation and tyranny, already begun with circumstances of Cruelty and perfidy scarcely paralleled in the most barbarous ages, and totally unworthy the Head of a civilized nation.

He has constrained our fellow Citizens taken Captive on the high Seas to bear Arms against their Country, to become the executioners of their friends and Brethren, or to fall themselves by their Hands.

He has excited domestic insurrections amongst us, and has endeavored to bring on the inhabitants of our frontiers the merciless Indian Savages, whose known rule of warfare, is an undistinguished destruction of all ages, sexes, and conditions.

In every stage of these Oppressions We have Petitioned for Redress in the most humble terms. Our repeated Petitions have been answered only by repeated injury. A Prince, whose character is thus marked by every act which may define a Tyrant, is unfit to be the ruler of a free People.

Nor have We been wanting in attentions to our British brethren. We have warned them from time to time of attempts by their legislature to extend an unwarrantable jurisdiction over us. We have reminded them of the circumstances of our emigration and settlement here. We have appealed to their native justice and magnanimity, and we have conjured them by the ties of our common kindred to disavow these usurpations, which, would inevitably interrupt our connections and correspondence. They too have been deaf to the voice of Justice and of consanguinity. We must, therefore, acquiesce in the necessity, which denounces our Separation, and hold them, as we hold the rest of mankind, Enemies in War, in Peace Friends.

We, therefore, the Representatives of the United States of America, in General Congress, Assembled, appealing to the Supreme Judge of the world for the rectitude of our intentions, do, in the Name, and by the Authority of the good People of these Colonies, solemnly publish and declare, That these United Colonies are, and of Right ought to be Free and Independent States; that they are Absolved from all Allegiance to the British Crown, and that all political connection between them and the State of Great Britain, is and ought to be totally dissolved, and that as Free and Independent States, they have full Power to levy War, conclude Peace, contract Alliances, establish Commerce, and to do all other Acts and Things which Independent States may of right do. And for the support of this Declaration, with a firm reliance on the protection of Divine Providence, we mutually pledge to each other our Lives, our Fortunes and our sacred Honor.

Creating the Constitution

Citizenship and You

It is May 1787, and the United States is facing a serious crisis. The government that helped guide the nation through the American Revolution is unable to deal with the challenges of leading a large country. War debts are piling up, the economy is failing, and unrest is growing all over the thirteen states.

In response to this crisis, many of the nation's most respected citizens have traveled to Philadelphia to serve as delegates to the Constitutional Convention. George Washington is here, as is Benjamin Franklin and James Madison. Their goal is to design a government that can hold the new nation together. Most delegates agree that a stronger national government is needed, but there is little agreement about what form this government should take. The debates are sure to be long and heated.

By late May, enough delegates have arrived so that the convention can begin. The future of the country is at stake. If the United States is to be a nation led by its citizens, those citizens will now have to work together to create a new kind of government.

Keep It Current

Items marked with this logo are periodically updated on the Internet. To keep up-to-date, go to www.phschool.com

What's Ahead in Chapter 5

In this chapter you will examine the Constitutional Convention to see how our nation's plan of government was created. You will also see why it was so difficult to get the Constitution approved by the states. Finally, you will examine the principles that have formed the basis of our government for over 200 years.

Section 1 **The Constitutional Convention**

Section 2 **The Struggle for Ratification**

Section 3 **The Supreme Law of the Land**

Citizen's Journal

Suppose you live in 1787 and have been chosen to travel to Philadelphia to represent your state at the Constitutional Convention. Write a paragraph stating what you think the goals of the convention should be.

The Constitutional Convention

SECTION PREVIEW

Objectives

- Explain how the delegates organized the Constitutional Convention.
- Summarize Madison's plan for the new government.
- Summarize the debate over how power would be shared by state and national governments.
- Describe the compromises that were made about representation in Congress.
- Explain the major elements of the executive and judicial branches created by the Constitution.

Building Civics Vocabulary

- The United States has a **bicameral,** or two-house, legislature.

 **Focus**

As you saw in Chapter 4, Shays' Rebellion raised doubts in the minds of many Americans about the young government under the Articles of Confederation. With no power to tax or to enforce laws, Congress seemed almost powerless to deal with the country's debts or to settle disputes between the states. Therefore, in 1787 Congress approved a convention "for the sole and express purpose of revising the Articles of Confederation."

Even before the convention began, most delegates agreed that a national government was needed, not just an alliance of states. Also, they recognized the need to guard against abuse of power. Many delegates agreed with Montesquieu's principle of separation of powers among three branches of government: legislative, executive, and

judicial. In addition, they agreed that the government's power must be limited by dividing power between the states and the national government.

Despite these areas of agreement, the delegates were sharply divided on other important questions, such as how many representatives each state should have in the national government and how much power the government should be given. As the delegates packed their bags and left for Philadelphia, they braced themselves for a long convention.

Getting Organized

The site of the Constitutional Convention was the Pennsylvania State House, where the Declaration of Independence had been signed in July 1776. Summer in Philadelphia meant heat, humidity, and flies; Thomas Jefferson is said to have joked that the Declaration was signed quickly because flies were biting the signers. Actually, the Declaration had been signed only after long, heated debate, and the convention of 1787 promised more of the same.

On Friday, May 25, the business of the convention began with the unanimous selection of George Washington as the presiding officer. However, the delegates realized that it would take more than Washington's popularity to keep the convention on course. Without clear rules, the meeting could end in confusion, and the young country might fall apart.

Setting the Rules Several of the rules the convention adopted were aimed at keeping the discussions secret. It was feared that if their debates were reported in the newspapers, delegates would not feel free to change their minds or to consider the common good of all the states rather than just the narrow interests of people back home. With these concerns in mind, they decided that no one should remove notes from the meeting room. They also agreed that conversations about the proceedings should take place only inside the State House, and that doors and windows were to be kept shut at all times.

Other rules covered voting procedures and behavior during meetings. Each state had one vote, regardless of its number of delegates. The debate rules allowed for each person's opinion to be heard. No one was to whisper, pass notes, or read while another delegate was speaking.

The delegates met six days a week from 10:00 A.M. until 4:00 P.M., without stopping for a meal. They also met with each other before and after the formal sessions. Although some of the 55 delegates left Philadelphia for brief times, an average of 40 were present on any given day.

Madison's Plan

As one of their first acts, the delegates voted not to revise the Articles of Confederation. Most of them believed that government under the Articles was so ineffective that a new plan was needed. Few delegates, though, had specific ideas about how to organize the new government.

One person who did have some definite ideas was Virginia's James Madison, who proposed a framework for a strong national government with legislative, executive, and judicial branches. The legislative branch would have two parts: a House of Representatives and a Senate. Members of the House would be elected directly by the people. Senators would be chosen by members of the House. The number of seats in the House and the Senate would be based on each state's population.

Madison's proposal, known as the Virginia Plan, dominated discussion for the entire convention. Madison was calling for the alliance of independent states to be replaced by a strong national government. Many of the delegates, however, feared that under Madison's plan the national government would be too strong, snatching away important powers of the state legislatures.

Sharing Power with the States

The states had become used to controlling all their own affairs. Many delegates feared

Convention delegates meet in the Pennsylvania State House. Standing at center is Washington, with James Madison on his right.

James Madison

If asked to name the persons most responsible for the founding of our nation, few Americans would mention the name of James Madison. Yet Madison played the leading role in building the lasting framework of our government, becoming known as the "Father of the Constitution."

Madison's role is not well known because much of his work was done out of the public eye. Convinced that good government is the result of careful thought, he spent years studying political ideas. He was determined to put the best of these ideas into the Constitution. At the Constitutional Convention, Madison presented proposals persistently and persuasively.

Madison's studious habits can be traced back to his childhood. Born on March 16, 1751, in Port Conway, Virginia, young James often suffered from illnesses, but his mind remained healthy and inquisitive. By the time he was eleven, he had read many of his father's books. A dedicated student, he graduated from the College of New Jersey at Princeton in only two years.

Sparked by the colonists' growing dissatisfaction with British rule, Madison entered politics in 1774. He helped write Virginia's constitution and represented his state in the Continental Congress.

Madison's experience in the Virginia legislature confirmed his belief that the states should be united under a strong government. At the Constitutional Convention, his proposed plan for a republic was based on the ideas of many thinkers whose writings he had studied over the years.

Crowning a career devoted to the new nation, Madison served as President from 1809 to 1817. Upon leaving public office, he returned home to edit the detailed notes he had taken at the convention. Madison left the most complete record we have of the meeting that led to the birth of our American government.

Recognizing Viewpoints

What actions demonstrated Madison's belief that good government is the result of careful thought and study?

that a strong national government might abuse its powers, treating the states in much the same way England had treated the colonies. Throughout much of the long, hot summer, delegates argued over how power would be shared between the national government and the states.

One issue was whether each state would have the power to either protect or abolish the slave trade. Several northern states wanted the national government to regulate all trade and to outlaw slavery. The southern states objected to this proposal because their plantations depended upon slave labor. Eventually the delegates compromised because they saw the urgent need to form a new government. They agreed that the national government could regulate trade in general but that it could not interfere with the slave trade until 1808.

Some delegates hoped that a national government might end slavery at a later time, but first that national government had to be created. Eventually, the delegates decided which powers would be given to the national government, which would be kept by the states, and which would be shared by both.

Compromises About Congress

Reaching agreement on the powers of the national government was only part of the struggle. The delegates also had to decide how that government would be organized. Since the core of a representative government is the legislature, the delegates focused mainly on issues relating to representation in Congress.

The major question was how many representatives each state would have in the legislature. In Madison's Virginia Plan each state's population would determine the number of its representatives. Objecting that they would always be outvoted by the large states, the small states supported a different plan proposed by William Paterson of New Jersey. Known as the New Jersey Plan, it called for a one-house legislature in which each state would have an equal number of votes.

As supporters of each plan argued back and forth, tempers flared in the June heat. The convention seemed to be going nowhere.

The Great Compromise Realizing that they were making no progress, the delegates considered a plan proposed by Roger Sherman of Connecticut. Like the Virginia

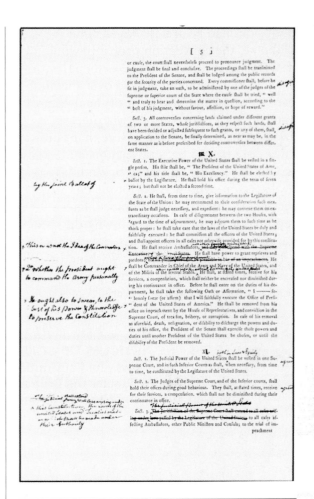

A page from a draft of the Constitution has notes by Virginia's George Mason. He suggested that the President take an oath to obey the Constitution.

Plan, it called for a bicameral, or two-house, legislature. The House of Representatives would be elected on the basis of state population. In the Senate, however, each state would have two senators, regardless of its population. This plan gave the large states more power in the House of Representatives, but each state had equal power in the Senate.

Although no one was completely satisfied with Sherman's plan, the delegates finally approved it by the narrow margin of one vote. The plan became known as the Great Compromise because each side gave up part of what it wanted in order to benefit all. If both sides had been unwilling to give and take, the convention probably would have failed.

Although they had argued over the number of representatives, most of the delegates agreed that a two-house legislature was a good idea. It would help ensure that fair laws were passed because each proposed law would have to be approved by both houses.

Jefferson, who was out of the country serving as ambassador to France, later reportedly asked Washington why the delegates had established a Senate in addition to a House of Representatives. Washington is said to have replied by asking, "Why do you pour your coffee into a saucer?"

"To cool it," Jefferson answered.

Washington replied, "Even so, we pour legislation into the senatorial saucer to cool it."

The Three-Fifths Compromise The Great Compromise kept the convention alive, but it did not settle the question of how to count state populations when determining representation in the House. Although slaves were treated as property, the southern states wanted to count each slave as a person when figuring state populations. The northern states objected that this would give the southern states more members in the House of Representatives and therefore more power.

CHART SKILL **FROM THE ARTICLES OF CONFEDERATION TO THE CONSTITUTION**
As this chart shows, the Constitution created a much stronger national government than had existed under the Articles of Confederation. **Government What are two powers that the national government gained under the Constitution?**

Government under the Articles of Confederation 1781	Government under the Constitution 1789
A loose alliance of independent states	A national government representing all citizens
A one-house legislature	A two-house legislature
No executive or judicial branches	Executive and judicial branches established
Only states can tax	Congress also given the power to tax
States may coin money	Only the national government may coin money
No regulation of trade between states	National government regulates trade between states
Most power held by states	Power shared by national and state governments

Once again the delegates compromised. They agreed to count each slave as three fifths of a person when a state's population was calculated.

The Executive and Judicial Branches

As you recall, under the Articles of Confederation there had been no executive branch to enforce the laws and no judicial branch to interpret the laws. The delegates agreed that these branches would be needed to provide for separation of powers.

The delegates decided that executive power should be given to one President rather than to a committee of leaders. They broadly defined the powers and duties of the President. In establishing the judicial branch, they created a Supreme Court that would have authority to interpret laws and would thus be able to settle conflicts between different states.

A Government by the People?

Although there was general agreement on the functions of each branch of government, the delegates argued about who should elect the President and the members of Congress. Should they be chosen by all the citizens or just by the members of the state legislatures?

Some delegates argued for direct election by the citizens because it would take into account the opinions of a wide variety of people. Madison said, "The people at large [were]...the fittest in itself." Many delegates, however, distrusted the people's judgment. Roger Sherman stated that average citizens "will never be sufficiently informed." Elbridge Gerry of Massachusetts declared that the people were easily swayed and not very thoughtful.

As part of the Great Compromise, the delegates decided that all eligible citizens— that is, white men with property—would elect members of the House, but state legislatures would select senators. The delegates determined that a group of electors known as the electoral college would select the President. Each state legislature could determine how that state's electors would be chosen.

The Signing

In mid-September the convention finally drew to a close, with 39 delegates signing the Constitution on September 17, 1787. Benjamin Franklin was impressed that the debate and the compromises had produced such a strong plan. On the final day of the convention, he stated, "Thus I consent, Sir, to this Constitution because I expect no better, and because I am not sure that it is not the best."

The delegates to the Constitutional Convention are often called "the Framers" because they framed, or shaped, our form of government. Over the years changes have been made in the Constitution, as the framers expected there would be. However, if they could see their work today, they would still recognize the basic plan of government they created over 200 years ago.

Section 1 Assessment

1. **Define** bicameral
2. Why did the delegates decide to keep their discussions secret?
3. Identify and explain the three main issues that arose during the debates at the Constitutional Convention.
4. What was the Great Compromise? Why was it important?
5. Explain the roles of the executive and judicial branches of the government.
6. **Analyze** Why do you think Benjamin Franklin stated that he could "expect no better" plan of government?

The Struggle for Ratification

SECTION PREVIEW

Objectives

- Compare the views of the Federalists and Anti-Federalists.
- Summarize the arguments presented in *The Federalist*.
- Explore reasons that the states finally ratified the Constitution.

Focus

The next step in forming a new government was for the states to vote on the plan. To go into effect, the Constitution had to be ratified, or approved, by at least nine state conventions. Only those states that ratified the new Constitution would be part of the new nation.

By calling for ratifying conventions, the framers bypassed the state legislatures. They suspected that most members of the state legislatures would vote against a Constitution that stripped away some of the states' power. The framers felt that ratifying conventions would give more people an opportunity to study the merits of the Constitution and might increase support for ratification.

While all discussions had been secret during the Constitutional Convention, the issues were now out in the open. When the Constitution was published in newspapers, a storm of debate arose. People argued in churches, meetinghouses, roadside inns, and town squares. Some strongly supported the plan while others loudly opposed it.

The Federalists

The supporters of the Constitution were known as Federalists because they supported a strong federal, or national, government. The Federalists argued that individual states might not be able to protect themselves against foreign nations. A strong national government, they declared, would provide protection, maintain order, regulate trade, and guarantee the rights of citizens. It would also ensure that the nation's debts were paid

In this 1788 cartoon, each state that ratifies the Constitution is shown as a "pillar" supporting a new national government.

Patrick Henry addresses a session of the Virginia House of Burgesses. A person familiar with Henry's speeches once declared, "He is by far the most powerful speaker I ever heard."

and that American money had a stable value at home and abroad.

The Anti-Federalists

The opponents of the Constitution, who were called Anti-Federalists, feared that a strong central government would endanger the people's liberties. According to them, a central government that met so far away from local communities could not truly be called a government by consent of the people. The Anti-Federalists believed that representatives should meet in a location close to the people whose interests they sought to protect.

What especially worried those who feared a strong national government was the statement in the Constitution giving Congress power to make laws "necessary and proper" to carry out its stated powers. Anti-Federalists argued that this wording left the door open to an abuse of power. A strong national government, they said, might eventually swallow up the state governments.

The Bill of Rights Issue The Anti-Federalists were also troubled by what was left out of the Constitution: a bill of rights. They feared that a strong national government might not respect citizens' rights. The Federalists responded that it was unnecessary to list the rights of citizens because the Constitution already carefully limited the government's powers.

A strong Anti-Federalist voice in this debate was that of Virginia's Patrick Henry. During the colonial period he had raised the cry: "Give me liberty or give me death!" His reputation as a fiery speaker and a Revolutionary War hero made him a tough opponent of the Federalists. Calling the Constitution "horridly defective," he led the fight in Virginia against ratification. At the Virginia ratifying convention he warned:

> **"**Mr. Chairman, the necessity for a bill of rights appears to me to be greater in this government than ever it was in any government before.... All rights not expressly reserved to the people are relinquished [given up] to rulers. **"**

The Federalist

Some leading Federalists responded to Patrick Henry and other Anti-Federalists in a series of pro-Constitution newspaper articles. James Madison, Alexander Hamilton, and John Jay wrote the articles, which were collected under the title *The Federalist*.

In *The Federalist*, Madison argued that the Constitution would protect the liberty of every citizen. With a national government representing all the people, no group would be able to ignore the rights of everyone else. Instead, to reach some of its goals, each group would have to compromise with other groups.

The Federalist also emphasized the problems America faced as a weak, young nation on a large continent. If the states did not unite under a strong national government, the forces of Spain, England, and France might overpower them.

Ratification

Support for the Constitution grew as many Americans were persuaded by the Federalists' effective campaign. Washington's and Franklin's support swayed people who admired those two great leaders. Many were won over after the Federalists agreed to propose a bill of rights if the Constitution was ratified.

Still, the debates in many state conventions dragged on for months. In many cases the Constitution was approved by only a few votes. Finally, in June 1788, the new

Facts & Quotes

A Farmer Speaks Out

At the Massachusetts ratifying convention, a farmer named Jonathan Smith spoke for the Federalist cause:

> **"**I am a plain man and get my living by the plow. I am not used to speak in public, but I beg your leave to say a few words...I have lived in a part of the country where I have known the worth of good government by the want [lack] of it. There was a black cloud [Shays' Rebellion] that rose in the east last winter and spread over the west...
>
> When I saw this Constitution, I found that it was a cure for these disorders...I got a copy of it and read it over and over. I had been a member of the convention to form our own state constitution, and had learnt something of the checks and balances of power, and I found them all here....
>
> Some gentlemen say, don't be in a hurry. Take time to consider, and don't take a leap in the dark. I say, take things in time; gather fruit when it is ripe. There is a time to sow and a time to reap. We sowed our seed when we sent men to the Federal Convention. Now is the harvest. Now is the time to reap the fruit of our labor. And if we don't do it now, I am afraid we shall never have another opportunity. **"**

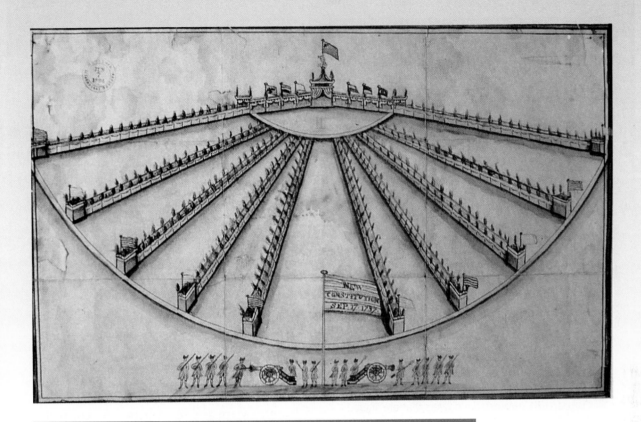

Over 6,000 citizens of New York City attended an outdoor banquet to celebrate their state's ratification of the Constitution in July 1788.

government was officially born when New Hampshire became the ninth state to ratify the Constitution.

The government would not last long, however, without the support of the remaining four states, which included more then 40 percent of the nation's people. The two key states were Virginia and New York. After bitter debate, Virginia ratified the document by only ten votes (89–79) and New York approved by the slim margin of three votes (30–27). By the spring of 1790, all 13 states had ratified the new Constitution.

The birth of our nation is really marked by the ratification of the Constitution, not by the signing of the Declaration of Independence. Only under the Constitution did Americans become united in one nation. What had once been a loose union of independent states had become the United States of America.

The Supreme Law of the Land

SECTION PREVIEW

Objectives

- Define the major goals of our government.
- Summarize the major sections of the Constitution.
- Explain the three main principles in the Constitution that limit the government's power.

Building Civics Vocabulary

- The President can **veto,** or reject, bills proposed by Congress.
- Powers given, or delegated, to Congress are known as **delegated powers.**
- **Amendments** are changes or additions.
- Under **federalism,** power is divided between the state and the federal governments.
- **Concurrent powers** are powers that are shared by federal and state governments.
- Powers given neither to Congress nor denied to the states are **reserved powers.**
- The system of **checks and balances** allows each branch of government to limit the powers of the other two.
- The House can **impeach,** or accuse, the President of wrongdoing.

★ Focus

The Constitution establishes our form of government, a republic. As you recall from Chapter 4, a republic is a government in which citizens elect their representatives. As the "supreme law of the land," the Constitution protects the rights of citizens by providing general rules that the national government and the state governments must follow.

The full text of the Constitution is found on pages 108–129.

The Goals of Our Government

The Constitution begins by stating the goals of our government. In the Preamble, or introduction, the framers listed six goals:

1. *"to form a more perfect union"*: The framers were seeking a better government than the one under the Articles of Confederation. Their main concern was to unite the 13 separate states under an effective national government.

2. *"establish justice"*: We have a legal system that seeks fair ways to settle disputes between individuals, between individuals and the government, between states, and

Providing relief from hurricanes and other disasters is one of the many ways in which our government promotes the general welfare of citizens.

between the national and state governments.

3. *"insure domestic tranquillity"*: Our government tries to establish a peaceful society in which people are protected from the unlawful acts of others.

4. *"provide for the common defense"*: Our government seeks to protect citizens from attacks by other countries.

5. *"promote the general welfare"*: Our government tries to create conditions that will benefit all Americans.

6. *"and secure the blessings of liberty to ourselves and our posterity"*: Our government seeks to give people the freedom to choose where they work, where they live, what they believe, and who shall represent them in government. However, our liberty as Americans does not leave us free to do whatever we want. Our actions should not interfere with the rights of others. The government protects the liberty of *all* citizens. It also protects future Americans— our posterity, or descendants.

The Articles

Following the Preamble, the framers laid out the plan for our government. This plan is organized into seven parts called articles. Some of the key ideas in the articles are described in the following paragraphs.

Article 1: The Legislative Branch

Article 1 describes the organization and powers of the national legislature, called the Congress of the United States. Congress is divided into two houses: the House of Representatives and the Senate.

The most important power of Congress is to make laws. A proposed law, called a bill, must gain a majority vote in both houses of Congress before it goes to the President for approval. If the President signs the bill, it becomes law. The President may veto, or reject, the bill; however, Congress has the final word. A vetoed bill can still become a law if

Congress votes on it again, with two thirds of the members of each house approving it.

The powers given, or delegated, to Congress are known as delegated powers. Look at the chart on page 102. Most of these delegated powers—such as the power to coin money, to declare war, and to regulate trade—are specifically listed in Article 1, Section 8. However, not all of Congress's powers are listed. Congress may also make laws that are "necessary and proper" for carrying out the powers that are listed.

By using the words "necessary and proper," the framers wanted to give the government flexibility to carry out its work and change with the times. However, this flexible wording—sometimes called "the elastic clause"—troubled the Anti-Federalists and continues to bother Americans who worry that Congress might abuse its powers. It is important to note, however, that Article 1 also limits the government's power by stating which actions Congress may not take.

Article 2: The Executive Branch

While the powers of the legislative branch are shared by hundreds of members of Congress, the framers gave the power of the executive branch to one person—the President. By establishing the office of President, they created something very new in the world: a leader who has some of the strengths of a monarch, but whose authority is based on the consent of the people. In order to continue in office after their four-year term, both the President and the Vice-President have to be re-elected.

The painful memory of the colonies' experience with King George of England was still fresh in the framers' minds. To avoid having another monarch, they made it clear that the President's job is to execute, or carry out, the laws—not to make them. The President may make treaties, but they are only binding if approved by the Senate. The President may also nominate judges, but the

CHART SKILL

SHARING THE POWER Under the Constitution, some powers are shared by the national and state governments. **Government If certain powers are not given to the national government or denied to state government, to which government do they belong?**

Powers of the National Government

Maintain army and navy

Declare war

Coin money

Regulate trade between states and with foreign nations

Make all laws necessary for carrying out delegated powers

Shared Powers

Enforce laws

Establish courts

Borrow money

Protect the safety of the people

Build roads

Collect taxes

Powers of the State Government

Conduct elections

Establish schools

Regulate businesses within a state

Establish local governments

Regulate marriages

Assume other powers not given to the national government or denied to the states

Senate has the right to reject the President's nominees.

The Constitution is far less specific on the office of President than it is on the national legislature. There had never been a President before. Most delegates to the Constitutional Convention believed that George Washington would be elected as the first President and that he could best create the office, setting an example for later Presidents.

Article 3: The Judicial Branch Although each state had its own courts, the framers wanted a national court system to settle disputes between states. The framers agreed that neither Congress nor the President should control the national courts. Accordingly, the President nominates judges, but the Senate must approve the nominations. Once appointed, judges may serve for life as long as they demonstrate "good behavior."

One of the most important contributions of the framers was the creation of the Supreme Court. This court has the final say in all cases involving the Constitution. Important cases on which lower courts disagree can be appealed to the Supreme Court for a final decision, thus ensuring that legal issues affecting the nation will not be left unsettled.

Article 4: The States To ensure that the rights of the states are respected, each state must honor the laws of other states. A New York marriage license, for instance, is valid in any other state. Requiring states to respect each other's laws helps preserve each state's rights and reduces the possibility of conflict between states.

Article 5: Amending the Constitution The framers knew that future Americans might want to change the Constitution. Therefore, they included in the Constitution instructions for making amendments, or changes. To ensure that each change reflects

In 1987, parades, speeches, and a shower of balloons over Philadelphia's Independence Hall marked the 200th anniversary of the signing of our Constitution.

the will of the people, three fourths of the states must approve an amendment. In Chapter 6 you will learn more about the amendment process.

Article 6: The Supremacy of the Constitution
Since both state and national governments may pass laws, the framers wanted to avoid any uncertainty about which laws take priority. Therefore, Article 6 requires officials in state and national government to take an oath to support the Constitution as "the supreme law of the land." No state law may violate the Constitution. Also, if a state law conflicts with a federal—or national—law, the federal law takes priority.

Article 7: Ratification
The last article of the Constitution establishes the procedure for ratification, or approval, of the Constitution.

Amendments to the Constitution
When you read the Constitution, you will see that a series of amendments follow the seven articles. The first ten amendments, ratified in 1791, are called the Bill of Rights and were added in response to the concerns of the Anti-Federalists. Since the approval of the Bill of Rights, only seventeen other amendments have been added. Clearly the Constitution has stood the test of time. You will read more about the Bill of Rights and the other amendments in Chapters 6 and 7.

Principles of Limited Government
The Constitution creates a government with powers limited by consent of the people. It is based on the idea of popular sovereignty—letting the people rule. Three main principles limit the government's power: federalism,

separation of powers, and checks and balances.

Federalism

Federalism The Constitution establishes a principle of federalism, the division of power between the states and the federal, or national, government. Under federalism, some powers belong only to the national government, some powers belong only to the states, and some are shared by both. The chart on page 102 shows how the powers are divided and shared.

Article 1 describes the delegated powers, those that belong to Congress. A number of these powers, such as the power to coin money or declare war, are denied to the states.

Some of the powers given to Congress are not denied to the states. For instance, the states, too, can collect taxes, establish courts, and borrow money. The powers shared by the federal and state governments are known as concurrent powers.

The Tenth Amendment declares that the states have reserved powers, those powers that the Constitution neither gives to Congress nor denies to the states. For example, two of the powers not mentioned in the Constitution that are reserved to the states are the authority to establish schools and to form police organizations.

By dividing power between the federal and state governments, the system of federalism gives the federal government the authority it needs while helping to protect each state's rights. This system also allows the federal government to deal with issues affecting all citizens, while each state government can better serve the particular needs of its people.

Separation of Powers Under our Constitution, power is not only divided between the state and federal governments; it is also divided within the federal government. Dividing power among the executive,

CHECKS AND BALANCES Under the system of checks and balances, each branch of government limits the power of the other two. **Government Which branch of government has the power to declare laws unconstitutional?**

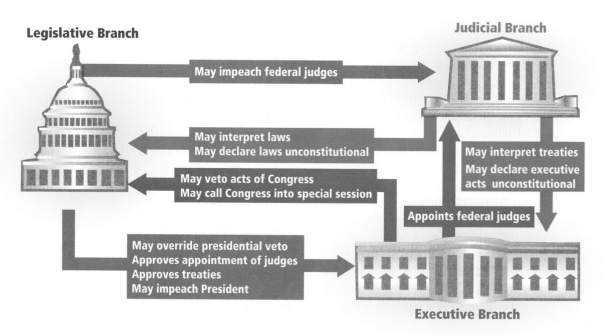

Legislative Branch

Judicial Branch

May impeach federal judges

May interpret laws
May declare laws unconstitutional

May veto acts of Congress
May call Congress into special session

May interpret treaties
May declare executive
acts unconstitutional

Appoints federal judges

May override presidential veto
Approves appointment of judges
Approves treaties
May impeach President

Executive Branch

legislative, and judicial branches helps prevent any one branch from abusing its power.

Checks and Balances Another way the Constitution protects against abuse of power in the federal government is through checks and balances, which is illustrated in the chart on page 104. This system gives each of the three branches of government ways to limit the powers of the other two. For instance, the House can impeach, or accuse, the President or other high officials of serious wrongdoing. If found guilty in a trial in the Senate, the official will be removed from office.

The President can check the actions of Congress by vetoing bills that are not in the best interest of the nation. Meanwhile, the judicial branch checks the power of the other two branches by determining whether laws passed by Congress or actions taken by the President are constitutional. By checking and balancing each other, the three branches of government ensure that they work together for the welfare of citizens.

Section 3 Assessment

1. **Define** veto, delegated powers, amendments, federalism, concurrent powers, reserved powers, checks and balances, impeach
2. Describe two goals listed in the Preamble to the Constitution.
3. Summarize Article 2 of the Constitution.
4. Describe one specific way the Constitution limits the power of the government.
5. **Analyze** How are the goals of the framers reflected in the Constitution?

Extending the Chapter

Global Views

The United States Constitution has been called "the most wonderful work ever struck off at a given time by the brain and purpose of man." Although the framers' plan was not the world's first constitution, up until then most were unwritten constitutions and based on custom or on the will of monarchs. Therefore, to the rest of the world it was quite remarkable that American citizens were using their knowledge and past experience in order to write their own plan of government.

The framers saw themselves as setting an example for self-government. Madison pro-claimed, "The happy union of these states is a wonder: their Constitution a miracle: their ex-ample the hope of liberty throughout the world." Hamilton declared that the Constitution was a model of "establishing good government from reflection and choice" rather than by "accident and force."

Indeed, the Constitution has set an example for many countries, particularly for former colonies in Latin America and Africa when they gained their independence. A number of countries have modeled their constitutions after the American document, spelling out rights and responsibilities of the government and the citizens. For many nations a written constitution has been a useful "rule book" that everyone must follow—from the highest government official to the "average citizen."

How to READ A FLOW CHART

In this chapter, you read about the plan of our government as established by the Constitution. You learned that the Constitution is organized into seven parts called articles. As you read, Article 5 defines the process for amending the Constitution. This article defines several different methods by which amendments can be proposed and then ratified. These different methods are illustrated in the flow chart on this page.

Explain the Skill

Flow charts are a useful way of illustrating a process with several steps, because they allow you to see the steps in a process, and to visualize how the steps relate to each other. Flow charts present information visually, using arrows to direct you through the steps of a system or process.

When reading a flow chart, first identify the process that the flow chart is describing. Then study the chart, following the arrows to discover how the different pieces of information in the chart are connected.

Analyze the Skill

Look at the flow chart on this page and begin by asking yourself: What process does this flow chart describe? After looking over the chart, you will see that it illustrates the amendment process described in Article 5 of the Constitution. In this flow chart, circles are used to represent steps in the amendment process.

Next, carefully read the information in each section of the chart. Start with the

headings above the circles. Then review the chart key, which tells you what the different colored arrows mean. Then read the information in each circle, following the arrows from one section of the chart to the other.

Skill Assessment

1. Who can propose amendments?
2. Who can ratify amendments?
3. How many different ways are there to propose and then ratify an amendment?
4. Now create a flow chart of your own. First list all the steps involved in writing a research report. Then create a flow chart illustrating this process.

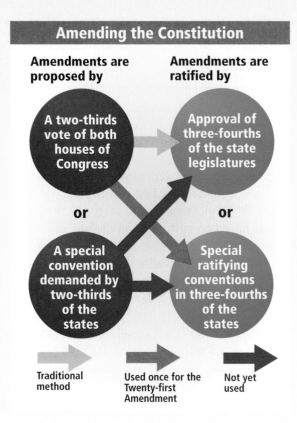

Amending the Constitution

Amendments are proposed by

Amendments are ratified by

A two-thirds vote of both houses of Congress

Approval of three-fourths of the state legislatures

or

or

A special convention demanded by two-thirds of the states

Special ratifying conventions in three-fourths of the states

Traditional method

Used once for the Twenty-first Amendment

Not yet used

CHAPTER 5 ASSESSMENT

Building Civics Vocabulary

The vocabulary terms in each pair listed below are related to each other. For each pair, explain what the two terms have in common. Also explain how they are different.

Example: *Impeach* and *veto* both refer to the system of checks and balances. However, the first is a check on the executive branch by the legislative branch, while the second is a check on the legislative branch by the executive branch.

1. *reserved powers* and *concurrent powers*
2. *federalism* and *checks and balances*

Reviewing Main Ideas and Skills

3. Why did many delegates to the Constitutional Convention think that a new form of government was needed?
4. Why did the delegates disagree strongly on these three main issues? **(a)** the powers of the state and national governments **(b)** representation in the national legislature **(c)** the election of the President and members of the national legislature
5. Explain how the delegates were able to settle each of the three main issues listed in question 4.
6. What were the Federalists' main arguments in favor of the Constitution? What were the Anti-Federalists' main arguments against it?
7. Describe in your own words the six goals stated in the Preamble.
8. **How to Read a Flow Chart** Look back at the flow chart on page 106. Which process of amending the Constitution has been used the most often? Which process has never been used?

Critical Thinking

9. **Identifying Main Ideas** Reread the "Extending the Chapter" section on page 105. How has our Constitution influenced other countries of the world?
10. **Drawing Conclusions** Why do you think that our Constitution has lasted for over 200 years? Do you think it will last for another 200 years? Why or why not?

Writing About Civics

11. **Writing an Amendment** If you could add one amendment to the Constitution, what would it be? Why do you think this amendment would help our country?

Citizenship Activities

12. **Working in Groups** Break into small groups and divide each group into Federalists and Anti-Federalists. Then stage a debate between these two sides on the issue of ratification of the Constitution. Present your debates to the class.

 Take It to the NET

Access the **Civics: Participating in Government** Internet site at **www.phschool.com** for the specific URLs to complete the activity.

Who were the men who created the Constitution of the United States? Use online research to write brief biographies of two of the signers. Where were the signers born? What were their economic backgrounds? How did they come to participate in the creation of the Constitution? Compare the two signers.

THE SIX BASIC PRINCIPLES

The classic textbook *Magruder's American Government* outlines the six basic principles of the Constitution. Below is a description of these principles:

 1 Popular Sovereignty

The Preamble to the Constitution begins with the bold phrase, "We the people. . . ." These words announce that in the United States, the people are sovereign. The government receives its power from the people and can govern only with their consent.

 2 Limited Government

Because the people are the ultimate source of all government power, the government has only as much authority as the people give it. Government's power is thus limited. Much of the Constitution, in fact, consists of specific limitations on government power.

 3 Separation of Powers

Government power is not only limited, but also divided. The Constitution assigns certain powers to each of the three branches: the legislative (Congress), executive (President), and judicial (federal courts). This separation of government's powers was intended to prevent the misuse of power.

 4 Checks and Balances

The system of checks and balances gives each of the three branches of government the ability to restrain the other two. Such a system makes government less efficient but also less likely to trample on the rights of citizens.

 5 Judicial Review

Who decides whether an act of government violates the Constitution? Historically, the courts have filled this function. The principle of judicial review means that federal courts have the power to review acts of the federal government and to cancel any acts that are unconstitutional, or violate a provision in the Constitution.

 6 Federalism

A federal system of government is one in which power is divided between a central government and smaller governments. This sharing of powers is intended to ensure that the central government is powerful enough to be effective yet not so powerful as to threaten states or individuals.

A Note on the Text of the Constitution

The complete text of the Constitution, including amendments, appears on the pages that follow. Spelling, capitalization, and punctuation have been modernized, and headings have been added. Portions of the Constitution altered by later amendments or that no longer apply have been crossed out. Commentary appears in the right column of each page.

Constitution

PREAMBLE

We the people of the United States, in order to form a more perfect union, establish justice, insure domestic tranquillity, provide for the common defense, promote the general welfare, and secure the blessings of liberty to ourselves and our posterity, do ordain and establish this Constitution for the United States of America.

Article I. Legislative Branch

Section 1. Legislative Powers; The Congress

All legislative powers herein granted shall be vested in a Congress of the United States, which shall consist of a Senate and House of Representatives.

Section 2. House of Representatives

1. Election of Members The House of Representatives shall be composed of members chosen every second year by the people of the several states, and the electors in each state shall have the qualifications requisite for electors of the most numerous branch of the state legislature.

2. Qualifications No person shall be a representative who shall not have attained to the age of twenty-five years, and been seven years a citizen of the United States, and who shall not, when elected, be an inhabitant of that state in which he shall be chosen.

3. Apportionment Representatives ~~and direct taxes~~ shall be apportioned among the several states which may be included within this Union, according to their respective numbers, ~~which shall be determined by adding to the whole number of free persons, including those bound to service for a term of years and excluding Indians not taxed, three fifths of all other persons.~~ The actual enumeration shall be made within three years after the first meeting of the Congress of the United States, and within every subsequent term of ten years, in such manner as they shall by law direct. The number of representatives shall not exceed one for every thirty thousand, but each state shall have at least one representative; ~~and until such enumeration shall be made, the state of New Hampshire shall be entitled to choose three, Massachusetts eight, Rhode Island and Providence Plantations one, Connecticut five, New York six, New Jersey four, Pennsylvania eight, Delaware one, Maryland six, Virginia ten, North Carolina five, South Carolina five, and Georgia three.~~

4. Filling Vacancies When vacancies happen in the representation from any state, the executive authority thereof shall issue writs of election to fill such vacancies.

5. Officers; Impeachment The House of Representatives shall choose their Speaker and other officers; and shall have the sole power of impeachment.

Commentary

The Preamble describes the purpose of the government set up by the Constitution. Americans expect their government to defend justice and liberty and provide peace and safety from foreign enemies.

The Constitution gives Congress the power to make laws. Congress is divided into the Senate and the House of Representatives.

Clause 1 *Electors* refers to voters. Members of the House of Representatives are elected every two years. Any citizen allowed to vote for members of the larger house of the state legislature can also vote for members of the House.

Clause 2 A member of the House of Representatives must be at least 25 years old, an American citizen for 7 years, and a resident of the state he or she represents.

Clause 3 The number of representatives each state elects is based on its population. An *enumeration*, or census, must be taken every 10 years to determine population. Today, the number of representatives in the House is fixed at 435.

This clause contains the famous Three-Fifths Compromise worked out at the Constitutional Convention. ***Persons bound to service*** meant indentured servants. ***All other persons*** meant slaves. All free people in a state were counted. However, only three fifths of the slaves were included in the population count. This three-fifths clause became meaningless when slaves were freed by the Thirteenth Amendment.

Clause 4 *Executive authority* means the governor of a state. If a member of the House leaves office before his or her term ends, the governor must call a special election to fill the seat.

Clause 5 The House elects a Speaker. Today, the Speaker is usually chosen by the party that has a majority in the House. Also, only the House has the power to *impeach*, or accuse, a federal official of wrongdoing.

Section 3. Senate

1. Composition; Term The Senate of the United States shall be composed of two senators from each state ~~chosen by the legislature thereof,~~ for six years, and each senator shall have one vote.

2. Classification; Filling Vacancies Immediately after they shall be assembled in consequence of the first election, they shall be divided as equally as may be into three classes. The seats of the senators of the first class shall be vacated at the expiration of the second year, of the second class at the expiration of the fourth year, and of the third class at the expiration of the sixth year, so that one third may be chosen every second year; ~~and if vacancies happen by resignation, or otherwise, during the recess of the legislature of any State, the executive thereof may make temporary appointments until the next meeting of the legislature, which shall then fill such vacancies.~~

3. Qualifications No person shall be a senator who shall not have attained to the age of thirty years, and been nine years a citizen of the United States, and who shall not, when elected, be an inhabitant of that state for which he shall be chosen.

4. President of the Senate The Vice President of the United States shall be president of the Senate, but shall have no vote, unless they be equally divided.

5. Other Officers The Senate shall choose their other officers, and also a president *pro tempore*, in the absence of the Vice President, or when he shall exercise the office of the President of the United States.

6. Impeachment Trials The Senate shall have the sole power to try all impeachments. When sitting for that purpose, they shall be on oath or affirmation. When the President of the United States is tried, the Chief Justice shall preside; and no person shall be convicted without the concurrence of two thirds of the members present.

7. Penalty on Conviction Judgment in cases of impeachment shall not extend further than to removal from office, and disqualification to hold and enjoy any office of honor, trust or profit under the United States: but the party convicted shall nevertheless be liable and subject to indictment, trial, judgment, and punishment, according to law.

Section 4. Elections and Meetings

1. Election of Congress The times, places, and manner of holding elections for senators and representatives, shall be prescribed in each state by the legislature thereof; but the Congress may at any time by law make or alter such regulations, except as to the places of choosing senators.

Clause 1 Each state has two senators. Senators serve for six-year terms. The Seventeenth Amendment changed the way senators were elected.

Clause 2 Every two years, one third of the senators run for re-election. Thus, the makeup of the Senate is never totally changed by any one election. The Seventeenth Amendment changed the way of filling *vacancies*, or empty seats. Today, the governor of a state must choose a senator to fill a vacancy that occurs between elections.

Clause 3 A senator must be at least 30 years old, an American citizen for 9 years, and a resident of the state he or she represents.

Clause 4 The Vice President presides over Senate meetings, but he or she can vote only to break a tie.

Clause 5 *Pro tempore* means temporary. The Senate chooses one of its members to serve as president *pro tempore* when the Vice President is absent.

Clause 6 The Senate acts as a jury if the House impeaches a federal official. The Chief Justice of the Supreme Court presides if the President is on trial. Two thirds of all senators present must vote for conviction, or finding the accused guilty. No President has ever been convicted. The House impeached President Andrew Johnson in 1868, but the Senate acquitted him of the charges. In 1998–99, President Bill Clinton became the second President to be impeached and acquitted.

Clause 7 If an official is found guilty by the Senate, he or she can be removed from office and barred from holding federal office in the future. These are the only punishments the Senate can impose. However, the convicted official can still be tried in a criminal court.

Clause 1 Each state legislature can decide when and how congressional elections take place, but Congress can overrule these decisions. In 1842, Congress required each state to set up congressional districts with one representative elected from each district. In 1872, Congress decided that congressional elections must be held in every state on the same date in even-numbered years.

THE CONSTITUTION

2. Sessions The Congress shall assemble at least once in every year, ~~and such meeting shall be on the first Monday in December, unless they shall by law appoint a different day.~~

Section 5. Legislative Proceedings

1. Organization Each house shall be the judge of the elections, returns, and qualifications of its own members, and a majority of each shall constitute a quorum to do business; but a smaller number may adjourn from day to day, and may be authorized to compel the attendance of absent members, in such manner, and under such penalties, as each house may provide.

2. Rules Each house may determine the rules of its proceedings, punish its members for disorderly behavior, and with the concurrence of two thirds, expel a member.

3. Record Each house shall keep a journal of its proceedings, and from time to time publish the same, excepting such parts as may in their judgment require secrecy; and the yeas and nays of the members of either house on any question shall, at the desire of one fifth of those present, be entered on the journal.

4. Adjournment Neither house, during the session of Congress, shall, without the consent of the other, adjourn for more than three days, nor to any other place than that in which the two houses shall be sitting.

Section 6. Compensation, Immunities, and Disabilities of Members

1. Salaries; Immunities The senators and representatives shall receive a compensation for their services, to be ascertained by law, and paid out of the Treasury of the United States. They shall in all cases, except treason, felony, and breach of the peace, be privileged from arrest during their attendance at the session of their respective houses, and in going to and returning from the same; and for any speech or debate in either house, they shall not be questioned in any other place.

2. Restrictions on Other Employment No senator or representative shall, during the time for which he was elected, be appointed to any civil office under the authority of the United States, which shall have been created, or the emoluments whereof shall have been increased during such time; and no person holding any office under the United States shall be a member of either house during his continuance in office.

Section 7. Revenue Bills, President's Veto

1. Revenue Bills All bills for raising revenue shall originate in the House of Representatives; but the Senate may propose or concur with amendments as on other bills.

2. How a Bill Becomes Law; the Veto Every bill which shall have passed the House of Representatives and the Senate shall, before it become a law, be presented to the President of the United States; if he approve, he shall sign it, but if not, he shall return it, with his objections, to that house in which it

Clause 2 Congress must meet at least once a year. The Twentieth Amendment moved the opening date of Congress to January 3.

Clause 1 Each house decides whether a member has the qualifications for office set by the Constitution. A *quorum* is the smallest number of members who must be present for business to be conducted. Each house can set its own rules about absent members.

Clause 2 Each house can make rules for the conduct of members. It can only expel a member by a two-thirds vote.

Clause 3 Each house keeps a record of its meetings. *The Congressional Record* is published every day with excerpts from speeches made in each house. It also records the votes of each member.

Clause 4 Neither house can *adjourn*, or stop meeting, for more than three days unless the other house approves. Both houses of Congress must meet in the same city.

Clause 1 *Compensation* means salary. Congress decides the salary for its members. While Congress is in session, a member is free from arrest in civil cases and cannot be sued for anything he or she says on the floor of Congress. This allows for freedom of debate. However, a member can be arrested for a criminal offense.

Clause 2 *Emolument* also means salary. A member of Congress cannot hold another federal office during his or her term. A former member of Congress cannot hold an office created while he or she was in Congress. An official in another branch of government cannot serve at the same time in Congress. This strengthens the separation of powers.

Clause 1 *Revenue* is money raised by the government through taxes. Tax bills must be introduced in the House. The Senate, however, can make changes in tax bills. This clause protects the principle that people can be taxed only with their consent.

Clause 2 A *bill,* or proposed law, that is passed by a majority of the House and Senate is sent to the President. If the President signs the bill, it becomes law.

A bill can also become law without the President's signature. The President can refuse to act on a bill. If Congress is in session at the time, the bill becomes law 10 days after the President receives it.

Constitution

shall have originated, who shall enter the objections at large on their journal, and proceed to reconsider it. If after such reconsideration two thirds of that house shall agree to pass the bill, it shall be sent, together with the objections, to the other house, by which it shall likewise be reconsidered, and if approved by two thirds of that house, it shall become a law. But in all such cases the votes of both houses shall be determined by yeas and nays, and the names of the persons voting for and against the bill shall be entered on the journal of each house respectively. If any bill shall not be returned by the President within ten days (Sundays excepted) after it shall have been presented to him, the same shall be a law, in like manner as if he had signed it, unless the Congress by their adjournment prevent its return, in which case it shall not be a law.

3. Resolutions Passed by Congress Every order, resolution, or vote to which the concurrence of the Senate and House of Representatives may be necessary (except on a question of adjournment) shall be presented to the President of the United States; and before the same shall take effect, shall be approved by him, or being disapproved by him, shall be repassed by two thirds of the Senate and House of Representatives, according to the rules and limitations prescribed in the case of a bill.

Section 8. Powers of Congress

The Congress shall have power

1. To lay and collect taxes, duties, imposts, and excises, to pay the debts and provide for the common defense and general welfare of the United States; but all duties, imposts and excises shall be uniform throughout the United States;

2. To borrow money on the credit of the United States;

3. To regulate commerce with foreign nations, and among the several states, and with the Indian tribes;

4. To establish an uniform rule of naturalization, and uniform laws on the subject of bankruptcies throughout the United States;

5. To coin money, regulate the value thereof, and of foreign coin, and fix the standard of weights and measures;

6. To provide for the punishment of counterfeiting the securities and current coin of the United States;

7. To establish post offices and post roads;

Commentary

The President can **veto**, or reject, a bill by sending it back to the house where it was introduced. Or if the President refuses to act on a bill and Congress adjourns within 10 days, then the bill dies. This way of killing a bill without taking action is called the **pocket veto**.

Congress can override the President's veto if each house of Congress passes the bill again by a two-thirds vote. This clause is an important part of the system of checks and balances.

Clause 3 Congress can pass resolutions or orders that have the same force as laws. Any such resolution or order must be signed by the President (except on questions of adjournment). Thus, this clause prevents Congress from bypassing the President simply by calling a bill by another name.

Clause 1 **Duties** are tariffs. **Imposts** are taxes in general. **Excises** are taxes on the production or sale of certain goods. Congress has the power to tax and spend tax money. Taxes must be the same in all parts of the country.

Clause 2 Congress can borrow money for the United States. The government often borrows money by selling bonds, or certificates that promise to pay the holder a certain sum of money on a certain date.

Clause 3 Only Congress has the power to regulate foreign and interstate trade, or trade between states. Disagreements over interstate trade were a major problem with the Articles of Confederation.

Clause 4 **Naturalization** is the process whereby a foreigner becomes a citizen. **Bankruptcy** is the condition in which a person or business cannot pay its debts. Congress has the power to pass laws on these two issues. The laws must be the same in all parts of the country.

Clause 5 Congress has the power to coin money and set its value. Congress has set up the National Bureau of Standards to regulate weights and measures.

Clause 6 **Counterfeiting** is the making of imitation money. **Securities** are bonds. Congress can make laws to punish counterfeiters.

Clause 7 Congress has the power to set up and control the delivery of mail.

8. To promote the progress of science and useful arts by securing for limited times to authors and inventors the exclusive right to their respective writings and discoveries;

9. To constitute tribunals inferior to the Supreme Court;

10. To define and punish piracies and felonies committed on the high seas and offenses against the law of nations;

11. To declare war, grant letters of marque and reprisal, and make rules concerning captures on land and water;

12. To raise and support armies, but no appropriation of money to that use shall be for a longer term than two years;

13. To provide and maintain a navy;

14. To make rules for the government and regulation of the land and naval forces;

15. To provide for calling forth the militia to execute the laws of the Union, suppress insurrections, and repel invasions;

16. To provide for organizing, arming, and disciplining the militia, and for governing such part of them as may be employed in the service of the United States, reserving to the states, respectively, the appointment of the officers, and the authority of training the militia according to the discipline prescribed by Congress;

17. To exercise exclusive legislation in all cases whatsoever, over such district (not exceeding ten miles square) as may, by cession of particular states, and the acceptance of Congress, become the seat of the government of the United States, and to exercise like authority over all places purchased by the consent of the legislature of the state in which the same shall be, for the erection of forts, magazines, arsenals, dock-yards, and other needful buildings; —and

18. To make all laws which shall be necessary and proper for carrying into execution the foregoing powers, and all other powers vested by this Constitution in the government of the United States, or in any department or officer thereof.

Section 9. Powers Denied to Congress

1. The Slave Trade ~~The migration or importation of such persons as any of the states now existing shall think proper to admit, shall not be prohibited by the Congress prior to the year one thousand eight hundred and eight, but a tax or duty may be imposed on such importation, not exceeding ten dollars for each person.~~

2. Writ of *Habeas Corpus* The privilege of the writ of habeas corpus shall not be suspended, unless when in cases of rebellion or invasion the public safety may require it.

Clause 8 Congress may pass copyright and patent laws. A *copyright* protects an author. A *patent* makes an inventor the sole owner of his or her work for a limited time.

Clause 9 Congress has the power to set up *inferior*, or lower, federal courts under the Supreme Court.

Clause 10 Congress can punish *piracy*, or the robbing of ships at sea.

Clause 11 Only Congress can declare war. Declarations of war are granted at the request of the President. *Letters of marque and reprisal* were documents issued by a government allowing merchant ships to arm themselves and attack ships of an enemy nation. They are no longer issued.

Clauses 12, 13, 14 These clauses place the army and navy under the control of Congress. Congress decides on the size of the armed forces and the amount of money to spend on the army and navy. It also has the power to write rules governing the armed forces.

Clauses 15, 16 The *militia* is a body of citizen soldiers. Congress can call up the militia to put down rebellions or fight foreign invaders. Each state has its own militia, today called the National Guard. Normally, the militia is under the command of a state's governor. However, it can be placed under the command of the President.

Clause 17 Congress controls the district around the national capital. In 1790, Congress made Washington, D.C., the nation's capital. In 1973, it gave residents of the District the right to elect local officials.

Clause 18 Clauses 1–17 list the powers delegated to Congress. The writers of the Constitution added Clause 18 so that Congress could deal with the changing needs of the nation. It gives Congress the power to make laws as needed to carry out the first 17 clauses. Clause 18 is sometimes called the elastic clause because it lets Congress stretch the meaning of its power.

Clause 1 *Such persons* means slaves. This clause resulted from a compromise between the supporters and the opponents of the slave trade. In 1808, as soon as Congress was permitted to abolish the slave trade, it did so.

Clause 2 A *writ of habeas corpus* is a court order requiring government officials to bring a prisoner to court and explain why he or she is being held. A writ of habeas corpus protects people from unlawful imprisonment. The government cannot suspend this right except in times of rebellion or invasion.

Constitution

3. Bills of Attainder; *Ex Post Facto* Laws No bill of attainder or ex post facto law shall be passed.

4. Apportionment of Direct Taxes No capitation, or other direct, tax shall be laid, unless in proportion to the census or enumeration herein before directed to be taken.

5. Taxes on Exports No tax or duty shall be laid on articles exported from any state.

6. Special Preference for Trade No preference shall be given by any regulation of commerce or revenue to the ports of one state over those of another; nor shall vessels bound to, or from, one state, be obliged to enter, clear, or pay duties in another.

7. Spending No money shall be drawn from the Treasury, but in consequence of appropriations made by law; and a regular statement and account of the receipts and expenditures of all public money shall be published from time to time.

8. Titles of Nobility No title of nobility shall be granted by the United States; and no person holding any office of profit or trust under them, shall, without the consent of the Congress, accept of any present, emolument, office, or title, of any kind whatever, from any king, prince or foreign state.

Section 10. Powers Denied to the States

1. Unconditional Prohibitions No state shall enter into any treaty, alliance, or confederation; grant letters of marque and reprisal; coin money; emit bills of credit; make any thing but gold and silver coin a tender in payment of debts; pass any bill of attainder, *ex post facto* law, or law impairing the obligation of contracts, or grant any title of nobility.

2. Powers Conditionally Denied No state shall, without the consent of the Congress, lay any imposts or duties on imports or exports, except what may be absolutely necessary for executing its inspection laws; and the net produce of all duties and imposts, laid by any state on imports or exports, shall be for the use of the Treasury of the United States; and all such laws shall be subject to the revision and control of the Congress.

3. Other Denied Powers No state shall, without the consent of Congress, lay any duty of tonnage, keep troops, or ships of war in time of peace, enter into any agreement or compact with another state, or with a foreign power, or engage in war, unless actually invaded, or in such imminent danger as will not admit of delay.

Commentary

Clause 3 A *bill of attainder* is a law declaring that a person is guilty of a particular crime. An *ex post facto law* punishes an act which was not illegal when it was committed. Congress cannot pass a bill of attainder or *ex post facto* laws.

Clause 4 A *capitation tax* is a tax placed directly on each person. *Direct taxes* are taxes on people or on land. They can be passed only if they are divided among the states according to population. The Sixteenth Amendment allowed Congress to tax income without regard to the population of the states.

Clause 5 This clause forbids Congress to tax exports. In 1787, southerners insisted on this clause because their economy depended on exports.

Clause 6 Congress cannot make laws that favor one state over another in trade and commerce. Also, states cannot place tariffs on interstate trade.

Clause 7 The federal government cannot spend money unless Congress *appropriates* it, or passes a law allowing it. This clause gives Congress an important check on the President by controlling the money he or she can spend. The government must publish a statement showing how it spends public funds.

Clause 8 The government cannot award titles of nobility, such as Duke or Duchess. American citizens cannot accept titles of nobility from foreign governments without the consent of Congress.

Clause 1 The writers of the Constitution did not want the states to act like separate nations. So they prohibited states from making treaties or coining money. Some powers denied to the federal government are also denied to the states. For example, states cannot pass *ex post facto* laws.

Clauses 2, 3 Powers listed here are forbidden to the states, but Congress can lift these prohibitions by passing laws that give these powers to the states.

Clause 2 forbids states from taxing imports and exports without the consent of Congress. States may charge inspection fees on goods entering the states. Any profit from these fees must be turned over to the United States Treasury.

Clause 3 forbids states from keeping an army or navy without the consent of Congress. States cannot make treaties or declare war unless an enemy invades or is about to invade.

Constitution

Article II. Executive Branch

Section 1. President and Vice President

1. Chief Executive; Term The executive power shall be vested in a President of the United States of America. He shall hold his office during the term of four years, and, together with the Vice President, chosen for the same term, be elected as follows:

2. Electoral College Each state shall appoint, in such manner as the legislature thereof may direct, a number of electors, equal to the whole number of senators and representatives to which the state may be entitled in the Congress: but no senator or representative, or person holding an office of trust or profit under the United States, shall be appointed an elector.

3. Former Electoral Method The electors shall meet in their respective states, and vote by ballot for two persons, of whom one at least shall not be an inhabitant of the same state with themselves. And they shall make a list of all the persons voted for, and of the number of votes for each; which list they shall sign and certify, and transmit sealed to the seat of the government of the United States, directed to the president of the Senate. The president of the Senate shall, in the presence of the Senate and House of Representatives, open all the certificates, and the votes shall then be counted. The person having the greatest number of votes shall be the President, if such number be a majority of the whole number of Electors appointed; and if there be more than one who have such majority, and have an equal number of votes, then the House of Representatives shall immediately choose by ballot one of them for President; and if no person have a majority, then from the five highest on the list the said House shall in like manner choose the President. But in choosing the President, the votes shall be taken by states, the representation from each state having one vote; a quorum for this purpose shall consist of a member or members from two thirds of the states, and a majority of all the states shall be necessary to a choice. In every case, after the choice of the President, the person having the greatest number of votes of the electors shall be the Vice President. But if there should remain two or more who have equal votes, the Senate shall choose from them by ballot the Vice President.

4. Time of Elections The Congress may determine the time of choosing the electors, and the day on which they shall give their votes; which day shall be the same throughout the United States.

5. Qualifications for President No person except a natural-born citizen, or a citizen of the United States at the time of the adoption of this Constitution, shall be eligible to the office of President; neither shall any person be eligible to that office who shall not have attained to the age of thirty-five years, and been fourteen years a resident within the United States.

Commentary

Clause 1 The President is responsible for *executing*, or carrying out, laws passed by Congress.

Clauses 2, 3 Some writers of the Constitution were afraid to allow the people to elect the President directly. Therefore, the Constitutional Convention set up the electoral college. Clause 2 directs each state to choose electors, or delegates to the electoral college, to vote for President. A state's electoral vote is equal to the combined number of senators and representatives. Each state may decide how to choose its electors. Members of Congress and federal officeholders may not serve as electors. This much of the original electoral college system is still in effect.

Clause 3 called upon each elector to vote for two candidates. The candidate who received a majority of the electoral votes would become President. The runner-up would become Vice President. If no candidate won a majority, the House would choose the President. The Senate would choose the Vice President.

The election of 1800 showed a problem with the original electoral college system. Thomas Jefferson was the Republican candidate for President, and Aaron Burr was the Republican candidate for Vice President. In the electoral college, the vote ended in a tie. The election was finally decided in the House, where Jefferson was chosen President. The Twelfth Amendment changed the electoral college system so that this could not happen again.

Clause 4 Under a law passed in 1792, electors are chosen on the Tuesday following the first Monday of November every four years. Electors from each state meet to vote in December.

Today, voters in each state choose *slates*, or groups, of electors who are pledged to a candidate for President. The candidate for President who wins the popular vote in each state wins that state's electoral vote.

Clause 5 The President must be a citizen of the United States from birth, at least 35 years old, and a resident of the country for 14 years. The first seven Presidents of the United States were born under British rule, but they were allowed to hold office because they were citizens at the time the Constitution was adopted.

6. Presidential Succession In case of the removal of the President from office, or of his death, resignation, or inability to discharge the powers and duties of the said office, the same shall devolve on the Vice President, and the Congress may by law provide for the case of removal, death, resignation or inability, both of the President and Vice President, declaring what officer shall then act as President, and such officer shall act accordingly, until the disability be removed, or a President shall be elected.

7. Salary The President shall, at stated times, receive for his services, a compensation, which shall neither be increased nor diminished during the period for which he shall have been elected, and he shall not receive within that period any other emolument from the United States, or any of them.

8. Oath of Office Before he enter on the execution of his office, he shall take the following oath or affirmation:—"I do solemnly swear (or affirm) that I will faithfully execute the office of the President of the United States, and will to the best of my ability, preserve, protect, and defend the Constitution of the United States."

Section 2. Powers of the President

1. Military Powers The President shall be commander in chief of the army and navy of the United States, and of the militia of the several states, when called into the actual service of the United States; he may require the opinion, in writing, of the principal officer in each of the executive departments, upon any subject relating to the duties of their respective offices, and he shall have power to grant reprieves and pardons for offenses against the United States, except in cases of impeachment.

2. Treaties; Appointments He shall have power, by and with the advice and consent of the Senate, to make treaties, provided two thirds of the senators present concur; and he shall nominate, and by and with the advice and consent of the Senate, shall appoint ambassadors, other public ministers and consuls, judges of the Supreme Court, and all other officers of the United States, whose appointments are not herein otherwise provided for, and which shall be established by law: but the Congress may by law vest the appointment of such inferior officers, as they think proper, in the President alone, in the courts of law, or in the heads of departments.

3. Temporary Appointments The President shall have power to fill up all vacancies that may happen during the recess of the Senate, by granting commissions which shall expire at the end of their next session.

Section 3. Duties of the President

He shall from time to time give to the Congress information of the state of the Union, and recommend to their consideration

Clause 6 The powers of the President pass to the Vice President if the President leaves office or cannot discharge his or her duties. The wording of this clause caused confusion the first time a President died in office. When President William Henry Harrison died, it was uncertain whether Vice President John Tyler should remain Vice President and act as President or whether he should be sworn in as President. Tyler persuaded a federal judge to swear him in. So he set the precedent that the Vice President assumes the office of President when it becomes vacant. The Twenty-fifth Amendment replaced this clause.

Clause 7 The President is paid a salary. It cannot be raised or lowered during his or her term of office. The President is not allowed to hold any other federal or state position while in office. Today, the President's salary is $400,000 a year.

Clause 8 Before taking office, the President must promise to protect and defend the Constitution. Usually, the Chief Justice of the United States administers the oath of office to the President.

Clause 1 The President is head of the armed forces and the state militias when they are called into national service. So the military is under *civilian*, or nonmilitary, control.

The President can get advice from the heads of executive departments. In most cases, the President has the power to grant a reprieve or pardon. A *reprieve* suspends punishment ordered by law. A *pardon* prevents prosecution for a crime or overrides the judgment of a court.

Clause 2 The President has the power to make treaties with other nations. Under the system of checks and balances, all treaties must be approved by two thirds of the Senate. Today, the President also makes agreements with foreign governments. These executive agreements do not need Senate approval.

The President has the power to appoint ambassadors to foreign countries and to appoint other high officials. The Senate must *confirm*, or approve, these appointments.

Clause 3 If the Senate is in *recess*, or not meeting, the President may fill vacant government posts by making temporary appointments.

The President must give Congress a report on the condition of the nation every year. This report is now called the State of the

such measures as he shall judge necessary and expedient; he may, on extraordinary occasions, convene both houses, or either of them, and in case of disagreement between them, with respect to the time of adjournment, he may adjourn them to such time as he shall think proper; he shall receive ambassadors and other public ministers; he shall take care that the laws be faithfully executed, and shall commission all the officers of the United States.

Union Address. The President has given this speech in person each January.

The President can call a special session of Congress and can adjourn Congress if necessary. The President has the power to receive, or recognize, foreign ambassadors.

The President must carry out the laws. Today, many government agencies oversee the execution of laws.

Section 4. Impeachment

The President, Vice President and all civil officers of the United States, shall be removed from office on impeachment for, and conviction of, treason, bribery, or other high crimes and misdemeanors.

Civil officers include federal judges and members of the Cabinet. *High crimes* are major crimes. *Misdemeanors* are lesser crimes. The President, Vice President, and others can be forced out of office if impeached and found guilty of certain crimes. Andrew Johnson and Bill Clinton are the only two Presidents to have been impeached.

Article III. Judicial Branch

Section 1. Courts, Terms of Office

The judicial power of the United States shall be vested in one Supreme Court, and in such inferior courts as the Congress may from time to time ordain and establish. The judges, both of the Supreme and inferior courts, shall hold their offices during good behavior, and shall, at stated times, receive for their services, a compensation, which shall not be diminished during their continuance in office.

Judicial power means the right of the courts to decide legal cases. The Constitution creates the Supreme Court but lets Congress decide on the size of the Supreme Court. Congress has the power to set up inferior, or lower, courts. The Judiciary Act of 1789 set up a system of district and circuit courts, or courts of appeal. All federal judges serve for life.

Section 2. Jurisdiction

1. Scope of Judicial Power The judicial power shall extend to all cases, in law and equity, arising under this Constitution, the laws of the United States, and treaties made, or which shall be made, under their authority;—to all cases affecting ambassadors, other public ministers and consuls;—to all cases of admiralty and maritime jurisdiction;—to controversies to which the United States shall be a party;—to controversies between two or more states; between a state and citizens of another state; —between citizens of different states;—between citizens of the same state claiming lands under grants of different states, and between a state, or the citizens thereof, and foreign states, citizens, or subjects.

Clause 1 *Jurisdiction* refers to the right of a court to hear a case. Federal courts have jurisdiction over cases that involve the Constitution, federal laws, treaties, foreign ambassadors and diplomats, naval and maritime laws, disagreements between states or between citizens from different states, and disputes between a state or citizen and a foreign state or citizen.

In *Marbury* v. *Madison*, the Supreme Court established the right to judge whether a law is constitutional.

2. Supreme Court In all cases affecting ambassadors, other public ministers and consuls, and those in which a state shall be a party, the Supreme Court shall have original jurisdiction. In all the other cases before mentioned, the Supreme Court shall have appellate jurisdiction, both as to law and fact, with such exceptions, and under such regulations as the Congress shall make.

Clause 2 *Original jurisdiction* means the power of a court to hear a case where it first arises. The Supreme Court has original jurisdiction over only a few cases, such as those involving foreign diplomats. More often, the Supreme Court acts as an appellate court. An *appellate* court does not decide guilt. It decides whether the lower court trial was properly conducted and reviews the lower court's decision.

3. Trial by Jury The trial of all crimes, except in cases of impeachment, shall be by jury; and such trial shall be held in the state where the said crimes shall have been committed; but when not committed within any state, the trial shall be at such place or places as the Congress may by law have directed.

Clause 3 This clause guarantees the right to a jury trial for anyone accused of a federal crime. The only exceptions are impeachment cases. The trial must be held in the state where the crime was committed.

Constitution

Commentary

Section 3. Treason

1. Definition Treason against the United States shall consist only in levying war against them, or in adhering to their enemies, giving them aid and comfort. No person shall be convicted of treason unless on the testimony of two witnesses to the same overt act, or on confession in open court.

2. Punishment The Congress shall have power to declare the punishment of treason, but no attainder of treason shall work corruption of blood or forfeiture except during the life of the person attained.

Article IV. Relations Among the States

Section 1. Full Faith and Credit

Full faith and credit shall be given in each state to the public acts, records, and judicial proceedings of every other state. And the Congress may by general laws prescribe the manner in which such acts, records, and proceedings shall be proved, and the effect thereof.

Section 2. Privileges and Immunities of Citizens

1. Privileges The citizens of each state shall be entitled to all privileges and immunities of citizens in the several states.

2. Extradition A person charged in any state with treason, felony, or other crime, who shall flee from justice, and be found in another state, shall on demand of the executive authority of the state from which he fled, be delivered up, to be removed to the state having jurisdiction of the crime.

3. Fugitive Slaves No person held to service or labor in one state, under the laws thereof, escaping into another, shall in consequence of any law or regulation therein, be discharged from such service or labor, but shall be delivered up on claim of the party to whom such service or labor may be due.

Section 3. New States and Territories

1. New States New states may be admitted by the Congress into this Union; but no new states shall be formed or erected within the jurisdiction of any other state; nor any state be formed by the junction of two or more states, or parts of states, without the consent of the legislatures of the states concerned as well as of the Congress.

2. Federal Lands The Congress shall have power to dispose of and make all needful rules and regulations respecting the territory or other property belonging to the United States; and nothing in this Constitution shall be so construed as to prejudice any claims of the United States, or of any particular state.

Clause 1 Treason is clearly defined. An ***overt act*** is an actual action. A person cannot be convicted of treason for what he or she thinks. A person can be convicted of treason only if he or she confesses or two witnesses testify to it.

Clause 2 Congress has the power to set the punishment for traitors. Congress may not punish the children of convicted traitors by taking away their civil rights or property.

Each state must recognize the official acts and records of any other state. For example, each state must recognize marriage certificates issued by another state. Congress can pass laws to ensure this.

Clause 1 All states must treat citizens of another state in the same way it treats its own citizens. However, the courts have allowed states to give residents certain privileges, such as lower tuition rates.

Clause 2 ***Extradition*** means the act of returning a suspected criminal or escaped prisoner to a state where he or she is wanted. State governors must return a suspect to another state. However, the Supreme Court has ruled that a governor cannot be forced to do so if he or she feels that justice will not be done.

Clause 3 ***Persons held to service or labor*** refers to slaves or indentured servants. This clause required states to return runaway slaves to their owners. The Thirteenth Amendment replaces this clause.

Clause 1 Congress has the power to admit new states to the Union. Existing states cannot be split up or joined together to form new states unless both Congress and the state legislatures approve. New states are equal to all other states.

Clause 2 Congress can make rules for managing and governing land owned by the United States. This includes territories not organized into states, and federal lands within a state.

Section 4. Protection Afforded to States by the Nation

The United States shall guarantee to every state in this Union a republican form of government, and shall protect each of them against invasion; and on application of the legislature, or of the executive (when the legislature cannot be convened) against domestic violence.

In a *republic,* voters choose representatives to govern them. The federal government must protect the states from foreign invasion and from *domestic,* or internal, disorder if asked to do so by a state.

Article V. Provisions for Amendment

The Congress, whenever two thirds of both houses shall deem it necessary, shall propose amendments to this Constitution, or, on the application of the legislatures of two thirds of the several states, shall call a convention for proposing amendments, which, in either case, shall be valid to all intents and purposes, as part of this Constitution, when ratified by the legislatures of three fourths of the several states, or by conventions in three fourths thereof, as the one or the other mode of ratification may be proposed by the Congress; provided that no amendment which may be made prior to the year one thousand eight hundred and eight shall in any manner affect the first and fourth clauses in the ninth section of the first Article; and that no state, without its consent, shall be deprived of its equal suffrage in the Senate.

The Constitution can be *amended*, or changed, if necessary. An amendment can be proposed by (1) a two-thirds vote of both houses of Congress or (2) a national convention called by Congress at the request of two thirds of the state legislatures. (This second method has never been used.) An amendment must be *ratified*, or approved, by (1) three fourths of the state legislatures or (2) special conventions in three fourths of the states. Congress decides which method will be used.

Article VI. National Debts, Supremacy of National Law, Oath

Section 1. Validity of Debts

All debts contracted and engagements entered into, before the adoption of this Constitution, shall be as valid against the United States under this Constitution, as under the Confederation.

The United States government promised to pay all debts and honor all agreements made under the Articles of Confederation.

Section 2. Supremacy of National Law

This Constitution, and the laws of the United States which shall be made in pursuance thereof, and all treaties made, or which shall be made, under the authority of the United States, shall be the supreme law of the land; and the judges in every state shall be bound thereby, anything in the constitution or laws of any state to the contrary notwithstanding.

The Constitution, federal laws, and treaties that the Senate has ratified are the *supreme,* or highest, law of the land. Thus, they outweigh state laws. A state judge must overturn a state law that conflicts with the Constitution or with a federal law.

Section 3. Oaths of Office

The senators and representatives before mentioned, and the members of the several state legislatures, and all executive and judicial officers, both of the United States and of the several states, shall be bound by oath or affirmation, to support this Constitution; but no religious test shall ever be required as a qualification to any office or public trust under the United States.

State and federal officeholders take an *oath,* or solemn promise, to support the Constitution. However, this clause forbids the use of religious tests for officeholders. During the colonial period, every colony except Rhode Island required a religious test for officeholders.

Article VII. Ratification of Constitution

The ratification of the conventions of nine states shall be sufficient for the establishment of this Constitution between the states so ratifying the same.

Done in convention by the unanimous consent of the states present the seventeenth day of September, in the year of our Lord one thousand seven hundred and eighty-seven, and of the independence of the United States of America the twelfth. In Witness whereof, we have hereunto subscribed our names.

During 1787 and 1788, states held special conventions. By October 1788, the required nine states had ratified the Constitution.

Attest:
William Jackson,
SECRETARY
George Washington,
PRESIDENT and
deputy from Virginia

NEW HAMPSHIRE
John Langdon
Nicholas Gilman

MASSACHUSETTS
Nathaniel Gorham
Rufus King

CONNECTICUT
William Samuel Johnson
Roger Sherman

NEW YORK
Alexander Hamilton

NEW JERSEY
William Livingston
David Brearley
William Paterson
Jonathan Dayton

PENNSYLVANIA
Benjamin Franklin
Thomas Mifflin
Robert Morris
George Clymer
Thomas Fitzsimons
Jared Ingersoll
James Wilson
Gouverneur Morris

DELAWARE
George Read
Gunning Bedford, Jr.
John Dickinson
Richard Bassett
Jacob Broom

MARYLAND
James McHenry
Dan of St. Thomas
  Jennifer
Daniel Carroll

VIRGINIA
John Blair
James Madison, Jr.

NORTH CAROLINA
William Blount
Richard Dobbs Spaight
Hugh Williamson

SOUTH CAROLINA
John Rutledge
Charles Cotesworth
  Pinckney
Charles Pinckney
Pierce Butler

GEORGIA
William Few
Abraham Baldwin

AMENDMENTS

First Amendment

(1791) Freedom of Religion, Speech, Press, Assembly, and Petition

Congress shall make no law respecting an establishment of religion, or prohibiting the free exercise thereof; or abridging the freedom of speech, or of the press; or the right of the people peaceably to assemble, and to petition the government for a redress of grievances.

First Amendment The First Amendment protects five basic rights: freedom of religion, speech, the press, assembly, and petition. Congress cannot set up an established, or official, church or religion for the nation. During the colonial period, most colonies had established churches. However, the authors of the First Amendment wanted to keep government and religion separate.

Congress may not *abridge*, or limit, the freedom to speak and write freely. The government may not censor, or review, books and newspapers before they are printed. This amendment also protects the right to assemble, or hold public meetings. *Petition* means ask. *Redress* means to correct. *Grievances* are wrongs. The people have the right to ask the government for wrongs to be corrected.

THE CONSTITUTION

Constitution

Second Amendment

(1791) Bearing Arms

A well-regulated militia being necessary to the security of a free state, the right of the people to keep and bear arms shall not be infringed.

Third Amendment

(1791) Quartering of Troops

No soldier shall, in time of peace, be quartered in any house, without the consent of the owner; nor in time of war, but in a manner to be prescribed by law.

Fourth Amendment

(1791) Searches and Seizures

The right of the people to be secure in their persons, houses, papers, and effects, against unreasonable searches and seizures, shall not be violated, and no warrants shall issue, but upon probable cause, supported by oath or affirmation, and particularly describing the place to be searched, and the persons or things to be seized.

Fifth Amendment

(1791) Criminal Proceedings; Due Process; Eminent Domain

No person shall be held to answer for a capital, or otherwise infamous, crime, unless on a presentment or indictment of a grand jury, except in cases arising in the land or naval forces, or in the militia, when in actual service in time of war or public danger; nor shall any person be subject for the same offense to be twice put in jeopardy of life and limb; nor shall be compelled, in any criminal case, to be a witness against himself; nor be deprived of life, liberty, or property, without due process of law; nor shall private property be taken for public use, without just compensation.

Commentary

Second Amendment State militia, such as the National Guard, have the right to bear arms, or keep weapons. Courts have generally ruled that the government can regulate the ownership of guns by private citizens.

Third Amendment During the colonial period, the British *quartered,* or housed, soldiers in private homes without the permission of the owners. This amendment limits the government's right to use private homes to house soldiers.

Fourth Amendment This amendment protects Americans from unreasonable searches and seizures. Search and seizure are permitted only if a judge has issued a *warrant*, or written court order. A warrant is issued only if there is probable cause. This means an officer must show that it is probable, or likely, that the search will produce evidence of a crime. A search warrant must name the exact place to be searched and the things to be seized.

In some cases, courts have ruled that searches can take place without a warrant. For example, police may search a person who is under arrest.

Fifth Amendment This amendment protects the rights of the accused. *Capital crimes* are those that can be punished with death. *Infamous crimes* are those that can be punished with prison or loss of rights. The federal government must obtain an *indictment*, or formal accusation, from a grand jury to prosecute anyone for such crimes. A *grand jury* is a panel of between 12 and 23 citizens who decide if the government has enough evidence to justify a trial. This procedure prevents the government from prosecuting people with little or no evidence of guilt. (Soldiers and the militia in wartime are not covered by this rule.)

Double jeopardy is forbidden by this amendment. This means that a person cannot be tried twice for the same crime. However, if a court sets aside a conviction because of a legal error, the accused can be tried again. A person on trial cannot be forced to *testify,* or give evidence, against himself or herself. A person accused of a crime is entitled to *due process of law*, or a fair hearing or trial.

Finally, the government cannot seize private property for public use without paying the owner a fair price for it.

Constitution

Sixth Amendment

(1791) Criminal Proceedings

In all criminal prosecutions, the accused shall enjoy the right to a speedy and public trial, by an impartial jury of the state and district wherein the crime shall have been committed, which district shall have been previously ascertained by law, and to be informed of the nature and cause of the accusation; to be confronted with the witnesses against him; to have compulsory process for obtaining witnesses in his favor, and to have the assistance of counsel for his defense.

Seventh Amendment

(1791) Civil Trials

In suits at common law, where the value in controversy shall exceed twenty dollars, the right of trial by jury shall be preserved, and no fact tried by a jury shall be otherwise re-examined in any court of the United States, than according to the rules of the common law.

Eighth Amendment

(1791) Punishment for Crimes

Excessive bail shall not be required, nor excessive fines imposed, nor cruel and unusual punishments inflicted.

Ninth Amendment

(1791) Unenumerated Rights

The enumeration in the Constitution, of certain rights, shall not be construed to deny or disparage others retained by the people.

Tenth Amendment

(1791) Powers Reserved to the States

The powers not delegated to the United States by the Constitution, nor prohibited by it to the states, are reserved to the states respectively, or to the people.

Eleventh Amendment

(1798) Suits Against States

The judicial power of the United States shall not be construed to extend to any suit in law or equity, commenced or prosecuted

Commentary

Sixth Amendment In criminal cases, the jury must be ***impartial***, or not favor either side. The accused is guaranteed the right to a trial by jury. The trial must be speedy. If the government purposely postpones the trial so that it becomes hard for the person to get a fair hearing, the charge may be dismissed. The accused must be told the charges against him or her and be allowed to question prosecution witnesses. Witnesses who can help the accused can be ordered to appear in court.

The accused must be allowed a lawyer. Since 1932, the federal government has been required to provide a lawyer if the accused cannot afford one. In 1963, the Supreme Court decided that states must also provide lawyers for a defendant too poor to pay for one.

Seventh Amendment ***Common law*** refers to rules of law established by judges in past cases. This amendment guarantees the right to a jury trial in lawsuits where the sum of money at stake is more than $20. An appeals court cannot change a verdict because it disagrees with the decision of the jury. It can set aside a verdict only if legal errors made the trial unfair.

Eighth Amendment ***Bail*** is money the accused leaves with the court as a pledge that he or she will appear for trial. If the accused does not appear for trial, the court keeps the money. ***Excessive*** means too high. This amendment forbids courts to set unreasonably high bail. The amount of bail usually depends on the seriousness of the charge and whether the accused is likely to appear for the trial. The amendment also forbids cruel and unusual punishments such as mental and physical abuse.

Ninth Amendment The people have rights that are not listed in the Constitution. This amendment was added because some people feared that the Bill of Rights would be used to limit rights to those actually listed.

Tenth Amendment This amendment limits the power of the federal government. Powers not given to the federal government belong to the states. The powers reserved to the states are not listed in the Constitution.

Eleventh Amendment This amendment changed part of Article 3, Section 2, Clause 1. As a result, a private citizen from

against one of the United States by citizens of another state, or by citizens or subjects of any foreign state.

Twelfth Amendment

(1804) Election of President and Vice President

The electors shall meet in their respective states, and vote by ballot for President and Vice President, one of whom, at least, shall not be an inhabitant of the same state with themselves; they shall name in their ballots the person voted for as President, and in distinct ballots the person voted for as Vice President, and they shall make distinct lists of all persons voted for as President, and of all persons voted for as Vice President, and of the number of votes for each, which lists they shall sign and certify, and transmit sealed to the seat of the government of the United States, directed to the president of the Senate; the president of the Senate shall, in the presence of the Senate and the House of Representatives, open all the certificates and the votes shall then be counted;—the person having the greatest number of votes for President shall be the President, if such number be a majority of the whole number of electors appointed; and if no person have such a majority, then from the persons having the highest numbers not exceeding three on the list of those voted for as President, the House of Representatives shall choose immediately, by ballot, the President. But in choosing the President, the votes shall be taken by states, the representation from each state having one vote; a quorum for this purpose shall consist of a member or members from two thirds of the states, and a majority of all the states shall be necessary to a choice. And if the House of Representatives shall not choose a President whenever the right of choice shall devolve upon them, ~~before the fourth day of March next following,~~ then the Vice President, shall act as President, as in the case of the death or other constitutional disability of the President.— The person having the greatest number of votes as Vice President, shall be the Vice President, if such number be a majority of the whole number of electors appointed, and if no person have a majority, then from the two highest numbers on the list, the Senate shall choose the Vice President; a quorum for the purpose shall consist of two thirds of the whole number of senators, and a majority of the whole number shall be necessary to a choice. But no person constitutionally ineligible to the office of President shall be eligible to that of Vice President of the United States.

Thirteenth Amendment

(1865) Slavery and Involuntary Servitude

Section 1. Outlawing Slavery Neither slavery nor involuntary servitude, except as a punishment for crime whereof the party shall have been duly convicted, shall exist within the United States, or any place subject to their jurisdiction.

Section 2. Enforcement Congress shall have power to enforce this article by appropriate legislation.

one state cannot sue the government of another state in federal court. However, a citizen can sue a state government in a state court.

Twelfth Amendment This amendment changed the way the electoral college voted. Before the amendment was adopted, each elector simply voted for two people. The candidate with the most votes became President. The runner-up became Vice President. In 1800, however, a tie vote resulted between Thomas Jefferson and Aaron Burr.

In such a case, the Constitution required the House of Representatives to elect the President. Federalists had a majority in the House. They tried to keep Jefferson out of office by voting for Burr. It took 36 ballots in the House before Jefferson was elected President.

To keep this from happening again, the Twelfth Amendment was passed and ratified in time for the election of 1804.

This amendment provides that each elector choose one candidate for President and one candidate for Vice President. If no candidate for President receives a majority of electoral votes, the House of Representatives chooses the President. If no candidate for Vice President receives a majority, the Senate elects the Vice President. The Vice President must be a person who is eligible to be President.

This system is still in use today. However, it is possible for a candidate to win the popular vote and lose in the electoral college. This happened in 1888 and in 2000.

Thirteenth Amendment The Emancipation Proclamation (1863) freed slaves only in areas controlled by the Confederacy. This amendment freed all slaves. It also forbids *involuntary servitude*, or labor done against one's will. However, it does not prevent prison wardens from making prisoners work. Congress can pass laws to carry out this amendment.

Constitution

Fourteenth Amendment
(1868) Rights of Citizens

Section 1. Citizenship All persons born or naturalized in the United States, and subject to the jurisdiction thereof, are citizens of the United States and of the state wherein they reside. No state shall make or enforce any law which shall abridge the privileges or immunities of citizens of the United States; nor shall any state deprive any person of life, liberty, or property, without due process of law; nor deny to any person within its jurisdiction the equal protection of the laws.

Section 2. Apportionment of Representatives Representatives shall be apportioned among the several states according to their respective numbers, counting the whole number of persons in each state, excluding Indians not taxed. But when the right to vote at any election for the choice of electors for President and Vice President of the United States, representatives in Congress, the executive and judicial officers of a state, or the members of the legislature thereof, is denied to any of the male inhabitants of such state, being twenty-one years of age, and citizens of the United States, or in any way abridged, except for participation in rebellion, or other crime, the basis of representation therein shall be reduced in the proportion which the number of such male citizens shall bear to the whole number of male citizens twenty-one years of age in such state.

Section 3. Former Confederate Officials No person shall be a senator or representative in Congress, or elector of President and Vice President, or hold any office, civil or military, under the United States, or under any state, who, having previously taken an oath, as a member of Congress, or as an officer of the United States, or as a member of any state legislature, or as an executive or judicial officer of any state, to support the Constitution of the United States, shall have engaged in insurrection or rebellion against the same, or given aid or comfort to the enemies thereof. But Congress may, by a vote of two thirds of each house, remove such disability.

Section 4. Public Debt The validity of the public debt of the United States, authorized by law, including debts incurred for payment of pensions and bounties for services in suppressing insurrection or rebellion, shall not be questioned. But neither the United States nor any state shall assume or pay any debt or obligation incurred in aid of insurrection or rebellion against the United States, or any claim for the loss or emancipation of any slave; but all such debts, obligations and claims shall be held illegal and void.

Section 5. Enforcement The Congress shall have power to enforce, by appropriate legislation, the provisions of this article.

Commentary

Fourteenth Amendment, Section 1 This section defines citizenship for the first time in the Constitution, and it extends citizenship to blacks. It also prohibits states from denying the rights and privileges of citizenship to any citizen. This section also forbids states to deny due process of law.

Section 1 guarantees all citizens "equal protection under the law." For a long time, however, the Fourteenth Amendment did not protect blacks from discrimination. After Reconstruction, separate facilities for blacks and whites sprang up. In 1954, the Supreme Court ruled that separate facilities for blacks and whites were by their nature unequal. This ruling, in the case of *Brown* v. *Board of Education*, made school segregation illegal.

Fourteenth Amendment, Section 2 This section replaced the three-fifths clause. It provides that representation in the House of Representatives is decided on the basis of the number of people in the state. It also provides that states which deny the vote to male citizens over age 21 will be punished by losing part of their representation in the House. This provision has never been enforced.

Despite this clause, black citizens were often prevented from voting. In the 1960s, federal laws were passed to end voting discrimination.

Fourteenth Amendment, Section 3 This section prohibited people who had been federal or state officials before the Civil War and who had joined the Confederate cause from serving again as government officials. In 1872, Congress restored the rights of former Confederate officials.

Fourteenth Amendment, Section 4 This section recognized that the United States must repay its debts from the Civil War. However, it forbade the repayment of debts of the Confederacy. This meant that people who had loaned money to the Confederacy would not be repaid. Also, states were not allowed to pay former slave owners for the loss of slaves.

Fourteenth Amendment, Section 5 Congress can pass laws to carry out this amendment.

Fifteenth Amendment

(1870) Right to Vote—Race, Color, Servitude

Section 1. Extending the Right to Vote The right of citizens of the United States to vote shall not be denied or abridged by the United States or by any state on account of race, color, or previous condition of servitude.

Section 2. Enforcement The Congress shall have power to enforce this article by appropriate legislation.

Fifteenth Amendment, Section 1 *Previous condition of servitude* refers to slavery. This amendment gave blacks, both former slaves and free blacks, the right to vote. In the late 1800s, southern states used grandfather clauses, literacy tests, and poll taxes to keep blacks from voting.

Fifteenth Amendment, Section 2 Congress can pass laws to carry out this amendment. The Twenty-fourth Amendment barred the use of poll taxes in national elections. The Voting Rights Act of 1965 gave federal officials the power to register voters where there was voting discrimination.

Sixteenth Amendment

(1913) Income Tax

The Congress shall have power to lay and collect taxes on incomes, from whatever source derived, without apportionment among the several states, and without regard to any census or enumeration.

Sixteenth Amendment Congress has the power to collect taxes on people's income. An income tax can be collected without regard to a state's population. This amendment changed Article 1, Section 9, Clause 4.

Seventeenth Amendment

(1913) Popular Election of Senators

Section 1. Method of Election The Senate of the United States shall be composed of two senators from each state, elected by the people thereof, for six years; and each senator shall have one vote. The electors in each state shall have the qualifications requisite for electors of the most numerous branch of the state legislatures.

Section 2. Vacancies When vacancies happen in the representation of any state in the Senate, the executive authority of such state shall issue writs of election to fill such vacancies: provided, that the legislature of any state may empower the executive thereof to make temporary appointments until the people fill the vacancies by election as the legislature may direct.

Section 3. Those Elected Under Previous Procedure This amendment shall not be so construed as to affect the election or term of any senator chosen before it becomes valid as part of the Constitution.

Seventeenth Amendment, Section 1 This amendment replaced Article 1, Section 2, Clause 1. Before it was adopted, state legislatures chose senators. This amendment provides that senators are directly elected by the people of each state.

Seventeenth Amendment, Section 2 When a Senate seat becomes vacant, the governor of the state must order an election to fill the seat. The state legislature can give the governor power to fill the seat until an election is held.

Seventeenth Amendment, Section 3 Senators who had already been elected by the state legislatures were not affected by this amendment.

Eighteenth Amendment

(1919) Prohibition of Intoxicating Liquors

Section 1. Ban on Alcohol After one year from the ratification of this article, the manufacture, sale, or transportation of intoxicating liquors within, the importation thereof into, or the exportation thereof from the United States and all territory subject to the jurisdiction thereof for beverage purposes is hereby prohibited.

Section 2. Enforcement The Congress and the several states shall have concurrent power to enforce this article by appropriate legislation.

Eighteenth Amendment, Section 1 This amendment, known as Prohibition, banned the making, selling, or transporting of alcoholic beverages in the United States. Later, the Twenty-first Amendment *repealed,* or canceled, this amendment.

Eighteenth Amendment, Section 2 Both the states and the federal government had the power to pass laws to enforce this amendment.

THE CONSTITUTION

Constitution

Section 3. Method of Ratification ~~This article shall be inopera-~~ ~~tive unless it shall have been ratified as an amendment to the~~ ~~Constitution by the legislatures of the several states, as provided~~ ~~in the Constitution, within seven years from the date of the sub-~~ ~~mission hereof to the states by Congress.~~

Nineteenth Amendment

(1920) Women's Suffrage

Section 1. The Right to Vote The right of citizens of the United States to vote shall not be denied or abridged by the United States or by any state on account of sex.

Section 2. Enforcement Congress shall have power to enforce this article by appropriate legislation.

Twentieth Amendment

(1933) Commencement of Terms; Sessions of Congress; Death or Disqualification of President-Elect

Section 1. Beginning of Terms The terms of the President and Vice President shall end at noon on the 20th day of January, and the terms of senators and representatives at noon on the 3d day of January, of the years in which such terms would have ended if this article had not been ratified; and the terms of their successors shall then begin.

Section 2. Congressional Sessions The Congress shall assemble at least once in every year, and such meeting shall begin at noon on the 3rd day of January, unless they shall by law appoint a different day.

Section 3. Presidential Succession If, at the time fixed for the beginning of the term of the President, the President-elect shall have died, the Vice President-elect shall become President. If a President shall not have been chosen before the time fixed for the beginning of his term, or if the President-elect shall have failed to qualify, then the Vice President-elect shall act as President until a President shall have qualified; and the Congress may by law provide for the case wherein neither a President-elect nor a Vice President-elect shall have qualified, declaring who shall then act as President, or the manner in which one who is to act shall be selected, and such person shall act accordingly until a President or Vice President shall have qualified.

Section 4. Elections Decided by Congress The Congress may by law provide for the case of the death of any of the persons from whom the House of Representatives may choose a President whenever the right of choice shall have devolved upon them, and for the case of the death of any of the persons from whom

Commentary

Eighteenth Amendment, Section 3 This amendment had to be approved within seven years. The Eighteenth Amendment was the first amendment to include a time limit for ratification.

Nineteenth Amendment, Section 1 Neither the federal government nor state governments can deny the right to vote on account of sex. Thus, women won ***suffrage,*** or the right to vote. Before 1920, some states had allowed women to vote in state elections.

Nineteenth Amendment, Section 2 Congress can pass laws to carry out this amendment.

Twentieth Amendment, Section 1 The date for the President and Vice President to take office is January 20. Members of Congress begin their terms of office on January 3. Before this amendment was adopted, these terms of office began on March 4.

Twentieth Amendment, Section 2 Congress must meet at least once a year. The new session of Congress begins on January 3. Before this amendment, members of Congress who had been defeated in November continued to hold office until the following March. Such members were known as lame ducks.

Twentieth Amendment, Section 3 If the President-elect dies before taking office, the Vice President-elect becomes President. If no President has been chosen by January 20 or if the elected candidate fails to qualify for office, the Vice President-elect acts as President, but only until a qualified President is chosen.

Finally, Congress has the power to choose a person to act as President if neither the President-elect nor Vice President-elect is qualified to take office.

Twentieth Amendment, Section 4 Congress can pass laws in cases where a presidential candidate dies while an election is being decided in the House. Congress has similar power in cases where a candidate for Vice President dies while an election is being decided in the Senate.

the Senate may choose a Vice President whenever the right of choice shall have devolved upon them.

Section 5. Date of Implementation ~~Sections 1 and 2 shall take effect on the 15th day of October following the ratification of this article.~~

Section 6. Ratification Period This article shall be inoperative unless it shall have been ratified as an amendment to the Constitution by the legislatures of three fourths of the several states within seven years from the date of its submission.

Twentieth Amendment, Section 5 Section 5 sets the date for the amendment to become effective.

Twentieth Amendment, Section 6 Section 6 sets a time limit for ratification.

Twenty-first Amendment
(1933) Repeal of Prohibition
Section 1. Repeal The eighteenth article of amendment to the Constitution of the United States is hereby repealed.

Section 2. State Laws The transportation or importation into any state, territory, or possession of the United States for delivery or use therein of intoxicating liquors, in violation of the laws thereof, is hereby prohibited.

Section 3. Ratification Period ~~This article shall be inoperative unless it shall have been ratified as an amendment to the Constitution by conventions in the several states, as provided in the Constitution, within seven years from the date of the submission hereof to the states by the Congress.~~

Twenty-first Amendment, Section 1 The Eighteenth Amendment is repealed, making it legal to make and sell alcoholic beverages. Prohibition ended December 5, 1933.

Twenty-first Amendment, Section 2 Each state was free to ban the making and selling of alcoholic drink within its borders. This section makes bringing liquor into a "dry" state a federal offense.

Twenty-first Amendment, Section 3 Special state conventions were called to ratify this amendment. This is the only time an amendment was ratified by state conventions rather than state legislatures.

Twenty-second Amendment
(1951) Presidential Tenure
Section 1. Two-Term Limit No person shall be elected to the office of the President more than twice, and no person who has held the office of President, or acted as President, for more than two years of a term to which some other person was elected President shall be elected to the office of the President more than once. ~~But this article shall not apply to any person holding the office of President when this article was proposed by the Congress, and shall not prevent any person who may be holding the office of President, or acting as President, during the term within which this article becomes operative from holding the office of President or acting as President during the remainder of such term.~~

Section 2. Ratification Period ~~This article shall be inoperative unless it shall have been ratified as an amendment to the Constitution by the legislatures of three fourths of the several states within seven years from the date of its submission to the states by the Congress.~~

Twenty-second Amendment, Section 1 Before Franklin Roosevelt became President, no President served more than two terms in office. Roosevelt broke with this custom and was elected to four terms. This amendment provides that no President may serve more than two terms. A President who has already served more than half of someone else's term can serve only one more full term. However, the amendment did not apply to Harry Truman, who had become President after Franklin Roosevelt's death in 1945.

Twenty-second Amendment, Section 2 A seven-year time limit is set for ratification.

Twenty-third Amendment

(1961) Presidential Electors for the District of Columbia

Section 1. Determining the Number of Electors The district constituting the seat of government of the United States shall appoint in such manner as the Congress may direct:

A number of electors of President and Vice President equal to the whole number of senators and representatives in Congress to which the district would be entitled if it were a state, but in no event more than the least populous state; they shall be in addition to those appointed by the states, but they shall be considered, for the purposes of the election of President and Vice President, to be electors appointed by a state; and they shall meet in the district and perform such duties as provided by the twelfth article of amendment.

Twenty-third Amendment, Section 1 This amendment gives residents of Washington, D.C., the right to vote in presidential elections. Until this amendment was adopted, people living in Washington, D.C., could not vote for President because the Constitution had made no provision for choosing electors from the nation's capital. Washington, D.C., has three electoral votes.

Section 2. Enforcement The Congress shall have power to enforce this article by appropriate legislation.

Twenty-third Amendment, Section 2 Congress can pass laws to carry out this amendment.

Twenty-fourth Amendment

(1964) Right to Vote in Federal Elections—Tax Payment

Section 1. Poll Tax Banned The right of citizens of the United States to vote in any primary or other election for President or Vice President, for electors for President or Vice President, or for senator or representative in Congress, shall not be denied or abridged by the United States or any state by reason of failure to pay any poll tax or other tax.

Twenty-fourth Amendment, Section 1 A *poll tax* is a tax on voters. This amendment bans poll taxes in national elections. Some states used poll taxes to keep African Americans from voting. In 1966, the Supreme Court struck down poll taxes in state elections, also.

Section 2. Enforcement The Congress shall have the power to enforce this article by appropriate legislation.

Twenty-fourth Amendment, Section 2 Congress can pass laws to carry out this amendment.

Twenty-fifth Amendment

(1967) Presidential Succession, Vice Presidential Vacancy, Presidential Inability

Section 1. President's Death or Resignation In case of the removal of the President from office or of his death or resignation, the Vice President shall become President.

Twenty-fifth Amendment, Section 1 If the President dies or resigns, the Vice President becomes President. This section clarifies Article 2, Section 1, Clause 6.

Section 2. Vacancies in Vice Presidency Whenever there is a vacancy in the office of the Vice President, the President shall nominate a Vice President who shall take office upon confirmation by a majority vote of both houses of Congress.

Twenty-fifth Amendment, Section 2 When a Vice President takes over the office of President, he or she appoints a Vice President who must be approved by a majority vote of both houses of Congress. This section was first applied after Vice President Spiro Agnew resigned in 1973. President Richard Nixon appointed Gerald Ford as Vice President.

Section 3. Disability of the President Whenever the President transmits to the president pro tempore of the Senate and the Speaker of the House of Representatives his written declaration that he is unable to discharge the powers and duties of his office, and until he transmits to them a written declaration to the contrary, such powers and duties shall be discharged by the Vice President as acting President.

Twenty-fifth Amendment, Section 3 If the President declares in writing that he or she is unable to perform the duties of office, the Vice President serves as acting President until the President recovers.

Section 4. Vice President as Acting President Whenever the Vice President and a majority of either the principal officers of the executive departments or of such other body as Congress may by law provide, transmit to the President pro tempore of the Senate and the Speaker of the House of Representatives their written declaration that the President is unable to discharge the powers and duties of his office, the Vice President shall immediately assume the powers and duties of the office as acting President.

Thereafter, when the President transmits to the president pro tempore of the Senate and the Speaker of the House of Representatives his written declaration that no inability exists, he shall resume the powers and duties of his office unless the Vice President and a majority of either the principal officers of the executive department or of such other body as Congress may by law provide, transmit within four days to the president pro tempore of the Senate and the Speaker of the House of Representatives their written declaration that the President is unable to discharge the powers and duties of his office. Thereupon Congress shall decide the issue, assembling within forty-eight hours for that purpose if not in session. If the Congress, within twenty-one days after receipt of the latter written declaration, or, if Congress is not in session, within twenty-one days after Congress is required to assemble, determines by two thirds vote of both Houses that the President is unable to discharge the powers and duties of his office, the Vice President shall continue to discharge the same as acting President; otherwise, the President shall resume the powers and duties of his office.

Twenty-fifth Amendment, Section 4 Two Presidents, Woodrow Wilson and Dwight Eisenhower, have fallen gravely ill while in office. The Constitution contained no provision for this kind of emergency.

Section 3 provided that the President can inform Congress that he or she is too sick to perform the duties of office. However, if the President is unconscious or refuses to admit to a disabling illness, Section 4 provides that the Vice President and Cabinet may declare the President disabled. The Vice President becomes acting President until the President can return to the duties of office. In case of a disagreement between the President and the Vice President and Cabinet over the President's ability to perform the duties of office, Congress must decide the issue. A two-thirds vote of both houses is needed to find the President is disabled or unable to fulfill the duties of office.

Twenty-sixth Amendment

(1971) Right to Vote—Age

Section 1. Lowering of Voting Age The right of citizens of the United States, who are eighteen years of age or older, shall not be denied or abridged by the United States or by any state on account of age.

Twenty-sixth Amendment, Section 1 In 1970, Congress passed a law allowing 18-year-olds to vote. However, the Supreme Court decided that Congress could not set a minimum age for state elections. So this amendment was passed and ratified.

Section 2. Enforcement The Congress shall have the power to enforce this article by appropriate legislation.

Twenty-sixth Amendment, Section 2 Congress can pass laws to carry out this amendment.

Twenty-seventh Amendment

(1992) Congressional Pay

No law, varying the compensation for the services of the senators and representatives, shall take effect until an election of representatives shall have intervened.

Twenty-seventh Amendment If members of Congress vote themselves a pay increase, it cannot go into effect until after the next congressional election. This amendment was proposed in 1789. In 1992, Michigan became the thirty-eighth state to ratify it.

The Bill of Rights

Citizenship and You

"What is so great about being an American citizen?" Mr. Walker's question surprised his students. For a moment the room was silent.

Finally Sharon raised her hand. "Well, we have rights," she said. "For one thing, we have freedom of speech."

Juan raised his hand and said, "People have a right to a trial, with lawyers, a judge, and a jury."

"And we have freedom of religion," Jessica added.

Mr. Walker nodded. "Those are all important rights," he said. He leaned against the desk and addressed the whole class. "As American citizens we have many rights—probably more than most of us can name. These rights are listed in a part of the Constitution called the Bill of Rights."

 Keep It Current

Items marked with this logo are periodically updated on the Internet. To keep up-to-date, go to **www.phschool.com**

What's Ahead in Chapter 6

Why is the Bill of Rights so important and how did it become part of the Constitution? This chapter will answer these questions and help you understand the value of your rights as an American citizen. You will also see that the story of the Bill of Rights is not just about history—it is an ongoing story in which you play a vital role.

Section 1 **Adding the Bill of Rights**

Section 2 **Protections in the Bill of Rights**

Section 3 **Interpreting the Bill of Rights**

Citizen's Journal

How would you have answered Mr. Walker's question to his class? Write a paragraph describing what you think are your most important rights as an American citizen.

Adding the Bill of Rights

SECTION PREVIEW

Objectives

- Describe the two methods that may be used to propose and to ratify an amendment.
- Summarize the debate in Congress over the Bill of Rights.
- Describe how the Bill of Rights became part of the Constitution.

 Focus

To understand how the Bill of Rights became part of the Constitution, you need to recall why a list of citizens' rights was left out of the original document. Quite simply, the framers thought that it was unnecessary. They believed that the Constitution already guarded against tyranny by limiting the government's power.

The Anti-Federalists disagreed and put up a stiff fight against ratification. If James Madison and other Federalists had not promised that a bill of rights could be added later, in the form of amendments, the Constitution might not have been ratified.

After the ratification, Madison was determined to fulfill his promise to the Anti-Federalists. Adding a bill of rights would be an important step toward gaining their support for the new government. The stage was set for the first changes in the Constitution and therefore the first test of the amendment process.

The Amendment Process

The Constitution requires that any amendment must be approved at both the national and state levels. First an amendment is approved at the national level—usually by Congress—and proposed to the states. Then the states either ratify it or reject it.

There are two ways to propose an amendment to the states. Congress may propose an amendment if it has been approved by a two-thirds vote in both the Senate and the House of Representatives. The 27 amendments that are part of our Constitution today were all proposed this way.

An amendment may also be proposed by a national convention called for by two thirds of the state legislatures. This method, however, has not yet been used.

Once an amendment is proposed, there are two ways for the states to ratify it. The usual route is approval by the legislatures of three fourths of the states. The other method is approval by special conventions in three fourths of the states. Congress chooses which method will be used. The amendment process can take months or even years to complete because any proposed change in the Constitution must gain such widespread support.

The Debate in Congress

In the case of the Bill of Rights, the amendment process began in Congress. Speaking to fellow members of the House in June 1789, Madison declared that many Americans believed that the articles of the Constitution did not adequately protect their rights. By proposing a bill of rights, he argued, Congress would be responding to the people's will and earning their trust, thereby laying a solid foundation for the new republic.

The newly-elected Congress, however, was impatient to begin passing laws that would set the young government firmly on its feet. Therefore, Madison agreed that a bill of rights could wait. He urged Congress, though, to prepare a bill of rights

George Mason wrote Virginia's Declaration of Rights, which became a model for the Bill of Rights added to the Constitution in 1791.

as soon as possible. By doing so, he declared, Congress would "make the Constitution better in the opinion of those who are opposed to it without weakening its frame... in the judgment of those who are attached to it."

Two months later, in August, members of Congress began preparing the amendments that they hoped would become the bill of rights. After some debate, they produced a list that drew on many earlier statements of individual rights, such as the Magna Carta, the English Bill of Rights, colonial charters, and state constitutions.

The next issue was where in the Constitution to place the bill of rights. Madison wanted to place the rights within the articles of the Constitution to show their relationship to limits already placed on the government.

As it turned out, a majority of members of Congress voted to attach the list of rights to the end of the document. Some Congress members wanted the Bill of Rights at the end because they did not want to give them the same importance as the original Constitution.

The Proposal and the Ratification

Following the debates, a committee of Congressmen wrote final versions of twelve amendments, including ten that protected citizens' rights. Congress approved the amendments and proposed them to the states in September of 1789.

The amendments were welcomed by people who had not trusted the new government. Only two failed to gain enough support: proposals to enlarge the size of the House and to limit when Congress might raise its salaries. By December 15, 1791, the states had ratified ten amendments protecting citizens' rights. The Bill of Rights had become part of the Constitution.

Section 1 Assessment

1. Describe the method by which all 27 amendments have been proposed.
2. What is one method of ratifying an amendment?
3. What was the main argument in favor of a bill of rights? What was the main argument against a bill of rights?
4. **Evaluate** If you had been a member of Congress in 1789, which would you have considered more important: getting the new government organized or proposing a bill of rights? Explain.

Protections in the Bill of Rights

 **Focus**

When the first ten amendments were added to the Constitution, they were intended to protect citizens' rights against actions by the national government. The Bill of Rights did not change any basic principles in the Constitution. Instead, these ten amendments spell out basic rights that are protected under our form of government. These rights fall into three main categories: **(1)** individual freedoms, **(2)** protections against government abuse of power, and **(3)** rights of citizens accused of crimes.

Protections of Individual Freedoms

Picture what your life might be like if the following were true: you could be arrested for criticizing a government official; the government could decide which books or magazines may be published and which movies or television shows you may watch; daily newspapers could publish no articles critical of the government and no political cartoons that poke fun at government officials; a person could be jailed because of religious beliefs.

Perhaps you are asking yourself, "What is the point of supposing things that could never happen?" The answer is that they do happen. Millions of people in the world today are denied the rights that we Americans often take for granted. These rights include a number of freedoms protected by the First Amendment.

Freedom of Religion The First Amendment provides for freedom of religion. Every American is free to follow the religion of his or her choice, or not to practice any religion at all. Also, the First Amendment establishes separation of church and state, the situation in which the government may not favor any religion or establish an official religion. This was the first time in history that a government had taken such a step. With separation of church and state, religion may never be used as a test for deciding who may hold office or who may vote.

Freedom of Speech When people say, "This is a free country, so I can say what I want," they are referring to freedom of speech, another right protected by the First Amendment. As an American you have the right to speak and write freely, to say what you believe.

Does freedom of speech mean that you may say anything, whenever and wherever

CHART SKILL THE BILL OF RIGHTS The first ten amendments to the Constitution are known as the Bill of Rights. **Government In your own words, summarize the overall goal of the Bill of Rights.**

Amendment	Subject
1st	Guarantees freedom of religion, of speech, and of the press; the right to assemble peacefully; and the right to petition the government.
2nd	Protects the right to possess firearms.
3rd	Declares that the government may not require people to house soldiers during peacetime.
4th	Protects people from unreasonable searches and seizures.
5th	Guarantees that no one may be deprived of life, liberty, or property without due process of law.
6th	Guarantees the right to a trial by jury in criminal cases.
7th	Guarantees the right to a trial by jury in most civil cases.
8th	Prohibits excessive bail, fines, and punishments.
9th	Declares that rights not mentioned in the Constitution belong to the people.
10th	Declares that powers not given to the national government belong to the states or to the people.

The full text and explanation of the Constitution can be found on pages 108–129.

you please? No. You are not free to slander another person, telling lies that damage his or her reputation. However, you are free to express opinions, no matter how unpopular, and to write articles, stories, and poems, no matter how much other people may dislike them or disagree with them.

Freedom of the Press As you read in Chapter 4, the belief in freedom of the press took root during the colonial period, especially through the Zenger case. That belief became a reality with the First Amendment, which prevents the government from deciding what may be printed.

Together with freedom of speech, freedom of the press guarantees that people may criticize the government without fearing arrest. In many countries today, the government controls newspapers and radio or tele-

vision stations. In the United States, the First Amendment helps guarantee that citizens can get information and hear different opinions.

Like freedom of speech, freedom of the press has its limits. For instance, a newspaper is not free to libel, or print lies about, a person because this would unfairly damage his or her reputation. Also, both freedom of speech and freedom of the press may be limited when what is said or written endangers the lives of citizens, as when a person falsely shouts "Fire" in a theater and causes a panic.

Freedom of Assembly Under the First Amendment, citizens also have the right to assemble, or meet together. For instance, a group may hold a demonstration to protest a new law as long as their demonstration is peaceful and does not violate the rights of other citizens.

"They can't say I'm not doing anything"

©1975 HERBLOCK

Freedom of the press applies not only to writings but also to political cartoons. This 1975 cartoon poked fun at President Gerald Ford.

Freedom of Petition

Perhaps you have heard people make statements such as, "I don't like that law, but there is nothing I can do about it." According to the First Amendment, there *is* something they can do about it. Any citizen or group of citizens has the right to ask a government representative to change a law, to make a new law, or in other ways to solve problems that arise. A citizen may make such a request by writing a letter, by telephoning, or by sending a petition—a request signed by many citizens— to a representative in Congress.

Protections Against Abuse of Power

The Second, Third, Fourth, and Fifth amendments all help protect citizens from abuse of power by police and judges, or by any other government officials. These amendments stem from the colonists' experience under the rule of England.

Gun Ownership The Second Amendment deals with the rights of citizens to own guns. The Amendment states:

> ❝A well-regulated militia being necessary to the security of a free state, the right of the people to keep and bear arms shall not be infringed.❞

When this amendment was written, the American Revolution was fresh in the minds of citizens. Americans remembered that militias, or groups of citizens armed to defend themselves, had played an important role in achieving victory over the powerful British. Now that the United States was forming a strong government of its own, many people felt this amendment provided a vital protection against abuses of government power.

Throughout our nation's history, citizens have debated the exact meaning of the Second Amendment. Do Americans have a constitutional right to own guns for personal use? Should the government have the right to restrict the sale and use of guns? These questions are still being debated today.

The Housing of Soldiers During the colonial period, England had allowed English soldiers to use colonists' homes as living quarters. The Third Amendment states that the government must obtain the owner's consent first. During wartime a citizen may have to provide soldiers with lodging, but only if Congress passes laws requiring it.

Unreasonable Searches and Seizures

"Open up! This is the police. We have a warrant to search your house!" You have probably seen movies in which police officers say this when entering the home of a suspect. Under the Fourth Amendment, officers cannot search a citizen or a citizen's home without a valid reason. Usually they must obtain a search warrant—written permission from a judge—to search citizens, their homes, or their belongings. To obtain a warrant, the police must convince a judge that they are likely to find evidence of a crime.

During the years leading to the American Revolution, as tensions between England and the colonies increased, Parliament allowed officers to make unlimited searches and seizures. Through the Fourth Amendment, Americans were guarding against any such abuse of power by the new government.

Protecting Property Rights May the government take away your property to build a freeway, subway, or other public project? Yes, it may. The government has the power of eminent domain (EM eh nehnt do MAYN), the power to take private property for public use. However, the Fifth Amendment protects citizens from an abuse of this power by requiring the government to pay owners a fair price for their property.

Protections of the Accused

When arresting a person suspected of a crime, a police officer makes a statement like the following.

> ❝You have the right to remain silent. Anything you say can and will be used against you in a court of law. You are entitled to have an attorney present when you are questioned. If you cannot afford an attorney, one will be provided for you at public expense. ❞

This statement is part of the Miranda warning, which is named after a man who was arrested without being informed of his rights. As a result of a Supreme Court decision in 1966, police officers must state the Miranda warning to anyone they arrest.

The rights of the accused are spelled out in the Fifth, Sixth, Seventh, and Eighth amendments. These amendments reflect English legal tradition dating back to the Magna Carta, which stated that no person could be deprived of life, liberty, or property except by "the law of the land." The Constitution continues English tradition by stating that citizens are entitled to due process of law, a process by which the government must treat accused persons fairly according to rules established by law. People accused of crimes have rights under the Constitution.

The Fifth Amendment The Miranda warning mentions the right to remain silent because the Fifth Amendment says that nobody may be forced to "be a witness against himself." This is why accused persons sometimes say, "I take the Fifth" or "I refuse to answer on the grounds that it

Accused Citizen Fights for Rights

In 1961 Clarence Gideon was charged with breaking and entering a Florida pool hall. When brought to trial in a Florida court, he pleaded innocent. However, he could not afford a lawyer, and the court refused to provide him with one. He was found guilty and sentenced to five years in prison.

Clarence Gideon was determined to prove that his rights had been violated. As he later wrote, "I always believed that the [main] reason of trial...was to reach the truth. My trial was far from the truth."

Gideon spent hours in the prison library studying law books. He read that the right to have a lawyer is stated in the Sixth Amendment. However, books about previous cases revealed disagreement over whether the right applied in state courts. Believing that it should apply in *any*

court, Gideon wrote a letter asking the Supreme Court to hear his case.

The issue of whether state courts should provide lawyers to represent the poor had already come before the Court several times. The Court had ruled that this right to a lawyer applies only to special circumstances. Gideon's situation did not seem special, but the Supreme Court agreed to re-examine the issue.

When the case came before the Court on January 14, 1963, all of the justices concluded that no court should deny a citizen the right to have a lawyer because he or she is too poor to afford one. It was a victory not only for Gideon but also for thousands of other Americans, who would now be guaranteed the right to have a lawyer if they were ever accused of a crime.

In winning his case before the Court, Gideon also won the right to a new trial in Florida. This time the court paid for a lawyer to represent him, and he was found not guilty. In learning about his rights and taking action to defend them, Gideon stands as an example that every citizen's voice can be heard.

Active Citizenship

How did Gideon's actions affect the rights of accused citizens throughout the nation?

may incriminate me [make me appear guilty]." In some countries, police use torture or other methods to pressure citizens into confessing to crimes. Under the Fifth Amendment, any confessions must be freely given, not forced.

The Fifth Amendment also states that persons suspected of committing serious crimes such as murder must be indicted (in DYE ted), or accused, by a grand jury. A grand jury determines whether there is enough evidence to put the person on trial.

Citizens are also protected from double jeopardy (JEP ur dee), being placed on trial twice for the same crime. Thus, a person who has been found "not guilty" of a crime in a federal court cannot be put on trial again for the same offense.

Right to Trial by Jury

A key element of due process of law is trial by jury. The Sixth Amendment guarantees a citizen's right to a speedy, public, and fair trial in any case involving a crime. A person may not be tried in secret or kept in jail for a long time awaiting trial. An accused person has the right to the advice of a lawyer. An accused person also has the right to know what the accusations are and the right to ask questions of any witnesses during the trial.

The Seventh Amendment permits jury trials in cases where there are conflicts over property or money—as long as the value in dispute is over twenty dollars. The Sixth and Seventh amendments reflect the belief that trial by jury is important if people are to have trust and confidence in the law. The work of the courts is open to public view and public participation. When people serve as jurors, they help to make sure that their fellow citizens are treated fairly.

Bail, Fines, and Punishments

The Eighth Amendment protects accused persons from unfair treatment both before and after a trial. Instead of having to stay in jail until the trial, an accused person may be allowed to deposit with the court a certain amount of money—called bail. This money is a pledge that the person will appear at the trial.

The Eighth Amendment forbids the amount of bail from being unfairly high. When the person appears at the trial, the bail is returned. This system protects the accused person from long-term imprisonment before being convicted of a crime. The Eighth Amendment also protects people from "cruel and unusual punishments." Whipping, branding, and other physical punishments were common in England and America during the 1700s. The debate continues today over whether the death penalty should be considered "cruel and unusual punishment."

Protections of Other Rights

One of the objections to adding a bill of rights had been that all rights could not possibly be included. James Madison, however, had provided a solution to this problem. Madison had suggested an amendment stating that citizens' rights are not limited to the ones listed in the Constitution. This proposal became the Ninth Amendment.

The Tenth Amendment settles a question arising from Article 1 of the Constitution. Article 1 describes which powers Congress has and does not have, and which powers are denied to the states. But who has the powers that the Constitution does *not* mention? The Tenth Amendment declares that those powers belong to the state governments or to the people.

Section 2 Assessment

1. **Define** separation of church and state, eminent domain, due process of law, double jeopardy
2. List the freedoms protected under the First Amendment.
3. Explain how the Third, Fourth, and Fifth amendments protect citizens from government abuse of power.
4. Explain how the Bill of Rights guarantees that the government cannot suddenly arrest a person and put him or her in prison without a reason.
5. According to the Tenth Amendment, who has the powers not mentioned in the Constitution?
6. **Synthesize** In what ways does the Bill of Rights reflect our American belief in freedom, justice, and equality?

Interpreting the Bill of Rights

Objectives

- Describe the role of the courts in settling disputes over citizens' rights.
- Summarize the Supreme Court's decision in the Tinker case.
- Review both sides of the Skokie case, and describe the Court's decision.
- Describe the continuing challenge of citizens in protecting our own rights.

 **Focus**

What happens when people disagree about the meaning of our rights under the Constitution? Consider freedom of the press and freedom of speech as examples. Is a school principal violating students' rights when he or she censors an article that was written for the school newspaper? Does a person have the right to make a speech that causes listeners to riot, causing injury to others and damaging public and private property?

The rights of citizens are often difficult to interpret. One reason is that the first ten amendments to the Constitution are broad descriptions of rights. They were not intended to explain how those rights apply to every situation. Another reason is that sometimes certain rights have to be weighed against other rights. For example, suppose a person wants to make a speech that may cause a violent reaction. The right of that person's free speech must be weighed against the importance of providing for the safety of other citizens.

The Role of the Courts

The people who tackle the difficult job of interpreting the meaning of citizens' rights are the judges in our nation's courts. As legal experts, they decide whether people's rights are being violated by the actions of other citizens. They also decide whether rights have been violated by any laws.

Usually cases involving citizens' rights are first brought before local judges. If necessary, the decisions of these judges may be examined by higher courts, such as state courts. A few cases that start out in local courts eventually reach the United States Supreme Court. These cases often have far-reaching consequences for the nation.

The Value of Case Studies You will now be reading about two challenging cases that reached the Supreme Court. Both cases involve First Amendment rights. The decisions of the Court are presented as case studies, which are descriptions of situations or conflicts, the issues involved, and the decisions made.

Case studies can help you see principles of the Constitution being put into action. You can see how an ideal, such as freedom of speech, applies to a real situation. As you read each case study, picture yourself as one of the nine justices, or judges, of the Supreme Court. Think about how you would decide the case.

The Tinker Case: Students and Free Speech

On December 16, 1965, two students in Des Moines, Iowa—13-year-old Mary Beth Tinker and 16-year-old Christopher Eckhardt—came to school wearing black armbands. The next day John Tinker, Mary Beth's 15-year-old brother, also wore a black armband to school. The students were protesting American involvement in the Vietnam War. Their small protest would

Mary Beth and John Tinker display the black armbands that the Supreme Court ruled were a form of speech protected by the First Amendment.

eventually cause the Supreme Court to wrestle with two questions: What is meant by "speech" in freedom of speech, and what rights do students have under the Constitution?

The Case When Des Moines officials first learned of the students' plan to protest, they announced that armbands would be forbidden. When the students wore armbands anyway, they were suspended. The Tinkers' parents argued that the school board was denying the students' right to freedom of speech. They declared that the students had not disrupted classes or interfered with other students' rights. School officials defended the armband rule, stating that it preserved discipline. They argued that schools were not places for political demonstrations.

The Court's Decision The case first came before a local court, which ruled that the armband rule was necessary to avoid disruption of classes. After a higher court also affirmed the school district's decision, the students had one last hope: the Supreme Court.

The Supreme Court heard the case and ruled in favor of the students. It held that armbands were a form of "speech" because they were symbols representing ideas. The justices also said that the protest was protected by the First Amendment because it had not interfered with other students' right to an education.

Most importantly, the Court emphasized that students *do* have a basic right to free speech. The Court declared:

> *"It can hardly be argued that students or teachers shed their constitutional rights to freedom of speech or expression at the schoolhouse gate... Students in school as well as out of school are "persons" under our Constitution.*

Think about the Court's ruling. Why is it important for students to have freedom of speech? How should that freedom be limited? What responsibilities go along with it?

The Skokie Case: Freedom for Nazis?

When may freedom of expression be limited? What other rights must be considered? What if a person or group expresses ideas that are very unpopular? All of these questions were involved in the Skokie case, one of the most controversial in our nation's history.

The Case The year was 1938. Members of dictator Adolf Hitler's Nazi party attacked the homes of Jews throughout Germany. Between 1938 and 1945, the Nazis forced millions of Jews and other people into camps to be starved, tortured, and killed.

The year was 1977. The place was Skokie, Illinois. The town's residents included 40,000 Jews. Many of these people had survived the horror of Nazi camps, but many of their relatives had not. In May a small group of uniformed men applied for a permit to march through Skokie. Each man's uniform displayed a large black swastika—the symbol of the Nazi party.

Shocked and enraged by the plans of these members of this Nazi group, Skokie officials wanted to prevent the march. They informed the Nazi group that it would have to obtain $350,000 of insurance before a permit to march would be issued. Town officials hoped that the cost of this insurance would dissuade the Nazis from wanting to march in Skokie.

When the Nazis planned a rally to protest the insurance requirement, the county court stated that the group could not hold a demonstration. The court forbade anyone to march in a Nazi uniform, display the swastika, or distribute material promoting hatred.

A long and painful court battle began. From the Illinois courts to the United States Supreme Court, judges faced a challenging question: does the First Amendment protect even Nazis and their message of hatred?

The case stirred nationwide interest. Many people argued that the First Amendment does not protect people who want to destroy freedom and spread violence. As one citizen stated, "Freedom of expression has no meaning when it defends those who would end this right for others." Another said, "In Germany they also started with a bunch of crazies...Anybody who advocates killing should not be allowed to rally."

Those who argued that Nazis do have a right to freedom of expression included members of the American Civil Liberties Union (ACLU), an organization devoted to defending citizens' rights under the First Amendment. ACLU lawyers asked a basic question: if the government may deny freedom of expression to one group, what will prevent it from denying that right to any other group? A Jewish member of the ACLU summed up this argument by saying, "The First Amendment has to be for everyone— or it will be for no one."

Clearly, the Skokie case presented a major challenge for the courts. There were powerful arguments and strong feelings on both sides.

The Court's Decision Because they were unwilling to accept the county court order, the Nazis took their case to the Illinois Supreme Court. However, that court refused

When should freedom of speech be limited? Courts have faced this difficult question in cases involving the American Nazi party and other groups that promote hatred.

to overrule the county court order or to rule on the fairness of the Skokie laws. Therefore, the Nazis asked the United States Supreme Court to hear their case.

On June 14, 1977, the Supreme Court ordered Illinois to hold a hearing on their ruling against the Nazis. The Court did not discuss either the county court order or the Skokie laws, but its decision led the Illinois and U.S. District courts to examine those laws closely in light of the First Amendment.

For almost a year, the Illinois and U.S. District courts struggled with the issue of limits on the Nazis' right to freedom of expression. The courts finally decided that the Skokie law requiring insurance violated the First Amendment. The courts stated that the insurance was too costly for most groups and therefore limited free speech and assembly.

Also, the law had not been applied equally. The town officials required the Nazis to pay for insurance, but other groups were allowed to hold rallies without insurance.

The courts also concluded that the Nazis had a right to distribute material expressing hatred. The First Amendment protects the expression of all ideas—even beliefs that threaten the basic principles of our nation. As Justice Oliver Wendell Holmes said, over 50 years before the Skokie case, our Constitution protects "the principle of free thought—not free thought for those who agree with us but freedom for the thought that we hate."

The courts discussed whether the Nazi uniform and swastika symbol were protected by the First Amendment. Earlier court decisions, particularly the Tinker case, had established that symbols were a form of speech. The issue was whether the hated swastika symbol would cause a violent reaction, threatening public safety. By planning to wear their swastikas in Skokie, were the Nazis guilty of trying to start a fight?

The courts heard strong testimony from Jews in Skokie about the meaning of the swastika to them. One concentration camp survivor angrily declared, "I do not know if I could control myself if I saw the swastika in a parade." Skokie attorneys argued that for Jews, seeing the swastika was just like being physically attacked.

The Illinois Supreme Court deeply sympathized with the Skokie residents but decided that the swastika could not be banned. Otherwise, the mere possibility of violence could be used to keep anyone from exercising the right to freedom of expression. The court reluctantly concluded that the Nazis could wear their symbol, just as war protestors could wear black armbands. The United States Supreme Court let the Illinois court's decision stand, thereby removing the last roadblock to the Nazi rally.

In the summer of 1978 the Nazis finally held two rallies, but not in Skokie. Both rallies were in Chicago, and the Nazis faced thousands of people demonstrating against them. A heavy guard of Chicago police officers was assigned to prevent any violence.

A Marketplace of Ideas The Skokie case showed that the First Amendment protects not only views that most citizens support but also unpopular beliefs. The First Amendment makes possible what Justice Holmes called "a marketplace of ideas," in which all views may be expressed. Holmes believed that people should be allowed to hear many different ideas. Then they can accept, or "buy," the good ones and reject the bad. According to Justice Holmes, the test of a good idea is "the power of the thought to get itself accepted in the competition of the market."

In our marketplace of ideas, a bookstore like this one invites people to read the opinions of many different authors on a wide range of subjects.

What do you think? Should any person be allowed to state his or her beliefs, even when those beliefs are very unpopular or encourage hatred and prejudice?

The Continuing Challenge

Protecting the rights of citizens is not just the responsibility of judges and laws. It is a continuing challenge that we all share. Another famous American judge, Learned Hand, made this point in the following way:

❝ *I often wonder whether we do not rest our hopes too much upon constitutions, upon laws, and upon courts. These are false hopes...*
Liberty lies in the hearts of men and women; when it dies there, no constitution, no law, no court can even do much to help it. While it lies there it needs no constitution, no law, no court to save it. ❞

As Judge Learned Hand emphasizes in his statement on the opposite page, the rights of American citizens are not protected just because they have been written down in our nation's Constitution. We as citizens of the United States—even while still students—play a key role in protecting our rights. By respecting each other's rights, we help guarantee that the Bill of Rights survives—not just as dry ink on faded parchment but as beliefs that we Americans live by.

Section 3 Assessment

1. Why is it often difficult to interpret the meaning of citizens' rights?
2. How do case studies help you understand the meaning of citizens' rights?
3. Describe the issues involved in the Tinker and Skokie cases, and explain how the cases were decided.
4. **Apply** You have looked at some of the issues judges have to deal with in cases involving freedom of expression. What issues would be involved when police arrest a murder suspect without obtaining permission to enter the suspect's home?

Extending the Chapter

Global Views

The Bill of Rights reflects our American belief that there are human rights no government should take away. In many countries today, governments ignore such basic rights as freedom of speech and trial by jury. People who criticize the government may be imprisoned without a trial. Many prisoners are tortured and killed.

Think about what it would be like to be imprisoned in your own home. It happened to Daw Aung San Suu Kyi, a leader of the movement to bring democracy and human rights to her native country of Myanmar. Suu Kyi was placed under house arrest by Myanmar's military government in 1989 and confined without a trial for six years. Even under these conditions she continued to work for change. For her courageous efforts, she was awarded the Nobel Peace Prize in 1991.

Daw Aung San Suu Kyi's story is just one example of the worldwide struggle to bring basic human rights to citizens of every country. A number of human rights organizations, such as Amnesty International, help political prisoners by writing petitions to government officials, protesting against the use of torture, and sending medicine, food, and clothing to prisoners. These organizations promote worldwide observance of the United Nations Universal Declaration of Human Rights, an international agreement on human rights.

The United Nations declaration lists many of the rights found in our Bill of Rights, such as freedom of speech, freedom of religion, and freedom from unfair arrest or imprisonment. The treatment of prisoners in some countries, however, shows that their governments only claim to support human rights. After all, human rights cannot be preserved by documents alone. People must be willing to abide by those agreements, treating each other with respect as fellow human beings.

DECISION MAKING SKILLS

How to EVALUATE SOURCES

"John was right again! That movie I saw last night was super." Many of the decisions you make, such as choosing what movie to see or selecting a summer job, are frequently based on information you get from other sources. Often, however, you do not have enough time to check the accuracy of every single piece of information. Therefore, you often base your decisions on information from sources you trust, such as a particular friend or a reference book.

Making good decisions involves knowing how to evaluate which sources of information are reliable, or trustworthy. A reliable source is one that you can depend on to provide accurate information. For instance, you think that John is a reliable source because his recommendations about movies have been good in the past.

Of course, information can come not only from what friends tell you but also from many other sources, such as books, magazines, newspapers, radio, television, and movies. Suppose that you have to form your own opinion about the Tinker case described on page 140. You want to get more information about the facts of the case and the legal issues before deciding. Suppose also that among the available sources is the one described here:

A movie about the Tinker case, made in 1970, portrays the students challenging the rule against armbands. The writers of the script interviewed the students' parents and the lawyers. The film credits list the writers and producers as members of an organization that opposed the Vietnam war.

How might you determine the reliability of the Tinker movie as a source? Here is one procedure you could follow.

Explain the Skill

One method to evaluate a source's reliability is to follow these steps. Notice how the steps relate to the example of the Tinker movie.

1. **Check the qualifications of the people providing the information.** Do they have training or knowledge that qualifies them to write or speak about the topic? Sometimes background on them may be found in the source itself. You can also check to see if the library or Internet has information about them. [We have no evidence that the writers of the Tinker movie are legal experts.]

2. **Check the reputations of the people providing the information.** Do they have a past history of being accurate? Have they received or won any awards? Might their beliefs or goals affect how they write or speak about this topic? [We do not know whether the writers have a record of accuracy. As opponents of the war, they might be presenting a one-sided story. They might not be accurately describing the legal issues involved in the case.]

3. **Check the methods the people used in preparing the source.** How did they get their information? Did they provide enough evidence to support their statements? Were their sources reliable? [The information in the movie is probably incomplete because no one seems to have interviewed the students. Also, it is probably one-sided because the school board and the principal do not seem to have been consulted.]

4. **Check to see if this source agrees with other sources known to be reliable on the topic.** When two or more sources agree with

what your source says, you can be fairly certain that the source you are using is reliable. [You could check records on the Tinker case, as well as articles that legal experts have written about the case.]

Analyze the Skill

Suppose the following sources on the Tinker case were available. Determine which source would be more reliable.

A. A collection of newspaper articles written in 1969 by a Pulitzer Prize-winning journalist. Her articles about the Tinker case include interviews with the three students and with members of the school board. She also relied on quotes from the minutes of school board meetings and on information from local newspapers. In addition, she examined the effect of the Supreme Court's past rulings on individual freedoms. Her explanation of the rulings refers to her sources throughout.

B. A book published in 1970 and written by a past president of the Des Moines school board. The author has also written several books calling for tougher discipline in public schools. The book includes quotes from board members, parents, and teachers regarding the armband protest. Interviews with the superintendent and the principal are included. The book contains summaries of lower court decisions in the case.

Skill Assessment

1. Which one of the two sources described above is likely to be more reliable on the topic of the Tinker case? Explain your answer.
2. Which of the following would be the best source to use to check the accuracy of information about issues in the Tinker case? **(a)** an interview with Mary Beth Tinker **(b)** the written record of the court proceedings **(c)** letters written by the school principal to a principal in another school district
3. Of the following, which one is the best sign of reliability? Explain your answer. **(a)** being published in a book **(b)** being written by someone who has received awards for journalism **(c)** being written by a person who observed the events being described.
4. What is meant by reliability?
5. What are four things you can do to check the reliability of a source?
6. Why is the skill of evaluating the reliability of a source useful for decision making?

How to USE PRIMARY SOURCES

In this chapter, you studied two Supreme Court cases dealing with citizens' First Amendment rights. In the section on the Tinker case, you read a passage from the Supreme Court's written ruling. This passage is an example of a primary source. Primary sources are records left by people who observed or were directly involved in the events being described.

Explain the Skill

On this page, you will read primary sources from a 1988 Supreme Court case. In this case, the Court considered whether or not school officials can decide what students may or may not write in school newspapers. The case involved faculty and students at Hazelwood East High School, near St. Louis, Missouri.

Analyze the Skill

Spectrum, the Hazelwood High School newspaper, was published by students in a class called Journalism II. In May 1983, the principal removed two pages from *Spectrum*, stating that these pages contained articles that were inappropriate for a school newspaper. Students in the Journalism II class objected, claiming that the removal of these articles violated their First Amendment rights. The students took their case all the way to the Supreme Court.

After hearing the case, the Supreme Court ruled that Principal Reynolds had *not* violated the students' First Amendment rights. Expressing the Court's opinion on the Hazelwood case, Justice Byron White wrote:

[Principal] Reynolds could reasonably have concluded that the students who had written and edited these articles had not sufficiently mastered those portions of the Journalism II curriculum that pertained [related] to the treatment of controversial issues....It was not unreasonable for the principal to have concluded that such frank talk was inappropriate in a school-sponsored publication distributed to 14-year-old freshmen....Accordingly, no violation of First Amendment rights occurred.

Justice William Brennan disagreed with the majority of the justices. He wrote:

When the young men and women of Hazelwood East High School registered for Journalism II, they expected a civics lesson. *Spectrum*, the newspaper they were to publish, was not just a class exercise in which students learned to prepare papers and hone writing skills, it was a forum established to give students an opportunity to express their views while gaining an appreciation of their rights and responsibilities under the First Amendment to the United States Constitution. ...In my view, the principal broke more than just a promise. He violated the First Amendment's prohibitions against censorship.

Skill Assessment

1. What reasons did Justice White give for supporting Principal Reynolds' decision to censor *Spectrum*?
2. Did Justice Brennan agree with Justice White? Explain.
3. In your opinion, should students be able to print whatever they want in a school newspaper? If not, in what cases should the freedom of a school newspaper be limited?

CHAPTER 6 ASSESSMENT

Building Civics Vocabulary

Each of the following vocabulary terms is related to a general type of protection provided by the Bill of Rights. Match each term with the appropriate type of protection. Then explain how the term relates to that type of protection.

Example: *Double jeopardy* relates to *protection of the accused* because the Bill of Rights protects a person from being tried more than once for the same crime.

1. *separation of church and state*
2. *eminent domain*
3. *due process of law*

(a) protection against abuse of power
(b) protection of individual rights
(c) protection of the accused

Reviewing Main Ideas and Skills

4. Explain how the amendment process works.

5. Why did James Madison think that Congress should add the Bill of Rights to the Constitution as soon as possible?

6. Describe the freedoms protected under the First Amendment and briefly explain why each one is important.

7. **How to Evaluate Sources** Suppose you want to learn more about the Hazelwood case discussed on the previous page. You find a book on the case written by Principal Reynolds. What steps would you take to judge the reliability of this source?

8. **How to Use Primary Sources** Reread the statement by Justice White on page 148. According to White, why were the principal's actions reasonable?

Critical Thinking

9. **Defending a Position** Why are the individual freedoms listed in the First Amendment important in a democratic government?

10. **Linking Past and Present** In 1789, many members of Congress felt the Bill of Rights was unnecessary. If they were alive today, do you think they would still hold the same view? Explain.

Writing About Civics

11. **Writing an Essay** Choose one right protected by the Bill of Rights. Write an essay explaining how this right has been important in your life. Use specific examples to support your explanation.

Citizenship Activities

12. **Working in Groups** In groups of three or four, prepare a skit in which one or more of the rights listed in the Bill of Rights is being violated. Following the skit, the class should identify the right or rights being violated and discuss what actions should have been taken to avoid violating those rights.

 Take It to the NET

Access the **Civics: Participating in Government** Internet site at **www.phschool.com** for the specific URLs to complete the activity.

Research current issues surrounding the Bill of Rights. Then select one of the amendments and prepare a short summary of a current debate. Discuss this debate in small groups.

CHAPTER 7

Our Living Constitution

Citizenship and You

One Monday morning Mrs. Taylor made a surprise announcement to her Civics class: they were going to elect a student committee to recommend rules for the class. At first the students responded enthusiastically, but then Mrs. Taylor stunned them by saying: "In order to vote for committee members, you must be a boy and you must be white."

Immediately students began to protest. Why were the girls not allowed to vote? Why could the African American, Hispanic American, and Asian American students not vote?

After listening to the objections, Mrs. Taylor replied, "Actually, I agree with you. It *is* unfair. But I wanted to make a point about our nation. For much of our history, most states allowed only white males to vote. Fortunately, this is no longer the case because the Constitution has been changed."

Our Constitution has survived for over two centuries because it is a "living" document that can respond to the needs of a growing and changing society. Despite changes in attitudes and conditions over the years, Americans have not had to create a whole new Constitution.

What's Ahead in Chapter 7

This chapter gives you a chance to explore the reasons our nation's Constitution has lasted so well. First you will read about the amendments that have brought our nation closer to the ideal of treating all people with equal respect. Then you will see the role the Supreme Court has played in making the Constitution a "living" document.

Section 1 Changing the Law of the Land

Section 2 A Flexible Framework

Keep It Current

Items marked with this logo are periodically updated on the Internet. To keep up-to-date, go to **www.phschool.com**

Citizen's Journal

Our Constitution is described as a "living" or flexible document. Write a paragraph explaining why you think this flexibility has been important to our nation. Then, after studying the chapter, reread your paragraph. Write a new paragraph, explaining how your understanding has grown.

Changing the Law of the Land

Objectives

- Explain how the laws concerning slavery have changed since the signing of the Constitution.
- Describe the amendments that insured the right to vote for African Americans.
- Summarize women's struggle for the right to vote.
- Explain why the voting age was lowered to eighteen.
- Describe how the amendment process gives Americans a voice in their government.

Building Civics Vocabulary

- The right to vote is also known as **suffrage**.

Focus

As you can see from the chart on the next page, since the Bill of Rights became part of the Constitution, 17 other amendments have been added. Most of these amendments reflect efforts by the people to change the Constitution to meet changing needs and attitudes. For example, over time there has been a great change in the attitude of Americans about who can be a citizen and who has the right to vote.

Originally, the Constitution let the states decide who was qualified to be a citizen, and most states granted citizenship only to white men who owned property. Today, however, anyone born or naturalized in the United States is a citizen, and any citizen who is at least eighteen years old may vote.

As you know, the Constitution begins with the words "we the people of the United States." Why is the meaning of "we the people" so much broader today than it was

in 1787? In the following pages you will step back into history to trace the changes in citizenship and voting rights that have taken place in this country over the years. In the process, you will see how the amendment process helps the Constitution adjust to changing times.

Abolishing Slavery

Among the people denied citizenship from the beginning were enslaved African Americans. Why did a country founded in the name of freedom permit slavery? Why was slavery eventually abolished by an amendment to the Constitution? The answers involve looking at the history of slavery in our nation.

Slavery and the Framers You may recall from Chapter 5 that the Constitutional Convention probably would have failed without a compromise on slavery. Southerners believed that their farming economy would collapse without slave labor. To ensure that both the northern and southern states would ratify the Constitution, the framers avoided making a decision on whether to abolish slavery. Nowhere in the Constitution is the word *slavery* even mentioned.

To avoid angering the southern states, the framers even tried to make slavery seem acceptable. They agreed that slaves could be counted as part of a state's population and that runaway slaves had to be returned to their owners. However, neither the northern nor southern states were completely satisfied by the compromises at the convention. Many Americans wondered whether a nation so divided over slavery could survive.

Tension Between North and South As new states joined the nation during the early 1800s, the North and the South competed for power in Congress. Although the more populous northern states controlled a majority in the House, the North argued that the three-fifths compromise gave southern states

AMENDMENTS 11–27 After the first ten amendments in the Bill of Rights, our Constitution has been amended only 17 more times. **History Which amendment lowered the voting age to 18? When was it passed?**

Amendment	Year Ratified	Subject
11th	1795	Lawsuits against the states
12th	1804	Separate voting for President and Vice President
13th	1865	Abolition of slavery
14th	1868	Citizenship and civil rights
15th	1870	Voting rights for African American men
16th	1913	Income tax
17th	1913	Direct election of senators
18th	1919	Prohibition of alcoholic beverages
19th	1920	Voting rights for women
20th	1933	Terms of the President, Vice President, and Congress
21st	1933	Repeal of Eighteenth Amendment
22nd	1951	President limited to two terms
23rd	1961	Electoral votes for the District of Columbia
24th	1964	Abolition of poll taxes
25th	1967	Presidential disability and succession
26th	1971	Voting age lowered to eighteen
27th	1992	Changing congressional salaries

The full text and explanation of the Constitution can be found on pages 108–129.

more representatives than they deserved. The South, in turn, feared that the North might use its political power to abolish slavery.

In 1820, Congress tried to head off serious conflict by passing the Missouri Compromise. This law divided new lands into "slave" territories and "free" territories. Nevertheless, Americans increasingly saw slavery as an "all or nothing" issue. On one side were those who defended the right to own slaves anywhere. On the other side were those who wanted slavery to be banned everywhere.

Since further efforts at compromise seemed hopeless, Congress later tried the principle of majority rule, allowing settlers in each territory to vote on whether to allow slavery there. However, this action only sparked conflict between pro-slavery and anti-slavery settlers.

A Controversial Court Decision In 1857, a tense nation awaited a Supreme Court decision on a case that many hoped would finally settle the slavery issue. A slave named Dred Scott had traveled with his owner to Illinois and the Wisconsin territory where slavery was illegal. After they returned to Missouri, Scott argued that his residence in a free territory had made him a free person. Now the Court had to decide whether or not Scott was free according to the Constitution.

On August 28, 1963, more than 200,000 Americans of all races gathered in Washington, D.C., to show their support for the struggle to guarantee African Americans the right to vote and other basic civil rights.

The Court ruled that according to the Constitution slaves were property and that Congress could not prevent owners from taking slaves anywhere they wished. This decision showed that the Constitution could be interpreted as allowing slavery.

The Thirteenth Amendment Although the defenders of slavery rejoiced at the Dred Scott decision, many Americans feared for the nation. In 1858, Abraham Lincoln warned, "I believe this government cannot endure permanently half *slave* and half *free*....It will become all one thing, or all the other."

Lincoln's warning proved true, but only after the Civil War took the lives of over 600,000 Americans. The North's victory paved the way for the Thirteenth Amendment, which abolished slavery in 1865.

African Americans and the Right to Vote

Although the Constitution now banned slavery, the struggle for citizenship and voting rights for African Americans had only begun. Even those who had been free long before the Civil War knew that freedom did not mean equality. For one thing, the states still had the power to decide who could be a citizen, and most states—both northern and southern—continued to deny citizenship to blacks.

The Fourteenth Amendment This amendment, adopted in 1868, ensured citizenship for African Americans. It takes the power to grant citizenship away from the states by providing that "All persons born or naturalized in the United States...are citizens of the United States and of the state wherein they reside." It also declares that no state may "deprive any person of life, liberty, or property without due process of law" or "deny to any person...the equal protection of the laws."

Why were these statements added when there was already a Bill of Rights? Actually, the first ten amendments say only that Congress must respect citizens' rights. The Fourteenth Amendment specifically requires the states to do so. Therefore, it has often been called the "second Bill of Rights."

The Fourteenth Amendment did not automatically ensure equal treatment. Although the Supreme Court ruled that state governments could not treat African Americans unfairly, it did not prevent private citizens, such as employers, from continuing to discriminate against them.

The Fifteenth Amendment

In some states being a citizen did not guarantee the right to vote. To keep states from denying voting rights to African Americans, the Fifteenth Amendment, added in 1870, declares that states may not deny the vote to any person on the basis of "race, color, or previous condition of servitude."

The Twenty-Fourth Amendment

Despite the Fifteenth Amendment, some states found a number of ways to prevent African Americans from voting, such as requiring citizens to pay a poll tax, or fee for voting. Many were unable to vote because they were too poor to pay the tax.

Not until the passage of the Twenty-fourth Amendment in 1964 were poll taxes declared illegal. This amendment, together with civil rights laws passed by Congress in the 1960s, was an important step toward protecting the rights of African Americans.

As you have just seen, changes in the Constitution do not guarantee that attitudes and conditions in society will change completely and immediately. It took more than 100 years for the nation to make real progress toward ending discrimination against African Americans and other racial groups.

Women and the Right to Vote

African Americans were not the only group left out of "we the people" in 1787. Women, too, faced a long struggle for full citizenship rights. Unlike slavery, women's rights did not even seem to be an issue in the minds of the framers. Traditional ideas about the role of women help to explain why most states denied them voting rights for many years.

Traditional Ideas About Women

Since long before the founding of our country, the only proper place for women was thought to be working in the home and caring for the family. Women were believed to be unable to handle many of the jobs that men performed. Even after large numbers of women took factory jobs during the 1800s, laws still treated them differently from men. Some laws allowed women to do only certain—usually low-paid—jobs.

People who held the traditional view disapproved of women voting or holding political office. They argued that politically active women would leave their family responsibilities behind, upsetting the stability of family life. They also thought that women were less intelligent than men and therefore less able to make political decisions.

Challenging the Traditional View

By the late 1800s, the tide had begun turning against the traditional view of women. Increasing numbers of women took jobs. Many women also became active in social issues in the cities and factories.

As women became more politically involved, they insisted on the right to vote, also known as suffrage. A declaration from the Seneca Falls women's rights convention in 1848 stated, "We hold these truths to be self evident: that all men *and women* are created equal." Nevertheless, by the turn of the century only a handful of states had granted suffrage to women.

During the late 1800s and early 1900s, supporters of women's right to vote, known as suffragists, gained the public's attention by marching, giving speeches, writing to government officials and newspapers, and even going

Suffragist Carrie Chapman Catt (front, center) leads a march in New York City in 1917. She was a leader in the campaign that resulted in the Nineteenth Amendment, giving women the right to vote.

on hunger strikes. The important economic role played by women factory workers also helped convince more and more Americans that women deserved to vote. A proposed amendment giving suffrage to women was introduced—but failed to pass—in almost every session of Congress for 40 years, from 1878 to 1918.

The Nineteenth Amendment Finally, the suffragists' determination paid off. A breakthrough came in January 1918 at an emotional session of the House of Representatives. The visitors' galleries were packed as the House prepared to vote. Several congressmen voted despite illness—one was even brought in on a stretcher. Another left his gravely ill wife, at her request, to cast his vote. This time the House approved the amendment. After Senate approval the following year, the Nineteenth Amendment was ratified by the states in 1920. Women were now truly part of "we the people."

Youth and the Right to Vote

The most recent voting rights amendment lowered the voting age to eighteen. From colonial times through the middle of the twentieth century, the voting age was twenty-one. However, as millions of young people served in World War II, and in the Korean and the Vietnam wars, many Americans came to believe that citizens old enough to fight and to die for their country should not be denied the right to vote.

Spurred on by growing public support for lowering the voting age, Congress passed a law in 1970 giving eighteen-year-olds the right to vote in national, state, and local elections. However, the Supreme Court later ruled that Congress could set the voting age only for national—not state or local—elections.

The Twenty-Sixth Amendment After the Court decision, it seemed that the only way to guarantee eighteen-year-olds the right to vote in all elections was by changing the Constitution. Aware of widespread public support for such an amendment, Congress overwhelmingly approved it in March 1971. The vote was 401–19 in the House and 94–0 in the Senate. It took just 107 days for the states to ratify the proposed change, making it the Twenty-sixth Amendment.

The Voice of the People

The voting rights amendments illustrate that the Constitution can be changed in response to new attitudes and conditions in society. Although the Thirteenth, Fourteenth, and Fifteenth amendments came about largely as a result of the Civil War, all the other changes in the Constitution were made through peaceful efforts of citizens. The United States is truly a government by the people because the citizens decide what will be "the law of the land."

The Constitution was most recently amended by the Twenty-seventh Amendment, ratified in 1992. This amendment states that if members of Congress vote to increase their salaries, the change cannot go into effect until after the next election. This way, if members of Congress vote themselves a pay raise, they are accountable to the voters for their actions.

Any citizen or group of citizens may propose a change in the Constitution. More than 5,000 amendments have been introduced in Congress, and efforts continue to this day. Recent proposals include an amendment that would allow official prayers to be said in public schools, and an amendment that would make it illegal to burn the flag of the United States.

Since not a year goes by without amendments being suggested and debated by citizens, you might be tempted to ask, "Is our Constitution truly a good plan of government?" A quick look back at history will provide the answer. If the framers had written a poor plan, we would have had hundreds, maybe thousands, of amendments by now—perhaps even a whole new constitution. Instead, we have had only 27 amendments. The voice of the people has been heard, and they have remained satisfied with the basic framework of the Constitution.

The voting age was lowered to 18 when people decided that citizens old enough to fight for their country are old enough to vote.

Section 1 Assessment

1. **Define** suffrage
2. Summarize the Supreme Court's ruling in the Dred Scott case.
3. How did the Fourteenth Amendment guarantee citizenship to African Americans?
4. Explain why a women's suffrage amendment was finally added to the Constitution.
5. Why was the voting age lowered to eighteen?
6. **Evaluate** Do you think that the voting age should be higher or lower than eighteen? If so, what age do you think it should be? Support your opinion with reasons.

A Flexible Framework

 Focus

Amendments enable the Constitution to change with the times. Now you will take a closer look at why, in fact, very few changes have been needed. The framers realized that specific instructions for running a government in 1787 might not work years later. By providing general principles, they gave later generations freedom to fill in the details. In this way, the Constitution does not have to be changed to meet every new issue the government might face.

The Role of the Supreme Court

You may be wondering, "If the Constitution does not spell out in detail how to follow the principles, who makes sure that they are being followed correctly?" This is where the courts, especially the Supreme Court, enter the picture. The Supreme Court has the final say over whether constitutional principles have been correctly followed by government officials and other citizens. By deciding whether a certain action violates the Constitution, the Court makes that action either legal or illegal. Supreme Court decisions must be obeyed, not only by private citizens but also by the President and by Congress.

However, a Court decision is not necessarily permanent. It may be overturned by an amendment that changes, removes, or adds a constitutional principle. For example, the Dred Scott decision was overturned when the Thirteenth Amendment abolished slavery.

A decision may also be overturned by a later Court decision. New evidence or new ideas may lead the Court to change an earlier interpretation of a constitutional principle.

Interpreting a Principle How has the Supreme Court applied broad constitutional principles to a changing society? One way to answer this question is to see how the Court's interpretation of one principle changed in the course of several important cases. A good example is the Fourteenth Amendment principle that each state must provide citizens with "equal protection of the laws."

Equal protection does not mean that everyone must be treated in exactly the same way, but only that people must be treated *fairly*. For instance, a bank does not have to lend money to every customer, but it must be fair in deciding who will receive loans. It may base its decision on a customer's ability to repay the money, but not on a customer's racial background.

Denying a loan to a person because of his or her race is, of course, an example of discrimination. Human history has been scarred by many forms of discrimination. The following cases focus on two forms that have been particularly common: racial discrimination and discrimination against women. As you read, think about the Supreme Court's important role in applying the general principles of our Constitution to these situations.

Equality and Segregation

The principle of equal protection was originally intended to prevent states from denying rights to African Americans. Over the years the Court has interpreted the meaning of equal protection in many situations that might involve racial discrimination.

Plessy v. Ferguson (1896) Although the Fourteenth Amendment had given blacks citizenship, many states passed laws requiring segregation, or separation, of blacks and whites in public places such as hotels, schools, restaurants, and trains. Did segregation violate the principle of equal protection?

The Court faced this question in 1896, when it heard a Louisiana case involving Homer Plessy, a black man who had refused to leave a "whites only" railroad car. Plessy argued that the Louisiana law requiring segregation violated his right to equal protection. In a famous decision, *Plessy* v. *Ferguson,* the Court ruled that the Louisiana law did not violate the Fourteenth Amendment as long as the cars for blacks and for whites were of equal quality. For more than 50 years after the decision, this "separate but equal" standard was accepted as a justification for laws that segregated blacks from whites.

Opposition to Segregation Not everyone, however, agreed that "separate but equal" facilities truly guaranteed "equal protection of the laws." Many schools and other facilities for black Americans were not as good as those for whites. Furthermore, even when the facilities were equal in quality, the fact of being separated by law made many black Americans feel that they were treated as inferior to whites. Could it really be said, then, that they were being treated equally?

By the early 1950s, many Americans were questioning the fairness of segregation. Among them was Thurgood Marshall, a lawyer for the National Association for the Advancement of Colored People (NAACP). He and other NAACP lawyers brought before the Court several cases involving facilities that were segregated but equal in quality. They knew that such cases would force the Court to decide whether "separate but equal" facilities truly represented "equal protection." At the center of one of these cases was a schoolgirl from Topeka, Kansas. Linda Brown was about to play a role in overturning a Supreme Court ruling that had permitted segregation for over half a century.

Facts & Quotes

A Flexible Constitution

Thomas Jefferson stressed that a plan of government must be able to change with the times:

66 Some men look at Constitutions with sanctimonious reverence and deem them, like the Ark of the Covenant [the Bible], too sacred to be touched. They ascribe [give credit] to the men of the preceding age a wisdom more than human, and suppose what they did to be beyond amendment....[L]aws and institutions must go hand in hand with the progress of the human mind. As that becomes more developed, more enlightened, as new discoveries are made, new truths disclosed, and manners and opinions change with the change of circumstances, institutions must advance also and keep pace with the times. 99

Thurgood Marshall

When President Lyndon Johnson appointed Thurgood Marshall to the Supreme Court in 1967, he said, "I believe he has already earned his place in history, but I think it will be greatly enhanced by his service on the Court."

Thirteen years earlier, Thurgood Marshall had gained national fame with his landmark victory in the case of *Brown* v. *Board of Education,* in which the Supreme Court declared segregation of public schools illegal. Marshall went on to argue a total of 32 civil rights cases before the Supreme Court, winning 29 of them.

As head of the NAACP's legal team, Marshall traveled the country arguing cases in state and federal courts. In victory after victory, he forced courts to adhere to the constitutional amendments passed to protect the rights of African Americans.

Serving as the nation's first African American Supreme Court Justice, Marshall continued to champion the cause of civil rights. During his 24 years on the Court, Marshall's opinions reflected his strong belief that the rights described in the Constitution must apply equally to all Americans.

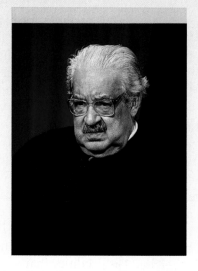

Looking at the role of the Constitution in his own lifelong fight for individual rights, Marshall stressed the importance of the changes Americans have made in this vital document. "I do not believe that the meaning of the Constitution was forever 'fixed' at the Philadelphia convention," said Marshall. "To the contrary [it took] several amendments, a civil war, and momentous social [change] to attain the system of constitutional government, and its respect for the individual freedoms and human rights, that we hold as fundamental today."

Recognizing Viewpoints

According to Thurgood Marshall, has the Constitution been improved since it was originally written? Explain your answer.

Brown v. Board of Education of Topeka (1954) Linda Brown lived only 7 blocks from a school for white children, but by law she was required to attend a school for black children 21 blocks away. Linda's parents thought she should be able to attend the neighborhood school. Therefore they took the school board to court, with the help of the NAACP. In arguing the case before the Supreme Court, Thurgood

Marshall presented evidence that separate schools had a harmful effect on both black and white children. Black children were made to feel inferior to whites, he argued, while white children learned to feel superior to African American children. Therefore, Marshall concluded, "separate but equal" schools could never be equal.

All of the justices on the Supreme Court were convinced by Marshall's reasoning. The

Court agreed that segregation of African Americans creates "a feeling of inferiority as to their status in the community that may affect their hearts and minds in a way unlikely ever to be undone." Separate educational facilities, the Court ruled, were "inherently [by their very nature], unequal" and therefore violated the principle of equal protection.

The decision in *Brown v. Board of Education of Topeka* overturned the decision in *Plessy* v. *Ferguson* and made all segregation laws unconstitutional. Thus, it is a significant example of how Supreme Court rulings can keep the Constitution flexible.

Equality and Affirmative Action

The Court's ruling gave a powerful constitutional weapon to Americans who were fighting racial discrimination. Spurred on by the Brown case and by increasing public pressure during the 1960s, Congress passed a series of laws—known as civil rights laws—to guard against racial discrimination. However, these laws could not undo the effects of years of discrimination against African Americans, Hispanic Americans, Asian Americans, and Native Americans, particularly in the workplace.

Over the years, many companies have discriminated against job applicants because of race. In these companies the racial background of employees has not reflected the mixture in the local population. For example, a business may have only white employees, even though half of the workers in the community are African Americans, Hispanic Americans, and Asian Americans.

Starting in the late 1960s, as a result of the civil rights movement, the government worked to correct the effects of unfair hiring practices. It required companies to take affirmative action, steps to counteract the effects of past racial discrimination and discrimination against women. Colleges and universities that seemed to favor white males

Linda Brown's case led to the Supreme Court's landmark decision declaring that school segregation was illegal.

when hiring staff and admitting students were required to take similar steps.

Some people have argued that affirmative action does not result in equal treatment but instead involves reverse discrimination. In other words, they say that affirmative action leads to discrimination against white male applicants. Faced with the question of whether affirmative action programs really do lead to fair treatment of applicants, the Court took another close look at the meaning of "equal protection."

Regents of the University of California v. Bakke (1978)

One school with an affirmative action program was the medical school of the University of California at Davis. The school reserved places in each

Traditional views on women's roles and rights have changed as more women, like this firefighter, have taken jobs previously held only by men.

entering class for African American, Hispanic American, Asian American, and Native American students. In 1973 and again in 1974 a white applicant, Allan Bakke, was rejected for admission, although some members of other racial and ethnic groups were admitted with lower grade-point averages, test scores, and interview ratings. Bakke took the university to court, arguing that he was a victim of reverse discrimination.

The Bakke case posed a challenge for the Supreme Court. Unlike the Brown case, the justices were sharply divided. Some thought the admissions program was a reasonable way to overcome effects of discrimination. The majority, however, agreed with Bakke.

The Court ruled that under the equal protection principle it was unconstitutional for an admissions program to discriminate against whites only because of their race. However, the Court stated that race could be *one* of the factors considered if the school wished to create a more diverse student body while treating white applicants fairly.

Affirmative action was challenged further in 1996 when California voters approved Proposition 209, a law that forbids state universities and employers from considering race or ethnicity when accepting students or hiring employees. The Supreme Court refused to review the case in 1997 when opponents tried to overturn the law.

Women and Equality

The Court has also applied the equal protection principle to other issues, such as whether companies may treat male employees differently from female employees. May a company hire only males for certain jobs or may they have different rules for women and men? The following case illustrates how the Court has addressed such questions.

Phillips v. Martin Marietta Corporation (1971)
Ida Phillips applied for a position with the Martin Marietta Corporation in Florida. Part of the corporation's screening process was to find out whether female applicants had young children. In the corporation's view, young children take up a lot of a woman's time and energy, thus interfering with her work performance. Women such as Ida Phillips, who had two pre-schoolers, were denied jobs for that reason.

When Ida Phillips was rejected for the job, she decided to take the corporation to court, arguing that she had not been treated equally. She charged the company with discriminating against women because male applicants were not questioned about their children and were hired whether they had young children or not.

The Court ruled in favor of Ida Phillips, declaring that the company could not have "one hiring policy for women and another for men."

A Framework for the Future

The cases you have just examined all show how the Supreme Court applies general principles of the Constitution to new situations or issues. A hundred years ago, most Americans could not have foreseen that racial discrimination against a white man would ever become an issue, as happened in the Bakke case. However, the equal protection principle can be applied just as well to racial discrimination of any type.

Similarly, the question of whether men and women should be treated equally in the workplace did not become a major issue until relatively recently. However, as more women have taken jobs outside the home, they have called attention to cases of unequal treatment. In response, the Supreme Court has applied the old principle of equal protection to this new situation.

The general principles of our living Constitution have guided our nation for over two centuries and can be expected to do so in the future. Judging from past history, amendments may be required from time to time, but the Constitution's sturdy framework of principles will most likely remain intact.

Section 2 Assessment

1. **Define** segregation, affirmative action
2. What powers does the Supreme Court have regarding the Constitution?
3. Explain how the cases of *Plessy* v. *Ferguson* and *Brown* v. *Board of Education of Topeka* show the flexibility of the Constitution.
4. Summarize the arguments for and against affirmative action.
5. What general principle of the Constitution did the Supreme Court apply to the case of *Phillips* v. *Martin Marietta*?
6. **Evaluate** What do you think would happen if the Constitution were a list of specific rules for the government to follow?

Extending the Chapter

Historical Views

Here is an item that you might find in a trivia quiz or a book of world records:

Question: What is the oldest written plan of government in the world today?

Answer: The United States Constitution.

This question and answer speak for the strength of our plan of government. Because it is limited to setting forth general principles and because it can be amended, our living Constitution has endured while constitutions of many other nations have been struck down by revolution or have been completely rewritten. For instance, since the French Revolution in 1789, France has had fifteen constitutions. By comparison, the basic framework of the United States Constitution remains the same.

The American Constitution is similar to a building constructed to withstand earthquakes. Such a building is designed to move with the motion of the earth, not against it. It can adjust to fairly strong movement without collapsing. In the same way, the American Constitution adjusts to the force of changing conditions and attitudes. Our Constitution stands as a tribute to the framers' foresight—their ability to plan for the future of our great nation.

Students' Rights

The dogs arrived without warning. The students sat quietly at their desks while the dogs sniffed up and down the aisles. Anyone who knew the school gossip guessed what the dogs were looking for.

People were saying that drug use at the junior and senior high schools in Highland, Indiana, had increased dramatically. Over a 20-day period, 13 students had been found with drugs or under the influence of drugs.

Concern among parents, faculty, and school officials had increased as each new incident became known. Furthermore, many students were saying that they felt pressure from friends to use drugs at school.

To fight what he believed to be a serious drug problem, Omer Renfrow, the superintendent of schools, decided to use trained dogs to conduct a drug investigation in March, 1979. The aim was to rid the junior and senior highs of illegal drugs and to discourage further drug use on campus.

Although the police were to be present during the procedure, they had agreed not to step in if drugs were found. Instead, they would allow school officials to discipline any students found with drugs.

Teachers were informed of the inspection that morning. Just before the end of

The dogs spent about five minutes in each room, sniffing near every student.

first period, dogs trained to detect the odor of marijuana were brought into each classroom. The dogs spent about five minutes in each room, sniffing near every student. When a dog found a suspicious odor, it alerted the trainer. With each alert, that student was asked to empty his or her pockets or purse.

The purse of one student, Diane Doe (not her real name), was searched, but no drugs were found. Because the dog continued to react, Diane was taken to the nurse's office where a more thorough "body search" was conducted. Still no drugs were found.

Diane sued those involved in the investigation. She claimed they had violated her Fourth Amendment right to be free of "unreasonable searches and seizures." Using drug-sniffing dogs in the schoolroom and searching her body without a search warrant was illegal, said Diane.

The United States District Court agreed that the body search, although done privately in the nurse's office, violated Diane's rights under the Fourth Amendment. However, the court also held that using drug-detecting dogs in a schoolroom and asking students merely to empty their pockets and purses if the dogs reacted was *not* unconstitutional.

The court explained that students do not "shed at the schoolhouse door rights guaranteed by either the Fourth Amendment or any other constitutional provision." However, said the court, a student's right to be free from unreasonable searches must be balanced against a school's responsibility to maintain order and discipline. Thus, a school may limit a student's rights in certain circumstances.

According to the court, a student's rights may be limited whenever school administrators or teachers are acting *in loco parentis*. Under this legal doctrine, school officials take on the rights and responsibilities that parents have in relation to their children.

There is "no question," the court said, that school officials have the authority of parents and thus have the duty to keep schools "free from activities harmful to [education] and to the individual students." Therefore, using trained dogs in the school and ordering stu-

dents suspected of having drugs to empty their pockets or purses are allowable

> **Students do not "shed at the schoolhouse door rights guaranteed by either the Fourth Amendment or any other constitutional provision."**

actions under the doctrine of *loco parentis*.

On the other hand, said the court, the more thorough search of Diane was an invasion of privacy forbidden by the Fourth Amendment because it caused more than the "mild inconvenience" of a pocket search. According to the court, "there is a core of privacy so vital to the student's personhood that it must be respected by a school official standing *in loco parentis*." Before such

a search can be done without a search warrant, there must be additional reasons to suspect that a person possesses drugs. Diane Doe was a good student and had never been in trouble before, so there was not good cause to suspect her.

Analyzing the Case

1. Why did the court decide that it was allowable to use trained dogs in the school?
2. Why was the body search of Diane unconstitutional even though the school officials were acting *in loco parentis*?
3. If drugs had been found on Diane during the body search, do you think the court would have decided the case the same way? Explain.
4. If you were a District Court judge, how would you have ruled in this case? Do you think the use of trained dogs to search for drugs in the school should have been allowed? Do you think Diane's Fourth Amendment rights were violated by the body search? Explain.

How to INTERPRET PHOTOGRAPHS

In this chapter, you learned that our Constitution has been amended a number of times to guarantee that equal rights are extended to all Americans. The Nineteenth Amendment, for example, gave women the right to vote. The photograph on page 156 documents a march that helped win support for this amendment. Photographs such as this one are considered primary sources.

Explain the Skill

As you have learned, primary sources, or records left by people who participated in or personally observed the events being described, can give you an inside view of important moments in history. You have studied several Supreme Court decisions, reading the actual words written by the justices who decided the cases.

Not all primary sources are written documents. Objects such as photographs, paintings, and videotapes can also provide direct sources of information about people, places, and events. The photograph on this page gives us a look at one person's experience with discrimination in employment.

Analyze the Skill

As with written primary sources, photographs need to be analyzed carefully. Look at the people in the photograph and pay attention to what they are doing. Take note of the setting. Try to determine whether the photograph is recent or from many years ago—clues to a photograph's age will include things like hair and clothing styles of people. Carefully examine all the elements of the photograph on this page.

Skill Assessment

1. Describe what you see in the photograph.
2. What do you think led the girl in the photograph to do what she is doing?
3. Do you think the Supreme Court's decision in *Phillips* v. *Martin Marietta Corporation* applies to the girl in this picture? Explain your answer.
4. Think about what the girl in this photograph is trying to achieve. What other actions could she take to promote her cause?
5. Find a photograph in a newspaper or news magazine. Write a paragraph analyzing it as primary source.

Building Civics Vocabulary

Match each vocabulary term with the event to which it relates. Explain the connection between the term and the event.

Example: *Segregation* is related to the case of *Brown* v. *Board of Education of Topeka* because in that case the Supreme Court decided that any laws permitting segregation are not allowed by the Constitution.

1. *suffrage*
2. *segregation*
3. *affirmative action*

(a) the case of *Plessy* v. *Ferguson*
(b) the case of the *Regents of the University of California* v. *Bakke*
(c) the passage of the Nineteenth Ammendment

Reviewing the Main Idea

4. Explain why slavery was not forbidden by the original Constitution.

5. Describe how African Americans gained citizenship and the right to vote.

6. How does the Supreme Court help ensure that our Constitution continues to apply to a changing society?

7. **How to Analyze Cases** Look back at the case on pages 164–165. According to the court's decision in the case, can a student be searched for drugs without a search warrant? Under what circumstances can such a search take place?

8. **How to Interpret Photographs** Look at the photograph on page 154. What does it tell you about the civil rights movement?

Critical Thinking

9. **Analyzing Ideas** What was the importance of the Supreme Court's decision in *Brown* v. *Board of Education of Topeka?*

10. **Identifying Main Ideas** Is a Supreme Court decision permanent? Explain.

11. **Drawing Conclusions** How have the general principles of the Constitution reduced the need for amendments? Explain how the *Bakke* and *Phillips* cases illustrate this.

Writing About Civics

12. **Writing an Essay** As you know, the Constitution alone cannot guarantee citizens' rights. Write an essay describing the role you believe citizens should play in protecting each other's rights.

Citizenship Activities

13. **Working in Groups** Create a bill of rights for your class. First, working in small groups, come up with two or three amendments that would help protect the rights of both students and teachers. Present your amendments to the class. As a class, debate each proposed amendment. Finally, vote on each amendment.

Take It to the NET

Access the **Civics: Participating in Government** Internet site at **www.phschool.com** for the specific URLs to complete the activity.

Research an amendment that interests you. Then, find an amendment currently under consideration and write a paragraph explaining your opinions about it.

Celebrating the 4th of July in an Internment Camp

During World War II, many Japanese Americans were imprisoned as security risks, even if they had shown no proof of disloyalty. In 1942, President Roosevelt issued an order placing more than 100,000 Japanese Americans in internment camps. In 1988, Congress officially apologized for the nation's actions and partially compensated the surviving internees. Mary Tsukamoto's family raised strawberries in California. In this excerpt, she describes the trauma of relocation that her family endured.

Before you read the selection, find the meaning of this word in a dictionary: internment camp.

A lot of little things just nagged at us and harassed us, and we were frightened, but even in that atmosphere I remember we frantically wanted to do what was American. We were Americans and loyal citizens, and we wanted to do what Americans should be doing....By May 1942, more than a hundred of our boys were already drafted....

Every little rule and regulation was imposed only on the Japanese people. There were Italian and German people in

"We were Americans and loyal citizens..."

the community, but it was just us that had travel restrictions and a curfew....

As we arrived [at the camp in Fresno, California], there were all these people peeking out from behind the fence wondering what group would be coming next, and, of course, looking for their friends too....

I remember another thing. We had our Fourth of July program. Because we couldn't think of anything to do, we decided to recite the Gettysburg Address as a verse choir. We had an artist draw a big picture of Abraham Lincoln with an American flag behind him. Some people had tears in their eyes; some people shook their heads and said it was so ridiculous to have that kind of thing

recited in a camp. It didn't make sense, but it was our heart's cry. We wanted so much to believe that this was a government by the people and for the people and that there was freedom and justice....

I know many Niseis [native-born Americans of Japanese ancestry] who say, that was all so long ago. Let's forget it and leave well enough alone. But I just say, we were the ones that went through it—the tears and the shame and the shock. We need to leave our legacy to our children. And also our legacy to America, from our tears, what we learned.

Source: John Tateishi, ed., And Justice for All: An Oral History of the Japanese American Detention Camps *(New York: Random House, 1984), pages 6–7, 11–15.*

Analyzing Primary Sources

1. Why did Japanese Americans during World War II feel the need to do "what was American"?

2. What kind of legacy does Mary Tsukamoto believe should be left to her children?

UNIT 2 ASSESSMENT

Reviewing Main Ideas

1. Discuss the roots of our American tradition of representative government.
2. Why did the founders of our nation want to limit the powers of the national government? In what ways does the Constitution limit the government's powers?
3. Explain why the Bill of Rights was added to the Constitution. Describe at least four protections provided in the Bill of Rights.
4. Explain how our Constitution has been able to adjust to changing attitudes and conditions in society.

Summarizing the Unit

The flow map below will help you organize the main ideas of Unit 2. Copy it onto a separate sheet of paper. Review the unit and complete the flow map by listing some of the important rights recognized by each of the societies or documents shown. Then choose one right from each list and explain why this right is important to you.

Foundations of Freedom

Ancient Greece and Rome	Magna Carta	English Bill of Rights

U.S. Constitution	Bill of Rights	Amendments 11–27

The Federal Government

Why Study Civics?

I describe the American form of government as a three horse team provided by the Constitution to the American people so that their field might be plowed. The three horses are, of course, the three branches of government—the Congress, the executive, and the courts.

—President Franklin D. Roosevelt

The Constitution established a federal government made up of the legislative, executive, and judicial branches. The framers divided power among these branches in order to prevent any one branch from abusing its power. The three branches also limit each other's power through a system of checks and balances. These checks and balances ensure that the branches work "as a three horse team" for the welfare of citizens.

What's Ahead in Unit 3

Unit 3 will examine the three branches of the federal government. You will see how each branch works, and how each checks and balances the power of the other two. You will also analyze the vital role you play in helping all three branches of our government work as an effective team.

The Legislative Branch

Citizenship and You

Diana Perez earned minimum wage at her supermarket job. This was an after-school job and she was happy having the extra spending money.

Then Diana got to know one her co-workers, Anne Petrini. Anne was the mother of two children and was supporting her family with the money she made at the supermarket. Anne often spoke about how hard it was to get by earning the minimum wage.

One day, Anne and Diana read in the newspaper that the Senate was considering a bill that would raise the minimum wage.

"We should write to our senators," Diana said.

"Do you really think that would help?" Anne asked.

"I'm not even sure raising the minimum wage is a good idea," added Christine, another co-worker. "The boss says that she can't afford to pay us more. If Congress raises the minimum wage, some of us might lose our jobs."

Anne, Diana, and Christine decided to find out more. Could Congress pass laws about how much a worker should be paid? Would a senator or representative pay attention to letters from citizens? How do members of Congress make up their minds about laws when people have strong feelings for and against them?

 Keep It Current

Items marked with this logo are periodically updated on the Internet. To keep up-to-date, go to www.phschool.com

What's Ahead in Chapter 8

In this chapter, you will read about the members of Congress and the lawmaking powers given to Congress by the Constitution. You will find out how Congress is organized and follow a bill as it makes its way through Congress.

Citizen's Journal

Suppose you worked in the supermarket and Anne and Diana asked you to join them in writing to your senators. Think about what you might write as you read this chapter. Then write a letter to your senators expressing your opinion on the proposal to increase the minimum wage.

The Members of Congress

 Focus

Congress is the legislative, or lawmaking, branch of the national government. It is made up of two houses, the Senate and the House of Representatives.

The most important job of Congress is to make laws. Laws do not simply state what you can and cannot do. A law can establish a national policy, a plan of action designed to achieve a certain goal. Laws, for example, spell out how the government raises and spends its money. They protect the environment and provide money for school lunches. Laws, as Diana Perez learned, can also determine how much workers are paid.

The Responsibilities of Lawmaking

We are often faced with important decisions in our lives. Can you remember a time when you had to make a decision? Your parents wanted you to decide one way, your friends wanted you to decide a different way, and you were caught in the middle trying to make up your mind what to do.

This is the kind of situation members of Congress face every day. A member has responsibilities to different groups of people. Often these groups make different demands. Lawmaking involves balancing many responsibilities and handling conflicting pressures.

Local versus National Needs Each member of Congress represents a group of citizens much smaller than the nation. One of a member's major responsibilities is to his or her constituents (kun STICH oo ents), the people he or she represents. Constituents expect senators and representatives to listen to their ideas about problems and issues and to be their voice in Congress.

In addition, a member of Congress has a responsibility to the whole nation. The laws Congress makes often affect all Americans. Sometimes, the needs of a member's constituents are in conflict with the needs of Americans in general. For example, a representative from a wheat-growing region may have to vote on a law that would please local wheat farmers but would anger the nation's consumers by raising the price of bread.

Political Parties A member of Congress also has a responsibility to his or her political party. A party is an organization of people who share certain ideas about what government should do. Most members of Congress today belong to either the Republican party or the Democratic party. Each party works to elect its candidates to Congress. In return, the party expects its members to support the party's position on an issue before Congress.

Activist Gets Congress to Listen

Fighting for her own rights and those of others is nothing new for Judith Heumann. "I have made it a pattern in my life," says Heumann, "to speak up against injustices whether to other people or to myself."

Ever since the disease of polio caused her to lose the use of her legs as a young child, Heumann has known discrimination firsthand. After graduating from college, her application to teach in the New York City Schools was turned down because she was in a wheelchair. A law suit against the city's Board of Education earned her the right to teach.

In the early 1980s, Heumann joined with activists across the United States working for passage of the Americans with Disabilities Act (ADA), a proposed law that would protect people with disabilities from discrimination and require that public buildings and mass transit systems be made accessible to disabled people.

Heumann talked to members of Congress and their staff. She sought support from civil rights organizations, women's groups, and religious groups. At a joint House and Senate hearing on the proposed law, she testified about the type of discrimination she had experienced as a disabled person.

In 1990, almost six years after Heumann and others began working for passage of the ADA, it became law. During those years, Heumann always remained confident. "You have to believe in your heart that the change that you want to occur has to occur. You have to be convinced that it is a genuine problem and that working with others you can convince people not only of the problem but also of the importance of the solution."

Recognized nationally for her successful leadership, Heumann was appointed the Department of Education's Assistant Secretary for Special Education and Rehabilitative Services during the Clinton administration.

Active Citizenship

What actions did Heumann take to help win passage of the ADA?

This responsibility may present a member of Congress with a difficult choice. The senator who received Diana Perez's letter about the bill, or proposed law, to increase the minimum wage was pressured from two sides. As a Republican, he felt he should follow his party's position and oppose the bill. However, most of the letters he had received from constituents were in support of the bill.

In his Washington, D.C. office, Representative Robert Matsui of California studies bills, meets constituents, and discusses issues with members of his staff.

Interest Groups A member of Congress may well want to run for re-election when his or her term of office ends. For this reason, members try to gain support and raise money for campaigns. They often get help from interest groups, groups of people who work together for similar interests or goals. Interest groups can supply both votes and money. Examples of well-known interest groups are the American Medical Association, the American Farm Bureau, and the National Rifle Association.

An interest group works to convince senators and representatives to support bills that help its members and to oppose bills that hurt them. This is done by hiring lobbyists, people who represent interest groups. For example, hotel and motel owners formed one interest group that opposed the minimum wage bill. They argued that it would increase their costs by forcing them to pay their workers more. Their lobbyists tried to convince members of Congress to oppose the bill.

Often a member of Congress supports the goals of a particular interest group. In

return, that group encourages its members to vote for him or her in the next election.

Factors in Decision Making A member of Congress votes on hundreds of bills every year. Each vote represents a decision the member must make. He or she must weigh conflicting information and arguments presented by constituents, fellow party members, and lobbyists.

A member must also search his or her own conscience and values. Predicting what the result of a bill will be in the long run can be difficult, but the member must consider that, too. All of these factors are part of the responsibilities of lawmaking.

Servants of the People In addition to being a lawmaker, a member of Congress plays a second important role as servant of the people. In this role, a member gives information and help to individual constituents who have special needs or problems. The owner of a small business, for example, may want to know the latest government rules that apply to her business. Many members of Congress place a great deal of emphasis on this role because it helps a member's constituents directly—and makes them more likely to vote for him or her for re-election.

Members of Congress at Work

In 1899, one senator reportedly joked, "God made a day 24 hours long for the ordinary man. After a man becomes a United States senator, he requires a day 48 hours long." These words still ring true for senators as well as for representatives. Although they work hard, it is almost impossible for them to do all that is required of them.

Members of Congress spend a great deal of time learning about the issues on which they must vote. In 2001, for example, members needed to know about issues ranging from use of American military apparatus and trade with the Middle East, to air pollution and child care.

Members of Congress try to be present on the floor of the House or Senate chamber as much as possible. There, they listen to and give speeches, and vote on bills.

Every day, members of Congress go to meetings. Every day, dozens of people compete for their time—a fellow member with questions about a bill, a lobbyist with arguments against one, a constituent visiting the Capitol. Between meetings, members prepare bills, study reports, and read many letters from constituents.

Congressional Staff Members of Congress rely heavily on their personal staffs—about 12,000 workers who help them do their jobs. Administrative assistants run a member's offices in his or her home state and in Washington, D.C. Legislative assistants study bills. Caseworkers handle requests from constituents.

Members and their staffs try to make their local offices a link between citizens and the government. Some local offices, for example, set up regular neighborhood meetings so that people can talk about issues that concern them. These opinions will be taken into account when bills are proposed and voted upon.

Representatives

You read in Chapter 5 that the House of Representatives is elected on the basis of population. The Constitution requires a census, an official count of the population made every ten years to find out how many representatives each state should have. Then Congress gives each state a fair proportion of the 435 seats in the House of Representatives. For example, the 2000 census determined that California, with the biggest population, should have 53 representatives. Vermont and Wyoming, with very small populations, have only one

representative each. States can gain or lose representatives after each census, but each state must have at least one representative.

The area that a member of the House represents is called a congressional district. Each state is divided into as many congressional districts as it has representatives in the House. By law, all congressional districts must have about the same number of people. Today, districts contain an average of 647,000 people.

The process of drawing district boundaries, which is controlled by state governments, can lead to controversy. Sometimes certain areas in a state have greater percentages of voters from one political party. Then districts can be created to favor one party over another. For example, if the Democratic party controls a state's legislature, it can draw boundaries in such a way that Democrats will be in the majority in most of the state's districts. This

Like other senators, Olympia Snowe of Maine attends meetings in her home state to keep in touch with constituents.

is a strategy that might be used to make sure that a majority of representatives from the state will be Democrats.

Term of Office Representatives serve for two years. All 435 representatives end their terms of office on January 3rd, every two years. They must run for re-election or retire. There is no limit to the number of times a representative can be re-elected.

If they wish to stay in office for more than two years, representatives must constantly work to earn the approval of the people in their districts. For this reason, a typical representative spends more than one fourth of his or her time working for constituents—writing letters, receiving visitors, and doing casework.

Senators

In the Senate, each state is represented by two senators. Thus, a senator pays attention to the interests of the state as a whole, not just one district. For example, a representative from a congressional district in central Illinois will be very interested in farm policies because most of the constituents grow crops and raise livestock. A senator from Illinois, in contrast, is concerned not only with farming, but also with all other parts of the state's economy, including manufacturing, banking, mining, and shipping.

Term of Office Senators are elected for terms of six years. One third of the senators are elected every two years. Unlike the terms of representatives, the terms of senators overlap. As a result, at any one time, there are a number of experienced senators in the Senate.

The framers of the Constitution hoped that longer, overlapping terms would make senators less sensitive to the shifting moods of the people than representatives, who face re-election every two years. As a more stable body, the Senate was expected to prevent quick, unwise changes in the law.

Requirements, Salary, and Benefits

The requirements for being a senator or a representative are similar. Senators and representatives must live in the states in which they are elected. Representatives must be at least 25 years old, and senators must be at least 30 years old. A representative must have been a citizen of the United States for at least seven years, but a senator must have been a citizen for at least nine years.

A member of Congress received an annual salary of $145,100 in 2001. In addition, a member receives benefits to help him or her do the job. For example, a member can have two offices, one in Washington, D.C., and one in his or her congressional district or state. A member receives allowances for running both offices and paying staff salaries, as well as money to travel home to meet with constituents. Members also have free use of the postal service to send mail, such as newsletters, to constituents.

Section 1 Assessment

1. **Define** policy, constituents, bill, interest groups, lobbyists, census, congressional district
2. How do interest groups try to influence members of Congress?
3. How do home offices help keep members of Congress in touch with their constituents?
4. What are some major differences between the jobs of senators and representatives?
5. What are some of the benefits received by members of Congress?
6. **Evaluate** Based on what you know about the area you live in, what do you think are some local needs your representative should take into account?

The Powers of Congress

SECTION PREVIEW

Objectives

■ Describe how Congress uses its powers to meet the goals stated in the Preamble to the Constitution.

■ Explain how limits on the power of Congress protect the rights of citizens.

Building Civics Vocabulary

■ A plan for raising and spending money is a **budget**.

Focus

Each year, our cities, states, and nation face many problems. Congress has the power to try to solve some of these problems. Others are left to local and state governments or to individuals and groups. For example, fixing the potholes in a street is the responsibility of a city. However, repairing the interstate highway, which runs between states, must be done by the national government.

Which problems Congress can try to solve is determined in part by the powers given it in the Constitution. As you will see, these powers are broad, but they have their limits.

Powers Given to Congress

In Chapter 5 you learned that the powers given to Congress are known as delegated powers. Most of these powers are listed in the Constitution, in Article 1, Section 8. In deciding which powers to give to Congress, the framers had the goals of the Preamble in mind. These goals are "to form a more perfect union, establish justice, insure domestic tranquility, provide for the common defense,

promote the general welfare, and secure the blessings of liberty." Each power reflects one or more of these goals.

Promoting the General Welfare The term *general welfare* refers to the needs of all the people of a nation. Congress promotes the general welfare by making laws that help people live better.

Many of these laws are based on the power of Congress to regulate commerce, or business, with foreign nations and between states. For example, a law sets up an agency which controls air traffic in the nation and writes and enforces rules for air safety. Another agency approves or disapproves increases in interstate telephone rates.

Congress can limit commerce in order to promote the general welfare. In 1808, Congress passed a law forbidding traders to bring African slaves into the United States. Today, a law says that companies that do

Many think that in its responsibility to promote the general welfare, Congress should provide more funds for nursery schools and day care.

not pay all their workers minimum wages may not ship their goods to other states.

Congress also has the power to collect taxes and to borrow money. Without money the government could not function. Any bill that has to do with raising money must begin in the House of Representatives. After a money bill has been introduced in the House, the Senate may then act on it by proposing amendments.

In addition, Congress has the power to decide how the money it collects will be spent. In this difficult task, Congress determines how much money will go to education, space programs, medical research, law enforcement and so on.

Congress is said to have the "power of the purse" because it has final approval of the government's budget, or plan for raising and spending money. With this power, Congress has the ability to act as a check on the executive branch. The President can do very little unless Congress provides the money.

Providing for Defense Congress has the power to establish and maintain an army and a navy to defend the nation. Congress also has the sole power to declare war. The last time Congress used this power was during World War II, when the United States declared war on Japan in 1941.

In the 1960s and early 1970s, Presidents Lyndon B. Johnson and Richard M. Nixon sent American troops into battle in the Vietnam War even though Congress did not declare war. In 1973, Congress passed a law called the War Powers Resolution, commonly known as the War Powers Act. That law limits the President's power to send troops into combat without approval by Congress. In the years since, however, Presidents and Congress have continued to debate the question of when congressional approval is needed to send American troops into battle.

Establishing Justice Congress has the power to create federal courts below the level of the Supreme Court. In addition, the appointment of judges to these courts and to the Supreme Court must be approved by the Senate.

Another power of Congress that helps to establish justice is the power to impeach, or accuse an official, such as the President or a federal judge, of serious wrongdoing. Only the House can impeach. The Senate, however, has the power to put the impeached official on trial. If found guilty, the official is removed from office. In our history, two Presidents have been impeached by the House—Andrew Johnson in 1868 and Bill Clinton in 1998. In both cases, the Senate voted not to convict the President.

Unlisted Powers Not all powers of Congress are specifically listed. A clause in the Constitution, often called the elastic clause, allows Congress to make all laws that are "necessary and proper" for carrying out the listed powers. For example, in order to coin money, Congress must set up a mint. The mint has power to design coins and bills, buy metal and paper, hire workers, and distribute the money to banks. None of these powers are listed in the Constitution. The elastic clause gives Congress room to stretch its powers. It makes the government flexible enough to carry out its work and change with the times.

Nonlegislative Powers Fulfilling the goals of the Preamble involves more than making laws. The Constitution grants Congress several important nonlegislative powers. You have already learned about the power to impeach, the power to approve treaties and appointments of federal judges, and the power to propose amendments to the Constitution. Congress also has the power to conduct investigations. It can gather information to help it make laws,

POWERS OF CONGRESS The Constitution gives Congress a wide range of powers. **Government What are two nonlegislative powers granted specifically to the Senate?**

Legislative Powers	Nonlegislative Powers
• Collect taxes	• Elect a President (House) and a Vice President (Senate) if no candidate gets a majority in the electoral college
• Borrow money	
• Regulate trade with foreign nations and among the states	• Confirm appointments and treaties made by the President (Senate)
• Make laws about naturalization	• Propose amendments to the Constitution
• Coin money and set a standard of weights and measures	• Call conventions to propose amendments if demanded by states
• Establish post offices and highways	
• Issue patents and copyrights	• Admit new states to the Union
• Declare war	• Bring impeachment charges (House)
• Create, maintain, and make rules for armed forces	• Try impeachment cases (Senate)
• Make laws for the District of Columbia	

and it can find out how the executive branch is enforcing laws.

Limits on the Powers of Congress

There are both general and specific limits to the powers of Congress. The general limits come from the system of checks and balances you read about in Chapter 5. The executive branch is able to veto proposed laws, and the judicial branch can declare laws unconstitutional.

The specific limits are listed in Article 1, Section 9 of the Constitution. The most important of these limits protect the rights of citizens.

In some countries, a person can be held in jail without having been charged with a crime and given a trial. In the United States, if you are held in jail without a charge, a lawyer or friend can get a writ of *habeas corpus* (HAY bee uhs KOR pus). This paper orders the police to bring you into court. The court then decides if the police have enough evidence to keep you in jail. If not, you must be released. The Constitution says that Congress cannot take away a citizen's right to a writ of *habeas corpus* except in times of invasion or civil war.

The Constitution also prevents Congress from passing bills of attainder. A bill of attainder is a law that convicts a person of a crime without a trial. In addition, Congress cannot pass *ex post facto* laws. Such a law makes a particular act a crime and then punishes people who committed the act before the law was passed. For example, you cannot be punished for something you do in April if a law against the act was not established until May.

These specific limits to the power of Congress were originally looked on as a kind of bill of rights. Together, they help to protect the rights of citizens in dealing with the police and the courts.

Section 2 Assessment

1. **Define** budget
2. Describe two powers that help Congress "promote the general welfare."
3. For what purposes does Congress conduct investigations?
4. Why are bills of attainder and *ex post facto* laws unfair?
5. **Evaluate** Do you think the framers were right in giving the power of the purse to Congress rather than to the President? Explain.

SECTION 3

How Congress Is Organized

SECTION PREVIEW

Objectives

- Describe the major congressional leadership posts and explain how they are filled.
- Summarize the role of committees in Congress.
- Explain the President's role in the lawmaking process.

Building Civics Vocabulary

- The **Speaker of the House** is the presiding officer in the House of Representatives.
- The **president pro tempore** presides over the Senate when the Vice President is absent.
- The party with more members in Congress is called the **majority party.**
- The party with fewer members is called the **minority party.**
- **Floor leaders** are the chief officers of each party in Congress.
- Assistant floor leaders are called **whips.**
- The President can stop a bill using a **pocket veto.** The President keeps the bill for ten days during which time Congress ends its session.

⭐ Focus

The terms, or meeting periods, of Congress have been numbered in order since the first Congress met in 1789. The 107th Congress began in 2001. Each two-year term of Congress is divided into two sessions, one for each year. Each house stays in session from January 3 until its members vote to end the session. Sessions often last until October.

The Constitution does not tell Congress how to make laws. When Congress first began meeting, any member could propose a bill at any time. Any other member could stop action on it by nonstop talking. Over time, Congress developed better ways to consider bills. One important way was to divide the work of preparing bills among committees, or small working groups. Another way was to choose leaders to oversee the process of committee work.

Leadership in Congress

The Constitution gives only a few directions about congressional leadership. First, it states that the House of Representatives must choose a presiding officer called the Speaker of the House. Second, it says that the Vice President of the United States is to serve as the presiding officer, or president, of the Senate. Finally, it directs the Senate to choose an officer called the president pro tempore (pro TEM puh REE), who will preside over the Senate when the Vice President is absent. This officer is also called president pro tem, for short.

The Constitution does not describe how the Speaker of the House or the president pro tem should be chosen. Early in the history of Congress, however, political parties gained control over who was elected to these positions.

Facts & Quotes

The Growth of Congress

The United States Congress celebrated its 212th anniversary in April 2001. The members of the 1st Congress would probably be amazed by the size and budget of our modern Congress.

	1st Congress	107th Congress
Members of House	65	435
Members of Senate	26	100
Standing Committees	0	36
Budget	$374,000	$3.1 billion

Today the Democratic and Republican parties make the decisions about leadership in Congress. In both the House and the Senate, the party with more members is called the majority party. The one with fewer members is called the minority party. In the first months of the 107th Congress, the Senate was split 50–50. Because the Vice President was a Republican, the Senate was considered to have a Republican majority. During the spring of 2001, Vermont Republican Senator James Jeffords switched parties to become an Independent, thus tipping the balance of power towards the Democrats.

Before a new Congress begins, members of each party hold meetings to select congressional leaders. The majority party in the House chooses the Speaker of the House. Likewise, the majority party in the Senate chooses the president pro tem.

Speaker of the House The Speaker is the most powerful member of the House. The Speaker presides over sessions, deciding the order of business and who may speak. The Speaker also appoints members of committees and refers bills to committees. These powers give the Speaker great influence over which bills pass or fail in the House.

President of the Senate As presiding officer of the Senate, the Vice President is in charge of sessions but cannot take part in debates and can vote only in case of a tie. Because the Vice President often is busy with executive duties, the president pro tem usually acts as the Senate's presiding officer.

Floor Leaders The chief officers of the majority and minority parties in each house are the floor leaders. They are responsible for guiding bills through Congress. Floor leaders work closely with committee leaders and party members to persuade them to accept compromises or trade-offs in order to win votes on bills.

Assistant floor leaders, called whips, aid floor leaders in each house. Whips try to persuade members to support the party's position on key issues and to be present when it is time to vote. On important issues, when close votes are expected, much depends on the skill of a party's floor leader and whip.

Working in Committees

More than 10,000 bills are introduced in a term of Congress. Because it would be impossible for a member to study each bill and decide how to vote, both the Senate and the House have set up a system of committees. Much of the most important work of lawmaking is done in the committees.

Introducing Bills Most bills start as ideas for solving problems. Many ideas for bills begin in Congress. Others come from individual citizens, special interest groups, and the executive branch. A group interested in wildlife may want a law to protect mountain lions. People who live near the airport might ask for a law to reduce noise. The President may call for a special police force to solve drug problems facing the nation.

Citizens, interest groups, and the executive branch can draw up bills. However, only a senator or a representative can introduce bills in Congress. A representative introduces a bill in the House by dropping it in a special box called a hopper. A senator introduces a bill by reading it aloud from the Senate floor. All bills introduced during a term are marked *HR* in the House and *S* in the Senate. They are given numbers in the order in which they are introduced. For example, when the minimum wage bill was introduced in the Senate in 1998, it was marked S.1805.

Standing Committees In both houses of Congress, a bill is sent to a standing committee for action. There are 17 permanent standing committees in the Senate and 19 in the House. Each committee deals with a certain area, such as education or banking.

Committees control the fate of bills. First, a standing committee carefully studies a bill. Next, it holds hearings, or public meetings, at which numerous speakers are often heard. The committee may propose changes in the bill. Finally, the committee decides whether to recommend that the entire House or Senate vote on the bill. If the committee does not recommend it, the bill dies, or goes no further.

Every committee has both Democratic and Republican members, but the majority of the members come from the majority party. The chairperson of every committee belongs to the majority party. These leaders have great power over bills because they decide which bills their committees will study. They also decide when and if the committees will meet and whether or not hearings will be held.

When the 107th Senate was evenly split, an even number of Democrats and Republicans served on committees. Each committee chairperson, however, was a Republican.

Select Committees Sometimes the House or Senate will form a select committee to deal with a problem not covered by any standing committee. For example, in 1998 the House of Representatives set up a select committee to determine whether China used technology from the United States to build advanced weapons.

Joint Committees A joint committee is made up of members of both the House and the Senate. Joint committees are usually select committees, formed to conduct investigations. Congress also has created a few standing joint committees, such as the Joint Committee on Atomic Energy.

Conference Committees Before a bill can go to the President to be signed, it must be passed by both houses. Sometimes a bill passes one house but is changed in the other.

HOW A BILL BECOMES A LAW A bill must pass through each house of Congress before reaching the President. **Government Describe the purpose of the conference committee.**

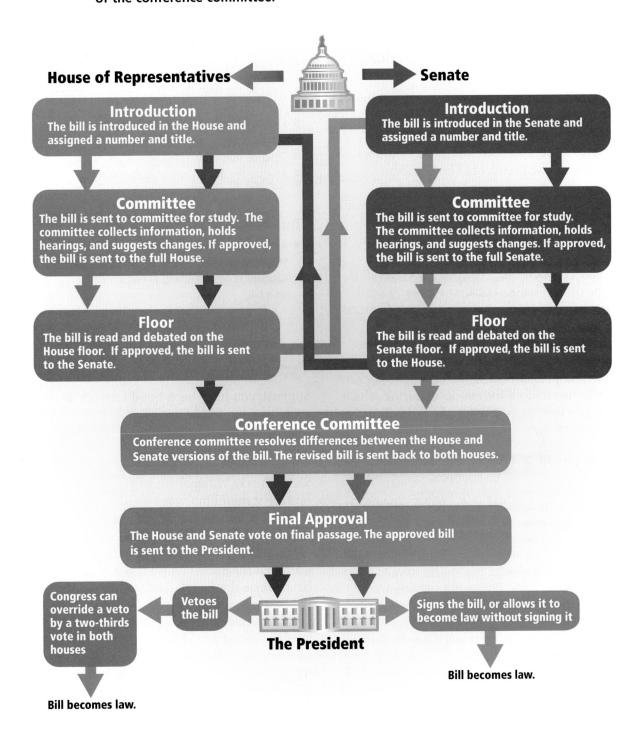

House of Representatives — **Senate**

Introduction
The bill is introduced in the House and assigned a number and title.

Introduction
The bill is introduced in the Senate and assigned a number and title.

Committee
The bill is sent to committee for study. The committee collects information, holds hearings, and suggests changes. If approved, the bill is sent to the full House.

Committee
The bill is sent to committee for study. The committee collects information, holds hearings, and suggests changes. If approved, the bill is sent to the full Senate.

Floor
The bill is read and debated on the House floor. If approved, the bill is sent to the Senate.

Floor
The bill is read and debated on the Senate floor. If approved, the bill is sent to the House.

Conference Committee
Conference committee resolves differences between the House and Senate versions of the bill. The revised bill is sent back to both houses.

Final Approval
The House and Senate vote on final passage. The approved bill is sent to the President.

Congress can override a veto by a two-thirds vote in both houses

Vetoes the bill

The President

Signs the bill, or allows it to become law without signing it

Bill becomes law.

Bill becomes law.

If the two houses cannot agree, a temporary joint committee—called a conference committee—is formed. This committee, made up of both senators and representatives, tries to settle the differences. The conference committee's version of the bill must then be passed by both houses in order for it to move on.

The President's Role

After the same bill has been passed by a majority vote in both houses of Congress, it is sent to the President. The President can sign the bill, making it "the law of the land." The bill will also become law if, while Congress is in session, the President holds the bill for ten days without either signing or vetoing it.

A President may veto, or reject, a bill in one of two ways. The first way is to send the bill back to Congress unsigned. Congress can override the veto by passing the bill again by a two-thirds vote of both houses. The second way a President can veto a bill is called a pocket veto. If the President pockets, or keeps, the bill for ten days, during which Congress ends its session, the bill will not become law.

Following a Bill in Congress

Focus

Suppose you have been hired to work as a summer intern for one of your state's senators. The senator is thinking of introducing a bill that would raise the minimum wage, but she needs some background information. She tells you "I need you to prepare a report on recent minimum wage legislation. I need to know about bills that became laws *and* bills that failed to pass Congress."

As you begin researching, you quickly learn that the minimum wage is a controversial issue. Since the Fair Labor Standards Act set the first minimum wage at 25 cents per hour in 1938, Americans have been debating whether increasing the minimum wage helps or hurts our economy. Some people argue that minimum wage increases help low-income workers support themselves and their families. Others disagree, insisting that increases in the minimum wage hurt workers. Businesses may not able to afford the wage increase, these opponents argue, and they may have to lay off workers.

So what has happened in the past when minimum wage bills have been introduced in Congress? To learn more about this, you decide to research the stories of several minimum wage bills as they moved through Congress.

Stopping a Bill

In March 1987, Senator Kennedy, a Democrat from Massachusetts, introduced the Minimum Wage Restoration Act, numbered S.837. The bill was assigned to the Labor and Human Resources Committee.

The Democrats were the majority party in the Senate at this time, so the chairperson of every committee was a Democrat. Senator Kennedy was chairman of the Labor and Human Resources Committee, and from this powerful position he was able to move the minimum wage legislation forward by scheduling hearings on the bill. At the hearings, committee members listened to testimony from supporters and opponents of S.837.

In July 1988, the Labor and Human Resources Committee sent S.837 to the full Senate. It recommended that the bill be approved. This is called reporting the bill.

The Senate began its debate on S.837. Senator Orrin Hatch, a Republican from Utah, felt the bill would be bad for the American economy. To try to block passage of the bill, Senator Hatch and some fellow Republicans started a filibuster, which is the use of long speeches to prevent a vote on a bill. Filibusters cannot happen in the House, where time limits are set for debates.

On September 22, the Democrats tried to stop the filibuster by calling for cloture (KLO chur), or agreement to end the debate on a bill. Cloture requires a three-fifths vote. At the final count only 53 senators voted in favor of cloture. The next day, the Democrats tried again but failed. Without an end to the filibuster, the Senate could not vote on the bill.

Even though they were the minority party in the Senate, the Republicans had stopped the bill.

Compromise Bills

In the next Congress, Senator Kennedy introduced S.4, a new minimum wage bill. This time, several changes were made in the bill. Some Republicans liked it better, and in April the Senate passed the bill.

Meanwhile, the House also passed a minimum wage bill, numbered H.R.2. Because the two bills were not exactly alike, a conference committee was formed to write a compromise bill. This bill was passed by both houses of Congress and sent to the President. President George Bush believed a minimum wage increase would hurt the economy. He vetoed the bill.

After failing to override the veto, Congress worked out a compromise bill that satisfied the President, who signed it into law in November. This law increased the minimum wage to $4.25 per hour in 1991.

The minimum wage remained at $4.25 until 1996. At this time, the Republicans were the majority party in both the House and the Senate. In May, Representative Bill

Senator Edward Kennedy's bills to raise the minimum wage have generated debate in Congress and around the nation.

Archer, a Republican from Texas, introduced H.R.3448, the Small Business Job Protection Act of 1996. One of this bill's provisions was a two-stage increase in the minimum wage—from $4.25 to $4.75 per hour in 1996, and from $4.75 to $5.15 in 1997.

The bill H.R.3448 was sent to the Committee on Ways and Means, which approved the bill by a vote of 33-3. The bill was then passed by the full House. Several weeks later, the Senate passed a similar bill. A conference committee worked out a compromise bill that was then passed by both houses of Congress. President Clinton signed the bill in August, making it law.

A Bill Dies in Committee

In 1998, Senator Edward Kennedy introduced S.1805, the Fair Minimum Wage Act. When introducing this bill in the Senate chamber, Kennedy explained its purpose to his colleagues:

❝ *The federal minimum wage is now $5.15 an hour. Our bill will raise it by $1.00 over the next two years—a 50 cent increase on January 1, 1999, and another 50 cent increase on January 1, 2000, so that the minimum wage will reach the level of $6.15 at the turn of the century.* ❞

 PROFILE OF MINIMUM WAGE EARNERS, 2000

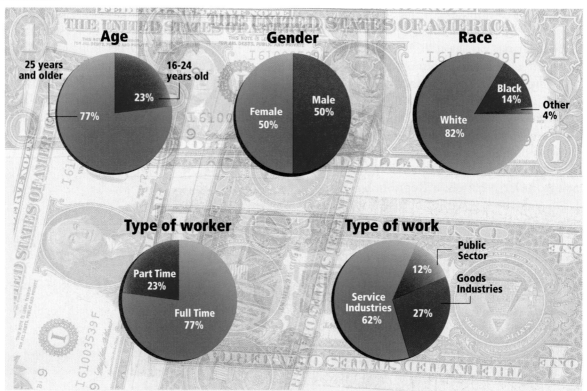

Age
- 25 years and older — 77%
- 16-24 years old — 23%

Gender
- Female 50%
- Male 50%

Race
- White 82%
- Black 14%
- Other 4%

Type of worker
- Part Time 23%
- Full Time 77%

Type of work
- Service Industries 62%
- Goods Industries 27%
- Public Sector 12%

Source: U.S. Bureau of Labor Statistics   Note: Percentages may not add up to 100 due to rounding.

 About 1 million people worked for the minimum wage of $5.15 an hour in 2000. **Economics** What percentage of minimum wage earners were over 25 years old in 2000?

The bill S.1805 was sent to the Labor and Human Resources Committee, chaired by Republican Senator Jim Jeffords of Vermont. It failed to gain the support of a majority of committee members. Therefore, the bill "died" when the 105th Congress ended.

Advantages of the Lawmaking Process

By following these minimum wage bills through Congress, you have learned a lot about lawmaking. Clearly, a bill must overcome many hurdles before becoming a law. You realize, however, that the framers wanted Congress to take its time. They wanted every bill to be studied and debated carefully. Any bill that makes it through this process has an excellent chance of being a good law.

Section 4 Assessment

1. **Define** filibuster, cloture
2. Explain how opponents of S.837 were able to block its passage in 1988.
3. How did the passage of a minimum wage bill in 1991 represent a compromise between Congress and the President?
4. Explain why the Fair Minimum Wage Act of 1998 was never voted on by the entire Senate.
5. Why did the framers set up so many hurdles in the lawmaking process?
6. **Evaluate** Do you think senators should be allowed to hold filibusters to prevent bills from coming to a vote? Explain.

Extending the Chapter

Global Views

The United States Congress is not the only body of its kind in the world today. There are many other democratic nations with legislatures that represent citizens in government. In many of these nations the legislature is called a parliament. Like Congress, a parliament often has two houses.

In some parliaments, such as the Spanish Cortes and the Japanese Diet, all the representatives are elected. In others, such as the British Parliament and the Canadian Parliament, some members are appointed or inherit their seats.

In the British Parliament, for example, one house—the House of Lords—is made up mainly of members with inherited titles of nobility. The other house of Parliament, which is called the House of Commons, is made up of representatives elected by the citizens. This house, which is subject to control by the voters, has the greater power.

Unlike the American system of government, a parliamentary system has no clear separation between the legislative and executive branches. The executive leaders, including the prime minister, are members of Parliament. They have a great deal of power because they both propose the laws and carry them out. The members of Parliament, however, must approve the laws. The Parliament also can force these leaders to resign by defeating their programs.

How to DETERMINE RELEVANCE

Suppose you wanted to buy a CD for a friend, a CD that he or she would be likely to keep. To make a good decision, what would you need to know? You might think about your friend's favorite group or type of music, as well as which CDs he or she already has. This information relates to your decision. However, you would not need to know which brand of CD player your friend has or which CDs are least expensive. These last two pieces of information would not help you choose the right CD.

Whenever you need to make a decision, some types of information are *relevant,* or related, to your subject. Others are not. To make a good decision, you need to determine which information is clearly connected to your subject. Stick to the subject. Do not get sidetracked by information that is *irrelevant,* or not clearly linked to your subject. If you start relying on irrelevant information, you will probably make a poor decision. In short, always ask yourself, "Does this information relate directly to my subject?"

Suppose that you are eighteen years old and have just taken a part-time job. You think your hourly pay is too low and want a new law to be passed that will raise the minimum wage. As you prepare to vote in your first national election, you look over the information on the candidates who want to represent your state in the Senate. Below is some information available to you:

> Democratic candidate Bill Smith is a former governor who is popular with voters, partly because of his good sense of humor. Republican candidate Jane Thickett has a nineteen-year-old daughter who supports raising farm workers' wages.

Mr. Smith actively campaigned for the Democratic presidential candidate, who supported an increase in the minimum wage.

You want to know which candidate is more likely to support an increase in the minimum wage. How might you determine whether each statement is relevant to the decision you must make?

Explain the Skill

One way to distinguish relevant information from irrelevant information is to follow these steps. As you examine the steps, notice how they might be applied to the three pieces of information you just read.

1. **Identify clearly the problem or issue you are examining.** Ask yourself, "What do I want to know or do?" (You want to know which candidate is more likely to support an increase in the minimum wage.)
2. **Identify the kinds of information that might relate to your chosen subject.** Such information might consist of details, examples, explanations, evidence, or definitions. (Examples of a candidate's position on the minimum wage and explanations of why a candidate either supports or opposes increasing the minimum wage would be relevant to the subject.)
3. **Examine each piece of information to determine whether it is relevant.** Judge whether each piece relates, or connects directly, to the subject. (The first two statements are not relevant. Neither the fact that Mr. Smith was a popular governor nor that Ms. Thickett's daughter supports higher farm worker wages is connected with the candidates' views. However, Mr. Smith's

support of the Democratic candidate *is* relevant. It shows that he probably agrees with that candidate's view on the minimum wage.)

Analyze the Skill

Below are more pieces of information. Examine each one to determine whether it is relevant to the subject of the candidates' views on the minimum wage.

A. Ms. Thickett has never been elected to any public office.

B. One of the current senators from your state, who is going to retire, consistently voted against increases in the minimum wage.

C. During an unsuccessful campaign for a seat in the House, Ms. Thickett declared that she would support an increase in the minimum wage only if it reduced the number of people on welfare.

D. As governor, Mr. Smith introduced a bill to raise the wages of workers in the state highway department.

E. Governor Smith's bill to increase highway workers' wages was rejected by the state legislature.

F. Most business leaders argue that a wage increase would force many stores out of business.

G. In a speech, Ms. Thickett pointed out that the minimum wage for American workers is much higher than wages in many other countries.

H. As governor, Mr. Smith wrote an article calling for greater efforts to reduce poverty in the state.

I. Both Ms. Thickett and Mr. Smith went to well-known law schools and later worked as lawyers.

Skill Assessment

When you have determined whether each piece of information is relevant to the candidates' views on the minimum wage, answer the following questions.

1. Given your concern, which candidate would you vote for? Explain why.
2. Identify a piece of information that is an *example* of a candidate's position on the minimum wage. Identify a piece of information that is an *explanation* of a candidate's position on the minimum wage.
3. What does the term *relevant* mean?
4. Which statements are most relevant to helping you decide which candidate is more likely to support a minimum wage increase? Explain your answer. **(a)** A, E, F **(b)** C, G, H **(c)** A, B, H
5. Which statements were irrelevant to your decision?
6. What are some general kinds of information that might be relevant to any subject?

How to ANALYZE CIRCLE GRAPHS

 Use the *Simulations and Data Graphing CD-ROM* to create and interpret graphs.

In this chapter, you learned about the legislative branch of our federal government. You read that there are 435 members of the House of Representatives and 100 Senators. As you would expect from a diverse nation such as ours, the 535 members of Congress represent a wide range of racial and ethnic groups. The circle graphs on this page provide some information about the members of our Congress.

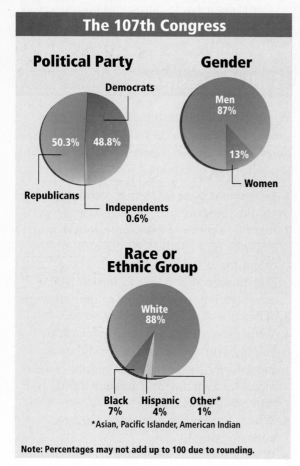

The 107th Congress

Political Party
Democrats
50.3% 48.8%
Republicans
Independents 0.6%

Gender
Men 87%
13%
Women

Race or Ethnic Group
White 88%
Black 7%
Hispanic 4%
Other* 1%
*Asian, Pacific Islander, American Indian

Note: Percentages may not add up to 100 due to rounding.

Source: *Congressional Quarterly Weekly*

Explain the Skill

Circle graphs are a useful way to show statistical information as parts or percentages of a whole. In a circle graph, the entire circle represents 100 percent of a certain group. The circle is then divided into sections, with each section representing a percentage of the whole. The sections of a circle graph are shaped almost like wedges of pie, and for this reason circle graphs are sometimes called pie graphs.

Analyze the Skill

The circle graphs on this page show statistical information about the 107th Congress, which took office in January 2001. To begin, identify the subject of the individual graphs by reading the label beside each graph. Then study each graph one at a time. Remember, each circle graph represents the entire Congress. The sections, or wedges, in each graph represent a certain percentage of the whole Congress.

Skill Assessment

1. Which party had a majority in the 107th Congress?
2. In the 107th Congress, what percentage of the members were women?
3. How would you describe the typical member of the 107th Congress?
4. Create a circle graph showing how many students in your class are male and how many are female.

CHAPTER 8 ASSESSMENT

Building Civics Vocabulary

The vocabulary terms in each pair listed below are related to each other. For each pair, explain how the two terms are related.

Example: *Impeach* is related to *delegated powers* because impeachment is one of the delegated powers of Congress.

1. *constituents* and *congressional district*
2. *interest groups* and *lobbyists*
3. *Speaker of the House* and *majority party*

Reviewing Main Ideas and Skills

4. How are the 435 seats in the House of Representatives divided among the states?

5. Describe two ways in which the Constitution specifically limits the powers of Congress.

6. How can Congress pass a law despite the President's veto?

7. **How to Determine Relevance** Explain the steps you could use to distinguish relevant information from irrelevant information. How do you think this process helps you to make good decisions?

8. **How to Analyze Circle Graphs** Look back at the circle graph on page 188. What percentage of minimum wage earners were men in 2000?

Critical Thinking

9. **Predicting Consequences** If you wrote a letter to your representative in the House, do you think it could influence his or her position on a bill? What factors might work in your favor?

10. **Drawing Conclusions** If the House of Representatives were abolished and the Senate were left as our only lawmaking body, would our government be less democratic? Why or why not?

Writing About Civics

11. **Giving Testimony** Suppose you have been invited to testify at a Labor and Human Resources Committee hearing on the minimum wage. A senator asks you, "What do you think the minimum wage should be and when, if ever, should it be increased?" Write a response to this question, offering arguments to support your position.

Citizenship Activities

12. **Your Local Community** Do some research on your representatives in Congress. You might look in your local newspaper, contact your representatives, or check the Internet—the House of Representatives' Web site is www.house.gov; the Senate's is www.senate.gov. Find out their positions on a current issue. Present your findings to the class. Share your position.

 Take It to the NET

Access the **Civics: Participating in Government** Internet site at **www.phschool.com** for the specific URLs to complete the activity.

Select a current piece of legislation. Follow links to find out more about the legislation. What is the purpose of the bill? Who is its sponsor? Prepare a letter or e-mail to your congressional representative expressing your opinion about the proposed legislation.

The Executive Branch

Citizenship and You

Have you ever wondered what it would be like to be President of the United States? Here is what several Presidents have said about the job.

Though I occupy a very high position, I am the hardest working man in the country. —James K. Polk (President, 1845–1849)

I have thoroughly enjoyed being President. But I believe I can also say that I am thoroughly alive to the tremendous responsibilities of my position. —Theodore Roosevelt (1901–1909)

The position is not a place to be enjoyed by a sensitive man. —William H. Taft (1909–1913)

Being a President is like riding a tiger. A man has to keep on riding or be swallowed. —Harry S. Truman (1945–1953)

No easy problems ever come to the President of the United States. If they are easy to solve, somebody else has solved them. —Dwight D. Eisenhower (1953–1961)

There is no experience you can get that can possibly prepare you adequately for the presidency. —John F. Kennedy (1961–1963)

Keep It Current

Items marked with this logo are periodically updated on the Internet. To keep up-to-date, go to **www.phschool.com**

What's Ahead in Chapter 9

In this chapter you will read about the duties of the President. You will also see how the executive branch is organized to help fulfill those duties. Finally, you will explore some of the ways in which Presidents have used their powers.

Section 1 **The Roles of the President**

Section 2 **The Organization of the Executive Branch**

Section 3 **Presidents and Power**

Citizen's Journal

When discussing their time in the White House, Presidents have often described the presidency as an extremely difficult job. Why do you think the presidency is such a demanding position? Write a paragraph explaining your opinion on this question.

The Roles of the President

SECTION PREVIEW

Objectives

- Explain how the Constitution limits the power of the President.
- Describe the President's role as head of the executive branch.
- Summarize the President's role in military affairs and foreign policy.
- Explain how the President influences the legislative and judicial branches.
- Identify presidential roles created by tradition.

Building Civics Vocabulary

- The **executive branch** is responsible for executing, or carrying out, the law.
- The President can issue **executive orders,** which are rules or regulations that executive branch employees must follow.
- **Foreign policy** is the set of plans that guides our nation's relationship with other countries.
- **Treaties** are formal agreements with other countries.
- **Ambassadors** are official representatives to foreign governments.
- **Executive agreements** are agreements with other countries that do not need Senate approval.
- The President helps set **domestic policy,** plans for dealing with national problems.

 **Focus**

Who is the leader of the United States? To most of us the answer seems clear: the President. As our highest elected official, the President represents all Americans, not just citizens of one state or congressional district. It is the President who usually meets with leaders of other nations and whose daily activities are closely followed by the television networks, newspapers, and news magazines.

Just about everyone knows who the President of the United States is.

How many Americans, though, have a clear picture of what the President does? The President is the head of the executive branch, the branch of government responsible for executing, or carrying out, the laws. However, carrying out laws passed by Congress is only part of the President's job. The most important duty is to set goals for the nation and to develop policies, which are methods for reaching those goals. In spite of having many advisors, the President alone is responsible for making the final decisions about many important issues facing the nation.

This heavy responsibility goes with an office that many think is the most powerful in the world. The office of President also has limits, though, which are set by the Constitution. To understand the powers and responsibilities of the presidency, as well as its limits, you need to look first at how the office was created.

Creating the Office of President

In creating the presidency, the framers did not want a leader with unlimited powers. The

Facts & Quotes

American Presidents

Of the 43 Presidents in the history of our nation:

42 were Protestant
36 were at least 50 years old when they took office
33 were college-educated
27 were lawyers
14 had previously served as Vice President
18 were Republicans
15 were Democrats

memory of the tyranny of the English king was fresh in the minds of many Americans. To calm the people's fears, the framers gave very few specific powers to the President. They also included ways to prevent abuse of power.

Term of Office One limit on the President's power is the term of office. The President is elected for a term of four years and must run for re-election in order to serve a second term. The Twenty-second Amendment says that no President may hold office for more than two terms.

Limited Power Another protection is the separation of powers among the three branches of government. The President may only carry out the laws. It is Congress that makes the laws. The Supreme Court has the power to decide if a law is constitutional.

The system of checks and balances also limits the President's power. Many presidential decisions must be approved by Congress. In cases of serious wrongdoing, Congress may remove the President from office. Furthermore, the Supreme Court can decide whether actions taken by the President are allowed by the Constitution.

Qualifications and Salary To be President, a person must be at least 35 years old and a natural-born citizen of the United States. He or she must have lived in the United States for at least 14 years. The President's yearly salary is set by Congress, rather than by the Constitution.

A Leader with Many Roles The framers knew that the nation needed a leader who could both carry out laws and represent the nation in meetings with leaders of other countries. However, the office of President was new in a world of nations led by monarchs.

Therefore, the framers did not describe exactly how the President should fulfill the duties of this new office. Expecting that

Acting as the nation's chief diplomat, President Reagan signed a weapons reduction treaty with Soviet leader Mikhail Gorbachev in 1987.

George Washington would be elected as the nation's first leader, they trusted that he would become a model of what a President should be. As Washington himself noted:

❝I walk on untrodden ground. There is scarcely any part of my conduct which may not hereafter be drawn into precedent [made an example of]. ❞

Through the examples of Washington and the Presidents who followed him, the roles of the President have become more clearly defined over the years.

The President as Chief Executive

The President serves as chief executive, or head of the executive branch. The Constitution states that the President must "take care that the laws be faithfully executed." To execute laws means to make sure that they are carried out. Although Congress makes the laws, it is up to executive branch officials to decide just how to carry out laws and other policies.

As leader of the executive branch, the President usually makes only the broadest decisions, leaving the details to other officials. One way in which the President gives direction is through executive orders, which are rules or regulations that government officials must follow. In 1948, for example, President Harry Truman gave an executive order to end segregation in the armed forces. After that, people of all races served together instead of in separate units.

The power to make executive orders, however, is limited. The President's orders may not violate the Constitution or laws passed by Congress.

As chief executive, the President also has the power to appoint about 4,000 executive branch officials. As a check on that power, Congress must confirm, or approve, many top appointments.

The President as Commander in Chief

The Constitution says that "the President shall be commander in chief of the army and navy of the United States." This statement points to the President's important role as leader of the armed forces. When the nation is at war, the President makes the most important decisions.

To protect American interests, the President may send troops to a foreign country even if Congress has not declared war. However, the War Powers Resolution, passed after the Vietnam War, says that such troops may not remain for more than 60 days without the approval of Congress.

The President as Chief Diplomat

The President is also our chief diplomat, the most important representative of the United States in relations with other nations. The President leads in making foreign policy, plans for guiding our nation's relationships with other countries. In general, foreign policy involves deciding how to support or oppose actions of other nations. Although they usually seek advice on foreign policy, Presidents must make the final decisions. President Truman made that point when he said, "I make foreign policy."

Foreign policy is clearly the President's "territory," but Congress may set limits. For instance, the President may make treaties, or formal agreements with other countries, but the Senate may reject any treaty. The President's appointments of ambassadors, the official representatives to foreign governments, must also be approved by the Senate.

The President does have freedom, though, to make executive agreements, agreements with other countries, which do not need Senate approval. Executive agreements may have a wide range of purposes. They may set goals for trade or make promises to give aid to other countries.

The President as Legislative Leader

You have read many times that Congress makes our nation's laws. The President, however, has a good deal of power to influence what those laws will be. The Constitution states that the President may recommend to Congress "such measures as he shall judge necessary and expedient." This means that Congress is expected to consider the President's ideas rather than act alone in making laws.

Early each year, the President gives a speech to both houses of Congress. In this State of the Union message, the President sets forth ideas about what America's foreign policy should be. The President also talks about problems at home, such as taxes, day care, and pollution. By describing these problems and giving ideas for solving them, the

Officials of all three branches of government gather to hear the President set forth his policies in his yearly State of the Union address to Congress.

President helps to set **domestic policy**, plans for dealing with national problems.

How does a President get Congress to turn foreign and domestic policy into laws? One way is by getting individual members of Congress to write bills. Another is by calling and meeting with members of Congress, urging them to support the President's program. Speeches to interest groups and to the public also help gain support for bills the President wants passed.

A powerful tool for influencing Congress is the veto. Often just the threat of a veto is enough to get Congress to change a bill to make it more to the President's liking. Congress has overridden about 4 percent of the more than 2,500 vetoes in our nation's history.

Another way in which the President acts as legislative leader is in making the budget. To put policy ideas into action costs money. Every year the President prepares a budget, a plan for how to raise and spend money to carry out the President's programs.

Of course, Congress does not pass all the laws the President asks for, and it almost always makes changes in the President's budget. However, Congress cannot ignore the President's power as legislative leader.

Finally, the President has the power to call special sessions of Congress if problems arise when Congress is not meeting. Today, however, Congress meets for almost the whole year, and the power is not much used.

The President's Judicial Powers

As part of the system of checks and balances, the President has several powers that affect the judicial branch. Most importantly, the President chooses Supreme Court justices and other federal judges. Of course, the President's power is balanced by the Senate which must confirm these appointments.

The President may limit the power of the judicial branch by putting off or reducing the punishment of someone convicted of a crime in federal courts. The President may even do away with the punishment by granting a pardon.

As chief diplomat, President Bill Clinton hosted the signing of a peace treaty between Israel and the Palestine Liberation Organization in 1993.

Roles Created by Tradition

Over the years, the President has taken on two other roles: party leader and chief of state. Neither role is mentioned in the Constitution, yet both are natural results of the President's position and power.

The President is a member of a political party, typically either the Democratic party or the Republican party. As our highest elected official, the President is seen as the leader of that party. The President's power and prestige can be used to support party goals or candidates.

As chief of state, though, the President speaks for the whole nation, expressing the values and goals of the American people. In this role, the President carries out many ceremonial duties, such as greeting visiting leaders and giving medals to citizens. As chief of state, the President stands for a national unity that overshadows differences between the political parties.

Section 1 Assessment

1. **Define** executive branch, executive orders, foreign policy, treaties, ambassadors, executive agreements, domestic policy
2. In creating the office of President, how did the framers guard against abuse of power?
3. Briefly describe four of the President's roles.
4. **Evaluate** Which of the President's roles do you think is the most difficult? Explain your answer.

The Organization of the Executive Branch

SECTION PREVIEW

Objectives
- Define the role of the Executive Office.
- Explain the importance of executive departments.
- Describe some of the major independent agencies.
- Explain the need for the civil service system.
- Explore the process of carrying out the law.

Building Civics Vocabulary
- A bureaucracy is an organization of government departments, agencies, and offices.
- An administration is the team of executive branch officials appointed by the President.
- The Cabinet is an important group of policy advisors to the President.

Focus

As our nation has grown, the President's duties have grown, too. Each year hundreds of laws must be carried out. Decisions must be made on a wide range of foreign and domestic policy issues. To fulfill their many duties, Presidents have needed more and more help. The executive branch has grown from a few hundred officials in George Washington's time to about 3 million employees today. It is now the largest branch of government.

As it has grown, the executive branch has become a huge bureaucracy. A bureaucracy (byoo RAH kruh see) is an organization of government departments, agencies, and offices. Most people who work in the bureaucracy are not chosen to work just for one President. They are hired as permanent employees.

To help direct the bureaucracy, the President appoints an administration, a team of executive branch officials. The nearly 2,000 members of the administration lead the three main parts of the executive branch: (1) the Executive Office of the President, (2) the executive departments, and (3) the independent agencies.

The Executive Office of the President

The Executive Office of the President is largely made up of people the President chooses to help make foreign and domestic policy. Unlike the other parts of the executive branch, the main job of the Executive Office is not to carry out laws directly, but to advise the President on important matters relating to the many presidential roles.

The White House Staff At the center of an administration is the White House staff. It includes the President's inner circle of trusted advisors and assistants. Some of these people see the President every day. They give advice and information about national security, the economy, and other subjects. The White House staff also helps guide the bureaucracy toward meeting the President's goals. Some Presidents like having several staff people report directly to them on issues relating to the executive departments and independent agencies. Other Presidents have depended on one powerful chief of staff to whom other staff members report.

The staff includes a chief of staff and other key advisors, press secretaries, legal experts, speechwriters, office workers, and researchers. The White House staff may truly be called "the President's people" because all of its members are appointed or hired by the President and do not need Senate approval.

The Vice President The Constitution gives the Vice President no duties aside from presiding over the Senate. It is the President who decides what the Vice President will do. Some Presidents ask the Vice President to

Madeleine Albright

From 1997 to 2001, Madeleine Albright was the first woman to serve as Secretary of State, the President's chief advisor on foreign affairs. "I believe," she says, "it is the responsibility of every free person to do what he or she can to advance the freedom of others."

Albright was born in 1936 in Czechoslovakia, the daughter of a diplomat. Her family fled its homeland when the German army invaded in the late 1930s. They lived in France and Yugoslavia before spending the remaining years of World War II in England.

After the war, Albright's family returned to Czechoslovakia, where her father resumed his diplomatic career. However, the family was soon on the move again after the Communists seized power in 1948. This time, the family moved to the United States.

By the time she was a teenager, Albright spoke five languages—French, Czech, Russian, Polish, and English. Interest in world affairs was a part of family life. "In my parent's home," she says, "we talked about international relations all the time, the way some families talk about sports...around the dinner table."

Albright says her own experiences as a refugee helped shape her views on how the United States

should respond to conflicts such as those that led to mass killings and ethnic cleansing in Bosnia and Kosovo in the late 1990s. "In today's world of deadly and mobile dangers," she says, "gross violations of human rights are everyone's business."

Speaking about women in the field of international relations, she said: "It is sad but still true that there are not enough women holding jobs in foreign affairs. Correcting this is not simply about fairness. Today's world needs the skills and experience that women bring to diplomacy."

Recognizing Viewpoints

How do you think Madeleine Albright's childhood experiences influenced her beliefs as Secretary of State?

play an active role, heading special commissions, making trips to other countries, and working with Congress. More often, the Vice President has been almost invisible. Fearing this fate, some leaders have refused to run for Vice President. In 1848, Daniel

Webster declared, "I do not propose to be buried until I am dead."

If the President dies, though, the Vice President may become President. Our nation's first Vice President, John Adams is reported to have said, "In this I am nothing, but I may be everything." Eight times in our nation's history the Vice President has risen to the highest office in the land because of the death of the President. The Vice President may also be asked to serve as "acting President" if the President falls seriously ill.

Since the Vice President may become President, the qualifications for the two offices are the same.

Special Advisory Groups The Executive Office of the President also includes several special groups that help the President make decisions on domestic and foreign policy. The three most important groups are the Office of Management and Budget (OMB), the National Security Council (NSC), and the Office of Homeland Security.

The OMB decides how much the President's policy goals will cost. The President may change the goals in light of the price tags provided by the OMB. Then the OMB prepares the budget that is sent to Congress.

The National Security Council plays a major role in helping the President make foreign policy. The NSC includes top military officers and advisors from other government agencies and departments concerned with foreign affairs and national defense.

The Office of Homeland Security was created in 2001 by President George W. Bush in response to the terrorist attacks on the World Trade Center and Pentagon on September 11, 2001. The Office is headed by a director who has Cabinet rank. The duty of the Office is to "lead, oversee, and coordinate a comprehensive national strategy to safeguard our country from terrorism." In this role, the Office must coordinate the anti-terrorist activities of many federal agencies, including the CIA, the FBI, the Coast Guard, and the Federal Aviation Administration.

The Executive Departments

Over the years, the number of executive departments has grown. Today they form the largest part of the executive branch. As the chart on page 204 shows, they do much of the work connected with carrying out the nation's laws and running government programs.

Each executive department helps fulfill one or more of the President's duties. The Department of State, for example, handles relations with other countries. It helps put the President's foreign policy decisions into action. The Department of Defense helps the President fulfill the duty of commander in chief by running the armed forces.

Executive Department Leadership The President appoints the head of each executive department. As a check on presidential power, each appointment must be approved by the Senate. The head of the Department of Justice is called the Attorney General. The other department heads are called secretaries, such as the Secretary of State and the Secretary of the Treasury. The department secretaries and the Attorney General form the core of the Cabinet, an important group of policy advisors to the President.

The Independent Agencies

The executive departments do not carry out all the duties of today's executive branch. Many tasks, from making rules about nuclear energy to providing farm loans, are carried out by approximately 60 independent agencies. There are three types of agencies: executive agencies, regulatory commissions, and government corporations.

Executive Agencies Executive agencies are under the direct control of the President, who can choose or remove their directors. Among the most important agencies are the National Aeronautics and Space Administration (NASA) and the Environmental Protection Agency (EPA).

Regulatory Commissions Congress has formed 12 regulatory commissions. Each one makes and carries out rules for a certain

EXECUTIVE DEPARTMENTS Much of the work of running government is done by the executive departments. **Government** Which executive department is in charge of managing our national parks?

Department of State (1789)

Carries out foreign policy.

Supervises ambassadors and other U.S. diplomats.

Represents the U.S. at the United Nations.

Department of Treasury (1789)

Collects federal taxes through the Internal Revenue Service (IRS).

Prints money and postage stamps; makes coins.

Protects the President and Vice President through the Secret Service.

Department of Defense
(1789, reorganized in 1947)

Maintains the Army, Navy, Marine Corps, and Air Force.

Does research on military weapons.

Builds and maintains military bases.

Department of Interior (1849)

Manages national parks and other federal lands.

Protects fish, wildlife, and other natural resources.

Department of Justice (1870)

Investigates and prosecutes violations of federal laws.

Operates federal prisons.

Runs the Federal Bureau of Investigation (FBI).

Represents the federal government in lawsuits.

Department of Agriculture (1862)

Provides assistance to farmers.

Inspects food processing plants.

Runs the food stamp and school lunch programs.

Works to control animal and plant diseases.

Department of Commerce (1903)

Provides assistance to American businesses.

Conducts the national census.

Issues patents and trademarks for inventions.

Maintains official weights and measures.

Source: U.S. Office of Personnel Management

Department of Labor (1903)

Enforces laws on minimum wage, job discrimination, and working conditions.

Helps run job training and unemployment programs.

Provides statistics on changes in prices and levels of employment.

Department of Health & Human Services (1953)

Directs Medicare program.

Runs the Food and Drug Administration (FDA).

Runs the Public Health Service.

Runs the Family Support Administration.

Department of Housing & Urban Development (1965)

Helps provide housing for low-income citizens.

Assists state and local governments in financing community development and housing projects.

Department of Transportation (1966)

Helps state and local governments maintain highways.

Enforces transportation safety standards.

Operates the United States Coast Guard.

Department of Energy (1977)

Conducts research on sources of energy.

Promotes the conservation of fuel and electricity, and directs programs to deal with possible shortages.

Department of Education (1953)

Provides assistance to elementary, high school, and college education programs.

Conducts research and provides statistics on education.

Promotes equal access to educational opportunities.

Department of Veterans' Affairs (1989)

Gives medical, educational, and financial help to people who have served in the armed forces.

President Clinton met often with his foreign policy team during the war in Kosovo in 1999.

business or economic activity. The Federal Communications Commission (FCC), for instance, makes rules for radio and television stations. The Consumer Product Safety Commission (CPSC) sets safety standards for products you might find around the house. The regulatory commissions also settle disputes between businesses they regulate.

The regulatory commissions are meant to be fairly free from political influences. The President chooses members of the boards which run the commissions. Each member has a long term so that no single President can choose all of a board's members.

Government Corporations Government corporations are like private businesses in that they try to make a profit. However, most of them provide public services that may be too risky or expensive for a private

business to undertake. The United States Postal Service is one example of a government corporation.

Political Battlegrounds Although the heads of the executive departments and many of the independent agencies are chosen by the President, these government bodies are not simply tools for putting presidential powers into action. Congress has an important say in how executive departments and agencies are run.

When members of Congress disagree with the President, executive departments and independent agencies can become settings for political battles. During President Clinton's second term, for example, Republican leaders in Congress proposed a bill that would eliminate two independent agencies—the Arms Control and Disarmament Agency and the United States Information Agency. The bill would also move a third independent agency—the United States Agency for International Development—under the authority of the State Department. Led by Senator Jesse Helms of North Carolina, this move was designed to streamline government bureaucracy.

At first, President Clinton opposed this measure. After Congress passed the bill, however, Clinton agreed to sign it, hoping to gain Republican support for foreign policy goals of his own. A conflict like this shows that the President must take into account the strength of Congress when making policy decisions.

The Civil Service System

As you might imagine, the executive branch includes a wide variety of employees, from budget experts at the OMB to rocket engineers at NASA. The President chooses less than

 INDEPENDENT AGENCIES The executive branch includes about 60 independent agencies. **Government** What is the purpose of the Federal Trade Commission?

Selected Executive Agencies	
Central Intelligence Agency (CIA) (1947)	Gathers information on matters of national security, both abroad and in the U.S.
Environmental Protection Agency (EPA) (1970)	Protects human health and the natural environment.
National Aeronautics and Space Administration (NASA) (1958)	Operates the space program; conducts research on flight both within and beyond the earth's atmosphere.
Federal Election Commission (FEC) (1971)	Enforces rules on campaigns for federal offices.
Selected Regulatory Commissions	
Federal Reserve System (FRS) (1913)	Directs the nation's banking system by managing the money supply.
Federal Trade Commission (FTC) (1914)	Protects consumers from unfair or misleading business practices.
National Labor Relations Board (NLRB) (1935)	Works to correct or prevent unfair labor practices by either employers or unions.
Equal Employment Opportunity Commission (EEOC) (1964)	Enforces laws against job discrimination based on race, color, religion, sex, national origin, age, or disability.
Selected Government Corporations	
Federal Deposit Insurance Corporation (FDIC) (1933)	Insures deposits at banks that are members of the Federal Reserve System and at non-member banks that meet certain standards.
Tennessee Valley Authority (TVA) (1933)	Develops the natural resources of the Tennessee Valley by controlling flooding and creating electric power.
United States Postal Service (1971)	Provides mail service.

The Environmental Protection Agency is responsible for carrying out environmental laws such as the Clean Air Act.

1 percent of the workers in the executive branch. How do all the others get their jobs?

For many years, government jobs were likely to go to friends and supporters of the President. Loyalty to the President was more important than knowing how to do the job.

In 1883, however, Congress set up the civil service system. Under this system most government workers, called civil servants, are hired on the basis of merit. There are tests for most kinds of jobs, and workers are hired from among those with the highest scores. The civil service system provides for a group of trained workers who stay on the job from administration to administration.

The Executive Branch in Action

As you have seen, carrying out laws is a big, complex job. The following example helps show how the executive branch works with legislators and the public to carry out laws.

When Congress passed the Clear Air Act in 1970, the Environmental Protection Agency (EPA), an executive agency, was put in charge of carrying out this law. Since then, part of the EPA's ongoing responsibility has been to create rules that meet the goals of the Clear Air Act.

In October 1998, the EPA proposed new rules designed to reduce several specific types of hazardous air pollution. Before these rules went into effect, however, the EPA consulted with members of Congress, administration officials, industry leaders, interest groups, and the public. Public hearings were held at which interested parties presented their views on the proposed rules. The EPA also studied how much it would cost for industries to meet the new pollution guidelines.

Finally, in May 1999, after this process of study and public participation, the new air pollution rules went into effect. This example gives you an idea of the work that goes into carrying out a single law. Of course, there are hundreds of other laws that the executive branch must carry out. It must also make many important decisions about domestic and foreign policy. This helps explain why the executive branch has become such a huge bureaucracy.

Section 2 Assessment

1. **Define** bureaucracy, administration, Cabinet
2. Describe the role of the National Security Council.
3. How does Congress exercise influence over executive departments?
4. How do government corporations differ from private businesses?
5. Why did Congress set up the civil service system?
6. **Evaluate** What do you think are the advantages and disadvantages of having a large executive branch bureaucracy?

Presidents and Power

SECTION PREVIEW

Objectives

- Describe some ways in which Presidents are able to act on their own.
- Summarize advantages and disadvantages of the power of Presidents to act on their own.
- Analyze some examples of the use of presidential power.

Building Civics Vocabulary

- **Executive privilege** gives the President the right to keep some information secret from Congress and the courts.

 **Focus**

As our first President, George Washington was the leader of a small nation of about 4 million people. Today, the President's actions affect our nation of about 281 million people. They also affect nations and peoples around the world.

In setting up the office of President, the framers could not have known how much the power and duties of the office would grow. Today, many people fear that too much power is in the hands of one leader. How much power should a President have? How free should a President be from checks and balances by Congress and the judicial branch?

Freedom to Take Action

In fact, the President has a good deal of freedom to take action to meet goals. For example, the President and presidential advisors do not need permission from Congress to hold talks with representatives of other countries. Many talks result in executive agreements, which do not need Senate approval. Other talks lead to treaties. Even though the Senate has the power to reject any treaty, once the President has committed the United States to a treaty, it is hard for the Senate to say no.

Another way the President can take independent action is by executive privilege, the right to keep some information secret from Congress and the courts. Executive privilege is based on the idea of separation of powers. It helps keep the other branches from interfering with the President's job. Sometimes, too, the nation's safety depends on secrecy. If the President has to tell Congress, the information is more likely to leak out and ruin the plan.

Seeking a Balance

Given the fact that the President has a good deal of freedom, an important question to ask is, "When should the President's powers be limited?" The answer depends on the situation and on the President's goals in that situation. In any situation, the possible advantages of the President acting independently have to be weighed against the possible disadvantages.

What are some reasons the President should be able to take action without talking with the other branches of government? One is that the President can act quickly in a crisis or take an opportunity that might be lost while waiting for approval by Congress. Furthermore, in some situations Congress may be seriously divided and not able to arrive at a decision.

Suppose, however, that a President often made important decisions without asking Congress or thinking about whether the actions were constitutional. How could we be sure that the President was acting in the best interests of the nation? Clearly, the need for

The American flag is raised over the Louisiana Territory, purchased from France by President Thomas Jefferson in 1803.

strong presidential leadership must be balanced against the need to protect ourselves against abuse of power.

Using Presidential Power

The following examples show how three Presidents have used their powers at certain times. As you read, think about the effects of each President's action. Was the President right to take that action?

Jefferson and the Louisiana Purchase
In 1803, President Thomas Jefferson had a great opportunity. Napoleon, the ruler of France, had offered to sell the huge Louisiana Territory for $15 million. By

Faced with possible impeachment, President Nixon resigned. Here he and his family bid farewell to Vice President Gerald Ford, who replaced him.

ing about Madison's advice, Jefferson accepted Napoleon's offer. The Senate ratified the treaty, and Congress agreed to pay France for the territory.

Truman and the Steel Mills In 1952, during the Korean War, President Harry Truman faced a problem. The steelworkers said they would not work unless certain demands were met. The steel-mill owners would not agree to their demands.

President Truman knew that steel was needed to make weapons for the soldiers in Korea. He gave an executive order placing the Secretary of Commerce in control of the mills for the time being. The steel companies said that the President had no right to take control of private property. Truman said that he was acting as commander in chief to protect American troops.

The case came before the Supreme Court. The Court ruled that the President had no power to take private property, even in a national emergency. His duty, the Court said, was to carry out laws passed by Congress, not to use executive orders to make his own laws.

Nixon and Watergate On August 9, 1974, President Richard Nixon left office as a result of the Watergate scandal. Nixon and members of his staff were accused of covering up White House involvement in a break-in at the Democratic National Committee Headquarters in the Watergate office building in Washington, D.C. The aim of the break-in was to help get Nixon re-elected by finding out about the Democrats' campaign plans.

After the burglars were caught in the act, newspaper reporters discovered that members of the White House staff had helped plan the burglary and later tried to cover up the crime. First a special Senate committee and later the House Judiciary Committee began an investigation of the President.

Investigators found that the President had taped all of his White House conversations.

buying Louisiana, Jefferson could double the size of the United States.

Although Jefferson thought that the purchase would be good for the young nation, he was troubled because the Constitution did not say that the President or Congress could buy territory. Jefferson thought that a constitutional amendment might solve the problem, but time was short. Napoleon was showing signs of changing his mind.

Knowing that he had to act quickly, Jefferson turned to his advisors, especially James Madison, who was then Secretary of State. Madison believed that the President's power to make treaties gave Jefferson the right to buy Louisiana. After carefully think-

When they asked to examine the tapes, however, Nixon refused to release them, claiming executive privilege. In July 1974, the Supreme Court ordered Nixon to turn over the tapes, saying that executive privilege is not an unlimited power, particularly if used to hide possible criminal actions. Based on the tapes and other facts, the House Judiciary Committee recommended that Nixon be impeached. Nixon resigned before the full House could vote.

Sharing the Power

The stories you have just read show that the President does not govern alone. Instead, power is shared among the three branches of government—the "three horse team" as President Franklin D. Roosevelt described them. The system of checks and balances helps to make sure that the government acts in the best interests of the people. In this way the "three horse team" works together for the good of the nation.

Section 3 Assessment

1. **Define** executive privilege
2. Describe three ways in which Presidents can take action on their own without consulting the other branches of government.
3. What are some advantages and disadvantages of the power of Presidents to take action on their own?
4. Why did President Jefferson hesitate before making the Louisiana Purchase?
5. **Evaluate** Do you think our system of government places too much power in the hands of the President? Support your opinion with reasons and examples.

Extending the Chapter

Global Views

As you know, ours is not the only nation with a representative government that includes both a legislature and a leader. However, just as there are differences between Congress and many other legislatures, there are also differences between the presidency and the role played by leaders of many other nations.

One difference lies in the fact that the President is both our chief of state and the leader of the government. In a number of other nations, each of these roles is filled by a different person. For instance, in Great Britain the head of state is the king or queen, who represents the nation at ceremonies but holds little political power. It is the British prime minister who leads the government, making decisions on foreign and domestic policy.

Another difference is in the way the leaders are chosen. In some parliamentary governments, such as Japan, the leader of the government is chosen by the legislature, not elected directly by the people. Such leaders usually stay in power only as long as their party has a majority in the legislature. They may be voted out of office at any time. Our Presidents, on the other hand, stay in office for a fixed term during which they may be removed from office only if convicted of crimes. Therefore, in our government the chief executive is more independent of the legislature.

How to DISTINGUISH FACT FROM OPINION

"Today Carol made a speech about school spirit in her campaign for student body president. It was a great speech."

Suppose you were trying to decide whom to vote for in a school election, and you overheard a comment like the one above. That information might influence your decision, but you would probably want to check it out first.

You could find out whether Carol really talked about school spirit by asking students who heard the speech. The statement that the candidate talked about school spirit is a *statement of fact,* a statement that can be either proved or disproved to everyone's satisfaction. In this case, the statement is true. However, suppose you were to say to someone, "Hi, my name is Mickey Mouse. I am over 60 years old." These statements of fact could easily be proved false.

The statement that the candidate's speech was "great," however, is a statement that is neither true nor false. Instead, it is an *opinion,* a personal belief that cannot be either proved or disproved. If you asked other students whether the speech was great, you would get different answers because people have different ideas about what is "great." There will always be disagreement about opinions.

Being able to tell the difference between statements of fact and opinions helps you judge the information you use in making decisions. When making a decision, you should have good reasons for trusting the information you use, whether that information is fact, opinion, or a combination of both.

Suppose you have an assignment to rate the Presidents of the United States, deciding which ones were good, average, and below average. In order to make your decision, you have gathered information on the Presidents.

Among the pieces of information are the following:

Thomas Jefferson's most important accomplishment was the purchase of the Louisiana Territory.

Andrew Johnson and Bill Clinton are the only Presidents who were ever impeached.

How might you decide what is a statement of fact and what is opinion?

Explain the Skill

One way to separate statements of fact from opinions is to follow these steps. Notice how the steps apply to the information that you just read.

1. **Recall the definitions of a fact and an opinion, as described above.**
2. **Apply definitions of fact and opinion to each piece of information.** When in doubt about whether a piece of information is a fact or an opinion, ask yourself, "Could it be proved or disproved to any reasonable person?" [Jefferson's purchase and the impeachment of Johnson and Clinton are statements of fact that can be checked in history books. However, saying that the purchase was "most important" is an opinion because there will always be disagreement about what is "important."]
3. **Determine the extent to which each piece of information fits the definition of fact or opinion.** Does it contain only fact, only opinion, or a combination of both? [The information about Jefferson is a combination of fact and opinion. The information about Johnson and Clinton is a statement of fact.]

Analyze the Skill

Examine the following information in order to identify statements of fact and opinions.

A. Woodrow Wilson was the most well-educated President.

B. During President Wilson's illness, his wife took on some of his duties as President.

C. William Howard Taft was the only person to hold the offices of President of the United States and Chief Justice of the Supreme Court.

D. After women were given the right to vote, Warren G. Harding was elected President because he was more handsome than his opponent.

E. Andrew Johnson was the only President who never spent a single day in a schoolroom.

F. Abraham Lincoln is the only President who actively took on the role of commander in chief.

G. President Lyndon Johnson selflessly gave up his political career in the interest of the nation's welfare by not running for re-election in 1968.

H. Richard Nixon would have been impeached if he had not resigned first.

I. John Tyler was the first Vice President to become President through the death of a President.

J. Approving the purchase of the Alaska Territory was the most important action that Andrew Johnson took as President.

K. When Ronald Reagan was re-elected to a second term, he was the oldest person to serve as President of the United States.

Skill Assessment

After you have identified the statements of fact and the opinions, answer the following questions.

1. Pick one of the statements that includes an opinion and rewrite it so that it only states facts.
2. Which of the following pairs of sentences includes only statements of fact? Explain your answer. **(a)** B and E **(b)** A and D **(c)** F and G
3. Which of the following sentences includes only opinion? Explain your answer. **(a)** D **(b)** I **(c)** A.
4. Which of the following sentences includes both statements of fact and opinion? Explain your answer. **(a)** D **(b)** A **(c)** C
5. What is the difference between a statement of fact and an opinion?
6. How does identifying facts and opinions help you in making good decisions?
7. Identify two times when it would be helpful for you to identify statements of fact and opinions. Explain why.

How to **USE AN ALMANAC**

In this chapter, you studied the powers and duties of the President of the United States. Suppose you wanted to find out more about our Presidents. For instance, who was the first President to take the Oath of Office in Washington, D.C.? How many Presidents have been assassinated? Information almanacs provide a quick and easy source of answers to questions such as these.

Explain the Skill

Information almanacs are books that are published each year. The original purpose of an almanac was to record and predict events in the natural world, such as the rising and setting of the sun and moon, weather patterns, and the movement of tides. Traditionally, farmers relied on almanacs to help them plan their farming operations. One almanac that was popular in colonial times was *Poor Richard's Almanac*, which Benjamin Franklin began publishing in 1733.

Today's information almanacs cover a much wider range of subjects. These books are filled with information on topics ranging from Academy Awards and Africa to zip codes and zoos.

Analyze the Skill

Almanacs are organized by topic. When you are searching for information in an almanac, begin with the table of contents. Here, you will find a list of topics along with the page numbers on which the topics are covered.

Here are some topics that might be listed in the table of contents of an almanac under the subject of United States Presidents.

Presidents, U.S.
Ages, 495
Assassinations and attempts, 517, 521
Biographies, 516–34
Birth, death dates, and sites, 495
Burial sites, 555
Cabinets, 203–5
Constitutional powers, 533
Families, 551
Internet addresses, 566
Portraits on currency, 387
Qualifications, 599
Salary, 176
Succession law, 538, 541
Vetoes, 95

Skill Assessment

On which page or pages of this almanac would you look to find answers to the following questions?

1. Which Presidents are pictured on our money?
2. Which Presidents, if any, were born in your home state? Buried in your state?
3. How much is a President paid?
4. How many children did President Lincoln have?
5. Who served as Secretary of State during President Carter's administration?
6. How old was George Washington when he became President?
7. Who was the first President to be assassinated?
8. How old do you have to be in order to be elected President?

CHAPTER 9 ASSESSMENT

Building Civics Vocabulary

The vocabulary terms in each pair listed below are related to each other. For each pair, explain how the two terms are related.

Example: *President* is related to *executive order* because it is the President who has the power to make an executive order.

1. *bureaucracy* and *executive branch*
2. *executive agreements* and *treaties*
3. *Cabinet* and *administration*

Reviewing Main Ideas and Skills

4. Describe three of the President's roles, and explain how the duties of each role require the President to work with Congress.

5. According to James Madison, what presidential power gave President Jefferson the right to purchase Louisiana?

6. **How to Distinguish Facts from Opinions** Which of the following are statements of fact? Which are opinions? **(a)** John F. Kennedy was the greatest President since World War II. **(b)** Under the Constitution, the President may be either a man or a woman. **(c)** George W. Bush was elected President in 2000.

7. **How to Use an Almanac** Look back at the list of topics on page 214. On what page would you find out about the qualifications for becoming President?

Critical Thinking

8. **Defending a Position** Some people argue that our federal government interferes too much with the lives of citizens by enforcing so many laws and regulations. Do you agree or disagree? Support your opinion.

9. **Linking Past and Present** How have the duties of the President grown since the time of President Washington?

Writing About Civics

10. **Writing an Essay** Look at the chart of executive departments on page 204. Choose one department and write an essay describing how the actions of this department affect your life.

Citizenship Activities

11. **Working in Groups** Working in small groups, create your own trivia game on Presidents of the United States. Write questions on small index cards and write the answers on the backs of the cards. Each group should come up with at least 10 questions. Some sources of interesting facts are almanacs, encyclopedias, and the Internet. Share your questions with your classmates and see if they can answer them.

 Take It to the NET

Access the **Civics: Participating in Government** Internet site at **www.phschool.com** for the specific URLs to complete the activity.

Use online information to research a current Cabinet department. What purpose does the department serve? Who is the department's leader? What part does the department play in current events? Use the information that you and your classmates have found to create a bulletin board display about the President's Cabinet.

The Judicial Branch

Citizenship and You

You are visiting the Supreme Court building in Washington, D.C. As you sit facing a long bench with nine dark leather chairs behind it, a clerk suddenly pounds a gavel and declares:

The Honorable, the Chief Justice and the Associate Justices of the Supreme Court of the United States!...

Everyone in the courtroom stands as the nine justices in black robes enter and take their seats behind the bench. You sit down quietly along with the rest of the audience.

A lawyer steps forward and begins arguing the first case of the day. Her client has been found guilty of first degree murder by a state court and sentenced to death. When he committed the crime, however, he was under the age of eighteen. The lawyer argues that a law allowing the death penalty for a person who has not yet reached adulthood is cruel and unusual punishment and therefore unconstitutional.

Next, the lawyer for the state presents his argument, justifying the state's law. The justices ask the lawyers many questions. Then the justices leave the courtroom to discuss their ruling privately. You wonder how the justices will decide this important case.

What's Ahead in Chapter 10

In this chapter you will read about the judicial branch of the federal government. Led by the Supreme Court, the judicial branch judges federal laws and interprets the Constitution. In doing so, it helps protect the rights of American citizens.

Keep It Current

Items marked with this logo are periodically updated on the Internet. To keep up-to-date, go to **www.phschool.com**

Citizen's Journal

Suppose you were a Supreme Court justice. In one paragraph, describe the beliefs and principles that would guide your decisions. Keep your answer in mind as you read this chapter.

The Role of the Federal Courts

SECTION PREVIEW

Objectives

- Explain the need for laws and a legal system.
- Describe the role of courts in our legal system.
- Compare the roles of state and federal courts.

Building Civics Vocabulary

- The **plaintiff** is an individual or a group of people who bring a complaint against another party to court.
- The party who defends against a complaint is the **defendant.**
- A government body called the **prosecution** brings a criminal charge against a defendant.
- Court decisions can establish a **precedent,** or guideline for how similar cases should be decided in the future.
- The court to which a legal case first goes has **original jurisdiction,** or the authority to hear a case first.
- Plaintiffs or defendants have the right to **appeal,** or ask a higher court to review their case.
- Courts with **appellate jurisdiction** have the authority to hear an appeal.

 **Focus**

The judicial branch of the federal government is made up of the Supreme Court and over 100 other federal courts. The most important members of the judicial branch are judges. Although they work quietly, away from the hubbub of politics that surrounds the President and members of Congress, the judges of the judicial branch have a very important role in our government.

Laws and Courts

In our society, disputes involving laws are resolved in the legal system. To understand the need for a legal system, consider the following example. A legislative body makes a law prohibiting one person from purposely damaging another's property. If a junior high student is then accused of throwing a baseball through someone else's window, several issues may have to be decided. Was the ball thrown on purpose? Has the law been broken? Is the accused person innocent or guilty? How shall the person who threw the baseball repay the person whose window was broken? These questions may be decided by the people involved in the incident, but if the matter is serious enough, it may have to be decided within the legal system.

The federal courts are part of a legal system that includes all the courts and laws in the United States. In this picture a trial is in progress.

What Courts Do

Legal conflicts in our country are resolved by courts of law. All courts perform the same basic function: to apply the law to an actual situation.

Courts in our legal system resolve two kinds of legal conflicts. In a criminal case, a court determines whether a person accused of breaking a law is innocent or guilty. If the person is found guilty, the court also decides what the punishment will be.

In a civil case, a court settles a disagreement. The disagreement can arise over such issues as who caused an auto accident or broke a contract, over a divorce, or over possible violations of constitutional rights. The federal courts hear both civil and criminal cases, and both kinds of cases can find their way to the Supreme Court.

The Parties in the Conflict Every court case involves two opposing sides, or parties. Who these parties are depends on whether the case is civil or criminal.

The typical civil case is brought to court by a party called the plaintiff, an individual or a group of people who bring a complaint against another party. The party who answers a complaint and defends against it is called the defendant. The defendant may be an individual, a group, or a government body.

Imagine that Mabel Edwards brought the Techno Corporation to court, claiming that the company had denied her a job because of her race. She would be the plaintiff in this civil case, and the company would be the defendant. The case would be called *Edwards v. The Techno Corporation*.

In contrast, a criminal case is always brought to court by the prosecution, a government body that brings a criminal charge against a defendant who is accused of breaking one of its laws. The prosecution is referred to as "The People" and is represented by a government lawyer known as a prosecutor.

Usually each party in a court case is represented by a lawyer. Here, two lawyers discuss their case with the judge.

What if Arlo Ashley was accused of robbing a convenience store in Lima, Ohio? The state of Ohio would bring him to court on charges of theft. In a criminal case, called *The People of the State of Ohio* v. *Ashley*, Arlo Ashley would be the defendant.

The Members of the Court In a court the job of a judge is to apply the law to the conflict between the plaintiff or prosecution and the defendant. This means determining which side's argument is most in keeping with the law. The judge directs the proceedings but must remain neutral and not take sides in the conflict.

Many legal cases also involve a jury, which decides the facts of a case—such as what happened and who did it. You may remember that a trial by jury is one of the rights guaranteed by the Constitution to a person accused of a crime.

Interpreting the Law In the process of hearing a case, a court may have to decide what the law in question means. For example, does a law banning "motor vehicles" in a park also ban radio-controlled model cars? A court may also have to decide if the law is allowed by the Constitution. This process of interpretation is an important job of the courts.

Although the legal system deals with individual cases, a court's decision in a case can have very broad effects. This is because a court's decision can establish a precedent, a guideline for how all similar cases should be decided in the future. A precedent makes the meaning of a law or the Constitution clearer. It also determines how the law should be applied, both inside and outside the legal system. For example, the Court's decision in *Brown* v. *Board of Education* established a precedent that made any law segregating blacks and whites unconstitutional.

State Courts and Federal Courts

Our legal system is made up of two separate but interconnected court systems—those of the states and that of the federal government. Although decisions that establish the broadest precedents are made in the highest federal courts, most legal cases begin in a lower court, often at the level of state government. To understand the federal court system, it helps to know about the state court system.

Each state has courts at different levels of government and courts for different purposes, such as traffic courts and juvenile courts. All of these courts are considered part of the state court system. Since most of the laws that govern our everyday actions are state and local laws, most legal disputes and violations of the law are decided in state courts.

Jurisdiction The court to which a legal case first goes has original jurisdiction, the authority to hear a case first. A court with original jurisdiction determines the facts in a case. Often this occurs during a trial conducted with a jury, but in certain cases a judge hears the case alone. Because they hold trials to resolve cases, courts with original jurisdiction are also called trial courts.

What happens if the court of original jurisdiction makes a decision that the plaintiff or defendant in the case believes is unjust? Then he or she has the right to appeal, to ask a higher court to review the decision and determine if justice was done. In each state, there are appeals courts set up just for the purpose of hearing cases appealed from lower state courts. These courts have appellate jurisdiction, the authority to hear an appeal.

An appeals court does not hold a trial, nor does it determine the facts in a case. Its

 A TYPICAL COURT SYSTEM
Most court systems have three levels. **Government Define the three levels of a typical court system.**

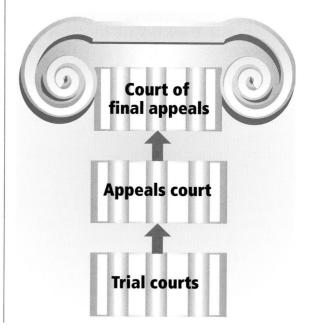

Court of final appeals

Appeals court

Trial courts

CASES HEARD BY FEDERAL COURTS The federal courts have jurisdiction over a wide range of cases. **Government** What kinds of federal law cases are heard by federal courts?

Cases Heard by Federal Courts

Cases that raise constitutional questions

Cases involving federal laws, such as treason and tax evasion

Cases in which the federal government is the defendant

Disagreements between states

Disagreements between people from different states when more than $75,000 is in dispute

Cases involving a foreign government and a state

Cases involving treaties signed by the United States

Cases involving American ships at sea

Cases involving ambassadors and other foreign representatives

Source: Administrative Office of the U.S. Courts

court of appeals is the state supreme court. Although state court systems differ, most have three levels: trial courts, appeals courts, and a court of final appeals. You will learn how state courts work in Chapter 11.

Cases Heard by Federal Courts If state courts have original jurisdiction over most legal disputes that occur in the United States, then what is the purpose of federal courts?

Federal courts hear two kinds of cases:

★ *Cases involving federal laws and issues beyond the authority of individual states.* In these cases, the federal courts have original jurisdiction. See the chart on this page for a list of these kinds of cases.
★ *Cases appealed from state supreme courts.* These cases must involve a federal law or a constitutional issue. They are heard only by the Supreme Court.

The authority to hear cases appealed from the state court systems gives the United States Supreme Court and the federal judicial branch the leadership role in our legal system. In this role, the Supreme Court sees that all 50 state court systems interpret the Constitution in the same way and that the rights of all Americans are protected.

purpose is to review the legal issues involved, to determine if the law was applied fairly and if due process of law was followed.

An appeals court may decide to affirm, or let stand, the lower court's decision. However, if it decides that the trial was unfair for some reason, it may reverse the lower court's decision. When that happens, the appeals court may order another trial, which is held in the court of original jurisdiction. When a plaintiff is declared innocent, however, the prosecution may not appeal because the Constitution prohibits double jeopardy—being tried again for the same crime after being declared innocent.

The appeals process may go beyond the first appeals court. In most states, the final

Section 1 Assessment

1. Define **plaintiff, defendant, prosecution, precedent, original jurisdiction, appeal, appellate jurisdiction**
2. What is the purpose of our legal system?
3. What two kinds of cases are heard by the federal courts?
4. Describe the levels of a typical state court system.
5. **Analyze** Explain how a court's decision about an individual case can affect our society as a whole.

The Organization of the Federal Courts

SECTION PREVIEW

Objectives
- Describe the relationship between district courts and courts of appeals.
- Explain the role of the Supreme Court.
- Recognize the roles of special federal courts.
- Summarize the responsibilities of federal judges.

 Focus

The Constitution creates the framework for the federal court system in Article III:

> The judicial power of the United States shall be vested in one Supreme Court, and in such inferior courts as the Congress may from time to time ordain and establish.

As you can see, the Constitution did not spell out how the inferior, or lower, courts would be set up. One of the first acts passed by the First Congress in 1789 was the Judiciary Act, which created the district courts and courts of appeals. Although many of the details of the Judiciary Act have since been changed, the federal court system it created is much the same more than 200 years later.

The District Courts

The workhorses of the federal court system are the 94 district courts scattered across the United States. Each state has at least one district court, and some larger states have as many as four. The number of judges in one district court ranges from 1 to 28, depending on the size of the district and its workload.

As courts of original jurisdiction, the district courts are the first to hear cases such as those involving kidnapping or a city's failure to obey federal air pollution standards.

Like a state trial court, witnesses are called, a jury normally decides the facts in the case, and one judge directs the proceedings and applies the law.

The Courts of Appeals

At the next highest level of the federal court system are the 12 United States courts of appeals, which handle appeals from the federal district courts. Each court of appeals takes cases from a group of district courts within a particular geographic area called a circuit. In fact, the courts of appeals are often called circuit courts. A thirteenth court of appeals has appellate jurisdiction over cases appealed from certain special federal courts and agencies of the executive branch. It is called the Court of Appeals for the Federal Circuit.

A court of appeals has no jury, calls no witnesses, and does not examine any evidence. Instead, lawyers for the defendant and the plaintiff or prosecution make arguments in front of a panel of three judges. The judges decide either to affirm the lower court's decision or to reverse it. Like state appeals courts, the courts of appeals are not concerned with guilt or innocence—only with whether the original trial was fair and whether the law was interpreted correctly.

The Supreme Court

The Supreme Court is the highest court in the federal court system. The major purpose of the Supreme Court is to serve as the final court of appeals for both the state and federal court systems.

The Supreme Court, however, does have original jurisdiction over a few special kinds of cases, including those involving representatives of foreign governments and disputes between state governments. The role of the Supreme Court in the legal system and in the federal government is so important that it will be discussed again in this chapter.

FEDERAL COURT CIRCUITS The 50 states are divided into 12 regional circuits.
Regions In which circuit is the state of Ohio?

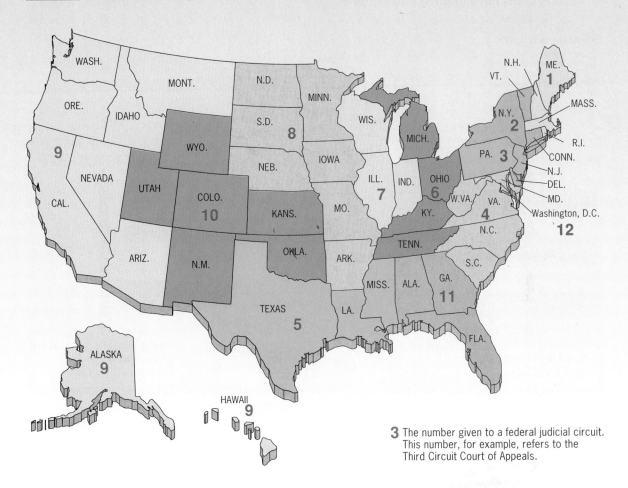

3 The number given to a federal judicial circuit. This number, for example, refers to the Third Circuit Court of Appeals.

Special Federal Courts

The chart on the next page shows additional federal courts. These special courts include the Court of Claims, the Court of Customs and Patent Appeals, and the Tax Court. Each of these courts was established by Congress for a special purpose. Appeals from some of these courts are sent directly to the Supreme Court; others must first pass through a court of appeals or a higher special court.

Federal Court Judges

Just as members of Congress do the work of the legislative branch, federal judges do the work of the judicial branch. A judge's role in government, however, is very different from that of a legislator.

A legislator is open to the influence of citizens, interest groups, other legislators, and the President. A judge, in contrast, must be impartial, favoring neither one party nor the other. A legislator seeks to solve broad problems by making laws, whereas a judge can only settle individual cases. By applying the law to specific cases, however, judges help define and clarify the work of legislators.

In part because judges' jobs are different from those of legislators, judges are selected

THE STATE AND FEDERAL COURT SYSTEMS Cases can reach the Supreme Court in several ways. **Government Over which types of cases does the Supreme Court have original jurisdiction?**

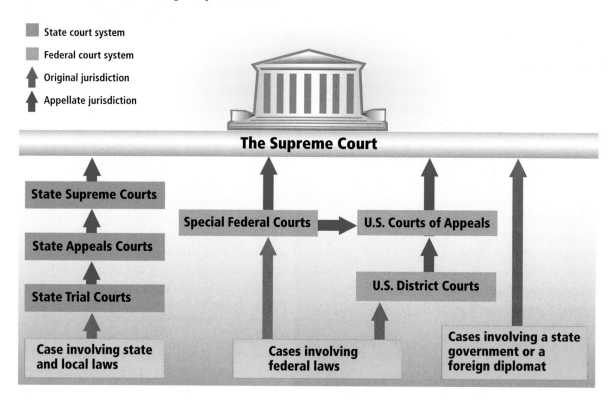

Key:
- State court system
- Federal court system
- Original jurisdiction
- Appellate jurisdiction

The Supreme Court

- State Supreme Courts
- State Appeals Courts
- State Trial Courts
- **Case involving state and local laws**

- Special Federal Courts → U.S. Courts of Appeals
- U.S. District Courts
- **Cases involving federal laws**

- **Cases involving a state government or a foreign diplomat**

in a very different way. All federal judges in the district courts, courts of appeals, and Supreme Court are appointed by the President and confirmed by the Senate. They serve life terms and can be removed from office only by the impeachment process.

Federal judges shoulder great responsibility. They must balance the rights of individuals with the interests of the nation as a whole. Often they are forced to make decisions which seem fair to one side but unfair to the other.

Of all federal judges, the nine Supreme Court justices have the most responsibility. From time to time the entire nation waits in anticipation for them to make a decision. Although they are only deciding a specific case, perhaps involving just one or two people, their decision may have very important consequences for the nation.

Section 2 Assessment

1. What kind of jurisdiction does a federal district court have? A federal court of appeals?
2. What is the major purpose of the Supreme Court?
3. Describe two major differences between a federal judge and a member of Congress.
4. **Analyze** Why are federal judges appointed instead of being elected?

The Supreme Court

Objectives

- Analyze the importance of judicial review.
- Summarize the Supreme Court's process of decision making.
- Examine the factors that can influence justices.
- Explain how and why the Court has changed throughout its history.
- Describe how the court's power is checked by the other branches of government.

Building Civics Vocabulary

- **Judicial review** is the power of the Supreme Court to overturn laws.
- **Judicial activism** is an effort by judges to play an active role in making policy.
- An effort by judges to avoid overturning laws is called **judicial restraint**.

Focus

❝*The Constitution is what the judges say it is.* **❞**

—*Chief Justice Charles Evans Hughes*

What are the rights of people accused of crimes? What kinds of punishment are "cruel and unusual"? What activities are protected by the right of free speech? When the Supreme Court is asked to decide cases that raise such constitutional questions, Americans can see the importance of the Court's role in our federal government.

Lower state and federal courts make rulings in cases that involve constitutional issues, but their rulings are not necessarily final. Only the Supreme Court has the final say about what the Constitution means and what laws it will allow. A Supreme Court decision establishes the broadest and longest-lasting kind of precedent in our legal system.

Judicial Review

One of the most important powers of the Supreme Court is judicial review, the power to overturn any law which the Court decides is in conflict with the Constitution. Judicial review gives the judicial branch final say over the validity of any law. Judicial review, however, is not spelled out in the Constitution. The Supreme Court asserted this power for itself early in its history.

As you have learned, every court of law is limited to dealing with individual cases. A court can interpret law only as it relates to the specific case it is hearing. The Supreme Court could not simply declare one day that it had the power of judicial review. It had to do so in relation to a particular case.

Marbury v. Madison In 1803, William Marbury sued James Madison, then serving as Secretary of State. Marbury demanded that Madison grant him a government job he had been promised by the previous President, John Adams. Marbury brought his case directly to the Supreme Court because the Judiciary Act of 1789 gave the Court original jurisdiction in such matters. Rather than decide whether Marbury should be given the job, the Supreme Court instead focused its attention on the law that had allowed Marbury to bring his case before the Court in the first place.

The problem, said the Court, was that Congress, in the Judiciary Act, had given the Court original jurisdiction in cases involving government officials. The Constitution, however, clearly gave the Supreme Court only appellate jurisdiction in such cases. Therefore, the Court decided, the part of the Judiciary Act that gave the Court original jurisdiction in Marbury's case was unconstitutional.

Chief Justice John Marshall wrote the Court's opinion on this decision. He argued that because the Supreme Court had a sworn duty to uphold the Constitution, it also had a responsibility to declare unconstitutional any law that violated the Constitution.

The Court's decision in *Marbury* v. *Madison* established a precedent that gave the Supreme Court one of its most important powers. Judicial review was extended in later cases to cover acts of the executive branch and of the states. Since 1803, over

1,000 state and local laws and over 100 federal laws have been overturned as a result of the Supreme Court's use of judicial review.

The Justices

If the justices of the Supreme Court are to use the power of judicial review in a way that defends the Constitution and promotes the common good, they must have the highest moral standards. They must also have a thorough knowledge of the law, the Constitution, and American history.

Although the Constitution lists no qualifications for the position of Supreme Court justice, the way justices are selected helps ensure that they will be qualified for the job. The President chooses a justice from among the most respected judges, lawyers, and legal scholars in the country. Then the Senate must approve the President's appointment.

Of the 108 justices who have served on the Court, all but four have been white men. Two of the exceptions are Thurgood Marshall and Clarence Thomas, African American men appointed in 1967 and 1991. The other two are Sandra Day O'Connor and Ruth Bader Ginsburg, white women appointed in 1981 and 1994. The Chief Justice earns $186,300 a year, and associate justices $178,300.

The Work of the Supreme Court

The decisions of the nine justices of the Supreme Court can affect the lives of millions of people. How do the justices make sure their decisions are carefully reasoned and fair?

Selecting Cases Each year, the Court chooses which cases to hear. By law, it must hear certain kinds of appeals from federal and state courts that involve the federal government or federal laws. It must also hear the few cases over which it has original

John Marshall, Chief Justice for 34 years, helped to shape the Supreme Court we know today. He wrote the opinion in *Marbury* v. *Madison*.

The Supreme Court justices in a recent portrait: (standing, left to right) Ruth Bader Ginsburg, David Souter, Clarence Thomas, Stephen Breyer; (sitting, left to right) Antonin Scalia, John Paul Stevens, Chief Justice William Rehnquist, Sandra Day O'Connor, Anthony Kennedy.

jurisdiction. The remainder of the cases it hears each year are chosen from among the more than 7,000 requests for appeal it receives from lower courts in both the state and federal court systems. The cases the Court chooses are generally those that raise the most important constitutional issues.

Hearing Arguments When a case is put on the Court's calendar, each side in the case submits briefs, or written arguments. The justices study the briefs and other records of the case carefully. Then attorneys for each side present oral arguments before the Court. There are strict time limits on these arguments: each attorney is given half an hour. The justices usually ask many questions of the attorneys to challenge and clarify their arguments.

Making a Decision After hearing oral arguments for a case, the Court meets in conference to discuss that case and vote on it. Only the justices are allowed to attend. The Chief Justice leads the discussion of each case, summarizing it and offering an opinion. Then each justice has an opportunity to comment. Finally, the Chief Justice calls for a vote. A simple majority decides the case, although justices may change their votes during the opinion-writing.

Writing Opinions Most Supreme Court decisions are accompanied by an opinion, a written statement explaining the reasons for the decision. A Supreme Court opinion shows exactly how the law must be applied, or how the Constitution must be interpreted in a specific situation.

The Court's opinion in a case, called the majority opinion, is written by one of the justices in the majority—the winning side of the vote. A draft of the opinion is circulated among the justices and often modified to keep the support of the other justices in the majority.

A justice who agrees with the majority opinion but has different reasons for supporting it may write a concurring opinion. A justice who does not agree with the majority's decision may write a dissenting opinion.

After all opinions have been written and finalized, the justices announce their final decision. Then copies of the opinions are distributed to news reporters.

Influences on Judicial Decision Making

What factors can influence how the justices vote when they decide a case? Like any judge, a justice is most concerned with the law and how it has been applied up to that point. The justices firmly believe that laws and the Constitution reflect the will of the people.

The justices, therefore, carefully review the laws involved in each case. They must consider all related precedents that have been established by any court. Precedent is always a factor in a justice's decision because a basic principle of the American legal system is to respect past judicial decisions. In this way we develop a consistent body of law.

The justices also try to determine the intentions of lawmakers at the time they made a particular law. For a constitutional question, for example, the justices may read historical documents such as *The Federalist* to try to determine the intent of the framers.

The issues the Court must decide—such as abortion, discrimination, and prayer in the schools—tend to be those about which people feel strongly. Although Supreme Court justices try to be impartial and to respect precedent, it can be difficult for them to put aside their personal views completely. The justices, after all, are only human.

Knowing that the personal views of Supreme Court justices can affect their decisions, Presidents will naturally try to appoint to the Court people who agree with their political views. A President hopes that if the appointee becomes a justice, he or she will favor the President's position on important issues.

A Changing Court

Throughout its history, the Supreme Court has gone through important changes in how it views its role in government and how it interprets the Constitution. These changes have been the result of shifts in public opinion and in the justices' own personal beliefs.

In Chapter 7 you read about cases that showed how the Supreme Court's decisions have changed over time. The Court's view of citizenship and voting rights, for example, has changed greatly in the past 150 years.

Since the 1950s, the Court has seemed to have had three different "personalities," each reflecting the views of the Chief Justice at the time. From 1953 to 1969, the Supreme Court was called the "Warren Court" after its Chief Justice, Earl Warren. The Warren Court was known for its active defense of the rights of people accused of crimes.

One of the Warren Court's noted decisions was in the case of *Miranda* v. *Arizona*. In this case, the Court ruled that when a person is arrested, police must inform him or her of the constitutional rights to remain silent and to have the advice of a lawyer. The decisions of the Warren Court are examples of what is called **judicial activism**, an effort by judges to take an active role in policy making by overturning laws relatively often.

From 1969 to 1986, Warren Burger was Chief Justice. The decisions of the "Burger Court" differed from those of the Warren

Facts & Quotes

The Conference Handshake

Before the justices meet to hear a case or to discuss a decision, each justice shakes hands with the other eight. This traditional practice, called the "conference handshake," was begun by Chief Justice Melville Fuller in the late 1800s. Its purpose is to remind the justices that differences of opinion do not mean that the Court cannot carry out its mission to promote "equal justice under law."

Louis Brandeis

Rarely has a Supreme Court justice been as outspoken an advocate of poor people and workers as was Justice Louis Brandeis. During his 22 years on the Supreme Court, Brandeis worked for social and economic reform, often dissenting from the majority vote to stand up for what he saw as being morally and legally correct.

Louis Dembitz Brandeis was born in 1856 in Louisville, Kentucky, the son of Jewish immigrants from what is now the Czech Republic. A brilliant student, Brandeis entered Harvard Law School when he was 18. He graduated in 1877 with the highest average in the law school's history.

With a friend, Brandeis began a successful law practice in Boston, which soon made him wealthy. However, Brandeis chose to protect the rights of the average American, often arguing cases without charging fees for his services. He supported public causes so actively that he soon became known throughout the nation as the "people's attorney."

In 1916, President Woodrow Wilson nominated Brandeis to the Supreme Court. Brandeis

became the first Jewish Supreme Court justice in the nation's history.

As a justice, Brandeis's commitment to protecting the rights of working people was reflected in his decisions on cases. Brandeis supported unions and small business, and he argued for a balance of economic power between owners and employees.

Above all, Brandeis was committed to promoting individual liberty. He believed that liberty is "the secret of happiness, and courage [is]...the secret of liberty."

Recognizing Viewpoints

What principles guided Brandeis during his years as a Supreme Court justice?

Court in that they were often characterized by judicial restraint, an effort by judges to avoid overturning laws and to leave policy-making up to the other two branches of government. The Burger Court, however, made one of the most controversial decisions of the twentieth century in the case of *Roe* v. *Wade*. In this case the Supreme Court said that no state could make a law that forbids a woman to have an abortion.

The Court today is often called the "Rehnquist Court," after Chief Justice William Rehnquist. The Rehnquist Court has made a number of important decisions limiting the federal government's authority over the states.

The Court and the Other Branches of Government

Judicial review gives the Supreme Court an important check on the power of the legislative and the executive branches. Although some people argue that appointed judges should not have what amounts to veto power over laws passed by elected legislators, nearly everyone agrees that the overall system of checks and balances prevents even the most active Court from abusing its power.

The President's Power One of the checks on the Supreme Court is the President's power to appoint justices. This extremely important power, however, can be exercised only when a justice dies or retires, creating an opening on the Court. President Carter, for example, was not able to appoint a single Supreme Court justice. President Reagan, in contrast, appointed three justices—Sandra Day O'Connor, Antonin Scalia, and Anthony Kennedy. President George H. W. Bush appointed David Souter and Clarence Thomas; President Clinton appointed Ruth Bader Ginsburg and Stephen Breyer.

The Power of Congress The Senate can check the power of both the President and the Supreme Court by refusing to confirm presidential appointments to the Supreme Court. In this way, Congress can weed out appointees who, it believes, are unsuited for the job, or who have beliefs contrary to those of the majority of Americans.

Public opinion can play an important role in the Senate's confirmation process because senators must be responsive to their constituents. Out of the 148 people who have been nominated by a President to be a Supreme Court justice, 30 have not been confirmed.

The Senate rejected Robert Bork's nomination as Supreme Court justice. He is shown during confirmation hearings in the Senate.

Occasionally, a Supreme Court appointee becomes the focus of a political battle between the other two branches of government. Such a battle occurred in 1987 when President Reagan appointed Robert Bork. After four months of hearings, the Senate refused to confirm Bork. His opponents convinced many Americans and a majority of senators that his views were outside of the mainstream.

In 1991 Clarence Thomas, appointed by President George H. W. Bush, also faced intense questioning by the Senate Judiciary Committee. Thomas, however, was confirmed in a close vote.

Another important way that Congress can check the power of the Court is to begin the process that could result in a constitutional amendment. If ratified by the states, an amendment proposed by Congress can nullify, or cancel out, a Supreme Court decision. When the Fourteenth Amendment was ratified in 1868, for example, it nullified the Supreme Court's decision in the Dred Scott case.

Citizen Participation Because of the system of checks and balances, no branch of government has final, or ultimate, power over another. Citizens, therefore, always have at least one avenue through which they can try to influence policies. If the Supreme Court, for example, makes a decision that goes against the wishes of a majority of Americans, citizens can always turn to Congress and the amendment process, or they can elect a President who promises to appoint justices whose ideas they like. If citizens wish to make such changes happen, however, they must do more than hold a view—they must participate in government.

Section 3 Assessment

1. **Define** judicial review, judicial activism, judicial restraint
2. How did the case *Marbury* v. *Madison* allow the Supreme Court to assert the power of judicial review?
3. When will a justice write a dissenting opinion?
4. For what was the Warren Court known?
5. What two checks does Congress have on the Supreme Court?
6. **Synthesize** Why is the Supreme Court called the "highest court in the land"?

Extending the Chapter

Global Views

The government of every nation in the world makes use of some kind of judicial system to apply and interpret its laws. Not every nation, however, has given its highest national court the kind of power exercised by the Supreme Court of the United States.

One hundred and fifty years ago, the Supreme Court was the only court of its kind in the world. It was then that the French writer Alexis de Tocqueville traveled to the United States to observe how our government worked. Later he wrote about the Supreme Court he had studied in America:

I am not aware that any nation of the globe has heretofore [up to now] organized a judicial power in the same manner as the

Americans...A more imposing judicial power was never constituted by any people.

Since de Tocqueville's time, many nations have used our Supreme Court as a model for creating their own national high court. Today, a number of nations, including Japan and Australia, have high courts with the power of judicial review—the authority to overturn laws made by legislatures.

In the remainder of the world's countries, in contrast, the final authority for deciding the validity of laws belongs to the legislature that creates the laws. This is true in Great Britain and many of the world's other democracies. Courts in these countries apply the laws and interpret them, but they cannot declare a law invalid.

Jerry Gault and Juvenile Rights

On June 15, 1964, fifteen-year-old Gerald Gault, called Jerry, was sentenced to six years of confinement in the Arizona Industrial School for juvenile delinquents. If Jerry had been over eighteen, his punishment would have been no greater than a fifty dollar fine or two months in jail.

Jerry's experience with the legal system had begun earlier that month. Jerry's neighbor, Mrs. Cook, reported to the police that Jerry and a friend had made "lewd and indecent" remarks to her over the telephone. Jerry was arrested, and after two hearings a juvenile court judge decided that Jerry had violated an Arizona law. The law prohibited anyone from using "vulgar, abusive, or obscene language" in the hearing of a woman or a child.

Neither Jerry nor his parents, however, had received official notice of the two hearings at which Jerry's guilt and punishment were determined. Mrs. Cook was not present at either hearing and was never questioned. Jerry confessed at his hearings that he was involved in the incident, but no lawyer was present to plead Jerry's case before the judge.

Mr. and Mrs. Gault filed a petition with the Arizona State Supreme Court asking that Jerry be released. They argued that their son had been denied the due process

> ### Mrs. Cook was not present at either hearing and was never questioned about the incident.

of law guaranteed by the Constitution. Jerry had not been told of his right to remain silent, said the Gaults, nor had he been properly informed of the charges against him. He was also denied both the right to question the person who accused him and the right to have the help of a lawyer.

The Arizona Supreme Court, however, denied the Gaults' request for Jerry's release. The court believed that ever since special courts for juveniles were estab-lished, "wide differences have been tolerated—indeed insisted upon—between the...rights [given] to adults and those of juveniles."

What the court was referring to was an established policy of treating juveniles in the criminal justice system differently from adults. This policy had developed out of a concern in the late 1800s that youths were being given long prison terms and mixed in jails with hardened adult criminals. Legal reformers had called for special juvenile courts and procedures to protect youngsters from such treatment. Concluding that the existence of a special juvenile justice system allowed youths to be treated differently, the court ruled that Jerry had not been denied his constitutional rights to due process.

Still convinced that their son had been treated unfairly, the Gaults appealed the Arizona court's decision to the United States Supreme Court. After reviewing the record, the Supreme Court reversed the Arizona court's decision. It said that Jerry had indeed been deprived of his constitutional rights in the juvenile court hearings. The Court stated that "neither man nor child can be allowed to stand condemned by methods that flout [ignore] constitutional requirements of due process."

The Court first of all rejected the state court's decision that proper notice, as required by the Sixth Amendment, had been given to the Gaults. The Court declared that due process "does not allow a hearing to be held in which a youth's freedom and his parents' right to custody are at stake" without official notice of all charges being given in advance.

The Court also concluded that Jerry had been deprived of his Fifth Amendment right to remain silent when questioned by authorities. The Court said that "it would indeed be surprising if the privilege against self-incrimination were available to hardened criminals but not to children." Because Jerry had not been informed of this right to remain silent, any confession he may have made could not be used as evidence against him, said the Court.

> ## "neither man nor child can be allowed to stand condemned by methods that flout [ignore] constitutional requirements of due process."

In addition, the Court ruled that Jerry had been denied his Sixth Amendment right to face and cross-examine all witnesses. In this case, Mrs. Cook, who had made the accusations, was not even present at either of Jerry's hearings in juvenile court. Due process, said the Court, requires that the right to cross-examine be given to juveniles as well as to adults.

Finally, the Supreme Court ruled that Jerry had been deprived of his Sixth Amendment right to have a lawyer assist him in his defense. The Court concluded that where freedom is in question, "the child requires the guiding hand of counsel at every step of the proceedings against him."

Analyzing the Case

1. According to the Supreme Court decision, which due process rights was Jerry denied?
2. Which two lower courts had their decisions reversed by the decision of the United States Supreme Court?
3. In your opinion, if Jerry had been given all of his due process rights but still had been found guilty of violating the law, should he have been given a six-year sentence? In general, do you think juveniles should be treated differently from adults?

How to ANALYZE NEWSPAPER EDITORIALS

As you learned in this chapter, the Supreme Court often hears cases about controversial issues. When such a case is before the Court, newspaper editors often print editorials about the case. In editorials, newspaper editors express their opinion on issues in the news.

Explain the Skill

On this page, you will read parts of two editorials, one from *The Los Angeles Times* and one from *The New York Times*. Both editorials deal with a series of 1999 Supreme Court cases in which the Court was asked to interpret the Americans with Disabilities Act (ADA). Though the cases were complex, the question before the Court was straightforward: Should people with treatable conditions such as high blood pressure be considered "disabled" and thus be entitled to special protection under the law?

Analyze the Skill

The Los Angeles Times printed an editorial on this issue on April 26, 1999.

> The Americans with Disabilities Act has made streets, offices, mass transportation and most public and private facilities accessible to countless numbers of people in wheelchairs....Now, the U.S. Supreme Court, in a series of cases slated for argument in the next two weeks, is invited to broaden the definition of "disabilities" to include common treatable impairments suffered by tens of millions, among them nearsightedness and high blood pressure. The court should decline the invitation....
>
> A part of the nation's civil rights legislation, the ADA was conceived as a weapon against prejudice and discrimination. It was not designed to create remedies for aggrieved [offended] employees or allow every form of common impairment to be treated as a protected disability. Going beyond the legislation's goal would serve nobody.

On April 20, the editors of *The New York Times* expressed their opinion on this issue.

> Nearly a decade after it was enthusiastically signed into law by President George H. W. Bush, the Americans with Disabilities Act faces a major review by the Supreme Court. Over the next two weeks, the justices are to hear four cases that will help define the true dimensions of the law. The Court's role should be to reaffirm the nation's commitment to fair treatment of people with some kind of physical or mental impairment....
>
> It may seem absurd to find that nearsightedness and hypertension [high blood pressure] are "disabilities" entitled to anti-discrimination protection. But the legislation calls for an expansive [broad] interpretation, and for a very good reason. What would be truly unfair would be for the Court to rule that people with corrected impairments are too disabled to hold a particular job but not disabled enough to bring suit under the Disabilities Act to show that they were improperly rejected.

Skill Assessment

1. Summarize the opinion presented in *The Los Angeles Times* editorial.
2. Summarize the opinion presented in *The New York Times* editorial.
3. How do the arguments presented in these editorials differ? Which do you agree with, and why?

CHAPTER 10 ASSESSMENT

Building Civics Vocabulary

The vocabulary terms in each pair listed below are related to each other. For each pair, explain how the two terms are related.

Example: The *plaintiff* and the *prosecution* both bring cases to court—the plaintiff to civil court and the prosecution to criminal court.

1. *original jurisdiction* and *appellate jurisdiction*
2. *plaintiff* and *defendant*
3. *prosecution* and *defendant*
4. *precedent* and *judicial restraint*

Reviewing Main Ideas and Skills

5. How are the state and federal court systems connected?
6. Describe the job of an appeals court.
7. Explain the power of judicial review. In which Supreme Court case was it established as a precedent?
8. What check does the President have on the power of the Supreme Court? What check does Congress have on the power of the Court?
9. **How to Analyze Newspaper Editorials** Select an editorial from your local newspaper. Summarize the issue being discussed and the opinion of the newspaper editors. State whether you agree or disagree with the editorial and give your reasons.

Critical Thinking

10. **Analyzing Ideas** What advantages would there be to electing Supreme Court justices instead of having Presidents appoint them? What would the disadvantages be?

11. **Linking Past and Present** Think about the Supreme Court cases discussed in this chapter and in previous chapters. Select one and describe how it impacts life in the United States today.

Writing About Civics

12. **Writing an Essay** Write a short essay describing the difference between judicial activism and judicial restraint. If you were a Supreme Court justice, which of these philosophies would you follow? Why?

Citizenship Activities

13. **Working in Groups** Working in groups of two or three, research a law that was declared unconstitutional by the Supreme Court. Good sources include the Internet, encyclopedias, and books on the Court. Prepare a presentation. Tell your classmates what the law was and why the Court declared it unconstitutional.

 Take It to the NET

Access the **Civics: Participating in Government** Internet site at **www.phschool.com** for the specific URLs to complete the activity.

Select a Supreme Court justice to research. Write a short biography of the justice you have selected. Share your biography with your classmates, then organize a class discussion comparing the justices' backgrounds and viewpoints.

A Congresswoman and Her Constituents

Representative Constance A. Morella, a Republican from Maryland, was elected to the House of Representatives in 1986. Her congressional district includes the Maryland suburbs of Washington, D.C. Morella taught college students for fifteen years, and proposed legislation to give students college scholarships in exchange for service in the Peace Corps. In addition to her interest in education, she has focused on such issues as technology around the world and benefits for federal workers.

Before you read the selection, find the meaning of this word in a dictionary: constituent.

I feel very fortunate to represent the very diverse eighth district of Maryland. The 654,000 people in my congressional district reflect a wide range of interests, with concerns that span every issue affected by the federal government....

Every member of Congress has at least two offices and two personal residences—one in the Washington, D.C., area and one in his or her congressional district. Most members of Congress use Fridays and the weekends to fly back to their home districts and meet with constituents....

Because I live only a half hour away from the Capitol, I drive back to my own district every evening. Every day, I try to participate in community functions, attend breakfast meetings, and meet those who visit my office....

Between my two offices, I receive several hundred letters and almost 1,000 phone calls a week—about twice the number of other representatives. I take my phone messages and mail very seriously. Unlike vague data from polls, personal and written contact gives me direct, reliable information on my constituents' opinions. Every piece of correspondence is answered in either Washington or the district office....

When I ran for Congress in 1986,...I found that getting

elected is difficult, but that the true challenge is doing the very best job possible of representing constituents....

I hope each of you will register to vote when you turn eighteen and then exercise that right regularly. I also expect many of you to consider running for office, either on local, state, or federal levels. Who knows, maybe someday you will be a member of Congress. It's the greatest honor any citizen could have.

Source: Perspectives: Readings on Contemporary American Government *(Alexandria, Va.: Close Up Foundation, 1993), pages 56–58.*

Analyzing Primary Sources

1. In what ways does Representative Morella keep in touch with her constituents?

2. In Representative Morella's opinion, what are some things citizens can do to be active politically?

UNIT 3 ASSESSMENT

Reviewing Main Ideas

1. The following are events in the life of a law. Write them in the correct time order.
   (a) The President signs the bill into law.
   (b) The citizen appeals the court decision to a federal court of appeals.
   (c) Both houses of Congress pass the bill.
   (d) A senator writes the proposed law as a bill.
   (e) The President proposes the law.
   (f) A federal district court finds a citizen guilty of violating the law.
   (g) The President gives an executive department authority to enforce the law.

2. For each of the following events, tell which branches of the federal government play an *active* role.
   (a) A Supreme Court justice is appointed and confirmed.
   (b) A law is declared unconstitutional.
   (c) A treaty is signed and approved.
   (d) War has not been declared, but troops are sent to a foreign country for two weeks.

3. Choose two of the three branches of the federal government. Describe the checks each branch has on the power of the other. What is the importance of each of these checks?

Summarizing the Unit

The tree map below will help you organize the main ideas of Unit 3. Copy it onto a separate sheet of paper. Review the unit and complete the tree map by naming the leader of each branch of government (the first one is done for you) and listing some of the powers granted to each branch. Then write a short essay describing why the framers chose to divide power between three branches of government.

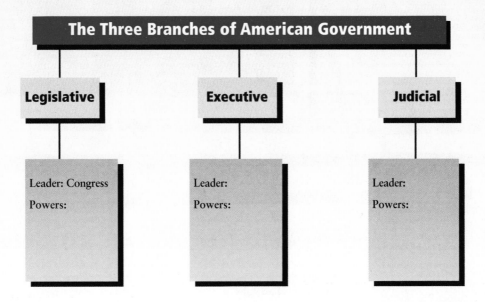

The Three Branches of American Government

Legislative	Executive	Judicial
Leader: Congress Powers:	Leader: Powers:	Leader: Powers:

TOWN OFFICES

State and Local Government

Why Study Civics?

The Powers not delegated to the United States by the Constitution, nor prohibited by it to the states, are reserved to the states respectively, or to the people.

—**Tenth Amendment to the United States Constitution**

The three branches of the federal government make and carry out many of the policies that affect you as a citizen. However, the federal government is only one level of government that responds to the needs of Americans. On another level, each of the 50 states has its own government. The states have also set up over 83,000 local governments. All three levels of government—federal, state, and local—share the costs and responsibilities for the many programs and services they provide for their citizens.

What's Ahead in Unit 4

In Unit 4 you will learn about how state and local governments are organized and what powers they have. You will also see that they offer you many opportunities to participate directly in the process of government.

Chapter 11 State Government
Chapter 12 Local Government

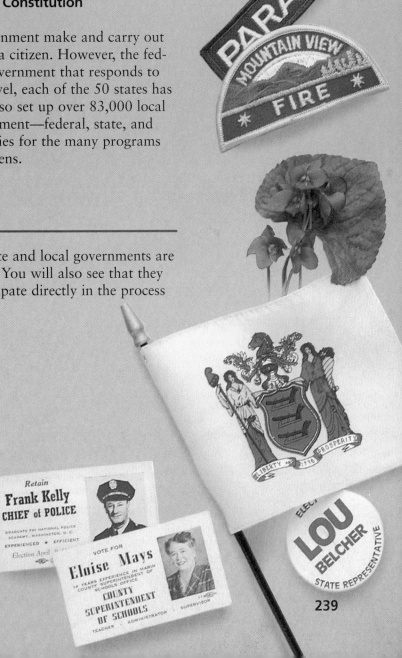

239

State Government

Citizenship and You

New Jersey is the most densely populated state in the nation. Each year, thousands of acres of the state's farmland and forests are replaced with development and suburban sprawl. Determined to preserve a significant amount of their state's remaining natural areas, environmental groups, farmers, local politicians, and students joined together in an effort to convince the state government to protect New Jersey's land.

The government responded. In July 1998, the New Jersey Legislature agreed to place an ambitious conservation plan on the ballot. In the next election, voters would be given the chance to approve the plan, which would use state money to buy and preserve up to 1 million acres of undeveloped land across the state. In November 1998, New Jersey voters approved the preservation plan by a 2 to 1 margin.

"This is really a legacy for the people of New Jersey," said New Jersey Governor Christine Todd Whitman. "Next time you fish or play baseball or pick pumpkins, pat yourselves on the back and say, this is the importance of voting."

 Keep It Current

Items marked with this logo are periodically updated on the Internet. To keep up-to-date, go to www.phschool.com

What's Ahead in Chapter 11

In this chapter you will learn about state governments, their powers, and how they are organized. You will discover that you can make a difference in the politics that affect your every day life.

Section 1   **Federalism: One Nation and Fifty States**

Section 2   **State Legislatures**

Section 3   **The State Executive Branch**

Section 4   **State Courts**

Citizen's Journal

Think about the effort made by people in New Jersey to preserve their state's undeveloped land. Write a paragraph describing an action that you believe should be taken in your own state. Explain how you think this action would improve life in your state.

Federalism: One Nation and Fifty States

SECTION PREVIEW

Objectives

- Summarize the powers of the states.
- Compare state constitutions to the federal Constitution.
- Analyze the need for balance between national and state government.

Building Civics Vocabulary

- State governments may provide **public assistance,** or programs that give help to people in need.
- **Constitutional initiative** is a process by which citizens in some states can propose a constitutional amendment.

 **Focus**

The national government is only one level of our government. Each of the 50 states also has its own government. If your public school system had problems, would you write a letter to the President? Probably not, because most of the laws and policies that affect the public schools are made by state and local governments, not by the government in Washington, D.C.

In fact, our state governments carry out much of the work of meeting the needs of citizens. These governments have major responsibility for public education, transportation, and health and safety. How do you know which tasks and services belong to the national government and which belong to the states? The answer to this question will give you a better picture of the role of state governments.

Powers of the States

Some delegates at the Constitutional Convention of 1787 argued that only a strong national government could handle the problems facing the country. Other delegates wanted the states to keep most of the power.

In trying to bring together these points of view and "to form a more perfect union," the framers settled on the system of federalism. Federalism divides some powers between the national and state governments while allowing them to share other powers. The Constitution lists what the powers of the national government are. They include the power to declare war, make treaties with other countries, and coin money.

The Constitution does not specifically list the powers of the states. Instead, the Tenth Amendment gives to the states or to the people all powers not given to the national government or denied to the states. Powers that the states alone hold include the power to set up local governments, conduct elections, set up public school systems, and oversee businesses. The states also make laws pro-

Facts & Quotes

State Mottoes

Every state has a motto. Here are a few examples.

Alaska: North to the Future
Florida: In God We Trust
Kentucky: United We Stand, Divided We Fall
New Hampshire: Live Free or Die
Texas: Friendship
West Virginia: Montani Semper Liberi (Mountaineers Are Always Free)
Wyoming: Equal Rights

tecting the health and safety of their residents, such as traffic laws.

The national government and state governments also share many powers. They both collect taxes, borrow money, set up courts, enforce laws, and punish lawbreakers. Both levels of government may also provide public assistance, government programs that give help to people in need. Often called welfare, this help can include money for people below a certain income level, food for the hungry, and services such as health care.

State Constitutions

Before the United States Constitution was written, each state already had its own constitution. In fact, those early constitutions became models for our national Constitution.

New states joined the union under rules stated in the Northwest Ordinance of 1787. Under those rules, when a territory wants to become a state, it must prepare a constitution, setting up its own plan of government. The constitution then has to be approved by the people of the territory and by Congress. Finally, Congress votes on whether to admit the state.

In 1954, citizens of Hawaii showed their desire for statehood by signing this long petition, which they rolled up and sent to Washington.

Content and Structure The federal Constitution contains about 3,500 words. The constitution of the state of Alabama has about 220,000 words. Why this great difference? One reason is that state constitutions are more detailed. For example, the federal Constitution simply states that the legislative branch of government has the power to levy and collect taxes. In contrast, many state constitutions list what kinds of taxes may be levied and how they may be collected.

Although different in length, most state constitutions are similar in form to the United States Constitution. All state constitutions begin with a preamble, describing the purposes of the state government. Each state constitution also includes a bill of rights,

similar to the federal Bill of Rights, listing the freedoms guaranteed to all the state's citizens. However, some state constitutions offer fuller protection for individual rights and freedoms. The Illinois constitution, for example, guarantees equal rights for women.

Like our federal Constitution, all state constitutions establish legislative, executive, and judicial branches of government. The powers of these state branches are much the same as those of the national government. However, state constitutions describe these powers in great detail.

Changes Because state constitutions are so detailed, they are often less flexible than the federal Constitution. Therefore, they are more likely to be changed as conditions and needs change. The most common way to change a state constitution is by amendment, usually proposed by the state legislature.

In 18 states, citizens may initiate, or begin, change by constitutional initiative, a process in which citizens propose an amendment by gathering a required number of signatures on a petition. When enough people have signed the petition, the amendment goes to the legislature for consideration or to the voters for approval.

A state can also rewrite its constitution. Rewriting a constitution most often requires a constitutional convention, which must first be approved by the voters in some states, or by the legislature in other states. The rewritten constitution must also go to the people for a vote. Of more than 230 state constitutional conventions in our nation's history, a little more than half have resulted in new constitutions.

Federalism in Action

Some people think of federalism as being like a layer cake. In this view, "layers" of government—national and state—are seen as separate, with different powers. In action, however, federalism is more like a marble cake, with the powers mixed and overlapping.

The way the powers of national government and state governments mix and overlap is not set, but continues to change. Some

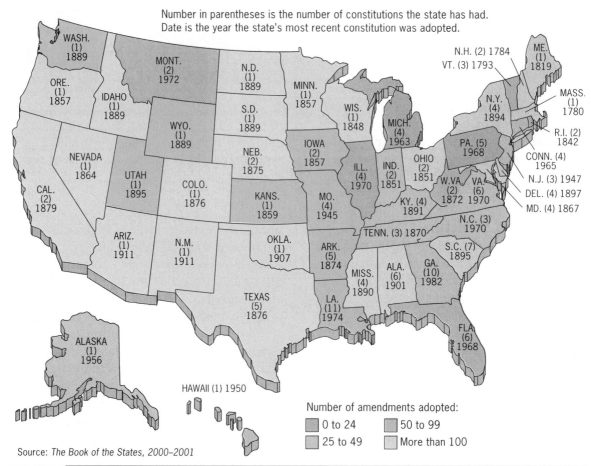

Number in parentheses is the number of constitutions the state has had.
Date is the year the state's most recent constitution was adopted.

Number of amendments adopted:
- 0 to 24
- 25 to 49
- 50 to 99
- More than 100

Source: *The Book of the States, 2000–2001*

STATE CONSTITUTIONS Unlike the United States Constitution, the constitutions of most states have been changed several times. **Regions Of the thirteen original states, which one has had only one state constitution?**

This photograph shows an example of federalism in action. When a tanker spilled millions of gallons of oil off the coast of Alaska in 1989, the state asked the federal government to help with the clean up.

people press to keep the national government out of what they see as the states' business. Others think that the national government should have greater power over the states in certain matters.

Power to the States Those in favor of states' rights point out that the states differ greatly, and therefore state governments can serve their people better than the national government can. State governments, they argue, should be allowed to fit laws and programs to the particular needs of their states. For example, states with large cities need more low-cost housing, health care, and public transportation than do states with mostly farmland.

People who favor states' rights also point out that citizens often feel closer to their state governments than to the federal government. James Madison recognized this point of view when he wrote that "the first and most natural attachment of the people will be to the governments of their respective States."

Dividing power can also make it easier for each level of government to do its job. When states take responsibility for local issues such as education, job training, and transportation, the national government can then focus its attention on its major responsibilities.

Finally, state governments can experiment with new programs which may later be adopted by other states or even by the national government. Oregon Senator Gordon Smith was asked why he felt the effort to clean up the Columbia River should be left to the state government. "Oregonians have long prided themselves on finding innovative solutions to local problems," he said. "Increasing the role of the federal government can only upset the progress being made at the local level."

Power to the National Government
Those who favor a strong role for the national government point out that state laws and services vary widely. As a result, the opportunities in different states are not always equal. In the past, as you read in Chapter 7, some states denied African Americans the right to vote and to attend school with whites.

Today some states might spend more money per student on education or offer more special programs, such as computer education, than other states. Thus, critics of states' rights argue, the national government needs to play a stronger role to ensure equal opportunity for people in all the states.

In addition, many citizens see that some problems are too big for individual states to solve. Following the terrorist attacks on the World Trade Center in New York and the Pentagon, near Washington, D.C., on September 11, 2001, everyone felt the need for better airport security. Congress debated whether the federal government should step in to take over the job of security at airports throughout the nation. Doing so represented a huge increase in the role of the federal government, which up to this point had simply set rules for private companies performing the work.

Whether it be providing airport security or building a dam to control floods, some tasks cost more than a state can afford. The state needs the help of the federal government to meet its citizens' needs. Sometimes, too, a problem involves several states. One example is in environmental issues. If one state's factories are causing pollution in another state, the national government might have to step in.

Seeking a Balance In general, the power of the national government has expanded as our nation has grown. As we begin the twenty-first century, citizens will have to continue seeking the most effective balance between national and state government. Do the problems facing our nation require the national government to take on added responsibilities? Or are there certain problems that are best handled by the states? If so, which ones? These are questions that you will have to help answer.

1. **Define** public assistance, constitutional initiative
2. Which powers do the states alone hold?
3. What current issues are examples of the "tug-of-war" for a stronger role between the national and state governments?
4. **Synthesize** Define federalism and explain why the Framers settled on this system of government for our nation.

State Legislatures

SECTION PREVIEW

Objectives
- Explain how the role of state legislatures has changed during our nation's history.
- Describe how state legislatures are organized.
- Summarize the powers of state legislatures.
- Identify ways in which citizens can influence state government.
- Explain how state governments are financed.

Building Civics Vocabulary
- Seats in state legislatures are **apportioned,** or divided among districts that are roughly equal in population.
- An **initiative** is a process by which citizens can propose laws.
- A **referendum** gives voters the chance to approve or reject a law.
- **Recall** is a process for removing elected officials from office.
- **Revenue** is income to government from taxes.
- Charges made on purchases of goods and services are **sales taxes.**
- An **excise tax** is a charge on certain goods, such as alcoholic beverages or tobacco.
- A tax on what individuals and businesses earn is an **income tax.**
- States can borrow money by selling **bonds,** which are loans. They are paid back, with interest, after a set period of time.

 Focus

Because your state legislators usually get less news coverage than members of Congress do, you might be less aware of the activities of lawmakers in your state. However, state legislators make most of the laws that affect your day-to-day life.

Indiana Governor Frank O'Bannon (seated, center) meets with Indiana state legislators at a bill signing. Serving in a state legislature can be a full-time job.

Who Are State Legislators?

For much of the first 100 years of our nation's history, the states were mostly rural, with small populations. The demands on state governments were not great. Legislators were citizens who would leave their jobs for a few weeks each year to go to legislative sessions. Most of these citizen legislators had jobs as farmers, lawyers, or business people.

Over time, however, the job of a state legislator grew more complex. The rapid growth of industries and cities led to new responsibilities for state government. As legislatures met more often and for longer sessions, citizen legislators found it difficult to balance their government duties with the demands of their jobs.

Today, many state legislators are full-time lawmakers. The typical legislator has studied political science, law, or public administration and has spent time in government service before running for office. Often state legislators plan on a life-long career in politics.

Qualifications and Terms Whether they serve full-time or part-time, state legislators have to meet certain qualifications. In most states, legislators must be United States citizens and live in the state and district they represent. Most states set the minimum age

for representatives at 21, and for senators at 25. Some states have lowered these ages to 18 and 21. In most states, senators serve four-year terms while representatives serve two-year terms.

Organization of State Legislatures

All states except Nebraska have a bicameral, or two-house, legislature with the upper house called the senate. The lower house is usually known as the house of representatives, although in some states the lower house is called the assembly, general assembly, or house of delegates.

As with Congress, the upper house of state legislatures is smaller than the lower house. However, in the lower house, the proportion of representatives to the state's population varies widely. For example, the lower house in New Hampshire has 400 members to serve a population of about 1.2 million, while California has 80 members to represent more than 33 million people.

Sessions State governments, like the national government, divide legislative terms into sessions. Most states hold annual sessions, while a few meet every other year. The majority of states limit the length of these sessions—anything from 20 days to 6 months. However, the governor may call special sessions to handle urgent business.

Representation Seats in state legislatures are apportioned, or divided among districts, on the basis of equal representation. That is, state legislators represent districts that are roughly equal in population.

Apportionment was not always determined according to equal representation. Seats in upper houses used to be apportioned on a geographical basis, like the United States Senate. Apportionment of many lower houses was also geographical. As a result, one legislator might have represented a rural district with a few hundred people, while another represented all the people in a large city.

The United States Supreme Court set up the present system of apportionment in the case of *Reynolds* v. *Sims* (1964). Pointing out that legislators should "represent people, not trees or acres," the Court ruled that the apportionment of both houses of state legislatures must be based on population. Today, most states reapportion seats in their legislatures every ten years, based on the results of the United States census.

Making Laws

The major job of a state legislature is to make laws. By and large, the process is the same as in Congress. Bills are introduced, discussed in committees, and debated on the floor. Both houses must agree on the final bill, which the governor must then approve.

Powers of the People A major difference between lawmaking in Congress and in state legislatures is that in some states citizens have a greater voice in the laws that are made. At the turn of the century, reformers known as "progressives" saw that powerful interest groups were having too much influence over state legislatures. The progressives wanted to "return the government to the people."

One of the progressives' ideas for giving lawmaking power to citizens is called the initiative, the process by which citizens can propose laws. In this process, which is similar to the constitutional initiative, citizens gather signatures on a petition. When enough people have signed the petition (usually 5 to 10 percent of the registered voters), the proposed law is put to a vote in a statewide election. If a majority of the voters approve the proposal, it becomes state law. The initiative is now permitted in 24 states.

Another way that citizens in some states participate in lawmaking is the referendum, the process by which a law proposed or passed by the state legislature is referred to the voters to approve or reject. Almost every state requires a referendum on constitutional amendments proposed by the legislature.

Both the initiative and referendum are ways that citizens can take lawmaking into their own hands. If enough people believe that a certain law is needed, or that a bad law should be removed, they can use the initiative or referendum.

Citizens in a number of states also have the power of recall, a process for removing elected officials from office. A recall effort is usually begun by a group of citizens who believe that an official is not doing a good job. They may think the official is dishonest, or they may simply disagree with his or her policies.

Citizens begin a recall by gathering voters' signatures on a petition. If, in the recall election that follows, a majority of voters agree with the recall, the official must leave office. The recall, like the initiative and the referendum, is an important way that citizens can directly influence state governments.

Checking the Other Branches In keeping with the principle of checks and balances, state legislatures have the power to oversee, or to check, the activities of the executive and the judicial branches. In many states, the legislature must approve officials and judges who are appointed by the chief executive, the governor.

State legislatures also must approve the governor's budget. In this process, the legislature examines how well executive agencies—the departments, committees, boards, and offices that carry out the work of the executive branch—are doing their jobs. State legislators also review how federal funds are spent in their state.

Legislatures in most states have the power to impeach, or bring charges against, executive and judicial officers and to determine their guilt or innocence. By and large, the impeachment process in the states is much the same as the process that is followed in Congress.

Financing State Government

State governments need money to meet the needs of citizens for such services as education, highways, health care, and environmental protection. Where does the money come from?

Taxes States raise more than 50 percent of their revenue, or income, from taxes. Most of state tax revenue comes from two sources: sales taxes and income taxes.

Most states have two kinds of sales taxes, or charges made on purchases of goods and services. The general sales tax places a charge on almost all goods sold in a state. This charge usually is a percentage of the price of a product. For example, if you buy a $15 book in a state with a 6 percent sales tax, you will have to pay a tax of 6 percent of $15, or 90 cents. Therefore, you will pay a total of $15.90.

A second kind of sales tax is the excise tax, a charge on certain goods, such as alcoholic beverages, gasoline, and tobacco. Most states also have an income tax, a tax on what individuals and businesses earn.

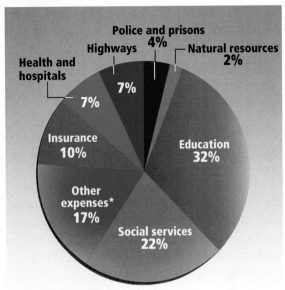

GRAPH SKILL

HOW THE STATES SPEND THEIR MONEY, 1999

- Police and prisons 4%
- Highways 7%
- Natural resources 2%
- Health and hospitals 7%
- Insurance 10%
- Other expenses* 17%
- Social services 22%
- Education 32%

*Includes administration
Note: Percentages may not add up to 100 due to rounding.
Source: U.S. Census Bureau

State spending supports a variety of important programs. **Economics To what service is the largest portion of state money dedicated?**

The income tax is a percentage of the money a person or business makes.

Other types of taxes also help states raise the money they need. For example, lumber and mining companies often must pay what is known as a severance tax on the timber, coal, gas, and oil they take from the land. All states also levy one or more of the taxes known as user fees. Charges for drivers' licenses and fees for fishing and hunting permits are examples of such fees.

States choose which taxes they wish to use. Montana, for example, has no sales tax, while Texas has no state income tax. Alaska, a state rich in natural resources, relies heavily on severance taxes.

Federal Funds Over time, state and local governments have increasingly turned to Congress for money. Federal money comes to the states in several forms. Two of the most widely used forms are categorical grants and block grants.

Categorical grants are given for specific purposes, such as a job training program or highway construction. These grants come with "strings attached"—certain conditions that must be met before the state may use the funds. In 1999, for example, many members of Congress wanted all 50 states to set a tough national standard for determining when a driver is legally drunk. To pressure the states into going along with their plan, supporters introduced bills in the House and Senate that would withhold millions of dollars of federal highway funds from states that did not adopt the tough new standard.

Block grants, on the other hand, are given for more general purposes. While a categorical grant might be for a special program such as health care for the homeless, a block grant might cover a broad area such as health care in general. The state can then decide which programs to use the block grant funds for. Many advocates of states' rights support block grants because they give governors and state legislatures more control over how money is spent in their state.

In 1996, Congress passed major welfare reform legislation, which was signed into law by President Clinton. One of the main provisions of this law was to convert the federal money sent to states for welfare programs from categorical grants to block grants. These block grants gave states more freedom to design their own welfare programs.

Other Sources of Revenue Sometimes states borrow money by selling bonds, certificates that people buy from the government. The government agrees to pay back the cost of the bond, plus interest, after a set period of time. States often use this method of raising revenue for such projects as building a school or convention center.

Some states also raise money through lotteries. About 60 percent of the money from lottery ticket sales goes toward prizes. The remaining 40 percent goes to the state, often to help pay for educational programs.

States with lotteries hope that the income they produce will fill the gap between tax revenues and the cost of state programs. However, even though you may hear about people winning multi-million-dollar prizes, lotteries have not fulfilled the states' dreams. Most states receive no more than 5 percent of their total revenue from a lottery. Further, some critics complain that any form of gambling is wrong, and the state should not encourage it. Others argue that the majority of lottery players are the people who can least afford to gamble—the poor.

Section 2 Assessment

1. **Define** apportioned, initiative, referendum, recall, revenue, sales taxes, excise tax, income tax, bonds
2. Why have citizen legislators been replaced by professional legislators in most states?
3. On what basis are seats in state legislatures apportioned?
4. Explain how the initiative and referendum allow citizens to participate in the lawmaking process.
5. Name two major sources of state revenue.
6. **Analyze** In what ways are state legislatures more directly responsive to citizens than is Congress?

The State Executive Branch

SECTION PREVIEW

Objectives

- Describe the powers of the governor.
- Compare state executive officials to the President's Cabinet.
- Explain the role of state executive agencies.

Building Civics Vocabulary

- The **item veto** gives governors the power to reject particular items, or parts, of a bill.

 **Focus**

The executive branch of state government is led by a governor and a group of executive officials. These officials help run the many agencies that enforce the laws and carry out the state's programs. Early state constitutions greatly limited the power of the governor. Over the years, however, many state constitutions have been changed in order to give the governor more power to take on the growing responsibilities of state government.

The Roles of the Governor

If the state and federal executive branches are similar, would it be correct to describe the governor as the "president of the state"? Presidents and governors do play similar roles. However, there are differences between the two offices, as well.

Chief Executive The governor's role of chief executive is similar to that of the President. He or she oversees the executive branch and makes sure laws are enforced. The governor is commander-in-chief of the

Jeanne Shaheen of New Hampshire is one of a number of women who have been elected to serve as the governors of states.

state militia, or National Guard, and can call on it in the event of a riot or disaster.

As chief executive, the governor has the power to appoint hundreds of officials to carry out the state's day-to-day work. However, as you will see, limits on governors' powers of appointment can greatly affect their ability to achieve their goals.

Perhaps the greatest source of executive power is the governor's budget-making role. Of course, the legislature must approve the governor's budget, and no state money may be spent without the legislature's approval. However, because the governor usually writes the budget, he or she still has a good deal of control over how much money various agencies get.

Legislative Leader Like the President, the governor also has legislative powers. To begin with, the governor may propose legislation in the form of a bill, a budget, or a speech to the state legislature. The governor can also influence lawmaking by talks with legislators or by whipping up public support, thus making clear what programs he or she wants lawmakers to set up and provide funds for.

Another legislative power of the governor is the veto. Further, in 43 states governors have the item veto, the power to reject particular parts, or items, of a bill. Presidents do not have this power. Congress passed the Line Item Veto Act in 1996, giving the President the item veto. Two years later, however, the Supreme Court ruled the Act unconstitutional.

A state legislature may override the governor's veto. However, the veto, or even the threat of a veto, gives the governor a good deal of power over the legislature because it usually takes more than 50 percent of the legislature to override it.

Judicial Role Like the President, a governor has certain judicial powers. For example, some state governors appoint certain state judges. The governor can also reduce or overturn the sentences of people convicted of crimes.

Qualifications and Terms In most states, a governor must be at least 25 or 30 years old, an American citizen, and a resident of the state. Terms of office are usually four years, and about half the states limit the number of terms a governor may serve in a row.

 THE DUTIES AND POWERS OF THE GOVERNOR The governor's role of chief executive is similar to that of the President. **Government** What are two ways the governor can influence the state legislature?

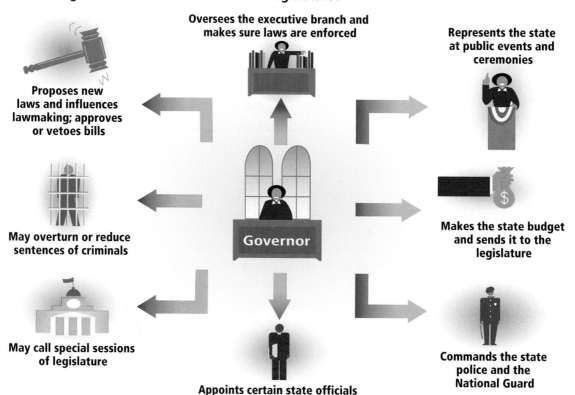

Oversees the executive branch and makes sure laws are enforced

Represents the state at public events and ceremonies

Proposes new laws and influences lawmaking; approves or vetoes bills

May overturn or reduce sentences of criminals

Makes the state budget and sends it to the legislature

May call special sessions of legislature

Governor

Commands the state police and the National Guard

Appoints certain state officials

This chart is based on the duties and powers of the governor of Texas. Other states' governors have similar duties and powers.

Tony Garza

"Before you become involved in any kind of public service, you should figure out what your personal priorities are and what is going to give you a sense of purpose in the political arena." So says Tony Garza, who has followed this advice himself during his career in local and state government.

In 1998, Garza was elected to the Railroad Commission of Texas, a state regulatory agency that oversees oil and gas, two of the state's most important natural resources. Prior to winning this election, Garza became the first Hispanic Republican to hold a statewide office in Texas when he joined then Governor George W. Bush's administration as Secretary of State in 1994. Before moving to the state capital, Garza served as a county judge and was an active

volunteer in the Brownsville community where he grew up.

"Being involved in one's community," says Garza, "is very important because government is supposed to be an extension of the community. Democracy works best when people feel a sense of community and want to participate through public service. Having a number of experiences as a volunteer on such issues as health care for the poor gave me a perspective that

is healthy to have in government. To represent people in government, it is important to have spent some time if not in their shoes then near their shoes, getting a sense of what their daily challenges are."

For students who want a career in public life, Garza has this advice. "First, get the tools. The most important tool is a good education. Second, find out what issues—environment, health care, economic development—are so important to you that you are willing to volunteer your time freely. This will give you a sense of self and help you know what is important to you."

Recognizing Viewpoints

According to Tony Garza, how can community volunteer work help prepare you for a career in government?

Other Executive Officials

A team of executive officials assists the governor. These officials include the lieutenant governor, who performs a role similar to that of the Vice President; the secretary of state, who has charge of official records and documents and supervises elections; the

attorney general, the state's chief legal officer; and the state treasurer, who oversees the state's financial affairs.

Some people have compared state executive officials to the President's Cabinet. However, Presidents can select their own Cabinet members, while many state executive officers are elected by the voters. Therefore, the governor may have to work with executive officials who do not share the same goals and may belong to a different political party.

State Executive Agencies

State executive agencies carry out the day-to-day work of the executive branch. Departments of health, revenue, and natural resources are examples of executive agencies.

To better understand what executive agencies do, take a look at one of the largest in every state—the agency in charge of education. This agency's major responsibility is to make sure that the state's education laws are carried out. One such law sets the number of school days in a year. Laws also set the subjects you have to study and how many classes you must take to graduate.

The state education agency works with local school districts to make sure that they meet these requirements. It also sets standards for teachers. The education agency makes sure that funds are being spent as the law requires.

As you have seen, keeping our states running takes many people, whether they be elected, appointed, or hired. In fact, our states employ millions of people.

Section 3 Assessment

1. **Define** item veto
2. In what ways are the roles of governor like those of President?
3. In what ways is the governor's team of executive officials unlike the President's Cabinet?
4. What is the purpose of the state executive agencies?
5. **Evaluate** Do you think governors should be allowed to appoint all other state executive officers? Why or why not?

State Courts

Objectives

- Describe the functions of the state court system.
- Compare the different methods of selecting state judges.
- Explore Supreme Court rulings on the balance between state and federal powers.

 Focus

We are all subject to two levels of law: state law and federal law. Just as federal courts interpret the United States Constitution and apply federal laws, state court systems interpret state constitutions and laws. State courts handle cases that are close to people's everyday lives, such as divorces, wills, drunk driving, robberies, and murders.

The organization of courts, and even their names, varies from state to state. The way judges are selected and the terms they serve vary, too. As you read about the state courts, keep in mind that this is a general description. As a citizen, you will want to know more about the special features of the court system in your own state.

What State Courts Do

Most state judicial systems have three levels. On the first level, the state's trial courts hear both civil cases and criminal cases. On the second level, state appeals courts review cases appealed from the trial courts. Cases that go beyond the first appeals court are heard in the state's supreme court, the highest court in the state system.

Like the federal judiciary, state courts act as a check on the two other branches of state government. For example, state courts may decide that a law passed by the state legislature violates the state constitution. Also like the federal judiciary, state courts have the duty of protecting the rights and freedoms guaranteed to each citizen by the state constitution.

Perhaps the best known tasks of the state courts involve hearing civil and criminal cases. State courts hear more than ten million cases each year. You will learn more about our civil and criminal courts in Unit 6.

Judges in State Courts

Judges are the foundation of the state court system. State court judges perform many of the same duties as federal judges. However, the way judges are selected and the lengths of their terms vary, depending on the state and on the level of court. The main differences, and the major debates, center on whether judges are elected or appointed, and whether they serve for life or for a fixed term.

Selection of Judges There are several advantages of having judges run for election. First, an elected judge is responsible to the public, whose lives and property may be directly affected by the judge's decisions. Second, election checks the power of a governor, who might want to appoint friends and supporters even if they are not well qualified to be judges.

Opponents of electing judges paint a different picture. They say that a judge must make decisions based on the law and the facts of the case, not on what might please the voters during an election campaign. Many people who hold this view believe that judges should be chosen on merit, or ability, alone, and should not have to face election.

Some states have adopted a method of choosing judges known as the Missouri Plan. Under this plan, the governor appoints a judge from a list prepared by a commission of judges, lawyers, and ordinary citizens. Then, in the next election, voters cast a

The state court systems handle heavy loads of civil and criminal cases. They also hear appeals and rule on the constitutionality of laws.

"yes" or "no" vote on whether they want the judge to stay in office.

Although the Missouri Plan does not satisfy the people who want strict merit selection, many people feel that it combines the best qualities of appointment and election. The governor is able to appoint judges from the best-qualified people, while the yes-or-no election gives the voters a voice.

Terms of Service The length of time judges spend in office depends on the state and on the level of the court. Most terms run from 4 to 15 years. In Rhode Island, though, judges have life appointments, while in some states judges serve until age 70.

Most judges may be removed by the voters at the end of their terms. State constitutions in most states also allow for judges to be impeached, and four states allow for the recall of judges. These powers, however, have rarely been used.

Most states have judicial action commissions to handle situations in which a judge might not be doing his or her job well. Such a commission looks into complaints against

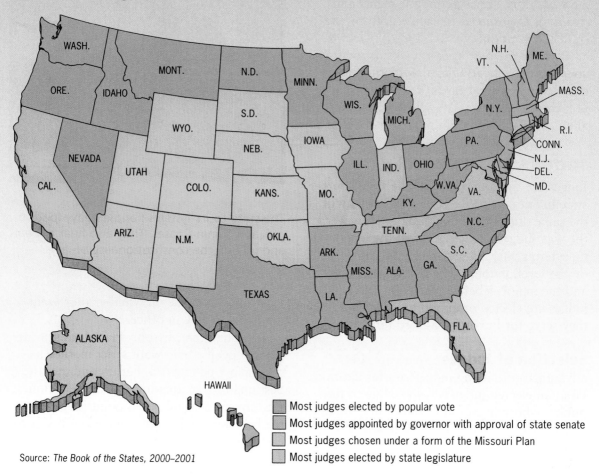

Source: *The Book of the States, 2000–2001*

■ Most judges elected by popular vote
■ Most judges appointed by governor with approval of state senate
■ Most judges chosen under a form of the Missouri Plan
■ Most judges elected by state legislature

the judge, holds hearings, reports on the judge's guilt or innocence, and decides penalties. Depending on how serious the act, a judge found guilty may face penalties ranging from a few days suspension to removal from the bench.

Case Study: Federalism and the Courts

As you may recall, some state constitutions offer greater rights and freedoms than the federal Constitution. This difference presents an interesting question about federalism. When an individual rights case comes up in

one of these states, which applies—the federal Constitution or the state constitution?

Two United States Supreme Court cases, one in Oregon and one in California, will help answer this question. In each case, the owners of a shopping mall took to court members of citizens' groups who had passed out leaflets and gathered signatures on petitions at the mall. The owners claimed that it was their right not to allow such political activity on their private property. In response, the citizens' groups stated that they were simply exercising their First Amendment rights to freedom of speech and to petition the government.

In its review of the Oregon case, the Supreme Court found that the owners of the shopping mall had a right to use their private property as they wanted. The Supreme Court, therefore, found in favor of the owners.

In the California case, *Pruneyard Shopping Center* v. *Robins*, on the other hand, the Supreme Court found for the citizens' groups. The Court pointed out that California's constitution offers greater protection of free speech than does the federal Constitution. Therefore, the decision in the Oregon case did not apply to California. Thus, the federal Constitution was applied in the Oregon case, while in California the state constitution, with its greater rights, was applied.

As you have seen in this chapter, the line between federal power and state power is not always an easy one to draw. These two court cases demonstrate the important role the judicial branch plays in deciding questions of federalism.

Section 4 Assessment

1. What is the basic structure of state court systems?
2. What is the Missouri Plan? Why was it used?
3. Why did the Supreme Court find for the citizens' group rather than the mall owners in *Pruneyard Shopping Center* v. *Robins*?
4. **Evaluate** Judges are selected in many different ways. What method of selecting judges do you support? Why?

Extending the Chapter

Global Views

Our system of federalism, although not unique, is quite unusual. A common form of government in the world is the unitary system, in which practically all political power lies with a central government.

To see how a unitary system operates, consider the government of Japan. In the area of education, for example, the Japanese national government makes most of the decisions, even deciding the subjects to be taught in school nationwide. Such an approach suits Japan. Geographically, it is a small country, and its people lack the diversity of backgrounds found in the United States.

The size of the United States and the diversity of its people would be difficult to serve with a unitary central government. A unitary government might not be able to manage all the problems now handled by the states. Therefore, the system of federalism suits our country. Federalism also gives citizens direct access to various levels of government. As a result, government can better serve individuals and the communities of which they are a part.

DECISION MAKING SKILLS

How to EVALUATE INFORMATION

Suppose you are in the following situation: You are sixteen, and your family will soon be moving to another state. You are trying to decide whether to take a driver's education class before you move. A friend says, "You might as well wait because in that state you have to be eighteen to get a driver's license." Therefore, you decide not to take the class. After you move, you find out that you made the wrong decision. The driving age in your new state is sixteen, too. You call your friend to complain: "If I hadn't listened to you, I would have been driving by now!"

To make good decisions, you need accurate, or true, information. That is why you should check the accuracy of any statements of fact before you rely on them. Remember, statements of fact are ones that can be proved either true or false.

Suppose that you are on a committee that is trying to decide how to prevent students from dropping out of school. You want to find out more about the problem. Before the first committee meeting, you read the following information in two magazine articles by educators who have done extensive research on the dropout problem:

Excerpt from Article A

High school dropouts pose a growing problem for American education. Some 3.8 million students—about 11 percent—now quit before graduation. In some urban areas the rate reaches 20 percent.

Dropouts who do manage somehow to find employment tend to work at low-paying, unskilled jobs. Many of the other teenagers who drop out turn to crime. An estimated 40 percent of prison inmates failed to complete high school.

Excerpt from Article B

According to one recently published study, it is estimated that 300,000 to 500,000 students across the nation drop out of high school each year.

Many dropouts do not realize that most states require persons under eighteen to be enrolled in school in order to get a work permit. Between October 1998 and October 1999, 276,000 teenage girls dropped out of high school. Those who found work discovered how little is available to them: low-paying, dead-end, no-room-for-growth jobs.

At the committee meeting, a school counselor makes the following statement: "A dropout has a poor chance of getting a skilled job." Your committee is trying to decide how to convince students to stay in school. The counselor's statement might help, but first you have to determine whether it is accurate. How might you check it out?

Explain the Skill

One way to check the accuracy of a statement is to follow these steps. As you read the steps, notice how they might be applied to the statement made by the counselor.

1. **Check whether the source of the statement is reliable, or trustworthy.** Is the person qualified to write or speak about the subject? Where did he or she get the information? [The counselor has experience in giving students advice on school problems and has probably done a lot of research on dropouts. You might ask the counselor what information he or she based the statement on.]

2. **Identify the general types of information that you would need in order to prove or disprove the statement.** Some types of information are statistics, descriptions, dates, names, and events. [You would look for statistics on unemployment and percentages of dropouts and graduates who hold skilled and unskilled jobs.]

3. **Identify reliable sources where these types of information might be found.** Determine which sources are likely to have accurate information on the subject. Some sources are the Internet, encyclopedias, almanacs, textbooks, dictionaries, magazines or newspapers, teachers, librarians, businesspeople, and government officials. [You could refer to the two articles you read, other articles or books, and businesspeople, who might have statistics on who is hired for skilled jobs.]

4. **Check two or more reliable sources to find information that either proves or disproves the statement.** Your final step is to look for specific information that either supports or disagrees with the statement. If two or more reliable sources support or agree with the statement, it is probably

accurate. [Articles A and B agree with the counselor's statement. Article B provides job statistics on teenage girls. You would still want to look for additional statistics, but the statement appears to be accurate.]

Analyze the Skill

Suppose that you are gathering information to convince students not to drop out. Using the excerpts from articles A and B, tell how accurate each of the following statements is.

A. Most dropouts return to earn a diploma by attending night classes.
(Source: a school principal)

B. Twenty-five percent of your classmates will drop out of school before graduation.
(Source: a television documentary)

C. Dropouts are not allowed to work until they are eighteen.
(Source: a dropout who was denied a job)

Skill Assessment

After determining whether each statement is accurate, answer the following questions.

1. For each statement, tell whether you think its source is likely to be reliable. Explain.
2. To what extent does each statement seem to be supported by excerpts A and B? Explain.
3. For each statement, explain what information you would need to prove or disprove it.
4. In addition to excerpts A and B, what sources would you use to check the accuracy of the statements? Explain why.
5. Why is it important to check whether your information is accurate?

How to ANALYZE NEWSPAPER ARTICLES

B4   THE REGION

Lawmakers OK Open-Space Plan

TRENTON—Legislation that could preserve up to 1 million acres of open space and farmland in New Jersey received final legislative approval late Thursday, ending several months of debate that pitted urban against rural lawmakers.

Governor Whitman, who proposed the

In the opening to this chapter, you read about the effort in New Jersey to preserve natural areas. Above is the beginning of a newspaper article on this issue which appeared in *The Record*, a local newspaper in northern New Jersey. Many Americans depend on local newspapers to keep them informed about their state government.

Explain the Skill

News stories follow a pattern. A headline tells what the story is about. The dateline shows where it was written—Trenton, New Jersey, in the case of the article above. If a story was not written by the newspaper's own reporters, the source appears on or above the dateline, or at the end of the article. The source might be a news-gathering agency such as the Associated Press (AP) or another newspaper.

The lead paragraph, or first paragraph of an article, summarizes the main facts of the story. The body, or remainder of the article, includes the rest of the details, as well as quotes from people involved with the issues being discussed. Good newspaper articles answer the basic questions Who? What? When? Where? Why? and How?

Analyze the Skill

Below is the beginning of an article from the *Herald-Times*, a local newspaper in Bloomington, Indiana. Gather as much information as you can from this article's headline, dateline, and lead paragraph.

B4   THE REGION

High Court Upholds Seat-Belt Law

Police warned they must have probable cause to stop motorists

INDIANAPOLIS (AP)—The Indiana Supreme Court ruled Tuesday that the state's new seat-belt law is constitutional, but emphasized that police may not stop motorists to enforce it unless they have reasonable suspicion that someone is not buckled up.

Skill Assessment

1. According to the headline, what is this article about?
2. Where was the article written?
3. What is the source of the article?
4. Summarize the information presented in the lead paragraph of the article.

CHAPTER 11 ASSESSMENT

Building Civics Vocabulary

The vocabulary terms in each pair listed below are related to each other. For each pair, explain how the two terms are related.

Example: *Amendment* is related to *constitutional initiative* because the constitutional initiative is a process by which citizens propose amendments to state constitutions.

1. *constitutional initiative* and *recall*
2. *initiative* and *referendum*
3. *revenue* and *sales taxes*

Reviewing Main Ideas and Skills

4. How do state constitutions differ from the federal Constitution?

5. How has the role of state legislator changed over the years?

6. What was the importance of the Supreme Court decision in *Reynolds* v. *Sims*?

7. What are some powers state legislatures have over the executive and judicial branches of state government?

8. What are some ways in which a governor can influence lawmaking?

9. Give the main arguments for and against each of the following: **(a)** Election of judges **(b)** Appointment of judges

10. **How to Evaluate Information** "In general, the states of the West have had fewer state constitutions than the states of the Southeast." Use the map on page 244 to determine whether or not this statement is accurate.

11. **How to Analyze Newspaper Articles** Select an article from your local newspaper. List the article's title, source (if one is given), and dateline. Summarize the content of the article.

Critical Thinking

12. **Analyzing Ideas** How can the case of *Pruneyard Shopping Center* v. *Robins* be seen as a case involving ideas of federalism?

13. **Defending a Position** "State governments can serve their people better than the national government can." Do you agree or disagree? Explain your answer.

Writing About Civics

14. **Writing an Article** Suppose you are a reporter for your local newspaper. Write a one-page article on a local issue. Include a headline and dateline with your article. Include the article in your portfolio.

Citizenship Activities

15. **Civic Participation** Write a letter to your governor. Ask him or her a question about an issue or problem that is important to your state. State your own opinion on this issue or problem. Share the reply you receive with the rest of the class.

 Take It to the NET

Access the **Civics: Participating in Government** Internet site at **www.phschool.com** for the specific URLs to complete the activity.

Use online resources to explore ten issues facing your state government. Rank them in order of how important you feel they are to your state and your neighboring states. Prepare to give your opinion on how each issue could be successfully resolved.

CHAPTER 12

Local Government

Citizenship and You

"No one has the right to force you to breathe smoke," says a Denver, Colorado resident. The city government backs up these words with laws banning cigarette smoking in many public places.

While hundreds of local governments across the nation have passed anti-smoking laws similar to Denver's, not everyone views anti-smoking laws in the same way. A citizen in North Carolina says, "We don't need to make a bunch of rules as to what people do with their private lives."

As these examples show, communities can be torn between respecting a person's right to smoke and protecting public health. Whatever their beliefs are on this issue, however, most local officials agree that laws about smoking should be set by local governments. Governments at this level have the best idea of what their citizens want. In fact, local governments were first formed to meet people's everyday needs—from fire fighting to garbage collection.

Keep It Current

Items marked with this logo are periodically updated on the Internet. To keep up-to-date, go to **www.phschool.com**

What's Ahead in Chapter 12

In this chapter, you will take a look at different kinds of local government. You will find out what they do and how they work with each other and with the state and federal governments for the good of our communities.

Section 1 **Types of Local Government**

Section 2 **Local Government Services and Revenue**

Section 3 **Conflict and Cooperation Between Governments**

Citizen's Journal

What do you think about the debate over anti-smoking laws? Do people have the right to smoke in public? Or is protecting non-smokers from second-hand cigarette smoke more important than an individual's right to smoke? Write a paragraph explaining your opinion on how local governments should deal with this issue.

Types of Local Government

Objectives

- Explore the origin and purpose of counties and townships.
- Describe the role of citizens in running a New England town.
- Explain why special districts are created.
- Contrast the mayor-council and council-manager plans of city government.

Building Civics Vocabulary

- A **board** is a group of people who manage the business of an organization.
- **Ordinances** are local laws.
- A government that serves the people of an urban area is called a **municipality**.

 **Focus**

You already know that the Constitution gives powers to the federal and state governments. What you may not know, though, is that it does not give any power to local governments, such as counties, cities, and towns. Local governments are created by the states and have only those powers that state governments give them. The powers that state governments give to local governments help meet the many needs of thousands of communities throughout the nation.

Nearly every day you see people who work for local governments—teachers, librarians, bus drivers, police officers, and others. Your daily life runs on the services of local governments, such as garbage collection, road repair, and water supply. Perhaps your family takes part in local government by voting in local elections or serving on committees. Local government is the level that is closest to you. It has the greatest effect on your everyday life.

Counties and Townships

Our oldest unit of local government is the county. Rooted in England, the county form of government came to North America with the English colonists. Colonies were divided into counties to carry out laws in rural areas. Because farmers lived far apart, county business was done at a place most people could reach within a day's wagon journey. This distance to the "county seat" set the boundaries of many counties.

Today, most counties help state governments keep law and order and collect taxes. Counties may also offer many other services, from libraries to health care.

County Officials Most counties are governed by county boards. A board is a group of people who manage the business of an organization. Most county boards, which are also called commissions, have three to five elected members, called commissioners or supervisors. Board members set up county programs and pass ordinances, which are local laws. The county board shares its power with other boards, which run hospitals, libraries, and other special programs.

Perhaps the best-known elected county official is the sheriff. The office of sheriff has its roots in England, just like the county form of government itself. The sheriff, with the help of deputies, runs the county jail and makes sure people obey the law. Sheriffs often work in rural areas not covered by city or state police. Other county officials may include the assessor, who figures property values; the treasurer, who sends the property tax bill; and the county clerk, who keeps official records such as marriage certificates.

Townships In the Middle Atlantic states and in the Midwest, counties are often

Although the existence of different levels of government—local, state, national—may seem confusing to some, each level has its own responsibilities and functions.

divided into townships. At first, townships were needed to help carry out duties such as setting up schools and repairing roads in rural areas far from the county seat. Over the years, though, cities have grown larger and transportation has improved, so most of these duties have been taken over by county and city governments. In many urban areas, townships just elect representatives to serve on the county board.

New England Towns

In New England, another form of rural government grew up—the town. When people from other countries came to the New England colonies, they were given land. Groups of settlers started a town by building villages with homes, a church, and a school. They also planted crops in the nearby farm-lands. The town was made up of both the village and the farmlands.

Citizens took an active part in local government in the early New England towns. The voters met once a year at town meetings to pass laws, set taxes, and decide how the money should be spent. This kind of town meeting still takes place today in some small New England towns. It is the closest thing we have to direct democracy.

At the yearly town meeting in a New England town, citizens elect a board of three to five members. The board carries on town business during the year. Other officials, such as the school board members, the town clerk, the assessor, and the treasurer, are chosen by the town board or elected by the voters. As you can see, towns in New England have most of the duties that counties have in other regions.

Like townships, New England towns have changed over the years. Because some towns have become large, it is not easy for all the citizens to gather together to decide things. Therefore, in many large towns the voters choose representatives to attend town meetings. Some towns have hired managers to take care of the town's business.

Special Districts

Sometimes it does not make sense for a community to handle certain matters alone. For example, it would not make sense for each community in a dry region to build its own water supply system. It would be too much work and cost too much money. In such a case, all the communities in the region ask the state to make a special water district to supply water to the whole region.

Running a large city poses very different challenges to local government leaders than does meeting the needs of a small town.

A special district is a unit of government that generally provides a single service. It can serve one community or cover parts or all of several communities. Special districts serve many needs. In cities, they provide subways and parks. Rural special districts protect people from fires or control insects. Most such districts are run by a board. One special district that you know about is your school district.

Cities

A government that serves people who live in an urban area is called a municipality. Most municipalities, especially those that serve large populations, are called cities. In some states, municipalities that serve small populations are called towns or villages.

As the population of the United States has grown, so also have the sizes of our cities. Today a mid-sized American city has between 25,000 and 250,000 citizens. Several cities have millions of people. Governments of large cities must meet many different needs, including services not heard of in earlier times, such as pollution control and drug abuse programs.

The boundaries and powers of a municipality—which can be a city, town, or village—are set by the state. Some communities write charters, or plans of government, that must be approved by the state. In other communities, the plan of government is set by state laws. No matter how they are formed, the governments of most municipalities follow one of three plans: mayor-council, council-manager, or commission.

The Mayor-Council Plan Like so much else in local government, the mayor-council plan comes from England. The mayor, like the English prime minister or the American President, is the executive. The council, like the English Parliament or the American Congress, is the legislative branch. About 35 percent of the cities in the United States use the mayor-council plan. Under this plan, the duties and powers of city officials depend on whether the city uses a weak-mayor plan or a strong-mayor plan.

Under the weak-mayor plan, the mayor does not have special executive powers. In fact, most of the power rests with the council. The council is elected by the people and acts as both a legislative and executive body. The council can choose the mayor from among its members. The council also chooses other officials, makes ordinances, and decides how money should be spent.

The weak-mayor plan dates back to the colonies. The early settlers did not trust the English government. When they formed their own city governments, they did not want to give too much power to one person.

During the first century of our nation's history, most cities used the weak-mayor plan. As cities grew in size, however, stronger leadership was needed in city hall. By the late 1800s, most large cities had switched to a strong-mayor plan. In this plan, the relationship between the mayor and the council is more like that between the President and Congress. The council makes ordinances, but the mayor is elected by the voters and is in charge of the budget, makes policies, and chooses city officials.

The Council-Manager Plan By the early 1900s, many cities were in the grasp of political groups called "machines." City officials did favors for the machine, such as giving jobs to politicians and friends. In return, the machine helped the officials get elected again. This arrangement often led to corruption. Officials looked after their own interests instead of looking after the interests of the public.

In an effort to create honest government, some people came up with the council-manager plan. The goal of this plan is to run government like a business.

In the council-manager plan, the council is chosen through an election in which candidates have no political ties. The council makes ordinances and hires a city manager to handle day-to-day city business. It is the manager, not the mayor, who prepares the budget and is in charge of people who work

 MAYOR-COUNCIL PLANS Mayors have different powers under different types of local government. **Government** Under the strong-mayor plan, how are the department heads chosen?

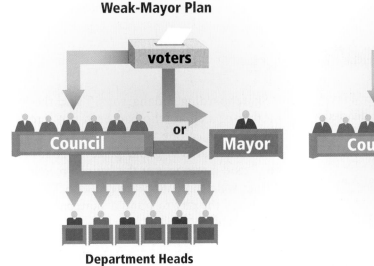

Weak-Mayor Plan

voters

Council or Mayor

Department Heads

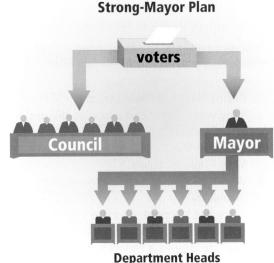

Strong-Mayor Plan

voters

Council Mayor

Department Heads

for the city. Because the manager is not elected, he or she is supposed to be free from political pressures. The council-manager plan is used in over two thousand cities today.

The Commission Plan Another reform of city government took place in Galveston, Texas, in 1900. The city was destroyed by a hurricane. The weak-mayor government that Galveston had at that time could not manage the rebuilding. Local citizens convinced the state to approve a new form of government called a commission plan. Under this plan, voters choose several commissioners who together make ordinances. In addition, each commissioner directs one of the city's departments, such as finance or public assistance.

The commission plan worked so well in rebuilding Galveston that hundreds of other cities decided to try it. However, the plan does not provide for a single leader to control the budget and make the departments work together. In the past few years Galveston and most other cities that tried the plan have decided not to use it any more.

No matter what the strengths and the weaknesses are of a plan of local government, its success or failure lies in the hands of its citizens. Today, most cities seek advice from groups made up of people who live there. Citizens *can* be heard in city hall.

Section 1 Assessment

1. **Define** board, ordinances, municipality
2. Why were American colonies divided into counties?
3. Describe the layout of a typical colonial New England town.
4. Why are special districts sometimes necessary?
5. For what purpose was the council-manager plan created?
6. **Analyze** Would a New England town government work in a large modern city? Why or why not?

Local Government Services and Revenue

SECTION PREVIEW

Objectives

- Summarize the role local governments play in providing public education.
- Describe the utilities provided by local government.
- Identify examples of health and welfare programs.
- Explain how zoning laws help local governments control land use.
- Examine local government's contribution to public safety.
- Analyze the ways local governments pay for the services they provide.

Building Civics Vocabulary

- **Utilities** are services needed by the public, such as water and electricity.
- **Zoning** laws divide a community into areas and tell how the land in each area can be used.
- A tax on land and buildings is a **property tax.**
- **Intergovernmental revenue** is money given by one level of government to another.

 **Focus**

"Skateboarding is dangerous!" said the mother of a child who had been run into by a skateboarder. She asked the city council to ban skateboards in public places. "That's not fair," said a teenager at the council meeting. "Then we'd have no place to skate." He asked the city to build a skatepark for skateboarders.

We ask local governments to help us in many ways. They provide utilities, or services needed by the public, such as water, gas, and electricity. They build parks, schools, and roads. They plan for community growth. Officials make hundreds of decisions in delivering these services. For example, they may have to decide whether a hole in a road that serves only two houses should be fixed or whether to cut water use during a dry spell.

Every time officials decide to handle a problem in a certain way, they are making policy. If the council bans skateboarding, it is making a public safety policy. Another policy might be to build a skatepark.

Policy decisions often depend on money. Because no government has all the money it needs, officials must decide which services to offer. The council might decide that it does not have enough money to build a skatepark, but it will allow skateboarders to use an empty parking lot. Perhaps the park could be built if skateboarders were charged money to use it.

Education

The service that local governments spend the most money on is education. Local governments—counties, cities, and school districts—are in charge of providing all public education from elementary school through high school. Some also are in charge of two-year colleges. Local school boards build schools and hire teachers and staff to run them. Many local boards have a strong say in what courses will be taught.

The federal and state governments are also important in public education. State officials set standards for school employees and buildings. State governments have a strong say in how schools are run because they pay about one third or more of schooling costs. The federal government helps to pay for buildings, school lunch programs, and programs for children with special needs.

Local vs. State Control Local and state governments often do not agree about which of them should have greater control over

state education money. State officials make sure state standards are met and that children in all school districts have equal opportunities. On the other hand, local control can be good for schools because local citizens know what the students need.

Utilities

You may not even notice some local government services. However, you would certainly notice if you no longer had them. These government services are the utilities: water, gas, electricity, sewage treatment plants, and garbage collection.

In many cases, water and sewage treatment plants are owned and run by local governments. Communities often arrange for

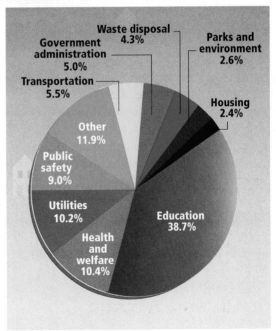

 LOCAL GOVERNMENT SPENDING, 1998–1999

Waste disposal 4.3%
Government administration 5.0%
Transportation 5.5%
Parks and environment 2.6%
Housing 2.4%
Other 11.9%
Public safety 9.0%
Utilities 10.2%
Health and welfare 10.4%
Education 38.7%

Source: U.S. Census Bureau

 Local governments are responsible for a wide variety of programs.
Government Which services received more than 10 percent of local government spending in 1998–1999?

One purpose of land-use planning is to prevent uncontrolled growth from destroying existing neighborhoods.

private companies to supply gas and electricity and to pick up garbage. The state makes rules to make sure the companies deliver good services at fair rates.

Utilities are best provided at the local level, where they can be planned to fit a community's needs. In Emmonak, Alaska, the ground freezes in winter. Sewer pipes are not put underground because they would freeze, too. Instead, sewer pipes made of materials that will not freeze are laid above ground—a method that fits the Arctic climate.

Health and Welfare

Millions of Americans are poor, too ill to work, or unable to find jobs or homes. Many people help the needy, but it is a very big job. Local governments play a part by offering health and child care, training people for jobs, and providing low-cost places to live.

Most programs giving public assistance, or welfare, are paid for by federal, state, and local governments together. However, local officials carry out the programs. The city of Atlanta, Georgia, for example, was recently recognized for its success in using federal funds to improve low-cost public housing in several Atlanta neighborhoods.

Communities also look after public health. In many cases, local officials carry out state health laws. Local health officials inspect restaurants, markets, hotels, and water to be sure that state and federal standards are met. Many communities also make sure that federal and state laws to control pollution are obeyed.

Land Use

Have you ever noticed that homes and businesses are in separate areas of your community? This is the result of zoning, local rules that divide a community into areas and tell how the land in each area can be used. For example, zoning may keep a factory from being built next to your home. Zoning is a tool used by local governments to plan and control the growth of their communities.

The people who plan communities think about where roads, parks, factories, and homes should be built. They must also think about how a new factory will affect the lives of people in the community. They must think about who will be using a park and whether it will need a playground or picnic tables. Will a new road bring too much traffic into downtown? Are there enough low-cost houses and apartments for families with low incomes? Planners must also look at how development affects the environment. Will the new factory have anti-pollution controls?

The Planning Process Planning is made up of many steps. A local government appoints a planning commission to set goals and get information about the community, such as its growth rate and types of businesses. Most commissions are made up of interested citizens, such as builders, environmentalists, and business leaders.

Commission members work with a staff that looks at requests from builders and reads reports about what building will do to the environment. The staff tells the commission what they think should be done about each request. Once the commission decides what to do, it presents the matter to the city council or county board, which makes the final decision.

Some of the most heated battles in planning are over how fast communities should grow. New businesses mean more jobs and more tax money. However, new businesses may bring in more people, who will need water, schools, and parks. New businesses may also bring more traffic and pollution.

By setting aside land for public parks, local governments help to meet the recreation needs of communities.

The city of Reno, Nevada grew rapidly during the 1980s and 1990s. This growth brought thousands of new jobs and lots of tax money to Reno. Local officials pointed out, however, that quick growth meant the city would also need more water. Reno gets its water from the Truckee River. The city could make land-use plans, but it could not make more water flow from the river. Planners must think about the resources they have as well as the short-term and long-term needs of citizens.

Public Safety

If you had an emergency, what would you do? You might call the police or fire department, or dial 911. Police officers and firefighters also look after the public safety in non-emergencies. The police help citizens stop crime by teaching them how to keep

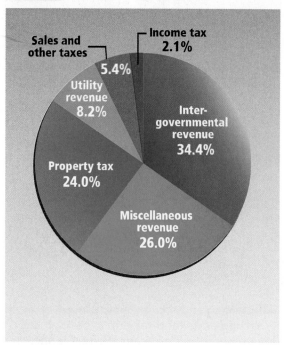

GRAPH SKILL

LOCAL GOVERNMENT REVENUE, 1998–1999

Sales and other taxes **5.4%**

Income tax **2.1%**

Utility revenue **8.2%**

Inter-governmental revenue **34.4%**

Property tax **24.0%**

Miscellaneous revenue **26.0%**

Source: U.S. Census Bureau

Local governments receive funding from local, state, and federal sources.
Government What percentage of local government revenue came from income and property taxes in 1998–1999?

people from breaking into their homes. The fire department checks for fire hazards, such as faulty wiring, and teaches safety rules to children.

Local governments also hire people to make sure that safety rules, called codes, are followed. A fire code may say that all buildings must have smoke alarms. Building codes make sure that new buildings are built safely.

Revenue: Paying for Services

To provide services to citizens, local governments need money. Like state governments, local governments depend on several sources of revenue.

Taxes About 25 percent of local government revenue comes from property tax, a tax on land and buildings. The county assessor decides how much the property is worth and charges the property owner a fixed percentage of that value. Many people feel property tax is fair because the more property that citizens own, the more services they use, such as water and fire protection.

Some communities bring in money through other taxes, such as a local sales tax. About 3,300 local governments in more than a dozen states put an income tax on the salaries of people who work there. The idea is to collect money from "daytime citizens" who use city services during the work day but live somewhere else.

Service Charges and Profits Cities often charge money for services such as inspecting buildings to see that they meet safety codes. Communities also get money from bridge tolls, park entrance fees, and parking meters.

Some local governments make money by running businesses. For instance, the city of Naperville, Illinois, runs a parking garage. It brings in money while providing parking spaces for people who work and shop in the city. Government-owned utilities, such as electric companies, also bring in money and give low-cost service to local citizens and businesses.

Borrowing When revenue from taxes, fees, and city-owned businesses is not enough to cover their costs, local governments can borrow money. For short-term needs, they may borrow from banks. To pay for big projects, such as school buildings, communities borrow money by selling bonds.

Sharing Revenue Local governments also receive intergovernmental revenue, money given by one level of government to another. Federal and state governments often

High School Volunteers Serve Their Community

Jonathan Carmenate, a student at Miami, Florida's William H. Turner Technical Arts High School, has been a member of Generation US for four years. Participation in this volunteer program has taught him that volunteer work is not just about giving—it's also about getting: "In addition to getting community service hours to help with school, I love service with a passion. In my eyes, there is nothing more uplifting than helping people."

Generation US is part of Intergenerational Programs, a service-learning program for the public schools in Miami-Dade County, Florida. Students from all over the county give their time to different volunteer projects.

Generation US works to bridge the gap between older and younger generations. It is a task force of older adults and younger people working together

to build understanding and talk about issues important to the community, such as youth violence. Generation US has worked to fight crime in their community. In recent years, students worked to pass new legislation for a "safe senior zone," an area providing the elderly with student escorts.

Dr. Ramona Frischman, the supervisor of Intergenerational Programs, believes that students who get involved in volunteering make a huge difference in their community. "Students

who volunteer learn more than would be possible from a book," she said. "Elders inspire the young people, and the program teaches people about love and respect for one another." Dr. Frischman is impressed with the number of students coming back to volunteer as young adults, graduate students, and professionals who feel that the program has changed their lives.

Jonathan Carmenate is glad to be contributing to an organization that is helping his community: "This program is very empowering. Senior citizens working together with students help them to save each other's lives. It makes a huge difference in Miami-Dade County, and that makes this part of the world a better place."

Active Citizenship

How are the volunteers of Generation US helping to improve their community?

give money to local communities. This money is called a grant. Grants are a way to make sure that services of national or state importance are provided at the local level.

Some grants are for special uses, such as

summer job programs for youth, or large building projects. Others are block grants for general uses such as education. Block grants allow local officials to decide how best to use the money.

Limits on Revenue Most communities face problems in paying for services. The demand for services is generally greater than the amount of money available to the community to pay for them. Sources of money may "run dry." Another problem is that the power to tax is controlled by the state. The state spells out what kinds of taxes may be collected and what the money may be used for.

Large cities can have a particularly difficult time balancing the money in the city treasury with the need for services. Philadelphia, Pennsylvania mayor Edward Rendell discussed this challenge when presenting his year 2000 budget to the city council. "In a city where our needs are so great, and where our resources remain so limited," Rendell told the council, "it is an absolutely critical part of our jobs to reject countless legitimate and worthy demands for public funds."

Section 2 Assessment

1. **Define** utilities, zoning, property tax, intergovernmental revenue
2. How do local governments help provide for public education?
3. What are the major factors considered by people who plan land use in communities?
4. What are some ways that local governments help protect public safety?
5. What are two ways by which a community might pay for a major project such as building a new airport or a new school?
6. **Evaluate** Local governments provide many services. Which two local government services do you think are most important? Explain.

Conflict and Cooperation Between Governments

SECTION PREVIEW

Objectives

- Explain how local governments cooperate and come into conflict with each other.
- Analyze relations between local and state governments.
- Describe the relationship between local, state, and federal governments.

Building Civics Vocabulary

- Some states have granted cities **home rule**, the right to create their own charter.

Focus

Look in your phone book and see how many levels of government are listed that serve you. Like most citizens, you probably live under at least four layers of government. Almost every town, city, and township lies inside a county. All these local governments must answer to their state governments. Of course, the nation as a whole is guided by the federal government. As the layers overlap, governments both cooperate and come into conflict.

Relations Between Local Governments

In 1954 a county official in the Detroit area became alarmed that the region's services were not keeping up with its growth. He met with officials of neighboring counties to figure out how to meet area-wide needs. Soon other regions were holding meetings, too. These groups became known as "councils of governments."

Other groups, such as the United States Conference of Mayors, are also ways of linking local governments. Officials from these groups talk about matters that affect them all, and they work together to look for solutions. Since cooperation would seem to help everyone, what causes conflicts between local governments?

Conflict One big cause of conflicts between local governments is economics. Communities often compete to attract new businesses, which pay new property taxes. Communities also compete to get federal money.

Another cause of conflicts is the effect of one community's policies on neighboring communities. One city may zone an area for new factories. However, when the pollution from that factory zone blows into a neighboring city, the stage is set for conflict.

Federal and state government relief workers pitch in with sandbags to help a local community protect itself against flood waters.

Cooperation Problems can also lead to cooperation. Sometimes communities work together to provide services that would cost too much for each to provide for itself. Townships have teamed up to answer emergency calls. Each township's fire department offers something different, such as clothing that protects people from fire or training for emergencies.

Small communities may also turn to counties for help. A county can build a jail or hospital to serve several small towns.

Relations Between Local and State Governments

Many states have a strong voice in deciding how local governments will be set up. Other states have granted cities and some counties home rule, the right to write their own charter. Whether or not they grant home rule, most states give communities some freedom to handle local matters.

Citizens of a local community are sometimes unhappy with federal and state decisions that affect their area.

Conflict The question of what is a local matter and what is also a state matter, however, can lead to conflict. For example, California wanted to build a sewage plant for the city of Arcata. The state had received federal money for the plant, but Arcata would have had to pay millions of dollars, too. Arcata came up with a plan for a cheaper sewage system, but the state said no. City officials spent two years going to meetings with state officials. Finally, Arcata won the right to build the system it wanted. When local and state laws come into conflict, however, state law is almost always enforced.

Cooperation Many state governments work directly with local governments to solve local problems. The city of Evanston turned to the Illinois Environmental Protection Agency for help in building a park over what had been a garbage dump.

The job was hard because rotten garbage is not a stable surface and makes a gas that can blow up if trapped. Together, city and state officials worked out plans to cover the garbage with a layer of clay and to build a vent for the gas to escape.

States often work with local governments to carry out state programs. When a state highway commission plans a road that will cut through a city it asks the advice of the city council. States also help local programs run smoothly. State officials help local officials in finance, law enforcement, health, and education. Also, states test and license local government workers such as teachers and doctors.

Relations Between Local, State, and Federal Governments

Money is the key to the relations of local governments to state and federal governments. The federal government gives grants and loans for housing, public assistance, and other uses. The idea is to use federal money at the local level to meet national goals. For example, the federal government gives grants for job-training programs. Such grants are often given to the states. Then the states decide how to divide up the money among local governments that run the programs. The federal government also gives aid directly to local governments.

Conflict Sometimes local officials come into conflict with federal and state officials over how to spend grant money. Most federal money for local governments can be used only in certain ways. Grants given to help meet a national goal may not match local needs. The states often have the power to decide who gets federal grants.

If local governments want the freedom to set their own policies, they may have to do without federal money. Unfortunately, most communities do not have enough money to do big projects without some federal help.

Cooperation Many problems affect all levels of government and are best solved by cooperation. If one factory dumps poisonous wastes, it is a local matter. However, poisonous wastes have polluted ground water, lakes, and rivers across the nation, so pollution has also become a nationwide concern. Federal, state, and local governments must all work together to clean up and stop pollution.

Local, state, and federal governments also cooperate in providing services, such as law enforcement. The Federal Bureau of Investigation (FBI) trains local police in the latest ways of fighting crime. Local police turn to the FBI for records of suspected criminals. Local, state, and federal officers work together to solve crimes like bank robbery and kidnapping.

The federal-state-local partnership is a good way to deal with nationwide issues. It also brings local problems to national attention because local officials can tell state and federal officials what their citizens want. Even though there are conflicts, they can lead to creative solutions. If you want to take part in finding solutions, local government is a good place to start.

Section 3 Assessment

1. **Define** home rule
2. What are some ways in which local governments compete and cooperate?
3. In what ways do state and local governments cooperate? How do they sometimes come into conflict?
4. Why do federal, state, and local governments often have to work together?
5. **Evaluate** Do you think competition between local governments is bad? Explain.

Extending the Chapter

Global Views

Local government powers vary from nation to nation. There are two main systems of city government outside the United States: the English and French systems. The English system is used in Great Britain, Australia, Canada, and New Zealand. It is similar to ours in that councils are voted for locally and mayors are elected by the councils. The local councils have broad power to deal with local issues.

The French system is found not only in France but also in many Latin American, African, Middle Eastern, and Asian countries in some form. Local governments have much less power in the French system. Local officials provide services such as water, electricity, and fire protection, but it is the national government that controls the money, education, and the police.

It is possible to have an even more centralized system, where local officials represent the national government. Such tight control is often found in communist countries such as China. In short, compared with other systems, our cities, towns, and counties have more freedom to set policies on local matters.

Banning Neighborhood Noise

Darien Mann's rock and roll band was loud. When Darien and his friends practiced in Darien's garage, many of the neighbors complained that they could not talk to each other without shouting. It made the neighbors even more angry that the four boys practiced late into the night.

Darien's next-door neighbors, the Macks, lived closest to the garage. They were disturbed by the noise more often than anyone else in the neighborhood.

One evening Mr. Mack thought the band was playing even louder than usual. He rang the Manns' doorbell and pounded on the door, but no one answered. In disgust, Mr. Mack returned home and called the police.

Los Angeles police officer Richard Hoefel and his partner answered the call at about 8 P.M. After months of complaints, the Mann house had become a regular stop on their beat. They could hear the band from half a block away.

The officers walked to the chain link fence in front of the Manns' garage and rapped on the gate with their flashlights to get the teenagers' attention. Officer Hoefel ordered the boys to meet him on the front porch.

Once they all were gathered together, Officer Hoefel

> **Thirteen months later, the Manns and the Macks were still arguing over the noise problem.**

explained the reason for the neighbor's complaint. He warned the group that if they did not stop making the noise he would have to arrest them for breaking the law. The Los Angeles Municipal Code has a "noise ordinance" which states that it is against the law for any person to make any "loud, unnecessary, and unusual noise which disturbs the peace and quiet of any neighborhood."

The officers talked with the band about ways they could avoid noise complaints in the future. The officers said that the band could rent a hall, soundproof the garage, or agree with the Macks about good times to practice. Because the boys seemed cooperative, Officer Hoefel decided to let them off with only a warning.

Thirteen months later, the Manns and the Macks were still arguing over the noise. An informal hearing before the city attorney failed to end the neighbors' differences. Darien and his band wanted to keep playing in the garage, and the Macks wanted the music to stop permanently.

To settle the matter once and for all, Darien Mann and his parents decided to bring a lawsuit against the City of Los Angeles. They wanted the municipal court to remove the noise ordinance from the municipal code. If the ordinance were removed from the books, Darien and his band would not be breaking the law

---

The Manns said that the wording of the law was not clear enough.

---

when they played their music late into the night.

In court, the Manns said that the wording of the law was not clear enough to tell if the law was being broken. They pointed out that because the level of noise banned by the law was not described in a scientific way, no one could tell how loud was too loud.

The Manns then said that if the law was not clear about what noise level was illegal, then the law could not be enforced. If this was true, the court had the

power to remove the law from the municipal code.

The city attorney defended the city's law. He pointed out that most laws are not scientifically exact. They must be flexible enough to be used in many different cases.

After thinking about both sides, the court ruled against the Manns. It agreed with the city attorney that it takes "common sense," not scientific measurement, to be able to know what is a "loud, unnecessary, and unusual" noise.

The court explained that it is often asked to decide if a law can be enforced. In such cases, it uses the "reasonable man test" to see if people can understand the law the way it is written.

When the court uses the reasonable man test, it puts itself in the shoes of an ordinary person. If the court believes that a reasonable man can understand what a particular law requires him to do or not to do, then the law is clear enough to be enforced.

The court also noted that the noise ordinance stated several factors for

courts to think about when deciding what the law means. Some of those factors were the time of night at which the noise occurred and how near the noise was to other people's homes.

Based on the reasonable man test and the wording of the law, the court ruled that the law was clear enough to be enforced against Darien and his band.

Analyzing the Case

1. What activities were made illegal by the Los Angeles Municipal Code noise ordinance?
2. What reasons did the Manns give to the court when they argued that the noise ordinance should be removed from the municipal code?
3. Do you think that it is fair for the City of Los Angeles to pass a noise ordinance that means people cannot play loud music in the privacy of their homes? Support your opinion.
4. Do you think the court would have ruled in the same way if the band had been playing loud classical music late at night? Support your opinion.

How to READ ORGANIZATION CHARTS

In this chapter you learned that the majority of American cities use the mayor-council plan of government. On page 267, two organization charts illustrate the two types of mayor-council plans. The other major type of city government—the council-manager plan—is illustrated on this page.

Explain the Skill

Organization charts are often used to show the various parts of an organization and to illustrate the different levels of power within an organization. In most organization charts, symbols are used to represent each section of an organization and arrows are used to indicate how the sections relate to each other. The official or group with the most power and authority is usually shown at the top of an organization chart.

Analyze the Skill

The organization chart on this page shows how the council-manager plan of city government works. As you read, the goal of this plan is to run government like a business, with the manager holding more executive power than the mayor. Supporters of this system hope that since the manager is not elected, he or she will not be influenced by political pressures.

Look at the chart one level at a time. As with other forms of local, state, and national government in our democracy, the power

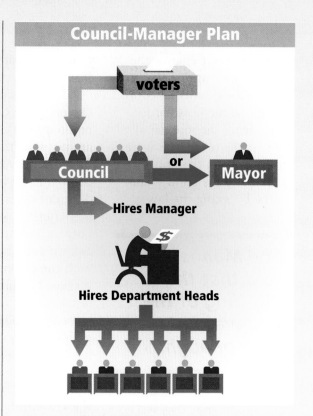

Council-Manager Plan

voters

Council or Mayor

Hires Manager

Hires Department Heads

begins with the voters, who select their elected officials. The city council then chooses a manager, who hires the heads of each government department.

Skill Assessment

1. Each level on the chart represents a level of organization. How many levels are there in this form of city government?

2. Under this system of government, who has more power, the mayor or the city council members? Explain your answer.

3. What are the two ways of selecting a mayor under the council-manager plan?

Building Civics Vocabulary

Match each vocabulary term with the lettered word or phrase most closely related to it. Then explain how the items in each pair are related.

Example: *Home rule* relates to *government structure* because cities and counties with home rule can choose their own government structure.

1. board
2. property tax
3. zoning
4. municipality
5. intergovernmental revenue
6. utilities

(a) land use
(b) city
(c) revenue
(d) commissioners
(e) water, gas, and electricity
(f) grants

Reviewing Main Ideas and Skills

7. Why are there different types of local government?

8. What are some difficulties local governments face in trying to provide services?

9. Why do federal, state, and local governments all become involved in meeting the needs of local communities?

10. **How to Read an Organization Chart** Look back at the organization charts on page 267. Aside from how the mayor is chosen, what is the major difference between the weak-mayor and strong-mayor plans?

Critical Thinking

11. **Comparing** How does the government of a traditional New England small town differ from the government of a large modern city?

12. **Defending a Position** "Of all levels of government, local government has the greatest effect on your everyday life." Do you agree with this statement? Support your answer.

Writing About Civics

13. **Writing a Letter** Suppose you are writing a letter to a friend in a foreign country. In your letter, explain the role of local government in the United States. Include specific examples of the types of powers held by local government.

Citizenship Activities

14. **Your Local Community** Bring to class a local newspaper. Find all the articles that involve local government and explain how each article is related to one or more of the services provided by local government.

Take It to the NET

Access the **Civics: Participating in Government** Internet site at **www.phschool.com** for the specific URLs to complete the activity.

Explore online information about the three levels of government—national, state and local. Take notes on an issue that all three levels of government address. Compare how they approach this issue. Which level do you think has the best approach? Why?

Closest to the People

Republican Christine Todd Whitman, the first female governor of New Jersey, was elected in 1993 and re-elected in 1997. In her first two years in office, she made good on her campaign promises by reducing New Jersey's income taxes by 30 percent. Whitman left the governorship in 2001 to become head of the Environmental Protection Agency under President George W. Bush.

Before you read the selection, find the meanings of these words in a dictionary: respectively, micromanage, undergird, devolution.

In recent years, as citizens and political leaders across the country have debated the proper role of government, the Tenth Amendment to the United States Constitution has gained greater attention. That amendment...declares: "The powers not delegated to the United States by the Constitution, nor prohibited by it to the States, are reserved to the States respectively, or to the people."

Our founding fathers had it right. The power closest to the people governs best. The states are eager to accept more responsibility from the federal government because we can respond better and more quickly to people's needs and concerns.

> **"Our founding fathers had it right. The power closest to the people governs best."**

We can adapt to real-life situations without being micromanaged from Washington. We can do this because we are closer to the people and their problems, and we take our responsibility to them very seriously....

Establishing priorities must be the direction of all in government. And a top priority must be to reshape government by shrinking the rate of growth in federal spending while providing necessary services. That obligation undergirds efforts to curb federal spending growth and move responsibility for public services out of the hands of the federal government and into the hands of the states.

Granted, this process—known as "devolution"—will force states to make some careful choices in administering these

programs. But governors and legislatures can and should be trusted to make responsible choices for their citizens....

Government should be a partnership where private interest and civic duty meet. That partnership must be built on confidence and trust—the citizens' confidence in government to provide needed services in an efficient manner and government's trust in the people to run their lives without pointless bureaucratic interference. The "devolution revolution" can help us restore trust by placing public services and programs at the state and local level....

Source: Perspectives: Readings on Contemporary American Government *(Alexandria, Va.: Close Up Foundation, 1997), pages 12-16.*

Analyzing Primary Sources

1. According to Whitman, why are state governments better equipped to respond to people's needs and concerns than the federal government?

2. What effect does Whitman think devolution will have on state legislatures and governors?

UNIT 4 ASSESSMENT

1. What are some of the ways that citizens can influence state and local government?
2. In what ways are the federal, state, and local governments similar in their organization?
3. Compare the powers and responsibilities of the President, the governor of a state, and the mayor of a city. How are they similar? How are they different?
4. How is the relationship between local and state governments similar to the relationship between the states and the federal government? How do the two relationships differ?
5. What are some advantages of having federal, state, and local levels of government? What are some disadvantages?

Summarizing the Unit

The double web graphic organizer below will help you organize the main ideas of Unit 4. Copy it onto a separate sheet of paper. Review the unit and complete the graphic organizer by naming examples of some of the powers held by state government, some held by local government, and some shared by state and local governments. (One of these has been done for you as an example.) Then write a short essay describing why it is important for state and local governments to work together.

STATE AND LOCAL GOVERNMENT POWERS

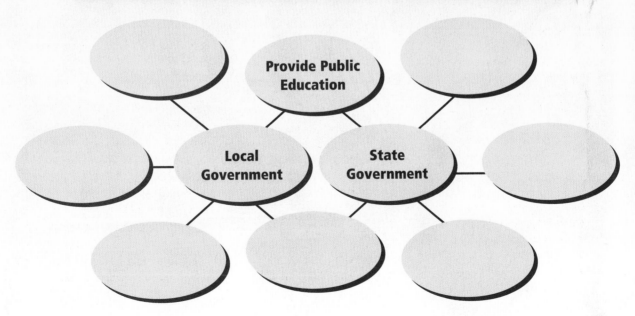

Provide Public Education

Local Government

State Government

UNIT 5

THE AMERICAN ECONOMIC SYSTEM

Why Study Civics?

Our economic system is...an instrument by which we add to the security and richness of life of every individual. It by no means comprises the whole purpose of life, but it is the foundation upon which can be built the finer things of the spirit.

—President Herbert Hoover

You have been learning about how governments at different levels protect our rights as citizens. Our freedom as individuals, however, depends on more than our democratic form of government. As Herbert Hoover reminds us, our economic system is a basic part of our free society.

What's Ahead in Unit 5

What is an economic system? How does our economy work? Why is money so important? What is the role of government in the economy? What role will you play in the economy? These are some of the questions you will explore as you read Unit 5.

What Is an Economy?

Citizenship and You

"Guess what, Mike!" Josh exclaimed. "The manager at Rick's Bikes just offered me a job! I could work after school and on the weekends and I'd make enough money to pay for movies and buy my own clothes. I could even start saving for that computer I want."

"Sounds good," Mike said. "But wouldn't you have to quit the soccer team?"

"I didn't think of that," Josh said. "The job would interfere with after-school practices. And a lot of our games are on weekends."

Josh has a problem. He wants to be on the soccer team *and* he wants to take an after-school job. Because Josh's time is limited, however, he won't be able to satisfy both of these wants. He has a tough decision to make.

Like Josh, societies have limited resources with which to satisfy their many wants. To solve this problem, they must make decisions. The system through which people in a society make choices about how to use their resources to produce goods and services is called an economy.

What's Ahead in Chapter 13

In this chapter you will read about economic wants, resources, and the decisions that must be made about using resources to satisfy wants. You will also find out about three different kinds of economic systems through which societies make these decisions.

Section 1 Why Societies Have Economies

Section 2 Basic Economic Decisions

Section 3 Three Types of Economies

Keep It Current

Items marked with this logo are periodically updated on the Internet. To keep up-to-date, go to **www.phschool.com**

Citizen's Journal

How do you decide how to spend your time after school and on weekends? Think of an instance when you had to choose between two or more different activities because you had a limited amount of time. What were your options? What did you choose? What factors influenced your decision?

Why Societies Have Economies

SECTION PREVIEW

Objectives
- Explore the factors that determine people's wants.
- Identify the resources people use to satisfy their wants.
- Summarize the links in the want-satisfaction chain.
- Describe the factors people consider when making economic choices.
- Explain how scarcity affects economic choices.

Building Civics Vocabulary
- The resources people have for producing goods and services are called **factors of production**.
- **Capital** is anything produced in an economy that is used to produce other goods and services.
- **Consumption** is the act of buying or using goods and services.
- **Opportunity cost** is the benefit given up when scarce resources are used for one purpose instead of the next best purpose.
- **Scarcity** means that resources are limited compared with the wants people have.

⭐ Focus

In reading about Josh on page 287, you came across the basic economic facts of life: in any society, people must make choices about how to use their resources to produce goods and services to satisfy their wants. Notice that there are several elements to think about when looking at these economic facts—wants, resources, production of goods and services, and choices. By looking at how each of the elements is related to the others, you will gain a clearer understanding of what an economy is and why every society has one.

People's Many Wants

Think about the first element: wants. Everyone has wants. Our most basic wants are for food, clothing, and shelter. However, people are rarely satisfied to have just their basic wants met. People also want to be able to move from place to place. They want to be entertained, to be educated, and to have health care when they are sick. In fact, people have an almost endless number of wants.

How Wants Differ Of course, your wants will differ from those of other people, depending on where you live and who you are. One important influence on your wants is your environment. If you live in Alaska, you will want to have warm clothes to wear and good heating for your house. In the warm weather of Phoenix, Arizona, are you likely to have the same wants?

In shopping for clothes that she likes and that she can afford, this young woman is fulfilling an "economic want."

Wants are also influenced by the societies in which we live and their cultures. Americans usually want to live in houses or apartments, while certain people in Tibet think that tents best fit their way of life.

Even when they live in the same environment and the same culture, different people want different things. Some people choose a vacation in the mountains, while others choose to go to the beach or on a tour of famous places. You may favor white basketball shoes, while your best friend wants black ones.

People's wants can also change. Think of the toys you wanted when you were a baby. How do they compare with the goods you want to have now?

Another important characteristic of wants is that many of them can be satisfied only for a short time. Do the jeans you wore last year still fit you, or do you need to buy a new pair? Understanding that many wants occur again and again is basic to learning what an economy is.

Using Resources

The resources people have for producing goods and services to satisfy their wants are called factors of production. According to economists—the people who study how economies work—the three basic factors of production in an economy are labor, land, and capital.

Labor One factor of production, labor, includes time and energy. If Josh takes the job at Rick's Bikes, he will be using his time and energy to help sell bicycles. His labor will also include the knowledge and skills he uses in his job.

Land Another factor of production, land, is made up of the many natural resources that are needed to help produce goods and

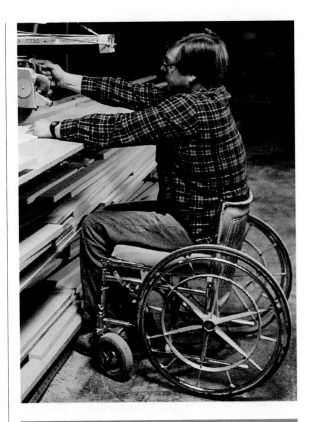

The skills and training as well as the time and energy a person puts into a job are part of the factor of production called labor.

services. Such resources include soil, minerals, water, timber, fish and wildlife, and energy sources.

Capital Finally, there is the factor of production called capital. Capital is anything produced in an economy that is used to produce other goods and services.

Capital includes any tools, machines, or buildings used to produce goods and services. When goods such as tools and factories are used as capital, they are called capital goods. For example, tools for fixing bicycles and a computer for keeping track of sales are capital goods to the owner of Rick's Bikes.

Although it is not a factor of production, money is sometimes referred to as financial capital. Financial capital is money that is available for investing or spending.

Production, Distribution, and Consumption

To produce the goods and services people want, the resources of labor, land, and capital must be combined in a process called production. That is why these resources are called factors of production. Farmers produce food by combining soil, water, and sunlight (land) with seeds and machinery (capital). They also use their knowledge, skills, time, and energy, as well as that of their workers (labor).

Production is followed by distribution, the process by which goods and services are made available to the people who want them. The truck that delivers bread to your market is part of the distribution process.

Finally, when goods and services have been produced and distributed, they are ready for consumption. Consumption is the act of buying or using goods and services.

The Want-Satisfaction Chain

Satisfying people's economic wants can be a very complex process. In our economy, millions of people work in hundreds of thousands of businesses that produce and distribute many different goods and services.

The steps in the process of satisfying wants can be thought of as links in a chain of activities. As you read the following

 THE WANT-SATISFACTION CHAIN The satisfaction of human wants can involve many steps. **Economics** In this want-satisfaction chain, what occurs in the "Production" step?

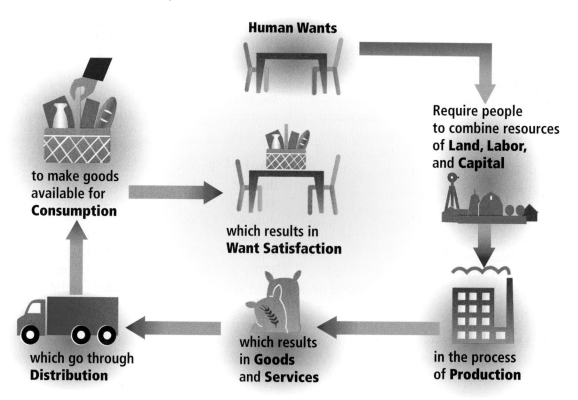

Human Wants

Require people to combine resources of **Land, Labor,** and **Capital**

in the process of **Production**

which results in **Goods** and **Services**

which go through **Distribution**

to make goods available for **Consumption**

which results in **Want Satisfaction**

description, look at the diagram of the want-satisfaction chain on page 290.

The process begins with a want. Suppose, for example, that you and some of your friends decide to get together one evening for a spaghetti dinner. Among the supplies that you will want to buy and cook is the pasta. The first link in this want-satisfaction chain, then, is your want for pasta.

The next link is made up of people who combine the resources of land, labor, and capital. In the case of your pasta, farmers use soil, water, seeds, farm machinery, and labor to produce wheat, which they sell to a grain milling company. The company combines labor and machinery to turn the wheat into flour, which it sells to a pasta maker. The pasta maker adds other ingredients and uses labor and machines to mix, roll, and cut the dough. This production process results in the pasta that you and your friends want.

However, your want is not yet satisfied. Once the pasta has been made, it must be sold to a grocery wholesaler who then sells and delivers it to a grocery store. This is the distribution link in the chain.

After the pasta has been distributed, you and your friends buy, cook, and eat it—the consumption link in the chain. At this point, you have achieved want satisfaction.

However, your want may be satisfied only for the time being. If you decide you want to eat pasta another time, the chain will have to repeat itself. The want-satisfaction chain is arranged in a circle to show that the process of satisfying wants happens over and over again.

Making Choices

A basic truth about all societies is that there are never enough resources to produce all the goods and services people want. As a result of this situation, people in all societies must make choices about which of their wants will be satisfied and which will not. These choices

The production process completed, these automobiles are awaiting distribution to dealers, who will sell them to consumers.

are economic choices, and the process of making them is what an economy is all about.

You will remember that Josh is trying to decide whether or not to take a job at Rick's Bikes. Josh has to make a choice because the job will use up the time, a limited resource, that he would otherwise use to satisfy his desire to play soccer. In order to decide, Josh will have to think about how he wants to use his time.

Benefits and Costs One part of making an economic decision is looking at the benefits you will receive from each of your possible choices. Josh's benefits from the bike store job will include one hundred and fifty dollars a week plus work experience and the satisfaction of having money of his own.

A second part involves looking at the costs of your choices. The major cost of any decision is giving up the benefits you would have received from the next best alternative. If Josh takes the job, for example, he will give up the benefits he would have received from using his time to play soccer.

Like Josh's decision, every economic decision has an opportunity cost, the benefit given up when scarce resources are used for one purpose instead of the next best purpose. If Josh decides that the opportunity cost of taking the job would be greater than its benefits, then Josh should refuse the Rick's Bikes offer.

Scarcity

Societies have always faced, and will continue to face, a problem like Josh's problem. This problem is known as scarcity, which means that resources are always limited compared with the number and variety of wants people have. Scarcity is a problem in both rich societies and poor ones. The idea of scarcity is based not on the total amount of resources in a society, but on the relationship between wants and the resources available to satisfy them.

The following example may help you understand scarcity. Japan does not have enough good farm land to grow all the food its people want. The United States has an abundance of good farm land. However, some of the land which could be used to grow food is also in demand for factories, houses, and shopping malls. You can see that in both Japan and the United States, land resources are scarce compared with the ways people want to use them.

Choices About Resource Use In any economy, each decision to use resources to produce one kind of good or service is, at the same time, a decision not to use the same resources to produce something else that people want. The farmers who grew the wheat for the spaghetti chose to use their limited resources of land, labor, and capital to grow wheat instead of some other crop such as corn, oats, or barley.

In a large economy such choices are made by businesses as well as by individuals. For example, a company that makes cars and trucks with a limited number of factories, machines, and workers will have to make choices about how many cars and trucks of each model to produce.

Governments also have to make choices about the use of resources. For example, how much of the federal government's resources should be used to build defense systems and how much to improve the schools or to build housing for families with low incomes? How much should be used to protect the environment and how much to meet the needs of the elderly?

Although the choices that individuals, businesses, and governments must make are different in many ways, they all have one thing in common. They involve making economic decisions about how to use limited resources to produce goods and services to satisfy people's unlimited wants.

Section 1 Assessment

1. **Define** factors of production, capital, consumption, opportunity cost, scarcity
2. What are some of the economic wants that everyone has?
3. What are the three basic factors of production?
4. After a good has been produced in the want-satisfaction chain, which process makes it available to people who want it?
5. What is one example of a choice governments must make about the use of resources?
6. What are two important parts of making an economic decision?
7. **Analyze** Explain why even in a wealthy society economic choices have to be made.

Basic Economic Decisions

SECTION PREVIEW

Objectives

- Analyze how people decide what and how much to produce.
- Explain how decisions are made about how to produce goods and services.
- Explore the role of society in deciding who will get what is produced.

Focus

Have you ever thought that a pizza is the result of economic decisions? A restaurant owner makes a choice to open a pizza business. The owner decides how many pizzas to make in a day, and how many people to hire to make the pizza and serve it to customers.

Like the restaurant owner, people in any economy face three major economic decisions:

- ★ *What* goods and services should be produced, and *how much* of them?
- ★ *How* should these goods and services be produced?
- ★ *Who* will get the goods and services that are produced?

Every day, these decisions are being made in every part of the economy.

What and How Much to Produce

In any economy, people must decide what to produce with the scarce resources they have. In our economy, this first major economic decision is made by the people who own or can get resources.

If his business is to succeed, this shopkeeper must make good decisions about what kinds of and how many pastries to bake.

A farmer who owns land and machinery may decide to produce wheat instead of barley. You might decide to use a resource you own—your labor—to mow lawns instead of sell bicycles. Any decision about what goods or services to produce is based on a prediction of what people will want to consume.

As an owner of resources decides what to produce, he or she also decides how much to produce. The amount of a good or a service that is produced will depend on a number of factors. For instance, farmers' decisions will be based on the amount of land they own or can rent, the amount of labor and machinery they can afford, and the amount of wheat or barley they think they can sell.

How to Produce Goods and Services

The second major economic decision is how to produce goods and services. In other words, in what way will land, labor, and capital be combined to produce the goods and services people want?

Farmers who produce wheat must make several choices about how to do it. Should they do all the work themselves, or should they hire workers to plant and care for the wheat? Should they rely more on workers or on machinery? Should they buy the farm machinery they decide to use, or should they rent it? In making decisions about how to produce, people usually want to choose the combination of resources that will be the least costly.

The Role of Technology In our economy, the desire to find the least costly way to produce goods and services has led to the growth of technology. In the early 1800s, cloth makers began using power looms. Although the new looms cost a lot of money, they could produce much more cloth much faster than the old handlooms could. Therefore, the cost of producing cloth soon dropped.

Since those early beginnings, technology has played an increasingly important part in decisions that people make about how to produce goods and provide services. For example, researchers have developed seeds that produce larger crops. Advances in electronics have given us robots to use in factories. Computers keep records, make calculations, and speed up many jobs. The Internet allows businesses to sell products and services to a wide audience online.

Who Will Get What Is Produced

Deciding who will get what is produced is the third basic choice that must be made in an economy. In other words, people must find a way to decide how all the goods and

Using robots and other technology can speed the production process. It also changes the training that workers need, as well as their responsibilities on the job.

BELIEFS IN ACTION

Michael Dell

Michael Dell has one word of advice for young people interested in starting a business. "Experiment," he says. "It's the fastest way to learn. Don't try to come up with a perfect plan, just get out there and do something. Try a lot of different things and see what works."

When Michael Dell was a first year student at the University of Texas in 1984, he decided to try an experiment of his own. His idea was to sell custom-built computers directly to customers, eliminating the costs that distributors and retail stores add to product price. This way, Dell believed he could sell computers more cheaply than his competitors and better meet his customers' needs.

Dell started his company with $1,000, selling his first computers out of his dorm room. Soon sales and profits were soaring. Today, the Dell Computer Corporation is a multibillion-dollar company, with thousands of employees and offices in over 30 countries around the world.

Dell plans to keep on experimenting with new ideas for years to come. He is always looking for new ways to use the Internet to interact with customers and he predicts that Internet technology will continue to reshape the way Americans do business.

"I believe," Dell says, "we're very much at the beginning of a new era for how our economy is going to work. Show me a business that's not on the Internet and I'll show you a business that's out of touch with the future."

Recognizing Viewpoints

According to Michael Dell, why is it important for young business owners to experiment?

services will be divided up. Because wants are always greater than the resources available to satisfy them, this choice is an important one and sometimes very difficult.

In the debate over who gets what goods and services, a number of questions arise. Should goods and services be divided equally among all people? Should people receive goods and services on the basis of what they say they want? Should a small group of people decide who is to receive which goods and services? Or should people who own more resources and produce more products get more goods and services than people who own and produce less?

What Is an Economy?   *Chapter 13*   **295**

The Role of Goals and Values Different societies have solved this problem in different ways, depending on their goals and values. A society that wanted to achieve complete equality among all of its people might develop a system for sharing its products equally among its citizens, even if it meant that some people worked harder than others for the same reward.

On the other hand, a society in which freedom was the highest value might solve the problem by letting citizens compete freely among themselves to try to get the goods and services they want, even if it meant that some people got more than they needed while others went hungry.

The goals and values of a society have a great influence on how that society makes all three basic economic decisions. In the next section you will read about three different economic systems that societies have developed for organizing their resources to produce and distribute the goods and services people want.

Section 2 Assessment

1. In our society, who decides what and how many goods and services to produce? What factors influence those decisions?
2. When making a decision about how to produce a product, what factors do people consider?
3. Describe three possible ways to determine who will get what is produced.
4. **Evaluate** How do you think our society decides who will get what is produced? What are some of the advantages and disadvantages of that method of decision making?

Three Types of Economies

SECTION PREVIEW

Objectives

- Compare the characteristics of a traditional economy, command economy, and market economy.
- Examine the way modern economies combine features of different economic systems.

Building Civics Vocabulary

- In a **traditional economy,** basic economic decisions are made according to long-established ways of behaving.
- In a **command economy,** the government or a central authority makes basic economic decisions.
- The **market economy** is a system in which private individuals make their own choices about production and consumption.
- **Profit** is the difference between what it costs to produce something and the price the buyer pays for it.
- To **invest** is to use money to help a business get started or grow.
- **Free enterprise** is a system in which individuals undertake economic activities with little or no control by the government.
- **Capitalism** is another name for the market system.
- A **mixed economy** has a mixture of the three basic economic systems.

 Focus

People do not make economic decisions all by themselves. Almost every economic task, from raising wheat to providing hospital services, requires that people work together. Also, people can rarely meet all their economic needs by themselves. Most people do one kind of work. They depend on the work of other people for most of the products and services that they use.

In human history, there have generally been three basic types of economic systems: the traditional economy, the command economy, and the market economy. These systems are three different ways a society can organize production, distribution, and consumption to solve the economic problem of scarcity.

A Traditional Economy

In a traditional economy, the basic economic decisions are made according to long-established ways of behaving that are unlikely to change. These customs are passed along from elders to youths.

For example, a tribe of hunters may follow certain customs. They will make camp at the same places and hunt the same game year after year. The roles that fathers, sons, mothers, and daughters play as they help each other in the hunt remain the same over the years.

Tradition answers the question of what and how much to produce. The people who belong to the tribe want to "produce" game, and they want enough of it to feed the whole tribe.

There are also customs that have to do with how to "produce" the game. Year after year the tribe members use the same weapons and methods to hunt the game, and the same methods to prepare and cook it.

The tribe's customs also determine who gets what is produced. When sharing the kill, each member might get an amount based on his or her role in the hunt. In another tribe, shares might be divided according to the number of members in a family.

Because individuals or families in a traditional economy usually own their own resources, such as land, tools, and labor, they have some freedom to make their own day-to-day decisions about when and how

Watering her pepper plants, this member of the Hopi people of Arizona plays a traditional role in her society's farming economy.

to use their resources. They may decide, for example, not to go on a hunt one day, but to gather fruit instead. They have little freedom, however, when it comes to making the basic economic decisions already set by tradition. As a result, there is very little change in the economy over time.

Today, few purely traditional economies remain in the world. A few societies in parts of Central and South America, Africa, and Asia still have economies that are mostly traditional.

In the command economy of ancient Egypt, the pharaoh had the power to decide that pyramids and monuments would be built and that slaves would build them.

A Command Economy

In a command economy, the government or a central authority owns or controls the factors of production and makes the basic economic decisions. In such a system, the government usually has charge of important parts of the economy, such as transportation, communication, banking, and manufacturing. Farms and many stores are government-controlled. The government may also set wages and decide who will work at which jobs.

Economic systems based on command principles have existed for thousands of years. From Egyptian pharaohs and medieval lords to communist nations such as the Soviet Union of the twentieth century, powerful rulers and governments have controlled the economies of their societies.

Government Decision Making In a command economy, a central planning group makes most of the decisions about how, what, and how much to produce. The result is that only those products that the government chooses will be available for people to consume.

Who gets what is produced in a command system depends on the goals and values of the central authority. A greedy dictator, for example, might choose to make himself and his friends rich. On the other hand, if the government's goal were to satisfy wants based on individual need, then each person might get food, clothes, and housing no matter how much or how little he or she earned.

A Market Economy

The third kind of economic system is the market economy, a system in which private individuals own the factors of production and are free to make their own choices about production, distribution, and consumption. The economy of the United States is based on the market system. Under this system, the American economy has become the strongest in the world.

In a market economy, all economic decisions are made through a kind of bargaining process that takes place in markets. As you learned in Chapter 2, a market is a place or situation in which buyers and sellers agree to exchange goods and services. In a market, the value of what you have to offer sets the value of what you can get. Therefore, no one person or group runs a market economy. Instead, everyone takes part in running it by freely making economic decisions.

Decision Making by Individuals In a market economy, people are not only free to decide how to use land, labor, and capital. They are also free to start their own businesses and to choose what jobs they want to work at. The major economic decisions about what and how much to produce and how to produce it are made by individuals, not by government command or by tradition.

In a sense, individuals also make the economic decisions about who will get what is produced in a market economy. People who make desirable products or who earn high wages for the work they do will be able to buy more goods and services than people who produce less desirable products or earn lower wages. People who own land and capital will also be able to afford more goods and services than people who do not.

In a market economy, the wants of individuals like this French shopper play a major role in determining what will be produced.

Competition and Profit Seeking

Competition plays an important part in a market economy. Producers compete to satisfy the wants of consumers. Workers compete for jobs. These individuals are all part of the process of making decisions in a market economy.

An incentive is the hope of reward that encourages a person to behave in a certain way. One of the chief incentives for people in a market economy is the potential to make a profit. Profit is the difference between what it costs to produce something and the price the buyer pays for it. In a market economy, people base their decisions about what and how much to produce largely on how much profit they think they will make.

The desire to make a profit also leads people to invest in a business. To invest

The greater choice now available to Polish shoppers reflects their government's decision to encourage free enterprise.

means to use your money to help a business get started or grow, with the hope that the business will earn a profit that you can share.

Free Enterprise and Capitalism
It is important to get to know two other names for the market economy. One of these is free enterprise. The term free enterprise refers to the system in which individuals in a market economy are free to undertake economic activities with little or no control by the government.

The other name for the market system is capitalism. Capitalism is a system in which people make their own decisions about how to save resources as capital, and how to use their capital to produce goods and provide services. The term capitalism calls attention to the fact that in a market economy capital is privately owned.

Modern-Day Economies
Describing economic systems as traditional, command, or market can be useful for under-

standing the way people in different societies make economic decisions. In today's world, however, every economy is a mixed economy, an economy that is a mixture of the three basic systems. Looking at the economies of the People's Republic of China and the United States will help you understand what a mixed economy is.

The Economy of China Before the late 1980s, the economy of China was a command economy. The central, one-party government had charge of the major resources and made the important economic decisions.

The government of China made economic plans, in which it set goals for what goods and how many of each would be produced during a certain period. These plans also set forth how resources were used in production.

In the late 1980s and 1990s, the Chinese government took steps toward making a

BASIC CHARACTERISTICS OF THE THREE ECONOMIC SYSTEMS Today's economies are a mixture of the three basic economic systems. **Economics** Which economic system offers the greatest individual freedom?

Traditional Economy
- **Decisions based on long-standing customs.**
- **Jobs passed down from generation to generation.**
- **Change occurs slowly if at all.**
- **Little individual freedom.**

Command Economy
- **Government or other central authority makes decisions and determines how resources are used.**
- **Change can occur relatively easily.**
- **Little individual freedom.**

Market Economy
- **Resources owned and controlled by individuals.**
- **Economic decisions made by individuals competing to earn profits.**
- **Individual freedom is considered very important.**

more mixed economy by adding some features of free enterprise to its economic system. In cities today, privately owned shops sell consumer goods, and new hotels and restaurants abound.

The Economy of the United States
The United States economy is considered a market—or free enterprise—system. Business owners are free to compete with each other to produce and distribute any goods and services they think they can sell. Americans are also free to buy and consume any goods and services they want and can afford.

However, there are elements of command in our economy as well. As you have seen in earlier chapters, our government provides, or "commands" the economy to provide, certain services such as education, mail services, and an army and navy for defense. Government also provides such goods as highways and airports. In the following chapters, you will read about many other ways in which citizens have asked the government to help take charge of and guide the American economy.

Section 3 Assessment

1. **Define** traditional economy, command economy, market economy, profit, invest, free enterprise, capitalism, mixed economy
2. Why is there little change or growth in a traditional economy?
3. Why can a command economy respond quickly to changing conditions?
4. What are some of the influences on decision making in a market economy?
5. Why is the United States economy considered to be a mixed economy?
6. **Evaluate** Suppose that you had lived in each of the three kinds of economic systems. Describe some of the major advantages and disadvantages that each of them would have had for you.

Extending the Chapter

Historical Views

In this chapter you have learned many of the important ideas of economics. Economics is a social science. It is "social" because it studies people. It is a science because it calls for carefully looking at, explaining, and predicting how people will act and what choices they will make.

Economics was born at about the same time as the United States. In fact, many people trace its beginnings back to 1776, when Scottish philosopher Adam Smith published *The Wealth of Nations*. Adam Smith was the first to describe and study the market economy. In the market system, Smith said, competition acts like an "invisible hand" that guides the economy.

Elements of the market system had been a part of many societies for centuries. Until Smith's book, however, very few people understood how the market system worked. By clearly explaining the benefits of competition and free enterprise, *The Wealth of Nations* gave people an exciting vision of the future. The basic economic freedoms Smith described were embraced by the newly formed United States and became the driving force behind our economy.

It is no accident, then, that economics was born in the same year that the colonies declared their independence. Both the new economic system and the new country were based on the idea that individuals should be free to make choices.

DECISION MAKING SKILLS

How to CHOOSE AND TAKE ACTION

This is a test. Your grade on the test will be determined by how fast you make the following decisions.

Will you take a part-time job during the school year?

Which sport or school club will you get involved in next year?

If you are thinking, "Stop! I need more information before I can choose," then you have passed the test. You have avoided making a snap decision.

Decision making, as you know, involves two main parts: choosing and taking action. You also know that to make a good decision you need good information. That is why you need to think critically—to judge which information is useful and accurate. Snap decisions, which are made without careful thinking, are often wrong and often regretted. The more serious the decision, the more time you should take to gather and judge information before making up your mind.

Explain the Skill

The lessons on pages 40 and 60 gave you some guidelines for choosing and taking action. One way to direct your thinking when making a decision is to change those guidelines into questions that you ask yourself. As you ask the questions, also ask yourself whether you have been thinking critically about the information available to you. The chart on this page is an example of a checklist of questions for decision making.

Analyze the Skill

Suppose that you are looking for a part-time job. Determine what your goal or goals are in seeking a job. Then imagine that you have gathered the following information about three possible jobs. Use the guidelines on page 40 and the checklist questions in this lesson to help you choose which one of the three jobs to apply for.

DECISION-MAKING CHECKLIST		
Choosing	**Critical Thinking**	**Taking Action**
✓ Do I know my goal or goals? ✓ Have I listed all the possible options? ✓ Have I predicted the consequences of each option? ✓ Can I list the good and bad points of each option? ✓ Have I chosen the best option?	*Do I know...* ✓ which sources I can trust? ✓ what relates to my subject? ✓ what are opinions and what are statements of fact? ✓ which statements are true?	✓ Do I know my action goal? ✓ Do I know what the resources and obstacles are? ✓ Have I listed what action I will take? ✓ Have I made changes in my plan as necessary? ✓ Have I judged how well my plan worked?

Information on Job 1

You see a flyer on the counter at the Burger Barn with a title that catches your attention: "Earn Money and Make New Friends." The flyer explains that jobs at the Burger Barn are fun. The employees are friendly and enjoy their work. They choose the hours that they will work and get free meals and uniforms.

The starting pay is $6 an hour. Every three months you will be eligible for a raise. If your performance is good for a year, you may be promoted to assistant manager.

Information on Job 2

Your best friend's older brother, Roy, works for King Grocery. He tells you that the grocery business is the best place to start because of the opportunities for advancement. He started out as a courtesy clerk, making $5.75 an hour bagging groceries. Once in a while he was asked to sweep the aisles. He says that the job was easy. His only problem was that he had to be available for work at any time. He missed some parties because his boss called up and said, "We need some extra help tonight."

However, after only a year Roy was promoted to service clerk and is now earning $7.00 an hour. He has been promised a position as food clerk when he turns eighteen, and he hopes that the company will later send him to management training school. His goal is to be a store manager by the time he is thirty.

Information on Job 3

When you ask the librarian at the local library about the Help Wanted sign at the checkout desk, he tells you that if you take the job, you will have a fixed schedule. Your work week will be 10 to 15 hours, including two or three hours on Saturday. Once in a while you will have to work on Sunday, for which you will get paid time and a half. The beginning salary will be $5.85 an hour.

Your duties will include putting the book carts in order and placing the books back on the shelves. You must know the Dewey decimal system of classifying books. Promotion to a job at the desk would add 35¢ to the hourly wage, more responsibilities, and a dress code. The librarian mentions that full-time summer jobs are available, too.

After you have chosen the job you prefer, imagine yourself applying for that job. Write down your action goal. List your resources and obstacles. Then list the steps you would take to reach your action goal.

Skill Assessment

1. What goal or goals did you set?
2. Write down two opinions and two statements of fact about the jobs. Why is it important to know which statements are opinion?
3. Give an example of some information that was relevant to your goal or goals. Explain how it was relevant. Give an example of some information that was irrelevant to your goal. Explain how it was irrelevant.
4. List the consequences of each job.
5. Which job option did you consider to be the best? Explain why.
6. What resources might help you reach your goal? What obstacles might you face?
7. What would you do to reach your goal?

How to INTERPRET A DIAGRAM

As you read in this chapter, satisfying people's economic wants can be a complex process. The want-satisfaction chain on page 290 helps illustrate some of the steps in this process. This want-satisfaction chain is an example of a diagram.

Explain the Skill

Diagrams are often used to show information about the relationships between ideas. They can show, for example, the order of steps in a process or how the parts of something are related to each other.

To interpret a diagram, you need to figure out why the parts of the diagram are arranged in the way that they are. Notice whether any arrows show movement from one part of the diagram to another. Also, be aware that diagrams often use a number of different shapes. For instance, one shape could stand for an action, while another could stand for the result of an action.

Analyze the Skill

The diagram on this page shows the relationship between some of the major concepts you learned about in this chapter. Read the diagram's title. Look over the different parts of the diagram and notice how arrows are used to show movement from one step of the process to the next. Also pay attention to different shapes used in the diagram. When you have studied the diagram, answer the questions.

Skill Assessment

1. What is the subject of this diagram?
2. What is created in the production process—capital, labor, and land, or goods and services? How can you tell by looking at the diagram?
3. According to the diagram, how are capital, labor, and land related to each other?
4. Why do you think the shape containing the word "production" is different from the other shapes?

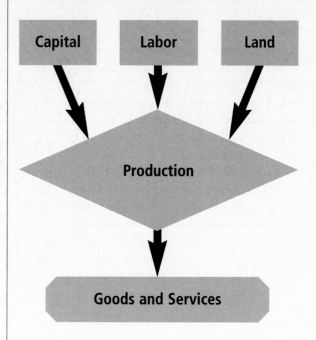

The Production Process

Capital Labor Land

Production

Goods and Services

CHAPTER 13 ASSESSMENT

Building Civics Vocabulary

The vocabulary terms in each pair listed below are related to each other. For each pair, explain how the terms are related.

Example: *Capitalism* is related to *free enterprise* because both terms are used to describe a market economy.

1. *scarcity* and *opportunity cost*
2. *factors of production* and *capital*
3. *free enterprise* and *profit*
4. *capitalism* and *invest*
5. *command economy* and *mixed economy*

Reviewing Main Ideas and Skills

6. Why do people in any economy have to make choices about what to produce and consume?

7. If you lived in a traditional economy, how would you be likely to decide on a job or career?

8. In a command economy, who decides how resources will be used and what goods and services will be produced?

9. In a market economy, what determines who gets the goods and services that are produced?

10. **How to Choose and Take Action** Suppose you have been offered three different summer jobs and you have to choose which one to take. Why is it important to predict the consequences of each option before making a decision?

11. **How to Interpret a Diagram** Look back at the want-satisfaction chain on page 290. Pick a product that you might want. Then create your own diagram, illustrating the steps in the process of satisfying your want.

Critical Thinking

12. **Making Decisions** Think of a difficult economic choice you have had to make. What was the most important factor you considered when you made your decision? Why?

13. **Analyzing Ideas** Describe the important freedoms that people have in a market economy.

Writing About Civics

14. **Writing an Essay** Suppose that you are the ruler of a society with a command economy. Write a one page essay describing how you would make the basic economic decisions for your society. Why? Include the essay in your portfolio.

Citizenship Activities

15. **Careers** In small groups, interview the manager of a local business such as a store or restaurant. Find out what kinds of decisions the person must make about how, how much, and what to produce. Ask how he or she makes those decisions. As a group, make a short oral report to the rest of the class about what you learned.

 Take It to the NET

Access the **Civics: Participating in Government** Internet site at **www.phschool.com** for the specific URLs to complete the activity.

Water is an everyday resource we often take for granted. Explore online information about water usage. Prepare a short presentation to the class on the current state of clean, drinkable water around the country or around the globe.

Basics of Our Economic System

Citizenship and You

The farmers' market is alive with activity. Eric and his friends are here because they love fresh strawberries, and it is now the middle of strawberry season. Many farmers are selling the sweet red berries in small paper or plastic baskets.

Eric notices that the prices for a basket of strawberries are almost all the same—50 cents a basket. One farmer, however, is charging 40 cents a basket. People are crowding around his stall. Another farmer is selling her strawberries for 60 cents a basket. Eric notices she has slightly fewer customers than the other farmers. He walks up to her stall and asks why her prices are higher.

"It costs me more to grow my strawberries," she answers. "I grow them without insecticides and I use organic fertilizer. I have to charge more to make a profit. But I think my strawberries taste better and are better for you."

Eric wonders which strawberries he and his friends should buy. He knows that choices made by individuals are what control a market economy. He sees that farmers make choices about how to grow their crops, and consumers make choices about what and how much to buy.

What's Ahead in Chapter 14

This chapter will help you understand economic choices. You will also find out what it means to own a business in the United States, and what it means to be a worker. As you learn more about how our market economy works, you will better understand how it affects you and your community.

Section 1 The Principles of Our Market Economy

Section 2 The Role of Businesses in the American Economy

Section 3 Labor in the American Economy

Keep It Current

Items marked with this logo are periodically updated on the Internet. To keep up-to-date, go to www.phschool.com

Citizen's Journal

Suppose you were a farmer selling strawberries at a farmers' market. What would your strategy be? To sell your strawberries at a lower price than your competitors? To sell the best-tasting strawberries? Explain your thinking.

The Principles of Our Market Economy

SECTION PREVIEW

Objectives

- Explain how goods, services, resources, and money flow through the economy.
- Summarize the laws of supply and demand.

Building Civics Vocabulary

- Producers pay **rent** in exchange for the use of land.
- **Interest** is payment for the use of capital.
- **Demand** is the amount of a product or service that buyers are willing and able to purchase at different prices.
- **Supply** is the amount of a product that producers are willing and able to offer at different prices.
- The **market price** is the price at which buyers and sellers agree to trade.

 Focus

In Chapter 13 you learned that the United States has a mixed economy that is based on the principles of a free enterprise, market system. In order to understand the American economy, then, it is important to take a closer look at the basic ways in which a market economy works.

The Circular Flow of Economic Activity

You rely on a steady flow of blood throughout your body to remain healthy. In a similar way, a healthy market economy depends on a steady flow of resources, goods, and services. An example will show how this flow occurs in our economy.

Suppose that your bicycle has a flat tire. At the bike shop you hand the clerk four dollars and receive a new inner tube. This simple kind of exchange is repeated millions of times each day by millions of Americans.

Buying something, however, is only one kind of exchange. Suppose that you also work part time for the bicycle shop. You exchange your labor for an hourly wage. These two exchanges—money for an inner tube and work for wages—are connected because you buy inner tubes with the money you earn from working.

By being a part of both exchanges, you have created a "flow" of labor, inner tubes, and money. This is an example of what economists call the circular flow of economic activity. The outside circle of the diagram below shows the flow of labor and inner tubes. The money (wages and cash) flowing in the inner circle only makes it easier for the exchange of labor and inner tubes to occur.

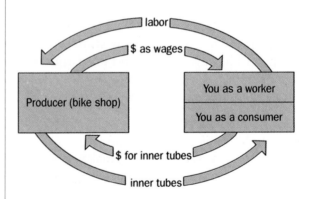

Expanding the Circular Flow This example of the circular flow of labor, inner tubes, and money involves just you and one business. In real life, people exchange their labor to buy goods and services from many businesses. The entire American economy, however, is based on a circular flow that is very similar to the one involving you and the bike shop.

Imagine, instead of the bike shop, every American business that produces goods or services. Together, all these businesses can be called producers. Then imagine, instead of you, all individuals in our society. The diagram below shows how goods, services, labor, and money flow through the United States economy.

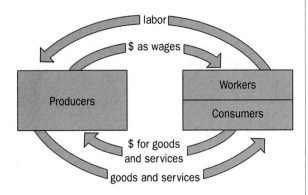

This circular flow diagram is not quite complete, however. Labor is only one of the resources that producers need to create goods. Producers also need land, which includes raw materials, and capital, which includes tools and machines used in production.

Producers exchange a certain kind of payment for the use of land and capital. Rent is the payment for the use of land. Interest is the payment for the use of capital. The payment for the use of labor is called wages. The diagram below shows the complete picture of the circular flow of economic activity.

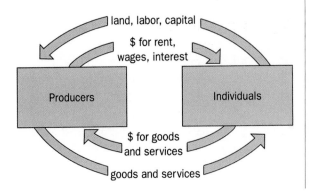

The exchange of labor, money, and bicycles that takes place in this bicycle shop is part of the circular flow of economic activity.

Supply and Demand

As goods, services, and money flow through the economy, producers and individuals act both as buyers and as sellers. You may recall that when buyers and sellers come together to exchange goods and services, they do so through what is called a market. Markets determine how much will be produced in a free enterprise economy. Markets also determine prices. How are markets able to do this?

In our free enterprise system, individuals are free to make choices about how to use resources to satisfy their needs. Producers compete to sell goods and services to consumers.

When there is free competition among sellers and among buyers, a market works according to what are called the laws of supply and demand. These "laws" are not made by legislatures. They are descriptions of what happens when many people make choices in a market.

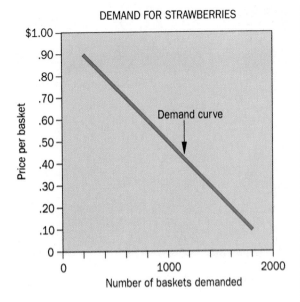

DEMAND FOR STRAWBERRIES

Price per basket / Number of baskets demanded

Demand curve

decide to buy strawberries, and the quantity demanded will be low.

The way the law of demand works for a particular product can be shown on a graph. The graph on the left, for example, shows what the quantity of strawberries demanded at the farmers' market is likely to be at different prices. The demand is described by the line on the graph, called the demand curve.

The Law of Supply A producer, like a buyer, balances costs and benefits when making decisions in a market. A producer's cost is determined by how much it costs to produce an item, such as a basket of strawberries. The price a buyer pays determines a producer's benefit. The higher the price, the higher the benefit to the producer.

Supply is defined as the amounts of a product that producers are willing and able to offer at different prices. When the price is high, more producers are willing to supply the product and to supply more of it. As a result, the amount supplied by producers as a whole will be high. When the price is low, fewer producers are willing to supply the product, and the quantity supplied will be low.

The Law of Demand Have you noticed that when the price of something is low, people will often buy more of it? Eric saw this happening at the farmers' market. People bought many strawberries from the farmer who was selling them for 40 cents a basket. In other words, people were demanding large amounts of strawberries at that price. Demand is defined as the amounts of a product or service buyers are willing and able to buy at different prices.

In deciding whether or not to buy an item, you balance its cost to you with the benefit you think you will receive from it. Will you enjoy the strawberries enough to buy a basket at 40 cents? Would the benefit be great enough for you to pay 80 cents? The lower the price of an item, and thus its cost to you, the more likely you are to decide to buy it.

At a low price, more people will want baskets of strawberries, and more people will be able to afford them. Also, more people will decide to buy more than one basket. In short, the quantity demanded by buyers will be high. At a high price, fewer people will

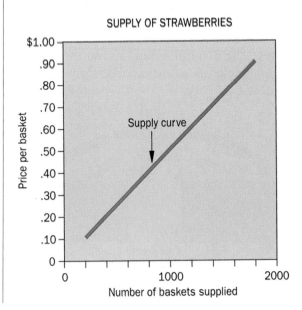

SUPPLY OF STRAWBERRIES

Price per basket / Number of baskets supplied

Supply curve

The way the law of supply works for a particular product can also be shown on a graph. The line on the graph on the bottom of the previous page is the supply curve. It shows what the quantity of strawberries supplied at the farmers' market is likely to be at different prices.

Supply and Demand Think for a moment about the farmers' market. Farmers want to sell at a high price. Buyers want to buy at a low price. You may be wondering how the price gets decided.

The law of demand and the law of supply work together in determining both the price of a product and the quantity that will be offered. As you have seen, price affects the amounts demanded and the amounts supplied in opposite ways. Another way of saying this is that the demand curve slopes down and the supply curve slopes up.

At higher prices, more of a product will be supplied but less will be demanded. At lower prices, less will be supplied but more demanded.

The quantity supplied and the quantity demanded, however, will tend to equal each

Interactive displays and advertising are aimed at increasing consumer demand for certain products, such as these notebook computers.

other in an ideal market. This balance takes place at a particular price called the market price. The market price is the price at which buyers and sellers agree to trade. If the demand and supply curves are placed on the same graph, the market price will be where the demand and supply curves intersect, or cross. The graph on the left shows supply, demand, and market price.

At the farmers' market today, the market price for strawberries is 50 cents a basket. At this price, all the producers together are supplying about 1,000 baskets, and consumers are demanding about 1,000 baskets. A market price of 50 cents, however, does not prevent some farmers from charging less than the market price and other farmers from charging more.

If all the farmers raised their price for strawberries to 90 cents a basket, many buyers

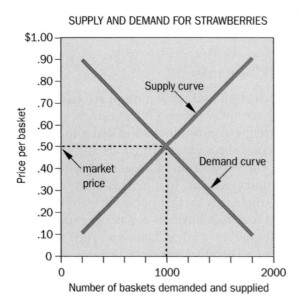

SUPPLY AND DEMAND FOR STRAWBERRIES

would decide the price was too high. The quantity demanded would fall, and farmers would find they could not sell all their strawberries at that price. They would have to lower their prices in order to encourage a higher demand. If all other factors remained the same, the price would settle back to 50 cents a basket.

Other Influences Of course, demand can be influenced by factors other than price. For example, the demand for basic products, such as milk and penicillin, will not change very much when the price changes, because people believe that they need milk and medicine at almost any price.

Advertising, styles of fashion, and the way consumers perceive a certain product can also have very important effects on the demand for that product. You might decide to buy a higher-priced pair of jeans, for instance, because that brand is more popular than a lower-priced brand.

Even though supply and demand can be affected by forces other than prices, the laws of supply and demand form one of the foundations of our market economy. They have an influence on all the basic economic decisions that Americans make.

Section 1 Assessment

1. **Define** rent, interest, demand, supply, market price
2. Describe in your own words the circular flow of economic activity.
3. What effect will a rise in the price of a product have on its demand and its supply?
4. **Apply** Think about the choices you have made as a consumer in the last week. What factors affected you?

The Role of Businesses in the American Economy

SECTION PREVIEW

Objectives
- Analyze the role of entrepreneurs in our economy.
- Describe how businesses use labor, land, and capital.
- Compare the three basic types of business ownership in the United States.
- Examine the rise of large corporations in the American economy.

Building Civics Vocabulary
- A person who starts a business is called an **entrepreneur**.
- A **sole proprietorship** is a business owned by an individual.
- A **partnership** is a type of business in which two or more people share ownership.
- A **corporation** is a business that is separate from the people who own it and legally acts as a single person.
- The shares of ownership in a corporation are called **stock**.

 Focus

Production and consumption are basic to any economy. As you have learned, people participate in production in order to be able to consume a variety of goods and services.

The production of goods and services is a complex process. In a market economy, most production is carried out by privately owned businesses. A business is any organization that combines labor, land, and capital in order to produce goods or services.

Ice Cream Makers Share Success

How many self-made millionaires learned their chosen business through the mail? According to Ben Cohen and Jerry Greenfield, that's exactly what they did. In 1978 the two childhood friends completed a correspondence course in ice-cream making, and later that year they opened their first Ben & Jerry's ice cream scoop shop in a converted gas station in downtown Burlington, Vermont. The business was an immediate success.

Today, these two entrepreneurs are known not only for their inventive ice cream flavors, but for their business philosophy as well. For them, success has meant giving back to the community. Following what Ben and Jerry call the "community-oriented"

approach to business, every year the company gives away a percentage of its earnings to help fund projects related to children and families, disadvantaged groups, and the environment.

In the mid 1990s the company's growth slowed somewhat as new competitors entered the ice cream market. Ben & Jerry's

began receiving pressure from stockholders to turn bigger profits.

In April 2000, Ben and Jerry sold the company to Unilever, a huge European food company. Because Unilever is an international company with a lot of money, it can sell Ben & Jerry's ice cream worldwide and increase profits.

Unilever promised to continue the policy of giving to charity. "We hope that, as part of Unilever, Ben & Jerry's will continue to expand its role in society," said Ben and Jerry.

Active Citizenship

Describe what Ben and Jerry mean by the "community-oriented" approach to business.

The Role of the Entrepreneur

Because businesses are so important in our economy, the people who start businesses play a very important role. A person who starts a business is called an entrepreneur (AHN truh preh NOOR).

An entrepreneur begins with an idea for a new product, a new way of producing something, or a better way of providing a service.

The entrepreneur then raises money for capital goods to start the business. This money can be the entrepreneur's own, or it can be borrowed from people or banks willing to invest in the business.

By deciding to start a business, the entrepreneur is usually taking a major risk. What if the business fails? The entrepreneur could lose all the money he or she invested in it. If the business does well, however, the entrepreneur stands to make a profit. This profit will be the income earned by the business, minus the costs of the resources it uses. The hope of earning a profit—the profit motive—is what motivates people in a capitalist economy to start and to run businesses.

Using the Factors of Production

In Chapter 13 you learned about three basic factors of production: labor, land, and capital. Some entrepreneurs are able to provide some factors of production themselves. Scott Sullivan, for example, is launching a small pie-baking business. He provides the labor by baking the pies himself. He provides the capital by using the pans and ovens in his own kitchen. All he needs to buy, with money he has saved, are ingredients such as fruit, flour, sugar, and shortening.

Payments for Resources Other entrepreneurs and business owners obtain the factors of production from other sources. Alice Ling is starting a larger pie-baking business. To set up a commercial kitchen, Alice borrows money from a bank to buy capital goods such as large ovens. In exchange for this loan, she pays the bank interest. Alice's kitchen is located on land owned by someone else. In exchange for the use of this land, Alice pays the owner rent. Finally, Alice hires workers as labor and pays them hourly wages. If she needs help in running her business, she will hire managers and pay them monthly salaries.

Through this example, you can see how businesses get each factor of production in exchange for a particular kind of payment. The diagram on this page shows these exchanges between businesses and the owners of resources. Some economists consider entrepreneurship to be a fourth factor of production. They point out that entrepreneurs provide ideas and take risks in return for payment in the form of profit.

How Businesses are Owned

When entrepreneurs such as Scott and Alice are planning their businesses, they must make an important decision. How will their businesses be owned? There are three basic types of business ownership in the United States: the sole proprietorship, the partnership, and the corporation. Each type has advantages and disadvantages.

Opening a sole proprietorship like this family-run Thai restaurant is a way many newcomers to the United States enter the economy.

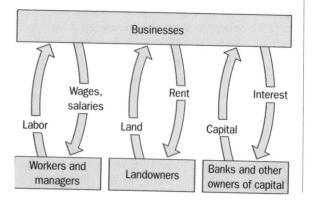

Businesses

Wages, salaries

Rent

Interest

Labor

Land

Capital

Workers and managers

Landowners

Banks and other owners of capital

The floor of the New York Stock Exchange is a tangle of telephones, TV monitors, and traders buying and selling shares in corporations.

The Sole Proprietorship Many entrepreneurs starting a small business, like Scott Sullivan, will establish a sole proprietorship, which is a business owned by an individual. Sole proprietorships are the most common form of business in the United States. About 70 percent of the businesses in this country are sole proprietorships. Most are small businesses such as restaurants, television repair shops, and small grocery stores.

The advantages of a sole proprietorship are many. The owner, or sole proprietor, has the freedom to decide how to run the business, and the profits belong to the owner alone. The owner also has the personal satisfaction of knowing that he or she made the business succeed.

There are also several disadvantages of a sole proprietorship. First, the owner has the whole responsibility for paying off loans and other business debts. Second, it can be hard for one owner to borrow enough money to expand the business beyond a certain size. Third, as a business grows it becomes increasingly difficult for one owner to handle all the responsibilities and decision making.

The Partnership A partnership is a type of business in which two or more people share ownership. Alice, for example, could set up her pie-baking business as a partnership if she knew someone who wanted to share the costs and help her run the business. In the United States, many law firms, medical groups, and accounting businesses are set up as partnerships.

The advantages and disadvantages of a partnership are similar to those of a sole proprietorship. The main difference is that risks and benefits are shared by more than

Facts & Quotes

American Corporations

Every year *Fortune* magazine publishes the Fortune 500, a list of the nation's largest corporations. Here are the companies that topped the 2000 list:

Company	Revenue (in millions)
1. General Motors	$189,058.0
2. Wal-Mart Stores	166,809.0
3. Exxon	163,881.0
4. Ford Motor Company	162,558.0
5. General Electric	111,630.0

By forming corporations and selling stock, early entrepreneurs could raise enough money to build factories like this cash register factory.

one person. An additional disadvantage of a partnership is the possibility of serious differences arising between the partners, which could damage or ruin the business.

The Corporation Sole proprietors and partners are closely linked to the businesses they own. The debts of their businesses, for example, are their personal debts. In contrast, a corporation is a business that is separate from the people who own it and legally acts as a single person. A corporation can have debts, hire workers, and make profits.

The ownership of a corporation is shared by more than one person. The shares of ownership in a corporation are called its stock, and people who buy stock are called stockholders.

Many corporations offer their stock for sale to the public. By selling stock, a corporation raises the money that is necessary to start, run, and expand the business. Millions of Americans buy stock as an investment because, as stockholders, they share the corporation's profits.

A corporation has unique advantages. It can raise large quantities of money to help it grow mainly through selling stock. Furthermore, stockholders are not responsible for the corporation's debts. If the corporation fails, a stockholder loses only the value of his or her stock.

Corporations also have several disadvantages compared to the two other forms of business ownership. Corporations are more difficult and more expensive to start. In addition, they are more limited by government regulations.

Corporations create more of the products, profits, and jobs in our economy than the other two forms of businesses combined. It is important to realize, however, that although most large businesses are corporations, not all corporations are large. Even

THE IMPORTANCE OF CORPORATIONS

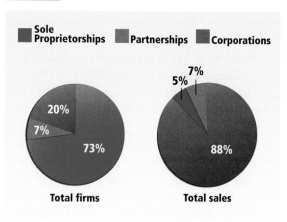

Total firms

Total sales

Source: Internal Revenue Service

Corporations dominate the American economy. **Economics What percentage of American firms are partnerships?**

Although many farms are still family owned, corporations have been playing a growing role in American agriculture.

some small businesses can benefit from the advantages of being a corporation.

The Rise of Big Business

Large businesses organized as corporations dominate our economy today. They make nearly 90 percent of the total sales in the American economy. However, large corporations did not always have such an important role in our economy.

In our country's early years, most businesses were small sole proprietorships. The economy was also very different. Many families were nearly self-sufficient, producing much of what they needed for themselves.

This situation changed dramatically during the 1800s. New inventions and manufacturing methods spurred growth and industrialization. Factories sprang up, producing more goods at lower prices. The population grew rapidly as immigrants poured into the country. People settled in cities, attracted by jobs in new industries.

People who lived in cities depended on businesses for the goods and services they wanted, and businesses did well. Successful sole proprietors turned their businesses into corporations in order to grow. Corporations could raise money more easily by selling stock and borrowing from banks. By the end of the 1800s, large corporations dominated the railroads, key manufacturing industries, and mining.

In the past 100 years, large corporations have become a major force in nearly every industry. Today, large corporations own most supermarkets and fast-food chains. They make most of our computers and automobiles. Large corporations even own many of America's farms.

One reason large corporations have grown in importance is that they can produce goods and provide services more efficiently than smaller firms. Large firms can better afford the expensive machinery needed to produce more goods in less time. They also have the resources to do scientific research to develop new products and production methods.

In the future, large businesses organized as corporations will probably continue to grow in importance. However, sole proprietorships, partnerships, and small corporations will always have an important role to play in our economy.

Section 2 Assessment

1. **Define** entrepreneur, sole proprietorship, partnership, corporation, stock
2. Why are entrepreneurs important to the American economic system?
3. What is the payment a business makes for the use of each factor of production?
4. What are the advantages and disadvantages of a sole proprietorship?
5. What factors led to the rise of large businesses during the 1800s?
6. **Analyze** Why are corporations considered a vitally important part of the American economy?

Labor in the American Economy

SECTION PREVIEW

Objectives

- Explain the growth of wage labor during the nineteenth century.
- Summarize the struggle between early labor unions and employers.
- Analyze the accomplishments of labor unions since 1930.
- Describe how the American labor force has changed throughout our history.

Building Civics Vocabulary

- **Labor unions** are organizations of workers that seek to improve wages and working conditions.
- **Collective bargaining** is the process by which representatives of unions and businesses negotiate.
- To **boycott** is to refuse to buy a product.
- In a **strike,** workers refuse to work unless employers meet certain demands.

Focus

Labor, as you know, is one of the factors of production. However, labor is different from the other factors of production in that it is provided by human beings who care about their working conditions and the rewards they receive for their labor.

Workers have a built-in conflict with entrepreneurs and business managers. On the one hand, business owners want to keep costs low and profits high. One way to do this is to keep wages low. Workers, on the other hand, want to earn the highest possible wages. You will see how this conflict between business and labor has had an important impact on the American economic system.

The Growth of Wage Labor

As you recall, many Americans were farmers when our country was young. Most of what they needed they produced themselves. They could do this because they owned a productive resource—land.

Unsafe working conditions and long hours, even for young children, led workers in the late nineteenth century to band together in labor unions.

Many other Americans were skilled craftspeople, such as shoemakers, blacksmiths, and tailors. Craftspeople either worked for themselves or for someone they knew personally. They also generally owned their own capital—the tools of their craft. Most Americans, therefore, had control over the conditions of their work.

In the nineteenth century, however, great changes began to occur. First, improvements in farm machinery meant there was less demand for workers on farms. Second, new machinery and manufacturing methods caused rapid industrialization. Because machines could produce more goods and could do it more cheaply than people making goods by hand, many craftspeople found themselves out of work.

As a result of these changes, more and more former craftspeople and farmhands, as well as arriving immigrants, turned to wage labor to make a living. Wage laborers worked in mines, in factories, and in smaller manufacturing workshops. They owned no land or tools. Instead, they exchanged their labor for payments called wages, and their employers controlled the conditions of their work.

Poor Working Conditions Many wage laborers were faced with a grim choice: to do whatever work was available at any wage or to starve. Business owners took advantage of this situation by paying very low wages. If a worker complained, he or she could be fired. There were plenty of other people wanting to take that worker's place.

The numbers of wage laborers grew steadily during the 1800s as factories increased in number. Most factory jobs were monotonous, low-paid, and dangerous. Wage laborers, many of them children as young as six years old, worked six days a week, 12 to 16 hours a day.

The Rise of Labor Unions

Compared to the power of the owner of a large business, an individual worker had little power over wages and working conditions. Workers began to realize that they could influence their employers only if they organized into groups fighting for common goals. As a result, workers began to form labor unions, which are organizations of workers that seek to improve wages and working conditions and to protect members' rights.

The first American unions began sprouting up in the 1790s. The movement grew, and by the early 1880s there were many small unions across the country. Most were organized as trade unions, made up of workers in one particular trade such as carpentry or cigarmaking. These were generally skilled workers, whose jobs required some special know-how. Because such workers could not be easily replaced, their employers were

 MEMBERSHIP IN AMERICAN LABOR UNIONS Union membership has fallen slowly since the 1970s. **Economics During which ten year period did union membership rise by over 10 million?**

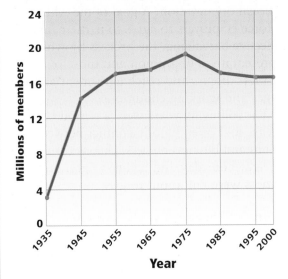

Source: Statistical Abstract of the U.S.

METHODS THAT EMPLOYERS AND UNIONS USE IN DISPUTES Workers and businesses have used a number of tactics in disputes over wages and working conditions. **Economics** What are three ways that businesses have responded to strikes by workers?

Union Tactics	Employer Tactics
Slowdowns	Strikebreakers
Sit-ins	Security forces
Strikes	Lockouts
Boycotts	Yellow-dog contracts
Demonstrations	Blacklists

more likely to listen to them to keep them from leaving.

The first important national union was The Noble Order of the Knights of Labor, which reached its height in 1886. The Knights of Labor tried to bring together the entire working class, both skilled and unskilled. However, these two groups of workers often disagreed, and finally the union broke up.

Soon after, a new union, the American Federation of Labor (AFL), gained power. Founded by Samuel Gompers in 1886, the AFL united smaller trade unions, made up of only skilled workers, into a more powerful national organization. A goal of the AFL was to force employers to agree to participate in collective bargaining, the process by which representatives of a union and those of a business discuss and reach agreement about wages and working conditions.

The following years were a period of intense and often bloody conflict between unions and business owners. Unions demanded an eight-hour day and higher wages, but the owners were not about to give in.

Labor's Weapons In the early days, unions used several methods to try to force reluctant employers to meet their demands. In a slowdown, workers stayed on the job but did their work much more slowly. In a sit-down strike, workers stopped working but refused to leave the factory, so the employer could not replace them with non-union workers. Sometimes union members would urge their members and the public to boycott, or refuse to buy, an employer's products.

Through the years, however, the major weapon of the unions has been the strike. In a strike, workers refuse to work unless employers meet certain demands. Hundreds of strikes occurred between 1886 and 1920. Some of the longest strikes involving the most unions were by textile, steel, and railroad unions. Most of these strikes were organized by AFL unions, but other unions had important roles as well.

The Weapons of Business Business owners responded to strikes in various ways. Typically they used strikebreakers, or "scabs"– non-union workers hired to replace the striking workers. If union workers tried to keep strikebreakers from entering the factory, business owners often hired private police to stop them. These private police also broke up union meetings and bothered union members in other ways. Often the business owners had the support of local police or state militias. Violence broke out during some strikes, causing many deaths.

In their struggle with the unions, employers used other methods as well. In lockouts, management refused to let union members enter the factory, and replaced them with scabs. Some employers forced workers to sign "yellow-dog contracts" in which they promised never to join the union. Finally, some employers circulated blacklists containing the names of union members and supporters, so that other employers would not hire them.

Gains and Losses The weapons used by both labor and management were basically economic. Sit-downs, slowdowns, boycotts, and strikes were all intended to interrupt production and reduce business profits. When employers used yellow-dog contracts, lockouts, blacklists, and strikebreakers, they took away union members' jobs and thus their ability to make a living.

By 1920, labor unions had achieved some important victories. A few industries had reduced the working day to 8 or 10 hours. Wages had increased for some workers. The federal government had established the Department of Labor to protect the rights of workers. In spite of these gains, however, labor suffered many crushing defeats and broken strikes.

Labor Unions Since 1930

After suffering setbacks in the 1920s, unions made important gains during the 1930s because the government began to fully recognize the right of unions to exist and to strike. In 1935, Congress passed the National Labor Relations Act, or Wagner Act. It required employers to bargain with unions. This act also outlawed several methods business owners had used to weaken unions.

More recent laws, such as the Taft-Hartley Act of 1947 and the Landrum-Griffin Act of 1959, have put limits on the powers of unions and union leaders.

However, the Wagner Act marked a turning point in the history of American labor. Unions felt that their rightful place in the American economy had finally been recognized.

Meanwhile, a new kind of union was gaining strength: the industrial union. An industrial union includes all workers in a particular industry—both skilled and unskilled. Soon, workers in such industries as steel, coal, and rubber had their own industrial unions. In 1935, some industrial unions within the AFL formed the Committee of Industrial Organizations (CIO). In 1938 these unions were expelled from the AFL and became independent as the CIO.

The Wagner Act and the creation of the CIO set the stage for the development of the modern labor movement. At first the AFL and the CIO were rivals, competing for members. In 1955, however, the two unions united to form the AFL-CIO.

 PERCENTAGE OF LABOR FORCE THAT BELONGED TO UNIONS IN 2000

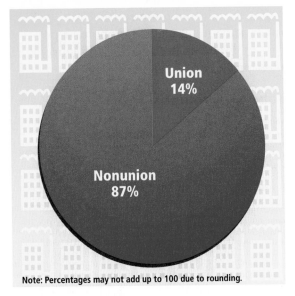

Union 14%

Nonunion 87%

Note: Percentages may not add up to 100 due to rounding.

Source: Bureau of Labor Statistics

 The majority of the people in the labor force do not belong to a union.
Economics What percentage of the labor force belonged to unions in 2000?

At the end of a successful collective bargaining session, union and business representatives sign an agreement, or contract.

Today, the AFL-CIO is the most powerful voice of organized labor in the United States. It has over 13 million members. Among its other activities, it plays an important political role by lobbying in Congress and working to elect pro-labor candidates to office.

Labor's Accomplishments In spite of setbacks and opposition, labor unions have made many gains for workers. Since the early 1930s, unions have helped win fairer wages for workers. They have been a major force in getting the government to pass laws creating social security, unemployment insurance, and a minimum wage. They have also worked for laws protecting workers' safety, banning child labor, and providing retraining for workers who have lost their jobs.

Today, only about one worker in seven is a union member, and union membership has declined in recent decades. Still, labor unions have played a key role in improving the lives of all workers.

Common Interests Unions today still go on strike and encourage boycotts. However, both workers and employers have learned to see their shared interests as well as their differences. Employers see that workers need safe working conditions. They also know that workers who are paid fairly produce more and are more likely to buy goods and services, thus contributing to a healthy economy.

Unions, on the other hand, recognize that members' jobs depend on businesses making profits. They have seen that when wages rise too high, profits may decline. Then businesses may fail or move to other states or foreign countries where labor costs are lower.

Today's Labor Force

As you have seen, the composition of the labor force—the number of people working at each type of job in the economy—has changed a great deal since the birth of our country. For example, farmers, who outnumbered any other kind of worker in 1776, today make up less than 3 percent of the American labor force. There are also more women in the labor force than ever before. Since the 1940s, women have been entering the labor force in ever-increasing numbers.

Another important change in the labor force has occurred over the last several decades. Manufacturing industries such as steelmaking, once the foundation of our economy, have declined in importance. As a result, these industries are employing a decreasing percentage of America's workers.

At the same time, businesses that offer services have grown in importance. These service-oriented businesses, such as banks, insurance companies, computer software firms, restaurants, movie theaters, and resorts, now employ a large and growing majority of American workers. These businesses make up what is called the service sector of the economy.

The change in focus of our economy, from manufacturing to service, has caused many problems for workers. When a steel factory closes, for example, its workers do not always have the training to find new jobs in the computer industry. Furthermore, service-sector businesses are often located in different parts of the country than the factories that are closing. Americans, therefore, face personal and economic change as our country shifts from an industrial economy to a service economy.

Section 3 Assessment

1. **Define** labor unions, collective bargaining, boycott, strike
2. What changes caused the growth of wage labor in the 1800s?
3. Describe the major weapons that unions and employers have used in their disputes.
4. What are three important gains that labor unions have made for workers since the 1930s?
5. What is one example of a service business?
6. **Apply** What are some of the ways the changes taking place in today's labor force may affect you as an adult?

Extending the Chapter

Global Views

In this chapter you have learned about the American economic system. Our economy, however, does not exist alone in the world. It influences, and is influenced by, a larger economy that spans the globe.

Evidence of a global economy is all around you. Many of the products you eat, use, and wear were grown or produced in another country. The global economy makes it possible for consumers all over the world to have a widening choice of goods and services to buy.

A global economy also means that the countries of the world are interconnected. Economic events in one country can have results far beyond that country's borders. For example, if farmers in Brazil produced less coffee, coffee drinkers in Europe and the United States would feel the effect in

the form of a shortage of coffee and higher coffee prices.

Similarly, your choices as an American consumer can affect the workers, farmers, and environments of other countries. Demand for certain electronic goods, for example, can provide jobs for people who produce those products in other countries. However, demands can sometimes have negative effects. In the twentieth century, demand for jewelry made of ivory encouraged the slaughter of many elephants in Africa.

In this century, the nations of the world will have to work together more closely than they often have in the past. A global economy means that we are all dependent on each other for our economic well-being.

How to READ CIRCULAR FLOW CHARTS

Flow charts are often used to show the steps in a process. In Chapter 8, for example, a flow chart was used to illustrate the steps in the process of how a bill becomes a law. In this chapter you have been studying a special kind of flow chart—a circular flow chart. Economists often use circular flow charts to explain how an economy works.

Explain the Skill

Circular flow charts illustrate how money, resources, goods, and services flow through an economy. The chart on page 308, for example, shows the flow of economic activity at a bicycle shop. The arrow from the bike shop to you as a worker shows wages, while the arrow from you as a consumer to the bike shop shows the money you spend. Follow the arrow from you as a worker to the bike shop and you will see labor. Follow the arrow from the bike shop to you as a consumer and you will see inner tubes. By following the circles, you see that labor is exchanged for an hourly wage, and money is exchanged for inner tubes.

Analyze the Skill

Look at the circular flow chart on this page. The two rectangles are used to represent two major economic groups—individuals and producers. Circles show the flow of money, land, labor, capital, goods, and services between the different groups in the economy. Use this circular flow chart to answer the following questions.

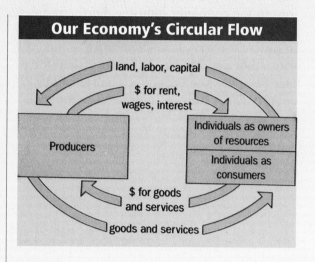

Our Economy's Circular Flow

land, labor, capital

$ for rent, wages, interest

Producers

Individuals as owners of resources

Individuals as consumers

$ for goods and services

goods and services

Skill Assessment

1. What two roles do individuals play in this circular flow chart?
2. Which circle shows the basic factors of production and what gets produced—the inside circle or the outside circle?
3. Which circle shows the flow of money through the economy?
4. Where do producers get the land, labor, and capital needed to produce goods and services?
5. Where do consumers get the goods and services they need?
6. Where do consumers get the money they need to pay for goods and services?
7. Where do producers get the money they need to pay for land, labor, and capital?
8. What are some other processes that could be illustrated by a circular flow chart?

CHAPTER 14 ASSESSMENT

Building Civics Vocabulary

The vocabulary terms in each pair listed below are related to each other. For each pair, explain how the terms are related.

Example: *Consumer* is related to *worker* because both terms describe roles individuals play in the economic system.

1. *demand* and *supply*
2. *rent* and *interest*
3. *stock* and *corporation*
4. *labor union* and *strike*

Reviewing Main Ideas and Skills

5. For a particular product, why does the quantity demanded usually decrease when the price increases? When is a higher price less likely to affect demand?

6. What does an entrepreneur hope to gain by starting a business? What does he or she contribute to the business?

7. What are the main advantages of each form of business ownership: sole proprietorship, partnership, and corporation?

8. **How to Read Circular Flow Charts** Look at the circular flow chart on page 308. What two exchanges are illustrated in this chart?

Critical Thinking

9. **Identifying Alternatives** You have invented a new type of soft drink. You want to start a business making, bottling, and selling your drink. What form of business ownership would you choose? Explain.

10. **Defending a Position** "Corporations are the most important form of business in our economy today." Do you agree with this statement? Support your position.

Writing About Civics

11. **Writing an Essay** Write an essay describing four purchases you have made recently and the prices you paid for each. Which items would you have bought even if the price were higher? At what price would you no longer have been willing to buy each item? What factors other than price influenced your decisions to buy? Include the essay in your portfolio.

Citizenship Activities

12. **Your Local Community** With a group, investigate a business in your community. Identify the producers and interview them to find out what goods or services they produce. Find out who the resource owners are and what resources they contribute. Find out who the consumers are. Make a circular flow diagram to show the information you have collected.

Take It to the NET

Access the **Civics: Participating in Government** Internet site at **www.phschool.com** for the specific URLs to complete the activity.

Economies can have both upswings and downswings, good times and bad. One of the hardest times for the United States was the Great Depression. Explore online information about the United States economy in the 1920s. Create a time line of the events that led to the Great Depression.

Money and Banking

Citizenship and You

The United States Bureau of Engraving and Printing began printing paper money during the Civil War, when there was a shortage of coins. Here are some facts about United States money today:

★ The Bureau of Engraving and Printing produces about 37 million paper bills a day with a total face value of nearly $700 million. It costs the government approximately 4.2 cents to produce each bill.

★ The United States dollar is the most widely held type of money in the world. As of July 2000, there was $540 billion in circulation worldwide. $365 billion of this was in $100 bills—the largest bill currently printed.

★ The United States Secret Service was created in 1865 to combat counterfeiting of United States money. Today, the government estimates that .03 percent of the United States bills in circulation are counterfeit.

★ Paper bills can wear out quickly from handling. The average life span of a $1 bill is about 18 months. $100 bills, which are handled less often, last an average of eight and a half years.

 Keep It Current

Items marked with this logo are periodically updated on the Internet. To keep up-to-date, go to www.phschool.com

What's Ahead in Chapter 15

In this chapter you will read about money—what it is, what it does, and how banks help us save it and use it. You will also be introduced to the way our banking system is regulated by the federal government. This information will give you a better understanding of your role in the American economy.

Section 1 **Money**

Section 2 **Our Banking System**

Section 3 **The Federal Reserve System**

Citizen's Journal

Suppose you were in charge of designing a new $500 bill. Whose portrait would you put on the front of the bill? What would you put on the back of the bill? Explain your choices. How would you design the bill so it could not be counterfeited?

SECTION PREVIEW

Objectives
- Describe the three basic functions of money.
- Summarize the characteristics of our money.
- Explain why our money has value.

Building Civics Vocabulary
- The coins and paper bills used as money in an economy are called **currency.**

Focus

Our market economy could not work without money. Like the blood in your body, money flows throughout our economic system, connecting and feeding all the vital parts. Without money, we would have to rely on bartering—exchanging goods and services. Such trading would be inconvenient in the economy we have today.

The Functions of Money

Money has three basic functions no matter what kind of economy it is used in. When you go to the store to buy a can of soda or a pen, why does the person behind the counter accept your money in exchange for real goods? After all, money is just some pieces of metal or paper. Your money is accepted because the owner of the store can spend it elsewhere to buy something he or she wants.

Exchanging money for cans of soda, pens, and other goods and services is an everyday event. It illustrates the first and most basic function of money. Money is a medium of exchange between individuals in an economy.

Money's second basic function is not as easy to see. Suppose you visit a shopping mall and discover a jacket on sale for $30. You know that this price is a "good deal," because you have checked the price of the same kind of jacket in other stores. You can compare the cost of the jacket in this store with its cost elsewhere because the price is expressed in the same way in every store—in terms of dollars and cents. Would it be as easy to know if the jacket was a good deal if the store owner offered to sell it to you for three cows, and other stores were charging six sheep?

Prices stated in money terms provide a standard which allows you to compare values of goods and services. The prices that you see every day reflect the second basic function of money. Money is a standard of value for goods and services.

The third function of money can be recognized when you decide to keep it instead of spending it. If you save money by hiding it in a dresser drawer or putting it in a bank, you are storing it for use in the future. Saving shows the third basic function of money. Money serves as a store of value, allowing you to buy goods or services sometime in the future.

Facts & Quotes

The First Penny

In 1787, the United States government issued the first American coin—the Fugio penny. On the front of this large copper coin, a chain made up of thirteen links encircles the words "We Are One." On the other side is stamped the advice "Mind Your Business."

Our economy could not work well without money. Unlike this French fur trapper and Native American fisherman in Canada during the 1600s, we would find it hard to get what we want only by trading goods.

The Characteristics of Our Money

The coins and paper bills used as money in an economy are called currency. Other kinds of objects have been used as money in the past such as salt, furs, grains, and gold. It is said that in Iceland several hundred years ago three dried fish could buy a pair of shoes.

These kinds of money all worked well in the economies in which they were used. None of them, however, could function very well as money in our economy today. Each of them lacks one or more of the six characteristics that make our currency the ideal kind of money for our economy.

1. *Our money is generally acceptable.* If you tried to pay for a can of soda with some salt, grain, or dried fish, would the clerk accept it? In our society, none of these goods can serve as a medium of exchange because they are not acceptable to everyone.

2. *Our money can be counted and measured accurately.* Consider the problem of pricing everything in terms of dried fish. One small dried fish might buy one hamburger. Two large dried fish might buy a T-shirt. This pricing is not a very accurate way of establishing standard values of products, because the size of dried fish is not standard. Imagine the arguments people would have over the size of the fish used as payment for a good.

3. *Our money is durable and not easily destroyed.* Dried fish, furs, and other objects used for money in the past did not always hold their value because they could be easily destroyed.

4. *Our money is convenient and easy to carry and use.* For hundreds of years, gold and silver in the form of standard-weight coins served as money all over the world. This kind of money worked well in an economy based on ocean trade. Unlike goods such as dried fish, gold and silver coins are durable and can be measured and counted accurately. However, gold and silver are not the ideal form of money in our economy because large amounts are very heavy and not easily transported.

5. *Our money is inexpensive to produce.* Today, gold and silver have a high value because they are expensive to find and mine.

6. *The supply of our money is easily controlled.* In a growing economy, there must be a continuous supply of money, with just the right amount available. It is difficult, however, to control gold and silver supplies to meet the demands for them, because new discoveries of these metals are hard to predict.

Think about the coins and bills you may have in your pocket. Are they generally acceptable, durable, and convenient? Are they easily measured and counted, and inexpensive to produce? Can their supply be controlled? You will find that our currency has all six of these characteristics.

The Value of Our Currency

The coins we use are generally made of a mixture of copper and nickel. The metal in each coin is worth less than the coin's face value. Our bills are just paper. Why, then, is this currency generally acceptable?

For the answer, look closely at a dollar bill. On the side with George Washington's picture on it, you will see the words, "This note is legal tender for all debts, public and private." This means that our money is money because the government says it is. The fact that our government stands behind our money gives us confidence that it will continue to have value in exchange for goods and services.

Section 1 Assessment

1. **Define** currency
2. What are the three functions of money?
3. What are the six characteristics of the money we use in our economy today?
4. Why does our currency have value?
5. **Analyze** Tobacco was used as money in parts of the South during colonial times. Which characteristics of our money today are not shared by tobacco?

Our Banking System

SECTION PREVIEW

Objectives
- Explore the role of banks in an economy.
- Compare different kinds of money.
- Summarize the services offered by banks.
- Explain the benefits of fractional reserve banking.
- Describe how banks make profits.
- Identify other financial institutions and the services they provide.

Building Civics Vocabulary
- The money in a checking account is called a **demand deposit**.
- A **loan** is an amount of money borrowed for a certain time period.

 **Focus**

Even though the money we use in our economy is durable and convenient, it can be easily lost or stolen. To overcome this limitation of currency, societies have created banks. Banks help us to save money and to exchange it for goods and services safely and conveniently. In this way, banks help businesses and individuals manage their money.

The Beginnings of Banking

Merchants and goldsmiths in Europe created banks during the Middle Ages. Banks became necessary as more goods were exchanged and larger amounts of money were needed in the growing European economy.

In a similar way, banks sprang up as they were needed in the young United States. The following story about the creation of a bank in the 1860s is fictitious. However, it shows how banks developed over time into institutions that could meet the needs of consumers and producers in a modern economy.

Hiram Wakefield was a goldsmith in Denver, Colorado, when he heard about the gold strike near Gemstone City, 50 miles to the west. He moved to the frontier town with his gold-weighing scale and his large safe. There he set up a new shop.

Soon Hiram's business was booming. Miners from the Gemstone City region brought their gold to be weighed, valued, and stored. When a miner brought in some gold for safekeeping, Hiram gave him a receipt which noted the value of that amount of gold. Then Hiram stored the gold in the safe.

The miners discovered that they could give any shopkeeper one of Hiram's receipts in exchange for the goods they wanted to buy. Business owners accepted these receipts because they could exchange them for gold if they wished.

Hiram further influenced the way his receipts were used in Gemstone City. He gave each miner both a receipt for the total value of the miner's gold stored in the safe and several "blank" receipts with which the miner could easily buy things. A miner completed a blank receipt by writing in a person's name and the amount of gold Hiram was to give to that person. The blank receipts became a form of money in Gemstone City.

Hiram soon discovered that miners only rarely came to exchange their receipts for all the actual gold they had on deposit in his safe. He also knew that some miners needed more gold than they had so they could buy supplies and continue to mine. Hiram decided, therefore, that he could safely lend some of the gold in his safe to miners who needed it. Miners who received these loans signed a note saying they would pay back the gold along with an added fee for borrowing it.

Hiram Wakefield had become the Gemstone City banker. His system of issuing blank receipts and loans is very similar to what banks do today.

Bankers in gold-mining communities such as Nome, Alaska, weighed and stored the gold that miners brought to them for safekeeping.

The Kinds of Money

When you think of money, you picture currency, such as quarters and dollar bills. Hiram Wakefield, however, had created a second kind of money—checks. The merchants of Gemstone City accepted the miners' checks—the blank receipts Hiram gave them—in exchange for goods and services, just as if they were currency.

Checks have all the characteristics of currency. They are generally accepted in exchange. By writing a specific amount on a check, a person states exactly how much money is to be paid. Although checks are not as durable as currency, the records banks keep for each check *are* durable. Checks are also easy to use and inexpensive to produce, and their supply can be controlled.

Checks can only exist in an economy if there are banks. In our economy, checks are used by people who have deposited money in a checking account at a bank. The money in a checking account is called a **demand deposit**. A person with a checking account can withdraw money from the bank "on demand" by writing a check.

Traveler's checks are a third kind of money we have in our economy today. Most traveler's checks are issued by banks. Printed on a traveler's check is the exact amount of money for which it can be cashed, usually $20, $50, or $100.

Banks and the Money Supply

Traveler's checks, demand deposits, and currency are the kinds of money that make up the United States' money supply. The money supply is the total amount of money available for use as a medium of exchange. As you will learn later in this chapter, the money supply goes up and down. It does, however, stay within certain bounds. In 1999, the money supply was about $1.12 trillion.

Look at the money supply table on this page. Over 50 percent of our nation's money supply is in demand deposits. Knowing that demand deposits are managed by banks, you can see how important banks are to the economy. Banks not only hold a great deal of our currency, they also have a role in every transaction that is made using a check.

Bank Services

Think back to the story of Hiram Wakefield. Hiram provided checking accounts for the miners, kept their gold safe, and made loans. Today, offering these same three services is the major function of banks in our economy.

Checking Accounts

When Bill and Wilma Kowalski first got married, they opened a checking account at Central National Bank by depositing money there. They found that using checks to pay for goods and to pay bills was an easy way to do business.

Using checks was also safe. The Kowalskis did not want to carry a lot of cash because it could be stolen. Checks, on the other hand, were useless to a thief because no one will accept a check unless it is written by the person whose name is printed on it.

THE PARTS OF THE MONEY SUPPLY, 2000

Kind of money	Approximate value (in billions)	Percent of money supply
Currency	$530	48%
Demand deposits (includes all checking accounts)	$550	51%
Traveler's checks	$8	1%
Total	$1,088	100%

Source: Federal Reserve Board

The majority of our nation's money supply is in demand deposits.
Economics In 2000, what was the total value of our money supply?

Loans from banks provide businesses with the money to put together big projects like this housing development.

Bill and Wilma also liked the fact that the checks provided a good record of how they spent their money. Each month the bank sent a record of their cancelled, or paid, checks. It also sent a statement telling how much money was in their account.

Savings Accounts Bill and Wilma also decided to save for the future. They opened a savings account at Central National Bank because they knew it was a safe place to keep their money. Unlike their checking account, the Kowalskis' savings account was not a demand deposit. They could not withdraw the money on demand. The bank reserved the right to require advance notice of a large withdrawal.

However, the bank paid the Kowalskis for keeping their money in a savings account because they were in effect lending the bank money it could use for other purposes. The payment the Kowalskis received from the bank is called interest. This kind of interest, received for the use of money, is not the same as the payment for the use of capital you learned about in Chapter 14.

People save for many reasons. The Kowalskis wanted to save for their daughter's college education and to have money in case of an emergency. Savings are an impor-

tant source of funds in our economy. With savings funds, banks can make loans to help people in the economy buy goods and services and to help businesses produce goods and services.

Loans To make some extra money, Bill and Wilma began designing Web sites for local businesses. They soon got so many requests for their services that they decided to quit their jobs and start their own Web design business. Bill and Wilma developed a plan for their new business. They figured they needed to borrow $25,000 to buy computer equipment and software.

The Kowalskis presented their business plan to Marcia Slatterly at Central National Bank. Marcia approved a loan of $25,000. A loan is an amount of money borrowed for a certain time period. The borrower agrees to pay back the amount of money borrowed plus a certain amount of interest.

The beginning of Bill and Wilma's business is the kind of story that takes place every day in banks throughout the United States. The home builder relies on bank loans for money for lumber and plumbing supplies. People also take out loans to buy a new car or to put braces on their children's teeth. People who take out loans have

Students Run School Bank

Students at New Albany High School do more than just talk about money and banking. Business students at this Indiana high school get hands-on banking experience working as tellers at a bank in their school.

The New Albany High School bank or BFC (Bulldog Financial Center) is a branch of National City Bank, a local banking institution. Set up in 1989 by business teachers, the school bank is used by both students and faculty.

Each year, twenty-six students are chosen to run the bank. The students receive several weeks of training to learn about their responsibilities as bank tellers. Student tellers set up bank accounts, cash checks, assist customers in making deposits and withdrawals, and complete loan applications. Students also keep track of loan payments and the amounts of money customers have in their accounts with monthly statements.

Business teacher Amy Pendleton says that having a school bank has been very beneficial for students: "It's very convenient to have a bank at school. Students get to deposit or cash their pay checks, or get loans if they forget their lunch money."

Students Amy Ledbetter and Carrie Eichenberger enjoyed working at the bank during their junior and senior

years. Carrie says that she came away with great leadership skills, and she learned how to delegate responsibility: "I worked as a bookkeeper my first year, and feel like working there was a reality-based education. It taught me about the real world."

Amy highly recommends that students get involved in learning about the economy, either through working at a school bank or in a business class. She discovered what she wants to do in life from working at the school bank: "I learned how to work with people, and use my creative skills. My experience helped me learn about marketing, which I plan to study in college next year."

Active Citizenship

How does working at the school bank help students at New Albany High learn about the economy?

decided that the benefit of having money now is greater than the cost of paying it back with interest later.

By making loans, banks serve an important function. They help businesses make use of productive resources, which causes the economy to grow. When a business gets a loan, that business often creates more jobs by hiring new workers. Bill and Wilma, for example, may create after-school jobs for young programmers.

A business that gets a loan may also help other businesses grow. When Bill and Wilma buy computer equipment, the makers and distributors of the equipment will benefit.

Fractional Reserve Banking

Making loans is perhaps the most important role of banks in our economy. The money banks lend comes from the deposits made by other customers.

Hiram Wakefield knew that what a miner cared about was that he could get back the correct amount of gold for his deposit. He also learned that all the miners would not want all their gold at the same time. At any particular time some miners would withdraw their deposits and others would make new deposits. These withdrawals and new deposits were just about equal, so the total amount of gold in his safe stayed about the same.

Hiram found that he needed to keep only a fraction of the miners' total deposits in his vault to meet the demands for withdrawals. Therefore, he could loan out a certain amount of the gold in his vault as long as he kept—or reserved—enough gold to pay depositors who demanded it.

Modern banking operates on the same principle of fractional reserve banking. Banks keep a percentage of checking and savings deposits in reserve. The rest of the money is available for loans and investments.

When bankers learned that they needed to keep only a fraction of their money on hand, it was an important discovery. Banks could then make the money they received from depositors do useful work instead of letting it sit in a dark vault. When the money deposited in banks is loaned to businesses and individuals, it helps those who need to borrow money. It also generates economic growth and creates an income for the bank in the form of interest payments on the loans.

The Business of Banking

Like other businesses in our economy, banks exist to make a profit. Most banks are corporations with stockholders who want a return on their investment. That is, they want their investment to grow, or become more valuable.

The largest source of revenue for most banks is interest on loans. Although banks pay customers interest on savings accounts, the amount of interest banks pay on savings is less than the amount of interest banks charge on loans. The difference in the interest paid out on savings and the interest paid to a bank by borrowers is a major part of a bank's income.

Other Financial Institutions

Banks are only one type of financial institution. There are also savings institutions, which include savings and loan associations and mutual savings banks, and credit unions. Each type was created for a particular purpose. In recent years, savings institutions and credit unions have become more similar to banks.

INSURED FINANCIAL INSTITUTIONS IN THE UNITED STATES, 2000

Type of institution	Number	Total value of assets (in billions)
Banks	8,476	$5,983
Savings institutions	1,625	$1,179
Credit unions	10,316	$438

Sources: FDIC and National Credit Union Administration

Banks are only one of several types of important financial institutions.
Economics Which type of institution had the second-greatest total value of deposits in 2000?

Savings and loan associations were meant to accept savings deposits and to make loans to families for buying land and houses. Today, most savings and loan associations also offer checking accounts, like banks.

A mutual savings bank is owned by its depositors, and any profits are paid to them. Mutual savings banks accept deposits, make loans, and allow checking accounts.

A credit union is a non-profit banking institution which serves only its members. The members often work for one organization such as a large company or a unit of government. Credit unions accept savings deposits and lend money. Credit unions also offer checking accounts called share drafts.

Our financial institutions provide important services to both producers and consumers. In this way they form a strong foundation for a healthy economy.

The Federal Reserve System

SECTION PREVIEW

Objectives
- Describe the reasons for the creation of the Federal Reserve System.
- Examine the organization of the Federal Reserve System.
- Summarize the functions of the Federal Reserve System.
- Analyze the importance of the money supply in our economy.

Building Civics Vocabulary
- A general rise in the prices of goods and services throughout the economy is called **inflation**.
- A slowdown of economic activity and production is called a **recession**.

 **Focus**

As you know, the economy of the United States is a mixed economy, with the government playing a significant role. One important way in which the federal government affects the economy is to regulate the banking industry and the nation's money supply. It performs these functions through the Federal Reserve System.

The Beginning of the Federal Reserve System

Several times in the late 1800s and early 1900s, the economy stopped growing for a period of time. There was widespread hardship as businesses closed and workers lost their jobs.

During these periods, people who had money deposited in banks began to panic because they feared that the banks, too, would go out of business. They wanted all their money in cash. Because banks operated on the fractional reserve principle, many did not have enough money on hand to meet such a great and sudden demand. Some banks ran out of money and had to close down, and many of their customers lost all their money.

After one of these financial panics occurred in 1907, the public demanded that the government step in and make rules for how banks should operate. They also thought that there should be a way for the federal government to assist banks when they needed help.

In 1913 Congress passed a bill creating the Federal Reserve System, which became the central bank of the United States. Often called "the Fed," the Federal Reserve System provides important services to banks all over the United States and regulates their activities.

How the Federal Reserve System Is Organized

The Federal Reserve System is an independent agency of the federal government. It is organized to remain beyond the reach of political influence so it can serve the needs of the nation as a whole.

FEDERAL RESERVE DISTRICTS The United States is divided into 12 Federal Reserve districts. **Regions In which Federal Reserve district is the city of Chicago located?**

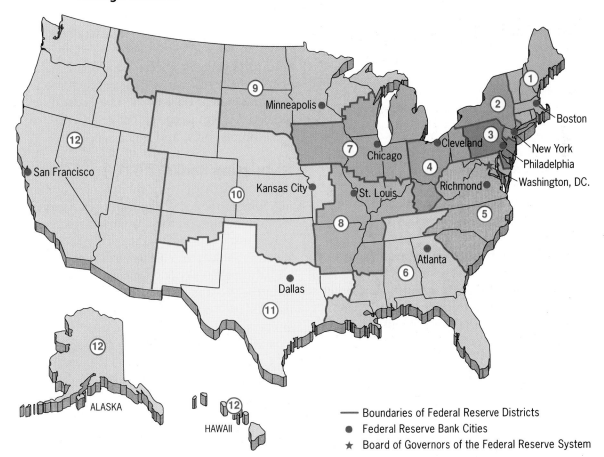

— Boundaries of Federal Reserve Districts
● Federal Reserve Bank Cities
★ Board of Governors of the Federal Reserve System

Federal Reserve Districts The lawmakers who created the Federal Reserve System wanted to keep the central bank in touch with the business needs of the country. Since the economic problems of one region may be different from those of another, Congress divided the United States into twelve geographic regions called Federal Reserve districts.

In each district there is a Federal Reserve Bank that supervises banking in that district and can pay attention to the economic problems of the area it serves. For example, the tenth district Federal Reserve Bank in Kansas City, which serves a farming region, is aware of the needs of farmers and of banks that make loans to farmers.

Running the Fed The most powerful people in the Fed are the seven members of the Board of Governors. They are appointed by the President for 14-year terms. The Board of Governors is responsible for running the Federal Reserve System as a whole.

The Functions of the Federal Reserve System

The Fed is not like any other bank. You cannot save money at the Fed; you cannot get a loan from the Fed; you cannot have a checking account at the Fed. The Fed, however, is important to you and to the value of your money. It is often called "the bankers' bank."

Providing Services An important day-to-day job of the Fed is to collect and to clear checks. If you pay for your new clothes with a check, the clothing store owner deposits the check in the store's bank. The store's bank then sends the check to the Fed, which sends it on to your bank. In this process, money is taken from your checking account and put into the clothing store's checking account. In a year, the Fed will process billions of checks. The diagram on page 339 shows how checks are collected and cleared.

The Fed also supplies currency to banks. If a bank needs currency to pay customers who are making withdrawals, it orders currency from the nearest Federal Reserve Bank. Look at a dollar bill. At the top of the side with George Washington's picture are the words "Federal Reserve Note." Each federal reserve note comes from one of the twelve Federal Reserve Banks.

The Government's Bank The Fed has the job of keeping the federal government's checking accounts. When people pay their taxes, the money is deposited in a government account at a Federal Reserve Bank. When the government pays for highways or airplanes, it writes checks on its Federal Reserve Bank accounts.

The Fed also keeps track of the federal government's debts. If the government borrows money, the lender—who may be an individual, a bank, or a business—receives a certificate called a government bond, bill, or note. This certificate tells how much money the government borrowed. The Federal Reserve System keeps records of all government bonds, bills, and notes.

Regulating Banks The Federal Reserve makes rules that govern the business of banking. One of the most important regulations sets a minimum on the amount of reserves a bank must keep on deposit with a Federal Reserve Bank. This rule ensures that banks will always have enough money available to meet the demand for withdrawals. To enforce its regulations, the Fed has a staff of bank examiners who visit banks from time to time to be sure they are following all the Fed's rules.

Congress has passed several laws that protect businesses and individuals doing business with banks. The Fed's job is to help put these laws into effect. One of the laws enforced by the Fed is the Truth in Lending Law, which requires banks and other financial institutions to tell you the full cost of borrowing money.

Making Loans to Banks

Banks sometimes need extra money. Usually this happens when bank customers want to borrow or withdraw large sums of money. The Fed will make loans to help out banks in these situations. Banks pay a special low rate of interest, called the discount rate, on funds borrowed from the Fed.

Controlling the Money Supply

The most powerful job of the Fed is to regulate the nation's money supply—the amount available for spending. The size of the money supply has a great influence on the health of the economy.

The largest and most changeable part of the money supply is made up of demand deposits. The amount of money in demand deposits is directly affected by the amount of money that banks lend to individuals, businesses, and governments. Because of this relationship, the Fed can control the money supply indirectly—by influencing the amount of money banks can lend and the amount that individuals, businesses, and governments will choose to borrow. The Fed can use three different methods to influence the amount of money loaned by banks.

First, the Fed can change its reserve requirement. If the Fed lowers the reserve requirement, banks have to keep less money on reserve at the Fed and will have more money available to make loans. In contrast, banks can make fewer loans if the reserve requirement is raised.

Second, the Fed can change the discount rate. If the Fed lowers the discount rate,

THE STORY OF A CHECK Checks allow money to be transferred from one bank to another. **Economics** What role does the Federal Reserve Bank play in the process shown by this chart?

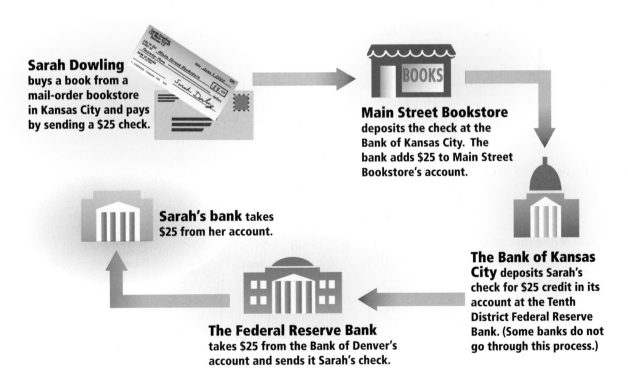

Sarah Dowling buys a book from a mail-order bookstore in Kansas City and pays by sending a $25 check.

Main Street Bookstore deposits the check at the Bank of Kansas City. The bank adds $25 to Main Street Bookstore's account.

The Bank of Kansas City deposits Sarah's check for $25 credit in its account at the Tenth District Federal Reserve Bank. (Some banks do not go through this process.)

Sarah's bank takes $25 from her account.

The Federal Reserve Bank takes $25 from the Bank of Denver's account and sends it Sarah's check.

THE SIX JOBS OF THE FEDERAL RESERVE SYSTEM

The Fed is often called the "banker's bank." **Economics** What are four services the Fed provides to banks?

1. **Provide services to banks, including clearing checks, wiring money, and supplying currency.**

2. **Serve as the bank for the federal government.**

3. **Make rules that govern the business of banking.**

4. **Make loans to banks.**

5. **Help foster a healthy economy.**

6. **Control the nation's money supply.**

banks pay less interest on money they borrow and can therefore charge a lower rate of interest to their borrowers. Lower interest rates will encourage more people to borrow more money. On the other hand, if the Fed raises the discount rate, banks will raise the rate of interest they charge their borrowers. In this case, people will tend to borrow less money.

Third, the Fed can buy and sell government bonds. Government bonds are certificates that the federal government issues in exchange for lending it money. A government bond can be bought or sold. It represents money owed to the holder of the bond certificate. If the Fed buys government bonds from banks, banks have more reserves and thus more money to lend. If the Fed sells government bonds to banks, banks pay for them from their reserves and thus have less money to lend.

Money and the Economy: The Delicate Balance

The money supply affects our economy in important ways because it is directly related to the amount of money people can spend in the economy. In order for the economy to be healthy, spending must be approximately equal to the economy's ability to produce goods and services. If this balance is not maintained, two different problems may result.

HOW THE FED AFFECTS THE MONEY SUPPLY AND THE ECONOMY The Fed tries to keep our economy running smoothly. **Economics** According to this chart, what does the money supply affect?

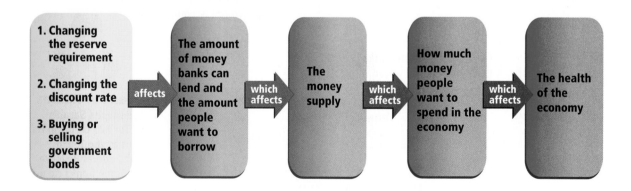

When there is more money in the economy than there are goods and services to spend it on, increased demand for goods and services will cause prices to rise. A general rise in the prices of goods and services throughout the economy is called inflation. Inflation reduces the buying power of people's money. If your income stays the same, you can buy less because of inflation.

When there is less money in the economy than goods and services to spend it on, the demand for goods and services decreases. This situation can cause businesses to cut back on production. Such a slowdown in economic activity and production is called a recession. A recession is bad for the country because it results in lower production, lower profits for businesses, and increased unemployment.

Controlling the money supply is therefore a delicate—and very important—balancing act. When prices begin to rise, the Fed may decide to discourage loans. With less money being loaned, spending slows and prices are less likely to rise. If a recession threatens to occur, the Fed will likely make it easier for banks to make loans. Increased lending will stimulate spending and increase production.

Through its ability to affect the money supply, the Fed can help keep the economy on a steady course. At the same time, the Fed helps keep our banking system safe and able to meet the needs of businesses and individuals.

Section 3 Assessment

1. **Define** inflation, recession
2. How did financial panics lead to the formation of the Federal Reserve System?
3. Why is the Federal Reserve System divided into districts?
4. Name three of the Fed's jobs.
5. Why is controlling the money supply important?
6. **Apply** Suppose you have an allowance of $10 a week. After a year of high inflation, your allowance is still $10 a week. What problem do you have? How will you try to convince your parents that you need a larger allowance?

Extending the Chapter

Global Views

Banks fill important needs in our economic system and in those of other countries. The services that banks can offer are so important, in fact, that several international organizations much like banks have been created to help countries participate in the global economy. The two most important international "banks," the International Monetary Fund and the World Bank, were created just after World War II.

The International Monetary Fund (IMF) was established mainly to facilitate and promote international trade. Most countries have their own kinds of currency, and so when countries buy goods from each other they must exchange different currencies. One of the jobs of the IMF is to help keep the rates of exchange between currencies stable and orderly.

The World Bank, officially called the International Bank for Reconstruction and Development, is closely linked to the IMF. The major job of the World Bank is to make loans to developing countries to help them improve their economies and raise the standards of living of their people.

How to ANALYZE CAUSE–EFFECT CHAINS

In this chapter you learned about the federal government's role in our economy. You read that the Federal Reserve Board can take a number of actions to affect the nation's economy. When the Fed buys or sells government bonds, for example, this action sets off a series of events that can impact the health of our economy. On page 340, a cause-effect chain is used to illustrate this chain of events. Arrows are used to link the Fed's action to the effects caused by the Fed's action.

Explain the Skill

A cause-effect chain offers economists an excellent way to present a series of linked events. A cause-effect chain begins with a specific action. The chain then uses arrows to show the series of effects caused by the first action. The chain ends with a final effect.

Suppose the Federal Reserve sets the goal of increasing economic activity in order to help the country climb out of a recession. It may decide to lower the discount rate. The Fed's action of lowering the discount rate, however, does not affect the rate of economic activity directly. Instead, this action ripples through the economy until the final goal is achieved. A cause-effect chain could be used to show how the Fed's action leads to the final goal.

Analyze the Skill

The diagram on this page is a double cause-effect chain, offering a side-by-side comparison of two possible chains of events. Both

chains begin with an action taken by the Federal Reserve. Follow each branch of this cause-effect chain, noting how the events in each chain lead to the ones that follow. When you have studied the diagram, answer the questions below.

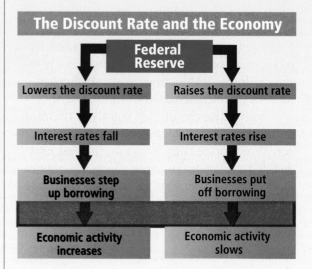

The Discount Rate and the Economy

Federal Reserve

Lowers the discount rate	Raises the discount rate
Interest rates fall	Interest rates rise
Businesses step up borrowing	Businesses put off borrowing
Economic activity increases	Economic activity slows

Skill Assessment

1. What is the first action, or cause, in each of the cause-effect chains?
2. What is the final effect in each cause-effect chain?
3. Is the rising of interest rates a cause, an effect, or both? Explain your answer.
4. How are the two chains in this diagram related?
5. How does this cause-effect chain help you to understand the relationship between events?

CHAPTER 15 ASSESSMENT

Building Civics Vocabulary

The vocabulary terms in each pair listed below are related to each other. For each pair, explain how the terms are related.

1. *currency* and *demand deposit*
2. *inflation* and *recession*

Reviewing Main Ideas and Skills

3. Why is money essential to our economy?

4. What is the money supply? What makes up the money supply?

5. Why do banks need to keep only a fraction of their deposits on reserve?

6. In what three ways can the Fed influence the money supply?

7. **How to Analyze Cause-Effect Chains** Re-read the section on page 336 entitled "The Beginning of the Federal Reserve System." Then create a cause-effect chain illustrating the steps leading to the creation of the Federal Reserve System. Begin your chain with "Recessions of the late 1800s and early 1900s." End your chain with "Congress creates Federal Reserve System."

Critical Thinking

8. **Linking Past and Present** Compare United States currency today to the gold and silver coins used by nations in the past. Why does today's currency serve our economy better than gold and silver coins could?

9. **Predicting Consequences** The leaders of the Federal Reserve System are appointed so that they will not be influenced by political pressures. What problems might arise if these leaders were elected instead of appointed?

Writing About Civics

10. **Writing a Business Plan** Suppose you want to start a business in your neighborhood. Choose a business and then write a one-page business plan, answering questions such as: What kind of business would you start? Who would your customers be? How much money will you need to start the business? How would you use the money? When would the business start to make money? How would you advertise your business?

Citizenship Activities

11. **Your Local Community** With a group of classmates, visit or call a local bank. Answer these questions: Does the bank charge a fee for its checking accounts? Does it pay interest on checking deposits when they are greater than a certain amount? What rate of interest does it pay on savings accounts? Then compare your findings with those of other groups. Of all the banks investigated by groups in your class, which bank would you do business with?

Take It to the NET

Access the **Civics: Participating in Government** Internet site at **www.phschool.com** for the specific URLs to complete the activity.

Explore online information about the history and functions of the Federal Reserve Board. Create a chart outlining the functions of the Federal Reserve Board. Your chart should include each function's impact on the economy of the United States.

Government's Role in Our Economy

Citizenship and You

At the electronics plant where Laura works, she cleans manufactured parts by dipping them into a chemical called a solvent. As she gets ready to dip a new batch of parts, she notices a man with a clipboard. Soon he walks up to her work station.

"I'm from a federal agency that protects the safety of workers," he says. "May I ask you some questions?"

"Sure," replies Laura. "Go ahead."

"How do you feel when you're working with this solvent?" asks the man.

"Well," Laura replies, "almost every day I get a headache—but it goes away pretty quickly. Sometimes I feel dizzy, too. Some of the other people I work with complain about the same things." Then Laura, curious, asks him why he is here. She finds out that his agency thinks that the solvent she works with may increase her chances of getting cancer. Laura feels a sudden rush of fear.

The man says the federal government is thinking of making rules that require businesses to protect workers who use the solvent. "It is even possible," he says, "that the government will ban the use of the solvent."

What's Ahead in Chapter 16

Making rules to protect workers is one of the ways that government takes actions that affect the economy. The word *intervention* is often used to describe such government actions. In this chapter, you will learn why and how government intervention occurs, and you will expand your understanding of government's role in the American economy.

Section 1 **Government Intervention in the Economy**

Section 2 **Government's Efforts to Solve Economic Problems**

Section 3 **Managing the Economy**

Keep It Current

Items marked with this logo are periodically updated on the Internet. To keep up-to-date, go to www.phschool.com

Citizen's Journal

Suppose you were the government inspector in the story on this page. Write a short report, giving your recommendations on what should be done about the chemical used in Laura's factory. Do you think new rules should be made? If so, describe them. If not, explain why new rules are not necessary.

Government Intervention in the Economy

SECTION PREVIEW

Objectives

- Explain how American values are reflected in our economic system.
- Identify the economic problems that Americans have asked government to solve.
- Describe the methods used by governments to correct or prevent economic problems.
- Analyze the debate over government intervention in the economy.

Focus

The government plays an important role in the American economy. In Chapter 15, for example, you learned how the Federal Reserve System controls the supply of money and regulates banks. Government shapes and controls our economy in other ways, too. It makes rules for how businesses should operate, spends nearly $2 trillion each year, and taxes individuals and corporations.

The federal government is both the largest consumer in the economy and the biggest employer. How and why did government's role in our economy become so important?

American Values and Economic Goals

Individual freedom is one of the basic values upon which our government is built. The framers of our Constitution believed that economic freedom, like political freedom, is a basic right of citizens. They held that producers and consumers should be free to own property, to make a profit, and to make their own choices about what to produce,

buy, and sell. In writing the Constitution, they had in mind a country with an economy based on a market system.

To make sure that the economy of the new nation would be strong and be able to grow, Article 1, Section 8 of the Constitution gave Congress the power to coin money, collect taxes, borrow money, set up a postal service, build roads, and regulate commerce. In other words, Congress was to lay a foundation on which a market economy could flourish.

The Constitution also gave Congress and the states the power to make "ground rules" for a market economy. These rules include laws that protect private property against theft and laws that say how corporations may be set up.

Once the foundations had been laid and the rules set, citizens expected government to play only a small role in the economy. Like the framers, they wanted businesses to be able to operate freely in our market economy.

At the same time, Americans believed strongly in the basic values of equality and justice. They hoped free enterprise would promote the common good and provide opportunities for all Americans to prosper.

The Limits of Free Enterprise

As the economy has developed, however, Americans have become increasingly aware that the free enterprise system may not always serve the common good. While it has made the United States one of the wealthiest countries in the world, it has also led to problems that cannot be solved by letting the market system work entirely on its own.

These problems have caused Americans to look to government for solutions. Six problems are listed below to help you understand why government has become involved in our economy. Later in this chapter you will read more about these problems and what government has done about them.

This famous photograph by Lewis Hine shows children working in a coal mine in 1910. Unsafe working conditions and the use of child labor led to increasing demands for government regulation.

1. *Businesses have sometimes earned profits unfairly.* They have driven competitors out of business or made secret agreements with competitors to fix prices at high levels. Businesses have also fooled consumers through false or misleading advertising.

2. *Conditions for workers have sometimes been unsafe and inhumane.* As you learned in Chapter 14, workers have sometimes been badly treated. Some have been required to work long hours with low pay, while others have had to use dangerous machinery or chemicals without protection.

3. *Unsafe products have harmed consumers.* Foods have sometimes spread diseases and caused other health problems. Household products have injured people, and toys have hurt children.

4. *Not all Americans have had economic security.* People who lose their jobs or cannot work due to sickness, injury, or old age have faced hunger and homelessness. Discrimination has made it hard for others to get jobs to support themselves.

5. *The economy has been unstable.* Periods of economic slowdown have put many people out of work and caused great hardship. Periods of inflation, when prices are rising faster than people's incomes, have reduced the buying power of people's incomes.

6. *The environment has been damaged.* Businesses and consumers have polluted the air, water, and land upon which we depend for our basic life needs. Many animals and plants are also in danger.

Americans have called on government to help solve each of these problems. As a result, governments at various levels have become increasingly involved in our market economy.

Methods Governments Use

What can governments do to correct or prevent economic problems? Local, state, and federal governments regularly take the following kinds of actions to make changes in the way the economy works.

1. *Governments regulate businesses.* They pass laws that set rules for business conduct. For example, they can limit the number of hours workers are required to work in one day, or set safety rules for airplanes. They can also set up regulatory agencies to enforce these laws.

Setting air traffic control standards is one way government regulates business to protect the public.

2. *Governments make direct payments to individuals.* They can give money to people who need help to pay for food, shelter, medical care, and other basic needs.

3. *Governments own resources and produce goods and services.* They can own land, such as the national forests. They also can run businesses that promote the common good, such as providing hydroelectric power from a government-built dam.

4. *Governments help pay for important economic activities.* They can give a sum of money to a private business to help it provide an important product or service. For example, the federal government has given money to help farmers, airlines, and builders of housing for the poor.

5. *Governments control the amount of money they spend and the amount they receive in taxes.* Taxes take money from the economy, and spending puts it back. By controlling the in-and-out flow of taxes and spending, governments can influence how the economy performs. In addition, the federal government can control the total supply of money.

6. *Governments make tax rules and collect special taxes.* They can change the rates at which people's incomes are taxed, and they can make tax rules that reward certain economic activities and punish others.

The Debate Over Government Intervention

We see that the market system alone does not always promote the common good. However, most people also see that there is a negative side to government intervention in the economy. Government regulations, for example, usually put some limits on individual freedom. They affect our freedom to buy and sell, to make a profit, and to do as we wish with our property.

Government intervention also has a huge price tag. The taxes that pay for government programs take large parts of most citizens' incomes. In addition, government does not always solve economic problems in the best way possible. People often complain that the government uses more time, more money, and more paperwork than necessary.

Because government intervention can both solve problems and cause problems, it often stirs great conflict. The question of how much to regulate business, for example, involves our most basic values. When freedom comes into conflict with equality and justice, as well as with the health of the public and the environment, people disagree about which values are more important to protect.

In our democratic society, there will always be debate over how much the government should get involved in the economy. Will a government rule do what it was meant to do? Who will gain or lose if government takes a certain action? What is the cost to taxpayers of a government action? These are questions you will have to ask yourself as you play your citizen role. Think about them as you read the rest of this chapter.

Section 1 Assessment

1. What basic economic powers did the Constitution give to Congress?
2. Name three economic problems that have caused citizens to ask government to become involved in the economy.
3. Give an example of government intervention in the economy.
4. What are two arguments against government intervention in the economy?
5. **Synthesize** How might your life be different today if there were little government intervention in the economy?

Government's Efforts to Solve Economic Problems

SECTION PREVIEW

Objectives

- Summarize the government's efforts to ensure fair business practices.
- Describe the steps that government has taken to protect workers and consumers.
- Examine government's attempt to provide economic security for Americans.
- Explain how government works to assure economic stability.
- Analyze government's role in protecting the environment.

Building Civics Vocabulary

- A **trust** is a group of companies organized to benefit from the high prices they all agree to charge.
- A single business that controls a market is often called a **monopoly.**
- The economy goes through the **business cycle,** repeated periods of growth and recession.
- Regulation of the money supply by the Federal Reserve System is called **monetary policy.**
- A government's decisions about the amount of money it spends and collects in taxes are called its **fiscal policy.**

Focus

The economic problems you have just read about raise a conflict in our basic values. On the one hand, we believe that individuals should have economic freedom. On the other hand, we believe that our economy should be fair and should promote the common good. Through the democratic process, citizens have asked government to solve each problem in a way that balances freedom with equality and justice.

Ensuring Fair Business Practices

The free enterprise system itself has no rules for how businesses should operate. Competition and supply and demand are supposed to keep prices fair.

Many business owners in the late 1800s, however, learned how to get rid of competition and thus make bigger profits. Large companies gathered greater and greater shares of the markets in which they operated.

By 1890, the steel, oil, sugar, meat, flour, and sewing machine industries were no longer competitive. In some industries, all but one or two large corporations were forced out of business. Other industries were controlled by a trust, a group of several companies organized to benefit from the high prices they all agree to charge. A trust or a single corporation that controls a market has what is called monopoly power—the power to control prices in a market. A single business with monopoly power is often called a monopoly.

Controlling Monopolies

During the 1870s and 1880s, Americans became angry about the growth of monopoly power. People demanded fairness—reasonable prices and the chance for small businesses to compete in any market. In response to public pressure, Congress passed the Sherman Antitrust Act in 1890. This act outlaws agreements among companies that limit competition.

In 1914, the Clayton Antitrust Act was passed to strengthen the Sherman Act. It outlaws many of the practices used by monopolies and trusts. In the same year, Congress created the Federal Trade Commission and gave it the power to break up companies with monopoly power.

Legal Monopolies

Monopoly power is not always opposed by the government. Businesses that provide services people need to have, such as electricity, water, and local phone service, are often allowed to have legal monopoly power. Such a business is called a public utility.

Governments allow some public utilities to be monopolies because competition by many small businesses in these service industries can be inefficient. Can you imagine ten different companies each putting up electrical lines in your neighborhood and competing for customers? To make sure that the prices public utilities charge for their services are fair, state and local governments often set the rates by law.

Banning False Advertising

In 1938, Congress outlawed "unfair or deceptive practices" in the way products are labeled

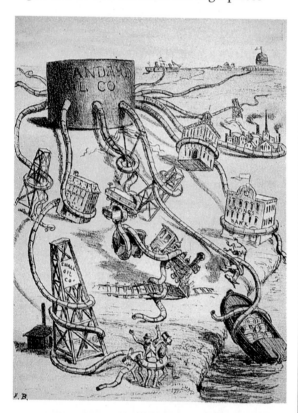

An 1884 cartoon, "The Monster Monopoly," attacked the Standard Oil Company, which almost completely controlled the oil industry.

To protect consumers, the government sets safety standards for many products—from fireproof pajamas for children to power tools for the home workshop.

and advertised. Ads, for example, may not say that a medicine can cure a disease when in fact it contains only sugar and alcohol.

Protecting Workers

You have learned that in the 1930s the federal government began to take an active role in protecting workers. Beginning with the National Labor Relations Act in 1935, and the Fair Labor Standards Act in 1938, the government has passed laws to limit working hours, set minimum wages, and require employers to bargain with unions.

Safe Working Conditions Workplace dangers, such as unprotected cutting blades on power tools, toxic chemicals, and disease-causing dust in the air, can threaten workers' health and lives. For over 100 years, labor unions have argued that business owners had a duty to make sure that working conditions were safe. Businesses, however, did not always want to pay the extra costs of safe equipment.

Congress created the Occupational Safety and Health Administration (OSHA) in 1971. This agency sets and enforces safety and health standards in the workplace.

Protecting Consumers

In 1906, Upton Sinclair published a novel called *The Jungle*, which described the meat-packing industry. Americans read about such horrors as sausage being made with dead rats, rat poison, and old, moldy meat. Shocked citizens demanded that the government take action to make sure that all food products were safe. Congress quickly passed the Meat Inspection Act, which regulated the production of meat products.

Since 1906, several laws have been passed to protect consumers from unsafe and harmful food and drug products. A federal agency, the Food and Drug Administration (FDA), was created in 1927. The FDA sees that foods, cosmetics, and drugs are safe and labeled correctly. It requires that new drugs be tested before they go on the market.

In 1972, the federal government took yet another step to protect consumer safety by creating the Consumer Product Safety Commission (CPSC). This government agency makes safety rules for products such as toys, tools, children's clothes, and household appliances.

Carol Browner

With the Florida Everglades just a bike ride away from her childhood home, Carol Browner's love of the natural environment began early. "I was shaped by growing up in an environment where nature was right there," she says.

As an adult, Brower has made protecting the environment a main focus of her career. As Secretary of the Florida Department of Environmental Regulations in the early 1990s, she worked with farmers, environmentalists, and the business community to find solutions to her state's environmental problems.

From 1993 to 2001, Browner tackled an even more difficult job as the head of the Environmental Protection Agency (EPA), the federal agency charged with protecting our nation's land, water, and air. Under Browner's leadership, the EPA accelerated the clean-up of toxic waste sites and worked to improve air and water quality.

Browner has been called a new kind of environmental activist because she believes that a balance can be struck between environmental protection and economic

development. "I am committed to the idea that economic progress and environmental protection can go hand in hand," she says. Browner believes all Americans share the same long-term goal: "To have a healthy environment, healthy people, as well as a healthy economy."

Browner has another, more personal, reason for working hard to protect the environment. "I want my son," she says, "to be able to grow up and enjoy the natural wonders of the United States in the same way that I have."

Recognizing Viewpoints

What beliefs have motivated Carol Browner's commitment to environmental protection?

Providing Economic Security

In 1929, the United States fell suddenly into a long period of economic hardship called the Great Depression. Factories closed down and banks failed. Within three years, 12 million people—24 percent of the workforce—were out of work.

The United States was faced with what seemed to many to be the failure of the free enterprise system. In 1932, Americans elected a new President, Franklin D. Roosevelt. He began a broad government program called the "New Deal." The New Deal was designed to get the economy moving again and help people in need. Roosevelt created agencies such as the Works Progress Administration (WPA), through which government put millions of unemployed people to work building bridges, roads, and public buildings.

The New Deal marked a turning point in our history. It greatly expanded the government's role in the economy. As a result, Americans became more likely to turn to government to solve economic problems.

Social Security In addition to giving people immediate help, a major goal of the New Deal was to give American families economic security. In other words, families were to have a minimum level of income in case of future hardship. The Social Security Act, passed in 1935, provides a monthly payment to workers or their families to replace the income lost when a person retires, becomes injured, or dies. It also provides for unemployment insurance. Through this program, workers who lose their jobs receive payments while they look for new jobs.

Public Assistance The Social Security Act was just the beginning. Since then, local, state, and federal governments have ex-panded their efforts to help people in need through public assistance programs. Public assistance helps poor families—not just people unable to work—by providing cash payments and various services. Food stamps, for example, are given to people with low incomes to help them buy food.

Maintaining Economic Stability

The hardships of the Great Depression were not easily forgotten. Following World War II, citizens asked government to find ways to prevent future depressions. Government was now to play a major role in trying to keep the economy stable and growing.

Economic instability has always been a part of the free enterprise system. Like a roller coaster ride, the economy goes through what is called the business cycle, a repeated series of "ups" of growth and "downs" of recession. During a period of economic growth, businesses increase their production of goods and services, and new jobs are created. Each period of growth is followed by a recession, or period of economic slow-down. In a recession, fewer goods are

Soup kitchens fed unemployed workers and their families during the Great Depression of the 1930s. Scenes like this pointed to the need for government to provide jobs to help rebuild the economy.

produced and unemployment increases. The Great Depression of the 1930s was a long, bad recession.

Because Americans want a stable economy, government tries to "flatten out" the ups and downs of the business cycle. It uses two major methods to reach this goal: monetary policy and fiscal policy.

Monetary Policy In Chapter 15 you learned that the Federal Reserve System regulates the money supply. Regulation of the money supply by the Federal Reserve System is called monetary policy.

If the economy is slowing down and a recession is feared, for example, the Fed may take action to increase the money supply. It may lower interest rates, lower the reserve requirement, or buy bonds from banks. Any of these actions will provide more money for banks to lend, encouraging consumers to spend more. Spending will cause businesses to produce more goods and services.

Fiscal Policy A government's decisions about the amount of money it spends and the amount it collects in taxes are called its fiscal policy. Although state governments have fiscal policies, the federal government's fiscal policy has a far greater effect on the economy.

Fiscal policy affects the economy because the role of the federal government as a spender and a taxer is so important. The federal government spends billions each year on highways, public assistance, employee salaries, weapons, and thousands of other products and services. Most of this money goes straight into the economy. Federal taxes, on the other hand, take about 25 percent or more of most people's income.

If the economy is entering a recession, the government may cut tax rates. Then people can spend more of their incomes on goods and services. This increased spending will stimulate production and may bring the economy out of the recession. The same goal may be achieved if government increases its spending. Increased government spending will help to create more jobs, also giving people more money to spend.

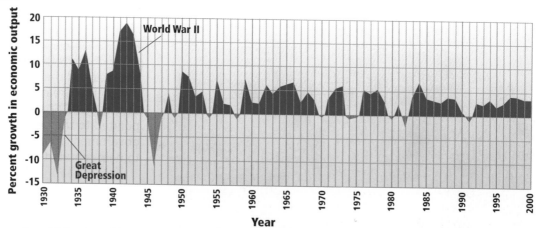

GRAPH SKILL

THE BUSINESS CYCLE 1930–2000

Source: U.S. Department of Commerce, Bureau of Economic Analysis

Our economy has gone through a series of ups and downs. **Economics** During what year did economic output reach the highest point shown on the graph?

Government workers protect the environment by inspecting dump sites to see whether toxic waste is being disposed of properly.

Protecting the Environment

By the 1960s, years of pouring toxic wastes into the rivers, the lakes, and the air had begun to cause big problems. Thick smog hung over cities and fish were dying. Our drinking water had poisons in it. Scientists warned that we were not just changing our environment but were rapidly destroying it as well. They said we were causing damage that could threaten our health and all life on earth.

Businesses were slow to take responsibility for the pollution they caused. They feared that trying to control or clean up their pollution would increase their costs and put them at a disadvantage compared to their competitors. As a result, citizens turned to the government.

Faced with growing citizen pressure, the Environmental Protection Act was passed in 1970. This act, though not the first to protect the environment, was certainly the most important. The Environmental Protection Agency (EPA) was created. The EPA controls pollution by making rules about what and how much can be dumped into our air, water, and soil.

Stepping in to protect the environment is one of the many ways you have seen in which government plays a role in our free enterprise economy. Most Americans value the freedom a market economy gives them. However, when faced with an economic problem—such as pollution, depressions, or unfair business practices—citizens ask our government to help promote the common good.

Section 2 Assessment

1. **Define** trust, monopoly, business cycle, monetary policy, fiscal policy
2. What are two methods government has used to ensure fair business practices?
3. What is the purpose of the Occupational Safety and Health Administration?
4. Why have consumers asked the federal government for protection?
5. What was the purpose of the Social Security Act of 1935?
6. What can the federal government do to try to bring the economy out of a recession?
7. What environmental problems led to the creation of the Environmental Protection Agency?
8. **Analyze** Explain how the Great Depression helped to greatly increase government intervention in the economy.

Managing the Economy

Objectives

- Explain how the government measures the health of the economy.
- Identify major programs funded by federal spending.
- Describe how the federal government raises money.
- Explain the balance between federal spending and federal income.
- Analyze the causes and dangers of the national debt.

Building Civics Vocabulary

- **Gross Domestic Product** is the total dollar value of all final goods and services produced within the country in a year.
- A **deficit** is the amount by which government spending is greater than government income.
- A **surplus** is the amount by which government income is greater than government spending.
- The total amount of money the government owes to lenders is the **national debt**.

 **Focus**

You have seen that the federal government has become deeply involved in solving problems in the economy. At the same time, American citizens have come to expect the federal government to keep our economy running smoothly. As a result, the federal government has taken on a role the framers of the Constitution could not have imagined. In addition to being the economy's biggest consumer and employer, the federal government has become the economy's chief manager.

As manager of the economy, the federal government has three major jobs. First, it keeps track of the economy's health. Second, it tries to adjust the economy's performance, using the fiscal and monetary policies you have already been introduced to. Third, it manages a huge sum of public money, deciding how to spend it and how to raise more of it from taxes. Like the manager of a large corporation, the government in its role as economic manager must be responsive to its "stockholders"—the citizens of the United States.

The Nation's Economic Health

The federal government is constantly checking on the health of the economy. Government agencies keep track of the number of people employed and unemployed, the number of new jobs created, the amount of money spent on imported goods and the amount received from exports. These figures, and many others like them, can be used to measure the economy's health. Like a doctor taking a patient's pulse and blood pressure, the government needs to measure the economy's health before it can decide how to maintain and improve it.

Inflation One of the most closely-watched signs of the economy's health is the rate of inflation. You may remember that inflation is a general rise in the price level of goods and services. The rate of inflation describes how fast prices are rising. During a period of inflation, money loses its buying power. If your income stays the same, you can afford to buy less and less. For this reason, inflation is one of the biggest worries of government, businesses, and consumers.

The rate of inflation is usually given as a yearly, or annual, percentage. If a set of goods cost $100 at one point, an annual inflation rate of 5 percent will increase the price of these goods to $105 a year later.

Inflation is difficult to control because as prices rise, workers demand higher pay to keep up. Businesses then spend more on labor costs and raise their prices even higher so they can still make a profit. A high rate of inflation is dangerous to the economy because people are very nervous about the future and slow down the economic activity of the country.

The federal government mainly uses monetary policy to keep inflation in line. When the inflation rate gets too high, the Fed often raises interest rates.

Gross Domestic Product A major goal of government is to help the economy grow. Government measures the economy's growth by calculating the gross domestic product (GDP). GDP is the total dollar value of all final goods and services produced within the country in a year.

Final goods are those that are complete and ready for sale. Goods used to make the final goods are not counted in the GDP because their values are included in the price of the final product. For example, the value of the plastic, glass, and steel used to make a car are included in the car's price.

A rising GDP, without rising prices, generally means that the economy is growing. A falling GDP generally means that

 GROSS DOMESTIC PRODUCT, 1991–2001

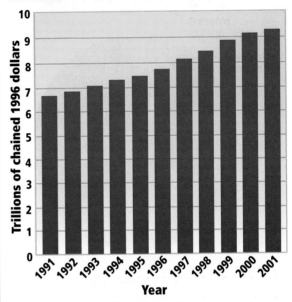

Year

Source: U.S. Bureau of Economic Analysis

 Our nation's economy grew steadily during the 1990s.
Economics In what year did the GDP first top $7 trillion?

the economy needs help, such as increased federal government spending.

The Federal Budget

In 2000, the federal government spent nearly $1.8 trillion. Much is spent on individuals for unemployment, medical care, and retirement. In addition, money is needed to pay for other government functions, such as national defense and federal highways. Federal spending has a big effect on the economy no matter what the money is used for.

Federal spending is planned ahead of time in great detail. The amount that each program, agency, department, and office will spend during a year is set by the federal budget. The federal budget is the government's plan for how it will raise and spend money. The budget estimates how much revenue

THE FEDERAL BUDGET FOR 2000: SPENDING $1.8 TRILLION

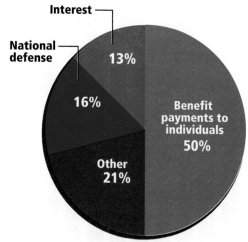

Interest —
National defense —
13%
16%
Benefit payments to individuals 50%
Other 21%

Source: U.S. Office of Management and Budget

Nearly half of all federal spending goes to benefit payments.
Economics What percentage of this federal budget goes to national defense?

will be received from taxes and how much money will be spent in a year.

The pie graph on this page shows the spending side of the federal budget for the year 2000. It is divided into the largest kinds of spending. Benefit payments to individuals include social security payments and public assistance, such as food stamps. Interest is the money the government pays for using money that it has borrowed.

Although $1.8 trillion is a huge sum of money, the federal government faces the same problem that individuals and businesses face in our economy—scarcity. People want more goods and services from the government than the government is able to provide. As a citizen, when you vote for elected representatives, you help make decisions about the quantity and quality of goods and services that the government will provide.

Sources of Federal Income

How does the federal government raise the money it spends? The pie graph on the next page shows that the federal government receives revenue, or income, from a variety of sources.

Income Taxes Governments at every level depend on taxes as a major part of their revenue. State and local governments, you may remember, receive most of their revenue from sales and property taxes. In contrast, the largest part of the federal government's revenue comes from income taxes.

Individuals pay two kinds of federal tax on their incomes: personal income tax and social security tax. The amount of personal income tax you pay is based on a percentage that increases as your income grows. In other words, the more money you earn, the greater the percentage of your income you pay in income tax.

The amount of social security tax you pay is also based on a percentage of your income. However, this percentage does not

Facts & Quotes

Taxes in America

Over 200 years ago, Benjamin Franklin said, "Nothing in this world is certain but death and taxes." How much tax you pay depends on how much money you earn. Here are the income tax rates for individuals in the United States as of 2000:

Income	Tax Rate
$0–$26,250	15%
$26,251–$63,550	28%
$63,551–$132,600	31%
$132,601–$288,350	36%
More than $288,350	39.6%

THE FEDERAL BUDGET FOR 2000: RAISING $2.0 TRILLION

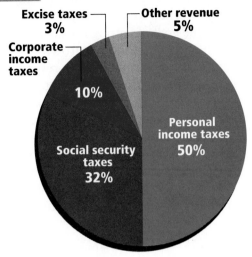

Excise taxes
3%

Other revenue
5%

Corporate
income
taxes
10%

Personal
income taxes
50%

Social security
taxes
32%

Source: U.S. Office of Management and Budget

Taxes account for the vast majority of government revenue. **Economics From which type of tax does the government raise the most money?**

Your personal income tax dollar goes to pay for a wide variety of government spending. Social security taxes, in contrast, pay for a specific kind of government spending—mainly the benefit payments established by the Social Security Act.

Social security and federal income taxes make up the largest part of most people's total tax bill. For this reason, income taxes are often the subject of conflict and debate.

Corporations must also pay income tax. Corporate income tax makes up about 10 percent of federal revenue.

Excise Taxes Taxes charged on specific products such as cigarettes, alcohol, gasoline, jewels, and furs are called excise taxes. Many excise taxes have two main purposes. In addition to raising money, they are intended to regulate certain kinds of consumption. For example, the excise tax on liquor is designed to discourage drinking by making liquor more expensive.

Tariffs, Fees, and Sales The federal government collects about four percent of its revenue from various other sources. The most important of these are tariffs, fees, and sales of government-owned land or resources. Tariffs are taxes on imported products. Fees are charges to users of certain services, such

vary according to income. Everyone's income is taxed at the same rate, except that any amount of income over $76,200, as of 2000, is not taxed.

Personal income taxes make up the single most important source of federal revenue.

TAX DEDUCTIONS FROM YOUR PAYCHECK Many paychecks use a chart format to show the taxes deducted from your earnings. **Economics Which tax accounted for the largest deduction from this paycheck?**

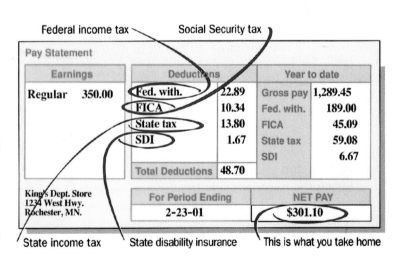

Federal income tax   Social Security tax

Pay Statement			
Earnings	**Deductions**		**Year to date**
Regular 350.00	Fed. with.	22.89	Gross pay 1,289.45
	FICA	10.34	Fed. with. 189.00
	State tax	13.80	FICA 45.09
	SDI	1.67	State tax 59.08
			SDI 6.67
	Total Deductions	48.70	

King's Dept. Store
1234 West Hwy.
Rochester, MN.

For Period Ending	NET PAY
2-23-01	$301.10

State income tax   State disability insurance   This is what you take home

THE NATIONAL DEBT, 1990–2000

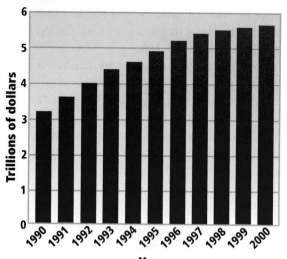

Trillions of dollars (y-axis: 0, 1, 2, 3, 4, 5, 6)

Year (x-axis: 1990, 1991, 1992, 1993, 1994, 1995, 1996, 1997, 1998, 1999, 2000)

Source: U.S. Office of Management and Budget

The national debt nearly doubled between 1990 and 2000. **Economics By approximately how much did the national debt grow between 1990 and 2000?**

as visitors to national parks. The resources the government may sell to make money include trees on national forest land, which are sold to lumber and paper companies.

Balancing the Budget The executive branch, Congress, interest groups, and the public all play a role in the federal budget-making process.

Throughout much of our history, the government has spent more money than it has taken in. In 1792, the federal government had its first budget deficit. A deficit is the amount by which government spending is greater than government income. Deficits occur when a government spends more money in a year than it takes in from taxes, tariffs, fees, and sales.

During the twentieth century, the government had 70 annual budget deficits. In 1994, for example, the government spent $1.4 trillion while taking in $1.2 trillion, resulting in a budget deficit of $200 billion.

To make up for a deficit, the government borrows money by selling bonds.

In the 1990s, President Clinton and Congress worked to limit government spending, with the goal of cutting the deficit. At the same time, strong economic growth led to an increase in the government's tax revenues. As a result, there was a federal budget surplus of $167 billion in 2000. A surplus is the amount by which government income is greater than government spending. An economic recession, combined with increased government spending during the war on terrorism following the attacks on September 11, 2001, likely means a return to deficit spending in the future.

The National Debt

The total amount of money the government owes to lenders is called the national debt. The national debt grew sharply during the 1980s and early 1990s, when the government borrowed money to cover large budget deficits. The debt stood at $5.7 trillion at the end of 2000.

The size of the national debt worries many people. They worry that the national debt may threaten the government's ability to pay for programs and manage the economy.

IF HE'S REALLY WORRIED—THERE'S A SIMPLE WAY OUT

Like any borrower, the federal government must pay interest on money it has borrowed. One danger of an increasing debt is that the interest that must be paid on it takes a larger and larger bite out of our federal budget. By having to set aside money to pay interest on the debt, the government has less money to pay for new programs to promote the common good.

Many proposals have been and will be made to try to reduce the national debt. These plans include raising taxes, cutting benefit payments to individuals, and cutting defense spending. Other plans support using money from the large surpluses alone to reduce the debt. Each plan has its supporters and its critics. Like any economic problem, the national debt requires citizens to become involved in deciding the best course of action for government and the economy.

Section 3 Assessment

1. **Define** gross domestic product, deficit, surplus, national debt
2. Why does the federal government closely watch the rate of inflation?
3. Why does the federal government face the problem of scarcity?
4. What is the major source of federal revenue?
5. Why is the national debt considered to be a problem?
6. **Analyze** What is an advantage of giving Congress, rather than the President, the final say in determining the federal budget? What is a disadvantage?

Extending the Chapter

Global Views

Government's role in our economy has grown over time. Today, the importance of its role is shown by the many ways in which the federal government helps manage the economy. The role of our government in our economy, however, is not nearly as great as the role government plays in many other countries.

You have already learned that in countries with command economies, the government has nearly complete control over the economy. In the world today, there are also countries in which the government has more control than in a market economy like ours, but less control than in a command economy. The economic system of many of these countries is known as social democracy.

In many social democracies, the government owns or controls at least some of the basic industries, such as transportation and banking. Businesses in the rest of the economy are privately owned. Under this system, individuals make many of the basic economic decisions, but a democratically elected government has some power to decide who gets what is produced. For example, in a social democracy like Sweden, health care and college educations are provided free, and every citizen is guaranteed both housing and a minimum income.

Social democracies are based on a strong belief in economic fairness and equality. In these societies, having one's basic needs met is considered a right. However, to achieve this goal, citizens in these countries must give up some freedom to make their own economic decisions.

A Question About False Advertising

Two women and a man are riding in an elevator. One woman turns to the other and says, "Guess what I happen to have."

"What?" asks the second woman.

"A leading anti-perspirant spray," says the first woman.

"Me, too," the second woman says, "but mine's Dry Ban."

"Mine helps keep me dry," says the first woman.

"So does my Dry Ban," claims the second. "Watch. Yours goes on like this."

The second woman takes off the man's glasses. He is very surprised. She sprays the first woman's deodorant on one of the lenses. A white, creamy deposit appears. Then she says, "Mine goes on like this." She sprays Dry Ban on the other lens and you see that the lens remains clear and dry.

"Uh...hmm...I see the difference," says the first woman. "I'll try it on my boss's glasses."

The commercial closes as an announcer says, "Clear Dry Ban helps keep you feeling clean and dry."

This commercial and four others like it ran on national television for 14 months during 1969 and 1970. Each of the ads showed that Dry Ban went on "clear and dry" instead of wet and creamy like the "leading spray." These television spots cost the Bristol-Meyers Company, makers of Dry Ban, $5.8 million.

In 1972 the Federal Trade Commission (FTC) brought a lawsuit against Bristol Meyers for showing the Dry Ban commercials.

> ## The FTC lawyers claimed that the product was actually "watery, wet, and runny."

It wanted to prevent Bristol-Meyers from showing similar commercials in the future.

The FTC is responsible for protecting the public from "false, misleading, and deceptive" activities in the advertising and sale of products. It may act as both a prosecutor and a court. The FTC's lawyers can bring legal actions against companies who break certain federal laws. Such cases are then decided by five FTC commissioners who act as judges.

The FTC lawyers claimed that although the product appeared to be clear and dry when shown in the television ads, it was actually "watery, wet, and runny" and left a white deposit when it dried.

The FTC lawyers supported their conclusions about the product in two ways. First, during the trial, the deodorant was sprayed on glass and on a person's arm. In both cases, a wetness appeared that soon dried, leaving a white powder.

Second, the FTC lawyers looked at the results of consumer surveys about the Dry Ban commercials. The

FTC lawyers argued that the surveys showed that people who saw the ads came away thinking that Dry Ban was a *dry* spray and that it left no visible residue. These impressions, they said, were false and misled people who saw the ads.

The FTC commissioners, however, ruled that the Dry Ban commercials were not false, misleading, or deceptive. Bristol-Meyers, they said, had operated within the law when it showed the ads on television.

The commissioners explained that they interpreted the consumer surveys differently from the FTC's lawyers. The commissioners believed that consumers did not think of Dry Ban as "dry" in a literal, or actual, way. They said that "consumers understood the commercials' message to be that Dry Ban was drier than the comparison product or that Dry Ban was relatively dry."

Moreover, said the commissioners, the commercials were meant to show only that Dry Ban "goes on" clear. It did not matter that the product did not stay clear after it dried.

The commissioners went on to say that there were real differences between the two products shown in the ads. Dry Ban is an alcohol-based product that does appear clear and dry when it is first sprayed on, although it dries to a powder after two or three minutes. In contrast, the "leading spray" in the commercials, Arrid, is oil-based and goes on as a white cream. Arrid was "ideally suited to play the role of a brand X," said the commissioners.

The commissioners also made the point that if the commercials were misleading, customers would try Dry Ban but never buy it again. A Dry Ban customer "standing in front of his TV set with a dripping armpit," said the commissioners, "is not likely...to go out and buy a second can of the stuff if ...it is a *literally* dry antiperspirant that he wants."

The commissioners said that because Dry Ban had $7.4 million in sales during the period the commercials ran, it was obvious that most customers were satisfied with the product and were buying it again and

again. They reasoned that any customer who bought the product more than once was not being misled by the ads, but was getting what he or she expected.

The FTC lawyers claimed that the product was actually "watery, wet, and runny."

If the commercials were misleading, customers would try Dry Ban but never buy it again.

Analyzing the Case

1. Why did the FTC's lawyers claim that the commercials were "false, misleading, and deceptive"?

2. Why did the commissioners decide that the commercials were not misleading?

3. Do you agree with the commissioners' opinion about the commercials? Explain.

4. If the FTC decides that a commercial is misleading, do you think the company should have to run another ad to set the record straight? Explain.

How to ANALYZE LINE GRAPHS

 Use the *Simulations and Data Graphing* CD-ROM to create and interpret graphs.

In this chapter you read about the federal budget—the government's plan for how it will raise and spend money. You learned that the government runs a deficit when its spending is greater than its income. When the government's income is greater than its spending, the government has a surplus. Line graphs are often used to chart changing levels of spending and income, and to illustrate the relationship between the two.

Explain the Skill

To analyze a line graph, begin by reading the graph's title and labels. The title will tell you the subject of the graph. The label on the horizontal axis usually shows the time period covered by the graph. The label on the vertical axis usually shows what is being measured. Next, study the line shown on the graph. Each point on the line shows you the quantity or level of something at a particular time. Finally, draw conclusions about the information shown on the graph.

Analyze the Skill

The graph on this page shows both federal spending and federal income from 1970 to 2000. Suppose you wanted to determine the level of government spending in 1980. On the green line—which shows government spending—find the point that matches up with the 1980 label on the horizontal axis. Then follow this point over to the vertical axis. You will see that government spending in 1980 was approximately $600 billion.

Since this line graph shows both spending and income, you can also use the graph to draw conclusions about the changing relationship between these two factors. For any year that the green "spending" line is above the red "income" line, you know that the government ran a deficit. In 1990, for example, you can see that spending was over $200 billion higher than income, meaning that the government had a deficit of over $200 billion in that year.

Skill Assessment

1. What was the approximate level of government spending in 1985?
2. In what year did government income first top $1 trillion?
3. Describe the relationship between income and spending between 1970 and 1995.
4. Between 1995 and 2000, what significant change took place in the relationship between spending and income? How can you tell?

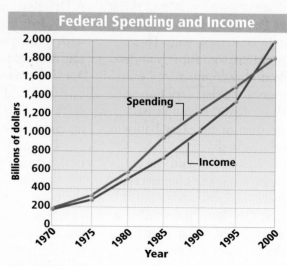

Federal Spending and Income

Source: U.S. Office of Management and Budget

CHAPTER 16 ASSESSMENT

Building Civics Vocabulary

The vocabulary terms in each pair listed below are related to each other. For each pair, explain how the two terms are related.

1. *trust* and *monopoly*
2. *monetary policy* and *business cycle*
3. *national debt* and *deficit*

Reviewing Main Ideas and Skills

4. What are some major ways in which the federal government provides economic security for Americans?

5. How do changes in the government's fiscal policy affect the economy?

6. What are the three major jobs of the federal government as manager of the economy?

7. Which of the following is not good for the economy? Why? **(a)** a rising GDP **(b)** a rising inflation rate **(c)** the creation of new jobs

8. **How to Analyze a Line Graph** Look at the line graph on page 364. Did the government have a deficit or surplus in 1995? What was the level of the deficit or surplus?

Critical Thinking

9. **Recognizing Points of View** Compare the arguments for and against government intervention in our economy. What is your position on this debate? Explain your point of view.

10. **Predicting Consequences** Suppose that a proposal has been made to increase income taxes in order to reduce the budget deficit and the national debt. What other effects might higher income taxes have on the economy?

Writing About Civics

11. **Writing a Speech** While debating the federal budget for the year 2000, Congress and the President argued over how to use the budget surplus. Should the money go to government programs? Should it be used to reduce the national debt? Should it be used to lower taxes? Suppose you are a member of Congress. Write a short speech explaining your opinion on this issue. Include the speech in your portfolio.

Citizenship Activities

12. **Your Local Community** With several classmates, go to a bicycle store in your community. Find out what safety features on bicycles are required by the federal government. Then write a short report about the regulations the government makes for the bicycle industry in order to protect consumers.

 Take It to the NET

Access the **Civics: Participating in Government** Internet site at **www.phschool.com** for the specific URLs to complete the activity.

During the Great Depression, many people lost their life savings and had no way of recovering their money. The Federal Deposit Insurance Corporation was created to help protect our money. Use online information to prepare a report to the class, explaining what the FDIC does and why. Do you think the FDIC is still important to Americans? Would Americans' savings be as safe without the FDIC?

Our Economy and You

Citizenship and You

Have you ever listened to a radio talk show? The following is a short segment from a show called "Managing Your Money." Kathy Clarke, a twenty-four-year-old travel agent, has called in to share her financial story with the talk show host:

Kathy: *My trouble began when I started using credit cards just after I moved out of my parents' house and into my own place.*

Host: *I gather that you used them a lot?*

Kathy: *Yes. You name it, I bought it—new clothes, a color TV, some luggage. I kept telling myself that I needed the stuff I was buying, and that I could save later.*

Host: *But later you had bills?*

Kathy: *Right. At first I thought I could handle them because I was expecting a raise at work. But the raise never came. Now I'm stuck with a growing pile of bills. I'm really in a panic.*

Keep It Current

Items marked with this logo are periodically updated on the Internet. To keep up-to-date, go to **www.phschool.com**

What's Ahead in Chapter 17

Kathy's story shows that people, acting as workers and consumers, make choices about money that dramatically affect their lives. In this chapter, you will look at personal money management. You will read about how to become a smart consumer and learn some methods for saving money. Finally, you will learn about planning for your future by exploring career options.

Section 1   **Managing Your Money**

Section 2   **Spending and Saving**

Section 3   **Careers: Planning for the Future**

Citizen's Journal

Suppose you were the host of "Managing Your Money." What advice would you give to Kathy? When you have finished reading the chapter, reread your advice. Make any changes or additions you think are important.

Managing Your Money

SECTION PREVIEW

Objectives
- Explore the different forms of personal income.
- Explain how a budget can help you make good financial decisions.

Building Civics Vocabulary
- **Fringe benefits** are indirect payments people receive for their work.
- People who own stock may receive **dividends,** or payments from the profits of companies in which they own stock.
- The amount of money a person has left after paying taxes is called **disposable income.**
- **Fixed expenses** are expenses that have to be paid regularly, usually every month.
- **Variable expenses** are expenses that change from month to month.

 **Focus**

Learning how to manage your money involves several steps. Understanding your income, knowing what your expenses will be, and determining your goals and values are all important steps in financial planning. Kathy Clarke got in trouble because she did not give enough thought to what her income and expenses were. Also, she did not understand credit well enough to see how using credit cards would affect her. Customers who charge their purchases with a credit card instead of paying with cash or a check often must pay additional interest. Once a month, the cardholder pays either the entire bill or a portion of the bill and interest.

Making a budget, or a plan for spending and saving, can help you to set your goals and reach them. Kathy realizes that in order to pay the money she owes on her credit cards, she needs to come up with a plan for managing her money.

Income: Knowing What You Have

There are many forms of income. You can earn income directly by working. If you own stock in a corporation, or have money in a savings account, you can earn income from these sources. Gifts of money and money earned by renting or selling property are also income.

Earned Income The pay that people receive for their work is known as earned income. Earned income comes in several forms: salary, wage, commission, and bonus.

At the time Kathy got into debt, she was earning $27,000 per year at the travel agency. Kathy received a salary, or payment at regular intervals—$1,038.46 every two weeks, before taxes.

Others in Kathy's office are paid in different ways. Mark Aguilar, a college student, works part time for a wage of $9 per hour. Mark's weekly income changes depending on how many hours he works.

Like many businesses that offer after-school and summer jobs, this record store pays employees by the hour.

TYPES OF INCOME Different forms of income offer different incentives to workers. **Economics In your opinion, which form of income has the most important advantages? Explain.**

Type	Description	Advantages	Disadvantages
Salary	Employee receives a fixed payment at regular intervals	Guaranteed pay whether business thrives or is slow	No extra pay for extra hours worked
Wage	Employee paid by the hour	Paid for all time worked	May face loss of income if business is slow and hours are cut back
Commission	Employee receives a percentage of the price of a good or service as payment for making the sale	Hard work rewarded with increased pay	Income not guaranteed; if business is slow, income could fall sharply
Bonus	Employee given additional money for excellent work performance	Good work rewarded with additional income	None
Piecework	Employee paid for each unit of a product he or she makes	Faster workers can make more money	Income can vary widely depending on work speed and availability of work

Joe Pelligrino has been a travel agent for 20 years. In addition to his salary, he gets a commission, or a percentage of money taken in on sales. Joe's commission is 20 percent of his sales. If he sells five or more tours in a month, he also receives a bonus, extra income as a reward for excellent work.

Kathy decides to look at her salary to see what she is making per hour. She discovers that because she is working many extra hours each month, she is actually making a low wage. Based on this information, Kathy manages to convince her boss to give her a raise.

Fringe Benefits In addition to salaries or wages, people often receive fringe benefits, or indirect payments for their work. Medical and dental care, sick leave, and vacation with pay are examples of fringe benefits provided for employees. These benefits mean that workers do not need to set aside part of their incomes to use for such purposes.

Other Income Kathy has a savings account at a local bank. She earns income in the form of interest on money in the account. People who own stock receive dividends, or payments from the profits of companies in which they own stock. People can also receive income from the sale or rental of their personal property, from gifts, and from money they inherit when a relative or friend dies.

To understand her income, Kathy now starts with her new, higher salary. She adds the interest on her savings account. Then she subtracts what she pays in taxes. The result is her disposable income, the amount of money left after taxes have been paid. Once Kathy knows how much money she has, she can make some choices about what to do with it.

Our Economy and You   Chapter 17   **369**

Paying for goods and services with credit cards is a common practice in stores, restaurants, and other businesses around the world.

Making Financial Choices

Choosing how to use your money involves making trade-offs, giving up one want in order to satisfy another. To make these choices wisely, you must look at your disposable income and at your current and future needs.

Goals and Values The choices people make about money are based on their goals and values. For Kathy, spending money on consumer goods was her goal. Consumer spending—buying clothes, a TV, and luggage—was more important to her than financial planning.

Some people choose to plan carefully in order to stay out of debt. Some plan to save for a particular goal, such as buying a house or going to college. Many people also choose to give money away. They may choose to give money to friends or family or people in need, or they plan to give to a cause or organization. All of these decisions reflect individual goals and values.

Kathy's credit card troubles have made her think about her values and her goals. She now sees the importance of good spending and saving habits. She knows she needs to take a look at her income and expenses and to make some decisions about what is most important.

Making a Budget Making a budget is a good way to decide how you want to spend and save. It helps you to be sure you set aside enough money for the things you need. It also helps keep you from buying more than you can afford.

Armed with good information about her income and with clear financial goals, Kathy sets out to make her personal budget. To do this, she asks herself the following questions:

★ What time period will my budget cover?
★ How much income will I be making during this time?
★ What will my expenses be during this time?
★ How much money should I set aside for each expense, and for savings and personal spending?
★ What expenses are most important to pay first?

Kathy decides that her first budget will cover one month. With her new raise, her disposable income is $1,800 a month.

Next, Kathy looks at her expenses. Some are fixed expenses, expenses that have to be paid regularly, usually every month, such as rent and car payments. Unless Kathy moves

Consumers make many choices about how to spend their disposable income. Entertainment, such as movies, is a variable expense.

into a cheaper apartment or sells her car, she cannot change those fixed expenses.

Kathy also has variable expenses, expenses that change from month to month. For Kathy, these variable expenses include food, clothes, entertainment, and her telephone bill. Cutting back on her variable expenses is a good way for Kathy to make progress in paying off her debt.

Finally, Kathy figures how much money she can save each month and how much she can put towards paying off her credit card debt. She then arrives at the following budget for the month:

rent	$750
car payment	$220
car insurance	$ 50
food	$180
personal (clothes, entertainment, etc.)	$120
utilities (electricity, gas, water)	$ 50
gasoline/transportation	$ 50
telephone	$ 50
savings	$125
credit card debt	$205
	$1,800

Making a budget gives Kathy a sense of confidence. She has made the choice to plan her spending and saving. If Kathy sticks to her current plan, she will be able to pay off her credit card debt. At that point she may want to take a new look at her budget. Budgets are not carved in stone. Whenever your income, expenses, or goals change, you can change your budget as well.

Section 1 Assessment

1. **Define** fringe benefits, dividends, disposable income, fixed expenses, variable expenses
2. What are four types of earned income?
3. Explain how a budget can help you to make good money management choices.
4. **Apply** Imagine that you earn $300 a month at an after-school job. You are still living at home. Make a budget showing how you would spend or save this money. Indicate whether each item is a fixed or a variable expense. Rank each budget item from most to least important.

Spending and Saving

SECTION PREVIEW

Objectives

- Identify important factors to consider when deciding whether or not to purchase a product.
- Compare advantages and disadvantages of different types of savings plans.
- Examine the role of insurance in financial planning.

Building Civics Vocabulary

- A **warranty** is a manufacturer's promise to repair a product if it breaks within a certain time from the date of purchase.
- The ability to turn savings back into cash is called **liquidity**.
- A **time deposit** is a savings plan with a set length of time that you must keep your money in the account.
- **Insurance** is a plan by which a company gives protection from the cost of injury or loss.
- **Liability insurance** protects a person from the costs of damage or injury to others.

Focus

You have seen that a budget is a plan of how much you will spend on goods and services, and how much you will save to use in the future. Even after you have created a budget, however, your decisions are not over. You will have many choices to make about which goods and services to buy. You will also need to think about what savings plan will be the best for you. Just as personal goals and values affect budget-making, goals and values will also affect your spending and savings decisions.

Making Spending Decisions

Mark Aguilar, the college student who works part time in Kathy's office, has to make a spending decision. He is trying to decide between buying a compact disc (CD) player and a new printer for his computer.

Mark listens to a lot of music. He knows that the sound quality of CDs is better than that of tapes. However, the computer printer he has now is old and breaks down often.

A mall is one place to compare products and make buying decisions.

He uses the printer both for school work and for his work at the travel agency, so he needs a printer he can count on.

Values and Pressures Values have a strong influence on a person's decisions about what to buy. Mark is faced with a conflict in values. Music is an important part of his life. However, he also values his education and his work, and he uses his computer for both.

To decide between a CD player and a printer, Mark must also be aware of factors other than his values. All consumers face certain pressures to buy. Being aware of these pressures can help Mark to weigh whether or not they should influence his decision.

Mark knows that his desire to buy a CD player is influenced by what his friends think. Most of his friends have CD players.

Mark also realizes that salespeople and advertisements have an influence on him. He says, "When I talk to salespeople, I get the feeling that tapes and records are from the Stone Age, and that music worth listening to comes from a CD." Mark has learned that a common sales method is to make consumers think that items they now own are not good enough.

Finally, Mark makes a decision. He would like to have a CD player, but he knows that there is nothing really wrong with the stereo system he has now. On the other hand, his printer is nearly past repair. If he does not replace it, he will not be able to do as good a job in school or at the travel agency. Mark decides to buy a printer instead of a CD player.

Choosing What to Buy Once you have decided to buy an item, the next decision is which one to buy. Often there is a wide selection of brands and models from which to choose. Wise shoppers consider a variety of factors when making buying decisions.

Considering the following factors can help you choose.

1. *Price.* Can you afford the product? Is its price about the same as the prices of other models of similar quality?

2. *Quality.* Will the product last? Is it well made? Does its quality match its price?

3. *Features.* Does the product have the features you need? Will you be paying for features you do not need?

4. *Warranty and Service.* Does the product have a **warranty**—a manufacturer's promise to repair the product if it breaks within a certain time from the date of purchase? Will the store repair or replace the product or give you your money back if it breaks down?

5. *Sales/Discounts.* Can you buy the same product at a lower price at a discount store or a special sale?

When Mark goes shopping he thinks about all these factors. He talks to salespeople at several stores and compares printers that have similar prices. He reads ads in the local paper to see if any printers are on sale. He also goes to the library to look at a consumer magazine, *Consumer Reports,* put out by a group called Consumers' Union. It lists the major products, their features, and their prices. It also gives the results of product tests.

Finally, Mark narrows his choices to two printers. Both are well made and have good warranties. One model costs about $400, the highest price that Mark had thought he would be willing to spend. The other model costs $500, but it has extra print features.

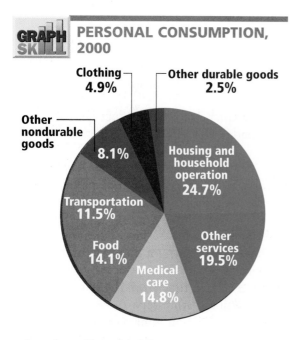

GRAPH SKILL PERSONAL CONSUMPTION, 2000

Clothing 4.9%
Other durable goods 2.5%
Other nondurable goods 8.1%
Housing and household operation 24.7%
Transportation 11.5%
Food 14.1%
Medical care 14.8%
Other services 19.5%

Source: Bureau of Economic Analysis

Housing and related expenses account for the largest percentage of personal consumption. **Economics What percentage of personal income was spent on transportation in 2000?**

Consumer Credit Mark is about to decide in favor of the less expensive printer. Then the salesperson suggests that Mark buy the more expensive printer. After all, it does have more features. She tells him that he will not have to pay the whole price at once. He can make a down payment, or pay part of the price. Then he can finance the rest through a credit arrangement with the computer store.

This credit plan—getting a loan from the store to cover the rest of the printer's cost—sounds good to Mark. However, he finds out that he would be paying 20 percent interest on the borrowed money. If he takes a year to pay this money back, he will end up spending nearly $600 on the printer, once interest payments are added in. Mark decides to buy the cheaper printer to avoid the cost of credit.

People often borrow money to pay for large purchases. Some borrow from banks, savings and loans, or credit unions. Others use a store credit plan, like the one the store offered Mark. Still others, like Kathy, use credit cards to pay off costs over time.

In borrowing money for purchases, it is important to pay attention to the real cost of the item—the purchase price plus interest. Consumers often "shop" for a loan. Sometimes a bank loan will cost less than a store's credit plan. In that case, a person might choose to borrow money from a bank for the purchase rather than use the store's plan.

Making Savings Decisions

People save for all sorts of reasons. Many save for that "rainy day" that comes along without warning. They want to have money set aside for car repairs or a long illness, for example. People save to buy homes, to finance vacations, or to pay for education. Saving can be an important way to help plan for the future. There are many ways to save money. When you are deciding which method would be best for you, think about the following factors: liquidity, income, and safety.

Liquidity One of the first questions to ask yourself when you begin to plan for savings is "How quickly do I need to be able to get at my money?" The ability to turn savings back into cash is called liquidity. Some savings plans are very "liquid." For example, if your savings are in a passbook account at a savings bank, you can withdraw part or all of the money immediately. However, if you have used your money to buy a house or a piece of land, you will not be able to use that money until you have sold the property.

Income Another factor to consider is the overall income you will earn from the money you save. If you choose to put your money in a savings account, your income will be the interest you earn on your deposit. You can also earn income from money you have set aside to invest—to buy property, such as a piece of land or stock in a corporation, with the hope of earning income from the profits.

Banks offer a number of savings plans, each with different possibilities for income. In general, banks pay higher interest rates on accounts that require you to leave your money in for a certain minimum amount of time. A time deposit is a savings plan with a set length of time that you must keep your money in the account. The bank charges a fee, called a penalty, if you withdraw money early.

Automatic teller machines make it possible for people to deposit and withdraw money from their accounts at all hours.

As you have seen in earlier chapters, you can also earn income by buying bonds. Government bonds and bonds issued by corporations pay a fixed rate of interest. With bonds, as with savings accounts, you can know ahead of time what income your savings money will earn.

People whose main goal is to make as much income as possible are more likely to invest their savings than to put them in a bank. They may buy stocks or invest in mutual funds. A mutual fund is a collection of money from many small investors, which experts invest in stocks and bonds. Another way to invest money is to buy real estate—land and buildings—in the hope that its value will increase.

When you are thinking about a savings or investment plan, you will have to make a trade-off between income and liquidity. In general, the higher the interest rate on a savings plan, the longer you will have to leave your money on deposit. Thus your savings will be less liquid. Investments in stock and real estate are usually hard to turn back into cash. Thus you will want to be sure that money you save or invest for a long period of time is not money you will need for that "rainy day."

Safety Of course you want your money to be safe. However, sometimes there is a trade-off between safety and income. Most deposits in banks and savings and loans companies are insured by the federal government. As long as your account does not have more than $100,000 in it, it is safe even if the bank or savings and loan fails. Government bonds are also considered safe investments. However, savings accounts and bonds have relatively low interest, and therefore low income.

In contrast, buying stocks in a corporation can be a risk. If the corporation makes big profits, your share of those profits, called dividends, may be higher than the amount you could earn from a savings account. The price of the stock may go up, too, and you could make money by selling it. However, if the corporation has a bad year, or if the economy has a recession, you could lose money on your stocks. Real estate investments involve a similar trade-off: safety against income.

Savings and You As a teenager, you may find that a passbook savings account best meets your needs. It is safe. It is also liquid—you can get money whenever you need it. Not having your money tied up for long periods of time is probably more important to you at this stage in your life than earning higher interest.

However, your life will be changing and so will your financial needs. Your income and expenses will most likely increase. Your goals may change as well. You may decide you want to do some long-term financial planning. It is always possible to change your savings plan to suit these changes in your life.

Insurance

Most people find it impossible to save enough money to cover a serious emergency. In order to protect themselves, people buy insurance, a plan by which a company gives protection from the cost of injury or loss. In return, the insured person makes regular payments, called premiums, to the company.

Insurance is based on a simple idea. If many people pay some money into an insurance plan, all the money, taken together, will be enough to pay the large costs of the few people who will need it. Many kinds of insurance are available. The four major kinds of insurance are described on the next page.

COMMON SAVINGS PLANS
There are a wide variety of savings plans to choose from. **Economics What are two ways you can make money by investing in stocks?**

Passbook savings	Pays a fixed interest rate; money can be withdrawn at any time.
Interest-bearing checking	Called NOW (Negotiable Order of Withdrawal) accounts; the owner can write checks on the account, which also earns interest.
Time deposit	Funds deposited for a set period of time; usually a penalty for early withdrawal. Interest rate dependent upon time limit on deposit.
Savings bond	Sold by the government. Common for bonds to be sold for half of their full value, reaching their full value after a period of time.
Stock	Shares in corporations. Owners of stock sometimes earn income from dividends. They make profits when they sell their stock for a higher price than they paid for it.
Mutual fund	Pooled funds of investors, managed by professional. Funds usually invested in stocks and bonds.
Real estate	Purchase of land and/or buildings. Income earned from rent. Profit made when real estate is sold for a higher price than was paid for it.
Insurance	Investment can be made in an insurance policy such as life insurance. After a set number of years, certain kinds of policies can be surrendered for cash value, plus interest.

Property insurance can help people rebuild their homes after hurricanes and other natural disasters.

3. *Liability insurance.* Many people carry liability insurance, which is insurance that protects a person from the costs of damage or injury to others. For example, if a tree in your yard falls onto a neighbor's roof, you are legally responsible for the damage. Liability insurance will pay to fix the roof. Most car insurance includes liability coverage.

4. *Health insurance.* Medical care can be very costly. The average worker would find it almost impossible to pay the bills for doctors, hospitals, and medicine out of salary and savings. Health insurance pays all or part of these costs.

Health insurance plans are included in the fringe benefits of many working people. The government gives health insurance, through Medicaid and Medicare, to many people who cannot afford it, and to senior citizens.

Having insurance, like saving and investing, is a way to set aside money from current income in order to meet needs you may have in the future. Making decisions about insurance will be part of the way you manage your money as an adult.

1. *Life insurance.* People buy life insurance to protect their families from loss of income. If the insured person dies, the money from the life insurance policy can help support his or her family.

2. *Property insurance.* Property insurance protects houses, cars, and other property. It pays to rebuild a house after a fire or to repair or replace a car after an accident. In some cases, property insurance pays for lost or stolen items.

Section 2 Assessment

1. **Define** warranty, liquidity, time deposit, insurance, liability insurance
2. List some factors to consider when buying a product. Explain why these factors are important.
3. Give three factors to consider when choosing a savings plan, and tell how they are related.
4. Why is insurance a part of the financial plan of many people?
5. **Apply** Decide on one savings plan that would be the best for you now and one that would be the worst. Give arguments to support each of your choices.

Careers: Planning for the Future

SECTION PREVIEW

Objectives

■ Explore the factors that will affect your future career search.

■ Examine ways to find out more about careers that interest you.

■ Identify qualities employers look for in employees.

■ Explain why career planning is an ongoing process.

Focus

In this chapter you have read about the importance of personal economic planning. You have learned about planning a budget and about making spending and saving decisions. Perhaps the most important planning you will do will be planning your career. How you choose to earn a living will affect all the other economic decisions you make in your life.

Thinking About Careers

Think for a moment about people who work in your community. How many ways do you see that people are making a living? Then think of all the people in the United States who are working at different jobs. Some of these people have had the same job for their whole working lives. Others have had several different careers.

There are thousands of careers for people to choose from. Furthermore, as our economy changes, career options change, too. When you begin to think about careers, it will be helpful to know what the changes in our economy may mean for you. Thinking about what you will have to offer to the working world will also help you to choose a career.

The Changing Economy In Chapter 14 you learned that the economy of the United States is changing dramatically. Most Americans used to work in farming and factory jobs. Today, however, over 70 percent of our work force performs service jobs.

New technology is also changing the career outlook. Computers, lasers, robots, and communication satellites are taking the place of some jobs and creating others. According to a 1999 report by the United States Department of Labor, high-tech industries will provide thousands of new jobs in the coming years.

> **"** Projections for the 1996–2006 period show high-tech and related employment growing more than twice as fast as employment in the economy as a whole. **"**

Many of these new jobs demand a much higher level of education than farm and factory jobs did. In fact, an increasing amount of special training is needed for many careers, such as engineering, accounting, computer programming, law, and medicine. Jobs in management and sales also call for education and training.

Asking Yourself Questions Evaluating your interests, talents, and personality can be an important step in finding your place in the job market. The school subjects you enjoy and do well in might give you some clues. What you like to do outside of school can also indicate things to look for in a career. Mark Aguilar's interest in music and in technology has led him to consider being a sound engineer.

In addition to looking at your interests and abilities, thinking about your life goals

Volunteering Helps Shape Career

Growing up in New Delhi, India, Annie Joseph often went with her mother, a biologist, to visit hospitals and clinics. She saw many patients suffering from diseases like leprosy and tuberculosis. "It was kind of overwhelming for a young child," she says, "but it first sparked my interest in science."

When Joseph was 10, her family moved to the United States. She grew up in Rustin, Louisiana, and attended college at Tulane University in New Orleans.

During her last year of college, Joseph volunteered for an organization called Amigos De Las Americas (Friends of the Americas). Her volunteer work took her to a remote village in northeastern Brazil, where many children regularly became ill from parasites and infectious diseases contracted from drinking contaminated water. Joseph worked with villagers to improve the community's water supply and sanitation systems. She also gave talks on reducing the spread of disease and improving nutrition.

By the end of her three months in Brazil, Joseph knew she had found her career. "That experience made me see that what I was interested in was public health."

To prepare for her chosen field, Joseph obtained a

master's degree in science and public health. She now works tracking trends in infectious disease in the United States, Europe and Asia.

In a few years, Joseph plans to return to school for a doctorate in immunology, the study of the immune system and how it protects the body. "One day," says Joseph, "I hope to work on the development of vaccines that prevent infectious diseases."

Thinking about her career to this point, Joseph sees her volunteer work as a key turning point. "When I was a volunteer in Brazil," she says, "I never imagined what an incredible sense of purpose this experience would add to my life."

Active Citizenship

How did Annie Joseph's volunteer work in Brazil help shape her current goals?

and personal values is an important part of a career search. Do you want to make a lot of money? Do you like a fast pace? Do you want to live in the country? Do you want your work to involve helping people? Answering these questions will help to guide your search by pointing you to careers that agree with your outlook on life and your personal goals.

Career Research

Once you have an idea of where your interests and abilities lie, you can begin to look at career fields. One way to learn about the possibilities is to do some research. Reading about career fields, the types of jobs they include, and the skills and abilities they require can help give you direction.

The library has information about careers. One example is the *Occupational Outlook Handbook,* which tells about hundreds of jobs, their requirements, and their future possibilities.

When you find a career field that interests you, try talking to someone who works in that field. Some questions you might ask are:

★ What do you actually do in this job?
★ What training and education does it require?
★ What do you like most about your job? What do you like least?
★ What job opportunities are available in this field now and in the future?
★ What is the salary range for this job?
★ Would I have to live in a certain region or city in order to get work in this field?

On-the-job experience can be a good way to find out whether or not a career is for you. Perhaps you can get a part-time or summer job in a field that interests you. You might work in an office, for example, to see what goes on day-to-day in a certain business. Many students volunteer in hospitals and day-care centers to see what careers in medicine and teaching are like.

Satisfying Employers

While you may be hunting for just the right job, employers are on the lookout for just the right employees. Understanding what an employer expects can help you prepare yourself to be successful in your work.

Three employers were asked what they expect from their employees. A personnel director at an aerospace company said:

❝ *You have to know the basic skills of reading, writing, and calculating. I want someone who is willing to learn—both on the job and outside of it. Our business is changing very fast, and we need people who are*

willing to learn new things—new computer programs, new management ideas, new uses of metals. We provide training, but we can't teach unwilling learners. ❞

A restaurant manager said:

❝ *My customers come first. They are not always right, but I need to treat*

CAREER OUTLOOK The government projects that many service industries will continue to grow rapidly. **Economics According to this chart, by how much will the demand for child care workers grow between 1996 and 2006?**

Fastest-growing jobs 1996–2006	Percent of increase
Computer support specialists & all other computer scientists	118%
Computer engineers	109%
Systems analysts	103%
Personal & home care aides	85%
Home health aides	76%
Medical assistants	74%
Teachers, special education	59%
Adjustment clerks	46%
Teacher aides	38%
Child care workers	36%
Social workers	32%

Fastest-declining jobs 1996–2006	Percent of decrease
Printers	-75%
Paste-up workers	-75%
Typesetting machine operators	-75%
Telephone installers & repairers	-74%
Computer operators	-50%
Central office operators	-47%
Directory assistance operators	-47%
Proofreaders	-38%
Textile machine operators	-34%
Welfare workers	-31%
Computer operators	-30%

Source: Bureau of Labor Statistics

them as if they are, or else they won't come back. People who work for me have to understand this and be able to maintain a positive attitude no matter what customers say and do. **"**

The manager of a photocopy sales and rental company said:

"*People who work for me have to get engaged in the job. They need to know customers' names. They need to know whom we buy supplies and equipment from. I have had to fire people who didn't seem to care very much. You can't do a good job if you don't care.* **"**

Most employers say that they want employees with a positive outlook and a "can do" approach. Persistence and effort are two important qualities for making a successful career.

Your Career Future

Doing career research can help you to feel more confident about your future. However, any decision you make today is not final. You will probably change career goals a number of times. In fact, most people change careers—or at least jobs within a career field—more than once. Planning a career is ongoing. It involves continuing to look at your interests, goals, skills, and experiences.

Section 3 Assessment

1. How are the educational requirements for jobs changing?
2. Describe how personal goals and values affect career decisions.
3. Describe three ways to find out about a career in the computer field.
4. Are the career decisions you make today "final"? Explain.
5. **Evaluate** Which qualities are most important for employees to have? Explain.

Extending the Chapter

Historical Views

Americans have not always had the wide range of career choices that exist today. The work most Americans did around 1900 was decided by family tradition and geography. If you were a male born in eastern Kentucky, you might have mined coal. If you were born in the steel towns of Ohio or Pennsylvania, you might have worked in a steel mill. In Oklahoma or Kansas you could have been a farmer.

Meanwhile, job opportunities for women were few. Women did not enter the work force in great numbers until World War II. Today, women make up 46 percent of the work force, and an increasing number of management jobs are held by women. These changes could hardly have been imagined at the start of the 1900s, when only single, young women were in the work force.

Many factors have contributed to the increase in career opportunities for Americans. The service sector has been growing, opening up new jobs. Education, including college, is much more widely available. People are more willing to move to other parts of the country to find jobs they like. Finally, barriers based on race and sex have been breaking down. All these changes have combined to give Americans career options and opportunities not even dreamed of at the turn of the century.

DECISION MAKING SKILLS

How to SET GOALS

Suppose your gym teacher led everyone out to a field and said, "Run a race." The class would be puzzled. No one would know where to go. In a way, making a decision is like running a race. You need a finish line—a clear goal to reach. In this lesson you will take a closer look at how to set clear goals.

Imagine that you have to decide which jacket to buy. With a fuzzy goal like "to buy a jacket," you could be in the store all day. However, a clear goal like "to buy an inexpensive blue jacket" points you in a direction and gives you a way to identify and judge options. It helps you limit your options to a reasonable number. In this case, you would look only at blue jackets.

Choosing a jacket is a decision in which you already have a goal. Many times, though, you are faced with options before you can think about a goal.

You are offered a part-time job. Should you take it or not? You see a bike you like. Should you buy it or keep your money in the bank? Friends invite you to a party on the same night that your family is planning a special dinner. What should you do?

Whether you start out with a fuzzy goal or with no goal at all, the first thing you need to do in decision making is to set a clear goal or goals.

Explain the Skill

The following steps can help you set clear goals. Notice how the steps relate to Mark Aguilar's decision in Section 2 of Chapter 17.

1. **Recognize your opportunity to make a decision.** Ask yourself, "What do I have to make a choice about?" You might begin your answer with "I have to decide whether..." or "I have to decide what..." [Mark might describe his situation in this way: "I have to decide whether to buy a compact disc player or a new printer. I do not have enough money to buy both. I would like to have better quality music, and my friends are pushing me to buy a CD player. However, my classes and my job are important, too, and I need a good printer for both."]

2. **Think of the qualities and values that are important to you.** (a) Suppose your problem is that you have a fuzzy goal. You need a better idea of what you want. Think of what qualities you might look for. For example, if you need to choose a bike, you could say to yourself: "I would like a bike that is black, costs less than $300, is a 21-speed, etc." The qualities you list will help you state a clearer goal. **(b)** Suppose your problem is that you have two or more options, and you do not know your goal yet. To identify a clear goal, you might ask yourself what good qualities each option has. Then ask yourself what good qualities the options have in common. You could start by saying, "What I like about all the options is that they are inexpensive, enjoyable, useful, easy to do, etc." The qualities that come to mind will help you state a goal by helping you identify what is important to you. Also, think about how your values and feelings might affect how you look at the options. Some might be pulling you toward one option, while others might be tugging you toward another one. Suppose one of your values is honesty, and another one is loyalty to friends. If you see a friend cheating on a test, these conflicting values might make it hard for you to decide what

to do. To help you state your goal, think about which values and feelings are most important to you. [Mark has two options but no goal. Mark might ask what qualities he likes about both machines. For instance, both are useful and are better than the machines he has. Mark also considers his values and feelings. His love of music and respect for his friends' opinions pull him toward the CD player, but the value he places on education and on his job pulls him toward the printer. He decides that his education and his job are most important in the long run.]

3. **Use the qualities and values to help you state your goal.** Look at the qualities and values that are most important to you. Your goal should be to choose whichever option most closely reflects them. Word your goal carefully so that later you can clearly tell if you achieve it. [Usefulness and improved performance were two qualities that Mark wanted. He especially valued anything that would help his education and his job. Therefore, his goal might be "to buy the machine that will be more useful and more of an improvement on what I already have." The new CD player will not be much of an improvement because his stereo is in good condition. However, the new printer will be a big improvement over the old one. Also, the printer will be more useful because he can use it for activities that he values more highly than listening to music.]

Analyze the Skill

Imagine that you are faced with a big spending decision. There are two or more things that you want to buy, but you only have enough money to buy one. Make a chart in which you include the following:

A. A description of what you will have to decide about.
B. A list of the qualities and values you think are important to keep in mind when choosing which thing to buy.
C. A clear statement of your goal.

Skill Assessment

After you have set your goal, answer the following questions.

1. What did you have to decide about?
2. What good qualities did the things you wanted to buy have in common?
3. What values did you consider? Which of these values was most important to you? Explain why.
4. What goal did you set? Explain why.
5. How would your goal help you in making a decision about which thing to buy?
6. Why is it important to set a clear goal?
7. Tell in your own words how to set a clear goal in decision making.

How to USE A LIBRARY CATALOG

As you learned in this chapter, people entering the workforce today have more career options than ever before. Which career is right for you? What qualifications do you need to get started in this career? One of the best places to look for answers to these questions is in your public library.

Explain the Skill

Most libraries today have computerized catalogs. These catalogs contain useful information on all the books in the library.

Suppose you go to the library to look for books with information on finding a job. The library computer allows you to search for books by title, author, or subject. You decide to search for books matching the subject "job hunting." The screen displays search results—a list of books that match your search. You click on the first one, which is titled *How to Win the Job You Really Want*. The graphic below displays the information a typical computer catalog would show you about this book.

Title:	How to Win the Job You Really Want
Author:	Weinberg, Janice
Published:	New York: H. Holt, 1994
Edition:	2nd ed.
Subject:	Job hunting
	Career development
	Vocational guidance
Material:	290 p. : ill.
Notes:	Includes bibliographical references and index
Call Number:	650.14 We

Analyze the Skill

Read the information presented by the library's computer catalog. This information can help you decide if the book will be useful to you.

The "Published" line tells you where the book was published, the publishing company, and the date of publication. From the "Material" line you learn the number of pages in the book. You also note the term "ill." indicating that the book is illustrated. If you decide you want to read this book, make a note of the call number, which tells you where on the library shelves the book is located.

Skill Assessment

1. Use the search results shown on this page to provide the following information about the book *How to Win the Job You Really Want*.
   (a) Author
   (b) Year published
   (c) Number of pages
   (d) Call number
2. What subjects does this book cover?
3. Does it have illustrations? Does it have an index?
4. Who might find this book useful?

CHAPTER 17 ASSESSMENT

Building Civics Vocabulary

For each pair below, explain how the first term is different from the vocabulary term that follows.

Example: A *passbook savings account* is different from a *time deposit* because a passbook savings account allows withdrawal at any time, while a time deposit specifies a length of time the money must be in the bank.

1. *earned income* and *fringe benefits*
2. *interest* and *dividends*
3. *salary* and *disposable income*

Reviewing Main Ideas and Skills

4. Explain the steps involved in making a budget. What factors should you consider in making this plan?
5. Describe some advantages and disadvantages of using credit.
6. Explain in your own words the idea on which insurance is based.
7. What kinds of jobs are vanishing from the American job market? What sort of jobs are replacing them?
8. **How to Set Goals** In your own words, explain some important steps a person should take when setting a goal.
9. **How to Use a Library Catalog** Look at the computer catalog graphic on the previous page. Create a similar graphic for this textbook. Copy down the headings in the left-hand column of the display and fill in as much information as you can. Next to the "Subject" heading, write three subjects you think fit this book.

Critical Thinking

10. **Making Decisions** Do you think Mark Aguilar made a good money management choice when he purchased a printer instead of a CD player? Explain.
11. **Ranking** Reread the quotes from employers on pages 380 and 381. Rank each employer, from the one you would most like to work for to the one you would least like to work for. Explain your thinking.

Writing About Civics

12. **Writing an Essay** Think of a career that interests you now. Write a short essay explaining how this career fits your goals, values, and talents.

Citizenship Activities

13. **Careers** With a partner, conduct practice job interviews. Each of you should take a turn playing employer and employee. Before each interview, both the employer and employee should prepare a list of questions they want to ask during the interview.

 Take It to the NET

Access the **Civics: Participating in Government** Internet site at **www.phschool.com** for the specific URLs to complete the activity.

As you have read, people use budgets to help them manage their money. So does the federal government. Explore online information about the federal budget and write a newspaper article analyzing the current federal budget. Summarize the government's spending and revenues. Explain to readers how the federal government's budget can impact their own income.

Something Else to Grow

Living on a family farm in Kentucky, 18-year-old Stan Ritchie balanced high school classes and backbreaking work raising tobacco and Charolais cattle. The farm gave Stan a daily course in economics. He managed tens of thousands of dollars—buying and selling cattle, tractors, and tobacco seedlings—and he worried about how changing consumer patterns would affect his future earnings. Stan hoped to buy his own farm after he graduated from high school.

Before you read the selection, find the meaning of this word in a dictionary: surplus.

I'd really like to run 200 head of cows and slowly but surely in the next two to five years I plan on having that. The tobacco side of it is a lot of labor if you raise 28,000 pounds like I'm doing....

I guess handling money just comes along with it. I started saving up money in savings accounts when I was very young, and I bought my first cow when I was ten years old. Then I was keeping the calves and building up. Along the way, I was just trying good management. When you sell your tobacco crop, if you have

17,000 pounds, you get $1.83 a pound. But you've got to pay bills with it or keep it back for your expenses on next year's crop and labor and all that stuff. And if you go buy new equipment, nothing's cheap....

If they want people not to be on unemployment, they better think about it before they destroy the tobacco industry. And really the tobacco companies are contributing to it themselves by going to South America. That's where generic cigarettes are made. When you buy generics for 80 cents to a dollar a pack and Marlboros for something like two dollars, people won't smoke [ours]....They need to give us something else to grow.

People will go to beef cattle, hogs, vegetables, or some other types of things to raise. But you can't raise too many, or there will be a big surplus of those and there won't be money in that either....

If you go to beef cattle though, then you're worrying about people wanting to stop eating beef....And if you don't eat that meat, people won't be able to sell cattle. If you knock out the tobacco and beef industry, you can't just dream up a job. Farmers have got to have money coming from something.

Source: Marcia A. Thompson, ed., Who Cares What I Think? American Teens Talk About Their Lives and Their Country (Alexandria, Va.: Close Up Foundation, 1994), pages 79–92.

Analyzing Primary Sources

1. How did Ritchie learn about economics first-hand growing up?
2. What problems did Ritchie feel might face farmers if the tobacco industry were shut down?

UNIT 5 ASSESSMENT

Reviewing Main Ideas

1. If you were to compare the federal government's budget with a personal budget you might make, how would they be alike? How would they be different?

2. Each situation below describes half of an exchange. For each, describe the other half.
   (a) a barber gives a haircut
   (b) a bank pays interest
   (c) a citizen pays taxes
   (d) a consumer pays interest to a bank
   (e) a worker works for an hour

3. Describe who in our society makes each of the following economic decisions. Also, describe what factors must be considered when each decision is being made.
   (a) whether to buy pizza or a hamburger
   (b) how much to spend on national defense
   (c) what wages to pay
   (d) whether to set up a business as a sole proprietorship or a corporation
   (e) what career to choose
   (f) whether or not to raise the reserve requirement for banks
   (g) how to save or invest money

Summarizing the Unit

The web graphic organizer below will help you organize the main ideas of Unit 5. Copy it onto a separate sheet of paper. Review the unit and complete the graphic by filling in examples of the roles that individuals, entrepreneurs, corporations, labor unions, banks, and the government play in our economy. Then write a short essay describing some of the specific roles you currently play in the American economy.

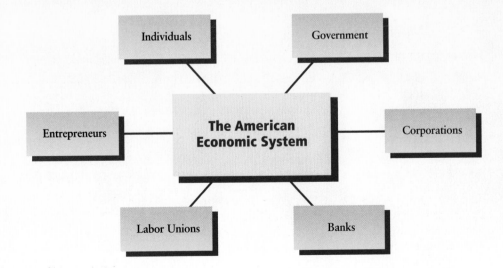

The American Legal System

If one man can be allowed to determine for himself what is law, every man can. That means first chaos, then tyranny. Legal process is an essential part of the democratic process.

—**Felix Frankfurter, Supreme Court Justice, 1946**

If everyone were allowed to make his or her own laws, would there be chaos, as Justice Frankfurter says? Why are the words *law* and *order* so often linked together?

What's Ahead in Unit 6

In Unit 6 you will be considering the role laws play in our society. The first step will be to explore some of the basic purposes and origins of our laws. Then you will examine how the criminal and juvenile justice systems deal with people who are accused of breaking the law. Finally, you will read about the ways our civil justice system helps people to settle conflicts in an orderly manner.

389

CHAPTER 18

Laws and Our Society

Citizenship and You

Have you read the book or seen the movie *Lord of the Flies*? As the story begins, a plane crash leaves a group of schoolboys stranded on a deserted island. Thousands of miles from the world they know, the boys must find a way to stay alive until help arrives.

Picture yourself in such a situation. You and the rest of the survivors face many problems that you must solve at once. Who will make decisions? Will the group need leaders during this emergency? How much power should the leaders have? What should be done with people who act selfishly and do not think about the needs of others? What responsibilities will each person have?

Books and movies have often used this dramatic setting to explore one of the necessities of society, the need for rules or laws. The survivors must make rules about how to live together. They must make laws to help handle conflicts and bring about order.

 Keep It Current

Items marked with this logo are periodically updated on the Internet. To keep up-to-date, go to www.phschool.com

What's Ahead in Chapter 18

In this chapter you will read about laws and their importance. You will take a closer look at why we have laws, where laws come from, and how laws affect your daily life.

Section 1 Why We Have Laws
Section 2 Where Our Laws Come From
Section 3 Kinds of Laws

Citizen's Journal

Suppose you were stranded with a group of people on a deserted island. What is one law you would suggest? What arguments would you make in support of your proposed law?

Why We Have Laws

SECTION PREVIEW

Objectives

- Explain how laws help bring order to society.
- Describe how laws protect safety, property, and individual freedoms.
- Explore ways that laws protect society as a whole.
- Define the common purpose of all laws.
- Analyze the link between laws and morals.

Building Civics Vocabulary

- **Laws** are rules of society that are enforced by government.
- Beliefs about what is fair and what is right or wrong are called **morals.**
- Breaking a law because it goes against personal morals is called **civil disobedience.**

 **Focus**

Throughout this book you have read about laws, rules of society that are enforced by governments. In some ways laws are like other rules, such as family, sports, or class rules. Rules set standards, or requirements. They also set penalties, or punishments, for failing to meet standards. A coach might have a rule that anyone who skips practice may not play in the next game.

Governments also set standards of behavior. An example is the law that requires drivers to stop at red lights. People who break this law usually must pay a fine.

Laws are different from other types of rules, however. Laws are the only rules that everyone in your community has to follow. A family rule against playing loud music after 9:00 P.M. applies only to your family, and your family decides what should be done if you break the rule. However, what if you broke a local law against playing loud music after midnight? You could be fined by your local government for disturbing the peace.

Why do governments make rules? In the following pages, you will explore some of the reasons why we have laws.

The Need for Order

One of the most basic purposes of laws is to bring order to society. One way laws bring order is by telling people what they may or may not do. Some of the most familiar do's and don'ts are traffic laws. Every driver must drive on the right side of the road and obey traffic signs. What would happen if people could drive on either side of the road? What if everyone tried to go through an intersection at the same time?

Another way laws help bring order is by setting standards in many areas. Some laws help make sure that supermarket scales, gasoline pumps, and other measuring devices are accurate. Others set standards for education, including courses of study and attendance requirements.

In many ways laws help bring order by telling people how something should be done. They tell how public officials should be elected, how evidence should be presented in trials, how building permits should be obtained, and so on.

Laws also spell out the proper ways to settle serious conflicts. Suppose a bicycle rider runs into you, knocking you down and causing you to break your leg. You and your family ask the rider's family to pay your medical bills, but they refuse. Laws help bring order by providing peaceful ways of settling such conflicts in court.

The Need to Protect People's Safety

Another purpose of laws is to protect people's lives. No society can run smoothly if

One purpose of laws is to protect people's safety. For example, there is a law requiring that new cars be put through crash tests.

people live in constant fear. Therefore, physical attacks such as murder and rape are against the law. These actions are punished by prison or even death.

Laws also protect the quality of people's lives. They especially look after the lives of people who are less able to protect themselves, such as children and the elderly. Laws hold parents responsible for the care of their children, including food, clothing, housing, and medical care. Laws help protect the elderly in many ways, such as guaranteeing retirement income and low-cost medical care.

The Need to Protect People's Property

Imagine what would happen if people were allowed to take anything that they wanted from each other. Laws against stealing are one way in which the government protects your property, whether it be money or anything else you own. If your bike is stolen, you can tell the police. They will try to find your bike and arrest the thief so that he or she can be punished.

Laws also give you rights if your property is damaged. Suppose you lend your video game system to a friend who spills a can of soda onto it. You ask him to pay for the damage, but he refuses. Laws give you the right to take him to court. A judge may order him to pay for the damage.

Property also includes ideas and inventions. Ideas for a new cereal, a board game, a new style of skateboard, or a labor-saving invention for the home are the property of the person or company who thought of them. A person also owns any work of art, music, or literature that he or she creates.

Any creation or invention can be protected by law. Examples of this protection are all around you. Books, CDs, videotapes, and games display the copyright symbol: ©. Brand names have the ® symbol standing for "registered trademark." Patent numbers are stamped on many products, from sports shoes to computers. Copyrights, trademarks, and patents are all warnings that it is against the law to copy creations or inventions without permission.

The Need to Protect Individual Freedoms

Americans have always treasured individual freedoms. As you know, these freedoms are protected by the Constitution—the highest

To guard public health, laws require that treatment plants need a discharge permit before releasing any pollutants.

law in the land. The Constitution, in the Bill of Rights, makes it illegal for the government to deny freedom of religion, freedom of speech, freedom of the press, and other basic freedoms.

The Constitution protects the basic rights and freedoms of individuals by limiting the government's power. The Constitution also guarantees, through the Fourteenth Amendment, that laws will be applied fairly and equally to all people.

The Need to Promote the Common Good

The Preamble of the Constitution declares that one of the goals of our government is to promote the general welfare, which means the common good of the people. Therefore, laws do not just protect the safety, property,

and freedoms of each individual. They also protect society as a whole.

Some laws protect the environment and everyone's health. Laws limit pollution to improve the quality of the air we breathe. They also regulate the safety of the water we drink, the food we eat, and the products we use. Laws cover everything from how restaurants prepare food to how nuclear power plants get rid of their wastes.

Laws also make sure that help is given to people who need it. Laws set up unemployment insurance and job-training programs that help people who have little or no income. Laws allow the government to give aid to victims of floods and other disasters. These and many other laws remind people of their responsibilities toward each other.

A Common Goal

You have just looked at several purposes of laws: to keep order; to protect the safety, property, and freedoms of individuals; and to promote the common good. However, any law may serve more than one purpose.

Laws that set speed limits, for instance, help preserve order and also protect people's safety. Laws that regulate the quality of food protect the safety of the individual. They also serve the common good by protecting everyone in our society. The purposes of law are closely tied to each other because all laws have a common goal: to encourage people to live together peacefully.

Laws and Morals

Most of us do not consciously think about the purposes of laws. However, we know that laws reflect many of the basic values and beliefs we share. Beliefs about what is fair and what is right or wrong are called morals. Most of us have similar morals. Our values and morals, rather than our laws, are the real glue that holds our nation together.

Most Americans obey laws because they want to. Theft and murder are against the law, but most people believe those actions are wrong anyway. Even if there were no laws, most people would never steal or commit murder. Laws are necessary, however, so that the government can take action against people who do act wrongly.

What happens, though, if a law goes against your beliefs? In a situation like that, some people disobey the law. Breaking a law because it goes against personal morals is called civil disobedience. For example, a person might refuse to pay income tax because he or she opposes government spending on nuclear weapons.

People who take part in civil disobedience willingly accept the punishment for breaking the law. In this way, they follow their morals while recognizing the need for order in society. There could be no order if everyone decided to disobey certain laws but was unwilling to accept the punishments. If people want to change a law, our democratic government provides ways to do so. In the meantime, we have a responsibility to each other to live by the laws we have.

Section 1 Assessment

1. **Define** laws, morals, civil disobedience
2. Describe four of the main reasons we have laws.
3. Which constitutional amendment states that laws must be applied fairly to all people?
4. Give one example of a law that protects both the individual and society as a whole.
5. Explain how laws are related to morals.
6. **Synthesize** Choose a law that you consider to be particularly important and predict what would happen if that law no longer existed.

Where Our Laws Come From

SECTION PREVIEW

Objectives
- Explain how laws made by legislatures differ from guidelines established by judges' decisions.
- Explore the history and importance of legal codes.
- Analyze our Constitution and state constitutions as sets of laws.
- Describe how laws are carried out by government agencies.
- Explain why laws are sometimes changed.

Building Civics Vocabulary
- **Statutes** are written laws made by legislatures.
- **Common law** is a body of law based on judges' decisions.
- A **legal code** is a written collection of laws.

 **Focus**

Where do our laws come from? Basically, they grow out of common values and beliefs in two ways: through rules written by legislatures and through decisions made by judges. Both of these sources of law have a long history, and both have played an important role in the development of American law.

Laws Made by Legislatures

When a certain need or problem arises, people often say that "there ought to be a law" to deal with it. If littering is a problem, your town or city council may pass a law setting a $500 fine for littering. Are too many people being injured in motorcycle accidents? Your state legislature may pass a law that riders must wear helmets. When the price of food goes up, Congress may pass a law increasing Social Security payments to the elderly.

All of these are statutes, written laws made by legislatures. Usually the term *statute* refers to laws made by Congress or by state legislatures. Laws made by city or town councils are typically called ordinances.

In making laws, elected officials are guided by the morals, values, beliefs, and customs shared by most of the people served by the government. Laws passed by Congress reflect basic values shared by most Americans. Whenever you see the words *federal law* or *federal statute*, you know that everyone in the nation has to obey that law.

Laws passed by a state or local government, however, only apply within that state or local community. Since customs and beliefs in one state or community may differ somewhat from those in another, their laws may differ, too. For instance, one state may allow lotteries while another does not.

The relationship between laws and common beliefs has always been a close one. For example, in ancient Rome, where many people believed in witchcraft, statutes made it illegal for anyone to cast spells that would do harm. Laws against witchcraft were even found in the American colonies. Today we have no such laws because most people do not believe in witchcraft.

Judges' Decisions

When people talk about "laws," they are usually referring to statutes and ordinances. However, "obeying the law" also means obeying decisions made by judges. Unlike legislatures, judges do not write laws. Instead, they wait for cases to come to them, and they decide each case based on laws that already exist. Those laws may be statutes and ordinances, or they may be earlier decisions made by judges in similar cases.

American judges have inherited from England a strong tradition of being guided by earlier court decisions. Hundreds of years before the colonists came to America, a system of laws had developed in England. Some of these laws were statutes made by Parliament, the English legislature. However, the English people also relied greatly on common law, a body of law based on judges' decisions.

Here is how common law worked. In making a decision on a case, an English judge would always consider general community customs and beliefs about what was fair. However, a judge would also need specific guidelines to follow in deciding each case. To find those guidelines, he looked at written records of how other judges had decided similar cases. If those decisions reflected the current beliefs of the community, the judge would follow them as a precedent, or guide.

Suppose, however, that community beliefs changed. Or perhaps a case came up that had no precedent. A judge would then make a new decision that reflected current beliefs and customs. The new ruling would be a precedent for future cases that were similar.

When the tradition of common law came to the United States, judges still followed

Facts & Quotes

It's the Law

Over the years legislatures have passed some unusual laws. Try to guess why each of the following laws was made.

★ A Kentucky city passed a law making it illegal for children to carry ice cream cones in their pockets.

★ According to a law in a small Illinois town: "It is illegal for anyone to give lighted cigars to dogs, cats, and other domesticated animals."

★ In one Washington city, the law states that anyone entering town with the intent to commit a crime must "stop at the city limits and telephone the chief of police as he is entering the town."

many of the decisions of English judges. Conditions and customs were not always the same in the United States as in England, however, and some decisions of American judges reflected unique aspects of life in the United States.

Under English common law, for example, it was illegal for a landowner to interfere with the natural flow of a stream. This law made sense in England. In the 1800s, Americans started using waterpower to run factories. American judges in some states, therefore, changed the common law ruling so that landowners could interfere with the flow of a stream by building dams to power factories.

Legal Codes

As you might imagine, thousands of laws have been made over the years. To help keep track of laws, lawmakers have organized many of them into legal codes. A legal code is a written collection of laws, often organized by subject. Traffic laws, for instance, are collected in your state's motor vehicle code, while laws relating to schools will be found in the state education code.

Codes provide a way to organize laws so that they are up-to-date and easy for people to find.

Legal codes have a long history. One of the earliest codes was made almost 4,000 years ago when the Babylonian king Hammurabi collected the laws of his people. The Code of Hammurabi was carved on stone tablets. It contained almost 300 laws. Some of these ideas we share today, such as family laws and criminal laws.

Another ancient legal code was the Justinian Code, created under the orders of the Roman emperor Justinian. This collection of Roman laws influenced the development of laws in Europe and the United States.

Legal codes played a key role in the growth of American government. When the colonies were being formed, there was a need for order. Codes such as the *Laws and Liberties of Massachusetts* provided lists of laws that everyone could know and follow.

Constitutions

Our United States Constitution and the constitutions of the states are also collections of laws. We do not usually think of constitutions

Government agencies decide how emission standards on cars should be carried out to meet the goals of anti-pollution laws.

as "laws" in the sense of rules or regulations, yet they include the basic rules by which our governments are run.

Constitutions tell how laws may be made and what the government can and cannot do. They also list the rights of citizens. As you know, state laws must follow the state constitution. Local, state, and federal laws must all follow the United States Constitution.

Regulations by Government Agencies

When Congress and the state legislatures make statutes, those laws usually set very general requirements. Government agencies then spell out how those requirements are to be met. Suppose that Congress passes a law requiring school cafeterias to provide healthy lunches. Officials of the Department of Agriculture set regulations about what should be in those lunches. If cafeteria workers do not follow those rules, they are breaking the law.

Agency regulations are reviewed by the legislature that made the laws. Any regulations that do not carry out the laws are changed.

Changing the Law

In our country, citizens have the final say on all laws. Through elected representatives, we can add, change, or remove any law. Changes might be as major as amending the Constitution or as minor as doing away with a local ordinance.

As you have already seen, sometimes laws become out of date as beliefs, values, or customs change. People may also change their ideas about what is fair or reasonable. If the majority of the people disagree with laws, the government will usually change them. One example, of course, was the change in the laws about voting rights for women. In short, the laws that last are those that are seen as fair, reasonable, and understandable by the majority of the people.

Section 2 Assessment

1. **Define** statutes, common law, legal code
2. What are the two main ways that our laws are made?
3. How are constitutions and codes similar and different?
4. Why do laws made by our legislatures sometimes become out of date?
5. **Evaluate** What is one law that you think should be changed? Explain why.

Kinds of Laws

SECTION PREVIEW

Objectives

- Explore the purpose and source of criminal law.
- Explain how civil law differs from criminal law.
- Describe how criminal and civil law can work together.

Building Civics Vocabulary

- A **crime** is any behavior that is illegal.
- **Criminal law** is the group of laws that tells which acts are crimes, how accused people should be tried, and how crimes should be punished.
- A **felony** is a crime for which the penalty is imprisonment for more than one year, a fine, or a combination of both.
- A **misdemeanor** is a crime for which the penalty is a jail sentence of not more than one year, a fine, or a combination of both.
- **Civil law** is the group of laws that help settle disagreements between people.

 **Focus**

Laws affect your life in many ways. You are reminded about laws even when you rent a videotape. Before the movie begins, a message in big letters appears on the screen:

> ### WARNING
> Federal law provides severe civil and criminal penalties for the unauthorized reproduction, distribution, or exhibition of copyrighted motion pictures, videotapes, or video discs.
>
> Criminal copyright infringement is investigated by the FBI and may constitute a felony with a maximum penalty of up to five years in jail and/or a $250,000 fine.

Why do you think the government might punish people for copying or selling videotapes? What does the warning mean by civil and criminal? You have probably heard the word *felony*, but what does it mean?

This section will explore the answers to these and other questions by looking at the two main types of law that affect you: criminal law and civil law. Both types help people live together peacefully.

Criminal Law

When people refer to "breaking the law," they are usually talking about crimes. A **crime** is any behavior that is illegal because the government considers it harmful to society. A crime may be an act, such as stealing. It may also be a failure to do something required by law, such as refusing to pay income taxes. Something cannot be a crime unless there is a specific written law against it. Each law must define a behavior and state how it may be punished. **Criminal law** refers to the group of laws that tell which acts are crimes, how accused persons should be tried in court, and how crimes should be punished.

The Purpose of Criminal Law The main purpose of criminal law is to protect society as a whole. Suppose that you catch a burglar leaving your home. The burglar returns the stolen money, and you agree not to tell the police. You might be satisfied just to get your money back. However, the government is not satisfied because it sees the burglar as a threat to the community's safety. That is why the act is a crime and must be reported.

To see how crimes harm society, imagine what would happen if the government did not punish people who commit them. If stealing was not against the law, there would be little to discourage some people from taking the property of others. Society would be harmed because everyone's property would be threatened. Suppose that people were allowed to copy and sell products

Under criminal law, people who purposely damage the property of others may be punished by fines or jail terms.

made by businesses, such as videotapes. Society would be hurt because businesses could not make a fair profit.

Penalties for Crimes Criminal laws must set fair and reasonable penalties. Some crimes deserve greater penalties than others. Also, most crimes have maximum and minimum penalties. This range allows people guilty of the same crime to receive different punishments, depending on the case. For instance, a first-time offender will probably receive a lighter penalty than someone who has committed many crimes.

Crimes are divided into two categories: felonies and misdemeanors. A felony is a serious crime for which the penalty can be imprisonment for more than one year. Felonies include such crimes as kidnapping and murder. A misdemeanor is a less serious crime for which the penalty is often a fine. Littering and driving without a license are examples of misdemeanors.

Sources of Criminal Law Would you feel comfortable if a single government leader could decide which types of behavior should be punished as crimes? Probably not. Too much power would be in the hands of one person. In the United States, no President, state governor, or judge may make a law that a certain act is a crime.

When people talk about "the government" making an act a crime, they are referring either to Congress, to state legislatures, or to local lawmakers such as city councils. At all three levels of government, criminal laws are passed, written down, and organized into codes. They are numbered and listed by subject so that they can be looked up easily.

Congress decides which types of behavior will be considered crimes anywhere in the United States. Each state legislature, though, can make its own criminal laws as long as they do not come into conflict with federal statutes or the Constitution.

Some types of behavior, such as gambling, may be illegal in one state but legal in another. Punishments may also differ. Drunk driving may be a felony in one state but a misdemeanor in another.

Civil Law

As you have seen, criminal law includes all the laws that the government can punish people for breaking. Civil law is the group of laws that help settle disagreements between people.

The Purpose of Civil Law Civil law provides a way for people to settle disagreements in court if they cannot or will not settle them privately. In civil cases, the government will not automatically get involved, as it does with crimes. An individual or group involved in the conflict must first ask for help by suing, or taking the matter to court.

By providing a system of civil law, the government is in effect saying, "If you

Sandra Day O'Connor

"There is no doubt that my appointment to the Supreme Court was a signal of hope to women throughout America that their dream of sharing in the power base might be fulfilled." So says Justice Sandra Day O'Connor, who in 1981 became the first woman appointed to our nation's highest court.

Raised on a cattle ranch in Arizona, O'Connor went on to academic excellence at Stanford University in California. In spite of graduating at the top of her law school class in 1952, however, O'Connor had a hard time finding her first job. "I interviewed with law firms in Los Angeles and San Francisco," she remembers, "but none had ever hired a woman before as a lawyer, and they were not prepared to do so."

O'Connor decided to start her own law practice in Arizona. After several years of successful practice, she became an assistant attorney general for the state. In 1969, she moved on to the Arizona state senate, where she was elected majority leader—the first female in the nation to be named majority leader of a state legislature. Following her legislative career, she became a state court judge.

As a Supreme Court justice, O'Connor has been a strong supporter of state's

rights and equality for women. When balancing the arguments presented before the Court, she relies on her experience in all three branches of government. "It undoubtedly has helped me understand and appreciate the importance and value of the federal system designed by the Framers of the Constitution."

Speaking recently with a group of young students, she was asked if being a woman influences her decisions as a judge. "I tend to think," she answered, "that probably at the end of the day, a wise old woman and a wise old man are going to reach the same answer."

Recognizing Viewpoints

Does Justice O'Connor feel her appointment to the Supreme Court has influenced other women? Explain.

disagree with someone and think you have been treated unfairly, first try to work it out yourselves. If that fails, there are laws that judges and juries may use to help settle the conflict."

Suppose, for example, you buy a CD player that breaks down the first time you use it. The store owner refuses to replace the machine, saying that you must have broken it. Under civil law, you have the right to sue the owner. That is, you may file a complaint with a court stating why you think the owner has been unfair to you. Both you and the owner might then tell your stories to a

When you set out to make a major purchase, it is reassuring to know that one purpose of civil law is to help make sure that buyers and sellers treat each other fairly.

judge or jury, who will make a decision based on rules of civil law.

Sources of Civil Law In criminal cases, the main question is, "Did the accused person commit a crime?" Judges and juries must compare the facts of the case with the statute that defines the crime. In civil cases, however, the main question is, "What is a fair way to settle this type of disagreement?" To answer that question, judges and juries often refer to earlier decisions that have been made in similar cases.

Decisions in civil cases may also be based on statutes. Most civil statutes sum up the unwritten laws on which judges have based their decisions over the years. For instance, in case after case judges have ruled that a seller has a duty to deliver goods and that a buyer must pay for them. Eventually, legislatures decided that this basic unwritten law should be spelled out as a written statute: "The obligation of the seller is to transfer and deliver and that of the buyer is to accept and pay in accordance with the contract."

Some civil statutes are collected and organized into legal codes. The example just mentioned comes from the Business and Commerce Code, which includes many laws that protect consumers.

Where Criminal Law and Civil Law Meet

Criminal law gives government the power to protect society as a whole by taking action against individuals who commit crimes. Civil law provides a way for individuals or groups within society to settle their conflicts in an orderly manner. Both types of laws help bring order to society and protect people's rights.

Sometimes situations involve both criminal and civil law. Suppose a drunk driver who has no insurance severely injures someone. Criminal law protects society by punishing the driver for drunk driving. However, it does not require the driver to pay the injured person's medical bills. That is where civil law enters the picture. If the driver refuses to pay, the injured person can sue. Under civil law, a court can force the driver to pay.

Think back to the warning that appears on videotapes. Criminal law protects society by fining or imprisoning a person who illegally copies and sells a company's tapes. However, punishing the criminal does not completely solve the company's problem. It has lost money it could have earned by selling tapes itself. Under civil law, the company can ask a court to force the criminal to pay the company the amount lost in sales.

Together, criminal and civil law look after our needs and rights. In Chapters 19 and 20 you will look at how our systems of criminal law and civil law work.

Section 3 Assessment

1. **Define** crime, criminal law, felony, misdemeanor, civil law
2. Why do some laws differ from state to state?
3. How are the sources of criminal and civil law similar? How are they different?
4. Why do we need both criminal and civil law?
5. **Evaluate** Which group of laws do you think is more important—criminal law or civil law? Explain your answer.

Extending the Chapter

Historical Views

Laws in our society have changed as Americans' beliefs about what is right and wrong have changed. Up until the early 1900s, for example, there were few child labor laws.

The change from a rural society to an urban one, however, brought changes in attitudes toward child labor. Instead of working at home or on a farm, many children worked in large factories. In 1900, one out of every five ten-to-fifteen-year-olds worked. As more people began to object to child labor, state legislatures passed laws limiting child labor. The goal was to protect the health and safety of children and to ensure time for schooling.

The growth of industry has also brought changes in laws on pollution. Until recently, few Americans worried about pollution of the air, water, and land. Now, however, the public has demanded that some forms of pollution be made crimes for which companies may be fined.

Another example of change is in laws protecting consumers. For many years American courts upheld laws based on the idea "let the buyer beware." If buyers bought a bad product, it was their fault for making a poor decision. Today, consumers expect the government to take action against sellers who make defective products or use false advertising. Changes in consumer law have given the buyer more protection than in the past.

As our society changes, some laws will also change. In most cases, new laws will be added. In some cases, acts that were previously crimes may be "decriminalized." For example, during the 1920s and early 1930s the sale and manufacture of alcoholic beverages was a federal crime. However, people found that prohibiting alcohol created more problems than it solved, and the law was changed. As you look to the future, what changes in our laws do you think lie ahead?

How to IDENTIFY AND JUDGE OPTIONS

Suppose that two of your friends have gotten into an argument. They plan to meet to fight it out. You know where and when the fight will take place. You worry that one or both of them might be seriously hurt. How will you decide what to do?

Decision making, as you know, has two main parts: choosing and taking action. The lesson in Chapter 17 provided some guidelines for the first step in choosing: goal setting. This lesson will help you with identifying and judging options.

Explain the Skill

Suppose that in deciding how to deal with the planned fight you have set two goals: to prevent anyone from getting seriously injured and to preserve your friendship with both friends. Copy the chart that appears on page 405. Allow plenty of space between the options. As you read the following guidelines for identifying and judging options, you will be answering questions and filling in the chart.

Have a Clear Idea of What You Want

Identify qualities and values that you think you should consider when deciding what to do. You will usually include the most important ones in the statement of your goal or goals. You can also list some qualities and values separately as other standards, or requirements, that your final choice must meet.

Suppose, for example, that you are deciding which people to invite to a party. You might look for certain qualities in guests, such as friendliness and a good sense of humor. You could also consider values, such as kindness, that might guide you in choosing guests. For example, your goal might be: "To invite people who are friendly and have a good sense of humor." This goal already

includes two standards. If you value kindness, you might add: "I will try to include some people who are not usually invited to parties."

Your goals in deciding how to deal with the planned fight might be to prevent anyone from getting seriously injured and to preserve your friendship with both friends. These goals already include some standards, such as the value of friendship. If you also value fairness, you might add another standard: "Do not play favorites." If you value honesty, you might add: "Do not lie to either friend." Whatever you finally decide to do would have to measure up to these goals and standards.

1. Write down another standard that you might use in deciding what to do about the fight. Add it to your chart.

2. How do clear goals and standards help you identify and judge options?

Identify Your Options Keeping in mind your goals and standards, identify ways to meet them. You can identify options by brainstorming. When you brainstorm, be sure to:

- Quickly list as many options as you can.

- Avoid criticizing the options you think of.

- Piggy-back options. In other words, use options you have already thought of to help you think of even more options.

One option is to meet with each friend and try to talk them out of the fight.

3. State at least two other options and add them to your chart. Leave plenty of space between options.

4. If you were to tell another student how to brainstorm, what advice would you give?

Decision to be made:	I need to decide what to do about the fight that my friends are planning to have.
My Goals:	To prevent anyone from getting seriously injured. To preserve my friendship with both friends.
My Standards:	Do not play favorites. Do not embarrass either friend.

Add another standard.

	Kinds of Information I Need		
Options	Effects on Friendship	Physical Risk to Me	**Add another kind of information.**
1. Meet with each friend.	+friends might appreciate my efforts. —Friends may get angry with me +probably will not embarrass either friend	+probably none	
2. Add another option.			
3. Add another option.			

Get Useful Information About Each Option

To choose the best option, you need information that is relevant, or related, to your decision. That information must also be reliable. Your search for useful information has three parts: (a) identifying which kinds of information you need, (b) finding that information, and (c) checking whether it is accurate.

Identify which kinds of information you need. To compare options, you will need certain types of information about each one. This might include *characteristics* of each option and *consequences,* or effects, of each option.

Look for information that relates to the type of decision you are making. In deciding which part-time job to take, for example, you might look at characteristics such as wages and schedules, and consequences such as effects on school activities. Ask yourself, "What do I need to know about each option?"

When considering options for dealing with the fight, you might consider consequences such as physical risks to you and effects on your friendship.

5. Name one other kind of information you might want. Explain how it would help you make a good choice. Then list it.

Collect the information you need. Find reliable sources of information about the characteristics and consequences of each option.

Perhaps you can rely on some of your own ideas and experiences. You can also get information from other sources that you trust. Suppose, for instance, that you are deciding which school activity to sign up for, and you want to know how much time each one will take. You might check with team or club members about practice schedules and meeting times.

You might recall that you once talked some friends out of fighting. They had agreed that it was a poor way to settle their disagreement. Therefore, you think that meeting with each friend might have a good effect.

6. For each of the options you listed in the chart, name at least three specific consequences or characteristics. Then add these pieces of information to your chart. Make sure that you have put at least one piece of information in each section of your chart.

Check whether the information is accurate. Even though you have collected information from reliable sources, take a closer look to make sure it is accurate. First, separate the statements of fact from the opinions because you will need to judge them differently.

In judging statements of fact, check whether they are true. Suppose you are deciding which video game to buy, and a friend who recently bought a game tells you prices from several stores. You might call the stores to check whether prices have changed.

In judging opinions, check whether they are reasonable. Suppose that a friend tells you a certain video game is "great." Does your friend have good reasons to back up that opinion? Keep in mind that statements about consequences are often opinions. When you look at a possible consequence, always

ask yourself, "How likely is this to happen?"

Suppose your brother tells you that trying to talk friends out of fighting will just make them angry. How reliable is his opinion? Based on your experience, you might consider this opinion unreliable and ignore it.

7. Give an example of information that you would *not* rely on when deciding what to do about the planned fight. Explain why you would not trust this information. Then look at your chart and cross out any information that you do not consider reliable.

Judge Each Option Identify the good and bad points of each option. Put a plus (+) next to each characteristic or consequence that meets one or more of your goals or standards. Put a minus (-) next to each one that does not.

You might think that some characteristics and consequences are more important than others and therefore give them greater weight. Next to important good points you might put two pluses. Next to important bad points you might put two minuses.

Give each option a fair look. If you are leaning toward one before carefully examining the others, look for any bad points you may have overlooked. This will help you to be as objective as possible.

In judging the option of meeting with each friend, you could put a plus next to "friends might appreciate my efforts."

8. Name one characteristic or consequence that you would consider positive and one that seems negative. Explain why. Then put a plus and a minus next to them on your chart. Judge the other pieces of information on your chart and mark each with a plus or minus.

Choose the Best Option Decide how best to reach your goal or goals by comparing the good and bad points of each option. In choosing the best option, keep in mind that some characteristics or consequences may be more important to you than others.

You might also consider how your choice could affect goals you have not listed, especially long-range goals. Suppose you have a goal to buy a car and are trying to decide whether to take a part-time job during the school year. If college is a long-range goal, you might consider the effect on your grades.

In judging the options for dealing with the fight, you might consider the effect on friendship to be most important.

9. Which option would you choose? Why?

Now that you have filled out your chart, you can see that it would not be practical to use a chart like this everytime you make a decision. After all, many decisions have to be made quickly. However, whenever you have enough time to think over an important decision, a chart can be a useful tool. Of course, whether or not you use a chart, you should always consider a number of possible options and think of their good points and bad points.

Analyze the Skill

Picture yourself in the following situation: You are standing in the lunch line at the cafeteria. An older student comes up to you and demands that you hand over your lunch money. You do not want to get hurt, so you hand over the money. "Thanks for the donation," the student says. "I'll be back tomorrow for another one."

First, describe exactly what it is you have to make a choice about. You might begin by saying, "I have to decide whether…" or "I have to decide what…" Next, set clear goals and standards. Then brainstorm and judge at least three options. Make a chart like the one on page 405 and fill it in as you move through the process. Finally, choose the best option. Be prepared to explain your choice.

Skill Assessment

After you have completed your chart and have chosen an option, answer these questions.

10. What goal or goals did you set?

11. What were three options you identified?

12. What kinds of information did you collect about each option?

13. Pick one of the options and tell what consequences you predicted.

14. Which option did you choose and why?

15. Suppose that one of the first options you think of seems to be a good one. Why is it useful to continue to think of other options?

How to INTERPRET SYMBOLS

A symbol is something that stands for something else. Symbols that stand for the United States, for example, include our flag, the bald eagle, and Uncle Sam. A dove and an olive branch are symbols of peace, and a lion is often used as a symbol of courage. The photograph on this page shows a statue of Themis, an ancient symbol of justice.

Explain the Skill

When interpreting a symbol, it is important to pay close attention to the different parts of the symbol. Each part often has a significance of its own that contributes to the overall meaning of the symbol.

Think of the United States flag, for example. As you know, the flag represents the entire nation. Within the flag, however, there are more specific symbols. The flag's thirteen stripes represent the thirteen original colonies. The flag's fifty stars stand for the fifty states that make up our nation today.

Analyze the Skill

In Greek mythology, Themis was a goddess of law and justice. She has been used as a symbol of justice ever since. Today, statues of Themis can be found at courthouses across the United States.

Study the photograph of the Themis statue shown on this page. As with the American flag, it is important to understand the meaning of each part of the symbol. Note that Themis is wearing a blindfold. In her left hand she holds a scale. She holds a sword in her right hand. Think about the meaning of each of these details and then answer the following questions.

Skill Assessment

1. Why do you think that the symbol of justice is usually shown with a blindfold over her eyes?
2. Why do you think that the symbol of justice is shown holding a scale in her hand?
3. For hundreds of years, the sword has been a symbol of government power and authority. Why do you think the symbol of justice carries a sword?
4. Think of another symbol commonly used to represent justice in the United States—two examples are shown on page 389. Describe the symbol and interpret its meaning.

Building Civics Vocabulary

The vocabulary terms in each pair listed below are related to each other. For each pair, explain what the two terms have in common. Also explain how they are different.

1. *laws* and *morals*
2. *common law* and *statutes*
3. *felony* and *misdemeanor*
4. *criminal law* and *civil law*

Reviewing Main Ideas and Skills

5. How do laws differ from other types of rules found within society?

6. Describe the two main sources of American law and explain how those sources differ.

7. Explain the importance of constitutions and legal codes.

8. Compare and contrast the purposes of criminal law and civil law.

9. **How to Identify and Judge Options** Suppose you are trying to make an important decision. Why is it helpful to know your goals before collecting information about options?

10. **How to Interpret Symbols** Look back at the painting of the American flag being raised on page 209. How has this national symbol changed since 1803? Why was it changed?

Critical Thinking

11. **Defending a Position** Suppose someone says to you, "To be a moral person, you only have to avoid breaking any laws." Do you agree with this statement? Defend your position.

12. **Making Predictions** What would the world be like without laws? Predict how your life would be different.

Writing About Civics

13. **Writing a Law** If you could pass a new law for your town, what would it be? What would the goal of your law be? What would the punishment be for breaking this law?

Citizenship Activities

14. **Civic Participation** With a group of three or four classmates, make a list of five school rules that you consider to be very important. Prepare an explanation of why those rules are necessary and make proposals for how they should be enforced. Each group should present its findings to the class.

Take It to the NET

Access the **Civics: Participating in Government** Internet site at **www.phschool.com** for the specific URLs to complete the activity.

Laws are vitally important to a society, but they can also be very complex and controversial. The courtroom is one place that laws are debated and applied. Explore online information about some famous trials that helped shape our legal system. Provide a summary of a trial and explain why you believe the trial was important.

CHAPTER 19

Criminal and Juvenile Justice

Citizenship and You

When Kate arrived home, something felt odd to her, but she couldn't figure it out. Then she walked into the family room. "Mom, where's the VCR?" she called back into the kitchen.

"Isn't it where it always is?" replied her mother, walking in with a worried look. She stared at the blank spot next to the television and said in a shaky voice, "Kate, I think we've been robbed."

Kate's father and brother ran to see for themselves. Then everyone rushed to a different part of the house.

Kate turned her doorknob slowly. She looked into her room. Her computer was gone, too.

Kate's mother called the police. An officer arrived soon after. He asked what had been taken.

"Looks like the burglar got in through here," said the officer, looking up at the half-open window above the kitchen sink.

"Will I get my computer back?" asked Kate.

"We'll do our best," said the officer, "But don't count on it. We don't recover many stolen items. And many burglars aren't caught."

What's Ahead in Chapter 19

In this chapter you will study the problem of crime in our society. You will also learn about how governments deal with adult criminals and with young people who break the law.

Section 1   Crime in American Society
Section 2   The Criminal Justice System
Section 3   The Juvenile Justice System

Keep It Current

Items marked with this logo are periodically updated on the Internet. To keep up-to-date, go to www.phschool.com

Citizen's Journal

Suppose someone conducting a survey asked you: Do you believe crime is a serious problem in the United States today? How would you respond? Explain your position.

Crime in American Society

Objectives

- Understand why crime is a major problem in the United States.
- Summarize the major types of crimes.
- Analyze important causes of crime.

Focus

A jogger is mugged in the park. A four-year-old is kidnapped from his front yard. A bank president flees the country, having stolen millions of dollars from depositors. These are the kinds of crimes you hear about all too often on the news. Other crimes take place every day. Cars are stolen, purses snatched. Crime is a major problem in the United States today.

The Problem of Crime

Crime touches many Americans every year. According to the Department of Justice, there was a property crime in one of every five American households in 1998. A violent crime happens in the United States about every 22 seconds, and a property crime takes place about every 3 seconds.

A 1999 poll showed that Americans see crime as one of the most important problems facing our country. Crime costs people, businesses, and governments billions of dollars every year.

Crime also makes people afraid. Because they fear crime, they change the ways they lead their lives. They put extra locks on their doors and do not go out at night. They are suspicious of strangers in their neighborhoods. When people and property are not safe, everyone becomes a victim of crime.

Although crime is a problem for all Americans, some places have more crime than others. In general, there is more crime in urban areas than there is in suburban or rural communities. In addition, poor neighborhoods often have more crime than wealthy ones.

The Types of Crimes

Serious crimes fall into several major groups. In the following paragraphs you will read about the kinds of crimes that cause the most concern among Americans.

Crimes Against People Acts that threaten, hurt, or end a person's life are crimes against people. They are also called

When people fear crime, they look for ways to protect themselves. Putting bars on windows is one way to try to prevent burglary.

violent crimes. Murder, rape, and assault are examples of violent crimes.

The most common violent crime is assault. Assault is an attack on a person for the purpose of causing injury to that person's body. Most people who assault another person use a weapon, such as a knife or gun.

Killing someone is known as homicide. When a killing is planned ahead of time, it is called murder. A killing that happens by accident or in a fit of anger is called manslaughter. Not all killings are crimes. Killing someone in self-defense is not against the law, if that is the only way to save your life.

Crimes Against Property Crimes against property happen more often than any other crimes. Most involve stealing.

There are three kinds of stealing. Larceny is taking anything of value that belongs to another person without using violence. Examples include shoplifting and stealing a car.

Robbery is a special kind of stealing. A robber takes something of value from another person by force or by threat of violence. Robbery is therefore both a crime against property and a crime against a person.

When a person breaks into a building and plans to do something illegal inside, that person is committing burglary. Burglary is a crime against property, but it may or may not involve stealing.

Other kinds of crimes against property include arson and vandalism. Arson is the act of setting fire to someone's property—such as a house, factory, or store—on purpose. Vandalism is purposely damaging property. Breaking windows and painting graffiti on walls are examples of vandalism.

White-Collar Crime White-collar crimes are illegal but nonviolent acts by white-collar, or professional, workers for personal or business gain. One white-collar crime is fraud, or taking someone else's property or money by cheating or lying. Another is embezzlement, stealing money that has been trusted to your care. If a bank employee put money from other people's bank accounts into his or her own account, that would be embezzlement. Stealing company secrets and not paying your taxes are other white-collar crimes.

Victimless Crimes Drug use and gambling are known as "victimless crimes," acts that hurt no one except the people who commit them. Our society calls them crimes because they go against common values or because people believe they hurt society as a whole.

Police sometimes draw lines around the body of the victim as part of their investigation at the scene of the crime.

There is disagreement over whether some victimless crimes should be crimes at all. Should there be laws against acts that do not hurt any innocent people?

On one side are people who say that making laws against activities such as gambling and using drugs only cuts down on the freedom of individuals. On the other side are people who argue that such acts really do hurt innocent people. They warn that gamblers and drug users are a bad influence, that their families suffer, and that they often turn to violent crime to pay for their habits.

Crimes Against Government Crimes against government include treason and terrorism. Treason is the betrayal of one's country by helping its enemies or by making war against it.

Terrorism is a crime in which people or groups of people use, or say they will use, violent acts in order to get what they want from government or society. Terrorists have kidnapped and murdered people, hijacked airplanes, and set off bombs, causing injury and death to hundreds of innocent people. The terrorist bombing of a federal government office building in Oklahoma City in 1995 caused the death of 169 people. On September 11, 2001, terrorists hijacked commercial airliners and crashed them into the World Trade Center in New York and the Pentagon near Washington, D.C. The number of people killed from these attacks was about 3,000.

The Causes of Crime

In the United States, millions of crimes are committed each year. People disagree about what causes so many people to break our society's rules.

Poverty Poverty and unemployment are closely connected to crime. When people cannot earn enough money to support themselves and their families, they may feel that society is not working very well for them. People who feel this way are more likely to break society's rules.

Rapid Social Change New technology and changes in the economy are bringing about great changes in the United States. Many Americans must learn new job skills or move to different parts of the country. Values are changing, too. It can be hard to get used to these changes. In the process, some people lose their sense of right and wrong.

Poor Parenting Some studies show that an unhappy family life can make a person much more likely to break laws. Children who have been hurt or neglected by their parents may suffer great emotional pain. As a result, some find it hard to control their behavior as adults.

Drug Abuse More and more of the crimes committed each year are drug-related. That is, the people who commit them are under the influence of drugs, are stealing to support their habit, or are selling drugs. Many people think that solving the drug-abuse problem in our society will also help solve the crime problem.

Permissive Courts Some people place much of the blame for crime on the way our courts treat criminals. Too few criminals are sent to prison, they say. Also, those criminals who do go to prison are let out too soon and go right back to committing crimes.

Not Enough Money for Police Crime will not be reduced, say many people, until the chances of getting caught are much higher. More money, they argue, should be given to police departments so that more police officers can be hired.

Violence in the Media Every day, millions of children and adults watch violent

Terrorism is one of the most serious criminal threats facing our society today. This memorial honors the victims of the 2001 terrorist attack on the World Trade Center in New York City.

acts on television. They see gangsters, police, and soldiers hurting and killing people. The same happens in movies and computer games. Many people believe that watching a great deal of violence causes people to be more violent themselves.

No Single Cause These and many other aspects of our modern society have been blamed for causing crime. People do not agree about which of these causes are most important. Experts do agree, however, that no single cause can explain our crime problem.

Section 1 Assessment

1. Why do Americans consider crime to be a major problem?
2. Name a kind of crime against a person and a kind of crime against property.
3. List three possible causes of crime.
4. **Analyze** In the beginning of this chapter, was Kate's mother correct in saying they had been robbed? Explain.

The Criminal Justice System

SECTION PREVIEW

Objectives

- Explain the role of police officers.
- Describe what happens when someone is arrested.
- Identify the steps in a typical criminal trial.
- Compare different types of correctional institutions.
- Examine the challenges facing the criminal justice system.
- Analyze several proposals for fighting crime.

Building Civics Vocabulary

- To make an arrest, the police must have probable cause, a good reason to believe that a suspect has been involved in a crime.
- A warrant is a legal paper, issued by a court, giving police permission to make an arrest, seizure, or search.
- Bail is money that a defendant gives the court as a promise that he or she will return for the trial.
- An indictment is a formal charge against a person accused of a crime.
- An arraignment is a court hearing in which the defendant is formally charged with a crime and enters a plea.
- Agreeing to plead guilty in exchange for a lesser charge or lighter sentence is called plea bargaining.
- Letting an inmate go free to serve the rest of his or her sentence outside of prison is called parole.

Focus

Police and other law enforcement agencies, courts, and jails and prisons make up our criminal justice system. Together, their job is to protect people against crime and to find and punish lawbreakers.

The criminal justice system faces a challenge. On the one hand, it must protect society against those who break the law. On the other hand, it must protect the rights of people who have been accused of crimes. Americans often disagree about how to balance these responsibilities. As a result, there is an ongoing debate about how best to solve our crime problem.

The Role of the Police

All levels of government have police officers. Most of them work for city police departments. A local police officer patrols neighborhoods, finds stolen property, investigates complaints, arrests lawbreakers, helps solve disputes, and writes traffic tickets.

The job of state police varies from state to state. In many states their major job is to protect automobile drivers and enforce traffic laws on state highways.

Federal law enforcement agencies such as the Federal Bureau of Investigation (FBI) help local police with such problems as gang wars and drug dealing. The FBI also enforces federal laws such as those against bank robbery and kidnapping.

Officers must know the law and what steps to follow when arresting people. They must be able to protect themselves and others from dangerous people. They have to make many quick decisions. Police officers come face to face with many of society's problems—child abuse, street fights, and drug dealing.

The police have great power. They can use weapons as part of their job. It is important, therefore, that they be trained to use their power wisely and legally.

GRAPH SKILL — ARRESTS FOR SERIOUS CRIMES IN 2000

Type of crime

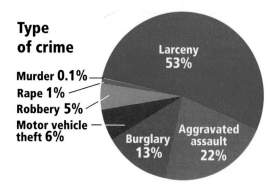

Larceny 53%
Murder 0.1%
Rape 1%
Robbery 5%
Motor vehicle theft 6%
Burglary 13%
Aggravated assault 22%

Age of person arrested

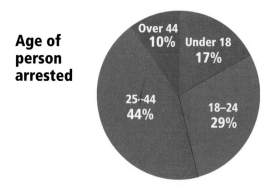

Over 44 10%
Under 18 17%
25–44 44%
18–24 29%

Note: Percentages may not add up to 100 due to rounding.

Source: Federal Bureau of Investigation

Nearly a fifth of the people arrested in 2000 were under 18 years old. **Government** What percentage of the arrests in 2000 were for motor vehicle theft?

What Happens to Someone Who Is Arrested

The purpose of our criminal justice system is to find and punish people who have committed crimes. In order to make sure that people's rights are protected, there are many steps to be taken in deciding whether a person is guilty. To follow those steps, suppose that Jack Jones broke into an electronics store and stole calculators and portable radios.

The Arrest Jack Jones enters the criminal justice system when he is arrested by a law enforcement official. When Jack is arrested, it means that he is no longer free to go. The police must have probable cause, a good reason to believe that a suspect has been involved in a crime. If the police see Jack commit the crime, or if someone reports that a person looking like Jack has committed the crime, then the police have probable cause.

A person can also be arrested if the police have a warrant for his or her arrest. A warrant is a legal paper, issued by a court, giving police permission to make an arrest, seizure, or search. To get a warrant the police must give evidence to a judge.

During the arrest, the officers must tell Jack that he has the constitutional right to remain silent and to have a lawyer present during questioning. This is part of the Miranda warning.

After the arrest, Jack is taken to a police station. The police record Jack's name, the time of the arrest, and the charges, or reason for the arrest. At this time, Jack has the right to make a phone call to a lawyer or to a friend who can arrange for a lawyer. Then he is placed in a jail cell.

Soon after this process has taken place, the case is given to a prosecuting attorney, or prosecutor. In the state court systems, the prosecutor will be the district attorney (DA) or an attorney on the DA's staff. The prosecutor will lead the government's case against Jack Jones. If the prosecutor decides that the case against Jack is too weak, the charges may be dropped, and the suspect released.

The Preliminary Hearing On the day of his arrest or soon after, Jack appears in court for a preliminary hearing. The suspect, Jack Jones, is now called the defendant. At this hearing, the prosecutor must show the judge that a crime has been committed, and that there is enough evidence against Jack to go ahead with the case. The judge may decide to dismiss the case if the prosecutor cannot show that there is enough evidence to believe that Jack committed the crime.

If the crime could lead to a jail or prison sentence, Jack has a right to the help of a lawyer, or attorney. If he does not have enough money to pay for a lawyer, the court will appoint one at this hearing. The lawyer may be either a private attorney whom the government will pay or a public defender. Public defenders are lawyers who work full time for the government defending criminal suspects who cannot afford to pay. The defendant's lawyer is called the defense attorney.

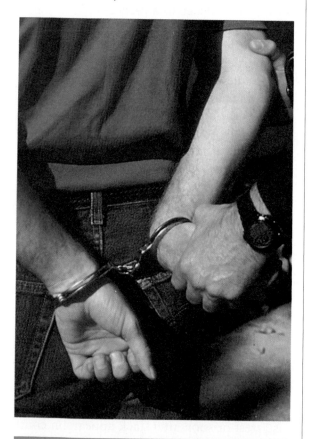

At the time of an arrest, the police must tell the suspect of the right to remain silent and to have the help of a lawyer.

In a misdemeanor case, the defendant may enter a plea of guilty, not guilty, or a plea of "no contest" at this first court hearing. For a felony, which is a crime that could send a person to prison for more than one year, the same types of pleas may be entered.

At this first appearance in court, the judge may set bail. Bail is money that a defendant gives the court as a kind of promise that he or she will return for the trial. If the defendant does not return, the court keeps the bail. The judge may also simply let the defendant go on his or her "own recognizance." This means that the defendant is considered to be a good risk to appear at the trial. A defendant who the judge decides is dangerous to society can be held in jail without bail.

Grand Jury The Constitution says that a grand jury must review cases involving serious federal crimes. Some states use grand juries, too. The grand jury is a group of from 16 to 23 citizens. Their job is to decide if there is probable cause for believing that the defendant committed the crime. The grand jury acts as a check on the government. It protects the rights of the individual, making sure there is enough evidence against him or her.

The grand jury may either return an indictment [in DIT ment] or refuse to indict. An indictment is a formal charge against the accused.

A defendant who is indicted must appear in court for a felony arraignment [uh RAIN ment], a court hearing in which the defendant is formally charged with a crime and enters a plea of guilty, not guilty, or no contest. If the defendant pleads guilty, no trial is needed. If the defendant pleads not guilty, the defense attorney will take the next step.

Pretrial Motions Suppose that Jack Jones has pleaded not guilty to the charges against him. There are important steps, called pre-

In this typical courtroom, an attorney addresses the spectators and jury as the judge looks on.

trial motions, that may be taken by Jack or his attorney before the actual trial begins.

One of the most important motions is the motion to keep evidence from being presented in court. Evidence may be kept back for many reasons. Sometimes the defense attorney may say that the police got the evidence through an illegal search. If the judge rules that key evidence cannot be used in the trial for this reason, the prosecution may have to drop the charges.

Some people believe it is wrong for the courts to throw out evidence that clearly shows a defendant's guilt. Although this rule protects the constitutional rights of the accused, it may result in people who have actually broken the law being set free.

Plea Bargaining Did you know that most criminal cases never go to trial? As you have

seen, some are dropped by the prosecutor or the grand jury, and some are dismissed by the judge. However, the main reason cases do not go to trial is that the defendant pleads guilty, and a trial is not needed.

Why would a defendant plead guilty? If you knew that you had broken the law and that the evidence against you was strong, you might want to make a deal with the prosecutor. Such a deal is called plea bargaining, agreeing to plead guilty in exchange for a lesser charge or a lighter sentence. As a result of plea bargaining, the defendant gets a milder punishment than he or she would probably have received in a trial. Meanwhile, the government saves the time and cost of a trial.

Although plea bargaining can be good for both sides, many people do not like it. Some people, including victims of crimes, think that because of plea bargaining, criminals get off with lighter punishments than they should. Other people, however, point out that prosecutors often "overcharge" defendants in the first place. Overcharging means to charge the accused person with more crimes or a more serious crime than he or she could probably be found guilty of.

Going to Trial

Suppose that, after all of these steps, Jack's case makes it to trial. What happens in the courtroom?

Jury Selection Citizens are called to serve on the jury. First they are questioned by both attorneys in the case. The attorneys are looking for people who will listen carefully to the evidence presented in court and then make up their minds fairly. Sometimes many people must be questioned before the attorneys agree on a group of jurors.

The Trial The rights of due process granted by the Constitution determine how a trial is run. The trial must be speedy and public.

The defendant—Jack—has the right to call witnesses and to question witnesses called by the prosecution. He has the right to be present in the courtroom, but he does not have to answer questions. The purpose of the trial is to decide upon the truth: is Jack innocent or guilty? This important question is answered by carefully studying the evidence.

Usually, statements made by witnesses are the most important evidence in a trial. A witness may be a person who saw the crime take place. A witness may also be anyone who knows anything about the defendant, the victim, or the crime.

The attorneys in the trial each call their own witnesses, asking them questions in court. After one attorney questions a witness, the other attorney may question that same witness.

At the end of the trial, the attorneys for each side make closing arguments. The judge then gives directions to the jury and sends it out to make its decision.

A jury must decide if the defendant is guilty "beyond a reasonable doubt." In other words, the jurors must have no important reasons to doubt that the defendant is guilty. If they are not sure beyond a reasonable doubt, they must find the defendant "not guilty." If the jury cannot agree, it is called a "hung jury," and the case may be tried again before another jury.

Sentencing If Jack is found guilty or pleads guilty, the final step in the courtroom is sentencing. Sentencing is deciding how the defendant will be punished.

In most cases, the law sets both the maximum and minimum sentences for each crime. Inside that range, the judge has the power to decide the exact sentence. In deciding on a sentence, the judge thinks about many factors, such as how much harm was done by the crime.

The judge also considers factors such as the criminal record, age, and attitude of the offender. For example, if the law calls for a sentence of five to ten years in prison for armed robbery, the judge may give a first-time offender who regrets the crime the lowest—or five-year—sentence.

Correctional Institutions

Having been convicted, Jack now enters what is called the corrections system. He may be sentenced to a community treatment program, a jail, or a prison.

Jails are run by cities and counties. They are used to hold people waiting for trial.

THE CONSTITUTION AND THE CRIMINAL JUSTICE SYSTEM

The Constitution provides several important protections for people accused of crimes. **Government Which amendment guarantees the right to confront witnesses?**

Article 1, Section 9
Forbids taking away the right of habeas corpus. Forbids bills of attainder and ex post facto laws.

Article 3, Section 2
Guarantees a trial by jury for those accused of federal crimes.

Amendment 4
Forbids unreasonable searches and seizures.

Amendment 5
Guarantees review and indictment by a grand jury and due process of law. Forbids double jeopardy and self-incrimination.

Amendment 6
Guarantees a speedy and public trial by jury, the right to confront witnesses, the right to be informed of charges, the right to counsel, and the right to force witnesses to appear in court.

Amendment 8
Forbids excessive bail, excessive fines, and cruel and unusual punishments.

Amendment 14
Guarantees due process of law in state courts, and equal protection of the laws in the state.

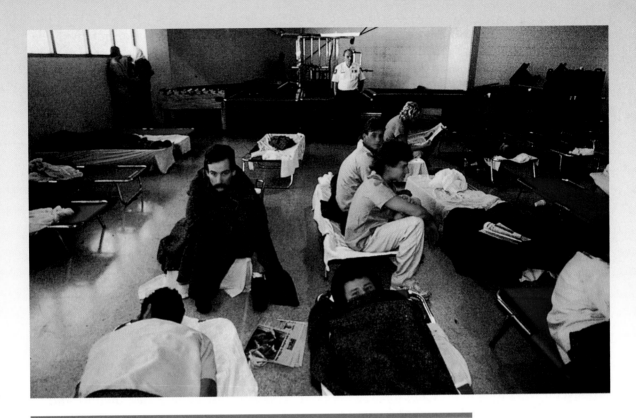

The growing number of prisoners puts a great strain on already overcrowded jails and prisons.

People convicted of misdemeanors may also serve time in a jail. Prisons are run by both state and federal governments. People convicted of serious crimes, such as murder and robbery, are usually sent to prisons. In prison they are called inmates.

An inmate's time in prison may be lowered for good behavior. Letting an inmate go free to serve the rest of his or her sentence outside of prison is called parole. A group called a parole board decides whether to let inmates go before their sentences are over.

At the end of 1999, there were over 1.4 million state and federal inmates and about 700,000 inmates in local jails. Our society spends a large amount of money running jails and prisons. In 1996, for example, state prisons spent a total of $22 billion, or about $20,100 annually per inmate.

Challenges Facing the Criminal Justice System

One of the biggest challenges facing our criminal justice system is the number of people the system must deal with each year. For example, there were an average of over 7 million arrests in the United States each year from 1990 to 1999. In many courts around the country, there are simply not enough judges and other court employees to quickly handle all the people waiting for trial.

Like the courts, prisons are also overcrowded. The number of people in prison nearly doubled during the 1990s, as arrests and average prison sentences both increased. New prison construction has not kept pace with the growing prison population. As a result, many prisons are overcrowded. A 1999 Department of Justice report stated that state prisons housed up to 17 percent more inmates than they were designed to hold. Federal prisons housed 32% beyond their capacities.

Proposals for Fighting Crime

Because of public pressure, Presidents, governors, and mayors have been giving top priority to fighting crime. These leaders have many ideas about how to solve our crime problem. However, few of them agree. What a person thinks is the best solution to crime often depends on what he or she sees as the major cause.

Preventing Crime Many people think we should work hardest at keeping crimes from taking place, rather than at dealing with people after they have broken the law. There are several ways to help prevent crime.

A growing number of communities are using methods such as community policing or the "Neighborhood Watch." In cities that use community policing, such as Winston-Salem,

NC, community members cooperate with the police and each other to prevent crime in their neighborhoods. In communities using a Neighborhood Watch, neighbors look out for each other's property. They report problems quickly to the police. Signs are put up to let criminals know they are more likely to get caught in that neighborhood.

Meanwhile, many people favor broader ways of fighting crime. They want to attack what they see as the root causes of crime: poverty and other social problems.

Being Tougher on Criminals Another view of the best way to fight crime is to be harder on criminals. For example, people have called for mandatory sentences—punishments that are set by law and that a judge must give no matter who the defendant is or the reason for the crime. Some states have passed mandatory sentencing laws. In some states anyone who uses a gun while carrying out a crime must be sent to prison.

Many people also favor the death penalty, or capital punishment, as a sentence for serious crimes such as murder. The death penalty, however, has many opponents.

Those who favor the death penalty believe that it helps keep people from committing murder. Those who oppose the death penalty point out that innocent people have been wrongly convicted of murder. Several death-row inmates have been freed from prison after being proven innocent with DNA evidence. The Supreme Court, however, has upheld state laws allowing the death penalty.

Rehabilitation Rehabilitation is the process of trying to teach prisoners how to live useful lives when they get out. Unfortunately, rehabilitation is not working very well. A large number of inmates break laws again after they are released. Many people, however, say that rehabilitation

Facts & Quotes

Behind Bars

As you have read, many factors go into determining the prison sentence for a convicted criminal. Here are the average sentences and average prison time served for selected crimes in the United States.

Crime	Average sentence	Average time served
Homicide	9 yrs., 5 mos.	4 yrs., 11 mos.
Kidnapping	11 yrs., 4 mos.	8 yrs., 1 month
Robbery	7 yrs., 7 mos.	5 yrs., 1 month
Assault	3 yrs., 3 mos.	2 yrs., 1 month

Source: U.S. Department of Justice

programs can be improved and become an important way of fighting crime.

Some rehabilitation programs go on within prison. Inmates, for example, may get counseling that helps them understand and change the way they act. Educational and job-training programs are also a part of prison rehabilitation. Inmates usually have a chance to obtain a high school diploma and take college level courses.

Rehabilitation may continue after the time in prison is over. Some ex-prisoners live in halfway houses for people who are returning to life outside prison. There they get support and help. They can test new skills in a job that brings in a steady income. Some people believe that skills training and help in finding a job can reduce the number of former inmates who commit crimes again and return to prison.

Our serious crime problem and our overcrowded prisons call out for new solutions. The more you know about the purpose and problems of the criminal justice system, the better you will be able to work with other citizens to solve these problems.

Section 2 Assessment

1. **Define** probable cause, warrant, bail, indictment, arraignment, plea bargaining, parole
2. Why is a police officer's job challenging?
3. What must the prosecutor prove during the preliminary hearing?
4. What must a jury decide in order to return a verdict of guilty?
5. What are two purposes of jails?
6. What factors have led to prison overcrowding?
7. List three possible ways of fighting crime.
8. **Analyze** What are some ways in which the criminal justice system tries to make sure that an innocent person is not mistakenly found guilty of a crime?

The Juvenile Justice System

SECTION PREVIEW

Objectives
- Summarize the origin and purpose of juvenile courts.
- Explain how juveniles are treated differently than adults in the courts.
- Explore various attempts to improve the juvenile justice system.

Building Civics Vocabulary
- A young person who is found guilty of a crime is called a **delinquent.**
- A **status offender** is a youth who is judged to be beyond the control of his or her parents or guardian.
- **Probation** is a sentence in which a person goes free, but must be under the supervision of a court official.

 Focus

In the early part of our country's history, children accused of crimes were treated like adults. They were thrown in jails with hardened criminals and given long prison terms if they were found guilty.

Some people objected to this harsh treatment of young offenders in courts and prisons. They argued that young people need special treatment. About 100 years ago, a group of reformers set out to create a separate justice system for juveniles, or young people.

Juvenile Courts

Juvenile courts are state courts set aside for young people. Their goal is to help juveniles in trouble, not to punish them.

One of the goals of the juvenile justice system is to provide counseling to help young offenders and their families.

The first juvenile court was opened in Illinois in 1899. Its purpose was to give personal attention to each youth. An understanding judge and social workers worked with each juvenile who got in trouble with the law. The Illinois juvenile court has served as a model for similar courts set up in other states.

Who enters the juvenile justice system? Most states say that a juvenile is a person under the age of 18, although a few states set the age at 16 or 17. A youth thought to have broken a criminal law is brought before a juvenile court. A juvenile who is found guilty of a crime is called a delinquent.

Children may also have to appear in juvenile court if they are charged with truancy—skipping school without permission—disobedience, or running away. These acts are not crimes. They are against the law only for young people. A youth who is found guilty of one of these acts is called a status offender. A status offender is a youth who is judged to be beyond the control of his or her parents or guardian.

Juvenile Court Procedure

What happens when Jenna Williams, a sixteen-year-old girl, is arrested for shoplifting makeup in a department store? As you will see in the following paragraphs, the steps she goes through are different from the ones for an adult charged with a crime.

Arrest and Intake When Jenna is arrested, the police now have the power to decide what to do with her. They might return her to her parents or give her case to a social service agency, an organization that helps children and families.

In Jenna's case the police do not send her home. Jenna has been charged with shoplifting before, and she has a history of running away from home. For these reasons, the police take her to a county detention home, or juvenile hall.

Next, Jenna goes through an informal court process called "intake," to decide if her case should be sent to juvenile court. A social worker asks Jenna questions and looks at her past record and family situation. Almost 25% of all cases are dismissed and the juvenile is sent home or directed to a social service agency. Because of Jenna's past record, however, the social worker sends her case to the next step in juvenile court.

The Initial Hearing At the first—or initial—hearing the judge must be convinced that a law was broken and that there is good evidence that the young person was the one

Students Discover the Importance of Jury Duty

Sixteen-year-old Gabriela Pangilinan was accused of drug possession and distribution. Her trial was about to begin. Luckily for her, this was just a classroom exercise.

Pangilinan was one of 30 juniors and seniors from South Boston High School in Boston, Massachusetts, taking part in Law Day—a series of activities designed to teach students the importance of jury duty. Pangilinan played the part of a juvenile defendant. The other students assumed the roles of potential jurors for her trial.

Guests in the classroom court included Federal Judge Lawrence Cohen and Federal Public Defender Owen Walker. They explained the jury selection process to the class. Then Walker, acting as lawyer for Pangilinan, helped his client question

potential student jurors, eliminating those that might be biased against her.

"The enactment of the jury selection process gave students a much better understanding of what jury duty is about," said the students' teacher, Charles Korzeniowski.

Later, the students took a trip to the federal courthouse in downtown Boston, where a satellite hook-up enabled them to join 800

students in classrooms across the nation. Together, these students took on the role of jurors as they watched a mock trial of a teenager.

Each class came up with its own verdict. Then, using the interactive satellite link, jurors from different classrooms discussed their decisions and their reasoning.

By day's end, the South Boston High students had a much better understanding of the legal system. "I was surprised at how much power jurors actually have," said Gabriela Pangilinan. "Now I am more willing to serve on a jury, because I see I can make a difference."

Active Citizenship

Do you think participation in activities like Law Day can help you learn about citizenship? Explain.

who did it. If there is not enough evidence, the juvenile is sent home.

The judge hearing Jenna's case decides that there is probable cause to believe that Jenna stole the makeup. The judge then sends Jenna back to juvenile hall, so that she

will not run away before her case is settled. In most states, a juvenile has no right to bail.

The Adjudicatory Hearing The third step, the adjudicatory hearing, takes the place of a trial. It is generally not public,

THE JUVENILE COURT PROCESS The justice system for young people is different than it is for adults. **Government** What are three sentences a youth might face after being found guilty in juvenile court?

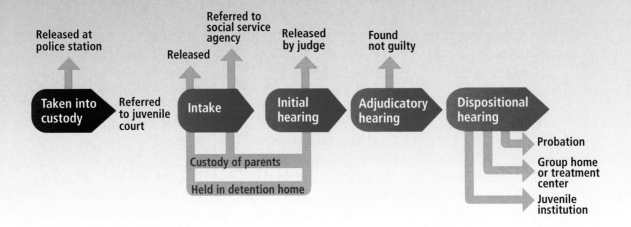

and there is no jury. The young person, however, may have an attorney.

Jenna has an attorney appointed by the court. The prosecutor presents the facts of the case. Jenna's attorney questions witnesses and asks Jenna to tell her side of the story. After the hearing, the judge makes a decision. In this case the judge finds Jenna to be a delinquent under the juvenile law of her state.

The Dispositional Hearing At the next step, the dispositional hearing, the judge decides on the sentence. The judge considers information about the youth's school situation, family, and past behavior.

The judge then decides on a sentence. Should the youth be sent to a state institution for juveniles, placed in a group home or community treatment program, or put on probation? **Probation** is a kind of sentence in which a person goes free but must be under the supervision of a court official called a probation officer.

Like many delinquents, Jenna is put on probation and given a probation officer to whom she must report regularly. She is also ordered to take part in individual and family counseling.

Aftercare The purpose of juvenile aftercare is to help young people after they have been released from an institution. Each youth is given a parole officer who can give advice and information about school, jobs, and other needed services.

Strengthening Juvenile Justice

Some people think that the juvenile justice system has been a big disappointment. They see overworked judges who make quick decisions without much knowledge of children or families. They see far too little money being spent on giving the help that troubled young people need to straighten out their lives.

Others say that the system is too easy on young criminals. They point to an increase in violent crimes committed by young people. In fact, about 17 percent of all people arrested for serious crimes are under eighteen. These critics want young offenders to be tried in regular criminal courts.

Other people have argued that juvenile courts should be done away with altogether. It is in the best interests of a young defendant, they say, to go to trial in a criminal court. There the defendant's rights to due process have much stronger protections.

Community-Based Programs Even though the juvenile justice system has in many ways failed to carry out its goals, there are many successful programs for juvenile offenders. One is the community residential treatment center. Youths live in small group homes instead of being locked up in a large state institution.

In a group home, counseling helps young people feel better about themselves and their future. Psychologists and social workers help them learn to get along better with other people in their lives.

Wilderness Programs Some delinquent youths take part in tough outdoor programs. The idea of these programs is that people's self-esteem grows as they find that they can do difficult tasks. In the wilderness, youths may discover that they have the power

within them to change the way they act and to affect the world around them in positive ways. Another purpose is to get them away from their neighborhoods and the influences that brought them trouble.

Keeping Kids from Becoming Criminals A large percentage of adults convicted of crimes were youths when they first got in trouble with the law. Therefore, the better our society is at preventing juvenile crime, the fewer adults the criminal justice system will have to deal with.

Section 3 Assessment

1. **Define** delinquent, status offender, probation
2. What was the purpose of the first juvenile court?
3. How does the adjudicatory hearing differ from an adult criminal trial? How is it similar?
4. How do wilderness programs help some juvenile delinquents?
5. **Evaluate** Do you think the juvenile justice system protects the rights of the accused as well as the criminal justice system? Explain.

Extending the Chapter

Historical Views

Many societies in the past—and some today—have given very harsh treatment to people accused of crimes. These people had little chance to challenge the charges or to gain help in defending themselves. Punishment was often painful and swift. For example, a person caught stealing might have a hand cut off. Only a few hundred years ago, European and American women who were thought to be witches were burned alive or drowned.

In the United States today, the accused have some of the most complete rights and safeguards in history. The rights of due process, as well as the many steps that police and courts must follow, help make sure that innocent people are not punished for crimes they did not commit. In addition, people who are convicted of crimes cannot be given cruel or unusual punishments, and they are generally given the chance to return to society as normal citizens.

How to ANALYZE AN AREA GRAPH

 Use the *Simulations and Data Graphing CD-ROM* to create and interpret graphs.

In this chapter, you read about crime in our society. The Federal Bureau of Investigation, or FBI, is one of several government agencies that keeps statistics on crime in the United States. These statistics help the government assess the effectiveness of crime-fighting efforts around the nation. The graph on this page is based on FBI crime statistics for 1997.

Explain the Skill

You have already studied line, circle, and bar graphs. Each provides a good way of displaying statistics visually. An area graph is another kind of graph. Area graphs are useful in showing smaller and smaller parts of the same original whole.

Suppose, for example, you wanted to create a graph showing how many people in your class will graduate from high school, and how many of those graduating from high school will graduate from college. This kind of information can be shown on an area graph. The largest circle in this area graph would represent your entire class. Inside this circle would be a smaller circle, representing all the students who will graduate from high school. The smallest circle would represent all the students who will graduate from college.

Analyze the Skill

Look at the area graph on this page, which deals with FBI crime statistics for 1997.

In that year, the FBI estimates that about 13 million serious crimes were committed. The graph's largest circle represents this total number.

Each of the smaller circles represents a percentage of the largest circle. The second-largest circle, for example, represents the percentage of serious crimes that were reported to the police.

Skill Assessment

1. Were a majority of the serious crimes committed in 1997 reported to the police? What percentage of the serious crimes were reported?
2. What percentage of serious crimes in 1997 resulted in the suspect being arrested?
3. Do all convictions for serious crimes lead to a prison sentence? Explain.

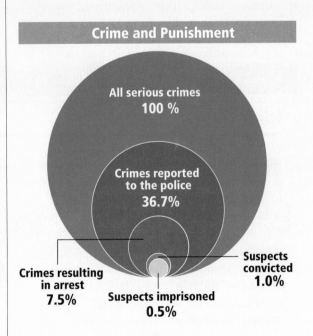

Crime and Punishment

All serious crimes
100 %

Crimes reported
to the police
36.7%

Crimes resulting
in arrest
7.5%

Suspects imprisoned
0.5%

Suspects
convicted
1.0%

Building Civics Vocabulary

The vocabulary terms in each pair listed below are related to each other. For each pair, explain what the terms have in common. Also explain how they are different.

1. *arraignment* and *indictment*
2. *probable cause* and *warrant*
3. *probation* and *parole*
4. *delinquent* and *status offender*

Reviewing Main Ideas and Skills

5. Why is robbery considered both a crime against a person and a crime against property?

6. Why do many people believe that some "victimless" crimes really do hurt innocent people?

7. What are the two responsibilities that the criminal justice system must balance?

8. What is the role of a grand jury?

9. What are some of the factors a judge considers when deciding the sentence of a lawbreaker?

10. **How to Analyze an Area Graph** Look back at the area graph on page 428. For every person imprisoned for a crime, how many serious crimes are committed?

Critical Thinking

11. **Making Decisions** Do you agree with the use of plea bargaining as a method of settling criminal cases quickly? Why or why not?

12. **Defending a Position** Do you think juveniles who commit serious crimes should be treated as adults? Explain.

Writing About Civics

13. **Writing an Editorial** As you read in this chapter, the death penalty is a controversial issue. Suppose you were an editor for your local newspaper. Write an editorial stating your opinion on the death penalty. Should it ever be used? If so, for what crimes? If not, why not? Include the editorial in your portfolio.

Citizenship Activities

14. **Working in Groups** In a small group, design your own treatment program for juvenile offenders. Your goal is to help youths in trouble with the law increase their self esteem and learn how to settle conflicts peacefully. Describe what you would have participants do, and how you would measure their success. Share your proposals with the class.

 Take It to the NET

Access the Civics: Participating in Government Internet site at **www.phschool.com** for the specific URLs to complete the activity.

Explore online information about crime rates, both in your area and across the nation. Prepare a chart showing the change in the overall national crime rate over the last few years. Write a paragraph explaining why you think these changes took place.

Civil Justice

Citizenship and You

First you hear it—the tinkling of bells. Soon a familiar scene is taking place. Children are forming a crooked line next to a brightly colored ice cream truck. The pictures of the frozen treats look mouthwatering, and excitement fills the air.

Whenever children gather near a busy street, though, accidents are likely to happen. A recent incident in Ohio illustrates this fact.

On a summer afternoon, five-year-old Tommy heard the sounds of an ice cream truck. Clutching a handful of change, Tommy dashed out of the house. Instead of using the crosswalk, he ran out into the street. Just then a car turned the corner and struck him.

Tommy was badly injured. The question of who should pay his medical bills became the subject of a serious dispute. Tommy's parents blamed the driver of the car, as well as the ice cream truck driver for parking in a dangerous location. Neither driver, however, would accept responsibility for the accident. Both of them said that Tommy should have used the crosswalk. How could this disagreement be settled? Tommy's parents realized that they might have to go to court.

Keep It Current

Items marked with this logo are periodically updated on the Internet. To keep up-to-date, go to **www.phschool.com**

What's Ahead in Chapter 20

In this chapter you will learn about the American civil justice system, which provides a way for people to settle conflicts in a fair, orderly manner. You will read about some types of cases that are decided in civil courts, how the civil justice system works, and what problems the system is facing.

Section 1   **The Role of Civil Law**

Section 2   **Civil Procedure**

Section 3   **Choices in Civil Justice**

Citizen's Journal

Suppose Tommy's case went to court and you were on the jury. Who do you think should pay Tommy's medical bills? Why? Write a paragraph explaining your decision to the other jurors.

The Role of Civil Law

Objectives

- Explain the main principles of civil law.
- Summarize several types of civil cases.
- Explore examples of how civil courts settle disputes.

Building Civics Vocabulary

- **Lawsuits** are cases in which a court is asked to settle a dispute.
- Under civil law, a person has a right to **compensation,** a payment that is meant to make up for the harm caused by another's acts.
- Money paid in an effort to compensate a loss is called **damages.**
- **Equity** is the use of general rules of fairness to settle conflicts.
- A court may issue an **injunction,** which is an order to do or not do a certain act.
- **Contracts** are legal agreements between buyers and sellers.

 Focus

Our civil justice system includes the judges, juries, and lawyers who help people settle conflicts according to the rules of civil law. In a typical year, Americans file more than a million lawsuits, or cases in which a court is asked to settle a dispute. Some people who file lawsuits believe that someone has injured them physically. Others believe that someone owes them money. Some think that their rights have been violated.

People who file lawsuits usually have two things in common. They believe that they have been harmed, and they want the courts to do something about it. Our civil justice system is based on the idea of re-sponsibility. Civil trials are one way to make people take responsibility for the harm they have caused others.

A civil case, like a criminal case, always has a plaintiff and a defendant. In a criminal case, the plaintiff is always the government. The defendant is the person or persons accused of a crime. In a civil case, however, the plaintiff is most often an individual. The defendant may be an individual, a group, a business, or even a government body. For instance, a person may sue the maker of a product that does not work. Someone may also sue the government to try to make it do or stop doing something.

Principles of Civil Law

As you already know, civil law has different purposes than criminal law. Criminal law protects society by punishing people who break the law. The main purpose of civil law, however, is not to punish wrongdoers but to settle disagreements fairly. Civil courts depend on two main principles for settling conflicts: the principle of compensation and the principle of equity.

Compensation Under civil law a person has a right to compensation, or being "made whole" for harm caused by another person's acts. Suppose someone breaks your bicycle, and you have to pay $45 to get it repaired. The person refuses to pay you back, so you decide to take him or her to court. The judge rules that the person must give you $45. This money is not a fine because it is not meant to be a punishment. Instead it is called damages, money that is paid in an effort to compensate, or make up for, a loss.

Sometimes the payment of damages completely makes up for a loss. For instance, if you get the $45 you paid to repair your bike, you are back in the same place you were before the bike was broken.

In many cases, though, the payment of damages cannot completely make up for the

Suppose a visitor is injured by slipping on skates that a child left in a dangerous spot. The next step could be a lawsuit against the parents.

harm done. An example would be money a court gives to a person left paralyzed by an auto accident. The money will not make the person able to walk again. Instead, it is an effort to soften the effects of the injury.

Equity Not every problem can be settled by the payment of money. Sometimes courts rely on equity, the use of general rules of fairness to settle conflicts. Suppose, for example, that bad-smelling fumes are coming from a nearby factory. Forcing the factory owners to pay money to everyone in town will not stop the smell. The dispute between the owners and the community has to be settled in a different way.

Under the rules of equity, a court may issue an injunction, an order to do or not do a certain act. For instance, a court could order the factory to keep the fumes from escaping. Unlike damages, which make up for past injuries, an injunction prevents future harm.

Some Types of Civil Cases

In almost every area of our lives, problems come up that can be settled in court through compensation or equity. Many civil cases, such as Tommy's, are personal injury cases. Personal injury cases can involve both physical and mental suffering. In some cases, such as those involving plane crashes, survivors may seek compensation for emotional stress. Also, relatives of a person killed in an accident may receive payments for mental suffering if the death was caused by someone else's carelessness.

In addition to personal injury cases, there are many other types of civil cases. Some kinds that you are most likely to hear about are property cases, consumer cases, housing cases, domestic relations cases, and probate cases.

Property Cases People often want payment for damage to their property. For instance, a car owner might sue a repair shop if the car comes back with a new dent. A homeowner might sue a neighbor whose tree fell over and damaged the homeowner's roof.

Before going to court, however, a person should carefully consider whether it is fair to blame someone else for the damage. If the case comes to trial, the plaintiff must prove that the defendant did the damage either on purpose or out of carelessness.

Another common type of property case involves charges of trespassing. In many trespassing cases, a plaintiff is trying to prove that the defendant knowingly and wrongfully crossed over his or her land. Property owners do have rights, of course, and signs saying "Private Property—Keep Out" are quite common. However, laws also protect people who have good reasons

In order to claim compensation for damage caused by a neighbor's fallen tree, the homeowner must prove that the tree's owner was guilty of negligence.

for crossing someone's property. For example, the person who reads your gas meter is not trespassing.

Property cases may be settled through compensation or through equity. Payment of money, for instance, may make up for damage to a person's roof. However, courts usually settle trespassing cases through equity. A court may issue an injunction ordering a defendant to stay off the plaintiff's land in the future.

Consumer Cases

"This computer you sold me broke down just one week after I took it home," declared Sharon. "I want my money back."

What happens if a product does not work as it was supposed to? What can consumers do if they are misled by an advertisement or by a salesperson? What guarantees must come with products you buy?

These questions and many others related to consumers' rights are covered in a collection of laws called the Uniform Commercial Code. Many of these laws set basic rules for contracts, legal agreements between buyers and sellers. The buyer promises to pay for a product or service, and the seller agrees that

it will meet certain standards. Conflicts arise when either a buyer or a seller says that the other has not lived up to the contract.

In Sharon's situation, for instance, if the computer store does not settle the problem, she may decide to sue the store. If the court finds that Sharon is not to blame, it may order the store to repair or replace the computer for free. In this way, Sharon's rights as a consumer are protected by law.

Housing Cases

Suppose that you live in an apartment building where the landlord refuses to repair some broken stairs. Do you have a legal right to do something about it?

Housing cases involve relationships between landlords and tenants. When you rent an apartment or a house, you usually sign a lease, an agreement stating the rights and responsibilities of the landlord and the tenant. The tenant agrees to pay rent every month, and the landlord agrees to keep the rental unit safe and in good repair.

Under civil law, a tenant and a landlord may take certain steps if either one believes that the other has not lived up to the lease. In some situations tenants can pay for needed repairs and take the cost out of the rent. If living conditions get too bad, tenants have the right to end their leases and move out without paying rent.

On the other hand, landlords who meet their responsibilities can force tenants to leave for not paying rent or violating other terms of the lease. In cases of housing law, the courts must consider the rights and responsibilities of both landlords and tenants.

Domestic Relations Cases Cases that concern family relationships are called domestic relations cases. Most domestic relations cases relate to divorce. The problems in divorce cases are often complicated and emotional. How will the couple divide up their property? Who will have custody of the children? Who will support them? In a divorce case, there are seldom easy answers.

Probate Cases Disagreements can also arise over how to divide up the property of a friend or relative who has died. Such cases are called probate cases.

Sometimes there is no will, a document that tells what is to be done with the dead person's money and other property. Usually, however, probate cases involve questions about whether the will can be trusted. Is the signature real? Was the person who made the will unfairly influenced or not thinking clearly? In probate cases, it may take years for the court to decide how to divide the property.

The Wide Range of Civil Cases

You have looked at just a few of the many types of civil cases. In fact, cases can arise over just about any area of people's lives—family relationships, school, jobs, recreation activities, and so on.

Civil courts can find ways to settle any type of disagreement. In some cases, such as property damage, the courts use compensation. Others, such as probate cases, are usually settled through equity. Sometimes courts

When buying a car, a customer signs a contract with the dealer. If either party breaks the terms of that contract, the other party may sue.

use a combination of compensation and equity. For instance, a person who dumps trash on your land may have to pay you back for the cost of removing it. In addition, the court may issue an injunction ordering the person never to dump trash there again.

Regardless of how civil cases are settled, they all have something in common. Their goal is to make a fair settlement and to place the responsibility where it belongs.

Section 1 Assessment

1. **Define** lawsuits, compensation, damages, equity, injunction, contracts
2. Compare the two main principles of civil law.
3. What are the main types of civil cases?
4. What is the goal of most civil case settlements?
5. **Analyze** How does our civil justice system help to make people responsible for their actions?

Civil Procedure

 Focus

Civil procedure is the process followed in taking a case through the civil justice system. The federal courts and many state courts have rules about how a disagreement must be brought to trial. The purpose of these rules is to settle disputes in a fair and orderly way.

Preparing for a Civil Trial

Think back to the accident described at the beginning of this chapter. Tommy's parents thought that one or both of the drivers were responsible. The parents hired a lawyer. The lawyer tried to get either of the two drivers to pay the medical bills. When that failed, she advised the parents to go to court.

Court Filings A civil lawsuit begins with a complaint, a legal document that charges someone with having caused harm. The complaint, which is filed with a court, describes the problem and suggests a possible solution—damages, equity, or both. By filing a complaint against each driver, Tommy and his parents became the plaintiffs in the case.

The defendant learns about the civil lawsuit when he or she receives a copy of the complaint and a summons, an order to appear in court. Next, the defendant is permitted to tell the court his or her side of the story.

The defendant's written response to a complaint is called an answer. In the answer

Facts & Quotes

Who's Responsible?

In September 1999, the Justice Department filed a massive civil lawsuit, accusing cigarette companies of misleading the public about the dangers of smoking. The lawsuit sought to recover billions of dollars that the government has spent providing health care to people with smoking-related illnesses. "The tobacco companies should answer to the taxpayers for their actions," said President Clinton when asked about the lawsuit.

Representatives of the tobacco industry, however, argue that people have long known about the health risks of smoking and should take responsibility for their choice to smoke. "We're right on the law," said a tobacco industry lawyer. "We're right on the facts. We will prevail in this lawsuit."

What do you think?

CIVIL CASES IN U.S. DISTRICT COURTS, 1988–2000

Year	Cases Begun	Non-jury Trials	Jury Trials
1988	239,000	5,422	4,329
1989	233,500	5,128	4,010
1990	217,900	4,772	3,829
1991	207,700	4,390	3,579
1992	226,900	4,378	3,410
1993	226,165	4,245	3,322
1994	236,391	4,380	2,987
1995	248,335	4,249	2,801
1996	269,132	4,401	2,646
1997	272,027	4,491	2,380
1998	256,787	4,125	2,148
1999	260,271	4,737	3,795
2000	259,517	4,529	3,404

Source: Judicial Business of the United States Courts

Only a small percentage of civil cases are heard by juries. **Government In what year shown on the chart were the fewest cases begun?**

1999 there were some 17,000 federal cases that were three or more years old. Delays in state courts are sometimes much longer.

One cause of delay is the time it takes to gather evidence, especially in complicated cases. Also, selecting a jury can take a long time because both sides have to approve the members. In addition, court rules make it possible for lawyers to delay trials in ways that will help their side.

High Costs Why are trials often expensive? For many civil trials people need the help of lawyers, who understand the law and know how to prepare the case. Lawyers' fees make up much of the cost of most civil cases.

In some cases, the lawyers are paid by the hour. When there is a great deal of evidence to gather and study, and many hours to spend in court, the fees can add up. In personal injury cases, like Tommy's, the lawyer's fee is often a large percentage of the money awarded by the judge or jury. Other costs include filing fees for court papers and payments for expert witnesses, such as doctors. Of course, there is also the cost in time and inconvenience to the parties themselves.

The Need for Alternatives

Many Americans know that trials are often long and costly. But did you know that most lawsuits never make it to trial? As the chart on this page shows, few cases actually get heard by a judge or jury. Plaintiffs often drop cases if they think they have little chance of winning. Sometimes what a trial will cost causes parties to settle out of court.

Also, the judge and lawyers involved in a case may strongly encourage the parties to find other ways of settling the conflict. In some states, courts will not even hear certain types of cases, such as those involving child custody, unless the parties have already tried to settle the conflict out of court.

In recent years, more and more people have been looking for ways of settling conflicts more quickly and cheaply. In the next section, you will explore some of the methods they have used.

Section 2 Assessment

1. **Define** complaint, answer, discovery, subpoena, deposition
2. How is evidence gathered for a trial?
3. How does the burden of proof in a civil trial differ from that in a criminal trial?
4. Why are civil trials often long and costly?
5. **Evaluate** What are the benefits and drawbacks of serving on a jury?
6. **Analyze** Why do you think that many states do not use juries in cases involving fairly small amounts of money?

Choices in Civil Justice

SECTION PREVIEW

Objectives

- Describe some alternatives to civil trials.
- Explore several ways to reduce the cost of civil trials.
- Summarize the arguments for and against large awards in civil cases.

Building Civics Vocabulary

- **Mediation** is a process by which people agree to use a third party to help them settle a conflict.
- **Arbitration** is the use of a third person to make a legal decision that is binding on all parties.
- **Small claims court** is a civil court that people may use to settle disputes involving small amounts of money.

 **Focus**

Many people go to court without being aware of the time and cost involved in a civil trial. Often they do not know about other ways to settle conflicts peacefully. In this section, you will look at some methods of settling disagreements without a civil trial. You will also see that even when people do have to go to court they can find ways to save time and money.

Avoiding Civil Trials

There are a number of ways to keep from going to trial. One possibility, of course, is for the people to discuss the problem themselves and come to an agreement. However, what happens if people cannot reach an agreement but still want to avoid a regular trial? Often they can bring in a third per-

son to help them settle the conflict. There are three main methods for doing this: mediation, arbitration, and "rent-a-judge" programs.

Mediation In 1994, major league baseball players went on strike, causing the cancellation of that year's World Series. After months of negotiations, players and team owners finally came to an agreement with the help of mediation.

Mediation is a process by which people agree to use a third party to help them settle a conflict. The third party, called a mediator, does not make a decision. Instead, mediation is a way to bring people together so that they can settle their own disagreement. When people ask for mediation, they are saying to the mediator, in effect, "Listen to each of us and help us reach a compromise."

In many states there are programs that train people to be mediators. Many mediation programs are sponsored by city or county courts, while others are run as private businesses. Mediation programs handle a variety of problems, including child custody, housing, and consumer problems. Mediation helps people solve their problems in an inexpensive and convenient way.

Mediation can also be used to settle conflicts between students. Schools in many states have successful mediation programs. Students in elementary schools as well as in junior and senior high schools act as official "conflict managers," helping their fellow students end disputes.

Arbitration For mediation to work, both sides must be willing to compromise. No one is legally required to obey an agreement reached by mediation. Therefore, people who want a conflict settled "once and for all" often turn to arbitration, the use of a third person to make a legal decision that is binding on all parties. In effect both sides are saying to the third person, or arbitrator,

"Listen to each of us. Then we will obey whatever decision you make."

Arbitration almost always costs less than a civil trial and is considerably faster. One reason is that the arbitrator is usually an expert on the subject in dispute. Therefore, it takes less time to hear a case and come to a decision. Another reason is that the parties save the expense of filing court papers. Also, people who choose arbitration are less likely to have cases that need lawyers.

Arbitration has become so successful that today the federal government and more than forty states have laws requiring that arbitrators' decisions be obeyed. Many courts will make arrangements for people to use arbitration. In certain conflicts involving public employees, such as firefighters or police officers, federal and state laws actually require arbitration.

Private Judges People can settle conflicts through private judges. Using this method, the two sides hire a person to hear and decide their case. This process is sometimes called "rent-a-judge."

Referees Another alternative is using a referee. A judge can appoint a referee who listens to both sides of a case and makes recommendations to the judge. A referee is usually a lawyer. In some places, when two sides agree to the use of a referee, they give up their right to a jury trial. In the end, though, a judge makes the final decision in the case.

Mock Trials Even after both sides in a conflict have filed court papers, they may change their minds and decide not to go to trial. In some cases this change of mind comes as a result of a "mock trial," a pre-

Mediation, which helps people avoid going to court, also provides students with a way to settle conflicts peacefully at school.

Judith Kaye

"I like to accomplish something every day," says Judith Kaye, Chief Judge of New York State's Court of Appeals. "It's important to me, at the end of the day, to say I've done something."

New York courts, like those in most states, face a growing number of cases—over 3.5 million new filings in 2000. As Judge Kaye explains, one of the biggest problems facing the state's legal system is the "sheer volume" of cases. "We must use every tool available to keep up with these enormous demands," she says.

Since being appointed Chief Judge in 1993, Kaye has led a successful drive to make the New York state court system more efficient. In the future, she hopes to see courtrooms using interactive computers and video conferencing to speed up the process of moving cases through the courts.

Additional reforms under Judge Kaye have helped make courthouses more "user friendly." For example, many New York

courthouses now have computerized booths that provide information about the courts in both English and Spanish.

While Judge Kaye is committed to improving the efficiency with which state courts serve the public, she is equally dedicated to raising the quality of those services. "We want to process cases faster, but we also want to process them better," explains Kaye. "A well-run court system does not just count its cases. It makes sure every case counts."

Recognizing Viewpoints

According to Judge Kaye, why is it important for New York's courts to become more efficient?

---

view of how the case would probably be settled if a civil trial were held.

A mock trial has been described as a "trial on fast-forward" because there are no witnesses, and no evidence is presented. Instead, the lawyers for each side summarize their case before a jury, which then gives an unofficial verdict. The two sides do not have to follow the jury's verdict. However, they get a very good idea of what the result would be if a real trial were held. With this in mind, the parties are often able to reach a compromise without having to spend months in court.

Cutting the Cost of Civil Trials

Although conflicts can often be settled out of court, there are still good reasons for having civil trials. Sometimes one or both sides are unwilling to compromise or to accept an arbitrator or referee. Perhaps they want to make sure that the verdict or settlement can be legally enforced in any state. Often a plaintiff thinks that he or she can get a better settlement by going to trial. In such situations, a civil trial may be the only solution. A trial, however, does not always have to involve a lot of time and money.

Small Claims Court When people have a conflict over a fairly small amount of money, they have a good chance of getting a quick, inexpensive trial if they use a special kind of court. Small claims court is a civil court that people may use when the amount of money they want to recover is small, usually not more than $3,000.

Most small claims courts are part of larger city or county courts. They are one answer to the question of how to cut the high costs of taking a case to court.

In small claims court, the whole trial may take less than an hour, and the costs are not much more than the filing fee—which is usually less than $100 in most states. Usually there are no lawyers or juries. Instead, both parties tell their stories directly to the judge. Either side can bring witnesses, but there are no formal rules for questioning them. The judge either decides the case on the spot or mails the decision to the parties in a day or two.

Prepaid Legal Plans Even when a dispute involves too much money to qualify for small claims court, the costs of going to trial can still be reduced. One method is prepaid legal plans, which are like insurance policies. For a fixed fee, these plans cover almost all of the costs of going to court, no matter how high.

Low-cost legal services help people who otherwise could not afford lawyers' fees and the other costs of going to court.

Storefront Law Offices Another trend in low-cost legal services is the "storefront law office." Storefront law offices provide legal services for low prices. These offices are often located in convenient places such as shopping malls. They often advertise on television.

Traditional lawyers generally charge their clients by the hour at rates that can range from $100 to $400 per hour or more. Storefront offices, however, usually have a printed "menu" of set prices for specific services, such as preparing legal papers. For example, the cost to prepare a simple will might be $150. Because customers are told the total fee for services ahead of time, they

In this cartoon the artist is making fun of the idea that every kind of dispute can be settled by bringing a lawsuit.

"If I make you drink your milk you'll sue me?"

are able to shop around and compare prices before selecting a lawyer.

Of course, when choosing a lawyer a person should not simply look for the least expensive one. A better guide is the advice of trusted friends who have had experience with various lawyers. A person should also look for a lawyer who is an expert in the kind of problem he or she has.

The Debate over Large Awards

Several years ago, a California family was seriously injured in a car accident when the gas tank of their car exploded after a collision. The family sued the manufacturer of their car, claiming the explosion could have been prevented if the car's design had included certain safety features. In 1999, a jury in Los Angeles agreed, ordering General Motors to pay damages of $4.9 billion—the largest verdict ever in a personal injury case.

Large awards in civil law suits are the subject of major public debate. Some people argue that such awards are needed to make up for serious losses. They also argue that

the largest awards are usually paid by those who can afford to pay them—insurance companies and large businesses.

Other people argue, however, that in the long run the average American consumer bears the burden of large awards. To cover their costs, businesses raise prices and insurance companies raise the rates that everyone who owns insurance must pay.

Also, some services are no longer provided because the cost of insurance is too high. For instance, many public swimming pools no longer have diving boards. Some schools do not allow certain "high-risk" sports, such as pole vaulting. Others no longer take students on field trips.

Both sides in the debate think that awards should be fair and reasonable. However, the question of what is fair and reasonable is often hard to answer. As the debate continues, a number of efforts have been made to limit the size of awards.

First of all, judges usually have the power to reduce the amount of an award made by a jury. In addition, laws have been passed that limit awards in certain types of cases. Under federal law, for example, airlines do not have to pay more than $1,250 per person for lost baggage, no matter how much it was worth. Another federal law limits the amount of damages a person may collect when injured by an accident at a nuclear power plant.

"No-fault" auto insurance plans are another way to avoid large awards. Under these plans, people hurt in auto accidents do not sue the person responsible for their injuries. Instead, their medical bills are paid directly by their own insurance companies. In many cases, this means that the parties do not have to go to court.

To Sue or Not to Sue?

As you have seen, the civil justice system is burdened with many cases. Civil trials are often long and costly. People may have to wait months before their trial can start. Once the trial has begun, months or even years may pass before the case is finally settled.

In short, people involved in a conflict should think carefully about what is the best way to settle it. Going to court may be the best solution in some cases. However, many judges and lawyers agree that people should first explore whether other methods might work, such as mediation, arbitration, or other alternatives. In many cases, going to court may be the last, not the first, resort.

Section 3 Assessment

1. **Define** mediation, arbitration, small claims court
2. Describe two of the ways in which people can settle conflicts without going to trial.
3. When people have to go to court, how might they reduce the cost?
4. Why do some people criticize large awards in civil cases?
5. **Evaluate** Give an example of a conflict that you think would be best settled in court. Give an example of one that you think would be best settled out of court. Give reasons to support your opinion.

Extending the Chapter

Historical Views

Americans often turn to the courts to make people take responsibility for the harm they have caused. This is nothing new.

In ancient Rome, for example, a larceny, or theft, victim could take the suspected thief to court. If found guilty, the thief was forced to pay a penalty of double the value of whatever he or she stole. Romans could also sue fellow citizens for insulting them or damaging their reputation.

In traditional Japanese society, by contrast, courts played a much less active role in resolving conflicts. Rather than relying on legal arguments and written law, Japanese people often turned to respected community members to help them find a peaceful solution to their disputes.

Some traditional methods of conflict resolution are still used in Japan today. Many local police stations, for example, provide "conciliation rooms" where parties are encouraged to resolve their disputes, often with the help of a mediator.

The influence of this traditional approach to conflict resolution can be seen in our society today. As you read in this chapter, overcrowded courts and increasing legal costs have encouraged many people to try mediation, arbitration, and other alternatives before taking their cases to court.

Personal Injury Suits

The batter swung, getting a piece of the fastball. The ball, however, flew back into the stands, hitting Mrs. Uzdavines on the side of the face.

Later, Mrs. Uzdavines explained that she had just at that instant turned to say something to her husband, who was sitting beside her. "It happened so fast," she said.

> ## *Mr. Uzdavines recalled counting at least six holes in the screen.*

Getting hit by a foul ball was the last thing Mrs. Uzdavines had expected that evening. She and her family had looked forward to an exciting baseball game at Shea Stadium in New York between the New York Mets and the Philadelphia Phillies.

They had really good seats, too—right behind home plate. They were less than forty feet from the batter. Fans in this area of the ballpark were supposed to be protected from any foul tips by a huge protective screen.

As it turned out, however, the screen had holes in it. Mr. Uzdavines recalled counting at least six holes in the screen when he returned to his seat after taking his wife to the first aid station. Aware of the holes, the entire family moved to safer seats for the rest of the game.

Mrs. Uzdavines's injury was emotionally as well as physically painful. She believed that the accident would not have occurred if the protective screen had been kept in good repair. She claimed it was the responsibility of the New York Mets management to see to it that the facilities at Shea Stadium were safe and in good condition for the baseball season. Therefore, Mrs. Uzdavines decided to file a civil lawsuit against the Mets for being careless in carrying out their responsibility.

The Mets, however, did not believe that their carelessness had caused the accident. In court, they argued that when people attend a

sporting event, they "assume the risk" that an object such as a baseball could fly into the crowd. It would be impossible, they said, for the operators of a baseball park to construct safety screens which could protect every person in every seat from such harm. Moreover, said the Mets, the fans are aware of this fact when they attend a game.

The court, however, ruled in favor of Mrs. Uzdavines. It said the Mets would have to pay her damages. The size of this sum of money would be determined later.

Explaining its decision, the court said that the Mets did have the responsibility to keep the safety net in good repair. The fans who were watching the game from behind home plate, it said, normally would have thought that they were seated in a safe place.

To reach this conclusion, the court looked to see how other courts in New York had decided this same kind of question. The court paid particular attention to a similar case, *Akins* v. *Glens Falls School District,* that had been decided just the year before.

In that case, Robin Akins had gone to watch a baseball game at her high school. The field was equipped with a backstop 24 feet high and 50 feet wide. Behind the backstop were bleachers which could seat about 120 people. In addition, two three-foot-high chain link fences ran from each end of the backstop along the base lines of the field.

Robin chose to watch the game from behind the chain link fence near third base. During the game, a foul ball struck Robin in the eye. She filed a civil suit against the school for failing to provide safe and proper screening along the base lines to protect spectators.

> **The Mets argued that when people attend a sporting event, they "assume the risk."**

The court deciding the *Akins* case said that the owner of a baseball field must provide a safety screen only in the most dangerous place—the area behind home plate. Because Robin chose not to sit behind the backstop, she had "assumed the risk" that she could be hit by a stray ball. Therefore, she could not hold the school responsible for her injury.

However, the court also said that any safety screen must be in good repair so that people sitting behind it are protected. The court deciding Mrs. Uzdavines's case took careful note of this part of the earlier decision. The New York Mets had not kept their safety screen in good repair. The court reasoned that while some fans want to watch a baseball game without a screen or net in front of them, those who choose to sit behind a screen have the right to expect that their seats are in a completely safe location.

Analyzing the Case

1. Why did the Mets believe that they were not responsible for Mrs. Uzdavines's injury?

2. What was the ruling in the Akins case that the court followed as precedent?

3. Do you think that the court made the correct decision in this case? Why or why not?

4. Do you think that the court would have decided the case differently if the net had been in good repair but the foul ball had torn a hole in the net before it hit Mrs. Uzdavines? Explain your answer.

How to **INTERPRET COMIC STRIPS**

As you read in this chapter, our courts are overcrowded with lawsuits. Some people feel that one reason for this is that many people file frivolous, or unnecessary, lawsuits in the hope of financial gain.

In one recent case, a woman went into a department store to buy a blender. She walked to the stack of blenders on display and decided to take a box from the bottom of the stack. The other blenders fell on her, and she sued the store, claiming it was responsible for the accident. It was three years before the case was resolved—the jury ruled in favor of the store.

Explain the Skill

The cartoon on page 444 makes fun of frivolous lawsuits. Many cartoonists use humor to make these types of observations or comments about life and politics in the United States and other nations. In the comic strip on this page, cartoonist Jim Unger pokes fun at how some Americans use the civil justice system.

Analyze the Skill

Comic strips often create a situation or tell a story with just a few words and pictures. Read the comic strip on this page and follow the story it tells.

From the pictures, we see that this husband and wife have just received a letter. From the dialogue, we learn that the letter is from a mailman who recently tripped on the couple's front step. In his last line, the husband reveals the contents of the letter. This last line, or "punch line," is funny, but it also sums up the serious message behind the cartoon.

Skill Assessment

1. Cartoonists often make a situation funny by taking it to extremes. What is extreme about this situation?
2. In the cartoonist's view, who is the innocent victim in this situation? How does the cartoonist show this?
3. What do you think is the main message the cartoonist is trying to get across?
4. Is the message of this comic strip similar to the message of the cartoon on 444? Explain.

CHAPTER 20 ASSESSMENT

Building Civics Vocabulary

The vocabulary terms in each pair listed below are related to each other. For each pair, explain what the two terms have in common. Also explain how they are different.

1. *damages* and *injunction*
2. *complaint* and *answer*
3. *arbitration* and *mediation*

Reviewing Main Ideas and Skills

4. Explain how both equity and compensation are ways of making people take responsibility for their actions.

5. Explain what discovery is in a civil procedure and why it is important.

6. How is a civil trial similar to and different from a criminal trial?

7. Pick two alternatives to regular civil trials and explain how they can be used to settle conflicts in a quicker, less costly way.

8. **How to Interpret Comic Strips** Look through this book and find a comic strip or cartoon that has a political message. Describe the cartoonist's message and explain how he or she gets this message across.

Critical Thinking

9. **Defending a Position** Do you think that large awards in civil cases are fair? Support your opinion with reasons.

10. **Understanding Causes and Effects** Your text states that civil lawsuits are often "long and costly." Why do lawsuits usually take a long time to settle? What causes them to be costly? Describe one effect that lengthy and costly trials have on the civil justice system.

Writing About Civics

11. **Writing a Complaint** Look back at the story about Tommy being hit by a car on page 431. Suppose you are the lawyer representing Tommy. Write a complaint to be filed with the civil court in your community. Describe the accident, who you think is responsible and why, and what settlement you are seeking.

Citizenship Activities

12. **Working in Groups** In groups of three or four, plan a mediation program that could be used to resolve conflicts between students in your school. Describe how the program would work. Decide what would have been done if a student refused to cooperate with a mediator. Then compare your plan with those of other groups.

Take It to the NET

Access the **Civics: Participating in Government** Internet site at **www.phschool.com** for the specific URLs to complete the activity.

Explore online information about recent important civil law cases. Write a report about three of these cases. For each case, examine both sides of the issue and, where applicable, explain what ruling has been made. Also explain how you think the outcomes of these cases could affect our everyday lives.

Don't Go the Way I Went!

At age thirteen, Katherine Olson began selling drugs and ran away from home. At first she liked the excitement of being a "gangster," but after witnessing a murder she became a police informant to protect her own life. Two narcotics officers helped bring her off the street and into the Fellowship of Lights, a shelter for runaway and homeless teens. Now Katherine wants to be a narcotics officer herself.

Before you read the selection, find the meanings of these words in a dictionary: homicide, narcotics.

I ended up joining the Fellowship of Lights because I had gotten really bad into dealing drugs. I was working out of this house where four [dealers] were dealing out of. One night, me and my best friend John and this other guy were talking to friends through a bedroom window when this guy named Marky called John over. Then I saw Marky shoot John. He knew I saw it. Somehow the police also found out that I saw it, and they were tracking me down. When they came to my house two days later looking for me, the people in the house thought I told the police.

When I went back, the [dealers] beat me up....I don't know why they didn't kill me....I called homicide the next day and decided to tell them everything that happened.

The next thing you know, I was helping the narcotics police....

I kept on helping these narcotics officers bust people by tipping them off with information. But then one of the guys that had gotten locked up got out of jail and came to my apartment. He held a gun to my head and was saying, "You're a snitch, you're Five-O, you called the cops, you got me busted!" So I ran and called the narcotics officers and asked them to come pick me up....

He told a lot of people that I was a snitch, though, and they believed it. It wasn't safe for me to go back there anymore, so they put me in the Fellowship of Lights....

Don't go the way I went! It may be fun, exciting, dangerous, and all that, but a lot of my friends didn't make it. Me and my best friend are the only—I guess you could say survivors. Everybody else is dead. I would tell [teens] to stay in high school, get an education, get a legal job.

Source: Marcia A. Thompson, ed., Who Cares What I Think? American Teens Talk About Their Lives and Their Country *(Alexandria, Va.: Close Up Foundation, 1994), pages 27–40.*

Analyzing Primary Sources

1. Why do you think Olson decided to join sides with the police?
2. What kinds of things does Olson urge young people to do and not do?

UNIT 6 ASSESSMENT

Reviewing Main Ideas

1. Name two purposes of laws and explain how those purposes relate to both criminal law and civil law.
2. How do the purposes of criminal and civil law differ?
3. Describe some problems facing the criminal and juvenile justice systems.
4. Describe some problems facing the civil justice system.

Summarizing the Unit

The tree map below will help you organize the main ideas of Unit 6. Copy it onto a separate sheet of paper. Review the unit and complete the graphic organizer by filling in the purpose of each justice system and giving examples of the challenges facing each system. Then pick three of these challenges and write a short essay describing potential solutions to each of the problems.

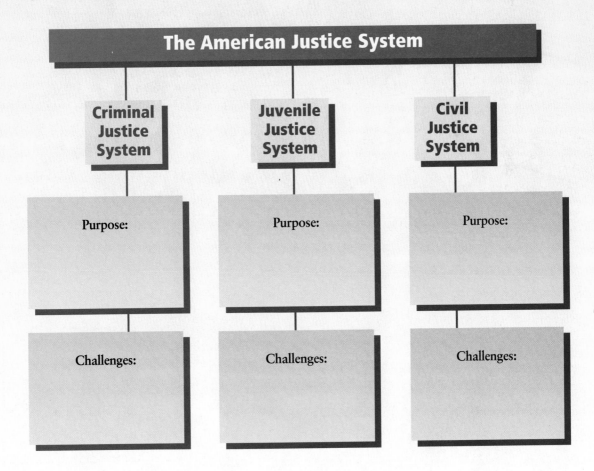

The American Justice System

Criminal Justice System — Purpose: — Challenges:

Juvenile Justice System — Purpose: — Challenges:

Civil Justice System — Purpose: — Challenges:

People Make a Difference

Why Study Civics?

Everyone who receives the protection of society owes a return for the benefit.

—**John Stuart Mill**

And so, my fellow Americans, ask not what your country can do for you; ask what you can do for your country.

—**President John F. Kennedy**

As you read these words, can you think of ways to participate in our democracy? You have seen that our government is built on the belief that people should govern themselves. As English philosopher Mill said, "we are indebted to our society for the protection it provides to us." What did he mean? How would you respond to President Kennedy's statement?

What's Ahead in Unit 7

In Unit 7 you will take a look at ways in which Americans, as a group and as individuals, make a difference in government. You will see how people can play their citizen roles through political parties, through voting and running for public office, and through helping solve the problems that face our society.

Chapter 21 Political Parties in Our Democracy

Chapter 22 Voting and Elections

Chapter 23 Confronting Society's Problems

Political Parties in Our Democracy

Citizenship and You

"Hey, isn't your eighteenth birthday next week?" Marta asked Tony.

"That's right," Tony replied.

"Great. That means you can vote in the next election if you register soon enough."

"I hadn't thought of that. I don't even know how to register. And how am I supposed to know who to vote for?"

"I don't know exactly how you register either," said Marta, "but I know you can register as a member of a political party if you want to. I think I'll probably register as a Republican."

"How come?"

"Well, my parents are Republicans and I liked the Republicans who ran in the last election. My dad even helped out with one candidate's campaign for representative."

"My mom's a Democrat, but she voted for several Republicans in the last election," Tony said. "I guess I need to find out more about what the parties stand for and what they do."

"It's up to you," replied Marta. "Let me know what you decide."

Keep It Current

Items marked with this logo are periodically updated on the Internet. To keep up-to-date, go to www.phschool.com

What's Ahead in Chapter 21

In this chapter, you will learn what a political party is and how parties help government and citizens. You will read about the two-party system in the United States and the similarities and differences between the two parties. Finally, you will study how we nominate candidates for public office.

Section 1   **The Role of Political Parties**

Section 2   **Our Two-Party System**

Section 3   **Choosing Candidates**

Citizen's Journal

Suppose you have just turned eighteen and you are going to register to vote. How would you decide with which party, if any, to register? To whom would you talk about your decision?

The Role of Political Parties

SECTION PREVIEW

Objectives

- Explain how political parties help government function.
- Describe ways that political parties link citizens to their government.

Building Civics Vocabulary

- A **political party** is an organization of citizens who wish to influence government by getting their members elected to office.
- Political parties **nominate** candidates, or name them to run for public office.
- A party's **platform** is a statement of its official stand on major public issues.
- A platform is made up of **planks,** or position statements on each specific issue in a party's platform.
- Party members often **canvass,** or go door-to-door seeking support for their candidates.

Focus

People want many things from government. They want their rights protected. They want to feel secure against poverty and unemployment. They want to be treated fairly in business, at work, and in the courts. They want a clean environment. Many want government to pass laws or to pay for specific programs that they believe are important, such as education for the handicapped, product safety, gun control, or finding a cure for cancer.

Alone, an individual may feel powerless to make his or her wants, needs, and ideas known. Acting together, however, groups of people can often have a greater effect than individuals acting alone. On page 81, you read about activists who formed a group to seek support for a monument honoring African American veterans of the Revolutionary War.

On a larger scale, people form groups called political parties in order to influence government. A political party is an organization of citizens who wish to influence and control government by getting their members elected to office. Party members share similar ideas about what they want government to do. If a party can put enough of its members into office, that party can have a major effect on the policies and programs of the government.

It has been said that parties are the oil that makes the machinery of American democracy work. Indeed, parties play a key role in government and provide opportunities for citizens to take part in the political process.

How Parties Help Government

You are probably aware of the active competition between the two main political parties in the United States, the Republican party and the Democratic party. You may even have heard Republicans criticizing Democrats or Democrats complaining about Republicans. Thomas Jefferson, who helped start the Democratic party, said, "If I could not get to heaven but with a party, I would not go there at all." Despite this criticism, are parties really useful? The answer is yes.

Parties help government at the local, state, and national levels in a number of ways. As you will see, they select candidates for many public offices. They set goals for the government and provide leadership to reach those goals. Political parties also keep an eye on each other, a function much like the checks and balances you learned about earlier.

At the 1996 Democratic National Convention in Chicago, party members nominated Bill Clinton to run for a second term as President.

Selecting Candidates A major way in which political parties help govern is to nominate, or name candidates to run for public office. Parties take the responsibility for finding and nominating qualified candidates.

There are about a half million elected positions in the local, state, and national governments of the United States. Some public offices, especially in local government, are nonpartisan, which means that the candidates do not declare themselves to be members of a political party when running for office. For example, judgeships and seats on school boards and city councils are often nonpartisan offices. However, most offices are partisan. The candidates for these offices run as members of political parties. If elected, they try to carry out the party's programs.

Setting Goals A political party establishes positions on issues and sets goals for government. Each party has a platform, a statement of a party's official stand on major public issues. The platform is made up of planks, position statements on each specific issue in a party's platform. These planks are often turned into government programs by party members who are elected to office.

Providing Leadership Parties help provide day-to-day leadership in government. Leadership is necessary to make the laws and carry out the programs that citizens want. You saw in Chapter 8 that party members in Congress select majority and minority floor leaders and whips to provide leadership in making laws. Parties work in much the same way in state legislatures, too.

Political parties also provide leadership in the executive branch of government. The political party of the executive—the President or governor—is referred to as the party "in office." The executive often appoints loyal members of the party in office to high government posts. They are then in a position to help shape government programs and policies.

Parties as "Watchdogs" Political parties also play an important "watchdog" role in government. After an election, the party not in power (the party "out of office" or the minority party in a legislature) makes sure that the public knows when the party in power is not living up to its promises.

Parties keep tabs on the behavior of members of the other party and are eager to report any wrongdoing. The watchdog function of parties helps government by making sure that members of the party in power are honest and hard-working.

How Parties Help Citizens

You have seen the ways in which political parties help make our government work. Parties also help citizens fulfill their responsibilities in our democracy. Parties link citizens to their government by making their voices heard and providing ways for them to participate. Parties also inform citizens and can help make political decision making easier.

Many volunteers are needed to run a campaign. These workers are making phone calls to ask voters to support their candidate.

Citizens' Voice in Government One reason why people form political parties is that parties provide a way for citizens to be heard. Edie Stevenson, the county chairperson of her political party, describes her experience:

❝ *When I accepted the job as county chair, few people in our county were aware of what the party stood for. So we wrote short statements of our policies on such topics as education and the environment. Then we held a series of community meetings. The people who came really spoke up about what was most important to them. We rewrote some of our statements based on what we learned about people's concerns. Our candidates discovered that the meetings were a good way to keep up on what people around here want from government.* ❞

Do political parties really reflect what citizens want? Edie's experience shows that at the local level parties can help give citizens a voice in government. At the state and national levels, party members help hammer out the party platform, debating and deciding on the issues.

Informing Citizens By writing policy statements, Edie's party was helping to provide citizens in her county with information—facts, figures, and party stands on various important issues. Some other ways parties inform citizens are by sending out mailings and giving information to newspapers, radio, and television.

A more personal way in which parties inform citizens is by arranging meetings with candidates. Party members and volunteers also canvass, or go door-to-door handing out information and asking people which candidates they support.

Parties canvass and provide information in order to encourage people to vote for their candidates. However, by making information available to voters, parties can also help simplify political decision making. If a voter agrees with a party's point of view or its stand on a particular issue, he or she can vote on the basis of the party. At election time Edie's party published "Voters' Tip Sheets"—the collection of statements they had prepared. They found that people who agreed with what the party stood for felt comfortable supporting most of the party's candidates.

Involving Citizens Political parties provide citizens with a variety of ways to get involved in the political process. To be successful, a party needs the help of many people, especially at election time. Campaign volunteers write letters and pamphlets and send them to voters. They raise money and hold picnics and other events at which candidates can meet voters. They make phone calls and canvass neighborhoods. On election day, volunteers remind people to vote and may even drive them to the polls.

As a citizen, it is both your right and responsibility to participate in government. Working through a party is one way to play your citizen role.

Section 1 Assessment

1. **Define** political party, nominate, platform, planks, canvass
2. List four ways in which political parties help government.
3. What are some ways in which political parties help citizens get involved in government?
4. **Analyze** How can political parties be seen as the oil that makes the machinery of American democracy work?

Our Two-Party System

SECTION PREVIEW

Objectives
- Summarize the history of political parties in the United States.
- Describe the role of third parties in our democracy.
- Compare the organization and basic beliefs of the two major parties.
- Explore how people choose which political party to support.
- Explain how party strength has changed.

Building Civics Vocabulary
- Communities are divided into **precincts,** or voting districts.
- The system in which party leaders do favors for local party supporters is called **patronage.**
- Voting a **straight ticket** means voting for the candidates of only one party.
- Voting a **split ticket** means voting for candidates of more than one party on the same ballot.
- **Independent voters** are people who do not support a particular political party.

Focus

Even though political parties are an important part of American government, they are not mentioned in the United States Constitution. In fact, George Washington feared that conflict between political parties might destroy the new democracy. He warned against "the baneful [harmful] effects of the Spirit of Party" in his farewell address in 1796.

However, even at the birth of our nation, Americans were banding together in groups, each with different ideas about the role of government. There were those who sup-

Party Symbols

You might recognize the donkey and the elephant as the symbols of the Democratic and Republican parties. Where do these symbols come from? They were first used by cartoonist Thomas Nast in 1874.

Nast got the idea for the donkey from Populist Ignatius Donnelly's comment, "The Democratic party is like a mule—without pride of ancestry nor hope of posterity [future generations]."

Nast first used the elephant to represent the Republican vote. Later it came to stand for the party itself. Why the elephant? Democrat Adlai Stevenson's opinion was that "the elephant has a thick skin, a head full of ivory, and . . . [it] proceeds best by grasping the tail of its predecessor."

ported a strong central government (Federalists) and those who feared it (Anti-Federalists). The first political parties arose out of these different views of the role of government.

A Brief History

Alexander Hamilton, President Washington's Secretary of the Treasury, led the first political party, the Federalist party. The Federalists, who wanted a strong national government, had the support of merchants and bankers. The party's power declined in the early 1800s.

The rival of the Federalists was the Democratic-Republican party, led by Thomas Jefferson. This party opposed a strong national government and supported the power of the individual states. The Democratic-Republican party had the support of farmers and frontier settlers. In 1828, under the leadership of Andrew Jackson, the party took the name the Democratic party. The Democrats gained support from immigrant workers as well as farmers.

The Whig party, organized in 1834, opposed the Democrats. The Whigs opposed a strong executive branch of government. The Whigs and the Democrats remained rivals until the early 1850s.

Democrats and Republicans Our current two-party system emerged in 1854. In that year the Republican party was born, replacing the Whigs as a major party. It was formed by groups opposed to slavery. It supported business interests and at first was purely a party of the North.

THE PRESIDENT'S POLITICAL PARTY For nearly 150 years, all our Presidents have been either Democrats or Republicans. **Government Which party controlled the presidency during the early 1800s?**

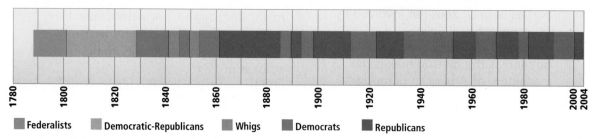

■ Federalists ■ Democratic-Republicans ■ Whigs ■ Democrats ■ Republicans

Source: 2001 World Almanac

In 1860, Abraham Lincoln became the first Republican President. The Republican party remained the majority party from the Civil War until the Great Depression of the 1930s. It dominated both the presidency and the Congress during those years.

A major shift in party power began in 1932 when Franklin D. Roosevelt, a Democrat, was elected President. Roosevelt's New Deal programs were designed to bring the country out of the depression. As the time line on the previous page shows, power shifted back and forth between Democrats and Republicans during the second half of the twentieth century.

The Role of Third Parties

Even though ours is a two-party system, third parties do arise, especially during presidential election years. Sometimes a third party forms to support a cause or idea. When the Republican party formed in opposition to slavery, it was actually a third party to the Democrats and the Whigs.

A second reason why a third party forms is to back a candidate, often one who splits from a main party. In 1912, former President Theodore Roosevelt failed to win the Republican nomination for President. With a strong following, Roosevelt formed the Progressive, or "Bull Moose," party. The Bull Moose party disappeared after Roosevelt lost the election.

Third party candidates face many problems. It may be difficult to get on the ballot because election laws in many states favor the two major parties. People often hold back from giving money because they doubt that a third party candidate can win. Also, even people who agree with the third party's ideas often decide that voting for its candidate would be wasting their vote.

The Importance of Third Parties
Even though third parties rarely win major elections, they still play an important role in

Senator Robert La Follette, the Progressive party's candidate for President in 1924, addresses women voters from the steps of his home.

American politics. A third party candidate can change the outcome of an election by drawing votes away from one of the main parties. In 2000, Green Party candidate Ralph Nader won many votes that probably would have gone to the Democratic candidate, Al Gore. As a result, Republican George W. Bush won the very close election.

Third parties can also play a key role by bringing up new ideas or pressing for action on certain issues. In the 1992 election, independent candidate Ross Perot made the national debt a major issue, forcing the Republican and Democratic candidates to talk about the problem more directly. Perot got 19 percent of the popular vote, the strongest showing for a third party presidential candidate in 80 years. Hoping to transform this support into a permanent political party, Perot formed the Reform Party in

SELECTED PARTY PLATFORM STATEMENTS The Democratic and Republican parties prepared these platforms for the 2000 elections. **Government How do the two parties differ on education?**

Democratic Party	Republican Party
$ The Economy	
"Democrats believe that in building upon…record-breaking prosperity and growth…we must not leave any community behind…. [We] are committed to building an America in which no neighborhood or town sees joblessness…."	"Budget surpluses are the result of over-taxation of the American people. The weak link in the chain of prosperity is the tax system. It not only burdens the American people; it threatens to slow, and perhaps to reverse…economic expansion…."
The Family	
"Government should be on the side of parents…. We should urge employers to make workplaces more parent-friendly…. [We] believe in making child care more affordable."	"The family is society's central core of energy…. It's why we advocate a family-friendly tax code; why we promote comp-time and flex-time to accommodate family needs; and why we advocate choice in childcare."
Education	
"[W]hat America needs are public schools that compete with one another and are held accountable for results, not private school vouchers that drain resources from public schools…."	"We endorse the principle of…expand[ing] parental choice and encourag[ing] competition by providing parents with information on their child's school, increasing the number of charter schools, and expanding education savings accounts…."
The United States in the World	
"We must maintain America's economic and military strength…. [W]e must deepen our key alliances, develop more constructive relationships with former enemies, and bring together diverse coalitions of nations to deal with new problems."	"[T]he United States will build and secure the peace. Republicans know what it takes to accomplish this: robust military forces, strong alliances, expanding trade, and resolute diplomacy."

1995. Perot ran as the Reform Party's candidate for President in 1996, receiving 8 percent of the vote.

Characteristics of Today's Parties

What do the major parties really stand for? One way to answer this question is to look at a party's platform. Generally, the Democratic party believes that the federal government should take responsibility for many social programs, such as aid to the poor. Democrats are more likely than Republicans to support tax increases, if needed, to pay for these programs. Over the years the Democratic party has also been more likely to support labor unions.

The Republican party generally supports reducing the power of federal government. Republicans tend to believe that state and local governments, as well as non-government organizations, should take more responsibility for social programs. They are also supporters of a strong military.

Political Parties Are Similar When you look at the two parties you can see differences. However, when the party in office or the majority party in the legislature changes, we do not usually have a radical change in government policies. Why not? The answer lies in the fact that, in many ways, our two major political parties are similar.

In Chapter 1 you learned about the American belief in equal respect and our values of freedom, justice, and equality for all. The two political parties have different historical traditions and see the role of government differently. However, the parties, like the American people they represent, hold the same basic beliefs and values.

Furthermore, in order to win elections, both parties need broad support. Each party tries to attract members from a broad spectrum of people—rich and poor, white collar and blue collar, rural and urban. To keep the support of all these different groups, both parties avoid taking extreme stands on issues. Each party also tries to attract the votes of the large number of voters who are not strongly committed to either party.

Party Organization The Democratic and Republican parties are also similar in the way they are set up. Both parties have local, state, and national organizations. These organizations work independently of each other. In other words, there is no single authority making decisions for the whole party.

Individual members at the local level are the most important part of any party. These members do the job of getting the party's candidates elected. Each community is di-

POLITICAL PARTY ORGANIZATION Individual members are the foundation of all political parties. **Government What group is at the top level of party organization?**

National Committee

State Committees

County and Local Committees

Precinct Organization

Party Members

vided into precincts, or voting districts. Precincts are made up of generally less than 1,000 voters who all vote at the same polling place. In each precinct, each party has a chairperson or captain who organizes volunteers to try to get as many party members as possible to vote.

Parties at the local level elect members to city and county committees. These committees may recommend candidates for office and are responsible for running local campaigns.

Each party is also organized at the state level. Most states have party committees, each with a chairperson. At state conventions, party leaders write the state party platform and nominate candidates for office. Party leaders also raise money and help with candidates' campaigns.

Voter registration tables like this one are a common sight around election time. Most states allow people to declare their party when they register.

Once every four years, each party holds a national convention. At the convention, delegates write the national party platform and nominate the candidates for President and Vice President.

Between national conventions, the national committee keeps the party running. During election years, the national committee helps the candidates for President and Vice President run their campaigns. It also works to elect members of Congress and to raise funds for the party.

Supporting a Party

Membership in a political party is not like membership in a club. You do not need to pay dues or attend meetings. All you need to do is think of yourself as a member. In some states, you can officially declare your party when you register to vote. Even so, you are free to vote for any party's candidates in general elections and to change your party registration whenever you wish.

How do you decide what party to support, or whether to support a party at all? One influence is your family. If you grow up listening to your parents talk about politics, you may come to share their views. The views of friends, co-workers, and teachers may also influence you. If people you respect support a party, you, too, may choose to back that party.

Your views on issues may also influence which political party you support. If you take a strong stand on an issue, you are more likely to back a party that shares your view. Also, if you like certain candidates and agree with their opinions, you may be attracted to their party.

Changes in Party Strength

Parties depend for their strength on their ability to elect their candidates. In order to be successful in elections, parties must have dedicated members to work on campaigns.

Historically, political parties have maintained their strength through a combination of three elements: (1) a system of patronage, (2) a central role in election campaigns, and (3) voter loyalty. Each of these elements has changed in recent years.

Patronage The system in which party leaders do favors for loyal supporters of the party is called patronage. Today, some patronage is still possible, especially at high levels. For example, the President often appoints loyal party members to cabinet positions. However, as you have learned, many people now get government jobs through the civil service system. As a result, the patronage system has decreased, though there are still 2,000 federal appointments and many state and local, as well.

Parties in Campaigns Another way in which party strength has changed is in the parties' role in campaigns. In earlier times, candidates for office worked within the party and depended on party support in their campaigns.

Today, candidates can more easily strike out on their own and run a campaign apart from the party. They can raise their own campaign funds, buy television ads, and print their own pamphlets. When candidates are less dependent on party help, they may be less bound to support the party's programs.

Voter Loyalty A third change that has weakened political parties is a change in voter loyalty. Only 40% of people now vote a straight ticket, the practice of voting for the candidates of only one party. Voters now tend to base their decisions on the appeal of a particular candidate or issue rather than on party loyalty. Many people now vote a split ticket, the practice of voting for candidates of more than one party on the same ballot.

As a result of split-ticket voting, parties can no longer count on a certain core of party votes in an election. In 1998, for example, Iowa voters re-elected Republican Senator Chuck Grassley while electing a Democrat, Tom Vilsack, as the state's new governor.

A 1999 poll found that 34 percent of American voters considered themselves Democrats, while 28 percent considered themselves Republicans. How do the rest of the voters think of themselves? Recent studies show that approximately 35 percent are independent voters, people who do not support a particular political party. This number is highest among young voters. However, a certain percentage of independent voters "leans" toward one party or the other.

Some observers claim that the influence of political parties is weakening—that "the party is over." Others believe that our two-party system will stay in place, but that the parties will change in response to changing times.

Section 2 Assessment

1. **Define** precincts, patronage, straight ticket, split ticket, independent voters
2. What were the basic beliefs of Thomas Jefferson's Democratic-Republican party?
3. Describe how third parties have played an important role in our political system.
4. In what ways are our two major political parties similar?
5. What are two things that might influence a person's choice of political parties?
6. What effect has the decrease in patronage had on political parties?
7. **Evaluate** Could you choose which party to support based on the excerpts on page 462? Why or why not?

Choosing Candidates

SECTION PREVIEW

Objectives

- Explain the process of nominating a candidate.
- Describe how political parties choose presidential candidates.

Building Civics Vocabulary

- **Self-nomination** means declaring that you are running for office.
- A **write-in candidate** asks voters to write his or her name on the ballot.
- A **caucus** is a meeting of party leaders to discuss issues or choose candidates.
- A **direct primary** is an election in which members of a political party choose candidates to run for office.
- A **closed primary** is a primary in which a voter must be registered as a party member in order to vote.
- An **open primary** is a primary in which voters do not need to declare a party before voting.

 **Focus**

The most important role of political parties is selecting, or nominating, the candidates who will run for office. Taking a look at the nominating process for candidates in general, and for presidential candidates in particular, is a good way to see parties in action.

Nominating Candidates

Suppose you want to run for office. The first step is to declare that you intend to run, or "throw your hat in the ring." After that, the nominating process ranges from simple to complex, depending on the office.

The simplest way to become a candidate is self-nomination, which means declaring that you are running for office. Self-nomination is still possible for many local offices. A self-nominee usually pays a small fee called a filing fee, as do other declared candidates. Another type of self-nominated candidate is a write-in candidate, one who asks voters to write his or her name on the ballot.

For some offices, a candidate may need to file a nominating petition. A number of voters must sign the petition saying that they support the nomination. Then the candidate pays the filing fee and begins the campaign. For other offices, candidates are chosen by delegates at party meetings called conventions. Parties hold local, state, and national conventions.

A few states select candidates or choose delegates to conventions at a caucus. A caucus is a meeting of party leaders to discuss issues or choose candidates. In earlier days, caucuses put great power in the hands of a few party leaders because the meetings were closed to ordinary members. Today a few state and local caucuses are still held, but they are very different. Most caucuses are open meetings.

Primaries Most candidates for state and federal office are now chosen in a direct primary. A direct primary is an election in which members of a political party choose candidates to run for office in the name of the party. The candidate with the most votes is then that party's nominee in the general election.

Most states use one of two kinds of direct primary: closed or open. A closed primary is a primary in which a voter must be registered as a party member and may vote only in that party's primary. Only Democrats may vote in the Democratic primary to choose Democratic candidates, and the same is true for Republicans. Voters registered as independent cannot vote in a closed primary. An open primary is a primary in which voters do not need to declare a party before voting, but may vote in only one party's primary.

Political Commitment Begins Early

The first Hispanic woman elected to the United States Congress, Ileana Ros-Lehtinen has been involved in politics from an early age. "I believe strongly that if you want to improve your community and nation," she says, "you must work hard for the principles in which you believe."

Ros-Lehtinen was born in Havana, Cuba in 1952. When she was seven years old, her family fled Cuba when a communist government led by Fidel Castro took power. The family settled in Miami, Florida.

As a student, Ros-Lehtinen joined the Young Republicans in Miami. "I was attracted by the party's basic support for individual freedom and its strong anti-communist stand," she explains.

While she worked as a teacher, Ros-Lehtinen became actively involved in politics, lobbying the Florida state legislature for better schools. Her lobbying efforts attracted the attention of Republican party leaders in the Miami area. They recruited her to run the Florida state legislature.

After winning election to the Florida House in 1982 and the Florida Senate four years later, Ros-Lehtinen decided to run for an open seat in the United States House of Representatives in 1989.

She won, and has represented Florida's Eighteenth District in the House since that time.

Ros-Lehtinen believes her family's experience as Cuban refugees helped make political party participation very important to her. "Parties give voters a way to express their differing viewpoints on important public policy issues," she says. "I am fully aware of how grateful we should be here in America that we have the right to vote and the ability to freely express our views to our elected officials. When you give up this precious right, you are letting others determine your future."

Active Citizenship

According to Ileana Ros-Lehtinen, why is political party involvement important?

Choosing Presidential Candidates

The primaries that receive the most attention take place once every four years to select the parties' candidates for President. Who runs for President? As you know, anyone over 35 years old and born in the United States may run for President. In fact, however, a candidate needs to be well known, to have experience in government, and to be able to raise enough money for the campaign.

Al Gore, seen here greeting students, finished first in New Hampshire's Democratic presidential primary in 2000. He went on to win later primaries and was nominated the party's candidate for President.

Most presidential candidates from the major parties have held elected office before seeking the nomination for President. Since World War II, 80 percent of Republican and Democratic candidates for President have been senators or governors. Also, since 1900, every President who has wanted to run for reelection has gained his party's nomination.

Paying for a Primary Campaign
In the presidential primaries, candidates raise much of their money from individuals. Federal laws, however, say that individuals may give only $1,000 to each candidate per election. Once candidates have raised at least $5,000 in each of 20 states, they can receive an equal amount from the federal government, up to a total of almost $31 million.

Choosing Delegates
Delegates to the national nominating conventions are chosen in one of two ways: through a presidential preference primary election or through a state-wide caucus or convention process. Each state has different rules for choosing delegates.

In a preference primary, voters show which candidates they prefer by voting either for the candidates themselves or for the delegates who support that candidate. In most primary states, delegates must promise to support a certain candidate at the national convention. In states without primaries, delegates are chosen by caucus or state convention.

In February or March of a presidential election year, candidates traditionally begin the race in New Hampshire, a primary state, and Iowa, a caucus state. How well a candidate does in these early tests will affect his or her ability to raise money and attract voters in later primaries and caucuses. As the process continues, some candidates drop out and others gain strength.

National Conventions
In a presidential election year, the parties hold their national conventions. Perhaps you have watched one on television. You have seen a large hall filled with people waving signs and banners and wearing campaign hats and buttons. Bands play, flags wave, and thousands of balloons fill the air. The delegates debate and discuss the candidates, listen to speeches, vote on the nominations, and hammer out the party platform.

At conventions in the early 1900s, several votes had to be taken before the delegates could decide a presidential nominee. Today, because of the primaries, almost all delegates are "pledged" to a candidate before the convention begins. Usually only one vote is needed to choose the candidate. Once the candidate for President has been chosen, the delegates most often approve that candidate's choice for Vice President.

Another task of the national convention is to approve the party platform. A committee writes the platform with advice from party leaders, including the candidates. Each plank is carefully worded to appeal to the widest possible audience. The delegates debate and finally approve a platform.

The convention winds up with acceptance speeches from the presidential and vice presidential candidates. These speeches are meant to bring the party together after months of primaries and four grueling days of discussions and—often—disagreements. The next step to gaining office will be the election campaign, leading up to the presidential election in November.

Section 3 Assessment

1. **Define** self-nomination, write-in candidate, caucus, direct primary, closed primary, open primary
2. Describe four ways in which candidates can be nominated.
3. Explain in your own words how presidential candidates are nominated.
4. **Evaluate** "The amount of money candidates spend on a campaign should not be limited." Do you agree or disagree? Why?

Extending the Chapter

Global Views

The United States has had two political parties for so long that many Americans cannot imagine another system. However, two-party systems are rare. They are found in Great Britain and the United States. In the rest of the world, multi-party or single-party systems are more common.

In most democratic countries, several political parties compete for power. Each party represents a different set of interests or ideas that are usually better defined than in a two-party system. Voters in Poland choose from more than 29 political parties in national elections. In Italy, more than 10 parties compete for votes. In both of these countries, voters have a wide range of choices.

A problem in some multi-party countries has been frequent changes in government. When no one party receives a majority of votes, two or more parties must join together to form a government that represents a majority of voters. If these parties cannot work together, the government soon falls apart. Italy, for example, has gone through over 50 changes of government since 1946.

Single-party systems are typical of communist countries and dictatorships. In many single-party countries only the ruling party is allowed. Opposition parties are outlawed. Supporters of single-party government argue that it builds national unity. Opponents say that single party governments grow corrupt and lazy without an opposition party to keep them honest and hard-working.

Most Americans see their two-party system as a good compromise between multi- and single-party systems. A two-party system can be more stable than a multi-party system. Also, having two parties means that there is always one party playing the watchdog role.

How to **ANALYZE ELECTION RESULTS**

 Use the *Simulations and Data Graphing* CD-ROM to create and interpret graphs.

As you read in this chapter, powerful third parties have arisen throughout our history. The chart below shows presidential election results for major third parties since 1832.

Major Third Party Election Results			
Party	**Year**	**Vote**	**Next Election**
Anti-Masonic	1832	7.8%	Supported Whigs
Free Soil	1848	10.1%	4.9%
American ("Know-Nothing")	1856	21.5%	Disappeared
Southern Democrat	1860	18.1%	Disappeared
Constitutional Union	1860	12.6%	Disappeared
Populist	1892	8.5%	Supported Democrats
Progressive ("Bull Moose")	1912	27.4%	.02%
Socialist	1912	6.0%	3.2%
Progressive	1924	16.6%	Disappeared
American Independent	1968	13.5%	1.4%
Independent	1992	18.9%	Became Reform Party
Reform	1996	8.4%	0.5%
Green	2000	2.7%	

Sources: New York Times Almanac, Federal Election Commission

Explain the Skill

Since the first presidential election in 1789, nine different third party candidates have won more than one million votes in a presidential election. While a third party candidate has never won a presidential election,

several have been able to influence election outcomes. The 2000 election results provide a good example of this.

Look at the chart on this page, which shows that in 2000 the Green Party candidate—Ralph Nader—received 2.7% of the popular vote. Some people feel that Nader's strong showing drew votes away from Al Gore, helping George W. Bush win the election.

Analyze the Skill

Study the chart on this page, which lists election results for 13 major third party presidential candidates. Beside the name of each party, the chart lists the year of the election and the percentage of the popular vote won by the party's candidate. The far right column tells you how the party did four years later in the next presidential election.

Each row of the chart gives information about one political party. Look at the chart to draw some general conclusions about third parties in American history.

Skill Assessment

1. Of all the third parties shown on the chart, which received the highest percentage of the vote in a presidential election? In what year did this occur?
2. What happened to the Southern Democrat party after the 1860 election?
3. How many of these third parties were able to win at least 10 percent of the vote in a presidential election? How many were able to win more than 10 percent two elections in a row?
4. In one sentence, summarize the pattern you see in these elections.

CHAPTER 21 ASSESSMENT

Building Civics Vocabulary

The vocabulary terms in each pair listed below are related to each other. For each pair, explain what the terms have in common. Also explain how they are different.

Example: A *caucus* and a *direct primary* are similar because they both are ways in which parties nominate candidates. They are different because a caucus is a meeting of party members, and a direct primary is an election to choose candidates to run for office.

1. *platform* and *plank*
2. *straight ticket* and *split ticket*
3. *closed primary* and *open primary*

Reviewing Main Ideas and Skills

4. How does a political party establish positions on issues and set goals for what the government should accomplish?

5. How can the party out of power act as a watchdog over the party in power?

6. In what ways do political parties inform citizens about various political issues?

7. Give two reasons why third parties are formed.

8. What tasks are accomplished at party national conventions?

9. **How to Analyze Election Results** Use the information from the chart on page 470 to create a chart of your own. Based on percentage of the vote received, create a chart ranking the five most successful third parties in American history. Include a column showing the year of each election.

Critical Thinking

10. **Analyzing Primary Sources** As you read on page 459, George Washington warned against "the baneful [harmful] effects of the spirit of party." What "baneful effects" was Washington worried about? Do you think he was right to be concerned?

11. **Linking Past and Present** What factors have caused the strength of the two major political parties to decline?

Writing About Civics

12. **Writing a Platform** If you were to write a platform for a political party, what would some of the main planks be? Explain your party's position on three important issues.

Citizenship Activities

13. **Working Together** Hold a mock national convention in your classroom. Divide the class into different delegate groups. Each group should choose one person to be a candidate. Develop a party platform that all the delegate groups can agree on, and select the final presidential and vice-presidential nominees.

 Take It to the NET

Access the Civics: Participating in Government Internet site at **www.phschool.com** for the specific URLs to complete the activity.

Explore online information about the differences in the political parties. You may wish to consider smaller, third parties. Choose a party whose stands on important issues you agree with. Debate the issues with your classmates, from the standpoint of that party.

Voting and Elections

Citizenship and You

Ian was cooking dinner when his mother arrived home from work. She had a smile on her face, and he knew she had some good news. "What's up, Mom?" he asked.

"I've decided to run for city council," she said.

"Really? Mom, that's great!" exclaimed Ian. "I can tell all my friends that my mother holds a government office!"

"Now wait a minute, Ian," she replied. "I haven't won the election yet. I'm just going to run. There are six other candidates, at least."

"Yeah, I know," said Ian. "What I meant to say is that I'm proud of you. It's a lot of work to run for office."

"Thanks. It's good to hear I have some support already," she said. "By the way, you'll turn eighteen before the election. That means you can vote for the first time. May I count on your vote?"

He said teasingly, "I haven't decided yet if you're the best candidate." His mother smiled and they both burst out laughing.

Keep It Current

Items marked with this logo are periodically updated on the Internet. To keep up-to-date, go to www.phschool.com

What's Ahead in Chapter 22

This chapter is about elections. As you read, you will first learn what it means to be a voter—sorting out messages from candidates, deciding how to vote, and finally marking your ballot. Then you will learn about how political candidates go about organizing and running their campaigns.

Section 1 **Being a Voter**

Section 2 **How Candidates and Groups Try to Influence Your Vote**

Section 3 **Campaigning for Office**

Citizen's Journal

Suppose someone you knew was running for a government office. Based on what you have learned so far, what is one piece of advice you would give that person? Why do you think this advice would be helpful?

Being a Voter

SECTION PREVIEW

Objectives

- Explain the purpose of general elections.
- Describe how and when elections are held, and who may vote in them.
- Explore the importance of becoming an informed voter.

Building Civics Vocabulary

- In a **general election** voters make final decisions about candidates and issues.
- **Registration** is the process of signing up to be a voter.

 **Focus**

At your age, you have the chance to play several citizen roles. You go to school, you obey laws, and you may do volunteer work. Soon, you will be old enough to play the most important citizen role in a democracy: the role of voter.

General Elections

You will have a chance to vote in two kinds of elections: primary elections and general elections. In Chapter 21 you learned that in a primary election members of political parties nominate candidates. A general election is an election in which voters make final decisions about candidates and issues.

About half a million federal, state, and local offices are filled in general elections. These offices include everything from President of the United States to member of a town council.

A general election may also offer citizens a chance to play a more direct part in government. Voters in many states, counties, and cities are asked to vote on certain ballot measures in a general election. Measures include initiatives, referendums, and recalls. They give each voter a voice in deciding what laws should be passed, how the government should raise money, and who should be removed from office.

In a typical general election, several hundred proposals for new laws, constitutional amendments, and new taxes or other ways of raising money appear on state ballots. In 2000, for example, citizens in California were asked to vote on eight proposals, ranging from providing housing for veterans to limiting state campaign contributions.

In addition to deciding about state-wide measures, voters across the country are often asked to vote on local ballot measures. These measures can involve new laws, public building projects, new taxes, and other government issues.

The Basics of Voting

Who may vote in a general election? The Constitution states that in order to vote you must be at least 18 years of age and a citizen of the United States. In addition, you must be a resident of the state in which you will vote. However, not everybody who meets these qualifications has the right to vote. In most states, prison inmates and people who are mentally incompetent are not allowed to vote.

Registration The process of signing up to be a voter is called registration. Registration was introduced in the late 1800s. It was meant to stop voter fraud, such as the same person voting more than once.

In a few states, voters are allowed to register at the polling place when they go to vote. In most states, however, you must register several weeks ahead of time. To make it easier, many cities and towns set up registration tables in libraries, church basements, and even shopping centers.

AVERAGE VOTER TURNOUT BY AGE GROUP: PRESIDENTIAL ELECTION YEARS 1984–1996

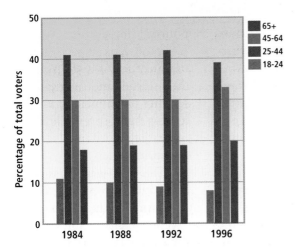

Percentage of total voters

Legend:
- 65+
- 45-64
- 25-44
- 18-24

Source: Federal Election Commission

The Twenty-sixth Amendment lowered the voting age from twenty-one to eighteen. **Citizenship Which age group had the highest voter turnout in the years shown?**

Each state makes its own laws about voter registration. In most states, local governments like counties and cities run the elections. They set the rules on voter registration and operate the polling places.

Voting—When and Where

An act of Congress set the Tuesday after the first Monday in November as the day for federal congressional and presidential elections. Most elections for state offices take place at the same time.

Primary elections and elections for local governments may take place at any time during the year, but most are set for the spring. Special elections to choose candidates to finish the terms of officeholders who have died, resigned, or been recalled also may be held at any time.

Voting takes place in what are called polling places. As a registered voter, you are assigned to a polling place near where you live. Each polling place serves a voting district or precinct—an area with between 200 and 1,000 voters. Your polling place may be a nearby school or church, or even a neighbor's garage.

How to Cast a Vote

On entering the polling place, you check in with an election official, who looks up your name to see that you are registered to vote there. Local election units within each state set up the ballot. As a result, there are different ways to cast a vote. Depending on where you live, you may pull a lever on an election machine, mark an X on a paper ballot, punch a hole in a card, or make your choice on a touchpad similar to an Automatic Teller Machine.

If you will not be able to get to a polling place on election day—you will be on vacation, for example—you can ask to have an absentee ballot sent to your home. In this case, you mark your ballot and then mail it in.

There is some debate over the varying kinds of voting methods. Some methods are considered to be easier and more accurate than others. The 2000 presidential election illustrated this point. Some of the Florida voters were given a "butterfly ballot," in which they punched out a hole to cast their votes. These ballots were confusing because of the way the boxes were lined up next to the candidates' names. After the election, many of these voters feared that they misread the ballot and voted for the wrong candidate by mistake. In addition, the hole-punch method was found to be inaccurate when voters didn't punch all the way through the ballot. Because this election was so close (President George W. Bush won by 500 votes out of 10 million votes cast in Florida), a confusing ballot may have affected the outcome.

Carolyn Jefferson-Jenkins

"**D**emocracy isn't something that runs by itself," says Carolyn Jefferson-Jenkins, the League of Women Voters' fifteenth president and first African American leader. "You can't switch government onto automatic pilot. You can't sit back and expect other people to do all the work. Each generation must reestablish the relationship between government and its citizens."

Several generations of activists have helped make the League of Women Voters one of the nation's oldest and most respected nonpartisan political organizations. Founded in 1920 by women's suffrage leader Carrie Chapman Catt, the League has spent the last 80-plus years working to educate voters and encourage participation in politics and government.

Today, Jefferson-Jenkins acknowledges that convincing people to become more active citizens is not always easy. During the 2000 presidential election, only 51 percent of all eligible voters went to the polls. In response to low voter turnout, League members have worked to pass laws to make voter registration easier and have lobbied for campaign finance reform to reduce the influence of special interest groups on

political decision making. Jefferson-Jenkins says her organization is also using the Internet and interactive satellite town meetings to help busy parents and others get more involved in running their country.

The long-term goal of all League programs, says Jefferson-Jenkins, is to "reengage citizens in civic life." This includes encouraging women and ethnic minorities to run for office. "In a healthy democracy," Jefferson-Jenkins says, "elected officeholders reflect the diversity of the citizens they represent."

Recognizing Viewpoints

Do you agree with Carolyn Jefferson-Jenkins' statement that democracy can't "run by itself"? Explain.

The debate over confusing ballots and potentially inaccurate methods of counting led politicians to discuss having more consistent voting methods. Some argue that each state should come up with one voting method, instead of letting each county use a different type of ballot.

States are also investigating new methods of voting. In 2000, Oregon became the first state to conduct an election totally by mail-in ballots. States are also looking into the use of the Internet for voting.

Becoming an Informed Voter

Going to your polling place and casting your vote is relatively easy. To vote wisely, however, you must become an informed voter. To prepare to vote on candidates for public office, you should find out all you can about them. What are their qualifications? Where do they stand on important issues? If they have held public office before, how good a job did they do?

You can get the answers to these questions from many sources. The candidates themselves can tell you how they stand on the issues. Public service organizations with no ties to political parties, such as the League of Women Voters, often put out excellent information. You can also count on newspapers to write stories on the candidates' records, backgrounds, and stands on the issues.

You can also learn a great deal about the candidates by going to hear them speak or watching news on television. If you have a chance to watch candidates debate each other, you can see how they answer questions and handle themselves in a tough situation.

You should also learn about initiatives and other ballot measures. Find out why a measure was proposed and what the outcomes might be if it is passed or turned down.

Having a complete picture of a ballot measure is very important. For example, at first glance you might vote against a 25-cent-per-gallon rise in the tax on gasoline because it would make driving your car cost more. However, if you learned that the money raised by the tax would go to building a highway that would shorten your drive to work by 10 miles, you might change your mind. Some states provide information on ballot measures, often in a voters' handbook sent to all registered voters.

Why Vote In recent years, only about half of all eligible citizens have actually voted in presidential elections. Even fewer have voted in most state and local elections.

Why have so many people chosen not to use their right to vote? Some people say they do not vote because the candidates are all pretty much the same. The government will follow the same policies no matter who wins, they say, so why bother to vote? Others choose not to vote because they think that no candidate truly represents them or understands their problems.

Sometimes people do not participate in elections because they think their vote cannot possibly affect the final outcome. How, they ask, can my one vote make a difference in a presidential race in which more than 90 million people cast ballots?

It is true that elections are almost never won by 1 or by even 100 votes. However, the 2000 presidential election came down to only about 500 votes in the deciding state of Florida. In the end, a very small percentage of the population determined the outcome of the race.

Furthermore, even if your candidate loses, your vote still matters. Through the ballot box you announce where you stand on the issues and what kind of representatives you want. By casting your vote you perform an important civic duty. You take part in the process of deciding who will lead our government and what policies those leaders will follow.

Section 1 Assessment

1. **Define** general election, registration
2. What are the benefits of voting at the local, state, and national level? Are there any drawbacks to voting?
3. What are the qualifications for voting in most states?
4. What should you find out about the candidates in order to become an informed voter?
5. **Evaluate** "Bad officials are elected by good citizens who do not vote." Do you agree or disagree? Explain your answer.

How Candidates and Groups Try to Influence Your Vote

SECTION PREVIEW

Objectives

- Describe ways that candidates get their messages to voters.
- Analyze the role of interest groups in the election process.
- Explain how candidates and interest groups try to influence the way people vote.
- Explore the importance of the media in election campaigns.

Building Civics Vocabulary

- Sending messages to large groups of people through the mail is called **direct mail**.
- Candidates get their message out through advertisements in the **media**—television, radio, newspapers, and magazines.
- A message that is meant to influence people's ideas, opinions, or actions is called **propaganda**.
- **Bias** means favoring one point of view over another.

Focus

The television screen shows a man walking down a quiet, tree-lined street holding the hands of his two young children. You hear an announcer saying, "Bob Kane has lived in our city all his life. He graduated from our public schools. His children attend those schools. He knows your problems and he knows what you want." Another television ad shows an empty jail cell. A frightened voice says, "What Bob Kane has done puts criminals back in our neighborhoods—not here, where they belong."

Before an election, you will see and hear many campaign messages. Each will try to influence how you vote. Some will give you information. Others, like these TV ads, will try to play on your fears and other feelings. In evaluating such messages, you should be aware that you cannot always trust what they say.

Messages from the Candidates

Candidates have many different methods to try to get you, the voter, to vote for them. Depending on the office for which they are running and the number of votes they must win, they may shake your hand in person or buy thousands of dollars' worth of television advertising time. As a voter, you will want to know about the many ways candidates try to get their messages to you.

Posters, Bumper Stickers, and Leaflets In the months before election day, you will see posters and stickers plastered on lampposts, billboards, windows, and car bumpers. You will also see people wearing buttons, pins, and caps with candidates' names on them. People running for office want to make their names known to the voters.

To give voters a better picture of the person behind the name, candidates use leaflets and flyers. Volunteers hand them out at shopping centers and put them under your door. Such leaflets give short biographical sketches of the candidates and tell where they stand on the major issues. All this information is written to appeal to as many voters as possible.

Personal Appearances Candidates running for a town council usually campaign in a personal way. The numbers of people who vote in such elections are so small—often fewer than 1,000—that candidates can meet most voters in person. They ring doorbells and hold neighborhood meetings, bringing their messages to citizens through conversations and speeches to small groups.

Representative Cynthia McKinney of Georgia made personal appearances a key part of her successful re-election campaign in 1998.

Even in elections for state and national offices, candidates appear in person to spread their messages among the voters. Your chance to "meet" someone running for state or national office usually comes at huge political rallies in public parks or auditoriums or at neighborhood political meetings. At these events, the candidates make speeches telling you why you should elect them and not the people running against them.

Direct Mail One of the best ways to get the attention of voters is by mail. With the help of computers, candidates can use direct mail, a way of sending messages to large groups of people through the mail. Direct mail allows candidates to target voters who have special interests. A candidate can send a message to senior citizens promising to support higher social security payments.

Advertisements in the Media

Candidates for state and national office must reach very large numbers of voters. They have found that one of the best ways to get their messages out is through advertisements in the media—television, radio, newspapers, and magazines.

However, using the media can be very expensive. A full-page advertisement in a major newspaper costs thousands of dollars. The cost of a few minutes on television can run into hundreds of thousands of dollars.

Since television time and newspaper space are so expensive, political advertisements are usually short and simple. They often give very little in the way of information. Instead, they try to grab your attention and to focus on a candidate's personality rather than qualifications and abilities. Many media ads depend on slogans, such as "Building a Better Tomorrow" or "It's Morning in America."

For these reasons, TV and newspaper ads are not a good source of information about what a candidate would do if elected. They rarely say much, for example, about how a candidate plans to fight the drug problem or improve the economy. However, some of these ads do tell voters what stands the candidates have taken on major issues.

These members of a special interest group, the American Association of Retired Persons, are helping "get out the vote" on issues that affect them.

Messages from Interest Groups

Candidates are not the only people trying to get your vote. Interest groups, too, put out their share of direct mail and media ads. Interest groups want to help elect candidates who agree with their views and to defeat candidates who have taken stands against them. Interest groups also work to pass or defeat ballot measures.

Interest groups try to achieve their election goals in two other ways. They endorse, or lend their names in support of, candidates and ballot measures. They also give money to campaigns.

The largest interest groups have political action committees (PACs) whose job is to carry out these election activities. PACs often work very hard for and against ballot measures. For example, when a 1999 ballot measure in Missouri asked voters to decide if citizens should be allowed to carry concealed handguns, the National Rifle Association campaigned in support of the measure while Handgun Control, Inc. worked to defeat it.

PACs also give large sums of money to campaigns for state and national office. United States senators running for re-election in 1998 received an average of more than $1 million each from PACs.

Since the early 1970s, the number of PACs in the United States has grown from just over 600 to over 4,000. Some PACs get their money from the people they represent—union members, employees of businesses, and corporation stockholders. Others use direct mail to find people who agree with their views and will send them large sums of money. The success of both methods of raising money has given PACs a large voice in campaigns.

Federal law limits the amount that PACs may give to each candidate. However, there are few rules for how much PACs may spend on running their own campaigns.

Many people believe that PACs have too much influence on the outcome of elections. They charge that the "special interests" that PACs represent are gaining too much power in government. Each interest group represents only a small percentage of Americans, or cares about only one issue, they say. Through PACs, however, interest groups can have a voice in who will hold office and make decisions on issues that affect everyone.

Although some people want limits placed on what PACs can do, other people are opposed to such limits. They argue that PACs are simply using their First Amendment right of free speech.

Recognizing Propaganda Techniques

Why do candidates and interest groups work so hard to get their messages across to voters? They all have the same goal: to influence the way you think and act. A message that is meant to influence people's ideas, opinions, or actions in a certain way is called propaganda.

Do you think of propaganda as lies or false information? Although propaganda can includes lies, it can also contain truthful—or mostly truthful—information. A message is called propaganda when it tells only one side of the story, distorts the truth, or appeals mostly to people's feelings.

Messages from candidates and PACs make use of many different kinds of propaganda. Six of the most common propaganda techniques used by candidates are described in the chart below.

When reading and listening to political messages, be aware of the kinds of propaganda techniques that might be at work. Recognizing them will help you decide how to act on the messages.

How News Media Report the Elections

In addition to running ads paid for by the candidates and interest groups, the media put out their own information about

---

PROPAGANDA TECHNIQUES Candidates use a variety of techniques to try to influence voters. **Government** Which one of these techniques do you think would be most effective in a presidential election? Why?

Glittering Generalities
Use words and phrases that sound appealing and that everyone agrees with.
Example: "I stand for freedom and the American way."

Card Stacking
Use only those facts that support your argument.
Example: "My opponent voted against raising Social Security." (You do not mention that she voted no because the proposed increase was too small.)

Plain Folks
Tell voters that you are just like them—an ordinary person with similar needs and ideas.
Example: "I've lived in this city all my life. My children go to the same schools as your children."

Name Calling
Attach negative labels to your opponent.
Example: "He's soft on crime."

Bandwagon
Appeals to desire to follow the crowd.
Example: "Polls show that more than 80 percent of voters support me."

Transfer
Connect yourself to a respected person, group, or symbol.
Example: "Remember what Abraham Lincoln said..."

candidates and issues. This information comes in two forms: editorials and news reporting.

In their editorials, the media give their opinions on ballot measures and candidates. News reporting, on the other hand, is supposed to stick to the facts.

Election News Election news reports give information about what a candidate says and does. They tell what a candidate said in last night's speech, for example, or what the candidate has promised to do for the schools.

Even though news reports give facts, not opinions, they can present these facts in ways that favor one candidate over another. In other words, bias, which means favoring one point of view, may show in the way the media report on elections.

For the most part, the news media usually try not to show bias. They do not want to be accused of favoring one candidate over another. However, reporters, news directors, and editors have their opinions, likes, and dislikes. Sometimes their feelings affect their work.

How can you spot bias in news reporting? Bias can show when stories about one candidate are given more time or space or better placement than stories about other candidates. If you were running for class president, how would you feel if a story about you got 10 lines on page 6 of the school newspaper, while your opponent was given half of the front page?

Another sign of bias is when the media play up the negative side of one candidate's personality or behavior. They may run stories, for example, about a candidate's bad temper or a divorce that took place years ago. Such stories, though they may not be lies, can give voters a bad impression of the candidate and influence the way they vote.

Opinion Polls Along with reporting on what candidates are doing and saying, the news media also present the results of opinion polls. Polls can show which candidate people favor at a certain time, why they like that candidate, and what issues they think are most important.

The basic idea behind a poll is that you do not have to talk to every person in a group to find out what the outcome of that group's vote will be. A poll asks questions of a sample, or small part, of the group. The answers given by the people in the sample are then taken to stand for how the whole group would answer if everyone were asked.

Polling, however, works only if the people are chosen at random, that is, by chance. Choosing a poll's sample by chance helps make sure that the views of the people in the sample will stand for those of the whole group.

Most of the major national polls use random sampling and ask fair questions. Polls are not always accurate, but they do give a sense of what the public is thinking.

However, not all polls reported in the news are based on random samples. A poll that gets answers from only certain kinds of people may not be very accurate. Such polls include those in which people send in

Facts & Quotes

Off to the Races

Early in our country's history, people noticed that race horses and candidates had a lot in common. They borrowed the vocabulary of horse racing to describe political campaigns and elections. To this day, we still call an election a "race" in which the candidates "run." A "dark horse" is a relatively unknown candidate who gets the nomination unexpectedly. The probable winner is called the "front runner." In a close race, as the votes are tallied, two candidates may be said to be "neck and neck."

"That's the worst set of opinions I've heard in my entire life."

answers to lists of questions in magazines or call in their answers by telephone.

Some people think that polls should not be used. They believe that polls can change the results of elections. They point to voters who say they will vote for a certain candidate mainly because that candidate is leading in the polls. In other words, those voters will jump on the candidate's "bandwagon."

Also, some voters may decide whether to vote or not based on the results of opinion polls. Studies suggest that if the polls show a huge gap between candidates, some people believe that the leading candidate will win, and they do not bother to vote.

The Impact of Television Today, many voters receive most of their information by watching the television news. For this reason, television has had a big impact on the way people see the candidates, understand the issues, and cast their votes.

Critics charge that television has made election issues seem unimportant because it covers the more exciting activities of the candidates, rather than paying attention to the major issues. These people also say that to make election news exciting and appealing,

television tries to reduce campaign stories to 20-second "sound-bites" that catch viewers' attention but give little or no information.

Television has also had a powerful impact on the way candidates run their campaigns. They make their messages short and simple to fit easily on the television news. They also plan campaign activities that will look good on TV.

Overall, television has created a new kind of political candidate. A person running for high office today must come across well on the screen. This "television" candidate, by and large, must be good looking, have a compelling personality, and be at ease in front of the camera. Otherwise, he or she may face a tough time in an election.

Even though network news is not always the best source of facts about the candidates and issues, good sources do exist. Public television, special network programs, newspapers, and magazines all provide fuller coverage. It may take more work to seek out good information. However, if being an informed voter is important to you, the effort will be worth it.

Section 2 Assessment

1. **Define** direct mail, media, propaganda, bias
2. List four methods candidates use to get their messages to voters.
3. What are the election aims of interest groups?
4. List the major propaganda techniques that might be used in campaign messages.
5. How may opinion polls affect the outcome of an election?
6. **Evaluate** Abraham Lincoln was one of our greatest Presidents. He was also awkward and tired-eyed. Do you think that Lincoln could become President today? Explain.

Campaigning for Office

SECTION PREVIEW

Objectives

- Explore how campaigns are planned and managed.
- Describe how campaigns are financed.
- Identify factors that help people win elections.
- Summarize the role of the Electoral College in presidential elections.

Building Civics Vocabulary

- An **incumbent** candidate already holds the office for which he or she is running.

 Focus

In the movie *The Candidate,* actor Robert Redford plays a man running for Congress. At one point the candidate says that he wants to "go where I want, say what I want, do what I want." His campaign advisor then writes a message on a matchbook and pushes it toward the candidate. The message reads, "You lose."

Campaigning for a major office is not something a person does alone. It is a highly organized, tightly controlled activity. To learn about how a campaign for a major office works, you will read about the way candidates run for the presidency. Keep in mind as you read that not all campaigns take as much planning and money as a presidential campaign. All of them, however, share a common goal—to get the candidate elected—and most use the same techniques to work toward that goal.

Planning and Running a Campaign

A person who is running for President in the November general election has already passed several major hurdles. After winning primary elections and caucuses in many states, the candidate has been nominated by his or her party at its national convention. He or she has chosen a running mate, raised a large amount of money, and built up an organization. Much work, however, still lies ahead.

A great deal of thought, planning, and hard work by many people goes into a presidential campaign. Paid staff members work with the candidate to plan and carry out the campaign. Thousands of workers put in long hours stuffing envelopes, making telephone calls, and ringing doorbells. The candidate's party contributes money, people, and other kinds of support. The final success or failure of the campaign depends not just on the candidate but also on the organization as a whole.

Campaign Organization Besides the candidate, the most important person in a campaign is the campaign manager. Along with a small group of assistants and advisors, the manager helps plan the broad outlines of the campaign: where to go, what issues to talk about, what image of the candidate to put forth. The manager also guides the work of other important members of the staff: fundraisers, speech writers, media advisors, and so on.

The manager also keeps in touch with the people who run the campaign in different parts of the country. These lower-level managers are in charge of the thousands of volunteers who work "in the field," handling the day-to-day campaign work that is needed to win the election.

Mary Matalin, deputy campaign manager of Republican President George Bush's 1992 re-election campaign, squares off with her husband and political opponent James Carville, former campaign manager for Democratic President Bill Clinton.

Finally, the manager is in charge of the workers who plan for the candidate to appear at meetings, picnics, and rallies. These "advance people" make sure that the candidate is in the right place at the right time, and that a big crowd is on hand.

Finding Out What the Public Thinks

A successful campaign must keep its finger on the pulse of the American public. How do people think things are going? What issues should the candidate be talking about? A presidential campaign usually has its own opinion poll taker who finds the answers to such questions.

The poll taker is able to find out which issues the voters think are important. Polls can also show what impact the campaign is having in different parts of the country and among different groups of voters.

Managing and Using the Media

Wherever they go, people who run for President are followed by planeloads and busloads of people from the media. Making certain that the news shows the candidate in the best light is the job of the campaign press secretary. The press secretary tells reporters about public appearances and gives them copies of speeches and policy positions.

The press secretary also helps make sure that the media is on hand when the candidate is "making news." A television news report on a candidate's visit to a children's hospital will be seen by thousands of people. Such media coverage is a good source of free publicity for the candidate.

One way for national candidates to get their message across to the public is by advertising in newspapers and on radio and television. A campaign hires media advisors to create these advertisements. Television ads, especially, can have a major impact on a campaign.

Media people have learned that saying bad things about the other candidate can sometimes work better than saying nice things about their own. They also know that it is often best to focus on image and style rather than issues and ideas.

Some critics say that this approach amounts to little more than "packaging and selling" the candidates. It is up to you, the voter, to view these ads carefully and to pay attention to the propaganda techniques being used.

Financing a Campaign

People who run for President and for other national and state offices have one thing in common—they need a lot of money. As Tip O'Neill, former Speaker of the House of Representatives, once said, "There are four parts to any campaign. The candidate, the issues of the candidate, the campaign organization, and the money to run the campaign with. Without money you can forget the other three." In 1998, for example, major party candidates for the Senate spent an average of over $3 million each.

Where do people get the money to run for office? Candidates for local, state, and national office get most of their money from individuals. Many candidates, especially

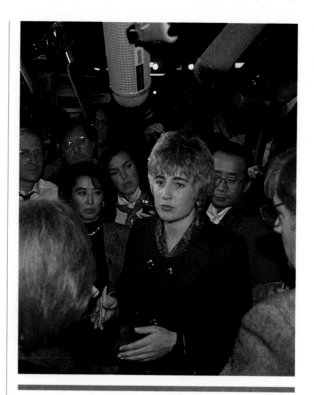

While serving as White House press secretary during the Clinton administration, Dee Dee Myers often fielded questions from television and newspaper reporters.

those for national and high state office, also get money from political parties and PACs.

In the early 1970s, the high costs of running for office began to worry people. They began to think that individuals, businesses, and interest groups that gave large sums of money might have too much influence on candidates.

In response, Congress passed several laws making rules for how campaigns for federal office can be paid for. The law now says that no one person may give more than $1,000 to a candidate. The law also says that candidates must report the name of anyone who has given them more than $200. As a result, the public can know where the money is coming from. Congress set up the Federal Election Commission (FEC) to carry out these and other rules.

Changes were also made in the way presidential campaigns are paid for. Citizens may now give $3 of their taxes each year to a presidential campaign fund. Every election year, the FEC offers money from this fund to each of the major candidates for the presidency. This system was first used in 1976. Once presidential candidates accept these public funds, they cannot accept or spend money from any other sources.

FEC rules allow a PAC to give up to $5,000 to a presidential candidate in the primary elections. However, in the general election, candidates who have accepted public tax money may not take money from PACs. Of course, as you have learned, this rule does not keep PACs from spending as much as they like on their own campaigns in support of certain candidates.

Many people complain that elections cost too much money. The high cost of running for even a local office, they say, keeps many good people from running at all. If costs continue to rise, people ask, will only the wealthy—and candidates backed by wealthy individuals and groups—be able to run and win?

Questions like these were behind the laws that limit contributions for federal elections. Some groups, however, would like to go further. They want to have all campaigns paid for entirely with public funds so that candidates do not have to raise funds privately.

How much should campaigns cost? Who should pay for them? The debate over these issues raises questions that by now should be familiar to you. Does our belief in equality mean that all candidates should have an equal opportunity to run and to get their messages across to the public? On the other hand, does our belief in freedom mean that every citizen should be free to give as much money to a candidate as he or she wishes?

Who Wins an Election?

It is a goal of our democracy to elect people who will be our best leaders and decision makers. Being a good leader and being able to make good decisions, however, are not all it takes to win an election. As you have seen, it is also important to look good on television, have a good organization, and be able to raise a lot of money, especially if you are running for national office. It also helps to have the backing of either the Democratic or Republican party.

One other factor is also very important. An incumbent, someone who already holds the office for which he or she is running, has a very good chance of winning. Incumbents win re-election far more often than they lose. In 2000, 399 incumbent members of the House of Representatives ran for re-election—392 of them won.

An incumbent has a name that voters know and a record to point to. Unless an incumbent has made major mistakes, a challenger usually faces a hard battle with only a small chance of winning.

The Electoral College

In the 2000 presidential election, more than 50 million people voted for George W. Bush. Did 50,456,141 people choose George W. Bush directly? No. They actually elected people from their states, called electors, who promised to cast votes for Bush. As set down in the Constitution, the President is chosen not by a vote of the people, but by electoral votes in what is called the Electoral College.

How does the Electoral College work? Each state has the same number of electors as it has members of Congress. Iowa, for example, with 5 representatives and 2 senators, has 7 electors. The District of Columbia has 3 electors. The Electoral College is made up of 538 electors, each with one vote.

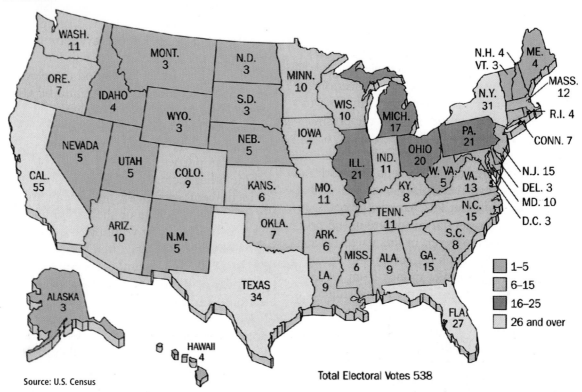

WASH. 11
MONT. 3
N.D. 3
MINN. 10
N.H. 4
VT. 3
ME. 4
ORE. 7
IDAHO 4
S.D. 3
WIS. 10
N.Y. 31
MASS. 12
R.I. 4
WYO. 3
IOWA 7
MICH. 17
PA. 21
CONN. 7
NEVADA 5
NEB. 5
ILL. 21
IND. 11
OHIO 20
W. VA. 5
VA. 13
N.J. 15
DEL. 3
MD. 10
D.C. 3
UTAH 5
COLO. 9
KANS. 6
MO. 11
KY. 8
CAL. 55
N.C. 15
ARIZ. 10
N.M. 5
OKLA. 7
TENN. 11
S.C. 8
ARK. 6
MISS. 6
ALA. 9
GA. 15
ALASKA 3
TEXAS 34
LA. 9
FLA. 27
HAWAII 4

1–5
6–15
16–25
26 and over

Source: U.S. Census

Total Electoral Votes 538

 The larger a state's population, the more electoral votes it has. **Place Which state has the most electoral votes?**

Before the presidential election, each political party in every state draws up a list of electors who promise to vote for the party's presidential candidate. In other words, each candidate has a "team" of electors in every state. On election day, when you vote for a certain candidate, you are really voting for that candidate's team of electors.

On election night, the whole nation waits to find out which states each candidate has "won." "Winning" or "carrying" a state, means that a candidate's whole team of electors has won in that state. That winning team then has the right to cast their electoral votes in the Electoral College.

A few weeks after the election, the official electoral voting takes place in each state.

An elector is not required by law to vote for the candidate to whom he or she is pledged, but nearly all do. The votes are then counted in Congress. To win, a candidate needs an absolute majority of electoral votes—270 or more.

Over the years, many people have charged that the "winner-take-all" method of awarding electoral votes from each state is not fair. They point out that candidates have gotten less than a majority of the votes nationwide but, by winning enough large states, have still been elected President. In 2000, for example, Al Gore received over 500,000 more popular votes than George W. Bush, but Bush was elected President with 271 electoral votes to Gore's 267. In most cases, however, the person who gets the majority of popular votes also gets the majority of electoral votes.

The drama of the 2000 election made many American political leaders question whether the Electoral College system is worth keeping, however. It is likely that Congress will continue to examine and debate methods of improving our electoral system.

Choosing a President every four years is an important process in our democracy. Citizen participation, however, is just as necessary in other elections, including those in states, counties, cities, and towns. Only by voting can Americans claim to live in a country where the government truly represents the will of the people.

Section 3 Assessment

1. **Define** incumbent
2. Who is in charge of the overall organization of a presidential candidate's election campaign?
3. Where do presidential candidates get most of their campaign money for the general election?
4. What is one advantage an incumbent has in an election?
5. Explain how presidential candidates win electoral votes.
6. **Evaluate** Do you think campaigns should be paid for entirely with public funds? Explain.

Extending the Chapter

Historical Views

Not only was the 2000 presidential election one of the closest elections in history, it was also the first election in which the U.S. Supreme Court made a decision that affected the outcome. The election was so close that the two major-party candidates, George W. Bush and Al Gore, needed to win the electoral votes in Florida in order to win the majority of the nation's electoral votes and the presidency. The vote totals in Florida were so close that precise counting was needed to find out who really got the most votes.

To complicate matters further, it turned out that many of the votes cast were not counted. All sorts of complaints arose including confusing ballots, inaccurate counting methods, and racial discrimination at the polling places.

The Florida counts indicated that Bush had a slight lead over Gore. But Gore and his supporters argued that the count was too close and the number of miscounted ballots were too great to declare the winner without a more accurate recount. They asked that the ballots be counted by hand.

Because elections are handled by each state, Florida officials were called on to decide whether there should be a recount. Florida's Secretary of State, Republican Katherine Harris, presided over the election results and declared that a recount by hand was unnecessary. Gore fought this decision by addressing the Florida State Supreme Court. The Florida court stated that the hand recount should occur.

In response, George W. Bush went to the United States Supreme Court to have this decision overturned. He argued that the Florida Supreme Court decision was illegal and that hand counts were less accurate than machine counts.

The Court was split 5–4, but the final decision was to stop the recount. The ruling was disappointing to some because it suggested that Supreme Court justices may rule in favor of a party, rather than according to the law.

Because of the U.S. Supreme Court decision, there was no official recount. Bush was declared the winner of the election soon after.

How to MAKE AN ACTION PLAN

Remember your first day at school? Maybe you were worried about not being able to find your way around. Perhaps you set yourself a goal: "I am going to make sure that I don't get lost." However, a goal will not do you much good unless you take steps to make sure you reach it. In decision making, you need to plan how to reach your goal, and then you must carry out that plan.

For carrying out everyday decisions, such as doing what you decided to do first after you get home from school, you can make a quick plan in your head. However, more difficult action plans often involve writing down the steps you must take to reach your goal. In previous lessons, you have concentrated on how to set a goal and how to choose from a number of options. In this lesson you can take a closer look at what to do after you have chosen an option.

Explain the Skill

The following guidelines can help you make a plan for carrying out a decision. Notice how the guidelines would apply if you decided to try to get elected to your school's student council.

1. **State your action goal.** Your action goal is to carry out the decision you just made. [If your decision was to run for student council, your action goal now is to get elected.]

2. **Identify resources (what will help you) and obstacles (what you will have to overcome).** Knowing what you can use and what problems you might face will help you decide what has to be done. Be sure to check the accuracy of any information you gather about possible resources and obstacles. [One resource, or strength, might be that most students in your class know you well. Being a member of some school clubs might also help you gather voter support. Some possible obstacles are not being well-known outside of your class or running against a former student council member. What other resources and obstacles can you think of?]

3. **List what you have to do to achieve your goal. Think about what needs to be done, who will do it, and when it will be done.** [As a student council candidate, you might list such tasks as thinking up campaign slogans and making posters. What are some other tasks involved in a campaign? In what order would the campaign tasks need to be done?]

4. **As you carry out your plan, check how well it is working and change it if necessary.** Make sure that what you planned to do is getting done. Check each item on your schedule to make sure it is getting done well and on time. Identify any problems with the plan, as well as any new resources and obstacles. Then make changes in your plan if necessary. [You and the friends helping you might use checklists, staff meetings, and opinion polls to keep track of the campaign's progress. Perhaps you might change your plan to account for new resources, such as more students volunteering to help, or new obstacles, such as a popular student entering the race.]

5. **Judge how well your plan worked.** Identify the results of what you did, including any unexpected results. Determine what you might do differently if you found yourself in a similar situation in the future. [After a campaign you might find out that posters with both your name and a campaign slogan on them were more effective than posters with just your name. Therefore, in any future campaign you might include slogans on all posters.]

Action Goal:	To get elected to the student council				
Resources I Have:	I am well-known within my class. My friend Jim will help.				
Resources I Need:	more volunteer campaign workers, poster materials (paper, cardboard, paint, brushes)				

Obstacles: 1. not well known outside of class 2. running against former council member	Ways to Overcome Obstacles: 1. have friends introduce me to other students 2. campaign theme: "new member—new ideas"

What to Do?	Who Does It?	By When?	Checked	Did it Work?
1. Recruit 10 volunteers	Jim and I	9/20	☑ (9/18)	Yes
2. Schedule staff meeting	Jim and I	9/25	☑ (9/24)	Yes
3. Campaign slogans	campaign staff	9/28	☑ (9/28)	Yes
4. Posters	campaign staff	9/30	☑ (10/1)	No

Analyze the Skill

Suppose there is a large open area near your school. Over the years, people have made it an unofficial park. You learn that the city council will vote next week on a plan to build houses there. You and your friends want to keep the land as a park. After considering many ways to do this, you decide to launch a campaign to make the area an official city park.

Now it is time to take action. What will you do to carry out this decision? Use a chart like the one above to make an action plan for saving the park.

Skill Assessment

After you have completed your action plan, answer the following questions.

1. What was your action goal?
2. What resources did you identify that might help you achieve your goal? How did you plan to make use of those resources?
3. What were some obstacles that you expected? How did you plan to overcome them?
4. In what order did you put the steps of your plan? Explain why.
5. Pick three steps you listed and explain why each was important. Tell how you and your friends would complete each step.
6. What would be some good ways of checking how your plan was working? Explain.
7. Suppose the proposal was changed so that a youth recreation center would be built in addition to houses. Would you stay with your plan, change it, or drop it? Explain.
8. Why are planning and taking action important parts of decision making?
9. How would you explain the process of making and carrying out a plan to a seventh-grade student?
10. Think of a decision you have made recently. How close did you come to your goal? What happened that you had not planned on and how did you deal with it? What would you do in a similar situation in the future?

How to **INTERPRET OPINION POLLS**

 Use the *Simulations and Data Graphing* CD-ROM to create and interpret graphs.

As you read in this chapter, public opinion polls play an important role in our election process. During election campaigns, one common opinion poll question is: "If the election were held today, which candidate would you support?" These polls give both candidates and voters an idea of who is most likely to win an election.

Explain the Skill

The chart on this page shows the results of another common poll question: "What do you think is the biggest problem facing our nation today?" Can you see why these poll results might be very valuable to a person running for government office? They help the candidate understand what the public is thinking. With this information, a candidate might choose to emphasize policies that address the problems about which voters are most concerned.

Analyze the Skill

The two public opinion polls shown here were conducted in 1997 and 2000. Problems are listed in the left-hand column. The percentage of people who thought that problem was the most important one facing our country is shown in the right-hand columns. In 1997, for example, six percent of the public considered taxes to be the nation's biggest problem. That number fell to four percent in 2000.

Not everyone polled named one of the problems shown here. Some named other problems, including health care,

What is the most important problem facing our nation today?		
	1997	2000
Moral/family decline	11%	12%
Crime/violence	16%	9%
Education	12%	17%
Poverty/homelessness	14%	6%
Drug abuse	12%	5%
Economy	8%	8%
Unemployment	8%	3%
Taxes	6%	4%
Federal budget deficit	5%	1%
Environment	3%	3%

international issues, welfare, and racism. Why did people come up with such a wide variety of responses? One answer is that when the economy is strong, as it was in the late 1990s, people tend to focus on non-economic problems. In 1992, by contrast, when the economy was in a recession, over fifty percent of the public listed "the economy" as the nation's biggest problem.

Skill Assessment

1. What percentage of people polled in 1997 felt that crime and violence was the most important problem facing our society? Did that figure change in 2000?
2. Suppose you were a candidate for the Senate. Based on the results of these polls, what issues would you emphasize in your campaign? Explain your answer.
3. If a poll taker asked you to name the most important problem facing our nation, what would you say? Would you choose one of the problems shown on this chart, or would you name a different problem? Explain your choice.

CHAPTER 22 ASSESSMENT

Building Civics Vocabulary

The vocabulary terms in each pair listed below are related to each other. For each pair, explain how the two terms are related.

1. *general election* and *registration*
2. *media* and *direct mail*
3. *propaganda* and *bias*

Reviewing Main Ideas and Skills

4. Why was voter registration introduced in the United States?
5. Why does PAC involvement in elections worry some people?
6. Describe the job of a campaign manager.
7. Why is it important for a candidate to have the media on hand when he or she is "making news"?
8. Why were laws passed that limit the amount of money that can be given to candidates running for federal office?
9. **How to Make an Action Plan** What is one goal you have for this school year? What steps will you take to reach this goal?
10. **How to Interpret Opinion Polls** Look back at the poll results shown on page 492. From 1997 to 2000, which problems had the largest increase in concern? Which had the largest decrease?

Critical Thinking

11. **Applying Information** What is one reason that people sometimes give for not voting? If you met someone who felt this way, what would you say to convince him or her that voting is important?

12. **Linking Past and Present** What are some ways that television has changed elections in the United States? Do you think television has a positive or negative impact on elections? Explain.

Writing About Civics

13. **Writing a Political Advertisement** Suppose you were running for public office. Write a radio advertisement designed to increase support for your campaign. Use at least two of the propaganda techniques shown on the chart on page 481.

Citizenship Activities

14. **Working Together** With a group, conduct an opinion poll among the students in your school to discover what they think about an issue affecting your school or community. Make a chart displaying your poll results. Present your charts to your class and explain what you learned from your poll.

 Take It to the NET

Access the **Civics: Participating in Government** Internet site at **www.phschool.com** for the specific URLs to complete the activity.

Explore online information about one of the interest groups that is currently involved in politics. What kinds of changes does this group want to bring about? How effective has the group been in its efforts? Provide a summary of your findings to the class. Include your opinion on how necessary interest groups are to our government today.

Confronting Society's Problems

Citizenship and You

The year: 1633. The place: Dorchester, Massachusetts, now part of Boston. The trouble: cows and goats had broken through the fences and were wrecking the village green.

John Maverick, a Dorchester minister, began to worry that the village green would be destroyed. He knew that he could not take care of the matter by himself. Furthermore, in 1633 Dorchester had no local government, no elected or appointed government officers to turn to. John Maverick decided to put the problem to members of the community. He asked them to come together to talk about it.

When the citizens of Dorchester met to discuss the problem of their village green, they were holding one of our country's first town meetings. Then, as today, citizens agreed to talk with one another and work together to solve shared problems.

Keep It Current

Items marked with this logo are periodically updated on the Internet. To keep up-to-date, go to **www.phschool.com**

What's Ahead in Chapter 23

Every society faces problems. In this chapter you will take a close look at two problems facing American society today—the rising cost of health care and the problem of how to dispose of trash from households and industries. By looking at these problems and how people are trying to solve them, you will get a better idea of the role citizens play in our democracy. You will see that even while we debate the actions government should take, we can find ways to make a difference as individuals.

Section 1   **Problems and Public Issues**

Section 2   **The Future of Health Care: An Issue for All Americans**

Section 3   **Waste: Managing Our Garbage and Trash**

Citizen's Journal

Suppose you were at the town meeting in Dorchester in 1633. How would you propose solving the problem of cows and goats on the village green?

Problems and Public Issues

SECTION PREVIEW

Objectives
- Identify the difference between private and public problems.
- Explain how issues arise when people try to solve problems.
- Explore ways that people attempt to solve public problems.

Building Civics Vocabulary
- An **issue** is a point of conflict or a matter to be debated.
- Government response to public issues is known as **public policy**.

 **Focus**

You have learned about the formal institutions in American politics—political parties, campaigns, and elections. Through these institutions we choose the people who speak for us in government. Some citizens think that once they have voted, they are "off the hook" and do not have to deal with the problems of society.

Just electing someone to public office, however, does not allow citizens to give up their responsibility to care, to be informed, and to face problems. As citizens, it is our right to call attention to problems that we see around us. It is also our duty as citizens in a democracy to take part in finding solutions.

Private or Public Problems?

What is a problem? It is an event or situation that troubles someone. A problem causes a person, or people, to feel uncom-

fortable or uncertain and to look for a solution. Here are three examples:

- You have homework due tomorrow and your favorite TV show is on tonight.

- Teachers at a local school say that too many students are wearing sloppy clothes to school.

- Automobile drivers age 16 to 21 have a much higher accident rate than do other groups of drivers.

What is your reaction to these situations? Would any of them trouble you? Why or why not?

The first situation might be troubling for you alone. In this sense, it is a private problem. You are the person who must decide to do or not do your homework. You must decide to watch or not watch the TV show. You make your decisions based on what you think is more important.

The second and third situations affect many people. Therefore, they are public—or social—problems. In these cases, people are troubled, annoyed, or upset by the situation. The teachers think that sloppy dress gets in the way of learning. People fear that young drivers make the roads unsafe.

A situation becomes a problem when it does not "fit" with a person's values. If the situation does not fit the accepted values of the community, it is a social problem. If enough people believe a situation needs to change, they will begin to take action.

How Issues Arise

Many people may agree that a certain situation is a problem. However, once someone offers a solution, people may not agree about whether it is a good—or the best—solution. Then issues arise. An issue is a point of conflict or a matter to be debated. Think about the issues that might arise from the following proposals.

Homelessness is a major problem in many American cities.

- To solve the problem of sloppy dress, the school district ought to make a rule that students must wear uniforms.

- To cut the accident rate of teenage drivers, all cars driven by this age group should have a mechanical device which limits speed to 55 mph.

What do you think about these proposals? Would you support or oppose them? What reasons would you give for your opinion?

Each proposed solution raises issues. The issues come up because people's values are different. Notice the key words *ought* and *should*. Those words are a sign that values are involved. In the first proposal, being neat is given a high value. Neatness becomes an issue, or point of conflict, when someone else gives a higher value to people's freedom to dress as they wish. In the

second proposal, equal treatment of all drivers is given a lower value than safety.

When people ask government to help solve a problem, the issues that arise are known as public issues. In the first case, the principal might ask the school board to make a rule that students must wear uniforms. In the second case, the state legislature might consider a bill to put speed-limiting devices on cars driven by young people.

Once government action is called for as part of a solution to a public problem, the issues then become the subject of public debate. Government response to public issues is known as public policy.

Issues and Choices

Each proposal on this page presents just one solution. Of course, social problems often

Teens Join to Fight Child Labor

Dianna English is speaking from experience when she says "kids are powerful and kids can do incredible things."

When she was thirteen, this Connecticut high school student first learned about Free the Children—a youth-run organization dedicated to ending child labor and protecting the rights of children worldwide. She started a chapter at her school and soon became one of the organization's most active members.

As head of the Windham High School chapter of Free the Children in 1999, Dianna gave speeches at schools around the nation, raising awareness of the child labor problem and inspiring other students to get involved in the search for solutions. She also lobbied Congress in support of the United Nations Convention on the Rights of Children.

Free the Children was founded in 1995 by Craig Kielburger, a student from Toronto, Canada. When he was 12 years old, Craig read a newspaper article about a 5-year-old Pakistani child who was forced to work at a rug factory. The story shocked Craig and he decided to take action.

Craig convinced friends and classmates to help him

form an organization to fight child labor. Free the Children now has over 5,000 members, with chapters in 20 countries. In addition to pressuring businesses and governments to oppose child labor, Free the Children has raised hundreds of thousands of dollars for the construction of schools in poor communities.

His experience with Free the Children has convinced Craig that young people can change the world. "We have proved the critics wrong," he says, "when they say the young aren't old enough, capable enough or smart enough to bring about change or to have a voice in society."

Active Citizenship

Does the work of Free the Children support Dianna's claim that "kids are powerful and kids can do incredible things"? Explain.

---

have more than one possible solution. Public debate over a given problem involves looking at several possibilities. In making public policy, government officials must make choices and trade-offs. You, too, must make choices when you are deciding which solution to support.

Take, for example, two other possible solutions to the accident rate problem:

- Raise the minimum age of drivers to 21.

- Take away the licenses of young drivers who are in accidents. Do not allow them to drive until age 21.

What conflicts of values might come up when citizens debate these possible solutions?

Raising the driving age may seem to be a simple solution, and it might satisfy people who want to see equal treatment for all drivers. However, is this policy fair to careful young drivers who are unlikely to cause an accident? Does it cause unfair hardship to youths who need to drive in order to get to school or to work?

In the case of the other solution, taking away a driver's license no matter who caused the accident may make young drivers more careful, but does the policy treat people equally? Would it be fair if you lost your license because someone else rear-ended your car?

Think about the three possible solutions to the accident rate problem. Which solution do you favor? What values influenced your decision? Can you think of any better solutions?

In the rest of this chapter you will be reading about two public problems. Ask yourself the following questions about each of the problems:

- What makes each situation a public problem? Who is troubled or upset? Why?

- What issues arise from proposed solutions to the problem? In other words, why do people disagree? What values are involved?

- Do you favor some solutions over others? Why?

These questions will help you to understand the problem and why people do not agree on how to solve it.

Also keep in mind how you might help solve each problem. Chapter 3 presented the idea that in our democracy, the office of citizen is the highest office in the land. In holding this office, American citizens are never "off the hook" when it comes to governing themselves.

Solving public problems requires the effort of the people we elect to public office. It

As American cities and their surrounding areas continue to grow, traffic becomes a more and more pressing problem.

also requires that individual citizens take responsibility. The key to finding and carrying out solutions to the public problems that face us lies in government, community, and individuals working together.

Section 1 Assessment

1. **Define** issue, public policy
2. How does a situation become a problem?
3. Why do issues come up when people are trying to solve problems?
4. What process is involved in solving a public problem?
5. **Apply** Tell about a private problem and a public problem that you are aware of. What makes them problems?

The Future of Health Care: An Issue for All Americans

SECTION PREVIEW

Objectives

- Explain why rising health care costs are a concern for all Americans.
- Explore the public policy issues behind the health care debate.
- Describe ways that individuals are helping to improve health care in their communities.

 Focus

When he was in his early twenties, Matthew Scott lost his left hand in a fireworks accident. Fourteen years later, he made medical history. In an operation lasting over fourteen hours, doctors in Louisville, Kentucky performed hand transplant surgery on Scott. That spring, Scott used his new hand to throw out the ceremonial first ball at a baseball game between the Philadelphia Phillies and the Atlanta Braves.

As this example illustrates, the United States is a world leader in cutting-edge medical techniques. Thanks largely to advances in the quality of health care in this country, average life expectancy for Americans rose from 63 years in 1940 to 77 years by the end of the twentieth century. As the quality of health care has risen, however, so have the costs.

On average, Americans spend about twice as much on health care as Europeans. Out of every $100 spent in the United States today, over $13 goes to health care. Americans now spend more than $1 trillion each year on health care, and the govern-ment estimates that this figure will double to $2.2 trillion by the year 2008.

Why have health care costs risen so rapidly in recent decades? One reason, as you read in Chapter 1, is that our population is getting older. People over the age of 65 require four times the health care services of people under 65. Another cause is the increasing use of computers, lasers, and other high tech medical equipment. These technologies have led to an increase in life expectancy, but they are often very expensive. In addition, treatment of relatively new diseases, especially acquired immune deficiency syndrome, or AIDS, has been very costly.

The Problem

You may not think of rising health care costs as an issue that affects your life right now. But everyone needs medical care sooner or later, and rising costs may mean that some people will not have access to quality care when they need it. In addition, rising costs can have a negative effect on our economy. Consider this example. Automobile maker General Motors reports that it charges an additional $1,500 per vehicle to cover the costs of health care for its employees and their families. For automobile makers in Japan, the figure is approximately $700 per vehicle. You can see why rising health care costs are a cause of concern for many American companies.

Americans Without Insurance As you read in Chapter 17, if faced with a medical emergency, the average American worker would find it almost impossible to pay the bills for doctors, hospitals, and medicine out of his or her salary alone. This is why many people consider health insurance a necessity. Health insurance policies allow people to set aside money from current income to cover the costs of medical care they may need in the future. As health care costs have skyrocketed, however, so has the cost of health insurance.

INSURED AND UNINSURED AMERICANS, 2000

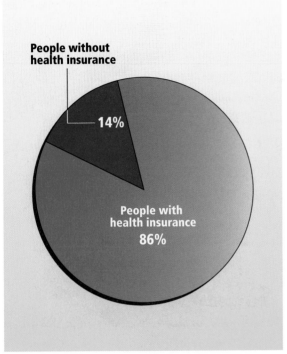

People without health insurance

14%

People with health insurance
86%

Source: Bureau of Labor Statistics and the Bureau of the Census

A 2000 government report found that 38.7 million Americans had no health insurance. **Economics What percentage of people had health insurance in 2000?**

Millions of Americans get health insurance through their jobs. Government programs provide health insurance to millions more—Medicaid offers insurance to many who cannot afford it; Medicare assists senior citizens with their health care bills. But what about the people who do not get health care through their jobs, yet do not qualify for government assistance? Many people in this category cannot afford to buy health insurance privately and are uninsured.

In 1999, the United States Census Bureau released a report stating that over 42 million Americans were without health insurance.

According to the report, people most likely to lack health insurance included young adults in the 18–24 age range and people who work part-time. When people don't have health insurance, they may not have access to high-quality medical care when faced with medical emergencies or life-threatening illnesses. This is one of the most serious problems resulting from the rising cost of health care.

Government Spending Another problem is the added strain rising heath care costs put on government budgets. The federal government spent over $300 billion on health care programs such as Medicare in 1999. That figure was expected to rise to well over $400 billion by the year 2004.

As you read in Chapter 16, the federal government struggled with annual budget deficits during most of the second half of the twentieth century. While the government was able to balance its budget in 1999 and 2000, rising health care costs could threaten this balance in the coming years.

Controlling Insurance Costs Rising health care costs have also affected the millions of Americans who get health insurance through their jobs or who purchase their own health insurance policies. Rising costs have affected both the cost and the quality of health insurance in the United States.

Until the early 1990s, nearly all health insurance policies were traditional "fee-for-service" policies. Under this system, when people needed medical attention, they went to doctors or hospitals of their choice, and then submitted their medical bills to their health insurance company for payment. As doctors' fees and the cost of medical procedures and medication rose, the cost of traditional health insurance soared—rising over 13 percent a year between 1988 and 1992. Many people could no longer afford health insurance. Companies were less likely to offer

This quilt bearing the names of more than 1,900 people who have died of AIDS was unfurled in Washington, D.C., in 1987. Treatment of AIDS has contributed to the rise in health care costs.

health insurance as a benefit to their employees. In response to this growing crisis, many people began turning to a new type of health insurance, known as "managed-care."

Have you heard the term HMO? A health maintenance organization (HMO) is the most common type of managed-care insurance company. When you join an HMO, you get all your medical care from a group of doctors, hospitals, and other medical care providers that work for the HMO. The HMO works to control the costs of medical care. Like any big business, HMOs have the ability to bargain for lower prices from suppliers, such as doctors and drug companies.

Proponents of managed-care say that it has been a success. By 1999, more than 100 million Americans got their health insurance from managed-care companies. Managed-care was given credit for slowing the growth of health insurance costs to an average of about 6 percent a year from 1993 to 1998.

Opponents say that managed-care companies have decreased the quality of medical care. Many people feel that HMOs and other managed-care plans force them to give up some of their freedom to choose their own doctors and treatments. Insurance companies, they argue, care more about profits than they do about providing quality medical care.

The Public Policy Issues

When it comes to public debate on health care, most Americans can agree on a few things. Costs continue to rise. Many people remain uninsured. Managed-care health plans generate a great deal of criticism. A 1999 poll found that 59 percent of Americans felt that the nation's health care system needs "major changes." Another 36 percent said it needs "minor changes." Only 3 percent of the people said they were "satisfied with the system the way it is." When it comes to finding specific solutions, however, there is much less agreement.

Attempts at Reform When President Bill Clinton took office in 1993, one of his major objectives was to reform the health care system in the United States. Clinton proposed a national health plan designed to guarantee basic health insurance coverage to all Americans. Under this plan, businesses would have been required to purchase insurance for their employees from a pool of managed-care insurance companies. The government would have provided coverage for anyone not covered through work. The plan never gained widespread support, largely because many people were concerned it would be extremely expensive, leading to tax increases.

Another common proposal is that the United States should adopt a government-sponsored health care system like the one in place in Canada. Under the system Canadians call "Medicare," the government uses tax dollars to provide health insurance to all its citizens. Bills to create a similar system in the United States have been introduced in Congress several times. Senator Paul Wellstone of Minnesota, for example, introduced the American Health Security Act in the 104th Congress. Under Wellstone's plan, the government would pay for health care services for all citizens and legal residents. An income tax increase would help finance the program. To justify the tax increase, Wellstone argued that health care is like education—it is a basic right to which all Americans are entitled.

Wellstone's bill, and most similar proposals, have consistently met with strong opposition from Congress and the public. People are worried about the high price tag. Government-sponsored health care would require tax increases, which take money from people's paychecks—and could hurt the economy. In addition, opponents argue, a government-run heath system would reduce our personal freedom by taking health care decisions away from individuals and giving them to the government.

The Debate Continues In his 1995 State of the Union Address, President Clinton talked about the difficulties of reaching agreement on a single plan that would solve all the problems in the nation's health care system. He told Congress: "Now, last year, we almost came to blows over health care…We bit off more than we could chew. So I'm asking you that we work together. Let's do it step by

Activists around the country have organized to support health care reform.

The American population may be getting older, but it is not slowing down. In 1998, Senator John Glenn, the first U.S. astronaut to orbit the earth, returned to space at age 77.

step." Reflecting this philosophy, health care reform efforts since 1995 have focused mainly on the two questions discussed below.

1. *How can we improve managed-care?* In the late 1990s, the public began putting pressure on Congress to pass a "patients' bill of rights"—legislation that would address some of the most common complaints about managed-care. People wanted their HMOs to guarantee payment for emergency care and they wanted greater access to doctors of their choice. Many also wanted the right to sue their HMOs if they felt the insurance company had prevented them from receiving medical care that they needed. While

Congress considered these issues, over 20 state legislatures passed laws protecting patients' rights.

2. *How can we extend coverage to the millions of uninsured Americans?* As you read above, the Census Bureau reported that more than 42 million Americans—about 16 percent of the population—lacked health insurance in 1999. Perhaps the most alarming finding in the report was that over 10 million children under the age of 18 were uninsured. Efforts are being made to combat this problem. In 1997, Congress created the Children's Health Insurance Programs, known as CHIP. The goal of CHIP is to provide health insurance to uninsured children. By mid-2000, over 2 million previously uninsured children were enrolled in CHIP health care programs. The government is also seeking ways to extend quality health care coverage to more low-income families and older Americans.

Making a Difference

You have seen that rising health care costs have created some major public policy issues. What can be done to control the rising costs of health care and health insurance? How can health insurance plans better meet the needs of all Americans? What, if anything, should the government do about people who cannot afford health insurance? While citizens and government officials study and debate these questions, Americans are not simply waiting for solutions. Every day, people in thousands of communities around the nation are taking action on their own.

Many communities, for example, have established health care clinics that provide services to people who cannot afford health insurance. In downtown Kansas City, Missouri, the Kansas City Free Health Clinic provides free health care to city residents. The clinic's mission is to "promote health and wellness by providing quality services, at no charge, to people without access to basic care." The clinic is run with the help of over 400 local volunteers. Volunteering at a clinic or hospital is one way many people get involved in meeting the health care needs of their fellow citizens.

As another example of how one person can made a difference, consider the story of Ganga Stone. While doing volunteer work with AIDS patients in New York City in 1985, Stone realized that many adults and children living with AIDS were having difficulty shopping and cooking for themselves. Stone decided to take action. She called restaurants around the city and convinced them to donate nutritious meals. She picked up the meals and delivered them by bicycle to the homes of people in need of food. The program, named God's Love We Deliver, grew quickly. By 1999, hundreds of volunteers were working to cook and deliver thousands of meals every day—free of charge—to people in need living with AIDS.

As you have seen, on both a local and national level, heath care is one of the issues that has the greatest impact on the quality of life in the United States. How can we improve our nation's health care system in the twenty-first century? As young Americans, you will play an important role in finding answers to this question.

Section 2 Assessment

1. What are two effects of rising health care costs in the United States?
2. What is the goal of the CHIP program?
3. What are some ways that people can make a difference in the field of health care?
4. **Evaluate** "The United States should adopt a government-run health care system, similar to the one in Canada." Do you agree or disagree? Explain.

Waste: Managing Our Garbage and Trash

SECTION PREVIEW

Objectives
- Explain why the problem of waste is both a space and a people problem.
- Identify issues that have arisen from proposed solutions to our waste problem.
- Describe ways that people can make a difference in solving the problem of waste.

 Focus

Several years ago, a barge left Islip, New York, loaded with more than 3,000 tons of garbage and trash. For almost two months the huge barge traveled along the eastern coast of the United States, but no state would allow it to unload. Neither would Mexico, Belize, nor the Bahamas.

Finally, the barge returned to Islip, swarming with flies and smelling rotten. After much bargaining, the garbage was finally burned over a period of twelve days in Brooklyn, New York.

Why was garbage sent to sea, only to come home to be burned? This story illustrates a situation facing Americans today—what to do with the huge amounts of garbage we produce.

Each day, the average American throws away more than four pounds of trash and garbage. This amounts to tons of trash and garbage per person over an average lifetime. Where does this waste all go? Most of us stuff our trash into plastic bags that we put out on the curb. From time to time, a truck comes by to collect the bags. As the truck

Much of the trash in American landfill sites consists of materials that could be recycled.

drives away, a large metal blade compacts the bags into small bale-like chunks. Our trash and garbage are out of sight—and out of mind. So what is the problem?

The Problem

Technically, garbage is kitchen waste. Trash is all other household waste, from gum wrappers to disposable diapers. Both terms, *garbage* and *trash,* are commonly used for all kinds of household waste. No matter what you call such waste, the problem of how to dispose of it is becoming staggering.

A Space Problem Every year, United States households throw away nearly 200 million tons of trash and garbage—enough to cover the state of Rhode Island with six inches of waste each year. Much of our trash, especially plastics, is not biodegradable, which means that over time it does not break down into natural substances. Such items do not just go away. They can last for hundreds of years.

For much of its history, the United States did not have to worry about what to do with its waste. Our country had a small population and lots of empty space. There was always plenty of extra land where waste could be put. Today, we do not have such new frontiers. Yet over 55 percent of our trash and garbage is still put in landfill sites, commonly called dumps. Using dumps has been inexpensive, and people have become used to paying very little for waste disposal.

Dumps across the nation are filling up, though. The number of operating landfill sites in the United States fell from 20,000 in 1977 to just over 5,000 by the end of 1998. Many of the sites closed because they reached full capacity, others because they failed to meet environmental regulations. Few new landfills are planned because finding space is getting more difficult. Most of the good landfill sites near cities have already been used. Many cities now have to send their trash to other areas, which increases the cost of trash disposal.

A People Problem The problem of waste in the United States is as much a people problem as it is a space problem. Not only does our population continue to grow, but many Americans have a "purchase-consume-dispose" way of looking at things. We often value convenience more highly than the safety of the environment, which can seem far away from our daily lives. Think of a fast-food restaurant, for example. The package your food comes in goes from counter to table to trash in a matter of minutes.

Another people-related problem is called the NIMBY attitude. NIMBY stands for Not in My Back Yard. People want to continue to pay low rates for trash collection. They also want to buy products in handy packages. However, when a city proposes opening a new dump site, the people who live in that area storm city hall in protest. They do not want the dump near where they live.

The same NIMBY attitude has kept cities from building new kinds of waste disposal plants, such as large incinerators to burn trash. The NIMBY view was largely responsible for keeping the Islip garbage barge from dumping its load.

The Public Policy Issues

As you have seen, the "frontier days" of being able just to toss things away are over. Local authorities, environmental experts, and concerned citizens agree that managing waste is becoming a crisis situation. Public issues center around three kinds of proposals: (1) recycling waste, (2) reducing the amounts of waste we put out, and (3) finding alternative means of disposal.

PER-PERSON, PER-DAY HOUSEHOLD WASTE Here is how Americans compare with citizens of some other countries in the amount of waste they generate. **Economics** Approximately how many pounds of waste does the average Japanese citizen produce each day?

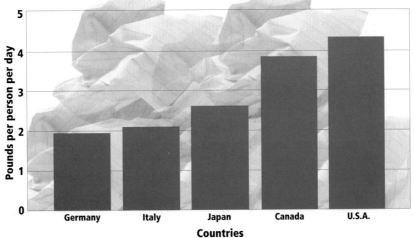

Source: Environmental Protection Agency

WHAT HAPPENS TO RECYCLED TRASH This chart shows some of the products that can be made from recycled materials. **Science and Technology Which recycled material can be used to pave streets?**

Plastic

- **Paintbrush bristles**
- **Filling in jackets and pillows**
- **Flowerpots**
- **Fences and boat docks**
- **Plastic strapping for shipping boxes**

Glass

- **Bottles (90%)**
- **"Glasphalt" used in street paving**

Paper

- **Corrugated boxes**
- **Copier paper**
- **Paper towels**
- **Napkins**

Aluminum

- **New cans (almost 100%)**

Recycling Waste Recycling, or returning trash to a form that can be used again, can help cut down the waste problem. The United States recycled 28 percent of its solid waste in 2001—up from just 6 percent in 1960 and 16 percent in 1990. In spite of this improvement, overall recycling rates in the United States are still considerably lower than they are in Japan and many European nations.

The major recycling issue is freedom of choice. Should states or local communities— and perhaps the federal government—pass laws that require recycling, or should individuals and businesses be free to choose whether or not they will recycle?

People who support recycling believe that the only way to solve the waste problem is for government to get involved. In some towns, there are laws that require people to recycle. People who do not must pay high fines. Other towns have raised the fee charged for garbage pick up. The idea is that if people must pay more, they are likely to try to cut down on the amount of their waste.

People against recycling laws claim that waste disposal is a matter of choice and should not be regulated. They believe that government should not get involved in ways that limit people's freedom and affect their daily habits.

Although some people think that recycling laws are the only way to make real progress in solving the waste problem, other solutions have helped, too. Many states now have deposit laws under which people get money back when they return used glass bottles and aluminum cans. Some states provide funds to help cities set up recycling programs. Further, many people are starting new businesses that are beginning to earn profits by recycling glass, metals, and tires.

Reducing Waste A major cause of the waste problem is packaging. In the United States, packaging accounts for about one third of the weight of trash and one half of the volume. The packaging we throw away amounts to about 600 pounds per person per year. New technology is producing new packaging that is not biodegradable and cannot be recycled. Some packages keep products safe and fresh for consumers. In other cases, however, packaging is merely used to attract the attention of consumers.

Adding to the difficulty of reducing waste is our desire for convenience. It seems so much easier to use disposable diapers, disposable razors, and cheap ball-point pens than to wash diapers and buy razor blades and pen refills. Until recently, few consumers have thought about the effects of such convenience on our waste problem.

When it comes to reducing waste, free enterprise is a major issue. Should government be able to decide what products a business can make or how much and what kind of packaging it can use? For example, should government make a law that all packaging materials must be biodegradable?

Some businesses argue that such a law would raise their costs, and then they would have to raise the prices of their goods. Another argument is that in a market economy, businesses respond to what consumers want. If consumers want disposable goods and fancy packages, businesses must make them or lose out on sales.

Alternative Means of Disposal As individuals and government are debating ways to cut down on the amount of waste, they are also looking for new means of waste disposal. One way is through waste-to-energy plants that burn garbage to produce electricity or steam. In the United States, 17 percent of all household waste is burned.

These plants are attractive to governments of large cities, where the dump shortage is at a crisis stage. However, the cost of building and running these plants is very high, and citizens are not eager to pay for them.

Public health and safety are also major issues in waste-to-energy plant development. Should communities go ahead and build plants in the face of possible health and safety hazards? Such plants can cut down on the amount of waste by 90 percent. However, some people worry that burning waste can create dioxins. Dioxins are chemicals that weaken the body's power to fight off sickness, increasing the chance of getting cancer. Critics also warn that the ash left over from burning is often poisonous and needs to be carefully disposed of so that it does not leak into water systems.

When people discuss a public problem like waste disposal, the solution almost always involves a trade-off. Is a proposed solution good enough, or will it create more problems than it solves?

Facts & Quotes

Litter's Life Span
Did you ever wonder what happens to trash left lying on the ground? Here is how long it takes for some common trash items to decompose.

- Paper — 2-4 weeks
- Cotton rags — 1-5 months
- Orange Peels — 6 months
- Cigarette butts — 10-12 years
- Plastic bags — 10-20 years
- Leather shoes — 25-40 years
- Aluminum cans — 200-500 years

Paper, cardboard, and other materials are being recycled at this facility in Seattle, which has one of the nation's most successful city-run recycling programs.

Making a Difference

Government has always played a major role in waste disposal in the United States. However, while we are debating what further action government should take, citizens—on their own and working together—have already begun to make a difference in solving this nationwide problem.

Schools have put on recycling and cleanup programs. These programs have not only cut down on waste. They have also taught students about their duties. Students who have taken part in such projects often go on to help their families begin recycling at home.

Entrepreneurs have seen opportunities to make "money out of garbage" by setting up recycling businesses. Ten northeastern states, for example, recently reported that recycling now contributes hundreds of millions of dollars and over 100,000 jobs to the region's economy.

Community-based groups are making a difference in towns and cities around the nation. In Pittsburgh, Pennsylvania, community members have formed the Green Neighborhood Initiative. A major goal of this project is to reduce waste and increase energy efficiency in Pittsburgh homes, schools, and businesses. In Lansing,

Michigan, citizens, business owners, and local government officials have formed a group called Sustainable Lansing. The group encourages waste reduction and recycling, which will help the city "meet the needs of the present without compromising the ability of future generations to meet their own needs."

As you have seen, many communities have begun to make progress on recycling and other waste reduction efforts. As our population and economy continue to grow, however, the problem of managing our garbage and trash will not simply go away. Every individual can make a difference in solving this problem.

Section 3 Assessment

1. Explain how the problem of waste is a people problem.
2. Why is free enterprise an issue in the debate over how to reduce the amount of waste?
3. What are some ways in which people are making a difference in solving the problem of waste?
4. **Evaluate** "All households should be allowed only one trash can full of waste each week." Do you agree or disagree with this statement? Why?

Extending the Chapter

Global Views

United States citizens and industries are the largest waste producers in the world, with Canadians not far behind. Although the countries of Western Europe produce only half the trash and garbage per person that Americans do, they have much less space for landfills. Thus, they, too, face a serious problem of how to get rid of their waste.

Industrialized countries have tried several solutions to the problem of disposing of waste. Many countries burn much of their waste. In Japan, Sweden, and Switzerland, about half of household waste is burned, compared with the United States figure of 17 percent. Now, however, there is growing concern about the pollution and poisonous ash that burning causes.

A more recent strategy is to export waste. Cities and industries have made contracts with entrepreneurs to remove their waste. Then where does it go? These entrepreneurs pay other countries—especially poor ones—to take the waste. A problem is that the chemicals in the waste threaten to pollute soil and water where the waste is dumped.

The export of waste alarms governments and environmentalists. The United States Environmental Protection Agency has ruled against exporting some types of poisonous waste. Several African countries have passed laws against importing waste. Still, the pressure on the industrial countries to get rid of their waste is very great.

Should there be a law against exporting waste? The people who support such a law say that it would force industrial countries to look for their own solutions at home instead of causing more problems around the world. One thing is clear: the problem of waste disposal is a global problem.

Cleaning up the Air

Home to some of the most spectacular scenery on earth, Arizona's Grand Canyon National Park is often called the "crown jewel" of America's national park system. Not long ago, however, many of the park's 5 million annual visitors were surprised to find one of America's natural wonders shrouded in a murky haze. Even on the clearest days this haze could dim visitors' views of the park's mile-deep canyons.

What was causing the problem? Fifteen miles from the Grand Canyon National Park sits a huge coal-fired electric power plant called the Navajo Generating Station. Every day three 77-story-high smokestacks at the power plant released air pollution in the form of sulfur dioxide. The haze resulting from these emissions was significantly reducing visibility in Grand Canyon. In addition, the National Park Service's air quality monitoring program had begun detecting significant increases in smog, the same pollutant that causes health problems in many urban areas. Concerned citizens decided it was time to take action. They turned to the law for help.

In 1970 Congress passed the Clean Air Act to protect the public from the harmful effects of air pollution. Seven years later the Clean Air Act was amended to add a new program to prevent "impairment [reduction] of visibility... which results from manmade air pollution." The goal of this amendment was to restore the scenic vistas in large national parks and wilderness areas to their natural state.

> *Every day three 77-story-high smokestacks at the power plant released air pollution in the form of sulfur dioxide.*

When Congress passed the Clean Air Act and the visibility amendment, it clearly indicated that citizens were welcome participants in the fight for clean air. "Congress wanted to empower private citizens to help the government enforce the law," says environmental lawyer Vickie Patton. To help accomplish this, Congress gave citizens the right to file lawsuits against the Environmental Protection Agency (EPA) as a way to force the government to take action.

This is exactly what several citizens groups did. In 1982, the Environmental Defense Fund and the National Parks and Conservation Association, two citizen-run environmental groups, filed a civil lawsuit against the EPA stating that it had failed to do enough to clean up the air in Grand Canyon National

Park and the surrounding area. At the time, a consultant to one of the citizens groups, Priscilla Robinson, stated that "EPA has never done anything about visibility. They have delayed and dragged their feet unless they were driven by a lawsuit." The citizens groups hoped the lawsuit would force EPA officials to act.

In 1984, after difficult and lengthy negotiations, EPA reached a settlement with the environmental groups. The agreement was approved by the court. As part of the settlement, the court ordered EPA to develop a plan to solve the visibility problem at the Grand Canyon. After studying the problem, EPA issued a report linking a "significant portion of the visibility impairment in the Grand Canyon National Park to emissions from the Navajo Generating Station."

The next step was to figure out a practical solution. Representatives of the Navajo Generating Station sat down with citizens and officials from the Arizona state government and EPA. Together, they created a pollution cleanup plan that all groups could accept. Finalized in 1991, the plan required the power plant's owners to spend millions of dollars to add scrubbers to the plant's smokestacks. The scrubbers would eliminate much of the sulfur dioxide before it left the smokestack. The new anti-pollution equipment was expected to result in a 90 percent reduction in haze-causing pollution. "This is a small piece of paper," said an EPA official referring to the clean-up plan, "but it represents the resolution of 20 years of dispute and disagreement."

> ## The citizen groups hoped the lawsuit would force EPA officials to act.

In 1997 the first scrubbers were installed at the Navajo Generating Plant. By the summer of 1999, twenty-two years after the laws for protecting air qual-

ity in the national parks were first passed, the project was complete. Citizens had used the courts to enforce the Clear Air Act. Visitors from around the world can begin looking forward to clearer skies at Grand Canyon National Park.

Analyzing the Case

1. How did Congress "empower" citizens groups to participate in enforcement of the Clean Air Act?
2. What did environmental groups hope to achieve by suing EPA?
3. What steps has the Navajo Generating Station taken to solve the air quality problem at the Grand Canyon?
4. Do you think citizens should be allowed to sue EPA to push for implementation of environmental laws such as the Clean Air Act? Why or why not?

SOCIAL STUDIES SKILLS

How to USE THE INTERNET FOR RESEARCH

In this chapter you read about an important issue in the United States today—health care. Where would you look to find out more about this issue? One answer is to search the Internet. The Internet is a network of computers that allows you access to the vast amount of information on the World Wide Web. The Web has countless Web sites on a wide range of subjects. There are methods for searching and sorting through all the information to find just what you need to know.

Search for:

Uninsured Children

1. Covering Kids Home
covering kids, a national health access initiative for low-income, uninsured children, is a $47 million program of The Robert Wood Johnson Foundation...

URL: http://www.coveringkids.org/

2. Understanding Differences in the Estimates of Uninsured Children
Understanding Different Estimates of Uninsured Children: Putting the Differences in Context. Acknowledgments: ASP would like to thank those...

URL: http://aspe.os.dhhs.gov/health/reports/uninsur3.htm

Explain the Skill

Search engines are Web sites that help you find information on a specific topic. When you use a search engine, you enter the subject and the search engine gives you a list of related Web sites.

When using a search engine, try to be specific. If you were to type in "Health Care," you would get thousands of responses. But if you type in "Uninsured Children" you get a narrower list of Web sites. Type in "Uninsured Children in California" and you get still more specific responses.

Analyze the Skill

Suppose you wanted to find out what is being done to help children who don't have health insurance. If you typed "Uninsured Children," you would get a list of Web sites like the ones shown on this page.

Each listing begins with the Web site's title. In some search engines, the listing gives a short description of the site. The listing also contains a link to the Web site and its URL, or site address.

To get the information, click on the links that seem most relevant. The URL can give you hints about the source. URLs with ".com" are commercial sites; URLs with ".org" are nonprofit organization sites; URLs with ".gov" are government sites; and URLs with ".edu" are school and university sites.

Skill Assessment

1. Based on the first search engine listing shown on this page, what do you think this Web page is about?

2. What is the URL of the second listing? What kind of organization put out this site?

3. Which of these two sites do you think would be most useful to you? Why?

CHAPTER 23 ASSESSMENT

Building Civics Vocabulary

The terms in each pair listed below are related to each other. For each pair, explain what the vocabulary term from the chapter has in common with the other term. Also explain how they are different.

1. *issue* and *problem*
2. *public policy* and *public issues*

Reviewing Main Ideas and Skills

3. What is the difference between a private problem and a public problem?
4. Why does solving public problems involve making choices?
5. Why do many people consider health insurance a necessity?
6. What are two reasons that health care costs are rising in the United States?
7. Why are many American cities running out of landfill space?
8. What are some solutions that have been effective in getting consumers and businesses to recycle their waste?
9. **How to Use the Internet for Research** Suppose you wanted to search the Internet to find information on waste management. What are three subjects you could type in a search engine to narrow your search?

Critical Thinking

10. **Solving Problems** Compare the advantages and disadvantages of burning garbage at waste-to-energy plants. Do you think burning garbage is a good solution to the waste problem? Why or why not?

11. **Predicting Consequences** Suppose the following rule was proposed at your school: To prevent alcohol use at school dances, all students should be searched at the door. What issues might arise from this proposed rule?

Writing About Civics

12. **Writing a Journal** Keep a list of everything you throw away for one day. How much of it could have been recycled? Would the amount of waste have been less if things had been packaged differently? Share your results with the class.

Citizenship Activities

13. **Your Local Community** Watch a local news program or check the newspaper to find a pressing public problem. Then answer the following questions.

   - What is the problem? What are some proposed solutions?
   - What public policies or citizen actions would you support?

 Take It to the NET
....

Access the **Civics: Participating in Government** Internet site at **www.phschool.com** for the specific URLs to complete the activity.

Even in an affluent society like that of the United States, not all citizens receive adequate nourishment. Examine online information about government guidelines for nutrition, and government and non-government efforts to provide adequate nutrition for all Americans. Deliver a short speech for the class, explaining the issue and offering possible solutions. Be prepared to answer questions from the class.

America Needs a Third Party

Ralph Nader is the founder of Public Citizen, a consumer advocacy organization that was established in 1971. Nader and Public Citizen have addressed such issues as food and drug safety, clean energy sources, transportation safety, and environmental conservation. In 1996 and 2000, Nader ran for President of the United States as the Green Party candidate.

Before you read the selection, find the meaning of this word in a dictionary: imagery.

The American electorate is faced with two major parties that serve up virtually identical political menus every four years....

Between 40 and 50 percent of eligible voters do not even bother to show up at the polls to select the federal government's chief executive....

For many of the stay-at-home voters, the dwindling differences between the two major parties provide little incentive to participate. Grassroots politics that once generated neighborhood discussion and participation has largely given way to mass media with corporate contributors financing expensive television advertising, which sells candidates in thirty-second

pops that stress empty imagery over substance....

This growing urge of the Democrats and the Republicans to imitate one another on major issues can only be cured by alternative parties that do not live off the corporate dole and are willing to raise the issues that count in people's lives....

In the fall of 1995, several leading California environmentalists asked if I would agree to their placing my name on the Green Party ballot for President. Reflecting on how well-corporatized government is rapidly shutting out civic participation, I agreed, but said I would not accept any campaign contributions or run in a traditional manner. My goal is to encourage a campaign dependent on self-reliant citizen muscle at the grass roots....

One thing politicians do understand is rejection. When voters are deciding how they wish to use their vote, they should ask themselves how best to send a clear message. The Greens and other progressives are in the early building stages of a people first, democratic political movement for future years. They deserve our attention because they are centering on the basic issues of representative government, one of whose purposes is to strengthen the tools of democracy, and the other, in the words of Thomas Jefferson, is to "curb the excesses of the monied interests."

Source: Perspectives: Readings on Contemporary American Government *(Alexandria, Va.: Close Up Foundation, 1997), pages 218–20.*

Analyzing Primary Sources

1. According to Nader, how have the growing similarities between the Republican and Democratic parties affected voter interest?

2. In Nader's view, how is the Green Party different from the traditional parties?

UNIT 7 ASSESSMENT

1. You have decided to run for President. Arrange the campaign events listed below in the order in which they could happen.
- **(a)** Receive 52.7% of the popular vote.
- **(b)** Accept federal campaign money.
- **(c)** Win the Illinois primary.
- **(d)** Receive 290 electoral college votes.
- **(e)** Accept your party's nomination at its national convention.

2. Suppose that there is a measure on the state ballot to ban the use of styrofoam containers by take-out restaurants. What role might each of the following play in the campaign?
- **(a)** An environmental interest group
- **(b)** A candidate for governor
- **(c)** You as a citizen
- **(d)** A political party

Summarizing the Unit

The flow map below will help you organize the main ideas of Unit 7. Copy it onto a separate sheet of paper. Each box lists a group of people or a subject that influences the democratic process. Review the unit and complete the graphic organizer by giving a brief summary of the role each group or subject plays in an election campaign. The first box has been completed for you as an example. When you have finished, choose one group or subject from the flow map and write a one-page essay explaining in detail why it is an important part of the democratic process.

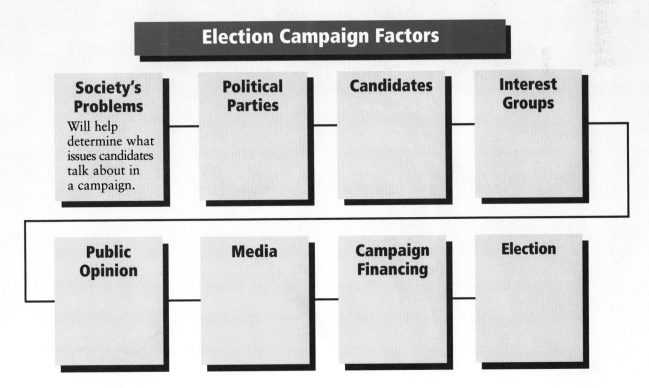

Election Campaign Factors

Society's Problems
Will help determine what issues candidates talk about in a campaign.

Political Parties

Candidates

Interest Groups

Public Opinion

Media

Campaign Financing

Election

UNIT 8

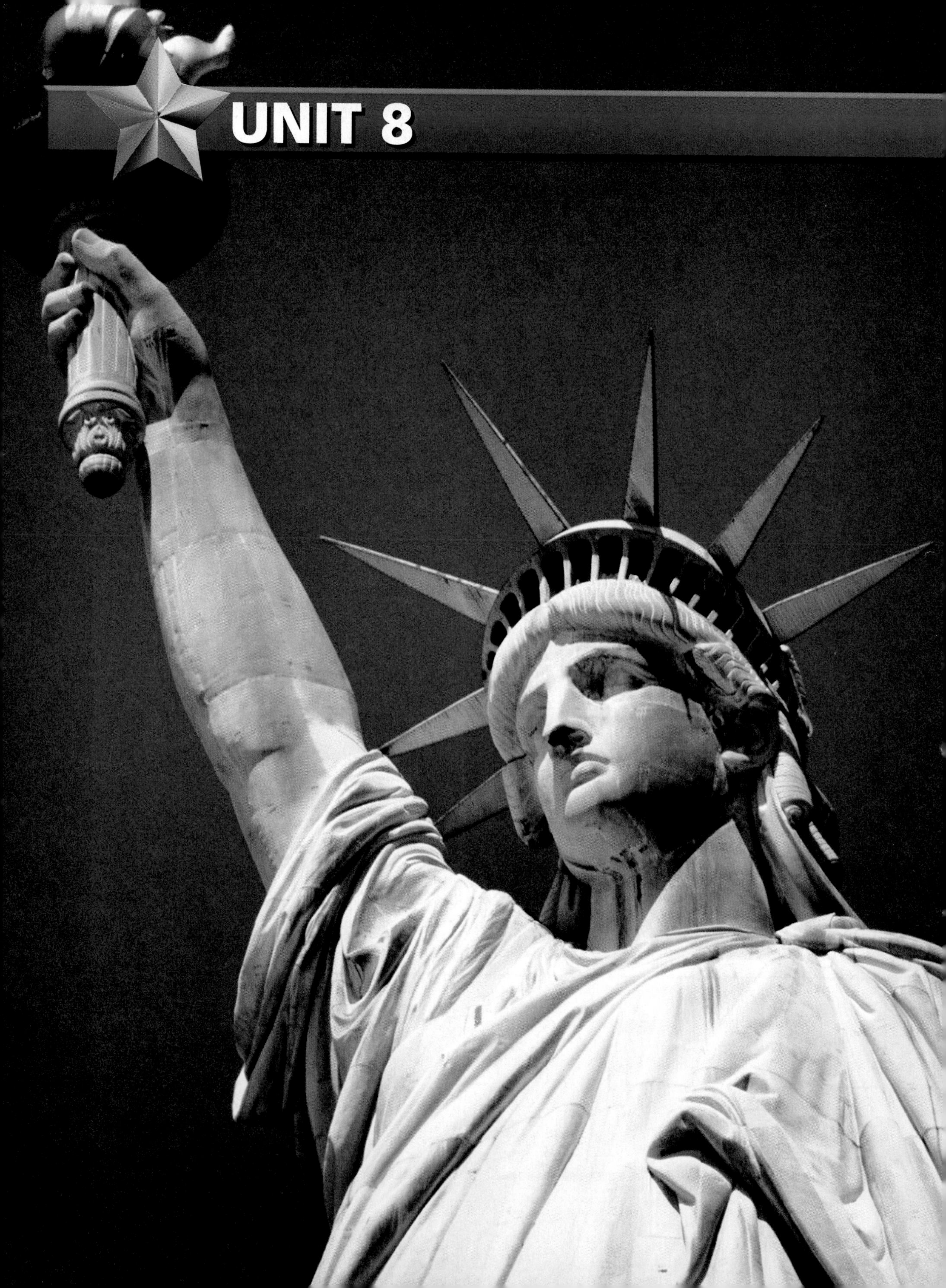

The United States and the World

Why Study Civics?

What we call foreign affairs is no longer foreign affairs. It's a local affair. Whatever happens in Indonesia is important in Indiana. We cannot escape each other. As long as any [nation] cannot enjoy the blessings of peace with justice, then indeed there is no peace anywhere.

—President Dwight D. Eisenhower

In this book, you have been learning what it means to be a citizen of the United States. As former President Eisenhower suggests, however, being a responsible citizen also means being a citizen of the world.

What's Ahead in Unit 8

This unit will introduce you to the world beyond the borders of the United States. First you will learn about nations and how they relate to each other. Then you will study our nation's foreign policy and role in world affairs. Finally, you will read about some of the serious problems that face all nations and that challenge Americans to act as citizens of both our nation and our world.

Chapter 24   **One Nation Among Many**

Chapter 25   **American Foreign Policy**

Chapter 26   **Making a Difference in the World**

One Nation Among Many

Citizenship and You

Today the United States is at war. That war— the war against terrorism—is a new and a different kind of war, against a new and a different kind of enemy. The conflict began with sudden and shocking violence on September 11, 2001. The government, acting with the full support of the American people, began to respond to that monstrous assault immediately by launching a bombing campaign on Taliban military and communications bases. President George W. Bush made it clear that these bombings were only the beginning of a relentless pursuit by the United States and many other nations working together to rid the world of terrorism and those who support it.

What's Ahead in Chapter 24

As the attacks of September 11, 2001, demonstrate, the actions of one nation can affect people in nations all over the world. The major purpose of this chapter is to help you see the United States as one nation among many. You will learn how nations differ, why conflicts occur, and what brings peace. Finally, you will see how developments in technology and the global economy are bringing many nations closer together.

Section 1   **The Nations of the World**

Section 2   **Relations Between and Within Nations**

Section 3   **The Challenge of Interdependence**

Keep It Current

Items marked with this logo are periodically updated on the Internet. To keep up-to-date, go to www.phschool.com

Citizen's Journal

Following the attacks of September 11, 2001, President Bush's advisors gave him a wide variety of recommendations. If you had been one of Bush's advisors, what would you have advised him to do? Explain the thinking behind your advice.

The Nations of the World

 **Focus**

Imagine that you are an astronaut looking back at the earth from far out in space. You see a beautiful blue sphere covered with oceans. In places the blue is broken by green and brown areas, the continents. Clouds swirl over both land and sea.

From space, you see the earth as a small globe, the shared home of more than six billion human beings. Now, look at the map of the world on page 594 of this book. How is that map different from an astronaut's view of our planet? In addition to being flat, the map shows the nations of the world and the borders that divide them. An astronaut cannot see these nations. Nevertheless, they are of great importance to the people living inside their borders.

What Is a Nation?

One way to define "nation" is as a group of people who share a language, a history, and an identity. By this definition, there may be more than one people within the borders of a country who call themselves a "nation."

In the eyes of the world, though, a group of people needs more than a sense of unity in order to be called a nation. They must form a political unit with a well-defined territory and a government that has authority over the people living there. In other words, they must have their own country. A strong sense of unity, of course, is still important and is a major reason why new nations emerge.

A good example of a new nation is Andorra, a tiny land in the Pyrenees mountains between France and Spain. The people of Andorra consider themselves to have their own identity that is neither French nor Spanish. In early 1993 they adopted their own constitution. Andorra, with a population of only 62,000, became a nation.

Characteristics of Nations Every nation has three basic characteristics. First, it has a territory with borders. The borders are the lines you see on the world map. The borders define the land area of the nation.

Second, a nation has a government. There are many kinds of national governments, including republics like our own, monarchies, and dictatorships.

Third, a nation has sovereignty, the power to make and carry out laws within the nation's borders. The government also has the power to deal with other nations. Having sovereignty means, for example, that a nation can regulate trade with other nations and decide who may enter its territory.

National Interest One thing common to all nations is a duty to try to protect the interests of the nation as a whole. Each nation has an interest in protecting itself from outside attack. It is also in each nation's interest to build a strong economy and to preserve order through its legal system.

To look after its national interest, a nation must have power. National power takes many forms. Some nations gain power because they have valuable natural resources. Some gain power through military strength. Some become powerful by building strong economies and becoming leaders in the use of new technology.

Nationalism People within a nation often feel a sense of nationalism, a pride in their shared history and a loyalty to their nation. Culture, language, religion, and political tradition can contribute to nationalism. Governments often try to stir feelings of nationalism through holidays, slogans, songs, and pledges.

The Different Histories of Nations

While nations share many characteristics, they are also different from one another in many ways. Some nations are rich, while others are poor. Nations have different climates, landscapes, languages, and religions.

One of the most important ways in which nations differ is in their histories. Some nations, such as China, have existed for thousands of years. Others, such as some of the nations in Africa, are less than 50 years old. Some have histories filled with fighting. Others have known more peace than war.

Colonies and Colonial Powers In the past, many nations in the Americas, Africa, and Asia were colonies. A colony is a territory ruled by a more powerful nation called a colonial power. Why did colonial powers want colonies? The reason is that colonies could supply crops such as rubber and coffee, and natural resources such as oil and copper. They were also a source of cheap labor for the colonial power.

Gates at a border crossing are a sign that every nation has the power to decide who may enter or leave its territory.

A few colonies, such as the 13 American colonies and Australia, were settled by large numbers of people from the colonial power. In their rush to get land, the newcomers killed or pushed aside the native peoples. In time, these people became a small minority in their own lands.

In most colonies, by contrast, the native peoples remained in the majority. Under colonial rule, however, their traditional ways of life were upset. A colonial power often forced its own language and laws on its colonies. It forced native peoples to leave their villages to work as miners, laborers, and plantation workers.

Independence Since 1776, when the 13 American colonies declared their independence, people in colonies all over the world have fought to free themselves. Most colonies in Latin America gained independence in the early 1800s. More than 80 colonies in Africa, Asia, and the Middle East became independent after World War II.

Some former colonies, such as the United States, have become strong and wealthy nations. However, many have not had that good fortune. Often the colonial powers left their colonies poorly prepared for nationhood.

Developed and Developing Nations

When people describe the nations of the world today, they often divide them into two groups: "developed nations" and "developing nations." These two groups of nations differ mainly in their standard of living, or the number and kinds of goods and services people can have.

The Developed World The developed nations have much in common. They are all heavily industrialized. They depend on factories and modern technology to turn out a wide range of goods and services. Most of their citizens live in towns and cities, and many of them work in service jobs. While the developed nations have only about 20 percent of the world's population, they have more than three quarters of the world's annual income.

The developed world has a relatively high standard of living. While there is poverty, hunger, and homelessness in nearly all developed nations, the poor are a minority of the population.

The Developing World In contrast, the majority of people in the developing world are poor. Many are hungry. People in developing nations are poor and hungry for many reasons. In some places poor soil and lack of rain make it hard for people to grow food. Some developing nations, such as India, do not have enough jobs for those who need work. Therefore, many Indians are hungry because they are too poor to buy enough food.

Another reason people in developing nations are poor is that it is hard for them to get an education. Many poor nations do not have enough schools for their children. As a result, about a quarter of the young children in developing countries do not attend school.

The Results of Having Been Colonies People in developing nations are poor for another reason. Most developing nations were once colonies. Their resources were used to increase the wealth of colonial powers rather than to improve the standard of living of their people.

When colonies won their independence, they had weak economies. They had few

RICH NATIONS AND POOR NATIONS

Nation	Per capita GDP, in dollars (2000)
United States	$36,200
Norway	27,700
Australia	23,200
Italy	22,100
Israel	18,900
South Korea	16,100
Iran	6,300
El Salvador	4,000
Indonesia	2,900
Vietnam	1,950
Kenya	1,500

Source: CIA World Factbook

One way to measure a nation's standard of living is to calculate its per capita gross domestic product—its GDP divided by its total population. This number is a rough estimate of how much the average person in a nation contributes to that nation's GDP. **Economics What was Vietnam's per capita GDP in 2000?**

people trained in engineering, banking, business, or government service. In addition, the new nations were left with economies that had been set up to export resources to the developed world. Changing those economies to meet the basic needs of their own people proved very difficult.

Many new countries also faced political problems. The colonial powers had created some colonies that included groups of people with different languages, religions, and histories. Once such colonies won their independence, these groups sometimes fought among themselves for power. In the African nation of Rwanda, a former colony of Belgium, civil war broke out in 1994. Fighting between two tribal groups—the Hutu and the Tutsis—left over 500,000 people dead.

Economic Development As the word *developing* suggests, the poorer nations are working to develop their economies. They have been aided in this huge task by the developed nations and by international organizations such as the United Nations, which you will learn about in Chapter 26. Many nations are still poor, and the gap between rich and poor nations has narrowed very slowly.

Some nations have had great success. One of them is South Korea. In 1963 the per capita gross domestic product (GDP) of South Korea was about $80. In other words, if the value of the goods and services produced in South Korea in 1963 had been divided among all South Koreans, each person would have received $80. By 1980, South Korea was becoming a worldwide exporter of manufactured goods, from cars and steel to shoes and clothing. By 1999, its GDP had reached $13,300 per person.

There are other success stories, as well. Sri Lanka, an island nation in the Indian Ocean, has made education an important part of its development plan. In spite of a continuing civil war that has lasted nearly two decades, 88 percent of Sri Lankans can

Local efforts, like this project started by a fishing community in the Philippines, help the economies of developing nations to grow.

read and write—one of the highest literacy rates among developing countries.

Economic development has improved life for many people in developing nations. Even so, 800 million people in the world, or about one person in seven, go to bed hungry every night. One challenge facing us in the years ahead is to help the developing nations meet the basic needs of their people.

Section 1 Assessment

1. **Define** sovereignty, nationalism, colony, standard of living
2. What are the characteristics of nations?
3. Why did colonial powers want colonies?
4. Why have the developing nations found it difficult to meet the needs of their people?
5. **Analyze** Compare nationalism with "school spirit."

Relations Between and Within Nations

SECTION PREVIEW

Objectives
- Describe the major causes of international conflict.
- Explore the types of competition between nations.
- Summarize the history of the Cold War.
- Examine ways that nations have cooperated since the end of the Cold War.

Building Civics Vocabulary
- Under **communism,** the central government owns and controls a nation's economic resources.
- The conflict between the United States and the Soviet Union following World War II became known as the **Cold War.**
- An **alliance** is a group of nations that have agreed to help or protect each other.
- **Détente** is a lessening of tensions.

 Focus

Like people, nations come into conflict, compete, and cooperate. Unfortunately, conflict and competition have shaped human history far more than has cooperation.

In this century alone, there have been two major world wars and dozens of smaller ones. Many of these "small wars" have been civil wars. Others have been conflicts between nations.

Types of Conflict

If you look in any daily newspaper, you will likely find a story about conflict within a nation or between nations somewhere in the world. Conflict is a struggle for something that two or more groups each want, such as land or power.

At the root of most conflicts is one group's belief that its interests are opposed by another group. A conflict may have one major cause, but there will probably also be others. Experts have identified four major causes conflict within or between nations.

Conflict Over Beliefs and Values Differing views on what is right or wrong may lead to conflict. There may be disagreement about the role of government in society, or over how businesses and property should be owned and used. The clash may be over whether there should be a national religion. Civil war broke out in the North African nation of Algeria during the 1990s, when Muslim religious groups fought for power against the ruling government.

Territorial and Environmental Conflict Disputes may arise over the control and use of land, water, oil, and other natural resources. A border dispute between the South American nations of Peru and Ecuador caused decades of conflict, before finally ending with a peace agreement in 1998.

Racial and Ethnic Conflict Conflict can occur between different racial or ethnic groups when one thinks it is superior, or because of long-term hatred. In southeastern Europe, ethnic hatred was a major cause of conflict between Muslims, Serbs, and Croats in the former nation of Yugoslavia during the 1990s.

Conflict Over Political Power This kind of conflict is about who makes decisions for a group of people. It might be a struggle to gain political power, or a protest or rebellion against a government that abuses its power. In the Asian nation of Pakistan in 1999, the Pakistani army seized power from an elected government. The

Thousands died as a result of the civil war in Bosnia between Serbs, Muslims, and Croats in the 1990s. Here a man digs a grave in the capital city of Sarajevo.

chief of Pakistan's army said he took power because the old government had been corrupt and had failed to serve the interests of the people of Pakistan.

Competition Between Nations

One common type is economic competition through trade. Such competition can benefit nations as their companies improve the way they do business. It can also be harmful if one nation believes that another is being unfair. A country may try to help its own farmers by refusing to buy farm products from another country. That country, in turn, may react by refusing to buy products from the first country. Both nations are hurt because trade decreases.

Nations also compete for military power. After World War II, the United States and the Soviet Union competed in a dangerous arms buildup. Today there is concern about the arms buildup in nations like Iraq, North Korea, and China. Such buildups can increase tensions that lead to conflict.

The Cold War and Its Aftermath

Conflict and competition between the United States and the Soviet Union had a great impact on the world for over 40 years. The arms buildup used many resources that could have been used for peaceful activities. The superpower rivalry also created tensions that no nation could escape. It forced people to live in fear of nuclear war.

Colin Powell

Growing up in New York City's South Bronx neighborhood, Colin Powell heard one message from his parents over and over—get a good education and do something with your life. He got the message.

Powell enlisted in the United States Army after graduating from college in 1958 and he rose quickly through the ranks. While serving in the Vietnam War, he received a Purple Heart and a Bronze Star. He was also awarded the Soldier's Medal for pulling several men from a burning helicopter.

A turning point in Powell's life came in 1972 when he was chosen to work in the White House. "I went from being just your average Army officer," explains Powell, "to somebody who was...meeting Presidents, seeing how policy is being made at the highest levels of government."

After rising to the rank of four-star general, Powell was appointed chairperson of the Joint Chiefs of Staff by President George H. W. Bush in 1989. He played a key role in planning military operations during the Persian Gulf War.

After retiring from the military in 1993, Powell wrote his autobiography, gave speeches, and worked for children's causes. In 2001, President George W.

Bush appointed Powell Secretary of State. He became the first African American to hold this high cabinet position.

In the future, Powell believes, democracy and economic strength will be more important than military might. He warns: "Nations seeking power through military strength, the development of nuclear weapons, terrorism, or tyrannical governments are mining 'fool's gold.' They can never...match...the military and economic power of the free world led by the United States."

Recognizing Viewpoints

What do you think Colin Powell means when he says that nations seeking power through nuclear weapons or terrorism are mining "fool's gold"?

The Beginnings of the Conflict During World War II, the United States and the Soviet Union were allies. By 1945 they were the two most powerful countries in the world.

After the war, conflict arose between the former allies. They could not agree on the future of Germany and Eastern Europe. By 1949 the Soviet Union had set up Communist governments in Poland, Hungary, Bulgaria, Romania, Czechoslovakia, and East Germany. Under communism, the central government owns and controls the economic resources. These nations, all on or near the Soviet border, were known as "satellites" of the Soviet Union.

Conflict between the United States and the Soviet Union was over more than territory. It was mainly a clash between two ideas about what was good for the world: communism and state control of the economy, or democracy and the free market economy. It was also a conflict between two military superpowers, each viewing the other as a danger to its national interest and even its survival.

The Growing Conflict The superpower conflict became known as the **Cold War,** a struggle much like a real war but with no armed battles. Instead, it was fought with words, warnings, and an arms buildup.

To protect their interests, the United States and the nations of Western Europe formed the North Atlantic Treaty Organization (NATO) in 1949. NATO is an **alliance,** a group of nations that have agreed to help or protect each other. A few years later the Soviet Union and the Eastern European nations formed the Warsaw Pact alliance. Each alliance built up its military power. Several times the Cold War led to the brink of nuclear war.

"Hot" Wars The Cold War broke into several "hot" wars between Soviet and American allies. In 1950 North Korea, backed by the Soviet Union and China, invaded South Korea. The United States and its allies helped South Korea fight off the attack.

The Cold War turned hot again in Vietnam. Between 1964 and 1973 the United States sent hundreds of thousands of troops to South Vietnam to prevent Communists from taking over its government. Despite American efforts, the Communist government of North Vietnam took over all of Vietnam in 1975.

The United States and the Soviet Union were on opposite sides of conflicts in Ethiopia, Afghanistan, and Nicaragua. However, at no time did Americans and Soviets fight each other, nor were nuclear weapons used.

The Cold War Ends In the 1970s the United States and the Soviet Union began to find ways to cooperate. The new relationship was called détente (day TAHNT), which means a lessoning of tensions. During this period, the two superpowers signed treaties to slow down the arms race, and they increased trade with each other.

Despite periods of tension in the early 1980s and renewed arms buildups, détente helped erode the distrust between the superpowers. In 1987 they signed a landmark agreement known as the Intermediate-Range Nuclear Forces (INF) treaty, an agreement to destroy thousands of nuclear missiles. After the signing, Soviet-American relations improved further.

Then, in late 1989, stunning political changes began to unfold in the Soviet Union and Eastern Europe. One by one the nations of Eastern Europe rid themselves of communist, one-party rule and began to switch to free market economies. The Warsaw Pact alliance dissolved. Then the Soviet Union itself began to unravel as its states called for independence and its economy stalled.

By the end of 1991 the Soviet Union had ceased to exist, and its Communist system had been rejected. The Cold War was over, and a major barrier to increased global cooperation had been overcome. Today the nations of Eastern Europe and the former states of the Soviet Union, which are now nations themselves, are struggling to build up their economies and to govern themselves.

Cooperation Between Nations

Much of the cooperation between nations has been through military alliances. However, economic interests have also brought nations together. Now that the Cold War has ended, nations are exploring new ways to cooperate. Major areas of cooperation between nations include trade, giving aid, and peacemaking.

Cooperation in Trade Many nations have formed regional trade organizations.

One of the oldest is the European Union (EU), formed by the nations of Western Europe to break down barriers to trade and travel in their region. In 1999, 11 EU countries adopted a new currency—the euro—as a single currency which could be used in all 11 nations.

The Association of Southeast Asian Nations (ASEAN), the Organization of American States (OAS), and the Organization of African Unity (OAU) are other examples of regional organizations. Each works for economic and political cooperation in its region. In 1993, Congress passed the North American Free Trade Agreement (NAFTA), which lowered trade barriers between Canada, Mexico, and the United States.

Cooperation in Providing Aid

With the end of the Cold War, the seven leading industrialized nations (United States, Canada, Britain, France, Germany, Italy, and Japan) decided as a group to help Russia and the other countries of the former Soviet Union.

EUROPE AND WESTERN ASIA AFTER THE COLD WAR The collapse of the Soviet Union led to the formation of many new countries. **Region Name five countries that were formerly states of the Soviet Union.**

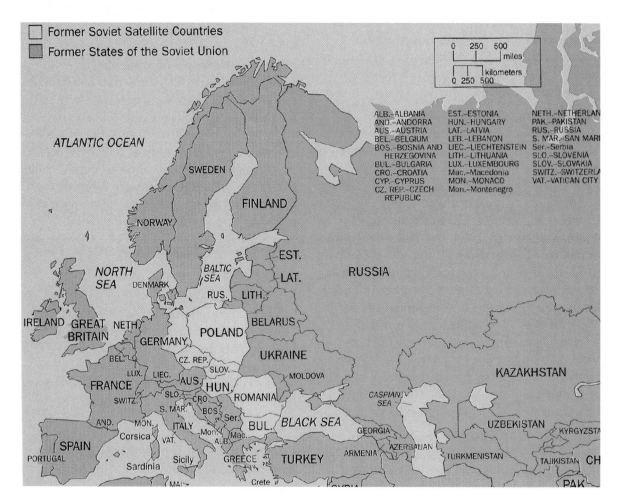

- ☐ Former Soviet Satellite Countries
- ■ Former States of the Soviet Union

0 250 500 miles
0 250 500 kilometers

ALB.–ALBANIA
AND.–ANDORRA
AUS.–AUSTRIA
BEL.–BELGIUM
BOS.–BOSNIA AND HERZEGOVINA
BUL.–BULGARIA
CRO.–CROATIA
CYP.–CYPRUS
CZ. REP.–CZECH REPUBLIC
EST.–ESTONIA
HUN.–HUNGARY
LAT.–LATVIA
LEB.–LEBANON
LIEC.–LIECHTENSTEIN
LITH.–LITHUANIA
LUX.–LUXEMBOURG
Mac.–Macedonia
MON.–MONACO
Mon.–Montenegro
NETH.–NETHERLAN
PAK.–PAKISTAN
RUS.–RUSSIA
S. MAR.–SAN MARI
Ser.–Serbia
SLO.–SLOVENIA
SLOV.–SLOVAKIA
SWITZ.–SWITZERLA
VAT.–VATICAN CITY

ATLANTIC OCEAN
SWEDEN
FINLAND
NORWAY
NORTH SEA
BALTIC SEA
EST.
LAT.
RUSSIA
DENMARK
RUS.
LITH.
IRELAND
GREAT BRITAIN
NETH.
BELARUS
GERMANY
POLAND
BEL.
CZ. REP.
UKRAINE
LUX.
LIEC.
SLOV.
AUS.
HUN.
MOLDOVA
KAZAKHSTAN
FRANCE
SWITZ.
SLO.
CRO
ROMANIA
CASPIAN SEA
SLO.
S. MAR.
BOS.
AND.
MON.
ITALY
Mon.
Ser.
Mac.
BUL.
BLACK SEA
GEORGIA
UZBEKISTAN
KYRGYZSTA
Corsica
VAT.
ALB.
AZERBAIJAN
SPAIN
PORTUGAL
Sardinia
Sicily
GREECE
TURKEY
ARMENIA
TURKMENISTAN
TAJIKISTAN
CH
Crete
PAK

The aid was to pay for importing food, dismantling nuclear weapons, and promoting democratic and free market reforms. Clearly, the rules of international relations have changed with the end of superpower conflict.

Nations also worked together to help refugees from the 1994 civil war in Rwanda. Over 1 million people had fled the country. People had little food, drank contaminated water, and lived in filthy surroundings. Thousands died from disease. Many governments—including the United States—came to their aid.

Cooperation for Peacemaking During the Cold War, international conflict was managed through a balance of power: the threat that one superpower's military strength might be used against the other's. Some experts claim that this balance of power helped keep peace.

Today, we are witnessing new paths to peacemaking. Peace may be promoted through cooperation among nations, the influence of a respected person, the act of a nation not involved in a dispute, or the economic pressures of many nations acting together. The following examples illustrate these possibilities.

- **The Gulf War** In August 1990, Iraq invaded Kuwait in a dispute over control of oil prices and Kuwait's oil fields. In November of 1990, the United Nations Security Council authorized the use of force if Iraq did not withdraw from Kuwait by January 15, 1991. Talks failed to resolve the crisis. As a result, troops from over 30 nations joined forces to defeat Iraq's army in Operation Desert Storm.

- **Kosovo** In 1999 tensions erupted in Kosovo, a province of Serbia. For several years the Kosovo Liberation Army (KLA) had been fighting a guerilla campaign for independence from Serbia. Vowing to defeat the KLA, the Serbian army launched an offensive in

In Operation Desert Storm, many nations cooperated to force Iraq to withdraw its troops from Kuwait in 1991.

Kosovo, destroying villages and forcing thousands of families from their homes. Diplomats from around the world tried to help the combatants find a peaceful settlement. When negotiations failed, NATO airplanes began bombing Serb military forces. After 11 weeks of heavy bombing, the Serbian military agreed to leave Kosovo. Negotiators then began trying to work out a long-term solution to the struggle for power in this region.

- **North Korea** In late 1993 and early 1994, North Korea refused to allow international inspectors to observe withdrawal of fuel rods from a nuclear reactor. Officials were concerned that the North Koreans would use the fuel rods to make nuclear weapons. In August 1994, former President Jimmy Carter was successful in getting North Korea to announce a freeze of its nuclear arms program. In the years since, North

Korea has agreed to limit its arms production in exchange for economic aid from the United States and other nations.

- **The Middle East** Since 1948 Israel has fought an on-again, off-again war with nearby Arab states and the Palestine Liberation Organization (PLO). The world held little hope for peace in the Middle East. In 1993 the foreign minister of Norway, a nation not involved in the crisis, held secret discussions with Israel and the PLO. Since that time, Israel and the PLO have signed several peace agreements, but obstacles to a lasting peace remain.

- **South Africa** Apartheid, South Africa's policy of denying blacks political and economic equality, had caused much conflict since it began in 1948. During the 1980s, the United States and other nations cut off most trade with South Africa. These protests pressured the government to do away with apartheid and allow free elections. In 1994 all South Africans of voting age voted in a nationwide election for the first time. Nelson Mandela, a black leader imprisoned for 27 years under apartheid, was elected President.

Section 2 Assessment

1. **Define** communism, Cold War, alliance, détente
2. What causes conflict within and between nations?
3. How can economic competition both benefit and harm nations?
4. How did the Cold War affect relations between nations?
5. What are some efforts at peacemaking since the end of the Cold War?
6. **Synthesize** What do you think nations should do to cooperate with each other more?

The Challenge of Interdependence

SECTION PREVIEW

Objectives
- Explain how the global economy makes nations dependent on each other.
- Describe how technology has linked people around the world.
- Explore what it means to think of the world as a system.

 Focus

You are an independent person. You make your own decisions about what to eat and what to wear. You decide with whom you want to be friends. However, you are also dependent on other people. You depend on your friends for advice, favors, and a friendly ear. Your friends, of course, depend on you for the same things. You are *inter*dependent. You depend on each other.

Nations are much the same. They are independent, but they also depend on each other for some of what they need and want. They rely on each other for help in dealing with earthquakes and floods. They use the same satellites for sending messages around the world. Nations also rely on each other to try to settle conflicts peacefully.

The Global Economy

Perhaps the most important way in which nations are dependent on each other is through world trade. As you learned in Chapter 14, connections among the economies of the world's nations have created a global economy.

In the global economy, nations depend on each other for products they cannot make or grow themselves. They also depend on each other for natural resources not found within their own borders. Although nations have traded for hundreds of years, in the last few decades there has a been a rapid increase in trade. Also, there are a growing number of multinational corporations, companies with factories and offices in many countries.

If you had been a European farmer 800 years ago, nearly all your food and clothing would have been produced within walking distance of your home. Today, in contrast, much of what you consume comes from other countries. For example, the beef in your hamburger may have come from Argentina. Your banana may have grown in Honduras or Costa Rica. Your television might have been made in Japan. People in other nations, in turn, depend on us for goods and services they want.

Once economic links have been made between nations, there can be problems if they are broken. For example, when Arab nations cut off the supply of oil to many countries in 1973, it seriously hurt the ones whose economies depended on Arab oil.

Local decisions may have far-reaching effects on our global economy. Consider what could happen if a multinational corporation based in Austin, Texas, decided to open a new factory in Thailand. This decision could give a boost to Thailand's economy and provide more of the company's products to people in Japan. However, it could also result in the company closing one of its older American factories and laying off those workers.

In a global economy a company like McDonald's, which is based in one nation, may do business in many others.

The Role of Technology

Interdependence is a result of improvements in the technologies of communication and transportation. Satellites, computers, planes, and the Internet have linked nations in ways that were wild dreams only 100 years ago.

Advances in technology have linked people, too. Americans with cable television can watch news broadcasts from India. People in Asian villages can hear news from around the world on radios.

A Smaller World Technology has made the world seem like a smaller place by creating better connections between people and nations. When Chinese students demonstrated for democracy in Beijing's Tiananmen Square in 1989, the world watched each day's events on television. The Chinese government tried to cut China off from the world news media. However, news continued to flow into and out of China by long

A view of our planet from space helps us see that the many nations and peoples of the world are really interconnected parts of one whole.

distance telephone links, fax machines, and satellite broadcasts.

As technology has shrunk time and distance, nations and people have become less separated from each other. We now have a better chance of understanding what humans share in common and of focusing on common goals rather than on opposing interests.

Our Shared Environment

The global economy and improvements in communication create connections between the world's nations. We are also connected simply because we all live on the same planet. We are interdependent because we share the same air and water. Pollution in one nation can affect every person and living thing on earth. As a result, the nations of the world are dependent on each other to protect an environment that knows no national boundaries.

Facts & Quotes

Food For Sale

As an industrial nation the United States plays an important role in the global economy. However, you might be surprised to learn that one of our biggest exports is food.

In fact, the United States is the world's leading producer and exporter of many important food products. In 1999, for example, 67 percent of the corn and 57 percent of the soybeans traded on the world market were grown in the United States. The United States is also the second largest exporter of wheat and the third largest exporter of rice.

The World as a System

Interdependence and warnings about global pollution have caused many people to conclude that "we're all in the same boat." They have begun to see the world not as a collection of independent nations, but as a system.

A system is any whole made up of interconnected parts. The most important characteristic of a system is that a change in any one part will affect every other part because the parts are all connected. In the case of the world, the "whole" is the planet on which we live, and the "parts" are nations, organizations, and individuals.

Physically, the earth has always been a system. Our planet has one atmosphere and interconnected oceans.

People and nations, however, have not always been aware that they, too, are important parts of the global system. One reason is that the world used to seem so big. People and nations could not easily see how their actions affected other people and nations far away.

Today it is easier to see how the parts of our system are connected. At the same time, we are continuing to create new links. The result is a closely interconnected, interdependent world—a world that is a system.

Section 3 Assessment

1. How has the global economy made nations more interdependent?
2. What role has technology played in increasing international interdependence?
3. How is the world an example of a system?
4. **Apply** Give an example of how your own actions might affect people in other nations.

Extending the Chapter

Global Views

During the 1960s, the first space flights carrying humans and television cameras into orbit gave people a new way of looking at our planet. They also suggested a comparison to Buckminster Fuller, an inventor and college professor. He compared the earth to a spaceship.

Like a spaceship, the earth is a closed system. Its living passengers depend completely on the system for what they need to live. Furthermore, everything the passengers create that is dangerous to life—such as toxic chemicals and air pollution—stays in the system. Social problems, such as poverty, hunger, and war, are also a danger to the system.

Fuller described "Spaceship Earth" as a very complex system that needs care and maintenance. He said that since we humans are able to understand our spaceship, it is up to us to help protect it.

Buckminster Fuller had special faith in young people. He said that since they are not confined by old ways of thinking, they can come up with new ideas and ways of doing things to keep our planet in good condition. Over 25 years ago he wrote a message to everyone who wants to preserve our spaceship's ability to support life: "Go to work, and above all cooperate and don't...try to gain at the expense of another."

DECISION MAKING SKILLS

How to USE AN ACTION PLAN

"Perform without fail what you resolve." These words of advice from Benjamin Franklin apply to anyone who has made a decision. Another way of putting this advice is, "After you decide what to do, *do* it."

You already know that decision making involves choosing and taking action. The lesson in Chapter 17 helped you set clear goals, and Chapter 18 provided tips on how to choose the best option. In Chapter 22 you looked at how to make an action plan. Here you will have an opportunity to put the whole process together.

Explain the Skill

When making an important decision, how can you keep track of all the things you have to do? One way is to make a checklist.

In the lesson on page 302 you saw a short checklist. Now that you know more about decision making, you can make a more detailed list. Copy the partial checklist that appears on page 537 and add items to complete it. If necessary, review previous lessons on the decision-making process and on critical-thinking skills helpful in decision making.

Analyze the Skill

After you have completed your checklist, you are ready to use it as a guide in making a decision. In this chapter you have read about competition between nations. One kind of competition between the United States and other nations is economic competition, which can lead to difficult decisions for American consumers. When comparing products, an American consumer might

wonder whether to buy an American product or one made by a foreign company.

Suppose your family is deciding which car to buy. After comparing the comfort of various cars, you narrow the options to one American model and one foreign model. Now you have to decide which car to buy.

Choosing Make a chart like the one on page 405 and fill it in as you move through the process of choosing. Use your critical-thinking skills to judge the following pieces of information that might relate to your decision:

A. The foreign car sells for $19,990, and the dealer offers a loan at 11% interest. The American car sells for $19,720, and the dealer offers a loan at 11.5%. Local banks offer 10%.

B. A consumer magazine says both cars have an "average" predicted reliability, which refers to how often repairs are needed.

C. Both cars get 15 miles per gallon in city driving. On the expressway, the foreign car gets 34 miles per gallon, and the American car gets 30 miles per gallon.

D. The American car is available now, but not in the color you want. The foreign car will be available in a month in the color you want.

E. A Department of Commerce official declared that "American businesses must be protected from too much competition from foreign imports." The official noted that "limits on foreign imports are fair because many nations severely limit American imports."

F. A trade official from a foreign country declared that many American cars are not selling well because they are not as well made as leading foreign cars. The official also said that stricter limits on imports

Decision-Making Checklist
Critical Thinking

Choosing	Critical Thinking	Taking Action
√ Do I have a clear goal? √ Do I know what my standards are? √ Have I brainstormed all my options? √ Have I identified which types of information I need about each option?	√ Have I checked how reliable my sources of information are? √ Do I know which kinds of information relate to my subject? √ Do I know which pieces of information are statements of fact and which are opinions?	√ Is my action goal clearly stated? √ Do I know what resources I can use? √ Do I know what problems I might face? √ Do I know what needs to be done to reach my action goal?

make it easier for American companies to raise prices and therefore hurt American consumers.

G. An American labor union leader states that limits on imports are necessary to boost sales of American products and protect American jobs.

H. Neighbors and friends are worried about the possible closing of a nearby factory that makes American cars. They urge you to "buy American."

I. Some foreign car companies have factories in the United States, which provide jobs for Americans.

Taking Action After you have made your choice, use a chart like the one on page 491 to make an action plan for buying the car. State your action goal, the resources and obstacles, what steps have to be taken to achieve the goal, and who will take those steps.

Skill Assessment

After making your choice and completing your action plan, answer these questions.

1. What goal or goals did you set?
2. What were two of your standards?
3. What types of information did you collect about each car?
4. Pick one of the cars and tell what characteristics and consequences you listed.
5. Pick two critical-thinking skills and explain how they helped you evaluate the pieces of information that you listed.
6. Which car did you choose? Explain why.
7. What resources might help you achieve your action goal? What obstacles might you face, and how might you overcome those obstacles ?
8. In what order did you put the steps of your plan for buying the car? Explain why.
9. Suppose that your family picks what seems to be a reasonable amount of money to offer for the car. However, after talking with the sales manager, the salesperson says that the offer is too low. Describe what you would do and explain why.
10. Explain how to judge options.
11. Explain why critical thinking is important in making good decisions.

How to ANALYZE SYSTEM DIAGRAMS

 Use the *Simulations and Data Graphing* CD-ROM to create and interpret graphs.

As you read in this chapter, today's world can be seen as a system—a whole made up of many interconnected parts, or nations. One important way that the nations of the world are connected is through global trade.

All around the world, global trade grew steadily in importance during the twentieth century. In the United States, for example, the total value of international trade rose from $2.2 billion in 1900, to $18 billion in 1950, to over $1.5 trillion by the end of the century.

Explain the Skill

System diagrams show how parts of a system are related. Such a diagram might be an electrical system for a building or an ecological system involving plants, animals, soil, and weather.

The diagram below shows how two countries—the United States and Japan—and two major international organizations—the European Union (EU) and OPEC—are connected to one another in the global economy. OPEC is the Organization of Petroleum Exporting Countries, a group of major oil exporting nations.

Analyze the Skill

Look at the system diagram on this page, which shows the flow of trade between the United States, Japan, the EU, and OPEC. The numbers indicate the value of goods traded in billions of dollars in 1998.

Look at the circle representing the United States. The arrow pointing from the United

States to Japan represents all the exports from the United States to Japan in 1998. The figure next to the arrow tells you the total value of those exports—$54.8 billion. The arrow pointing from Japan to the United States tells you that U.S. imports from Japan totaled $119.8 billion. Because the United States imported more from Japan than it exported to Japan, the United States had a *trade deficit* with Japan in 1998. In contrast, Japan had a *trade surplus* with the United States.

Skill Assessment

1. Which nations are shown on this diagram? Which international organizations?
2. Based on the total value of imports and exports, which nation or organization was the major trading partner of the United States?
3. With which nation or organization did the United States have the largest trade deficit in 1998?

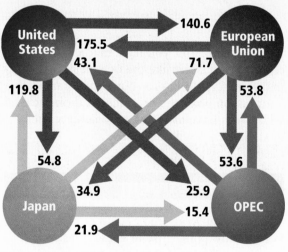

Flow of Trade, 1998 (in billions of dollars)

Source: United Nations 1998 International Trade Statistics Yearbook

CHAPTER 24 ASSESSMENT

Building Civics Vocabulary

The vocabulary terms in each pair listed below are related to each other. For each pair, explain how the two terms are related.

1. *sovereignty* and *nationalism*
2. *Cold War* and *détente*

Reviewing Main Ideas and Skills

3. In what ways can a nation build its power in order to protect its national interest?

4. How did colonial powers benefit from having colonies? How did the colonies suffer?

5. Explain some of the reasons why the United States and the Soviet Union came into conflict after World War II. Why did that conflict end?

6. Explain what it means for two nations to be interdependent. Give an example.

7. How does the environment make nations interdependent?

8. **How to Use an Action Plan** When working with an action plan, why should you check how well your plan is working while you are carrying it out?

9. **How to Analyze System Diagrams** Look back at the system diagram on page 538. Did Japan have a trade deficit or a trade surplus with the EU in 1998? How can you tell?

Critical Thinking

10. **Analyzing Visual Evidence** Look at the photograph on page 533. What does this photograph show? How does it help illustrate the global economy?

11. **Linking Past and Present** In what ways is the world a "smaller" place than it was 100 years ago?

Writing About Civics

12. **Writing a List** Labels on many common items tell you where the item was made. A VCR may have a label that says "Made in Japan." Check the labels on clothing, shoes, appliances, and other items. Make a list of at least ten different items along with the country each was made in. What can you conclude about the importance of global trade?

Citizenship Activities

13. **Working Together** With a small group, present a report on the United States' relationship over the past ten years with a foreign country. Tell why we have cooperated with, competed with, or come into conflict with that nation. Discuss what you believe should be done to ensure good relations in the future.

Take It to the NET

Access the **Civics: Participating in Government** Internet site at **www.phschool.com** for the specific URLs to complete the activity.

The United Nations was created in an attempt to foster understanding between nations and solve world problems. Examine online information about what the United Nations is and how it operates. Create a time line of the history of the United Nations and some of the major issues that it has confronted.

CHAPTER 25

American Foreign Policy

Citizenship and You

The date is September 12, 2001—the day after a horrible and deadly terrorist attack on the United States that has killed thousands of innocent Americans at the World Trade Center, the Pentagon, and on four hijacked planes. Throughout the country, Americans remain in a state of shock, horror, and mourning. Many look to the government to explain what has happened and to reassure them that they are safe.

Meanwhile, one by one, people enter a room and take seats around a huge table. Several of them are wearing military uniforms hung with medals. Finally the President arrives. He greets the people gathered in the room—the members of the National Security Council.

President Bush begins by asking each member of the council to update him on what actions have been taken to protect the country from further attacks. The remainder of the meeting is spent discussing both short- and long-term actions that must be taken. In the face of an incredible crisis, the President and the Security Council must act quickly and carefully to make important decisions about with military and diplomatic actions to take at home and abroad.

What's Ahead in Chapter 25

The President is in the middle of an important process—the making of foreign policy. In this chapter you will learn what foreign policy is and how it is made. You will also read about how our foreign policy has changed over time to reflect the changing role of the United States in the world.

Section 1 **What Is Foreign Policy?**

Section 2 **Making Foreign Policy**

Section 3 **Foreign Policy in Action**

Keep It Current

Items marked with this logo are periodically updated on the Internet. To keep up-to-date, go to www.phschool.com

Citizen's Journal

Suppose you were a member of the President's National Security Council. How would you suggest fighting the war on terrorism both at home and abroad? Defend your position.

What Is Foreign Policy?

SECTION PREVIEW

Objectives

- Summarize the main goals of American foreign policy.
- Describe the tools the United States uses to achieve its foreign policy goals.

Building Civics Vocabulary

- American armed forces defend against **aggression,** an attack or threat of attack by another country.
- Keeping a strong defense to discourage aggression by other nations is called **deterrence.**
- **Diplomacy** is the relations and communications carried out between nations.
- At a **summit meeting,** the President talks about important issues with heads of other governments.
- Military and economic help to other countries is called **foreign aid.**
- **Sanctions** stop or limit trade with another nation in order to change its behavior.
- Information about another country and what its government plans to do is called **intelligence.**

Focus

The United States is one nation among many in the world. One of the main duties of any government is making a plan for relating to other nations. A government's foreign policy is a plan that outlines the goals it hopes to meet in its relations with other countries. Foreign policy also sets forth the ways these goals are to be met.

Goals of Foreign Policy

What do Americans hope for in relations with other countries? To think about that question, you might ask yourself what we, as individual Americans, want in our relations with the people around us.

First of all, we want to be respected. We want others to treat us as equals. We would like to live in a safe place, free from the fear of harm. As adults, we would like to be able to earn a living.

These goals are like the goals we have as a nation. In general, the foreign policy goals of the United States are to protect citizens' safety, to promote prosperity, and to work for peace and democracy in other countries.

National Security You learned in Chapter 24 that government leaders naturally try to protect the interests of their country. Acting in the national interest involves making sure the nation is safe. National security, or the ability to keep the nation safe from attack or harm, is the chief goal of American foreign policy. Because war is the greatest danger to any nation, national security mainly focuses on the threat of war.

World Peace A second goal of American foreign policy is to get countries to work together as a way to keep out of war. In today's world, wars anywhere can be a threat to people everywhere. People fear that other countries may be drawn into the fighting. They fear that nuclear weapons may be used and the world destroyed.

Trade Increasing trade is a third goal of United States foreign policy. Trade is good for the United States economy. Trade creates markets for American goods and services, earning profits for our businesses. It also brings us goods from other countries.

Trade also brings greater interdependence and therefore cooperation. Maintaining good trading relations helps the United

In 1978 President Jimmy Carter worked for world peace by helping the leaders of Egypt and Israel settle some of their differences.

States meet its goals of national security and world peace. The profit and products nations gain from trade give them a good reason to avoid war with their trading partners.

Human Rights and Democracy Another goal of American foreign policy is to encourage all countries to respect the human rights of freedom, justice, and equality. Americans believe that democracy, in which citizens have the final say in their government, is the best way to protect human rights. Thus, they want to help people in other countries who are trying to form or keep democratic governments.

History shows that countries in which human rights are denied can be a threat to world peace. When citizens do not have the right to take part in their own government, revolutions and civil wars are likely to break out, and other countries are likely to be drawn in. Therefore, encouraging human

rights and democracy is also a way to meet our foreign policy goals of peace and security.

Tools of Foreign Policy

How does a country go about meeting its foreign policy goals? The United States uses several tools, such as defense, alliances, diplomacy, trade measures, and intelligence, in its relations with other nations.

Defense Defense is an important tool of American foreign policy. It helps the government maintain national security. American armed forces, with modern weapons, aircraft, and ships, are the means by which we defend ourselves against aggression, an attack or threat of attack by another country.

A key part of United States foreign policy has been deterrence, keeping a strong defense to discourage aggression by other nations. In

Chapter 24 you read about the arms race between the United States and the Soviet Union. Both sides claimed that they were building weapons as deterrence against aggression.

Sometimes it is not clear whether a nation is using its armed forces for defense or aggression. When the Soviets sent their army into Afghanistan in 1979, they said they were just helping the Afghan government defend against anti-communist forces. The United States accused the Soviets of aggression—of using its military power to take over an independent nation.

In 1989, when American forces overthrew Panama's dictator, Manuel Noriega, Latin American leaders accused the United States of aggression. President George H. W. Bush said the invasion's purpose was to protect American interests, especially the Panama Canal, and to help Panama get rid of a corrupt leader.

Alliances The United States also meets its foreign policy goals by forming military, political, or economic alliances with other countries. In Chapter 24 you read about NATO, a military alliance created to protect Western Europe from Soviet aggression. NATO members pooled military forces into one army in order to better defend themselves if attacked.

An example of a political alliance is the Organization of American States (OAS), made up of countries in North, Central, and South America. The OAS helps its members work together peacefully, trying to settle disputes before they become violent. The OAS also reports on human rights and helps to keep elections fair and honest.

The United States is a member of several economic alliances. One is the Organization for Economic Cooperation and Development (OECD). The 27 members of the OECD, mostly Western European countries, agree to help each other's economic well-being through trade. They also work together in giving aid to developing nations.

Diplomacy Can you remember settling a disagreement with someone by talking it out? In a similar way, the American government tries to settle disagreements with other countries peacefully. To do so, it depends mostly on a third tool of foreign policy, diplomacy. Diplomacy is the relations and communications carried out between countries. When countries disagree, they send representatives called diplomats to talk about the issues.

The United States uses diplomacy not only to settle disagreements but also to accomplish tasks such as building a canal or space station. Alliances and trade agreements are also made through diplomacy. Diplomacy often results in formal agreements known as treaties.

Usually, diplomacy is carried out by members of the Department of State. Sometimes, however, there is a summit meeting, a meeting at which the President talks about important issues with heads of other governments. In 1999, President Clinton traveled to China for a summit meeting with Chinese President Jiang Zemin at which the two leaders discussed military and economic issues.

Foreign Aid Another tool used to meet foreign policy goals is foreign aid, a program of giving military and economic help to other countries. After World War II the United States gave aid to European countries to help them rebuild factories, farms, cities, and homes destroyed in the war. Since the end of World War II, the United States has given or loaned almost $500 billion in foreign aid to over 100 countries.

Foreign aid can support American policy goals by strengthening governments and political groups that are friendly to the United States. In some cases this military aid has helped countries that are trying to put down rebellions within their borders. Sometimes the United States has sent weapons to rebels who are struggling against governments considered unfriendly to American interests.

Money and equipment are not the only forms of foreign aid. Peace Corps volunteers like this one in Ecuador give help to developing nations.

Economic aid takes many forms. The United States might help pay for a hospital, or a dam to control floods or produce electricity. Aid might be loans or grants to help a country start a new industry.

Sending experts and teachers to work in developing countries is also a form of aid. The United States also sends aid in a crisis such as a flood or earthquake. Aid helps nations' economies to grow and is seen as a way to reduce the chance of revolution and war.

Foreign aid has caused bitter debates in Congress and the nation. Americans disagree over how much and what kind of aid to give. Some say that giving help to other countries is our duty as a rich and powerful country. They say that if we do not give aid, poorer nations will turn to other governments— governments that are not necessarily friendly to the United States—for help. Another argument for economic aid is that it helps the United States. Countries that receive our aid can then buy American products.

Those who oppose aid do so for two main reasons. Some say that we should solve problems at home first and not send so much money out of the country.

Other critics say that the kind of aid we give does more harm than good. They charge that our military aid has sometimes helped governments that violate human rights. Just because a group is friendly to the United States, they say, is not a good reason to give it money and weapons. Critics also believe that some kinds of economic aid give the United States too much control over how other countries develop.

Trade Measures Another tool of foreign policy is trade measures, or the terms under which the United States trades with other countries. One trade measure is a quota, which states how much of a foreign product can be sold in the United States. Another measure is a tariff, a tax on foreign products sold in the United States. Trade measures also include limits on what products United States firms can sell abroad, such as weapons, or whether untested foreign products, such as drugs, can be brought into the United States.

In recent years a foreign policy tool has been sanctions—measures to stop or limit trade with another nation in order to change its behavior. In 1998, for example, India and Pakistan conducted underground nuclear weapons tests. To demonstrate its disapproval of the tests, the United States imposed economic sanctions on both nations.

The United States has two main goals in regulating trade with other countries. One is to get other countries to buy American goods. The other is to get our trading partners to support us in other foreign policy goals, such as stopping human rights violations and reducing possible threats to peace.

Intelligence Information about another country and what its government plans to do is called intelligence. Most countries work hard to gather intelligence in order to help them meet the goal of national security.

The Central Intelligence Agency (CIA) and other agencies gather information for the United States government. The CIA focuses mostly on countries it thinks might be unfriendly, and tries to learn what the governments of these countries intend to do. It also tries to predict how these governments will react to what the United States does.

Much of intelligence is secret. Information is sometimes gathered by spying. Sometimes intelligence agencies have helped overturn the government of a country. In Chile in 1973, for example, the CIA took part in overthrowing the government of Salvador Allende. The United States government thought Allende was not favorable to our national interest. Like defense, diplomacy, foreign aid, and trade measures, intelligence is an important tool of foreign policy.

Section 1 Assessment

1. **Define** aggression, deterrence, diplomacy, summit meeting, foreign aid, sanctions, intelligence
2. Why is world peace a goal of American foreign policy?
3. How does the United States use diplomacy as a tool of foreign policy?
4. **Synthesize** Explain how the foreign policy goal of promoting trade relates to the goals of national security and world peace.

Making Foreign Policy

SECTION PREVIEW

Objectives

- Describe the role the President and executive branch departments play in making foreign policy.
- Examine the powers Congress has over foreign policy.
- Explain how private groups and citizens can help shape foreign policy.

 Focus

Sarah was upset. She had learned that whales might become extinct because they were being hunted. Every year there were fewer and fewer whales left. "There must be something we can do," she thought.

Sarah found out that in 1946 countries that hunted whales, including the United States, had formed the International Whaling Commission (IWC). The goal of the IWC was to protect whales.

The IWC set limits on the number of whales that could be killed. Even so, by the 1980s there were so few whales left that the IWC decided to ban whaling for a while. However, Iceland, whose economy depended on whaling, refused to go along with the ban.

"How can we stop Iceland from hunting whales?" asked Sarah. She wondered if people in the government could help.

"Why don't you start by writing our representative in Congress?" suggested Sarah's father. So she did.

Sarah is one person hoping to affect American foreign policy. Like Sarah, many people and organizations have ideas about America's relations with other countries.

They want the government to take action to help achieve their goals.

Who decides how the United States should behave toward other countries? Who decides what action to take? As you will see, many people both inside and outside of government play a role in foreign policy.

The Executive Branch

Sarah was only one of many people who spoke out against whaling. The issue came to the attention of the President. The Constitution gives the President the major responsibility for making foreign policy. Since most foreign policy issues touch many parts of American life, from jobs to the environment, many departments and agencies of the executive branch get involved in foreign policy decisions.

The President The President shapes foreign policy both as commander in chief of the armed forces and as the nation's chief diplomat. The President sets defense policies, meets with leaders of other countries, and makes treaties and executive agreements. The President also appoints ambassadors to represent the United States in other countries and makes budget proposals to Congress for defense spending and foreign aid.

The President does not make foreign policy decisions alone, however. In the case of Iceland and whaling, the President might begin by asking the chief of staff to look into the matter. The chief of staff would then raise the question at a meeting with other members of the White House staff. Once the White House staff has talked over the problem, the chief of staff might send a letter to the Secretary of State, asking for information and perhaps some recommendations.

The Department of State The Department of State advises the President on foreign policy. It also carries out foreign

President George H. W. Bush visited American troops during the Persian Gulf War in 1991.

policy once that policy has been made. The Secretary of State works closely with the President and represents the United States in many diplomatic meetings. The Secretary is assisted by experts on different parts of the world, such as the Middle East or Europe, and by experts on foreign policy.

The Department of State also has nearly 16,000 officials working in other countries. These officials are known as foreign service officers. They include ambassadors, who represent our country in embassies, or diplomatic offices, around the world. They also include consuls, who help American business people and travelers abroad.

Members of the foreign service carry out our foreign policy. They also give the State Department information about the countries in which they serve.

When the President asked the Secretary of State to look into the whaling issue, here are some of the State Department offices and officials who took part.

- The Bureau of European Affairs has an Icelandic "desk" that keeps track of our relations with Iceland. The desk officer gave reports from our ambassador in Iceland. The Prime Minister of Iceland claimed that his country would take only a limited number of whales each year for a scientific study.

- The Bureau of Oceans and International Environmental and Scientific Affairs gave evidence that Iceland's "study" is really an excuse to keep whaling.

- The Bureau of Legislative Affairs of the State Department tells the Secretary of State what actions are allowed by Congress. Congress had given the President power to use trade measures in this case.

Facts & Quotes

Diplomatic Immunity

To help foreign relations run smoothly, nations have agreed on certain ways to treat diplomats. Some of these are:

- A diplomat is entitled to "diplomatic immunity," meaning he or she cannot be arrested by the country in which he or she serves.
- An embassy is treated as part of the diplomat's home country. Soldiers or police cannot enter unless invited.
- Packages sent home by diplomats cannot be seized or searched.
- At ceremonies, diplomats are seated according to strict rules of rank.

The Department of Defense

The Department of Defense also plays a part in making foreign policy. It advises the President on matters such as what weapons to make and where to place bases and troops. The President and the Secretary of Defense work closely with the Joint Chiefs of Staff—the heads of the Army, Navy, Air Force, and Marines.

The United States Navy has bases in Iceland. These bases make a contribution to Iceland's economy, and the Department of Defense believes they are needed. The Secretary of Defense could warn the President that if trade were cut off, Iceland might close these bases.

The National Security Council

The National Security Council (NSC) advises the President on the country's safety. The NSC includes the President and Vice President and the secretaries of state and defense. The director of the CIA and the head of the Joint Chiefs of Staff, as well as other experts, also attend NSC meetings. The President calls a meeting of the NSC when a crisis comes up somewhere and American security seems in danger.

The President's National Security Advisor is the director of the NSC. Like the Secretary of Defense, he or she would consider how changing our trade policy with Iceland could affect NATO and our bases.

Other Executive Departments and Agencies

Depending on the problem, the President may seek help from other executive departments and agencies. In the whaling case, for instance, the Department of Commerce played an important role.

One division of the Department of Commerce is responsible for protecting marine mammals and representing the United States on the International Whaling Commission.

The Department of Defense, with headquarters in the vast Pentagon building, has an important role in making and carrying out American foreign policy.

Congress

Although the President plays the major role in making and carrying out foreign policy, Congress also has some power over foreign policy. The Senate has the power to approve or reject treaties. The President's choices for the diplomatic corps must also be approved by the Senate. Furthermore, only Congress can declare war.

Congress has power over foreign policy because it controls the federal budget, including spending on defense and foreign aid. The executive and legislative branches sometimes have conflicts over foreign policy. In 1999 President Clinton clashed with the Senate over the Comprehensive Test Ban Treaty—a treaty to prohibit nuclear weapons tests worldwide. Clinton urged senators to ratify the treaty, saying it would help prevent the spread of nuclear weapons. Republican senators, however, argued the agreement would weaken national security. The Senate voted to reject the treaty.

Several congressional committees are important in making foreign policy. Those most directly involved are the Senate Foreign Relations Committee, the House International Relations Committee, and the Armed Services committees in both houses.

These committees hold hearings and write and study bills that affect our relations with other countries. The Secretary of State and other executive branch officials are often asked to come before these committees to answer questions.

Private Groups

Private organizations and individuals can also shape foreign policy. Sarah had read about the whaling problem in a magazine published by an environmental protection group. Many groups have special interests that are affected by foreign policy. These groups want to have a voice in what that policy will be.

Business Groups You saw in Chapter 24 that countries around the world are linked by trade. Businesses that trade with other nations have a direct interest in foreign policy. Restaurant owners, for example, might want to buy Icelandic fish because of its low cost. During the whaling controversy, however, environmental organizations convinced several major American restaurant chains to boycott Icelandic fish. This action hurt Iceland's economy, causing Iceland's leaders to rethink their whaling policy.

Labor Groups Today, Americans are buying more foreign-made goods than we

Youth Gain Understanding

In Alexandria, Virginia, Sarah Lin is an only child. In Bern, Switzerland, she has several brothers, sisters, and parents. She gained her new "families" while on a summer exchange with Youth For Understanding, an organization that arranges for high school students to go to school in foreign countries.

Sarah traveled with three different families around Switzerland. She learned about their lives and values and saw how their schools and government work. Sarah feels that living in Switzerland changed how she thinks about the world: "The experience changed who I am, how I do things, and how I think. It opened my eyes to the way Swiss people live. I learned why people do what they do, and why they are the way they are."

Because Sarah's summer was such a good experience, the Lin family decided to host a foreign student. They wanted to continue to learn about the world through others.

Jasmin Koeber, from Nuremberg, Germany, came to live with the Lin family for a year. She went to school with Sarah, took classes with American students, and got to know Americans as friends.

Because Sarah was born in China, Jasmin also learned about that country as well.

"Living here in the U.S.A. has led to an expanded view of the world for me," said Jasmin. "Becoming part of another family helped me learn more about myself."

Sarah's experience left her wanting to find out more about the world as well. "I want to visit more places and meet more people and learn as much about the world as possible," said Sarah. "I want to take the best of everything I find in the world and incorporate it into my life."

Active Citizenship

According to Sarah and Jasmin, what are the benefits of learning about other countries?

---

are selling to other countries. The result has been the loss of many jobs in the United States. Labor groups, therefore, try to get executive branch policymakers and members of Congress to protect jobs by limiting or taxing certain imports and by putting pressure on our trading partners to buy more American products.

Political Groups Many other organizations, such as the environmental group that got Sarah interested in the whaling issue, try to affect foreign policy. Anti-nuclear groups want the United States to stop sending nuclear weapons to support NATO forces in Europe. Church groups and human rights groups also get involved.

The United States is home to people of diverse backgrounds, some of whom try to shape policy toward areas of the world they care about. For example, many Cuban Americans who fled Cuba's government have influenced American policy towards that country. Although the United States recently eased its policy of restricting trade and travel to Cuba, the strong support of Cuban Americans has kept the basic policy in place.

Individuals Individuals can also play a role in foreign policy. Americans who keep up with international news, and who study, travel, or work abroad, learn about foreign countries and our government's policies toward them. Being better informed helps citizens make better decisions on foreign policy.

There are many ways that citizens who care about foreign policy can make a difference. Running for office or voting for a candidate who shares your views are two important ways. Letting your senator or representative know what you think about the issues is another way. Members of Congress want to know how citizens feel about matters of foreign policy, especially if an issue puts American troops in harm's way.

In the whaling matter, Iceland agreed to go along with the IWC ban. It decided not to risk losing the American market for its fish. In this case, citizens' groups and individuals played an important role in getting our government to put pressure on Iceland.

Section 2 Assessment

1. Briefly tell what responsibilities the President has in foreign policy.
2. In what ways does Congress help shape foreign policy?
3. Why do business and labor groups take a special interest in foreign policy?
4. **Synthesize** Why do you think so many government groups and private groups try to affect foreign policy?

Foreign Policy in Action

SECTION PREVIEW

Objectives

- Explain the major changes in American foreign policy between the American Revolution and World War II.
- Describe American foreign policy during the Cold War.
- Explore world events that brought the Cold War to an end.
- Explain how the rise of new economic powers affects American foreign policy.
- Summarize the foreign policy challenges that the United States will face in the future.

Building Civics Vocabulary

- **Isolationism** is a foreign policy that seeks to limit our relations with other countries.
- **Neutrality** is a policy of not taking sides in wars between other countries.
- **Containment** was a policy of using military power and money to prevent the spread of communism.

 Focus

You have read about the goals of American foreign policy and the tools our leaders use to meet these goals. Although the goals have stayed largely the same over the years, the role that the United States plays in the world is continually changing. At times we have followed isolationism, a foreign policy that seeks to limit our relations with other countries as much as possible. During other periods, the United States has tried to meet its goals by taking an active part in affairs around the world.

Early Isolationism

In its early years, the United States had a mostly isolationist foreign policy. A farming country with very little industry, we had just fought a costly war for independence. President George Washington believed that the young country could not afford to take part in European alliances and wars. He chose a position of neutrality, a policy of not taking sides in wars between other countries.

This neutrality served two foreign policy aims. It kept the United States out of war. It also allowed America to continue to trade with both sides in a war.

Staying isolated was not easy to do. European countries were expanding into Latin America, competing with our economic interests and threatening American security. In 1823 President James Monroe responded to the threat with the Monroe Doctrine. He warned European nations not to create more colonies in the Western Hemisphere. Monroe promised that in return, America would stay out of European affairs. Monroe saw this position as a way to protect American interests and still stay isolated from Europe.

Foreign Policy and Expansion

The policy of isolationism was again tested as Americans began to move west, seeking more land. Expansion forced the United States into contact—and sometimes conflict—with Mexico, France, Spain, Great Britain, and Russia, which held claims to these lands.

The United States used several foreign policy tools to help it grow in size. Sometimes it gained land through purchase or treaty. At other times, it used its armed forces to win land in war or by threat of war.

Meanwhile, American businesses were expanding across the Pacific, beginning to trade with Japan, China, and other Asian countries. The United States built military bases in Hawaii and the Far East to protect this trade and prevent European countries from setting up colonies.

American business also expanded into Central and South America. The policy of isolationism did not apply to that part of the world, which the United States, still following the Monroe Doctrine, viewed as being in its own backyard. Many times, the United States sent its armed forces into Latin America. Most often, the goal was to protect economic interests or national security.

World War I and Return to Isolationism

World War I forced the United States to change its policy of isolationism toward Europe. Although at first President Woodrow Wilson took a position of neutrality, German aggression caused Congress to declare war in 1917. President Wilson said that the goal in entering the war was to make the world "safe for democracy." He believed that this would be the "war to end war," leading to lasting world peace.

After the war, Wilson helped found the League of Nations, a new organization intended to help keep peace. However, Congress was eager to withdraw from European affairs and return to isolationism. It refused to approve American membership in the League.

World War II: The End of Isolationism

The efforts of the League of Nations failed to keep peace, and within 20 years the world was again at war. When World War II began in Europe, the United States tried to stay out of the conflict. However, when the Japanese bombed the American Navy at Pearl Harbor, Hawaii, in 1941, the United States declared war.

When the war ended in 1945, the United States was the richest and most powerful country in the world. It believed it could play a key part in keeping world peace. American leaders met with Soviet and European leaders to make a peace plan. The United States also helped to found the United Nations, an international organization you will learn more about in the next chapter.

From Containment to Cooperation

The end of World War II marked the end of the belief that the United States should try to stay out of conflicts between other nations. American leaders saw that our own national security went hand-in-hand with global security. Trouble anywhere in the world could mean trouble for the United States. Therefore, the goal of world peace took center stage in foreign policy.

As you read in Chapter 24, many Americans thought that the Soviet Union and the spread of communism were the main dangers to the goal of peace. Already the Soviets had taken control of several Eastern European countries. When the Communists, backed by the Soviets, tried to take over Greece and Turkey, President Harry Truman sent American military aid to help those countries defend themselves.

Truman's action was the beginning of a new foreign policy of **containment,** a policy of using military power and money to prevent the spread of communism. At first, the government's main tool of containment was economic aid. By giving economic aid, the United States hoped to strengthen the economies of European countries so that they could hold out against Soviet aggression.

Later, the United States came to depend more and more on military strength and deterrence to support the policy of containment. As you saw, the Cold War was fought with words and warnings, and sometimes

Afghan residents pick up food packets of U.S. humanitarian aid dropped by U.S. planes in the fall of 2001. The food packets were intended to help the Afghan people while the United States and Britain waged a war against terrorists and the country's Taliban rulers. The Taliban, a religious fundamentalist group, had taken control of Afghanistan following a failed attempt by the Soviet Union to take over the country.

confrontation. The Cuban missile crisis and the wars in Korea and Vietnam are examples of confrontations that grew out of the effort to contain communism.

By the mid-1960s, it was clear the Soviet Union was gaining nuclear strength nearly equal to that of the United States. In Chapter 24 you read about détente in the 1970s, when the superpowers turned to treaties and diplomacy to ease the tensions caused by the military buildup. Through the 1980s, leaders continued to see that depending on military strength alone would not guarantee national security. Even though both the United States and the Soviet Union continued building up arms, the spirit of cooperation grew.

As the Communist government of East Germany crumbled in late 1989, the hated Berlin Wall could no longer keep East and West apart.

The End of the Cold War

As the 1980s gave way to the 1990s, the improving relationship between the superpowers was overshadowed by some breathtaking events. First, Communist governments fell in Poland and other Eastern European countries. Then the Soviet Union itself began to fall apart. Suddenly, the ground on which forty-five years of American foreign policy had been built had shifted greatly. No longer could Americans picture the world as a cold-war battleground, with Communist nations united against democracies.

The Breakup of the Soviet Union

Changes had begun to take place in the Soviet Union in the mid-1980s. Mikhail Gorbachev, the new head of the Soviet Communist party, undertook reforms, known as perestroika, aimed at improving the economy. Perestroika loosened some government controls over the economy and encouraged some private business. Gorbachev also announced a policy of glasnost, or "openness" between government and citizens.

Gorbachev's policies gave the people of the Soviet Union a taste of freedom—and they wanted more. Citizens grew impatient with the slow pace of change, and nationalist feelings erupted among the diverse peoples of the fifteen Soviet republics.

By the end of 1991, every Soviet republic had declared its independence and the Communist central government had been dissolved. The Soviet Union ceased to exist.

As an independent nation, Russia began making the transition from communism to democracy and a market economy. In June 1991, Boris Yeltsin was elected president in Russia's first popular election. Relations between Russia and the United States continued to improve. In 1993, Presidents Bush and Yeltsin signed a major nuclear arms reduction treaty.

Throughout the 1990s, however, Russia's economy remained stuck in a deep recession. Reflecting the new spirit of cooperation between Russia and the United States, the United States began helping its longtime rival. Along with other nations, the United States gave Russia billions of dollars of financial aid during the 1990s.

Eastern Europe As the Soviet Union began to collapse, dramatic changes took place in Eastern Europe as well. In 1989, Hungary declared itself an independent republic. Voters in Poland elected the first non-Communist government in the region since World War II. In Czechoslovakia, after masses of citizens marched in the streets,

In late 1991, amid rallies like this one in Ukraine, Soviet republics declared themselves independent states. A paint-splattered poster of Lenin represents rejection of Soviet communism. By the end of that year the Soviet Union ceased to exist—a startling development that raised new foreign policy issues for the United States.

Communist leaders gave up power. In November 1989, the Berlin Wall, symbol of the Cold War, was torn down by the people of Germany.

The United States began helping the nations of Eastern Europe establish democratic governments and market economies. As with Russia, the United States developed friendly relations with its former enemies. In 1999, three former Communist nations (the Czech Republic, Poland, and Hungary) were invited to join NATO.

As you have seen, the end of the Cold War caused dramatic changes in American foreign policy. The United States was left as the world's only superpower. How should the United States use this power to promote peace and economic growth around the world? This question will continue to challenge American policymakers for years to come.

Relations with China Some observers of the startling events in Eastern Europe and the Soviet Union spoke of the "death of communism." However, the world's most populous country—China—was still ruled by a communist government.

Trade has increased between China and the United States, but China's treatment of its own citizens has hurt relations between the two countries. Americans were outraged when Chinese troops crushed a student-led democratic movement in June 1989, killing hundreds of protestors in Beijing's Tiananmen Square.

There has been debate over how to react to these human rights violations. Should we punish China by cutting off diplomatic relations and trade? Or should we maintain such contacts as ways of influencing Chinese leaders?

Changes in Economic Power

The United States also faces changes in economic power around the world. As other countries have gained strength, American leaders have had to rethink policies.

Japan has become a great economic power. While the United States buys many Japanese products, Japan buys far fewer American goods and services. An important goal of foreign policy is to balance this trade. Meanwhile, China's rapidly growing economy is making it a strong force in international trade.

The countries of Western Europe have also gained economic strength. You have read about the European Union (EU) and its efforts to break down trade barriers between its member nations. This alliance gives the countries of the EU power to compete with the United States.

Another source of economic power outside the United States is the oil-rich countries. Foreign policy toward the Middle East will continue to be greatly affected by our need to assure a continuing oil supply.

Clearly the United States will have to make new policies to deal with changes in economic power. Neither isolationism nor military strength can meet the challenges posed by the changing world economy.

Regional Challenges

American leaders often have to make foreign policy fit the issues and needs of different regions in the world. Four regions that will continue to pose major challenges for United States foreign policy are Latin America, Eastern Europe, the Middle East, and Africa.

Latin America During the Cold War the United States used aid, diplomacy, and military intervention to stop the spread of communism in Latin America. By the early 1990s most Latin American countries were governed through fragile democracies. What is the best way for the United States to support these democratic governments? How can the United States help the nations of Latin America improve their economies?

As you read in Chapter 24, the United States, Canada, and Mexico signed the North American Free Trade Agreement in 1993, lowering trade barriers between the three nations. Should the United States now pursue free trade agreements with all the nations of Latin America, making North and South America into one huge market similar to the European Union?

Eastern Europe Since the end of the Cold War, the Czech Republic, Hungary, and Poland have made great strides toward democratic government and free market economies. The standard of living in Eastern Europe, however, is still well below that in Western Europe. Wars in Bosnia and Serbia have left serious ethnic divisions that will need to be healed. Three former Soviet states— Ukraine, Kazakhstan, and Belarus—still have nuclear weapons, and their economies are lagging. Should we try to help these countries and, if so, how?

The Middle East In 2000, violence broke out once again between Israelis and Palestinians. Then, in 2001, Ariel Sharon was elected Israel's prime minister. Sharon took a much tougher stance on negotiating peace with the Palestinians than the previous prime minister, Ehud Barak. It will take a great effort to overcome the long history of religious and political conflict in the region. American policymakers need to decide how best to promote a lasting peace.

Africa Many countries of Africa are among the poorest in the world. For example, the per capita GDP of Chad was only $1,000 in 1999. Many also suffer from political instability. During the 1990s, civil wars raged in Sudan, Rwanda, the Congo Republic, and Algeria, leaving hundreds of thousands dead. The new democracy in South Africa appears to be a bright star on the horizon. It faces a challenge, though, in expanding economic opportunity for black South Africans.

Foreign policy questions for Africa are similar to those for other parts of the developing world. Should the United States become involved? What actions will promote peace, economic growth, and democracy?

Leading the War on Terrorism

The United States emerged from the Cold War as the world's strongest economic and military power. The threat from another superpower no longer exists, but in its place is the threat of terrorism. After the terrorist attacks on New York and the Pentagon on September 11, 2001, the United States vowed to work with allies throughout the world to halt future terrorist attacks as well as to stop the flow of money to terrorist organizations.

While Americans may debate how best to fight the threat of terrorism, most agree that returning to a policy of isolation is not a workable foreign policy in an interdependent and dangerous world. Neither is relying on economic or military power. Foreign policy decisions are likely to be more difficult, now that the enemy is no longer easy to identify. Each problem will have to be handled case by case, but at least the end of the superpower conflict has removed a major barrier to cooperation. The United States can begin to establish a new role.

Section 3 Assessment

1. **Define** isolationism, neutrality, containment
2. Why did the United States choose a policy of isolationism early in its history?
3. What foreign policy tools did the United States use to carry out the policy of containment?
4. What challenges face the United States in the post-Cold War world?
5. **Evaluation**. "The United States should return to an isolationist foreign policy." Do you agree or disagree? Why?

Extending the Chapter

Global Views

While the danger of world war may have declined since the end of the Cold War, another danger—that of international terrorism—is as serious a threat as ever. Dealing with this threat will be one of the major challenges facing the United States in the future.

On October 12, 2000, a small boat full of explosives was crashed into the American warship U.S.S. *Cole* while it was anchored in a harbor in Yemen in the Middle East. The explosion killed 17 American sailors and wounded 42.

Less than a year later on September 11, 2001, approximately 3,000 Americans were killed when terrorists crashed hijacked commercial airplanes into the World Trade Center in New York City and the Pentagon in Washington, D.C. Investigators believe that Osama bin Laden was responsible for both of these attacks as well as the bombings of American embassies in Kenya and Tanzania.

President George W. Bush has declared that the United States is committed to combating international terrorism. As former President Clinton said, "This is not just America's fight. It's a universal one, between those who want to build a world of peace…and those who would tear everything down."

Becoming a Political Refugee

In her hearing before the Immigration and Naturalization Service (INS) Margaret Njoroge, a young woman from Kenya, stated: "These are not joyful stories for me to write or to remember. They represent life and death experiences which no one should or would want to face."

At the time of Margaret's hearing in 1998, she was living in the United States on a temporary student visa. She was about to graduate, however, and under the terms of her student visa, she was required to return home right after graduation. Fearing that her life would be threatened if she went back to Kenya, Margaret asked the INS to allow her to stay in the United States. Before the INS could decide if she would be allowed to stay, Margaret had to tell INS officials why she believed she would be in danger if she returned to Kenya.

Six years earlier, Margaret reported, her family had been forced out of their house in the Rift Valley province in western Kenya because of violent clashes between the Kalenjin, the dominant ethnic group in that area, and the Kikuyu and other less powerful tribes. Margaret and her family are Kikuyu.

In 1992, shortly after Kenya moved to create a multi-party political system, Margaret's family faced more serious threats. Just before Kenya was to hold its first multi-party elections, the Kalenjin began to terrorize the Kikuyu to force them out of the region. Young Kalenjin men told Margaret and her family that unless they voted for the candidates from President Daniel Arap Moi's party they might be harmed.

> **Margaret asked the INS to allow her to stay in the United States.**

Accused of working against the Moi government and fearing for his life, Margaret's husband fled the country. Her father's stores were burned. Kalenjin men committed violent attacks on Margaret's family and her Kikuyu neighbors.

After fleeing the Rift Valley province along with her family, Margaret was unable to find a job. In 1997, she received a scholarship to attend an American university where she completed a masters degree.

Although recalling the terrible times in her homeland was very hard for Margaret, she said that "In some ways I am glad to have the opportunity to tell these stories." To help her present her case, Margaret hired an immigration lawyer. She was able to find a non-profit legal firm that aided her in preparing the documents she needed to submit.

Margaret's lawyer explained that a federal law

gave her the legal basis for staying in the country. This law is the Immigration and Nationality Act. It says that the United States government shall not send an alien back to his or her native country if that person's "life or freedom would be threatened in such country on account of race, religion, nationality, membership in a particular social group, or political opinion."

Congress passed this law in response to what it saw as a need to protect those threatened by persecution in their homelands. The law's purpose is to support the traditional role of the United States as a safe place for "the oppressed of other nations."

The law says that for an alien to be allowed to stay in the United States, he or she must first be classified as a "refugee." A refugee is someone who lives outside of his or her native country and is unable to return to that country because of "a well-founded fear of persecution."

For a person to be called a refugee, the law says that the person must be able to offer "reasonably specific information" that shows a real threat of personal harm. The person's fear of harm cannot be based on just a general concern for his or her safety.

> **The law's purpose is to support the traditional role of the United States as a safe place for "the oppressed of other nations."**

The main question the INS had to decide was whether Margaret fit the strict definition of a "refugee." At her hearing with the INS, an INS officer questioned her about everything she had written in her sworn statement. She told how she feared for her life if she returned to Kenya, based on what had happened to her father and other members of her family there. She pointed out that activists and others who had spoken out for political reform in Kenya had been jailed or persecuted by the government. She also presented reports from experts on Kenyan politics and history about the current situation in the country.

The INS concluded that the evidence Margaret presented made for a "very solid case." About a month after her hearing, Margaret received a letter from INS officials granting her refugee status and stating that she would be eligible for permanent residence status after one year.

Analyzing the Case

1. What law did Margaret depend on to allow her to remain in the United States?
2. Under what conditions can someone classify as a "refugee"?
3. Do you think the INS should make it easy or difficult for an alien to remain in the United States as a refugee? Explain your view.

How to INTERPRET GRAPHICS

As you read in this chapter and Chapter 24, both the United States and the Soviet Union built huge arsenals of nuclear weapons during the Cold War. While several arms treaties have led to an overall reduction in the number of nuclear missiles, the United States and Russia still maintain large nuclear arsenals. As of 2000, the United States had an estimated 12,000 nuclear bombs—down from an all-time high of 32,000 in 1966.

Other countries, including Great Britain, France, China, India, and Pakistan have also developed nuclear weapons. These nations hope that their nuclear weapons will discourage other countries from attacking them. It is the tremendous destructive power of nuclear weapons that makes them an effective deterrent to attack. The graphic on this page helps illustrate the destructive power of nuclear weapons.

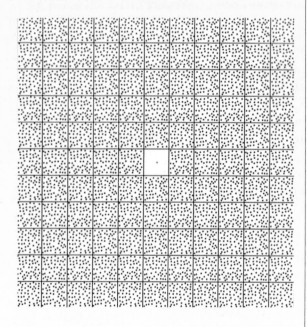

Explain the Skill

A graphic is a visual way of showing an object, idea, or relationship. We see graphics all around us—maps, logos, posters, and illustrations. Graphics communicate in a vivid way without words.

For example, look at the map of the United States on page 488 of this book. This map shows how many electoral votes each state has. Using colors and numbers, the graphic shows the relative political power of different states. Now look at the graphic on this page.

Analyze the Skill

The single dot in the center square of this graphic represents all of the weapon power used in World War II, including the two atomic bombs dropped on Japan. The other dots represent the weapon power of all nuclear weapons at the height of the Cold War. The weapon power in two squares could destroy all medium and large cities on earth. Think about what this graphic is intended to show, and then answer the following questions.

Skill Assessment

1. What does the dot in the center square of this graphic represent?
2. What do the other 6,000 dots represent?
3. What does this graphic say to you?
4. How does this graphic relate to the policy goals of national security and world peace?

CHAPTER 25 ASSESSMENT

Building Civics Vocabulary

The terms in each pair listed below are related to each other. For each pair, explain what the terms have in common and how they are different.

1. *aggression* and *deterrence*
2. *diplomacy* and *summit meeting*
3. *isolationism* and *neutrality*
4. *containment* and *deterrence*

Reviewing Main Ideas and Skills

5. How does trading with foreign countries benefit the United States economy?
6. How do alliances help the United States meet its foreign policy goals?
7. Why do countries work so hard to gather intelligence about one another?
8. How do the foreign policy powers of Congress check the foreign policy powers of the executive branch?
9. How did the end of the Cold War affect American foreign policy?
10. **How to Interpret a Graphic** Look back at the graphic on page 560. Write a title for this graphic. Explain why you chose this title.

Critical Thinking

11. **Identifying Main Ideas** How does foreign aid support United States foreign policy goals? What are some criticisms of United States foreign aid programs?
12. **Linking Past and Present** Why did George Washington decide on a foreign policy position of neutrality toward European conflicts? What world events caused the United States to change this policy?

Writing About Civics

13. **Writing a Letter** Of all the United States' foreign policy goals, which do you think is the most important? Write a letter to your Representative or Senator telling him or her which foreign policy goal you believe Congress should focus on. Explain your reasons.

Citizenship Activities

14. **Working Together** In groups of three or four, choose a foreign country with which the United States has ongoing foreign relations. Collect newspaper and magazine articles about our relations with this country. What do the articles tell you about United States foreign policies toward this country? Do you agree with the policies? What tools is the United States using to fulfill its foreign policy goals? Prepare a short report to give to the class.

Take It to the NET

Access the **Civics: Participating in Government** Internet site at **www.phschool.com** for the specific URLs to complete the activity.

United States foreign policy is a complex field that is shaped by a number of issues. Examine online information about foreign policy issues to create a report of current events. What are the current "hot spots" and how, in your opinion, should the United States react to these situations?

CHAPTER 26

Making a Difference in the World

Citizenship and You

At the Johnson house, the television was switched on to the six o'clock news. The screen filled with the image of a huge American cargo plane being unloaded at an airport in Bangladesh. "Shipments of food from the United States and other countries," said the reporter, "are desperately needed to help people survive the terrible flooding in this part of Asia."

The Johnsons hardly had time to take in the sight of flooded villages and hungry children before they were transported back to the network news center in New York. "In other news today," the anchorwoman was saying, "scientists at an international conference in Toronto, Canada, discussed the possibility that air pollution is heating up Earth's atmosphere. Changes in climate could threaten not only human health but also food and water supplies throughout the world. The scientists urged all nations to take action against pollution."

Mrs. Johnson turned toward her husband and their children. "You know," she said, "sometimes I feel like tuning out the news and escaping from the world's problems. The more I learn, though, the more I see that we can't escape. They are our problems, too, and we have to face them. We can't afford not to."

What's Ahead in Chapter 26

In this chapter you will explore some of the problems facing our world. You will also be looking at how organizations and individuals are making a difference in dealing with those problems.

Section 1   **Global Problems for Spaceship Earth**
Section 2   **Organizations Facing the Problems**
Section 3   **How Individuals Can Make a Difference**

Keep It Current

Items marked with this logo are periodically updated on the Internet. To keep up-to-date, go to www.phschool.com

Citizen's Journal

What is one world problem you have heard about recently in the news? When you heard about this world problem, did you feel that it was your problem, too? Why or why not?

Global Problems for Spaceship Earth

SECTION PREVIEW

Objectives

■ Explain why the world faces a shortage of natural resources.
■ Explore pollution problems that are threatening Earth.
■ Describe the global threats of arms buildups, terrorism, and human rights violations.
■ Analyze ways that nations can cooperate in solving global problems.

Building Civics Vocabulary

■ A **renewable resource** is a resource that can be replaced after being used.
■ A **nonrenewable resource** is a resource that cannot be replaced once it has been used.
■ Cutting and burning forests to clear land for farms or cattle grazing is called **deforestation**.
■ **Terrorism** is the use or threat of violence to spread fear, usually for the purpose of reaching political goals.

 Focus

The world is getting used to warnings. Scientists and government officials point to a "population explosion" that is straining Earth's supply of fresh water and food. "Acid rain" pollutes lakes and rivers. Many scientists think that air pollution will cause a dangerous rise in Earth's temperature. Meanwhile, we must continue to slow down the arms race and try to keep a nuclear war from happening.

How are limited resources, pollution, and the arms race alike? They are all global problems—problems that affect the whole world and that can be solved only by countries working together. It is becoming clear to people everywhere that decisions made in one country can have effects on other countries. Sometimes those effects are good, and sometimes they cause great harm.

As you read about some of the major problems facing all of us who live on Earth, you will see why no one person or country can solve them alone. You will see why we Americans cannot afford to say, "Those are your problems, not ours." As you read, think about your duty to life on our planet. How might you help to make a difference?

Limited Natural Resources

How much longer will the world's oil last? What can be done about the lack of water in many places? Questions like these point to one of the major problems facing the world: Earth has limited natural resources.

Our main natural resources are water, air, soil, trees and other plants, animals, sunlight, and minerals. To understand why we are running short, you first need to know the difference between renewable and nonrenewable resources.

A renewable resource is a resource that can be replaced after being used. Trees are a renewable resource because new ones can be planted to replace those cut down. However, just because some resources are renewable does not mean that there will always be enough of them. Often it takes a long time to replace a resource. You can cut down a tree in minutes, but it takes years to grow a new one. If people do not plant new trees, the world may run out of wood.

A nonrenewable resource is a resource that cannot be replaced once it has been used. Metals, coal, and oil are nonrenewable resources. At some point they may all be used up. The metals in some products may be used again. The same is not true of fossil fuels such as coal and oil. Once they are

WORLD POPULATION, 1950-2050 The world population is expected to top 9 billion by the year 2050. **Regions What is expected to happen to the population of developed nations over the next 45 years?**

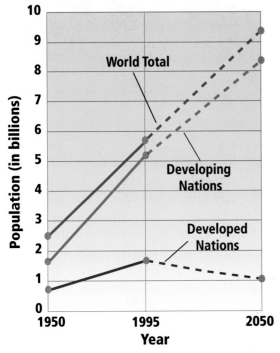

Dotted lines indicate projected population figures.

Source: United Nations Population Division

burned up, they are gone forever. You can plant a new tree, but you cannot "grow" more coal, oil, or metals.

Another problem is that resources are not spread evenly around the world. Some countries are "water-rich" because they get plenty of rainfall. Countries in dry parts of the world are "water-poor." Some countries have enough oil or coal, but others must buy most of the oil and coal they need.

Population growth also puts pressure on resources. The number of people in the world is growing, but the supply of many resources is staying the same or shrinking. For instance, there are three times as many people in the world today as in 1900, but the amount of fresh water has stayed about the same.

People's life-styles also put a strain on resources. Developed nations use up oil and coal to make gasoline and electric power for factories and houses. The United States consumes over eight times as much energy as all the countries on the African continent combined.

Meanwhile, people in developing nations want to improve their standard of living. To meet their needs, as well as our own, we must try to find new resources and not waste the ones we have, or else learn to do without.

Pollution

Human beings can live on Earth because it has land, water, and air. Too often, people are careless with these resources. We are polluting the environment. That is, we are making it unclean and unhealthy.

Pollution is a hard problem to tackle. One reason is that we do not know enough about its causes. When the first factories and cars were built, people did not know how they would affect the land, water, and air. Even today scientists do not know the effects of many new products, such as pesticides. Also, after a product is found to be harmful, months or years may be needed to undo the damage it has caused.

Perhaps an even greater roadblock to reducing pollution is the fact that many people think that the effort is too hard or costs too much. For instance, everyone knows that carpooling or taking a bus helps to cut down air pollution, but people still like to drive their own cars. Farmers are finding that using pesticides is the easiest way of killing insects and protecting their crops. Meanwhile, companies say it costs them too much to try to limit the amount of smoke coming from their factories.

However, scientists fear for Earth. They warn that problems such as toxic chemicals,

The burning of Amazon rain forests, like air pollution from cars and factories, releases large amounts of carbon dioxide, which may cause a dangerous warming of Earth's atmosphere.

acid rain, the greenhouse effect, and the weakening of the ozone layer are threatening the world.

Toxic Chemicals Millions of tons of chemicals are produced each year throughout the world. There are over 70,000 different ones in everyday use. They are found in many products—from household cleansers to weed killers. Many are helpful in households, farming, and industry, but some can also be toxic, or poisonous, to people and the environment. Chemicals can get into rivers, lakes, and wells.

Toxic chemicals are a global problem because rivers polluted by chemicals often flow from one country to another. Also, multinational corporations have factories in many countries around the world. In India, for example, gas leaking from an American factory killed over 2,000 people in 1984.

Acid Rain Perhaps you have heard news reports about acid rain. When coal and oil are burned, they give off chemicals that mix with water in the air to form acids. These acids fall to the ground as acid rain—polluted fog, rain, and snow. Scientists have found that acid rain kills fish and damages forests.

Acid rain is a global problem because the wind blows pollution from factory smokestacks across borders. Canada says that half of the acid rain falling on its lakes, farms, and forests comes from American factories. In short, the problem cannot be solved unless countries work together.

The Greenhouse Effect Many scientists believe that Earth is slowly getting warmer. They say one cause of this warming is that factories and cars burn fossil fuels. Another possible cause is deforestation, cutting and burning forests to clear land for farms and cattle grazing. Deforestation is taking place in many parts of the world, including the huge Amazon River Basin in South America.

Burning fossil fuels and forests is said to cause global warming by adding to the blanket of carbon dioxide in the air. Carbon dioxide traps the sun's heat, much as a garden greenhouse does. Many scientists believe that too much carbon dioxide will dangerously increase this "greenhouse effect." Rising temperatures could cause droughts. They might also melt glaciers and ice caps, raising the sea level and flooding coastal cities.

Some scientists do not think that Earth is getting warmer. However, most believe that we must take steps to cut down the amount of carbon dioxide in the air. If we do nothing now, we may find later that it is too late.

The Weakened Ozone Layer High in the air a layer of ozone gas protects Earth against most of the sun's ultraviolet rays, which can cause skin cancer and eye damage. Without this layer, most plants and animals probably could not live.

Scientists have discovered that the layer of ozone is getting thinner, and holes are opening in it. The main cause is chlorofluorocarbons (CFCs) used in refrigerators and air conditioners, spray cans, and many take-out food packages. In the air, CFCs cause a chemical reaction that cuts down the amount of ozone. For this reason, most countries have banned the use of certain CFCs.

The Arms Buildup

Nations must also face the challenge of preventing war, especially nuclear war. The end of the Cold War has not removed the need for arms control. A number of countries now have the power to wage a nuclear war that could destroy life on Earth as we know it. Also, some countries have large amounts of nerve gas and other chemical weapons.

To defend against a missile attack from an enemy state, the United States is working to develop a national missile defense system—a system capable of shooting down missiles headed toward the United States. Some feel this system will be vital to our national security in the new century. Others oppose the system, fearing it will set off a new arms race. Once our system is in place, they argue, other nations will respond by developing more sophisticated missiles or missile shields of their own.

Terrorism

Terrorism is the use or threat of violence to spread fear, usually for the purpose of reaching political goals. Even before the devastating terrorist attacks on New York and the Pentagon on September 11, 2001, Americans viewed terrorism as one of the gravest threats to the United States. (See the poll results below.)

Following those attacks, many countries around the world pledged to work with the United States to put an end to terrorism. As a result, intelligence agencies from the United

Facts & Quotes

World Problems

Which international problem poses the greatest threat to the United States? Here are the results of a 1999 poll that asked Americans that question. The numbers to the right of each issue list the percentage of people who felt that issue posed a "critical threat" to our country.

Issue	Critical Threat
International terrorism	84%
Chemical/biological weapons	76%
Unfriendly nations becoming nuclear powers	75%
AIDS and other potential epidemics	72%
Development of China as a world power	57%
Economic competition from Japan	45%
Global warming	43%
Military power of Russia	34%
Regional ethnic conflicts	43%
Economic competition from Europe	24%

One way governments violate human rights is by secretly jailing or executing people. This woman protests her son's disappearance.

in one country affect other countries when refugees flee across borders. Perhaps more important is the fact that more and more people are beginning to believe that every person in the world has certain basic rights.

Many countries have accepted an agreement called the Universal Declaration of Human Rights, which lists political rights, such as the right to vote and the right of free speech. It also lists economic rights, such as freedom from hunger, and social rights, such as the right to marry and start a family.

In spite of the declaration, some governments continue to violate the human rights of their citizens. To stay in power, their leaders arrest citizens who speak out against the government. They keep them in prison or put them to death without a trial. Prisoners are often tortured, either by order of the government or because the police are not well supervised.

One nation whose violations of human rights have received worldwide attention is China. As you have read, the Chinese government brutally crushed student-led pro-democracy demonstrations in Beijing's Tiananmen Square in 1989. In the years since, the Chinese government has jailed many citizens for their religious or political views. China's human rights abuses have drawn criticism from governments and organizations around the world.

People who seek to protect human rights face two challenges. One is to find out where the violations are taking place. The other is to find ways to make governments stop the violations.

Working Toward Solutions

What needs to be done to solve global problems? First, we need more information about the causes and effects of the problems, especially pollution problems such as acid rain and the greenhouse effect. As American inventor Buckminster Fuller noted, "Now there is one outstandingly

States and many other countries have begun to share information in their efforts to track down, arrest, and punish international terrorists. New technologies make this sharing of information among governments easier and more efficient. However, these same technologies also make it easier for terrorist groups to plan and carry out their deadly missions. Even with intense effort and cooperation on the part of many government agencies, the prevention of future terrorist attacks will require all citizens to be on the alert for warning signs and potential terrorist plots.

Violations of Human Rights

Human rights has also become a global issue. One reason is that violations of human rights

important fact regarding Spaceship Earth, and that is that no instruction book came with it."

Secondly, we need to work together in looking for solutions. Getting cooperation, however, is a problem in itself. Nations must first respect each other's sovereignty. No country wants others telling it what to do with its money or natural resources.

Countries must also share the blame for the problems that face the world, instead of pointing fingers at each other. They must look beyond their own short-term goals to see the "big picture." Each country must see that in the long run, what is best for the world is also best for that country.

Resources and Pollution It is not easy to get people to think in terms of what is best for the world in the long run. One reason is that developing nations are in a hurry to "catch up." They want to improve their economies by building factories and clearing land for farming and other uses.

People in developing nations are angry when other people try to tell them what they should and should not do. They point out that the developed nations wasted resources and polluted the environment when their own economies were growing. Besides, they say, many scientists think that factories and cars in the developed world are still the major cause of pollution.

World reactions to deforestation in the Amazon are a good example of conflicting views on the use of resources. For a long time, Brazil allowed people to clear rain forests for farming and cattle ranching. During the 1990s, the Brazilian rain forest was destroyed at the rate of 13,000 acres per day. On average, an area of rain forest comparable to eight football fields was cleared every minute. Environmentalists have blamed Brazil for letting this happen. However, some Brazilians see clearing the rain forest as a form of economic development.

If Brazil does not protect its forests, though, its economy may be hurt in the long run. The soil of the cleared land is poor. Furthermore, the economy could benefit from the many animals and plants that grow naturally in the rain forests and which can be used for foods, medicines, and other products.

Meanwhile, the burning sends carbon dioxide into the air, which may add to the greenhouse effect. Brazil's government is now trying to limit deforestation because it sees that the rain forests are more valuable to the country and to the world if most of them are left standing.

Nations must share responsibility for solving problems related to pollution and limited resources. Instead of blaming each other, they must help each other grow and prosper in ways that protect the environment and use Earth's resources wisely.

Facing Threats to Security People in every country fear nuclear war, but governments are not rushing into arms control agreements. As each country wants to protect its own security, it is careful about reducing its military power or trusting other countries. Since the end of the Cold War, the United States and Russia have each sent inspectors to check whether the other side was following the terms of arms control treaties.

Countries must try to weigh the need for security against the danger of an uncontrolled arms race. Also, governments must think about the risks of selling arms to other countries. Another thing they should do is weigh the need for more military spending against the need for spending in other areas, such as improving their economies and protecting the environment.

Terrorism, of course, is another threat to security. Facing this threat means more than adding guards and security devices at airports. Governments must also try to deal with some of the causes of terrorism, such as poverty, injustice, and racism.

Protecting Human Rights In dealing with human rights issues, we must accept the fact that not everyone agrees about what human rights are. Different countries have different views about which rights belong to every person and which ones are most important. For example, some countries stress economic rights, while in the United States we think that political rights are most important.

People must also try to understand the pressures that can lead to human rights violations. For example, a government that is struggling to stay in power may ban free speech and freedom of the press to silence opponents. All nations must work together to make sure that respect for human rights can go hand-in-hand with national security and economic growth.

Section 1 Assessment

1. **Define** renewable resource, nonrenewable resource, deforestation, terrorism
2. What are some reasons why the world may run out of natural resources?
3. Describe three types of pollution and explain why they are global problems.
4. Why have the arms buildup, terrorism, and human rights become international issues?
5. Why is it sometimes hard for nations to cooperate with each other? What can be done to encourage cooperation?
6. **Evaluate** Do you think the developed nations have a greater responsibility to deal with global problems than the developing nations? Explain.

Organizations Facing the Problems

Objectives
- Examine how the United Nations is organized to deal with global problems.
- Explain how nongovernmental organizations are helping to solve global problems.
- Explore factors that can weaken or strengthen the impact of international organizations.

 Focus

How do people from different countries work together to solve problems facing the world? In many cases, representatives from two or more countries meet to talk about problems. International economic conferences and summit meetings of world leaders are examples of such meetings. However, as nations have grown more interdependent, permanent organizations have also been set up to deal with the world's problems.

In this section you will look at the role of the largest organization of governments, the United Nations. You will also see how private groups are helping to solve global problems.

The United Nations

The United Nations, or UN, has 189 member nations—almost every nation in the world. Its constitution, the United Nations Charter, sets forth the rules and purposes of the UN. The UN was created in 1945, at the end of World War II. Its goals are to preserve world peace, to promote justice, and to encourage international cooperation. Since 1951, the headquarters of the UN has been New York City.

The UN has six main parts: the Security Council, the General Assembly, the Secretariat, the Economic and Social Council, the International Court of Justice, and the Trusteeship Council. As you will see, in some ways the UN is like a national government. However, it is not a "super-government." It does not have sovereignty over its member nations.

Security Council The most powerful arm of the UN is the Security Council. It has power to take action to keep the peace and help settle conflicts that break out.

The Security Council was created with five permanent members: the United States, the Soviet Union, Great Britain, China, and France. They were the five most powerful countries at the end of World War II. Russia now holds the Soviet seat. Ten other members are elected to two-year terms by the General Assembly. For an action to be approved, nine votes out of fifteen are needed.

When the UN was created, none of the "Big Five" countries wanted to give up any of its power. Therefore, each has veto power in the Security Council. If a proposal is vetoed by one of the "Big Five," it is defeated, no matter how many members voted for it.

When a war breaks out, the Security Council may send a peace-keeping force to the trouble spot. The job of these UN soldiers is usually not to fight, but to help settle the conflict and make sure that both sides go along with the agreement. The Security Council may also ask member nations to stop

CHART SKILL **THE UNITED NATIONS** UN agencies deal with a wide variety of global issues. **Science and Technology** Which UN agency focuses on health care issues?

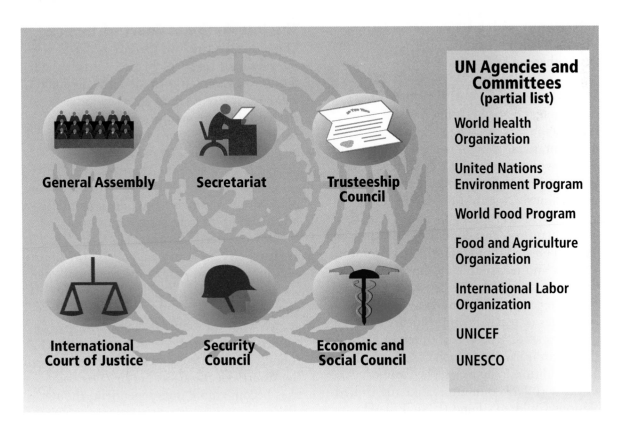

General Assembly   Secretariat   Trusteeship Council

International Court of Justice   Security Council   Economic and Social Council

UN Agencies and Committees
(partial list)

World Health Organization

United Nations Environment Program

World Food Program

Food and Agriculture Organization

International Labor Organization

UNICEF

UNESCO

trading with the warring countries or perhaps to break diplomatic relations with them.

General Assembly Every member nation has a vote in the General Assembly. Problems anywhere in the world can be discussed there. The General Assembly also decides how the UN will spend its money.

The General Assembly cannot make laws that must be obeyed. It can only make resolutions, or recommendations. However, General Assembly resolutions can lead to international agreements. For instance, over 160 nations have signed the Montreal Protocol—an agreement to end the production of CFCs and other ozone-depleting chemicals.

Secretariat Like any government, the UN needs a bureaucracy to carry out its daily tasks. People from over 150 countries work in the UN bureaucracy, called the Secretariat. They translate documents, prepare reports, and provide services to UN councils and agencies. The Secretariat has 25,000 workers in New York and in UN offices in Geneva, Vienna, Nairobi, Rome, and The Hague in the Netherlands.

Economic and Social Council The Economic and Social Council works to improve standards of living. The Council has representatives from 54 countries and works closely with a number of UN agencies, such as the United Nations Educational, Scientific, and Cultural Organization (UNESCO).

UNESCO supports education, science, art and culture, and communications. It has helped developing nations set up radio stations and newspapers. It has scientific projects to study Earth's crust, atmosphere, and water supply. UNESCO also sets up exchanges of teachers and students between countries so that people of different nationalities can learn about each other's cultures.

In addition to agencies, the Council works with UN committees, like the United Nations Children's Fund (UNICEF). The

One purpose of the UN is to provide relief during emergencies. Here, UN trucks deliver bags of rice to a refugee camp in Thailand.

goal of UNICEF is to give food and health care to needy children throughout the world.

The International Court of Justice
The judicial branch of the UN is the International Court of Justice. Often called the World Court, it is made up of 15 judges from 15 different countries. The judges, elected by the General Assembly and the Security Council, hear cases on international disputes. The "Big Five" countries have permanent seats on the Court.

World Court judges work with a growing body of international law. Like common law, it is made up of long-standing customs, such as allowing freedom of travel on the seas. Treaties, UN declarations, and World Court decisions are also part of international law.

The judges' decisions are by majority vote. However, a country does not have to accept what the Court decides. Only 62 countries have agreed to accept all Court rulings. The United States does not accept all the Court's decisions as binding. As countries become more interdependent, though,

Ginetta Sagan

It was February 1945. For five years, Ginetta Sagan had been helping political prisoners escape from German prisons in war-time Italy. Then everything changed. This brave 20-year-old from Milan—nicknamed "Topolino" (Little Mouse) by her co-workers in the Italian resistance movement—was herself caught and taken to prison. She was beaten, starved and tortured by military police. With the help of friends dressed as German soldiers, she escaped after two months. But she never forgot her time in prison.

Ginetta Sagan dedicated her life to working with Amnesty International (AI), a group that documents human rights abuses and struggles to free political prisoners. AI also seeks prompt and fair trials for prisoners and an end to torture and executions.

After the war, Sagan came to the United States.

She started the first AI chapter in the western United States, and over the next two decades her tireless work led to the establishment of 75 new groups.

Each chapter of AI "adopts" political prisoners in certain countries and begins working for their release. "When people have been jailed without trial or due process for their political beliefs, religious beliefs, or because of their racial or ethnic background, they become AI adoptees," explained Sagan. AI volunteers then write letters to government officials, hold rallies, and raise money to support the prisoners they have adopted. "They are members of the human race," Sagan said, "and we should not abandon them."

In her long career as a human rights activist, Sagan worked to document human rights violations and free victims of torture all over the world. According to Sagan, "It is important that people speak up against repression and persecution and not remain indifferent. After all, fear is very contagious, but so is courage."

Recognizing Viewpoints

Do you think Ginetta Sagan's experience in prison influenced her choice to work with Amnesty International? Explain.

---

the Court may play a growing role in getting them to settle conflicts peacefully.

The Trusteeship Council When the UN was formed after World War II, there were still some territories that did not have governments. The job of the Trusteeship Council was to help govern them until they were ready to become independent nations. Today all of the original 11 trust territories are independent or have become parts of other nations. Therefore, the Trusteeship Council has suspended operation.

Nongovernmental Organizations

The UN and other organizations of governments are not the only groups working on global problems. There are also private nongovernmental organizations, or NGOs. They meet many challenges—from protecting human rights to working for arms control.

Some NGOs protect political and economic rights. Amnesty International, for instance, calls attention to violations of the rights of political prisoners. CARE and the Red Cross help victims of war and natural disasters. A wide variety of religious organizations work on issues such as protecting human rights and combating hunger and disease.

Private groups deal with other global problems, as well. Greenpeace, an environmental group, takes on many challenges—from preventing pollution of the oceans to stopping the unnecessary killing of whales and other animals. A group called Doctors Without Borders was awarded the 1999 Nobel Peace Prize for its dedication to providing medical care to war and disaster victims worldwide.

Many Americans have become involved in groups that are trying to solve world problems. What these people share is an awareness that "global issues" and "local issues" are becoming one and the same.

The Impact of Organizations

For organizations to be successful in facing global problems, countries have to be willing to work together. There has to be some "give and take." However, there is a limit to what each country is willing to give up. Nations are not likely to give up any of their political power. When a country's security is at stake, it usually wants to make its own decisions.

It is not surprising, then, that the UN has had trouble stopping conflicts. When a war breaks out, UN peace-keeping forces are sent only if both sides agree. Also, a dispute can come before the World Court only if the parties involved agree.

Countries are most willing to work together when it does not mean giving up power. For this reason, the UN and other worldwide organizations have had some of their greatest success dealing with economic, rather than political, problems. Teams of experts teach farmers better ways of preparing fields and raising crops. International agencies help countries build dams and railroads, start businesses, and enter into world trade.

Countries tend to cooperate best in smaller, regional organizations, such as NATO and the Organization of African Unity. Members of such groups usually have more in common than do members of worldwide organizations like the UN. As countries gain more experience in working together, though, and as people's awareness of the world's problems increases, the countries of the world may become more willing to turn to worldwide organizations to help them solve global problems.

Section 2 Assessment

1. Explain what roles the United Nations plays in dealing with global problems.
2. Give two examples of how nongovernmental organizations play an important role in solving global problems.
3. What encourages governments to work together? What can get in the way of cooperation between governments?
4. **Evaluate** Do you think that all UN members should have to follow resolutions passed by the General Assembly? Explain.

SECTION 3

How Individuals Can Make a Difference

SECTION PREVIEW

Objectives
- Describe how people can use their skills to deal with global problems.
- Explore examples of people who have made a difference in the world.
- List several small actions that can help solve global problems.

 Focus

"The world has so many problems. I don't see how I can make a difference." Many people have this feeling. Yet every day, in every country, individuals are taking steps to help solve the world's problems.

The organizations you have just read about are simply groups of people putting their skills together. The world's future really depends on individuals—working within groups and on their own. In the following pages you will see some ways in which individuals have made a difference in the world.

Using Skills

Imagine yourself in the crowd shown in the photo below. Some of the world's best rock musicians were putting on a huge concert called Live Aid. Their goal was to make people aware that a long drought was causing millions of Africans to starve to death.

Over a billion people around the world saw the concert and heard its message on television and radio. They gave more than $100 million to send food to East Africa. Like the concert performers, writers, actors, and news reporters can use their skills to bring problems to the attention of millions of people.

Skills can be used not only to inform people about problems but also to find solutions. Scientists, for instance, play a key role in finding ways to control pollution and save resources. At international meetings, they share what they have learned about ozone, acid rain, and other important subjects. Scientists are also helping farmers in developing nations. They are studying ways to raise crops without hurting the environment.

Musicians performing a benefit concert to help starving people in Africa are one example of how individuals can use their skills to deal with world problems.

Medical workers can also use their skills to meet international needs. For example, after an earthquake in Turkey in 1999, medical teams from the United States and many other countries rushed to the region in order to treat injured people.

Of course, you do not have to be a musician, writer, scientist, or medical worker. Almost any skill you have or learn you can use to make a difference in the world.

Making Connections

In 1944 a Swedish businessman named Raoul Wallenberg risked his life by entering Hungary to save Jews there from being sent to Nazi death camps. He talked the Swedish government into giving Jews official-looking "passports" and helped pay for shelters where escaping Jews could stay. In this way, he helped save the lives of more than 100,000 Jews.

Wallenberg's story shows that people with connections to businesses and governments can use those resources to do good. Another example is the American businessman Armand Hammer, whose business contacts helped the United States improve relations with the Soviet Union and China.

Hammer was also able to use his money and connections to give aid in times of crisis. He sent medical teams to help victims of an earthquake in Armenia and radiation accidents in the Soviet Union and Brazil. He also helped pay for art and education projects around the world.

Volunteering Time

Obviously, you do not need to be a business leader with worldwide connections in order to make a difference. Any time and effort you give can be important. Your commitment might be a few hours of volunteer work, or it might be a lifetime, as in the case of Mother Teresa.

By serving the poor, Mother Teresa showed how one person can help solve problems facing people throughout the world.

A tireless Roman Catholic nun, Mother Teresa began her work in the slums of Calcutta, India. With other nuns who came to work with her, she provided shelter and schooling for children and gave food and medicine to sick and needy people. She also picked up dying people off the streets to give them a place to die in dignity.

Mother Teresa's struggle to help poor people received worldwide attention. In 1979 she won the Nobel Peace Prize. However, Mother Teresa was humble, always seeing herself as just one person working together with many others. She inspired millions of people who used to think they were not "important enough" to make a difference.

Taking Everyday Steps

Using skills, donating money, and volunteering time are not the only ways to make a difference. Every day you can take small but important steps to help solve the large problems facing the world. One obvious step, for example, is to make use of daily opportunities to save resources and reduce pollution.

One way you can save resources is by recycling or reusing glass, cans, newspapers, cardboard, and grocery bags. You can save energy by turning off the house lights and heaters when they are not being used. Installing a low-flow shower head saves water. Carpooling and using public transportation not only save oil but also reduce pollution. Small steps like these can make a big difference when many people take them together.

You Can Make a Difference

In this book you have studied citizenship and what citizens have done to help their communities, their country, and the world. You have learned something about making decisions and taking action to carry them out. You can use these skills to work on problems facing the whole world, from pollution to hunger to war. As an American, you have the right and the opportunity to join with others in making our country, and the world, a better place.

Section 3 Assessment

1. How have people used their skills to deal with global problems?
2. How did both Raoul Wallenberg and Armand Hammer help other people?
3. Why is Mother Teresa a good example of how one person can make a difference?
4. What are some ways that individuals can help save resources and reduce pollution?
5. **Analyze** Which global problem or problems did Mother Teresa face? Which did Armand Hammer face? Explain.

Extending the Chapter

Global Views

You will be taking on many responsibilities as a citizen in the twenty-first century. Perhaps you are wondering, "What will life be like in the future?" Researchers known as "futurists" are exploring that question by looking at where trends might lead us.

Some futurists are hopeful. They think that space colonies and new supplies of energy will solve the problems of hunger, poverty, and pollution. Others, however, warn that pollution will get worse and that many more people will starve as populations grow and resources run out.

Many futurists think that lifestyles will change over the next hundred years. They say that people will be less interested in making and buying goods and services and will try harder to protect the environment. Perhaps computers will allow most people to work at home. As the cost of housing rises, people may have to live in large groups of up to a dozen people.

Futurists also make political predictions. Some think that a nuclear war will break out, while others believe that countries will form a worldwide democratic government.

What do you think about these views? Think about which ones are likely to happen. Then ask yourself what you hope the future will be and what steps we might take to reach that future.

How to INTERPRET MAPS

In this chapter you read about the ozone layer—a thin layer of gas high in the atmosphere which protects Earth from the sun's dangerous ultraviolet rays. In the mid-1980s, scientists began to detect a thinning of the ozone layer over the South Pole. Scientists discovered that the main cause of this loss of ozone was the use of chlorofluorocarbons (CFCs), a chemical used in air conditioners and other common products.

Faced with this clear threat to Earth's health, many nations took action together. In 1987, 57 nations signed the Montreal Protocol, an international agreement to ban the use of CFC's. By 2001, 172 nations had signed the agreement. Scientists have since reported a decline in the amount of chemical compounds that lead to the destruction of the ozone layer. They expect the rate of ozone loss to peak early in this century and then to decline slowly throughout the following decades. A full recovery of the ozone layer may occur within a century.

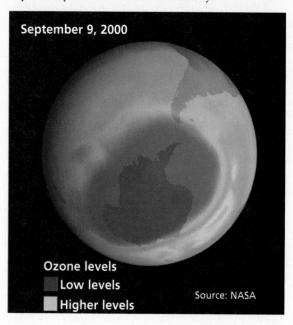

September 9, 2000

Ozone levels
Low levels
Higher levels

Source: NASA

Explain the Skill

The map on his page illustrates the serious environmental problem that caused world leaders to ban the use of CFCs. The map shows the loss of ozone as of September 9, 2000.

It would be difficult to study global problems without maps. Maps can show not only geographic and political features, but also information on such topics as population growth, economic development, and global pollution. A map, for example, could be used to show the levels of deforestation in rainforests around the world.

Analyze the Skill

Most maps of the world have the North Pole at the top and the South Pole at the bottom. The map on this page is drawn from a different point view. It shows what the world would look like if seen from above the South Pole. The large continent near the center the map is Antarctica. The continent near the top edge is South America.

This map focuses on the South Pole because that is where the loss of ozone has been most severe. The map key tells us that there were low levels of ozone over the area shown in purple. Ozone levels were higher over the area shown in yellow.

Skill Assessment

1. What is the subject of this map?
2. In one sentence tell what this map shows about its subject.
3. How do you think this map might change over the next fifty years? Why will it change?

Building Civics Vocabulary

The vocabulary terms in each pair listed below are related to each other. For each pair, explain what the terms have in common. Also explain how they are different.

1. *renewable resource* and *nonrenewable resource*
2. *terrorism* and *deforestation*

Reviewing Main Ideas and Skills

3. Why do people in developed nations use so much more energy resources than those living in developing nations?

4. Describe two of the roadblocks to solving the pollution problem.

5. Give two examples of how human rights are being violated.

6. Why is the UN not always successful in settling international disputes and stopping armed conflicts between nations?

7. How does the UN differ from organizations such as the Red Cross and CARE?

8. Describe some ways in which individuals can help solve global problems.

9. **How to Interpret Maps** Look back at the map on page 578. In 2000, which continents were affected by ozone loss?

Critical Thinking

10. **Identifying Main Ideas** What are the causes of deforestation in the Amazon River Basin? What long-term effects will continuing destruction of the rainforest have on Earth?

11. **Defending a Position** "Only large, organized groups can hope to make any difference at all with issues such as hunger, poverty, war, and pollution." Do you agree or disagree? Give reasons for your answer.

Writing About Civics

12. **Writing a Declaration** What kinds of human rights should all people throughout the world be entitled to? Develop a list of basic human rights that you think everyone in the world should have. Write an introduction to your declaration of human rights.

Citizenship Activities

13. **Working Together** Organize a mock UN session to discuss a global problem, with students representing major developed and developing nations. Think about possible conflicts between the nations and how they might compromise to solve this global problem.

 Take It to the NET

Access the **Civics: Participating in Government** Internet site at **www.phschool.com** for the specific URLs to complete the activity.

Explore online information about environmental issues around the world. Choose one of these issues to analyze. What caused the problem? In what ways is the problem global as well as local? Who should be involved in providing a solution? Write an editorial on the topic, as if for a newspaper editorial page. Be sure to include your own strong opinions on the above questions.

A Rainbow Nation

In April 1994, South Africa held the first multiracial election in its 342-year history. Prior to the election, the white minority had ruled the black majority through a system of racial segregation known as apartheid. Nelson Mandela, an anti-apartheid activist who served 27 years in prison, was elected the first black president of South Africa. At his inauguration on May 10, 1994, Mandela shared his vision of South Africa as "a rainbow nation at peace with itself and the world."

Before you read the selection, find the meanings of these words in a dictionary: confer, emancipation, deprivation, covenant.

Today, all of us do, by our presence here, and by our celebrations in other parts of our country and the world, confer glory and hope to new-born liberty.

Out of the experience of an extraordinary human disaster that lasted too long, must be born a society of which all humanity will be proud.

Our daily deeds as ordinary South Africans must produce an actual South African reality that will reinforce humanity's belief in justice, strengthen its confidence in the nobility of the human soul and sustain all our hopes for a glorious life for all....

We, the people of South Africa, feel fulfilled that humanity has taken us back into its bosom, that we, who were outlaws not so long ago, have today been given the rare privilege to be host to the nations of the world on our own soil.

We thank all our distinguished international guests for having come to take possession with the people of our country of what is, after all, a common victory for justice, for peace, for human dignity....

We have, at last, achieved our political emancipation. We pledge ourselves to liberate all our people from the continuing bondage of poverty, deprivation, suffering, gender and other discrimination....

We have triumphed in the effort to implant hope in the breasts of the millions of our people. We enter into a covenant that we shall build the society in which all South Africans, both black and white, will be able to walk tall, without any fear in their hearts, assured of their inalienable right to human dignity—a rainbow nation at peace with itself and the world.

Source: Inauguration Speech from A LONG WALK TO FREEDOM by Nelson Mandela. Copyright ©1994 by Nelson Rolihlahla Mandela. By permission of Little, Brown and Company (Inc.).

Analyzing Primary Sources

1. Why do you think Mandela refers to South Africans of the apartheid years as "outlaws"?

2. What kinds of goals does Mandela set for himself and South Africans in the years to come?

Reviewing Main Ideas

1. Explain how developed nations differ from developing nations. Why does this difference often make it hard for nations to cooperate in solving global problems?
2. Describe some common types of foreign policy issues. In making foreign policy, why should our government consider the needs of other nations rather than just our own needs?
3. Choose one global problem. Discuss how American foreign policy could help solve it.
4. Explain how the UN is both similar to and different from national governments.

Summarizing the Unit

The web graphic organizer below will help you organize the main ideas of Unit 8. Copy it onto a separate sheet of paper. Review the unit and complete the graphic organizer by giving examples of how each group or organization plays a role in dealing with global issues. The "United Nations" rectangle has been partially completed for you as an example. When you have finished, choose one group or organization from the web graphic organizer and write a one-page essay explaining in detail how it can make a difference in solving global problems.

United States President

United Nations
• Encourages International Cooperation

United States Congress

Global Issues

Individuals

Regional Trade Organizations

Military Alliances

Nongovernmental Organizations

SUPREME COURT CASES

These pages provide summaries of key Supreme Court rulings over the course of the nation's history. For additional material and links to Supreme Court cases, see Civics: Participating in Government *Companion Web site at* **www.phschool.com**

Baker v. Carr, 1962

(14th Amendment, Equal Protection Clause) Rapid population growth in Nashville and reluctance of the rural-dominated Tennessee legislature to redraw State legislature districts led Mayor Baker of Nashville to ask for federal court help. The federal district court refused to enter the "political thicket" of State legislature re-districting and the case was appealed. The Court directed a trial to be held in a Tennessee federal court. The case led to the 1964 Westberry decision, which created the "one man, one vote" equal representation concept.

Bethel School District #403 v. Fraser, 1986

(1st Amendment, freedom of speech) A high school student gave a sexually suggestive political speech at a high school assembly to elect student officers. The school administration strongly disciplined the student, Fraser, who argued that school rules unfairly limited his freedom of political speech. Fraser's view was upheld in State court. Washington appealed to the Supreme Court, which found that "It does not follow, however, that simply because the use of an offensive form of expression may not be prohibited to adults making what the speaker considers a political point, the same latitude must be permitted to children in a public school."

Bob Jones University v. United States, 1983

(14th Amendment in conflict with 1st Amendment) Bob Jones University, a private school, denied admission to applicants in an interracial marriage or who "espouse" interracial marriage or dating. The Internal Revenue Service then denied tax exempt status to the school because of racial discrimination. The university appealed, claiming that their policy was based on the Bible. The Court upheld the IRS ruling, stating that "...Government has a fundamental overriding interest in eradicating racial discrimination in education."

Brown v. Board of Education of Topeka, 1954

(14th Amendment, Equal Protection Clause) Probably no 20th century Supreme Court decision so deeply stirred and changed life in the United States as Brown. A 10-year-old Topeka girl was not permitted to attend her neighborhood school because she was an African American. The Court heard arguments about whether segregation itself was a violation of the Equal Protection Clause and found that it was, commenting that "in the field of public education the doctrine of 'separate

but equal' has no place.... Segregation is a denial of the equal protection of the laws." The decision overturned Plessy, 1896.

California v. Greenwood, 1988

(4th Amendment, illegal evidence) Acting on a tip that Billy Greenwood was selling narcotics, police examined trash bags that had been picked up from Greenwood's house. Items associated with drug use were found in the garbage and were listed in the application for a search warrant. The subsequent search revealed further evidence that was used in a trial to obtain a conviction. When Greenwood appealed the "warrantless search," the Court said that garbage bags left in the street are accessible to "animals, children, scavengers, snoops, and other members of the public." Greenwood could not reasonably have expected that the contents of the garbage would remain private. The evidence was admissible.

The Civil Rights Cases, 1883

(14th Amendment, Equal Protection Clause) The Civil Rights Acts of 1875 included punishments for businesses that practiced discrimination. The Court ruled on a number of cases involving the Acts in 1883, finding that the Constitution, "while prohibiting discrimination by governments, made no provisions...for acts of racial discrimination by private individuals." The decision limited the impact of the Equal Protection Clause, giving tacit approval for segregation in the private sector.

Dennis v. United States, 1951

(1st Amendment, freedom of speech) The Smith Act of 1940 made it a crime for any person to work for the violent overthrow of the United States in peacetime or war. Eleven Communist party leaders, including Dennis, had been convicted of violating the Smith Act, and they appealed. The Court upheld the Act. Much modified by later decisions, the Dennis case focused on anti-government speech as an area of controversy.

Dred Scott v. Sandford, 1857

(6th Amendment, individual rights) This decision upheld property rights over human rights by saying that Dred Scott, a slave, could not become a free man just because he had traveled in "free soil" States with his master. A badly divided nation was further fragmented by the decision. "Free soil" federal laws and the Missouri Compromise line of 1820 were held unconstitutional because they deprived a slave owner of the right to his "property" without just compensation. This narrow reading of the Constitution, a landmark case of the Court, was most clearly stated by Chief Justice Roger B. Taney, a States' rights advocate.

Edwards v. South Carolina, 1963

(1st Amendment, freedom of speech and assembly) A group of mostly African-American civil rights activists held a rally at the South Carolina State Capitol, protesting segregation. A hostile crowd gathered and the rally leaders were arrested and convicted for "breach of the peace." The Court overturned the convictions, saying that "The Fourteenth Amendment does not permit a State to make criminal the peaceful expression of unpopular views."

Engel v. Vitale, 1962

(1st Amendment, Establishment Clause) The State Board of Regents of New York required the recitation of a 22-word nonsectarian prayer at the beginning of each school day. A group of parents filed suit against the required prayer, claiming it violated their 1st Amendment rights. The Court found New York's action to be unconstitutional, observing, "There can be no doubt that...religious beliefs [are] embodied in the Regent's prayer."

Escobedo v. Illinois, 1964

(6th Amendment, right to counsel) In a case involving a murder confession by a person known to Chicago-area police and who was not afforded counsel while under interrogation, the Court extended the "exclusionary rule" to illegal confessions in State court proceedings. Carefully defining an "Escobedo Rule," the Court said, "where...the investigation is no longer a general inquiry...but has begun to focus on a particular suspect...(and where) the suspect has been taken into custody...the suspect has requested...his lawyer, and the police have not...warned him of his right to remain silent, the accused has been denied...counsel in violation of the Sixth Amendment."

Ex Parte Milligan, 1866

(Article II, executive powers) An Indiana man was arrested, treated as a prisoner of war, and imprisoned by a military court during the Civil War under presidential order. He claimed that his rights to a fair trial were interfered with and that military courts had no authority outside of "conquered territory." He was released because "the Constitution...is a law for rulers and people, equally in war and peace, and covers...all...men, at all times, and under all circumstances." The Court held that presidential powers to suspend the writ of habeas corpus in time of war did not extend to creating another court system run by the military.

Furman v. Georgia, 1972

(8th Amendment, capital punishment) Three different death penalty cases, including Furman, raised the question of racial imbalances in the use of death sentences by State courts. Furman had been convicted and sentenced to death in Georgia. In deciding to overturn existing State death-penalty laws, the Court noted that there was an "apparent arbitrariness of the use of the sentence...." Many States rewrote their death-penalty statutes and these were generally upheld in Gregg v. Georgia, 1976.

Gibbons v. Ogden, 1824

(Article I, Section 8, Commerce Clause) This decision involved a careful examination of the power of Congress to "regulate interstate commerce." Aaron Ogden's exclusive New York ferry license gave him the right to operate steamboats to and from New York. He said that Thomas Gibbon's federal "coasting license" did not include "landing rights" in New York City. Federal and State regulation of commerce conflicted. The Court strengthened the power of the United States to regulate any interstate business relationship. Federal regulation of television, pipelines, and banking are all based on Gibbons.

Gideon v. Wainwright, 1963

Decision: Gideon won a new trial and was found not guilty with the help of a court-appointed attorney. The "Gideon Rule" upheld the 6th Amendment's guarantee of counsel for all poor persons facing a felony charge, a further incorporation of Bill of Rights guarantees into State constitutions.

Gitlow v. New York, 1925

(1st Amendment, freedom of speech) For the first time, the Court considered whether the 1st and 14th amendments had influence on State laws. The case, involving "criminal anarchy" under New York law, was the first consideration of what came to be known as the "incorporation" doctrine, under which, it was argued, the provisions of the 1st Amendment were "incorporated" by the 14th Amendment. Although New York law was not overruled in the case, the decision clearly indicated that the Supreme Court could make such a ruling. Another important incorporation case is Powell v. Alabama, 1932.

Gregg v. Georgia, 1976

Decision: The Court upheld the Georgia death sentence, finding that it did not violate the cruel and unusual punishment clause of the 8th Amendment. The Court stated for the first time that "punishment of death does not invariably violate the Constitution."

Griswold v. Connecticut, 1965

(14th Amendment, Due Process Clause) A Connecticut law forbade the use of "any drug, medicinal article, or instrument for the purpose of preventing conception." Griswold, director of Planned Parenthood in New Haven, was arrested for counseling married persons and after conviction, appealed. The Court overturned the Connecticut law, saying that "various guarantees (of the Constitution) create zones of privacy..." and questioning, "...would we allow the police to search the sacred precincts of marital bedrooms...?"

The decision is significant for raising for more careful inspection the concept of "unenumerated rights" in the 9th Amendment, later central to Roe, 1973.

Hazelwood School District v. Kuhlmeier, 1988

Decision: The Court upheld the principal's action because the school official acted as the publisher of the newspaper. "1st Amendment rights of students…are not automatically coextensive with the rights of adults in other settings…." School officials had full control over school-sponsored activities "so long as their actions are reasonably related to legitimate pedagogical concerns…"

Heart of Atlanta Motel, Inc. v. United States, 1964

Decision: The Court upheld the law, saying, "If it is interstate commerce that feels the pinch, it does not matter how 'local' the operation which applies the squeeze…. The power of Congress to promote interstate commerce also includes the power to regulate the local incidents thereof, including local activities…which have a substantial and harmful effect upon that commerce." Segregation by race of private facilities engaged in interstate commerce was found unconstitutional.

In Re Gault, 1966

(14th Amendment, Due Process Clause) Prior to the Gault case, proceedings against juvenile offenders were generally handled as "family law," not "criminal law" and provided few due process guarantees. Gerald Gault was assigned to six years in a State juvenile detention facility for an alleged obscene phone call. He was not provided counsel and not permitted to confront or cross-examine the principal witness. The Court overturned the juvenile proceedings and required that States provide juveniles "some of the due process guarantees of adults," including a right to a phone call, to counsel, to cross-examine, to confront their accuser, and to be advised of their right to silence.

Island Trees School District v. Pico, 1982

(1st Amendment, freedom of speech) A number of books were removed by the school board from the library at Island Trees High School, New York. When a group of students sued to have the books returned, the case reached the Supreme Court. The Court reversed the decision of the school board, saying that though school boards "possess significant discretion to determine the content of their school libraries…that discretion may not be exercised in a narrowly partisan or political manner."

Katz v. United States, 1967

(4th Amendment, electronic surveillance) The Court reversed Olmstead, 1928, in this decision about wiretapping. Arrested for illegal gambling after using a public phone to transmit information about betting, Katz claimed that the electronic bug, used without a warrant, was a violation of his 4th Amendment rights. The Court expanded the protections of the 4th Amendment, observing that persons, not just property, are protected against illegal searches. Whatever a citizen "seeks to preserve as private, even in an area accessible to the public, may be constitutionally protected."

Korematsu v. United States, 1944

Decision: The Court upheld the military order, noting that "pressing public necessity [World War II] may sometimes justify the existence of restrictions which curtail the civil rights of a single racial group…" but added that "racial antagonism never can…[justify such restrictions]." Only Japanese Americans were interned during World War II.

Lemon v. Kurzman, 1971

(1st Amendment, Establishment Clause) In overturning State laws regarding aid to church-supported schools in this and a similar Rhode Island case, the Court created the Lemon test limiting "…excessive government entanglement with religion." The Court noted that any State law about aid to religion must meet three criteria: (1) purpose of the aid must be clearly secular, not religious, (2) its primary effect must neither advance nor inhibit religion, and (3) it must avoid "excessive entanglement of government with religion."

Marbury v. Madison, 1803

(Article III, judicial powers) Chief Justice Marshall established "judicial review" as a power of the Supreme Court. After defeat in the 1800 election, President Adams appointed many Federalists to the federal courts, but the commissions were not delivered. New Secretary of State James Madison refused to deliver them. Marbury sued in the Supreme Court. The Court declared a portion of the Judiciary Act of 1789 unconstitutional, thereby declaring the Court's power to find acts of Congress unconstitutional.

Massachusetts v. Sheppard, 1984

(4th Amendment, illegal evidence) A search in Massachusetts was based on a warrant issued on an improper form. Sheppard argued that the search was illegal and the evidence was inadmissible under Mapp, 1961. Massachusetts argued that the police acted in "good faith," believing that the warrant was correct. The Court agreed with Massachusetts, noting that the exclusionary rule should not be applied when the officer conducting the search had acted with the reasonable belief that he was following proper procedures. This was the first of several exceptions to the Exclusionary Rule handed down by the Court in the 1980s, including Nix, 1984, and United States v. Leon, 1984.

McCulloch v. Maryland, 1819

(Article I, Section 8, Necessary and Proper Clause) Called the "Bank of the United States" case. A Maryland law required federally chartered banks to use only a special paper to print money, which amounted to a tax. James McCulloch, the cashier of the Baltimore branch of the bank, refused to use the paper, claiming that States could not tax the Federal Government. The Court declared the Maryland law unconstitutional, commenting "…the power to tax implies the power to destroy."

Miller v. California, 1973

(1st Amendment, freedom of the press) In Miller, the Court upheld a stringent application of California obscenity law by Newport Beach, California, and attempted to define what is obscene. The "Miller Rule" included three criteria: (1) That the average person would, applying contemporary community standards, find that the work appealed to the prurient interest; (2) that the work depicts or describes, in an offensive way, sexual conduct defined by State law; and (3) that "the work, taken as a whole, lacks serious literary, artistic, political or scientific value…."

Miranda v. Arizona, 1966

(5th, 6th, and 14th amendments, rights of the accused) Arrested for kidnapping and sexual assault, Ernesto Miranda signed a confession including a statement that he had "full knowledge of [his] legal rights…." After conviction, he appealed, claiming that without counsel and without warnings, the confession was illegally gained. The Court agreed with Miranda that "he must be warned prior to any questioning that he has the right to remain silent, that anything he says can be used against him in a court of law, that he has a right to…an attorney and that if he cannot afford an attorney one will be appointed for him…." Although later modified by Nix, 1984, and other cases, Miranda firmly upheld citizen rights to fair trial in State courts.

Cruzan v. Director, Missouri Dept. of Health, 1990

(9th Amendment, right to die) A Missouri woman was in a coma from an automobile accident in 1983. Her family, facing astronomical medical bills and deciding that "her life had ended in 1987," directed the health care providers to end intravenous feeding. The State of Missouri opposed the family's decision. The family went to court and the Supreme Court ruled that States could require "clear and convincing" evidence that Cruzan would have wanted to die, although the Court did not require other States to meet the Missouri standard. Following the ruling, another hearing was held in Missouri at which "clear and convincing evidence" was presented to a judge. The intravenous feeding was ended and Cruzan died on December 26, 1990.

Mueller v. Allen, 1983

Decision: The Court upheld the law, stating that it met the Lemon test (Lemon, 1971), and that the deduction was available to all parents with children in school. Although it was of greater benefit to parents of children in private schools, each parent had the choice of which school their children attended.

New Jersey v. T.L.O., 1985

Decision: The court set a new standard for searches in schools in this case, stating that the school had a "le-gitimate need to maintain an environment in which learning can take place," and that to do this "requires some easing of the restrictions to which searches by public authorities are ordinarily subject…." The Court thus created a "reasonable suspicion" rule for school searches, a change from the "probable cause" requirement in the wider society.

New York Times v. United States, 1971

Decision: The Court cited the 1st Amendment guarantee of a free press and refused to uphold the injunction against publication, observing that it is the obligation of the government to prove that actual harm to the nation's security would be caused by the publication. The decision limited "prior restraint" of the press.

Nix v. Williams, 1984

(4th Amendment, illegal evidence) A man was convicted of murdering a 10-year-old girl after he led officers to the body. He had been arrested, but not advised of his rights, in a distant city, and in transit, he had conversed with a police officer. Williams agreed that the child should have a proper burial and directed the officer to the body. Later, on appeal, Williams's attorneys argued that the body should not be admitted as evidence because the questioning was illegal. The Court disagreed, observing that search parties were within two and one-half miles of the body. "Evidence otherwise excluded may be admissible when it would have been discovered anyway." The decision was one of several "exceptions to the exclusionary rule" handed down by the Court in the 1980s.

Olmstead v. United States, 1928

(4th Amendment, electronic surveillance) Olmstead was engaged in the illegal sale of alcohol. Much of the evidence against him was gained through a wiretap made without a warrant. Olmstead argued that he had "a reasonable expectation of privacy," and that the Weeks decision of 1914 should be applied to exclude the evidence gained by the wiretap. The Court disagreed, saying that Olmstead intended "to project his voice to those quite outside…and that…nothing tangible was taken." Reversed by subsequent decisions, this case contains the first usage of the concept of "reasonable expectation of privacy" that would mark later 4th Amendment decisions.

Plessy v. Ferguson, 1896

(14th Amendment, Equal Protection Clause) A Louisiana law required separate seating for white and African-American citizens on public railroads, a form of segregation. Herman Plessy argued that his right to "equal protection of the laws" was violated. The Court held that segregation was permitted if facilities were equal. The Court interpreted the 14th Amendment as "not intended to give Negroes social equality but only political and civil equality…." The Louisiana law was seen as a "reasonable exercise of (State) police power…" Segregated public facilities were permitted until Plessy was overturned by the Brown v. Board of Education case of 1954.

Powell v. Alabama, 1932

(6th Amendment, right to counsel) The case involved the "Scottsboro Boys," seven "young negro men" accused of sexual assault. This case was a landmark in the development of a "fundamentals of fairness" doctrine of the Court over the next 40 years. The Scottsboro boys were quickly prosecuted without the benefit of counsel and sentenced to death. The Court overturned the decision, stating that poor people facing the death penalty in State courts must be provided counsel, and commenting, "...there are certain principles of Justice which adhere to the very idea of free government, which no [State] may disregard." The case was another step toward incorporation of the Bill of Rights into State constitutions.

Regents of the University of California v. Bakke, 1978

Decision: The Court ruled narrowly, providing an admission for Bakke, but not overturning "affirmative action," preferring to take discrimination questions on a case-by-case basis.

Reynolds v. United States, 1878

(1st Amendment, Free Exercise Clause) Called the "Mormon Case," this decision involved George Reynolds, an "old order" Mormon with multiple wives. An anti-Mormon law forbidding bigamy was passed by Congress, and Reynolds was prosecuted. He claimed that his religious belief overrode federal laws and that the law was unconstitutional. The Court ruled that "freedom of religion means freedom to hold an opinion or belief, but not to take action...subversive to good order."

Roe v. Wade, 1973

(9th Amendment, right to privacy) A Texas woman challenged a State law forbidding the artificial termination of a pregnancy, saying that she "had a fundamental right to privacy." The Court upheld a woman's right to choose in this case, noting that the State's "important and legitimate interest in protecting the potentiality of human life" became "compelling" at the end of the first trimester, and that before then "...the attending physician, in consultation with his patient, is free to determine, without regulation by the State, that...the patient's pregnancy should be terminated." The decision struck down State regulation of abortion in the first three months of pregnancy and was modified by Webster, 1989.

Rostker v. Goldberg, 1981

Decision: The Court did not support the challenge, observing that "the purpose of registration was to prepare for draft of combat troops" and that "Congress and the Executive have decided that women should not serve in combat." Since the matter of using women in combat had received considerable attention in Congress, with debates, hearings, and committee actions, the Court agreed that Congress did not act unthinkingly or reflexively.

Roth v. United States, 1957

(1st Amendment, freedom of the press) A New York man named Roth operated a business that used the mail to invite people to buy materials considered obscene by postal inspectors. The Court, in its first consideration of censorship of obscenity, created the "prevailing community standards" rule, which required a consideration of the work as a whole. In its decision, the Court defined as obscene that which offended "the average person, applying contemporary community standards." In a case decided the same day, the Court applied the same "test" to State obscenity laws.

Schenck v. United States, 1919

(1st Amendment, freedom of speech) Charles Schenck was an officer of an antiwar political group who was arrested for alleged violations of the Espionage Act of 1917, which made active opposition to the war a crime. He had urged thousands of young men called to service by the draft act to resist and to avoid induction. The Court limited free speech in time of war, stating that Schenck's words, under the circumstances, presented a "clear and present danger...." Although later decisions modified the decision, the Schenck case created a precedent that 1st Amendment guarantees were not absolute.

School District of Abington Township, Pennsylvania v. Schempp, 1963

(1st Amendment, Establishment Clause) A Pennsylvania State law required reading from the Bible each day at school as an all-school activity. Some parents objected and sought legal remedy. When the case reached the Court, it agreed with the parents, saying that the Establishment Clause and Free Exercise Clause both forbade States from engaging in religious activity. The Court created a rule holding that if the purpose and effect of a law "is the advancement or inhibition of religion," it "exceeds the scope of legislative power."

South Dakota v. Dole, 1986

Decision: The Court upheld the right of the National Government to limit highway funds to States that did not qualify under the rules of "entitlement." All States that wished to continue to receive full federal highway aid were required to raise the legal age to purchase and consume alcohol to 21 years. In recent years the Federal Government has attached similar strings to federal aid in a number of instances, including mandating maximum speed limits on interstate highways.

Texas v. Johnson, 1989

(1st Amendment, freedom of speech) Dousing with kerosene and burning a U.S. flag taken from the flagpole at the 1984 Republican National Convention in Dallas, Gregory Johnson led a protest against national policies outside the convention center. He was arrested and convicted under a Texas law prohibiting the desecration of the Texas and United States flags. Johnson's conviction was overturned in the highest criminal court in Texas, and the State appealed. The Court ruled the Texas law placed an unconstitutional limit on "freedom of expression," noting that "…nothing in our precedents suggests that a state may foster its own view of the flag by prohibiting expressive conduct relating to it."

Thompson v. Oklahoma, 1988

(8th Amendment, capital punishment) An Oklahoma youth was 15 years old when he committed a capital murder. At age 16 he was sentenced to death for the slaying. In hearing an appeal of the case, the Court overturned the death sentence, holding that "[t]he Eighth and Fourteenth Amendments prohibit the execution of a person who was under 16 years of age at the time of his or her offense." A death penalty was cruel and unusual punishment for a 15 year old.

Tinker v. Des Moines Public Schools, 1969

Decision: The Court agreed with the Tinkers, upholding students' 1st Amendment rights, noting that students do not abandon their civil rights "at the schoolhouse gate…" and that the wearing of black armbands was "…silent, passive expression of opinion.…" Schools would need to show evidence of the possibility of "substantial disruption" before free speech could be limited at school.

United States v. Nixon, 1974

Decision: The Court overruled the President and ordered him to surrender the tapes, thereby limiting executive privilege. The President's "generalized interest in confidentiality…" was subordinate to "the fundamental demands of due process of law in the fair administration of criminal justice."

Walz v. Tax Commission of the City of New York, 1970

(1st Amendment, Establishment Clause) State and local governments routinely exempt church property from taxes. Walz claimed that such exemptions were a "support of religion," a subsidy by government. The Court disagreed, noting that such exemptions were just an example of a "benevolent neutrality" between government and churches, not a support of religion. Governments must avoid taxing churches, because taxation would give government a "control" over religion, prohibited by the "wall of separation of church and state" noted in Everson, 1947.

Webster v. Reproductive Health Services, 1989

(9th Amendment, right to privacy) A 1986 Missouri law stated that (1) life began at conception, (2) unborn children have rights, (3) public funds could not be used for abortions not necessary to save the life of the mother, and (4) public funds could not be used for abortion counseling. Health care providers in Missouri filed suit, challenging the law, claiming it was in conflict with Roe, 1973 and intruded into "privacy questions." A 5–4 Court upheld the Missouri law, stating that the people of Missouri, through their legislature, could put limits on the use of public funds. The Webster decision narrowed the protection of Roe.

Weeks v. United States, 1914

(4th Amendment, illegal evidence) A search without proper warrant was made in San Francisco and evidence was used by a postal inspector to prosecute Mr. Weeks. Weeks claimed that the evidence was gained by an illegal search, and thus was inadmissible. The Court agreed, applying for the first time an "exclusionary rule" for illegally gained evidence in federal courts. The decision stated "…if letters and private documents can thus be seized and used as evidence…his right to be secure against such searches…is of no value, and…might as well be stricken from the Constitution." See also Mapp v. Ohio, 1961; Massachusetts v. Sheppard, 1984; and Nix v.Williams, 1984.

West Virginia Board of Education v. Barnette, 1943

Decision: The Court held that a compulsory flag salute violated the 1st Amendment's exercise of religion clause and was, therefore, unconstitutional. "…no official, high or petty, can prescribe what shall be orthodox in politics, nationalism, religion, or other matters of opinion.…"

Westside Community Schools v. Mergens, 1990

(1st Amendment, Establishment Clause) A request by Bridget Mergens to form a student Christian religious group at school was denied by an Omaha high school principal. Mergens took legal action, claiming that a 1984 federal law required "equal access" for student religious groups. The Court ordered the school to permit the club, stating, "a high school does not have to permit any extracurricular activities, but when it does, the school is bound by the…Act of 1984. Allowing students to meet on campus and discuss religion is constitutional because it does not amount to a 'State sponsorship of a religion.'"

Wisconsin v. Yoder, 1972

(1st Amendment, Free Exercise Clause) Members of the Amish religious sect in Wisconsin objected to sending their children to public schools after the eighth grade, claiming that such exposure of the children to another culture would endanger the group's self-sufficient agrarian lifestyle essential to their religious faith. The Court agreed with the Amish, while noting that the Court must move carefully to weigh the State's "legitimate social concern when faced with religious claim for exemption from generally applicable educational requirements."

PRESIDENTS *of the United States*

1

George Washington
(1732–1799)
Years in office: 1789–1797
No political party
Elected from: Virginia
Vice Pres.: John Adams

2

John Adams
(1735–1826)
Years in office: 1797–1801
Federalist
Elected from: Massachusetts
Vice Pres.: Thomas Jefferson

3

Thomas Jefferson
(1743–1826)
Years in office: 1801–1809
Democratic Republican
Elected from: Virginia
Vice Pres.: Aaron Burr, George Clinton

4

James Madison
(1751–1836)
Years in office: 1809–1817
Democratic Republican
Elected from: Virginia
Vice Pres.: George Clinton,
    Elbridge Gerry

5

James Monroe
(1758–1831)
Years in office: 1817–1825
National Republican
Elected from: Virginia
Vice Pres.: Daniel Tompkins

6

John Quincy Adams
(1767–1848)
Years in office: 1825–1829
National Republican
Elected from: Massachusetts
Vice Pres.: John Calhoun

7

Andrew Jackson
(1767–1845)
Years in office: 1829–1837
Democrat
Elected from: Tennessee
Vice Pres.: John Calhoun,
    Martin Van Buren

8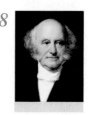

Martin Van Buren
(1782–1862)
Years in office: 1837–1841
Democrat
Elected from: New York
Vice Pres.: Richard Johnson

9 **William Henry Harrison***
(1773–1841)
Years in office: 1841
Whig
Elected from: Ohio
Vice Pres.: John Tyler

10 **John Tyler**
(1790–1862)
Years in office: 1841–1845
Whig
Elected from: Virginia
Vice Pres.: none

11 **James K. Polk**
(1795–1849)
Years in office: 1845–1849
Democrat
Elected from: Tennessee
Vice Pres.: George Dallas

12 **Zachary Taylor***
(1784–1850)
Years in office: 1849–1850
Whig
Elected from: Louisiana
Vice Pres.: Millard FIllmore

13 **Millard Fillmore**
(1800–1874)
Years in office: 1850–1853
Whig
Elected from: New York
Vice Pres.: none

14 **Franklin Pierce**
(1804–1869)
Years in office: 1853–1857
Democrat
Elected from: New Hampshire
Vice Pres.: William King

15 **James Buchanan**
(1791–1868)
Years in office: 1857–1861
Democrat
Elected from: Pennsylvania
Vice Pres.: John Breckinridge

16 **Abraham Lincoln****
(1809–1865)
Years in office: 1861–1865
Republican
Elected from: Illinois
Vice Pres.: Hannibal Hamlin,
Andrew Johnson

17 **Andrew Johnson**
(1808–1875)
Years in office: 1865–1869
Republican
Elected from: Tennessee
Vice Pres.: none

18 **Ulysses S. Grant**
(1822–1885)
Years in office: 1869–1877
Republican
Elected from: Illinois
Vice Pres.: Schuyler Colfax,
Henry Wilson

19 **Rutherford B. Hayes**
(1822–1893)
Years in office: 1877–1881
Republican
Elected from: Ohio
Vice Pres.: William Wheeler

20 **James A. Garfield****
(1831–1881)
Years in office: 1881
Republican
Elected from: Ohio
Vice Pres.: Chester A. Arthur

21  **Chester A. Arthur**
(1830–1886)
Years in office: 1881–1885
Republican
Elected from: New York
Vice Pres.: none

22  **Grover Cleveland**
(1837–1908)
Years in office: 1885–1889
Democrat
Elected from: New York
Vice Pres.: Thomas Hendricks

23  **Benjamin Harrison**
(1833–1901)
Years in office: 1889–1893
Republican
Elected from: Indiana
Vice Pres.: Levi Morton

24  **Grover Cleveland**
(1837–1908)
Years in office: 1893–1897
Democrat
Elected from: New York
Vice Pres.: Adlai Stevenson

25  **William McKinley****
(1843–1901)
Years in office: 1897–1901
Republican
Elected from: Ohio
Vice Pres.: Garret Hobart,
Theodore Roosevelt

26  **Theodore Roosevelt**
(1858–1919)
Years in office: 1901–1909
Republican
Elected from: New York
Vice Pres.: Charles Fairbanks

27  **William Howard Taft**
(1857–1930)
Years in office: 1909–1913
Republican
Elected from: Ohio
Vice Pres.: James Sherman

28  **Woodrow Wilson**
(1856–1924)
Years in office: 1913–1921
Democrat
Elected from: New Jersey
Vice Pres.: Thomas Marshall

29  **Warren G. Harding***
(1865–1923)
Years in office: 1921–1923
Republican
Elected from: Ohio
Vice Pres.: Calvin Coolidge

30  **Calvin Coolidge**
(1872–1933)
Years in office: 1923–1929
Republican
Elected from: Massachusetts
Vice Pres.: Charles Dawes

31  **Herbert C. Hoover**
(1874–1964)
Years in office: 1929–1933
Republican
Elected from: New York
Vice Pres.: Charles Curtis

32  **Franklin D. Roosevelt***
(1882–1945)
Years in office: 1933–1945
Democrat
Elected from: New York
Vice Pres.: John Garner, Henry
Wallace, Harry S. Truman

33 **Harry S. Truman**
(1884–1972)
Years in office: 1945–1953
Democrat
Elected from: Missouri
Vice Pres.: Alben Barkley

 *34* **Dwight D. Eisenhower**
(1890–1969)
Years in office: 1953–1961
Republican
Elected from: New York
Vice Pres.: Richard M. Nixon

 *35* **John F. Kennedy****
(1917–1963)
Years in office: 1961–1963
Democrat
Elected from: Massachusetts
Vice Pres.: Lyndon B. Johnson

 *36* **Lyndon B. Johnson**
(1908–1973)
Years in office: 1963–1969
Democrat
Elected from: Texas
Vice Pres.: Hubert Humphrey

 *37* **Richard M. Nixon*****
(1913–1994)
Years in office: 1969–1974
Republican
Elected from: New York
Vice Pres.: Spiro Agnew,
  Gerald R. Ford

 *38* **Gerald R. Ford**
(1913–)
Years in office: 1974–1977
Republican
Elected from: Michigan
Vice Pres.: Nelson Rockefeller

 *39* **Jimmy Carter**
(1924–)
Years in office: 1977–1981
Democrat
Elected from: Georgia
Vice Pres.: Walter F. Mondale

 *40* **Ronald W. Reagan**
(1911–)
Years in office: 1981–1989
Republican
Elected from: California
Vice Pres.: George H.W. Bush

 *41* **George H.W. Bush**
(1924–)
Years in office: 1989–1993
Republican
Elected from: Texas
Vice Pres.: J. Danforth Quayle

 *42* **William J. Clinton**
(1946–)
Years in office: 1993–2000
Democrat
Elected from: Arkansas
Vice Pres.: Albert Gore, Jr.

 *43* **George W. Bush**
(1946–)
Years in office: 2001–
Republican
Elected from: Texas
Vice Pres.: Richard Cheney

*Died in office
**Assassinated
***Resigned

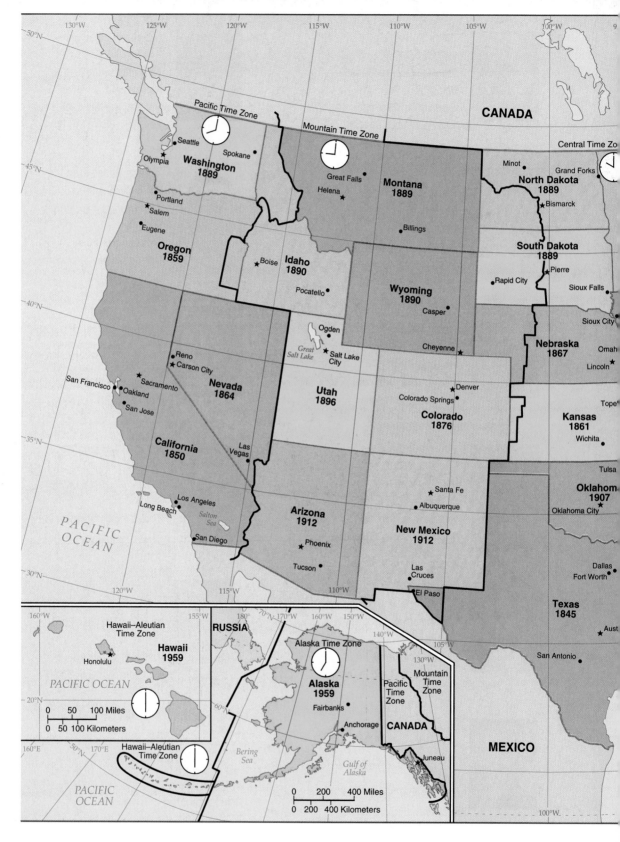

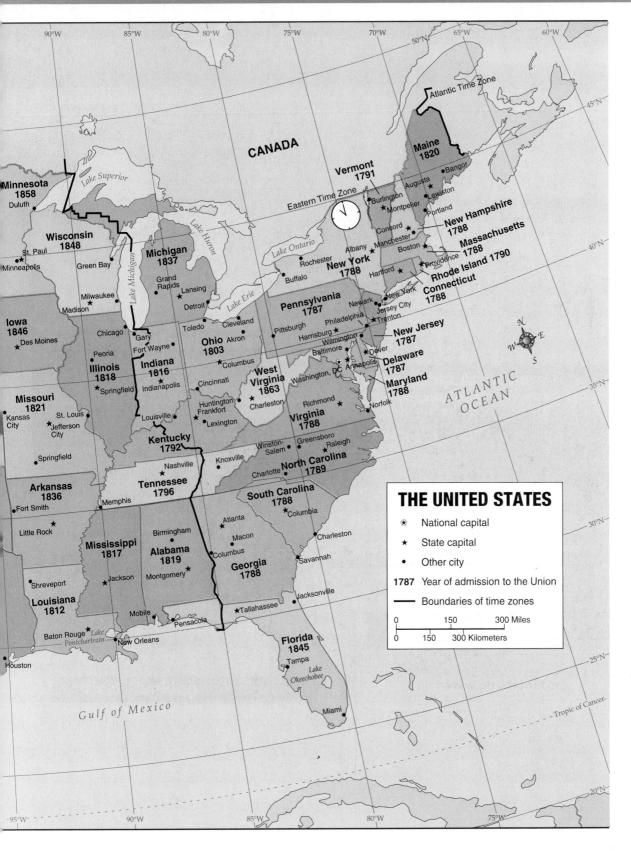

90°W   85°W   80°W   75°W   70°W   50°N   65°W   60°W

Atlantic Time Zone

45°N

CANADA

**Maine
1820**
• Bangor

**Vermont
1791**
Augusta ★
• Lewiston

Eastern Time Zone
Burlington •
Montpelier ★
• Portland

**New Hampshire
1788**

**Minnesota
1858**
• Duluth

Lake Superior

Concord ★
Manchester •

**Massachusetts
1788**

**Wisconsin
1848**

Lake Huron

Lake Michigan

**Michigan
1837**
Grand
Rapids •
• Lansing ★

Rochester •
Albany ★
Boston ★
**New York
1788**
• Buffalo
Hartford ★
Providence ★
Rhode Island 1790
**Connecticut
1788**

40°N

St. Paul ★
• Minneapolis
Green Bay •
Milwaukee •
Madison ★

• Detroit

Lake Ontario

Lake Erie
Cleveland •

New York •
Newark •
Jersey City •

**Iowa
1846**
★ Des Moines

Chicago •
Gary •
Fort Wayne •
Toledo •
**Ohio
1803** Akron •
Columbus ★

**Pennsylvania
1787**
Pittsburgh •
Harrisburg ★
Philadelphia •
Trenton ★
**New Jersey
1787**

**Illinois
1818**
Peoria •
★ Springfield

**Indiana
1816**
Indianapolis ★

Cincinnati •

Baltimore •
Wilmington •
Dover ★
**Delaware
1787**

**Missouri
1821**
Kansas
City •
★ St. Louis
• Jefferson
City

Louisville •
Frankfort ★
• Lexington

**West
Virginia
1863**
Charleston ★
Washington, D.C. ⊛
Annapolis ★
**Maryland
1788**
• Norfolk

35°N

ATLANTIC
OCEAN

• Springfield

**Kentucky
1792**

Huntington •

**Virginia
1788**
Richmond ★

N
W E
S

**Arkansas
1836**
• Fort Smith
• Little Rock

Nashville ★
**Tennessee
1796**
Knoxville •

Winston-
Salem •
Greensboro •
Raleigh ★
**North Carolina
1789**
Charlotte •

Memphis •

**South Carolina
1788**
★ Columbia

30°N

**Mississippi
1817**

Birmingham •
Atlanta ★
• Macon
Columbus •

Charleston •

**Alabama
1819**
Jackson ★
Montgomery ★

**Georgia
1788**

• Savannah

**Louisiana
1812**
• Shreveport

• Jacksonville

Baton Rouge ★
Lake
Pontchartrain
New Orleans •
Mobile •
Pensacola •
★ Tallahassee

• Houston

**Florida
1845**
Tampa •
Lake
Okeechobee

25°N

THE UNITED STATES

⊛   National capital

★   State capital

•   Other city

1787   Year of admission to the Union

━━━   Boundaries of time zones

0   150   300 Miles

0   150   300 Kilometers

Gulf of Mexico

• Miami

Tropic of Cancer

20°N

95°W   90°W   85°W   80°W   75°W

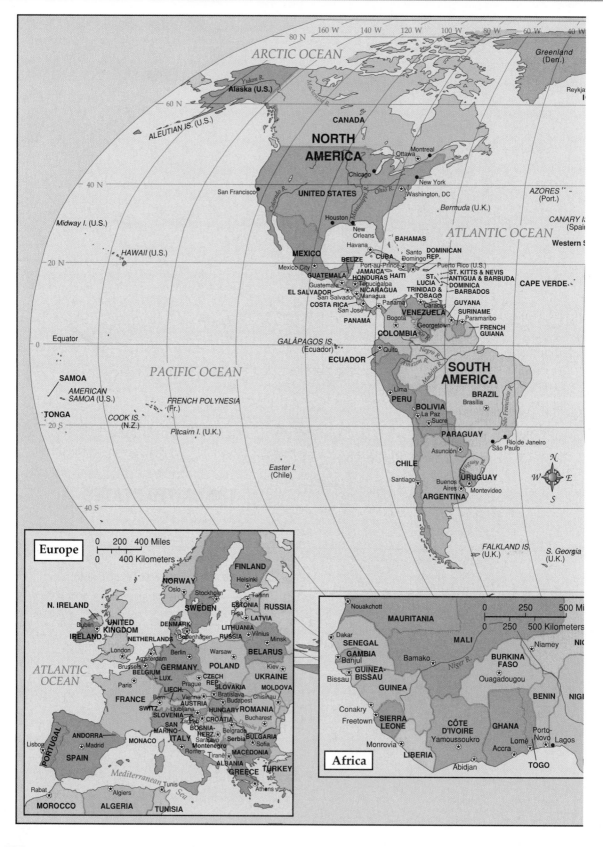

160 W   140 W   120 W   100 W   80 W   60 W   40 W

80 N

ARCTIC OCEAN

Greenland
(Den.)

Yukon R.

60 N

Alaska (U.S.)

Reykja

CANADA

ALEUTIAN IS. (U.S.)

NORTH
AMERICA

Montreal

40 N

Ottawa

Chicago

New York

San Francisco

Colorado R.

Ohio R.

Washington, DC

AZORES
(Port.)

Mississippi R.

UNITED STATES

Bermuda (U.K.)

ATLANTIC OCEAN

CANARY I.
(Spain)

Houston

Midway I. (U.S.)

New
Orleans

BAHAMAS

Western S

20 N

HAWAII (U.S.)

Havana

Santo

DOMINICAN

Mexico City

CUBA

Domingo

REP.

MEXICO

BELIZE

Port-au-Prince

Puerto Rico (U.S.)

ST. KITTS & NEVIS

GUATEMALA

JAMAICA

HAITI

ANTIGUA & BARBUDA

CAPE VERDE

HONDURAS

ST.

DOMINICA

Guatemala

Tegucigalpa

LUCIA

TRINIDAD &

BARBADOS

EL SALVADOR

NICARAGUA

TOBAGO

San Salvador

Managua

COSTA RICA

Panamá

GUYANA

San José

VENEZUELA

SURINAME

PANAMÁ

Bogotá

Caracas

Paramaribo

FRENCH

Georgetown

GUIANA

0

Equator

GALÁPAGOS IS.
(Ecuador)

COLOMBIA

Negro R.

Quito

ECUADOR

Amazon R.

Madeira R.

PACIFIC OCEAN

SOUTH
AMERICA

SAMOA

Lima

BRAZIL

São Francisco R.

AMERICAN
SAMOA (U.S.)

FRENCH POLYNESIA
(Fr.)

PERU

BOLIVIA

Brasília

TONGA

COOK IS.
(N.Z.)

La Paz

20 S

Pitcairn I. (U.K.)

Sucre

PARAGUAY

Rio de Janeiro

São Paulo

Asunción

Uruguay R.

Easter I.
(Chile)

CHILE

N

URUGUAY

W   E

40 S

Santiago

Buenos
Aires

Montevideo

S

ARGENTINA

FALKLAND IS.
(U.K.)

S. Georgia
(U.K.)

Europe

0   200   400 Miles

0   400 Kilometers

FINLAND

NORWAY

Helsinki

Oslo

N. IRELAND

Stockholm

Tallinn

ESTONIA

RUSSIA

SWEDEN

Riga

LATVIA

Dublin

UNITED

DENMARK

LITHUANIA

IRELAND

KINGDOM

Vilnius

Minsk

NETHERLANDS

Copenhagen

RUSSIA

London

Amsterdam

Berlin

Warsaw

BELARUS

ATLANTIC
OCEAN

Brussels

Kiev

Paris

BELGIUM

GERMANY

POLAND

UKRAINE

LUX.

Prague

CZECH

LIECH.

Bern

REP.

SLOVAKIA

MOLDOVA

FRANCE

Vienna

Bratislava

Chisinau

SWITZ.

Ljubljana

AUSTRIA

HUNGARY

ROMANIA

SLOVENIA

Zagreb

Budapest

Bucharest

SAN

CROATIA

Danube R.

MARINO

BOSNIA-

Belgrade

BULGARIA

Lisbon

PORTUGAL

ANDORRA

HERZ.

MONACO

ITALY

Sarajevo

Serbia

Sofia

Madrid

Rome

Montenegro

MACEDONIA

SPAIN

Tiranë

ALBANIA

Mediterranean Sea

Tunis

GREECE

TURKEY

Rabat

Algiers

Athens

MOROCCO

ALGERIA

TUNISIA

Africa

0   250   500 Mi

0   250   500 Kilometers

Nouakchott

MAURITANIA

Dakar

MALI

SENEGAL

Niamey

NI

GAMBIA

Bamako

BURKINA

Banjul

Niger R.

FASO

GUINEA-

BISSAU

Bissau

GUINEA

Ouagadougou

BENIN

NIG

Conakry

CÔTE

GHANA

Porto-

Freetown

SIERRA

D'IVOIRE

Novo

Lagos

LEONE

Yamoussoukro

Lomé

Monrovia

Accra

LIBERIA

TOGO

Abidjan

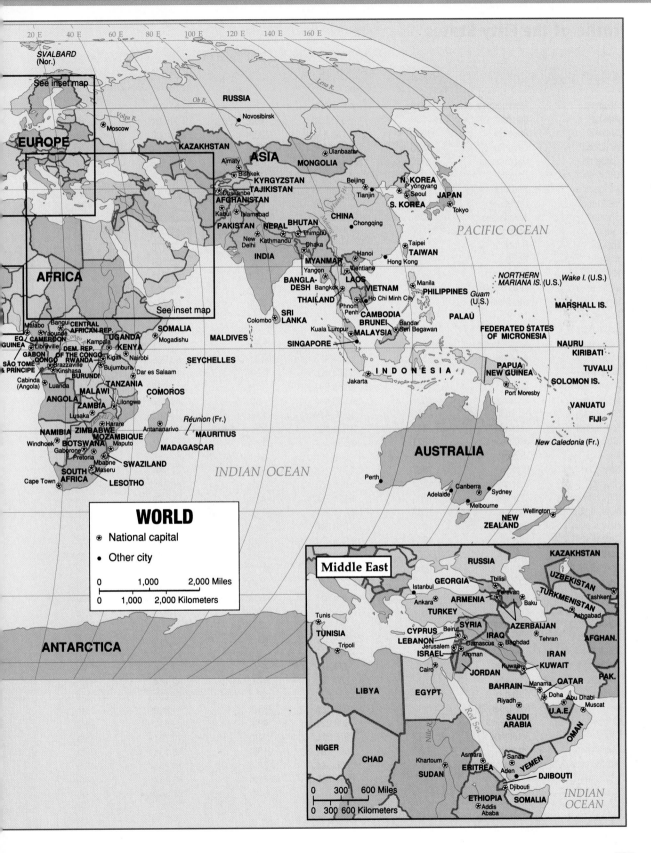

20 E 40 E 60 E 80 E 100 E 120 E 140 E 160 E

SVALBARD (Nor.)

See inset map

EUROPE

RUSSIA

Novosibirsk

Moscow

Volga R.

Ob R.

Lena R.

KAZAKHSTAN

ASIA

Ulanbaatar

MONGOLIA

Almaty

Bishkek

KYRGYZSTAN

Dushanbe

TAJIKISTAN

AFGHANISTAN

Beijing

Tianjin

N. KOREA

P'yongyang

Seoul

S. KOREA

JAPAN

Tokyo

Huang He

Kabul Islamabad

PAKISTAN NEPAL BHUTAN

CHINA

Chongqing

PACIFIC OCEAN

New Delhi Kathmandu Thimphu

INDIA Dhaka

Mekong R.

Hanoi

Taipei

TAIWAN

Hong Kong

AFRICA

See inset map

MYANMAR

Yangon

LAOS

Vientiane

Manila

NORTHERN MARIANA IS. (U.S.) Wake I. (U.S.)

BANGLA-DESH Bangkok

THAILAND

VIETNAM

Ho Chi Minh City

PHILIPPINES

Guam (U.S.)

MARSHALL IS.

SRI LANKA

Colombo

Phnom Penh

CAMBODIA

BRUNEI Bandar Seri Begawan

PALAU

FEDERATED STATES OF MICRONESIA

Malabo Bangui CENTRAL AFRICAN REP.

SOMALIA

Mogadishu

MALDIVES

Kuala Lumpur

MALAYSIA

EQ. GUINEA CAMEROON Yaoundé UGANDA KENYA

SINGAPORE

NAURU

KIRIBATI

GABON DEM. REP. OF THE CONGO RWANDA Kampala Kigali Nairobi

SEYCHELLES

TUVALU

SÃO TOMÉ & PRÍNCIPE Libreville Brazzaville Kinshasa BURUNDI Bujumbura Dar es Salaam

INDONESIA

PAPUA NEW GUINEA

SOLOMON IS.

Cabinda (Angola) Luanda TANZANIA

Jakarta

Port Moresby

VANUATU

ANGOLA ZAMBIA MALAWI COMOROS

Réunion (Fr.)

FIJI

Lusaka Harare Lilongwe

Antananarivo

MAURITIUS

New Caledonia (Fr.)

NAMIBIA ZIMBABWE MOZAMBIQUE

MADAGASCAR

Windhoek BOTSWANA Maputo

AUSTRALIA

Gaborone Pretoria

INDIAN OCEAN

Perth

Cape Town SOUTH AFRICA Mbabane SWAZILAND Maseru LESOTHO

Adelaide Canberra Sydney

Melbourne

Wellington

NEW ZEALAND

WORLD

⊛ National capital

• Other city

0   1,000   2,000 Miles

0 1,000 2,000 Kilometers

ANTARCTICA

Middle East

RUSSIA

KAZAKHSTAN

Istanbul

GEORGIA Tbilisi

UZBEKISTAN

Ankara

ARMENIA Yerevan Baku

TURKMENISTAN Tashkent

TURKEY

AZERBAIJAN

Ashgabad

Tunis

CYPRUS Beirut SYRIA IRAQ Tehran

AFGHAN.

TUNISIA

LEBANON Damascus Baghdad

Tripoli

Jerusalem Amman

ISRAEL

IRAN

PAK.

Cairo

JORDAN Kuwait KUWAIT

LIBYA EGYPT BAHRAIN Manama QATAR

Riyadh Doha Abu Dhabi Muscat

U.A.E.

SAUDI ARABIA

OMAN

NIGER CHAD

Nile R.

Red Sea

Khartoum Asmara Sanaa

SUDAN ERITREA Aden YEMEN

Djibouti DJIBOUTI

INDIAN OCEAN

ETHIOPIA SOMALIA

Addis Ababa

0   300   600 Miles

0 300 600 Kilometers

Profile of the Fifty States

State	Capital	Entered Union	Population (2000)	Population Rank	Land Area (Square Miles)	Land Area Rank
Alabama	Montgomery	1819	4,447,100	23rd	51,705	29th
Alaska	Juneau	1959	626,932	48th	591,004	1st
Arizona	Phoenix	1912	5,130,632	20th	114,000	6th
Arkansas	Little Rock	1836	2,673,400	33rd	53,187	27th
California	Sacramento	1850	33,871,648	1st	158,706	3rd
Colorado	Denver	1876	4,301,261	24th	104,091	8th
Connecticut	Hartford	1788	3,405,565	28th	5,018	48th
Delaware	Dover	1787	783,600	45th	2,044	49th
Florida	Tallahassee	1845	15,982,378	4th	58,664	22nd
Georgia	Atlanta	1788	8,186,453	10th	58,910	21st
Hawaii	Honolulu	1959	1,211,537	42nd	6,470	47th
Idaho	Boise	1890	1,293,953	39th	83,564	13th
Illinois	Springfield	1818	12,419,293	5th	56,345	24th
Indiana	Indianapolis	1816	6,080,485	14th	36,185	38th
Iowa	Des Moines	1846	2,926,324	30th	56,275	25th
Kansas	Topeka	1861	2,688,418	32nd	82,277	14th
Kentucky	Frankfort	1792	4,041,769	25th	40,409	37th
Louisiana	Baton Rouge	1812	4,468,976	22nd	47,751	31st
Maine	Augusta	1820	1,274,923	40th	33,265	39th
Maryland	Annapolis	1788	5,296,486	19th	10,460	42nd
Massachusetts	Boston	1788	6,349,097	13th	8,284	45th
Michigan	Lansing	1837	9,938,444	8th	58,527	23rd
Minnesota	St. Paul	1858	4,919,479	21st	84,402	12th
Mississippi	Jackson	1817	2,844,658	31st	47,689	32nd
Missouri	Jefferson City	1821	5,595,211	17th	69,697	19th
Montana	Helena	1889	902,195	44th	147,046	4th
Nebraska	Lincoln	1867	1,711,263	37th	77,355	15th
Nevada	Carson City	1864	1,998,257	35th	110,561	7th
New Hampshire	Concord	1788	1,235,786	41st	9,279	44th
New Jersey	Trenton	1787	8,414,350	9th	7,787	46th
New Mexico	Santa Fe	1912	1,819,046	36th	121,593	5th
New York	Albany	1788	18,976,457	3rd	49,108	30th
North Carolina	Raleigh	1789	8,049,313	11th	52,669	28th
North Dakota	Bismarck	1889	642,200	47th	70,703	17th
Ohio	Columbus	1803	11,353,140	7th	41,330	35th
Oklahoma	Oklahoma City	1907	3,450,654	27th	69,956	18th
Oregon	Salem	1859	3,421,399	29th	97,073	10th
Pennsylvania	Harrisburg	1787	12,281,054	6th	45,308	33rd
Rhode Island	Providence	1790	1,048,319	43rd	1,212	50th
South Carolina	Columbia	1788	4,012,012	26th	31,113	40th
South Dakota	Pierre	1889	754,844	46th	77,116	16th
Tennessee	Nashville	1796	5,689,283	16th	42,144	34th
Texas	Austin	1845	20,851,820	2nd	266,807	2nd
Utah	Salt Lake City	1896	2,233,169	34th	84,899	11th
Vermont	Montpelier	1791	608,827	49th	9,614	43rd
Virginia	Richmond	1788	7,078,515	12th	40,767	36th
Washington	Olympia	1889	5,894,121	15th	68,138	20th
West Virginia	Charleston	1863	1,808,344	38th	24,231	41st
Wisconsin	Madison	1848	5,363,675	18th	56,153	26th
Wyoming	Cheyenne	1890	493,782	50th	97,809	9th

Sources: *World Almanac, Statistical Abstract of the United States, U.S. Census Bureau*

Glossary

This glossary defines all key terms. The page number given after each definition refers to the text page on which the term appears in blue.

Pronunciation Key

Certain glossary terms and other words have been respelled in the text and in this glossary as an aid to pronunciation. The term *entrepreneur,* for example, has been respelled AHN–truh–preh–NOOR. The small capital letters mean that the first syllable should be spoken with a minor stress. The large capital letters mean that the last syllable should be spoken with a major stress. The vowel sounds shown by the letters *ah, uh, eh,* and *oo* in the respelling correspond to the vowel sounds in the pronunciation key below.

Pronounce	as in	Pronounce	as in
a	hat	j	jet
ah	father	ng	ring
ar	tar	o	frog
ay	say	ō, oh	no
ayr	air	oo	soon
e, eh	hen	or	for
ee	bee	ow	plow
eer	deer	oy	boy
er	her	sh	she
ew	new	th	thick
g	go	u, uh	sun
i, ih	him	z	zebra
ī	kite	zh	measure

A

administration A team of executive branch officials appointed by each President (page 201)

affirmative action Steps to counteract effects of past racial discrimination and discrimination against women (page 161)

aggression An attack or threat of attack by another country (page 543)

alien A citizen of one country who lives in another country (page 46)

alliance A group of nations that have agreed to help or protect each other (page 529)

ambassadors Official representatives to foreign countries (page 198)

amendments Changes to the Constitution (p. 102)

answer The defendant's written response to a complaint (page 437)

appeal To ask a higher court to review a decision and determine if justice was done (page 221)

appellate jurisdiction (a-PEL-et JOO-ris-DIK-shun) A court's authority to hear an appeal of a decision by another court (page 221)

apportioned Divided among districts (page 248)

arbitration The use of a third person to make a legal decision that is binding on all parties (page 440)

arraignment (uh-RAIN-ment) A court hearing in which the defendant is formally charged with a crime and enters a plea of guilty or not guilty (page 418)

B

bail Money that a defendant gives the court as a kind of promise that he or she will return for trial (page 418)

beliefs Certain ideas that people trust are true (page 15)

bias A favoring of one point of view (page 482)

bicameral (bī-KAM-er-uhl) Two–house, as in a legislature with two houses (page 93)

bill A proposed law (page 175)

board A group of people who manage the business of an organization (page 264)

bonds Certificates that people buy from the government, which agrees to pay back the cost of the bond, plus interest, after a set period of time (page 250)

boycott To refuse to buy a certain company's products (page 320)

budget A plan for raising and spending money (page 180)

bureaucracy (byoo-RAH-kru-see) An organization of government departments, agencies, and offices (page 201)

business cycle A repeated series of "ups" of growth and "downs" of recession (page 354)

C

Cabinet An important group of policy advisors to the President, made up of the executive department heads and a few other officials (page 203) candidate A person running for office (page 53)

canvass To go door–to–door handing out political information and asking people which candidate they support (page 458)

capital Anything produced in an economy that is saved to be used to produce other goods and services (page 289)

capitalism Another name for market economy; a system in which people make their own decisions about how to save resources as capital and how to use their capital to produce goods and services (page 300)

caucus (KAW-kus) meeting of party leaders to discuss issues or choose candidates (page 466)

census An official count of the population made every ten years to find out how many representatives each state should have (page 177)

charter A document giving permission to create a government (page 70)

checks and balances The system that gives each of the three branches of government ways to limit the powers of the other two (page 105)

citizen A person with certain rights and duties under a government; a person who by birth or by choice owes allegiance, or loyalty, to a nation (page 46)

civil disobedience Breaking a law because it goes against personal morals (page 395)

civil law The group of laws that help settle disagreements between people (page 400)

closed primary A primary election in which a voter must be registered as a member of a party and may vote only for candidates of that party (page 466)

cloture (KLŌ-chur) Agreement to end the debate on a bill in the Senate (page 187)

Cold War A struggle between the superpowers, much like a real war but with no armed battles (page 529)

collective bargaining The process by which representatives of a union and of a business discuss and reach agreement about wages and working conditions (page 320)

colony A territory ruled by a more powerful nation called a colonial power (page 523)

command economy An economic system in which the government or a central authority owns or controls the factors of production and makes the basic economic decisions (page 298)

common good, the The well–being of all members of society (page 51)

common law A body of law based on judges' decisions (page 396)

communism A system under which the government owns all land, businesses, and resources (page 528)

compact A written agreement to make and obey laws for the welfare of the group (page 80)

compensation Being "made whole" for harm caused by another person's acts (page 432)

complaint A legal document that charges someone with having caused harm (page 436)

concurrent powers The powers shared by the federal and state governments (page 104)

congressional district The area that a member of the House represents (page 177)

constituents The people a member of Congress represents (page 174)

constitution A plan of government (page 80)

constitutional initiative A process in which citizens can propose an amendment by gathering a required number of signatures on a petition (page 244)

consumer A person who uses, or consumes, goods and services to satisfy his or her wants (page 35)

consumption The act of buying or using goods or services (page 290)

containment A policy of using military power and money to prevent the spread of communism (page 553)

contracts Legal agreements between buyers and sellers (page 434)

corporation A business that is separate from the people who own it and legally acts as a single person (page 316)

crime Any behavior that is illegal because the government considers it harmful to society (page 399)

criminal law The group of laws that tell which acts are crimes, how accused persons should be tried in court, and how crimes should be punished (page 399)

currency The coins and paper bills used as money in an economy (page 329)

D

damages Money that is paid in an effort to compensate, or make up, for a loss (page 432)

defendant The party who answers a complaint and defends against it in a court case (page 219)

deficit The amount by which government spending is greater than government income (page 359)

deforestation Cutting and burning forests to clear land for farms and cattle grazing (page 566)

delegated powers The powers given to Congress rather than to the states (page 101)

delinquent A juvenile who is found guilty of a crime (page 424)

demand The amounts of a product or service buyers are willing and able to buy at different prices (page 310)

demand deposit The money in a checking account (page 332)

democracy A system of government in which the power is shared by all the people (page 38)

deposition The record of answers to questions asked of a witness in person before a trial (page 437)

détente (day-TAHNT) A lessening of tensions between the superpowers (page 529)

deterrence Keeping a strong defense to discourage aggression by other nations (page 543)

dictatorship A government controlled by one person, called a dictator, who usually takes power by force, rather than by inheriting it (page 38)

diplomacy The relations and communications carried out between countries (page 544)

direct democracy A form of government in which laws are made directly by the citizens (page 75)

direct mail A way of sending messages to large groups of people through the mail (page 479)

direct primary An election in which members of a political party choose candidates to run for office in the name of the party (page 466)

discovery The process of gathering evidence before a trial (page 437)

discrimination The unfair treatment of a group of people. (page 10)

disposable income The amount of money left after taxes have been paid (page 369)

diversity Differences (page 7)

dividends Payments from the profits of companies in which a person owns stock (page 369)

domestic policy Plans for dealing with national problems (page 199)

double jeopardy Being placed on trial twice for the same crime (page 139)

due process of law A process by which the government must treat accused persons fairly according to rules established by law (page 137)

E

economy A system for producing and distributing goods and services to fulfill people's wants (page 35)

eminent domain (EM-ih-nehnt do-MAYN) The power of the government to take private property for public use (page 137)

entrepreneur (AHN-truh-preh-NOOR) A person who starts a business (page 313)

equality The condition of everyone having the same rights and opportunities (page 16)

equity The use of general rules of fairness to settle conflicts in a civil court case (page 433)

excise tax (EK-sīz taks) A charge on certain goods, such as alcoholic beverages, gasoline, and tobacco (page 249)

executive agreements Agreements with other countries that do not need Senate approval (page 198)

executive branch The branch of government responsible for executing or enforcing the laws (page 196)

executive orders Rules or regulations that executive branch employees must follow (page 198)

executive privilege The President's right to keep some information secret from Congress and the courts (page 209)

F

factors of production The resources people have for producing goods and services to satisfy their wants (page 289)

federalism The division of power between the states and the federal, or national, government (page 104)

felony A crime for which the penalty is imprisonment for more than one year, a fine, or a combination of both. Felonies include crimes such as kidnapping and murder. (page 400)

filibuster (FIL-ih-BUS-ter) The use of long speeches to prevent a vote on a bill in the Senate (page 187)

fiscal policy A government's decisions about the amount of money it spends and the amount it collects in taxes (page 355)

fixed expenses Expenses that remain the same from month to month (page 370)

floor leaders Officers who guide through Congress the bills that their party supports (page 183)

foreign aid A program of giving military and economic help to other nations (page 544)

foreign policy Plans for guiding our nation's relationships with other countries (page 198)

free enterprise The system in which individuals in a market economy are free to undertake economic activities with little or no control by the government (page 300)

freedom The ability to say what you want, go where you want, and do what you want (page 17)

fringe benefits Indirect payments for work (page 369)

G

general election An election in which voters make final decisions about candidates and issues (page 474)

goods Physical products, such as food and clothing (page 35)

gross domestic product (GDP) The total dollar value of all final goods and services produced and sold in the country in a year (page 357)

H

heritage The traditions passed down from generation to generation (page 70)

home rule The right of a city or county to choose its own form of government (page 275)

I

immigrants People who move from one country to make their homes in another. (page 8)

impeach To accuse the President or other high government officials of serious wrongdoing (page 105)

income tax A tax on what individuals and businesses earn (page 249)

incumbent Someone who already holds the office for which he or she is running (page 487)

independent voters People who say they do not support a political party (page 465)

indictment A formal charge against a person accused of a crime (page 418)

inflation A general rise in the prices of goods and services throughout the economy (page 341)

initiative The process by which citizens can propose laws (page 248)

injunction A civil court order to do or not do a certain act (page 433)

insurance A plan by which a company gives protection from the cost of injury or loss (page 376)

intelligence Information about another nation and what its government plans to do (page 546)

interest Payment for the use of capital (page 309)

interest groups Groups of people who work together for similar interests or goals (page 176)

intergovernmental revenue Money given by one level of government to another (page 272)

invest To use money to help a business get started or grow, with the hope that the business will earn a profit (page 299)

isolationism A foreign policy that seeks to limit our relations with other countries as much as possible (page 551)

issue A point of conflict or a matter to be debated (page 496)

item veto A state governor's power to reject particular parts, or items, of a bill (page 252)

J

judicial activism An effort by judges to take an active role in policymaking by overturning laws relatively often (page 229)

judicial restraint An effort by judges to avoid overturning laws and to leave policymaking up to the other two branches of government (page 229)

judicial review The Supreme Court's power to overturn any law that it decides is in conflict with the Constitution (page 225)

jury of peers A group of ordinary citizens who hear a court case and decide whether the accused person is innocent or guilty (page 50)

justice Fairness; the idea that every person deserves to be treated fairly (page 18)

L

labor unions Organizations of workers that seek to improve wages and working conditions and to protect members' rights (page 319)

laws Rules of society that are enforced by governments (page 392)

lawsuits Cases in which a court is asked to settle a dispute (page 432)

legal code A written collection of laws, often organized by subject (page 397)

legislature A group of people chosen to make laws (page 70)

liability insurance Insurance that protects a person from the costs of damage or injury to others (page 377)

liquidity (li-KWID-i-tee) The ability to turn savings back into cash (page 375)

loan An amount of money borrowed for a certain time period (page 333)

lobbyists People who represent interest groups (page 176)

M

majority party The political party with more members in the House or Senate (page 183)

market A place or situation in which an exchange of goods or services takes place, such as stores, shops, or stock exchanges (page 35)

market economy An economic system in which private individuals own the factors of production and are free to make their own choices about production, distribution, and consumption (page 298)

market price The price at which buyers and sellers agree to trade (page 311)

media Television, radio, newspapers and magazines (page 479)

mediation A process by which people agree to use a third party to help them settle a conflict out of court (page 440)

minority party The political party with fewer members in the House or Senate (page 183)

misdemeanor A crime for which the penalty is a jail sentence of not more than one year, a fine, or a combination of both. Littering and driving without a license are examples of misdemeanors. (page 400)

mixed economy An economy that is a mixture of the characteristics of two or more of the three basic systems (page 300)

monarchy A form of government in which all or most of the power is in the hands of one individual, the monarch. The monarch's authority is hereditary. (page 38)

monetary policy Regulation of the money supply by the Federal Reserve System (page 354)

money Anything that is generally accepted as payment for a good or service (page 36)

monopoly A single business with the power to control prices in a market (page 350)

morals Beliefs about what is fair and what is right or wrong (page 394)

municipality A government that serves people who live in an urban area (page 266)

N

national debt The total amount of money the government owes to lenders (page 360)

nationalism A feeling of pride in shared history and loyalty to a nation, which is shared by its citizens (page 523)

natural rights Rights that people are born with and that no government can take away, such as the rights to life, liberty, and property (page 76)

naturalized To have gone through the process of becoming a citizen. Naturalization is a process which applies to a person not born a citizen of the United States. (page 46)

neutrality A policy of not taking sides in wars between other nations (page 552)

nominate To name candidates to run for public office (page 457)

nonrenewable resource A resource that cannot be replaced once it has been used (page 564)

O

open primary A primary election in which voters do not need to declare a party before voting, but may vote for the candidates of only one party (page 466)

opportunity cost The benefit given up when scarce resources are used for one purpose instead of the next best purpose (page 292)

ordinances Local laws (page 264)

original jurisdiction A court's authority to hear a case first (page 220)

P

parole Letting an inmate go free to serve the rest of his or her sentence outside of prison (page 421)

partnership A type of business in which two or more people share ownership (page 315)

patronage (PAY-truh-nij) The system in which party leaders do favors for loyal supporters of the party (page 465)

plaintiff An individual or a group of people who bring a complaint against another party in a civil case (page 219)

planks Position statements on each specific issue in a party's platform (page 457)

platform A statement of a party's official stand on major public issues (page 457)

plea bargaining Agreeing to plead guilty in exchange for a lesser charge or a lighter sentence (page 419)

pocket veto A way in which the President can veto a bill by pocketing, or keeping, the bill for ten days, during which Congress ends its session (page 186)

policy A plan of action designed to achieve a certain goal (page 174)

political party An organization of citizens who wish to influence and control government by getting their members elected to office (page 456)

precedent A guideline for how all similar court cases should be decided in the future (page 220)

precincts Voting districts (page 464)

president pro tempore (pro TEM-puh-REE) An officer who presides over the Senate when the Vice–President is absent. [Also known as president pro tem.] (page 183)

price The amount a person must pay for a good or service (page 36)

probable cause A good reason to believe that a suspect has been involved in a crime (page 417)

probation A kind of sentence in which a person goes free but must be under the supervision of a court official called a probation officer (page 426)

profit The difference between what it costs to produce something and the price the buyer pays for it (page 299)

propaganda A message that is meant to influence people's ideas, opinions, or actions in a certain way (page 481)

property tax A tax on land and buildings (page 272)

prosecution A government body that brings a charge against a defendant who is accused of breaking one of its laws (page 219)

public assistance Government programs that give help to people in need (page 243)

public policy Government response to public issues (page 497)

R

racism The belief that members of one's own race are superior to those of other races (page 11)

ratification Approval, as in approval of an amendment to the Constitution (page 82)

recall A process for removing elected officials from office (page 248)

recession A slowdown in economic activity and production (page 341)

referendum The process by which a law proposed or passed by a state legislature is referred to the voters to approve or reject (page 248)

registration Signing up to be a voter (page 474)

renewable resource A resource that can be replaced after being used (page 564)

rent Payment for the use of land (page 309)

representatives People who are chosen to speak and act for their fellow citizens in government (page 47)

republic A government in which citizens elect representatives to make laws (page 75)

reserved powers Those powers that the Constitution neither gives to Congress nor denies to the states (page 104)

revenue Income (page 249)

rule of law The concept of a government of laws (page 49)

rules Specific expectations about what our behavior should be (page 26)

S

sales taxes Charges on purchases of goods and services, usually a percentage of the price (page 249)

sanctions Measures to stop or limit trade with another nation in order to change its behavior (page 545)

scarcity The problem that resources are always limited in comparison with the number and variety of wants people have (page 292)

segregation Separation, as in separation of one racial group from another (page 159)

self-nomination Declaring that you are running for office (page 466)

separation of church and state The situation in which government may not favor any religion or establish an official state religion (page 134)

separation of powers Dividing government power among legislative, executive, and judicial branches (page 76)

services Work that you will pay to have done, such as cleaning or repair work (page 35)

small claims court A civil court that people may use when the amount of money they want to recover is small, usually not more than $1,000 or $2,000 (page 443)

social institutions Systems of values and rules that determine how our society is organized. Five major institutions in our society are the family, religion, education, the economy, and government. (page 28)

social roles Roles people play in real life, such as mother, husband, worker, friend, or consumer (page 55)

socialization (soh-shul-i-ZAY-shun) The process of learning how to participate in a group; learning to accept the values in a group and learning the rules for behavior within it (page 27)

sole proprietorship A business owned by an individual (page 315)

sovereignty A nation's power to make and carry out laws within its borders (page 522)

Speaker of the House The presiding officer of the House of Representatives (page 183)

split ticket The practice of voting for candidates of more than one party on the same ballot (page 465)

standard of living The number and kinds of goods and services people can have (page 524)

status offender A youth who is judged to be beyond the control of his or her parents or guardian (page 424)

statutes Written laws made by legislatures (page 396)

stock Shares of ownership in a corporation (page 315)

straight ticket The practice of voting for the candidates of only one party (page 465)

strike The situation in which workers refuse to work unless employers meet certain demands (page 320)

subpoena A court order to produce a witness or document (page 437)

suffrage The right to vote (page 155)

summit meeting A meeting at which the President talks about important issues with heads of other governments (page 544)

supply Amounts of a product that producers are willing to offer at different prices (page 310)

T

terrorism The use or threat of violence to spread fear, usually for the purpose of reaching political goals (page 567)

time deposit A savings plan with a set length of time that money must be kept in the account and a penalty for withdrawing early (page 375)

traditional economy An economic system in which the basic economic decisions are made according to long-established ways of behaving that are unlikely to change (page 297)

treaties Formal agreements with other countries (page 198)

trust A group of several companies organized to benefit from the high prices they all agree to charge (page 350)

tyranny Abuse of power (page 74)

U

utilities Services needed by the public, such as water, gas, and electricity (page 268)

V

values Standards of behavior; guidelines for how people should treat each other (page 15)

variable expenses Expenses that change from month to month (page 371)

veto To reject, as in to reject a bill (page 101)

W

wants Desires for goods and services (page 35)

warrant A legal paper, issued by a court, giving police permission to make an arrest, seizure, or search (page 417)

warranty A manufacturer's promise to repair a product if it breaks within a certain time from the date of purchase (page 373)

whips Assistant floor leaders in each house of Congress (page 183)

witnesses People who have seen events or heard conversations related to a court case, or who have special information that may help settle a case (page 50)

write-in candidate A candidate who asks voters to write his or her name on the ballot (page 466)

Z

zoning Local rules that divide a community into areas and tell how the land in each area can be used (page 271)

Index

Note: Entries with a page number followed by a *c* indicate a chart or graph on that page; *m* indicates a map; and *p* indicates a picture.

A

abortion, 229
absentee ballot, 475
abuse of power, 136–137. *See also* tyranny.
accused, rights of, 137–139, 232–233, 416, 419–420
acid rain, 564, 566, 568, 575
acquired immune deficiency syndrome. *See* AIDS.
activities. *See* career activities; citizenship activities; community activities; Internet activities; portfolio activities.
Adams, John, 74–76, 79, 202–203, 225, 588, 588*p*
Adams, John Quincy, 588, 588*p*
adjudicatory hearing, 425–426
administration, 201
advertising
    effect on demand, 312
    false or misleading, 347, 350–351, 362–363, 403
    political, 479, 486
affirmative action, 161–162
Afghanistan, 529, 544, 553*p*, 557
Africa, 523–524, 556–557
African Americans, 10–11
    contributions to Black Patriots Monument and, 81
    equal protection and, 159–161, 245
    on Supreme Court, 226
    voting rights and, 64, 154–155, 154*p*
aggression, 543–544
Agriculture, Department of, 204*c*, 386, 398
AIDS, 500, 502*p*, 505
airport security, 246
Akins v. Glens Falls School District, 447
Alabama, 243, 596
Alaska, 13, 242, 245*p*, 249–250, 270, 288, 596
Albright, Madeleine, 202
alcohol, 403
Algeria, 526, 556
aliens, 46, 559
Allende, Salvador, 546
alliance, 529, 544
almanac, using. *See* social studies skills.
alternatives, identifying. *See* critical thinking skills.
aluminum, recycling, 508*c*
Amazon rain forests, 566, 566*p*, 569
ambassadors, 198, 547
amendment process
    state constitution, 243–244
    U.S. Constitution, 102-103, 106*c*, 132
amendments, 103, 120-129, 135*c*, 153*c*. *See also* Constitution, U.S.; specific amendments.
American Association of Retired Persons (AARP), 480*p*
American Civil Liberties Union (ACLU), 142
American Farm Bureau, 176
American Federation of Labor (AFL), 320–321
American Federation of Labor-Congress of Industrial Organizations (AFL–CIO), 321–322

American Health Security Act, 503
American Indians. *See* Native Americans.
American Medical Association, 176
American Nazi party, 142–144, 143*p*
Americans with Disabilities Act, 175
Amigos De Las Americas, 379
Amnesty International, 145, 573–574
Andorra, 522
Anglican Church. *See* Church of England.
answer (legal term), 436
Anti-Federalists, 97–98, 101, 103, 132–133, 460
antitrust laws, 350
apartheid101, 103, 132–133, 460
Anti, 532, 580
appeal, 220–221
appeals court
    federal, 221, 222
    state, 220–221, 254
appellate jurisdiction, 220–221, 226
apportionment, 248
Arab-Israeli conflict, 532, 556
arbitration, 440–441
area graphs, analyzing. *See* social studies skills.
Argentina, 489, 533
Arizona, 11, 232–233, 288, 297*p*, 401, 512–513, 596
Arkansas, 596
armed forces, 49–50, 50*p*, 198
Armenia, 576
arms control, 531-532, 567, 569
Arms Control and Disarmament Agency, 205
arms race, 529, 544, 564, 567, 569
arms, right to bear, 136
Army, United States, 528
arraignment, 418
arrests, 417, 417*c*, 424
arson, 413
Arthur, Chester A., 590, 590*p*
Articles of Confederation, 80–82
    decision to replace, 91, 100
    structure of government under, 94-95, 94*c*
    weaknesses of, 83, 90
Articles, Constitutional, 101–103, 109–120
Asia, 524
Asian Americans, 12, 161, 162. *See also* specific nationalities.
Asian "exclusion" laws, 12
assault, 413
assembly, freedom of, 135, 142–144
assessment, 23, 43, 63, 65, 85, 107, 149, 167, 169, 193, 215, 235, 237, 261, 281, 283, 305, 325, 343, 365, 385, 387, 409, 429, 449, 451, 471, 493, 515, 517, 539, 561, 579, 581
assessor, county, 264, 272
Association of Southeast Asian Nations (ASEAN), 530
Athens, Greece, 75
Atlanta, Georgia, 270
Attorney General, 203
Austin, Texas, 533
Australia, 231, 489, 523, 578
Austria, 489

B

"baby boom," 6–7
Bahamas, 505
bail, 139, 418, 425

INDEX

INDEX

INDEX

INDEX

Acknowledgments

Cover Design

Suzanne Schineller

Staff Credits

The people who made up the *Civics: Participating in Government* team—representing editorial, on-line services/multimedia development, product marketing, and production services—are listed below.

Margaret Broucek, Mary Hanisco, Lance Hatch, Grace Massey, Elizabeth Pearson, Robin Santel, Tracy St. Pierre, Mark Tricca, and Merce Wilczek.

Additional Credits

Katharine Ingram, Debra Reardon, Nancy Rogier.

Program Development, Design, and Production

Editorial and Project Management: Pearson Education Development Group.
Production: Pearson Education Development Group.
Charts and Graphs: Paula Jo Smith.

Photography

Unit 1: xvi Terry Ashe/TIME Magazine; **1** "Goddess of Liberty": New York State Historical Association, Cooperstown; Daguerreotype of Frederick Douglas: The National Portrait Gallery, Smithsonian Institution; photography by Curt Fisher.

Chapter 1: 2 Bob Daemmrich/Stock Boston; **6** Jim Leynse/SABA; **7** Larry Manning/Woodfin Camp & Associates; **9** The Bettman Archive; **10** Danny Lyon/Magnum Photos; **13** Paul Gregory; **14** Scala/Art Resource; **17** David Madison; **18** Tim Davis.

Chapter 2: 24 Tom Sobolik/Black Star; **27** Tim Davis; **30** Tim Davis; **31** Courtesy of Interfaith Food Shuttle; **32** Pamela Price/Picture Group; **37** A. Ramey/Woodfin Camp and Associates

Chapter 3: 44 J. L. Atlan/Sygma; **49** Lionel Delevingne/Stock Boston; **52** Zigy Kaluzny/Liaison Network; **57** Lester Sloan/Woodfin Camp & Associates; **64** Fred Ward/Black Star.

Unit 2: 66 Robert Rathe/Stock Boston; **67** TIME cover of March 19, 1965: Time Inc. Magazines cover illustration by Ben Shahn; photography by Curt Fisher.

Chapter 4: 68 Cary Wolinsky/Stock, Boston; **72** The Granger Collection; **73** L Rare Book Division, The New York Public Library, Aster, Lenox and Tilden Foundations; **73** R Culver Pictures, Inc.; **75** Bibliotheque Nationale, Paris; **76** The Bettman Archive; **77** By permission of the Houghton Library, Harvard University; **78** Library of Congress; **79** The Historical Society of Pennsylvania; **81** Courtesy of Wayne Smith; **82** Culver Pictures, Inc.; **85** The Historical Society of Pennsylvania.

Chapter 5: 88 Michael O'Neill; **91** Commissioned by the PA, DE, NJ State Societies, Daughters of the American Revolution. Independence National Historic Park Collection. Copyright Louis Glanzman.; **92** The Thomas Gilcrease Institute of American History and Art, Tulsa, Oklahoma; **93** Henry E. Huntington Library and Art Gallery; **96** The Bettman Archive; **97** Library of Congress; **99** New York Historical Society, New York City; **100** Cary Wolinsky/Stock Boston; **103** Sal DiMarco/Black Star.

Chapter 6: 130 Simon Nathan/The Stock Market; **133** The Bettman Archive; **138** Flip Schulke/Black Star; **141** UPI/Bettmann Newsphotos; **143** Arnold Zann/Black Star; **144** Elliott Smith; **147** John Coletti/Stock Boston.

Chapter 7: 150 Sylvia Johnson/Woodfin Camp & Associates; **154** Steve Schapiro/Black Star; **156** AP/World Wide Photos; **157** Vernon Merritt/Black Star; **160** Arthur Grace/ SYGMA; **161** Carl Iwasaki/Life Magazine © 1953 Time Inc.; **162** Ellis Herwig/Stock Boston; **164** Dennis Brack/Black Star; **167** Tim Davis; **168** Independence National Historical Park Collection, painting by C. W. Peale.

Unit 3: 170 Catherine Karnow/Woodfin Camp & Associates; **171** East, Route 66 sign: Terry Moore/Woodfin Camp & Associates; Photography by Curt Fischer.

Chapter 8: 172 Steve Weber/Stock Boston; **175** Courtesy Judith Heumann; **176** Richard A. Bloom/SABA; **177** Joan Seidel/APWideworld; **179** Ann States/SABA; **187** Mark Reinstein/Photoreporters; **191** Karp.

Chapter 9: 194 Stacy Pick/Stock Boston; **197** Brad Markel/Gamma-Liaison; **199** Dennis Brack/Black Star; **200** Reuters/Bettmann; **202** Richard Ellis/SYGMA; **205** APWideworld; **207** Webb/Magnum; **209** From the collection of the Louisiana State Museum; **210** Nixon Project/National Archives.

Chapter 10: 216 Steve Elmore/The Stock Market; **218** Michael Heron/Woodfin Camp & Associates; **219** Comstock; **226** The Supreme Court Historical Society; **227** Collection, The Supreme Court Historical Society; **229** UPI/Bettman Newsphotos; **230** Shepard Sherbell/Picture Group; **232** Tim Davis; **236** Panoramic Visions

Unit 4: 238 Donald Dietz/Stock Boston; **239** photography by Curt Fischer.

Chapter 11: 240 Bob Daemmrich/Stock Boston; **243** By permission of Honolulu Star Bulletin; **245** Al Grillo/Picture Group; **247** The Office of Governor Frank O'Bannon; **251** The Office of Governor Jeanne Shaheen; **253** Courtesy of Office of Tony Garza; **255** Luis Villota/The Stock Market; **259** Lawfer.

Chapter 12: 262 John M. Roberts/The Stock Market; **265** Reprinted by permission: Tribune Media Services; **266** David Pollock/The Stock Market; **270** Leo Touchet/Woodfin Camp & Associates; **271** Tim Davis; **273** Courtesy of Miami-Dade County Public Schools; **275** Marv Wolf/After-Image; **276** Bohdan Hrynewych/Stock Boston; **278** Tim Davis; **282** New York Historical Society, New York City.

Unit 5: 284 James R. Holland/Stock Boston; **285** Toy bank: Strong Museum, Rochester, New York; Daguerreotype of man posing with tools of goldminer: Minnesota Historical Society; photography by Curt Fisher.

Chapter 13: 286 Craig Aurness/West Light; **288** Michal Heron/The Stock Market; **289** Charles Gupton/Stock Boston; **291** Tom Carroll/International Stock; **293** Herb Snitzer/Stock Boston; **294** Ted Horowitz/The Stock Market; **295** James Leynse / SABA; **297** Terry E. Eiler/Stock, Boston; **298** Wendy Stone/Bruce Coleman Inc.; **299** Martine Franck/Magnum; **300** Filip Horvat/SABA.

Chapter 14: 306 Julie Houck/Stock Boston; **308** Peter L. Chapman/Stock Boston; **311** Porter Gifford/Liaison Network; **313** James McGoon; **314** Tim Davis; **315** Nubar Alexanian/ Woodfin Camp & Associates; **316** Courtesy NCR Corporation; **317** Cotton Coulson/Woodfin Camp & Associates; **318** International Museum of Photography at George Eastman House; **322** Bob Abraham, Hawaii.

Chapter 15: 326 Erich Hartmann/Magnum Photos, Inc.; **329** Rare Book Division, New York Public Library; Astor, Lenox and Tilden Foundations; **331** Culver Pictures; **333** Bill Ross/West Light; **334** Courtesy of New Albany High School.

Chapter 16: 344 Bill Gillette/Stock Boston; **347** Library of Congress–Lewis W. Hine photograph; **348** Ron Watts/Black Star; **350** The Granger Collection; **351** Tim Davis; **352** Delaney/Environmental Protection Agency; **353** D.B. Owen/Black Star; **355** Fred Ward/Black Star; **360** Chuck Brooks/ **362** Tim Davis.

Chapter 17: 366 Leonard Freed/Magnum Photos, Inc.; **368** Chuck Savage/The Stock Market; **370** Brian Smith/Stock Boston; **371** Tim Davis; **372** Bill Pugliano/Liaison Network ; **373** © 1990 Sidney Harris; **375** Chris Jones/The Stock Market; **377** Paul Howell/Liaison Network; **379** Richard Chase; **383** Lawfer; **386** Chuck Nacke/Picture Group.

Unit 6: 388 Tim Davis; **389** "Nevada Sheriff's Department"; Butler's Uniforms, San Francisco, CA; "Judge Jack Puffenberger, Toledo Municipal Court"; Hart Associates; "Warning, Member Neighborhood Crime Watch": © The Sign Center, San Diego, CA; photography by Curt Fischer.

Chapter 18: 390 Jennie Jones/Comstock; **393** NHTSA/U.S. Department of Transportation; **394** Jeff Zaruba/The Stock Market; **397** Lynn Johnson/Black Star; **398** Charles Feil/Stock Boston; **400** Frank Siteman/Stock Boston; **401** APWideworld ; **402** MugShots/The Stock Market; **407** Richard Hutchings Photography; **409** Spencer Grant/Liaison Network.

Chapter 19: 410 James Marshall/The Stock Market; **412** Tim Davis; **413** R.P. Kingston/Stock Boston; **415** J.Pat Carter/Liaison Agency; **418** Tim Davis; **419** David Young Wolff/Stone; **421** James Kamp/Black Star; **424** Steve Chenn/West Light; **425** Courtesy of South Boston High School.

Chapter 20: 430 Anne Heimann/The Stock Market; **433** Tim Davis; **434** Nik Kleinberg/Stock Boston; **435** Frank Siteman/Stock Boston; **437** Jim Pickerell/Black Star; **438** Bob Daemmrich/Stock Boston; **441** Mark Peterson/SABA; **442** Courtesy of the Office of Judge Judith Kaye; **443** Daniel S. Brody/Stock Boston; **446** Jeffrey E. Blackman/The Stock Market; **450** Courtesy Justice Richard Neely.

Unit 7: 452 Berenholtz/The Stock Market; **453** photography by Curt Fischer.

Chapter 21: 454 AFP/Corbis; **457** Haviv/SABA; **458** Dennis Brack/Black Star; **461** UPI/Bettmann Newsphotos; **464** Lisa Quinones/Black Star; **467** Courtesy of the office of Congresswoman Ileana Ros-Lehtinen; **468** AFP/Corbis.

Chapter 22: 472 David Ryan/Photo 20-20; **475** Mark Richards/Picture Group; **477** Courtesy of the League of Women Voters; **479** Ric Feld/APWideworld; **480** Kenneth Jarecke/Woodfin Camp & Associates; **485** Chris Pizello/AP-Wideworld; **486** Najlah Feanny/SABA.

Chapter 23: 494 Paul Sakuma/APWideworld; **497** Andrew Holbrooke/Black Star; **498** Free the Children; **499** Richard Howard/Black Star; **502** © 1987 Matt Herron; **503** Downing; **504** Kraft/SYGMA; **506** Peter Menzel/Stock Boston; **510** David Sears/Gamma-Liaison; **512** Tom Bean/The Stock Market; **516** Gene Pierce/SYGMA

Unit 8: 518 Roy Morsh/The Stock Market; **519** photography by Curt Fischer.

Chapter 24: 520 Gordon Gillespie/Northsport.com; **523** Cary Wolinsky/Stock Boston; **525** Joe Viesti/Viesti Associates, Inc.; **527** Christopher Morris/Time/Black Star; **528** Stone/SYGMA; **531** Delahaye/Sipa Press; **533** Jason Laure/Woodfin Camp & Associates; **534** NASA.

Chapter 25: 540 Charles Krebs/The Stock Market; **543** D.B. Owen/Black Star; **545** Pedro Meyer/Black Star; **547** Atlan/SYGMA; **549** Dennis Brack/Black Star; **550** Courtesy of Joan Carey; **553** Steve McCurry/Magnum; **554** Robert Wallis/SIPA Press; **555** A.F.P. Photo; **558** Elliott Smith.

Chapter 26: 562 Peter Morgan/Picture Group; **566** Claus Meyer/Black Star; **568** Owen Franken/Stock Boston; **572** Joe Urban/Picture Group; **573** Courtesy of Ginetta Sagan; **575** Jacques Chenet/Woodfin Camp & Associates; **576** Susan Meiselas/Magnum; **578** Copyright ©2000 by The National Aeronautics and Space Administration; **580** Antonio Ribeiro/ Liaison Agency

Presidents of the United States: 591 Eric Draper/The White House (George W. Bush)

Special thanks to The Paper Pile of San Anselmo, California, for their help in finding memorabilia for the unit opener pages.

Text Credits

Unit 3: 234 Public Safety Comes First. Copyright ©2000. Reprinted with permission by *The Los Angeles Times*; **234** Defining 'Disability' Down. Copyright ©2000. Reprinted with permission by *The New York Times*.

Unit 5: 313 Reprinted with the permission of Simon & Schuster, Inc. from BEN & JERRY'S DOUBLE DIP by Ben Cohen and Jerry Greenfield. Copyright ©1997 by Ben Cohen and Jerry Greenfield.

Note: Every effort has been made to locate the copyright owner of material used in this textbook. Omissions brought to our attention will be corrected in subsequent editions.

ACKNOWLEDGMENTS